国家数智财经行业产教融合共同体推荐教材
十四五 高等院校财务会计类专业重构系列教材

大数据技术
在财务会计中的应用

（Hive分析）

主　编◎蒋道霞　张卫平　蔡清龙
副主编◎苏　畅　顾　航　秦媛媛　赵瑞晓

立信会计出版社
LIXIN ACCOUNTING PUBLISHING HOUSE

图书在版编目（CIP）数据

大数据技术在财务会计中的应用：Hive 分析／蒋道霞，张卫平，蔡清龙主编. -- 上海：立信会计出版社，2024. 8. -- ISBN 978-7-5429-7717-5

Ⅰ．F234.4-39

中国国家版本馆 CIP 数据核字第 2024Z4A467 号

责任编辑　　王秀宇
美术编辑　　北京任燕飞工作室

大数据技术在财务会计中的应用（Hive 分析）
DASHUJU JISHU ZAI CAIWU KUAIJI ZHONG DE YINGYONG

出版发行	立信会计出版社		
地　　址	上海市中山西路 2230 号	邮政编码	200235
电　　话	(021)64411389	传　　真	(021)64411325
网　　址	www.lixinaph.com	电子邮箱	lixinaph2019@126.com
网上书店	http://lixin.jd.com		http://lxkjcbs.tmall.com
经　　销	各地新华书店		
印　　刷	浙江天地海印刷有限公司		
开　　本	787 毫米×1092 毫米　1/16		
印　　张	22.25		
字　　数	500 千字		
版　　次	2024 年 8 月第 1 版		
印　　次	2024 年 8 月第 1 次		
书　　号	ISBN 978-7-5429-7717-5/F		
定　　价	49.80 元		

如有印订差错，请与本社联系调换

前言

随着大数据技术和人工智能技术的发展，Hadoop 大数据生态系统中的各项技术逐渐成为大数据开发领域的事实标准，特别是 Hadoop 大数据生态系统中各项技术的开源特性，使其核心技术和各种解决方案得到了广泛的应用。大数据蕴藏着巨大的价值，对大数据的运用和价值挖掘给社会和企业带来新的机遇和变革。随着大数据对时代的引领，会计工作模式也发生了巨大改变，运用大数据技术对企业财务数据进行分析已经成为企业的一项重要工作。为适应新技术的发展，教育部《职业教育专业目录(2021 年)》专业名称中原本与财务相关的专业，更新命名为大数据与财务管理、大数据与会计、大数据与审计、统计与大数据分析、财税大数据应用等，学习大数据技术已经成为财务、会计工作人员的必修课。财务数据可以揭示企业财务状况，如企业的偿债能力、盈利能力、营运能力等。运用大数据技术，企业可以获得更详细的分析结果，挖掘难以察觉的现象之间的相关性，有利于在运营上作出更好的决策。

目前，市场上关于大数据技术在财务会计中应用的图书较多，但是基于 Hadoop 大数据平台深入剖析大数据离线批处理计算领域和用数据仓库 Hive 技术进行数据处理的大数据框架技术原理和案例的图书却很少。本书以实战操作为主，通过详细介绍 Hadoop 大数据平台的常用技术，实际部署大数据分析环境，通过大量大数据存储和财务分析案例，帮助读者更加全面、深入、透彻地理解大数据技术和主流框架在财务分析中的应用，提高读者对各种大数据框架的整合能力，进而提高读者的财务大数据项目实战能力。

本书特色如下。

1. 图解及案例丰富，方便学生理解

为了方便读者的理解，本书在介绍每种技术框架时都配有大量的框架架构图和执行流程图，并为相关的技术框架配有详细的数据处理案例。这些框架架构图和执行流程图的原件和案例源码收录于随书资料中。

2. 用大数据技术解决实际问题，弱化学习难度

本书涵盖 Hadoop 大数据常用热门技术、关系型数据库 MySQL、数据仓库 Hive 和数据迁移工具 Sqoop 的整合使用，通过实际的财务分析案例，消化技术运用。

3. 将基本原理融于操作过程，强化技术技能

本书每讲解一个大数据技术，都会先对其基本原理进行详细介绍，对大数据环境部署过程进行详细操作，图文并茂，便于读者理解基本原理，最重要的是便于读者通过项目案例学会工具的使用。

4. 精选专业数据分析案例，提高应用能力

本书对每种技术框架都配有财务会计相关的典型案例，具有较强的实用性。每个案例项目都是独立的，方便读者随时查阅和参考。本书中大数据处理应用案例引入了Hive在财务报表分析中的应用、Hive在贷款数据分析的应用。这些案例是编者将Hadoop中的HDFS技术和HiveQL技术融合运用于财务报表分析、贷款数据分析所开发的实际项目，本书对其进行了一定的简化，具有很高的实际应用价值和参考价值。应用案例整合了本书中所涉及的大数据技术，便于读者融会贯通地运用本书中所学习的知识和技术解决工作中的实际问题。读者对应用案例稍加修改，便可用于实际的专业数据分析中。

本书共有9个单元，即大数据及其在会计工作中的应用、虚拟机的安装与CentOS 7的使用、Hadoop大数据处理平台的安装与配置、大数据存储技术HDFS、大数据并行计算技术MapReduce、数据仓库Hive的安装部署、数据仓库Hive在数据处理中的应用、Hive在会计和金融数据分析中应用的综合案例、大数据迁移工具Sqoop。学习时，学生应在了解基本理论的前提下，进行大数据环境的构建和运用，重点是运用大数据技术解决实际的会计分析问题。

为了方便阅读，本书附带随书资料，包括：①书中所有案例项目源码。②书中所有的插图文件。③教材配套PPT、微课视频。④教材配套在线课程。

读者若需要教材资源，可通过访问配套课程网站下载。

本书的适用对象包括大数据技术专业中高职学生、大数据与财务管理专业中高职学生、大数据与会计专业中高职学生、大数据与审计专业中高职学生、统计与大数据分析专业中高职学生、财税大数据应用专业中高职学生等。

编者对阅读本书的建议如下：没有大数据基础的读者，建议按照顺序从单元1开始阅读，并练习、掌握每一个案例；有一定大数据专业基础的读者，可以根据自身实际情况，选择性地阅读各个单元的项目案例。对于本书涉及的每个大数据应用案例，读者可以先自行思考实现方式，再阅读相关的项目案例，这样有助于达到事半功倍的学习效果；读者可以先阅读本书涉及的大数据项目案例，再阅读各单元对应的原理细节，这样理解起来会更加深刻；学生可以借助华为大数据实验平台、青椒课堂等学习平台，也可以直接使用Hive环境学习HiveQL。

尽管编者对技术有着很高的追求，但是大数据领域中各种技术涉及的知识点众多，财务管理、会计、审计、统计各专业的应用非常广泛，因此一本书籍很难涵盖所有的知识点和

功能点。如果编者有书写不妥的地方,恳请大家批评指正,并提出改进建议。我们的联系方式为:邮箱56301672@qq.com,微信15996198776。

对于本书的编写与出版,编者要感谢国内外开源分布式大数据资源网站,感谢新道科技股份有限公司及北京红亚华宇科技有限公司提供的大数据分析案例,感谢我们的团队以及许许多多一起合作过和交流过的朋友们,感谢CSDN博客的粉丝,感谢出版社各位编辑的辛勤劳作。

编 者

2024年8月

目录

单元 1　大数据及其在会计工作中的应用 …………………………………… 1
　　任务 1.1　认识大数据 ………………………………………………………… 2
　　任务 1.2　大数据在会计工作中的应用 ……………………………………… 4
　　任务 1.3　大数据处理架构 Hadoop ………………………………………… 6
　　单元总结 ………………………………………………………………………… 10
　　单元习题 ………………………………………………………………………… 10

单元 2　虚拟机的安装与 CentOS 7 的使用 ………………………………… 11
　　任务 2.1　虚拟机 VMware 的安装 …………………………………………… 12
　　任务 2.2　CentOS 7 的安装与配置 …………………………………………… 22
　　任务 2.3　WinSCP 的安装与使用 …………………………………………… 54
　　任务 2.4　Xshell 的安装与使用 ……………………………………………… 63
　　单元总结 ………………………………………………………………………… 71
　　单元习题 ………………………………………………………………………… 71

单元 3　Hadoop 大数据处理平台的安装与配置 …………………………… 73
　　任务 3.1　Hadoop 的安装模式 ………………………………………………… 73
　　任务 3.2　JDK 的安装和配置 ………………………………………………… 75
　　任务 3.3　Hadoop 的本地模式安装和配置 …………………………………… 79
　　任务 3.4　Hadoop 的伪分布模式安装和配置 ………………………………… 86
　　任务 3.5　Hadoop 的完全分布模式安装 ……………………………………… 95
　　单元总结 ………………………………………………………………………… 122
　　单元习题 ………………………………………………………………………… 122

单元 4　大数据存储技术 HDFS ……………………………………………… 123
　　任务 4.1　Hadoop HDFS 架构和容错 ………………………………………… 123
　　任务 4.2　Hadoop HDFS 文件管理 …………………………………………… 130

任务 4.3　Hadoop HDFS 命令 ······ 133
单元总结 ······ 152
单元习题 ······ 152

单元 5　大数据并行计算技术 MapReduce ······ 154
任务 5.1　MapReduce 的原理和部署结构 ······ 154
任务 5.2　MapReduce 的工作机制 ······ 156
单元总结 ······ 160
单元习题 ······ 160

单元 6　数据仓库 Hive 的安装部署 ······ 161
任务 6.1　Hive 的架构和部署模式 ······ 161
任务 6.2　安装并配置 MySQL 数据库 ······ 166
任务 6.3　Hive 的环境安装与配置 ······ 175
单元总结 ······ 184
单元习题 ······ 184

单元 7　数据仓库 Hive 在数据处理中的应用 ······ 185
任务 7.1　Hive 命令说明 ······ 186
任务 7.2　Hive 数据定义 ······ 188
任务 7.3　Hive 数据操作 ······ 220
任务 7.4　Hive 数据查询 ······ 233
任务 7.5　Hive 视图 ······ 252
任务 7.6　Hive 函数 ······ 257
单元总结 ······ 263
单元习题 ······ 263

单元 8　Hive 在财务报表分析和贷款数据分析中应用的综合案例 ······ 265
任务 8.1　Hive 在财务报表分析中的应用 ······ 265
任务 8.2　Hive 在贷款数据分析中的应用 ······ 305
单元总结 ······ 320
单元习题 ······ 320

单元 9　大数据迁移工具 Sqoop ·· 321
任务 9.1　Sqoop 的工作原理 ·· 321
任务 9.2　Sqoop 的安装和配置 ·· 324
任务 9.3　用 Sqoop 导入、导出数据 ·· 330
单元总结 ··· 341
单元习题 ··· 342

参考文献 ·· 343

单元 1

大数据及其在会计工作中的应用

随着信息技术的发展,硬件成本不断降低,网络带宽获得大幅提升,这些都为大量数据的传输和存储提供了基础;智能终端的普及及物联网的发展让更多的人和物连接到互联网中,成为数据的生产者,互联网上数据信息正以前所未有的速度增长和积累。数据已经成为一种重要的生产要素,在信息化发展的新阶段,大数据应运而生。大数据引领着新时代的工业革命,大数据时代已经来临。大数据蕴藏着巨大的价值,对大数据的运用和价值挖掘给社会和企业带来新的机遇和变革。在大数据时代下,会计工作模式发生了巨大改变。对企业财务数据进行分析是企业的一项重要工作。财务数据可以揭示企业财务状况,如企业的偿债能力、盈利能力、营运能力等。运用大数据技术,企业可以获得更详细的分析结果,挖掘难以察觉的现象之间的相关性,从而在运营上作出更好的决策。

学习目标

知识目标

1. 了解大数据定义、大数据特征和大数据关键技术。
2. 了解大数据应用领域、大数据在企业中的应用架构。
3. 了解大数据在会计工作中的应用。
4. 了解大数据在会计工作应用中的问题和解决对策。

技能目标

1. 能明确在企业中大数据的技术架构模式,熟悉大数据的数据采集、存储、分析和结果呈现等基本处理流程。
2. 明确大数据在企业中的应用架构,了解 Hadoop 生态系统各组件功能。
3. 养成将大数据技术运用于自己专业的科学思维,探索大数据技术运用新举措。
4. 养成运用学习资源和学习工具开展自主学习和终身学习的习惯。

单元任务

任务 1.1 认识大数据。
任务 1.2 大数据在会计工作中的应用。
任务 1.3 大数据处理架构 Hadoop。

任务 1.1　认识大数据

任务描述

要将大数据技术应用于财务会计，就要认识大数据，了解大数据的定义和特征、大数据应用及大数据关键技术，思考如何运用大数据解决会计专业问题。

关键步骤

(1) 熟悉大数据的定义和特征。
(2) 了解大数据的应用与发展。
(3) 了解大数据技术。

1.1.1　大数据的定义和特征

1.1.1.1　大数据的定义

"大数据"概念最早出现在 1980 年，由著名的未来学家阿尔文·托夫勒在其著作《第三次浪潮》中提出。2009 年，美国互联网数据中心证实了大数据时代的来临。关于大数据的确切定义，目前尚无统一公认的说法。著名研究机构 Gartner 给出的定义是：大数据是需要新处理模式才能具有更强的决策力、洞察发现力和流程优化能力来适应海量、高增长率和多样化的信息资产。全球领先的管理咨询公司麦肯锡给出的大数据定义是：一种规模大到在获取、存储、管理、分析方面大大超出了传统数据库软件工具能力范围的数据集合，具有海量的数据规模、快速的数据流转、多样的数据类型和低价值密度四大特征。IBM 公司增加了一个真实性(veracity)特征。维克托·迈尔·舍恩伯格和肯尼斯·库克耶编写的《大数据时代》中指出：大数据不用传统的随机分析法(即抽样调查)这样的捷径，而是采用所有数据进行分析处理。全球最大的数据中心 IDC 则侧重从技术角度说明其概念：大数据处理技术代表了新一代的技术架构，这种架构通过高速获取数据并对其进行分析和挖掘，从海量且形式各异的数据源中更有效地抽取出富含价值的信息。

1.1.1.2　大数据的特征

大数据具有 5V 特点，分别是 Volume(体量)巨大、处理 Velocity(速度快)、Variety(类型)繁多、Value(价值)密度低、数据 Veracity(真实)。下面具体说明 5V 特点。

(1) Volume：体量巨大，采集、存储和计算的量都非常大。大数据的起始计量单位通常是 PB、EB 或 ZB。数据存储单位换算关系如表 1.1.1 所示。

(2) Velocity：处理速度快，因为要保证数据的时效性，数据增长和处理必须要迅速。例如，搜索引擎要求几分钟前的新闻能够被用户查询到，个性化推荐算法要求尽可能实时完成推荐。这是大数据区别于传统数据挖掘的显著特征。

(3) Variety：类型繁多，种类和来源多样化，包括结构化、半结构化和非结构化数据，具体表现为网络日志、音频、视频、图片、地理位置信息等。多类型的数据对数据处理能力提出了更高要求。

表 1.1.1 数据存储单位换算关系

单位	换算关系	单位	换算关系
B(Byte 字节)	1 Byte = 8 Bit	PB(Petabyte 拍字节)	1 PB = 1 024 TB
KB(Kilobyte 千字节)	1 KB = 1 024 B	EB(Exabyte 艾字节)	1 EB = 1 024 PB
MB(Megabyte 兆字节)	1 MB = 1 024 KB	ZB(Zettabyte 泽字节)	1 ZB = 1 024 EB
GB(Gigabyte 吉字节)	1 GB = 1 024 MB	YB(Yottabyte 尧字节)	1 YB = 1 024 ZB
TB(Trillionbyte 太字节)	1 TB = 1 024 GB		

（4）Value：数据价值密度相对较低。随着互联网以及物联网的广泛应用，信息感知无处不在，信息海量，但有价值的信息密度较低，如何结合业务逻辑并通过强大的机器算法来挖掘数据价值，是大数据时代需要解决的问题。

（5）Veracity：数据真实，数据的准确性和可信赖度高，即数据的质量高。

1.1.2 大数据的应用与发展

大数据时代引领未来，数据已经渗透每一个行业和业务领域。大数据技术已经广泛应用在零售、金融、医疗、教育、农业、环境、智慧城市等领域。

党的十八届五中全会将大数据上升为国家战略。中共中央总书记习近平强调，大数据发展日新月异，我们应该审时度势、精心谋划、超前布局、力争主动，深入了解大数据发展现状和趋势及其对经济社会发展的影响，分析我国大数据发展取得的成绩和存在的问题，推动实施国家大数据战略，加快完善数字基础设施，推进数据资源整合和开放共享，保障数据安全，加快建设数字中国，更好服务我国经济社会发展和人民生活改善。要推动大数据技术产业创新发展，构建以数据为关键要素的数字经济，运用大数据提升国家治理现代化水平，运用大数据促进保障和改善民生，切实保障国家数据安全。

大数据正在以前所未有的形式影响着人们的生活和工作，大数据环境下各行各业面临的机遇和挑战并存，如何发挥大数据的优势，提高对大数据的应用能力，是各行业发展必须研究的重要课题。对大数据进行分析和处理，可以更加深层次地了解事物的本质特征，了解业务与业务之间的关联性，从而挖掘数据潜在的附加值，为经营管理工作提供有效的决策数据。

1.1.3 大数据技术

大数据技术是指伴随着大数据的采集、存储、分析和应用，一系列使用非传统工具对大量的结构化、半结构化和非结构化数据进行处理，从而获得分析和预测结果的一系列数据处理和分析技术。

大数据的基本处理流程主要包括数据采集、存储、分析和结果呈现等环节。数据采集是将分散在各处的数据，采用相应的设备或软件进行采集。数据无处不在，如互联网网站、政务系统、零售系统、办公系统、自动化生产系统、监控摄像头、传感器等，每时每刻都在不断产生数据。采集到的数据通常无法直接用于后续的数据分析，因为来源众多、类型多样的数据,不可避免地存在数据缺失和语义模糊等问题,必须采取数据预处理过程,把数据变成一个可用的状态。数据经过预处理后,首先会被存放到文件系统或数据库系统中进行存储与管理,其次由用户采用数据挖掘工具对数据进行分析处理,最后用可视化工具为用户呈现结果。在整个数据处理过程中,还必须注意隐私保护和数据安全问题。

从数据分析全流程的角度,大数据技术主要包括数据采集与预处理、数据存储和管理、数据处理与分析、数据安全和隐私保护等几个层面的内容。

任务1.2 大数据在会计工作中的应用

任务描述

思考会计中有哪些业务可以用大数据思维和大数据平台去完成,从而提升会计数据分析和会计数据挖掘的水平,解决会计中存在的实际问题,提高大数据认识和运用水平。

关键步骤

(1) 了解大数据可以应用在哪些会计工作中。
(2) 了解大数据应用在会计工作中存在的问题和解决对策。

大数据时代给各行各业的发展都带来了契机,大数据在会计工作中的应用范围也越来越广,以下简单列举大数据在会计工作中应用,并分析大数据应用在会计工作中存在的问题和解决对策。

1.2.1 大数据在会计工作中的应用举例

1.2.1.1 应用大数据思维和技术,研究重点数据

大数据汇集了众多的小数据,小数据是由会计工作人员通过各种渠道和方式获取的,这些小数据有的是原始的,有的是经过加工之后得到的,也有的是因为某些因素而虚拟出的,这些数据的真实性有待考量。而这时就需要会计工作人员通过大数据技术以及相应的工具,对这些数据信息进行深层的分析和挖掘,以确保数据信息的真实性和准确性,将数据与相关业务流程进行结合,根据业务发生的流程与实际数据进行一一对应,深挖数据信息,从而为管理层提供准确、可靠、有价值的数据,提高经营管理水平。

1.2.1.2 根据业务特点,应用大数据技术挖掘数据本质

数据信息都是有源头的,在对数据进行分析和处理的过程中,会计工作人员应结合业务的基本特点,利用大数据技术找出业务与数据之间的内在关系,并从中提取有价值的数据。在此过程中,会计工作人员要了解业务的相关流程,并根据其特点来挖掘数据的本质。

1.2.1.3 依据大数据,查找资金的流向

资金是发展的命脉,而资金流是经营管理中的核心内容。在实际的会计工作中,会计工作人员要以资金的流向数据作为根本的研究点,对资金流进行严格的监督,一旦发现异

常资金流,要及时地找寻原因,以降低资金异常带来的风险。强化资金流的监管,对相关业务流程进行严格控制,从资金的预决算一直到项目的完成,都要做好追踪和监督工作,企业应利用大数据相关技术,对资金的流向进行全方位、多角度的监督。

1.2.1.4　根据大数据基础,进行趋势研究

会计数据是会计事项的真实反映,利用大数据技术以及相关的模型、算式等对会计数据进行分析,以此进行发展趋势的研究正变得越来越重要。会计工作人员利用大数据相关工具对已经产生的会计数据进行分析,以分析结果为根本出发点,对未来的会计工作进行规划,有助于确保会计工作的有效性。另外,企业可以根据会计数据的分析结果进行相应的完善,根据行业的基本数据信息,寻找一些易变数据,并以此为出发点,做好相应的规划工作,以确保经营管理能够稳健发展。

1.2.1.5　利用大数据,构建大数据平台

在实际的会计工作中,会计工作人员要能立足会计工作自身,结合大数据思维以及相关技术手段,收集并整理数据,以完成对大数据平台的构建,并在大数据平台基础上,实现对重点数据的定位和判断,以提升数据的价值性;对于数据信息的来源,要不断提升判断和辨别的能力,以确保其真实性和可靠性;将会计工作中的财务数据与业务数据进行有效结合,并利用算法工具,深挖数据的信息。同时,会计工作人员要加强对数据分析的针对性,探寻数据间存在的关联性,并进一步分析会计工作中潜在的各类风险,对各类风险外在的表现特征进行系统归纳和科学总结,为会计工作决策和管理提供有价值的数据参考。

1.2.1.6　提高大数据认识和运用水平

众所周知,在实际的会计工作中,会计信息数据量非常庞大,其中包含的数据并非都是准确的,因此如何从众多的数据中提取有价值的数据信息,对会计工作而言是一项重要的工作内容。在传统手工会计时代,人们往往通过手工进行查找,耗时耗力且工作质量不高。在大数据时代,会计工作人员可以利用大数据的相关技术,发挥其在会计工作中的分析和判断作用,从根本上提升会计的工作效率以及工作质量。

1.2.2　大数据应用在会计工作中存在的问题和解决对策

1.2.2.1　大数据应用在会计工作中存在的问题

1) 会计人员认知水平落后

在传统会计工作模式下,会计人员的思维模式较为简单,工作方法也较为落后,且人工处理大数据信息,很难保证会计数据的真实性。在大数据时代下,大数据思维有其自身独特的内容,而这对会计从业人员也提出了较高的要求,除了要具备使用大数据相关技术的能力,同时还要具有大数据思维。与传统的会计数据相比,现阶段的会计数据骤增,而这些数据的真伪很难辨别。会计人员必须建立大数据思维,并不断提升对大数据的认识水平,利用大数据工具和方法来处理会计数据,从众多的数据中获取有价值的数据,以帮助决策者制定有效的决策。

2) 数据复杂,储存成本大

现阶段,会计数据量猛增,会计人员如果不能快速地对数据进行识别和判断,就需要对

数据进行存储,而存储就需要有较大的存储空间,这对计算机的软件和硬件都提出了更高的要求,同时也在无形中提高了数据的存储成本。鉴于上述问题,构建完善的数据共享平台是非常有必要的,利用互联网云计算等平台,对庞大的数据进行存储,不仅能够节省成本,而且也能实现数据信息的实时共享。

3) 缺乏大数据管理会计人才

大数据时代背景下,管理会计人才在会计工作的发展中起着至关重要的作用。大数据飞速发展,而管理会计人才相对匮乏,具有综合能力的专业型管理会计人才少之又少。具体表现在:其一,在管理会计工作的过程中,对会计人才的培养力度严重不足,会计人员结构的设置不科学,会计人员的年龄普遍偏高,而这一部分人群思想较为保守,很难适应和接受大数据思维,甚至对大数据思维存在着抵触情绪,这与大数据时代的发展相违背;其二,管理会计工作人员对大数据的认识不够完善,在实际的工作中,对大数据相关技术以及工具的利用不足,最终影响大数据技术的发挥。

1.2.2.2 大数据对会计应用问题的解决对策

在大数据时代下,会计人员要从根本上建立大数据思维,提高大数据的应用水平,同时辅之以相应的考核机制,以不断强化对大数据的应用能力。对大数据在会计工作的实际应用中发现的问题,要及时采取有效的对策,结合会计工作情况,提出有针对性的建议并不断完善,以不断提升管理会计工作人员对大数据的应用能力;要不断加强对在岗的会计工作人员的培训,以使其建立全新的思维模式,同时提升其大数据的应用水平;要引进优秀的会计管理人才,引导并推动大数据在会计工作中的有效应用,以此来提升会计人员的整体水平,提高会计工作的效率,为经营管理工作奠定坚实的人才基础。

大数据时代下,会计工作必须转变传统的思维定式以及工作模式,以大数据技术为根本出发点,将大数据算法、工具等应用到实际的会计工作中,以提升会计工作效率和工作质量,确保会计工作的真实性和可靠性,为管理决策的制定提供数据支撑。

任务 1.3　大数据处理架构 Hadoop

任务描述

要将大数据应用于会计,需要了解大数据技术 Hadoop 的生态系统,了解 Hadoop 各组件的功能,思考用 Hadoop 的哪个组件可能解决会计数据的分布式存储和数据分析。

关键步骤

(1) 了解 Hadoop 和 Hadoop 生态系统的概念和功能。

(2) 了解 Hadoop 生态系统中各组件的功能。

(3) 了解大数据在企业中的应用架构模式。

Hadoop 是一个开源的、可运行于大规模集群上的分布式计算平台,它实现了

MapReduce 计算模型和分布式文件系统(hadoop distributed file system，HDFS)等功能，在业内得到广泛的应用，同时也成为大数据的代名词。借助于 Hadoop，程序员可以轻松地编写分布式并行程序，并将其运行于计算机集群上，完成海量数据的存储与处理分析。

1.3.1　认识 Hadoop

Hadoop 是 Apache 软件基金会旗下的一个开源分布式计算平台，为用户提供了系统底层细节透明的分布式基础架构。

1.3.1.1　Hadoop 的定义

Hadoop 是基于 Java 语言开发的，具有很好的跨平台特性，可部署在廉价的计算机集群中用于数据的存储和计算。Hadoop 的核心是分布式文件系统 HDFS 和 MapReduce。HDFS 是面向普通硬件环境的分布文件系统，具有较高的读写速度、很好的容错性和可伸缩性，支持大规模数据的分布式存储，其冗余数据存储的方式很好地保证了数据的安全性。MapReduce 允许用户在不了解分布式文件系统底层细节的情况下开发并行应用程序。用户采用 MapReduce 来整合分布式文件系统上的数据，可保证分析和处理数据的高效性。借助于 Hadoop，程序员可以轻松地编写分布式并行应用程序，将其运行于廉价计算机集群上，完成海量数据的存储与计算。Hadoop 被公认为行业大数据标准开源软件，在分布式环境下提供海量数据处理能力。几乎所有主流厂商都围绕 Hadoop 提供开发工具、开源软件、商业化工具和技术服务，如谷歌、雅虎、微软、思科、淘宝等都支持 Hadoop。国内采用 Hadoop 的公司主要有百度、淘宝、网易、华为、中国移动等。Hadoop 具有高可靠性、高效性、高可扩展性、高容错性、低成本、Linux 平台、支持多种语言等特性。

1.3.1.2　Hadoop 生态系统

Hadoop 的项目结构不断丰富发展，已经形成一个丰富的 Hadoop 生态系统，目前已包含多个子项目，除了 HDFS 和 MapReduce 两大核心，Hadoop 生态系统还包括 HBase、Hive、Pig、Tez、Spark、Zookeeper、Flume、Sqoop、Ambari 等功能组件。Hadoop 2.0 中还新增了一些重要的组件，即 HDFS HA 和分布式资源调度管理框架 YARN。Hadoop 生态系统如图 1.3.1 所示。

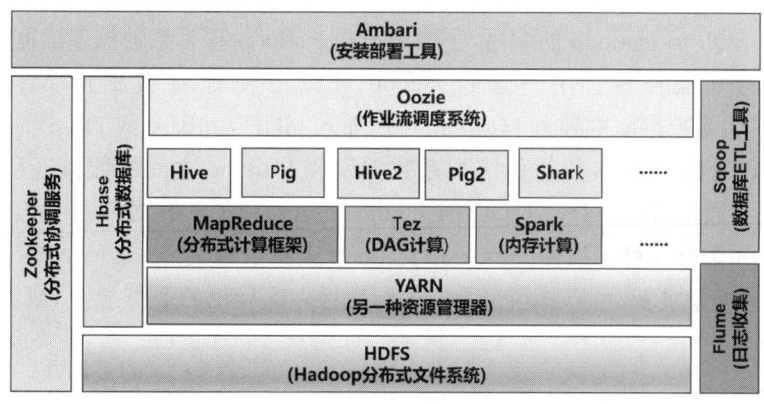

图 1.3.1　Hadoop 生态系统

接下来，本书选择了与后续单元中会计分析相关的几个组件加以介绍。

1) HDFS

HDFS 分布式文件系统是 Hadoop 项目的两大核心之一，具有处理超大数据、流式处理、可以运行在廉价商用服务器上等优点。HDFS 在设计之初就是要运行在廉价的大型服务器集群上的，因此在设计上它就把硬件故障作为一种常态来考虑，可以保证在部分硬件发生故障的情况下仍然能够保证文件系统的整体可用性和可靠性。HDFS 放宽了一部分 POSIX(portable operating system interface of UNIX)约束，从而实现以流的形式访问文件系统中的数据。HDFS 在访问应用程序数据时，具有很高的吞吐率，因此对于超大数据集的应用程序而言，选择 HDFS 作为底层数据存储是较好的选择。

2) MapReduce

MapReduce 是一种编程模型，用于大规模数据集(大于 1 TB)的并行运算，它将复杂的、运行于大规模集群上的并行计算过程高度地抽象到了两个函数——Map 和 Reduce 上，并且允许用户在不了解分布式系统底层细节的情况下开发并行应用程序，并将其运行于廉价计算机集群上，完成海量数据的处理。MapReduce 能把输入的数据集切分为若干独立的数据块，分发给一个主节点管理下的各个分节点来共同并行完成；最后，通过整合各个节点的中间结果得到最后结果。

3) Hive

Hive 是一个基于 Hadoop 的数据仓库工具，可以用于对 Hadoop 文件中的数据集进行数据整理、特殊查询和分析存储。Hive 的学习门槛较低，因为它提供了类似于关系数据库 SQL 语言的查询语言——HiveQL。用户可以通过 HiveQL 语句快速实现简单的 MapReduce 统计，Hive 自身可以将 HiveQL 语句转换为 MapReduce 任务进行运行，而不必开发专门的 MapReduce 应用，因而十分适合数据仓库的统计分析。

4) Zookeeper

Zookeeper 是一个高效和可靠的协同工作系统，能提供分布式锁之类的基本服务(如统一命名服务、状态同步服务、集群管理、分布式应用配置项的管理等)，用于构建分布式应用，减轻分布式应用程序所承担的协调任务。Zookeeper 使用 Java 编写，很容易编程接入，它使用了一个和文件树结构相似的数据模型，可以使用 Java 或者 C 来进行编程接入。

5) Sqoop

Sqoop 是 SQL-to-Hadoop 的缩写，主要用来在 Hadoop 和关系数据库之间交换数据，可以改进数据的互操作性。用户通过 Sqoop 可以方便地将数据从 MySQL、Oracle、PostgreSQL 等关系数据库中导入 Hadoop(可以导入 HDFS、HBase 或 Hive)，或者将数据从 Hadoop 导出到关系数据库，使得传统关系数据库和 Hadoop 之间的数据迁移变得非常方便。Sqoop 主要通过 JDBC(Java DataBase Connectivity)和关系数据库进行交互，理论上，支持 JDBC 的关系数据库都可以使 Sqoop 和 Hadoop 进行数据交互。Sqoop 是专门为大数据集设计的，支持增量更新，可以将新记录添加到最近一次导出的数据源上，或者指定上次修改的时间戳。

6) Spark

Spark 是基于内存计算的大数据并行计算框架，适用于各种各样的分布式平台系统，是一个可应用于大规模数据处理的统一分析引擎。与 MapReduce 相比，Spark 在计算时产生的中间结果存储在内存中，计算速度更快；Spark 在执行数据处理时，只需要将数据加载到内存中，之后直接在内存中加载中间结果数据集即可，减少了磁盘的 I/O 开销。

1.3.2 大数据在企业中的应用架构

在企业中对大量数据源抓取并进行分析，最典型的应用包括数据分析、数据实时查询、数据挖掘三种。从底层数据源得到数据后，为支持上层的三种应用，要通过中间的大数据层，即整个 Hadoop 相关技术来支撑。大数据层提供了整个 Hadoop 软件框架技术，不同的 Hadoop 组件可实现不同的企业分析，最底层用 Hadoop 平台中的分布式文件存储 HDFS 来满足企业大量的数据存储需求，存储完成后进行数据分析。数据分析需要对许多数据进行批量处理，批量处理最典型的工具是 MapReduce，此外，还可以利用 Hadoop 平台中的数据仓库 Hive 和 Pig 来实现离线数据分析。对于数据实时查询，可以利用 HBase 数据库，HBase 可支持几十亿行数据存储，是非常好的分布式面向列的存储。数据挖掘可利用 Hadoop 平台中的 Mahout 组件，Mahout 可把大量的数据挖掘、机器分析和商务智能算法用 MapReduce 实现，而且都是开源算法，可直接使用。Hadoop 在企业中的应用架构如图 1.3.2 所示。

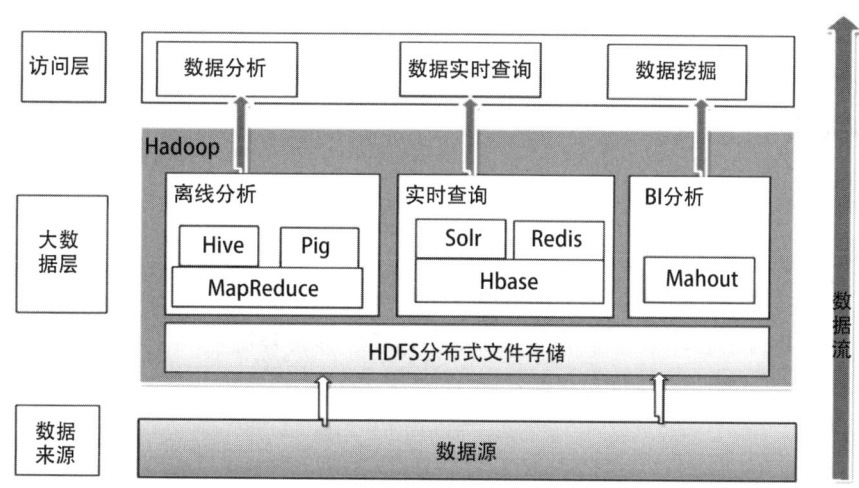

图 1.3.2　Hadoop 在企业中的应用架构

企业中最有价值的数据主要有客户数据、财务数据和生产数据。通过对客户数据的分析，企业可以在现有客户中挖掘出更有价值的客户并重点关注。财务数据的分析是企业的一项重要工作。财务数据可以揭示企业财务状况，如企业的偿债能力、盈利能力、营运能力等。运用大数据技术，企业可以获得更详细的分析结果，挖掘难以察觉的现象之间的相关性，有利于在运营上作出更好的决策。生产数据并不单单指产品生产流程中各种生产设备的数据，也包括服务类的企业在项目实施过程中可收集到的相关信息。挖掘生产数据中的信息，企业可以发现流程中出现滞后的环节，从而进行调整优化，提升企业的工作效率和服务水平。

单元总结

本单元首先学习了大数据的定义、大数据5V特征和大数据的技术;其次总结了大数据在会计工作中的典型应用,如应用大数据思维和技术研究会计重点数据、应用大数据技术挖掘数据本质、查找资金的流向、进行趋势研究、构建大数据平台等,提出大数据在会计工作应用中的问题和解决对策;最后学习了Hadoop生态系统各组件的功能和大数据在企业中的应用架构。

单元习题

一、选择题

1. 下列选项中,属于hadoop生态圈组件的有(　　)。
   A. HDFS　　　　B. Hive　　　　C. Redis　　　　D. Hbase
2. 大数据的数据特点主要有(　　)。
   A. 容量大,种类多
   B. 价值密度低
   C. 数据增长率低
   D. 数据可以是采集的,也可以是凭空捏造的

二、简答题

1. 什么是大数据?
2. 简述大数据的5V特征。
3. 大数据容量单位有哪些?
4. 请举例说明大数据在会计工作中的应用。
5. 目前大数据在会计工作应用中存在哪些问题?如何解决?

单元 2
虚拟机的安装与 CentOS 7 的使用

Hadoop 被公认为行业大数据标准开源软件,它具备在大规模计算机集群中对海量数据进行处理的能力。由于其良好的性能,Hadoop 大数据处理平台在大数据企业中应用广泛。本单元为完成 Hadoop 大数据处理平台的安装作准备,首先在 Windows 系统中安装虚拟机 VMware;其次在 VMware 上安装 CentOS 7,并对 CentOS 7 进行了主机名、IP 地址、映射关系、防火墙、SSH 免密码登录等配置,重点学习 CentOS 7 常用操作命令的功能与使用;最后为便于操作 CentOS 7 系统,又安装了 WinSCP 和 Xshell。

学习目标

知识目标
1. 了解虚拟机 VMware 的作用。
2. 了解 CentOS 7 系统功能和优点。
3. 掌握 CentOS 7 常用操作命令功能。
4. 了解 WinSCP 工具的功能。
5. 了解 Xshell 工具的功能。

技能目标
1. 掌握虚拟机 VMware 的安装。
2. 掌握 CentOS 7 系统的安装与配置。
3. 掌握 CentOS 7 常用操作命令的使用。
4. 掌握 WinSCP 工具的安装与使用。
5. 掌握 Xshell 工具的安装与使用。

单元任务

任务 2.1 虚拟机 VMware 的安装。
任务 2.2 CentOS 7 的安装与配置。
任务 2.3 WinSCP 的安装与使用。
任务 2.4 Xshell 的安装与使用。

任务 2.1 虚拟机 VMware 的安装

任务描述

要将大数据技术应用于会计业务,就必须构建大数据环境,即安装 Hadoop 平台。目前通用的操作系统是 Windows,而 Hadoop 通常要安装在 Linux 系统中。本任务要在 Windows 系统中安装虚拟机 VMware,为安装 CentOS 7 做好准备。

关键步骤

(1) 了解虚拟机的概念和工作原理。
(2) 了解使用虚拟机的优势。
(3) 熟练掌握虚拟机的安装和配置过程。

2.1.1 认识虚拟机

2.1.1.1 虚拟机概述

虚拟机(virtual machine,VM)是指通过软件模拟的具有完整硬件系统功能的、运行在一个完全隔离环境中的完整计算机系统。实体计算机能够完成的工作在虚拟机中都能够实现。在计算机中创建虚拟机时,需要将实体机的部分硬盘和内存容量作为虚拟机的硬盘和内存容量。每个虚拟机都有独立的 CMOS、硬盘和操作系统,用户可以像使用实体机一样对虚拟机进行操作。虚拟机的实现方法是在一台物理机上安装虚拟机,一个虚拟机可跑多个程序,虚拟机技术示意图如图 2.1.1 所示。

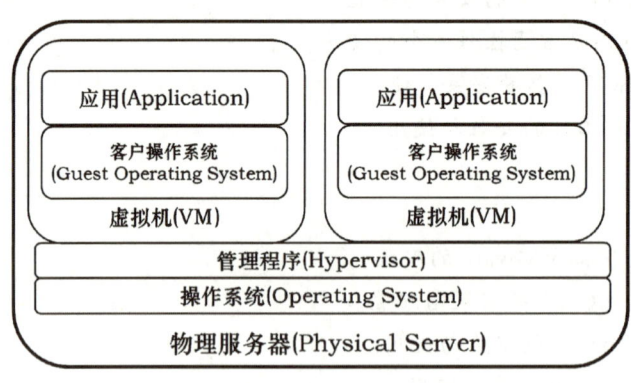

图 2.1.1 虚拟机技术示意图

2.1.1.2 虚拟机的优势

不管是在企业还是在日常学习中,虚拟机都可以发挥它的巨大优势。安装多个虚拟机部署服务实现集群的效果,可大大减少购买服务器的开销。当不需要该服务器的时候,用

户可以随时将其删除,灵活分配系统资源。虚拟机的优势具体如下:

(1) 操作灵活。虚拟化的最大优势在于从同一个控制台操作多个显示器或者系统,如 Linux 和 Windows,允许用户在操作系统之间切换。VM 模拟同时使用多台计算机的体验,对于具有多系统需求的复杂服务器有着很好的支持。此外,这些系统彼此完全独立,这为所有的操作增加了一层安全性。

(2) 减少开销、节省成本。服务器虚拟化最直接的好处也许就是无需购买那么多物理服务器,这样就可以节省成本。在大多数数据中心中,有些服务器以其最大容量运转,而其他服务器却很少使用或用于需求不高的应用程序。借助虚拟化,对硬件要求较低的操作系统和应用程序可以在同一台服务器上运行,从而节省了服务器硬件成本。其最终结果是,可以更高效地使用服务器,因此减少使用所需的物理服务器。

(3) 灾难恢复。虚拟机会定期制作其操作历史的副本,因此在发生硬件故障时数据丢失的风险很小。此外,虚拟环境中的硬件开销可以忽略不计,因此服务器一开始就具有较低的系统故障风险。

常用的虚拟机软件有 VMware,VirtualBox,KVM 等多种。其中,VMware 是一款领先的虚拟化软件,为用户提供强大的虚拟机平台。通过使用 VMware,用户可以在一台物理计算机上同时运行多个虚拟操作系统,实现资源的高效利用和隔离。它提供了灵活的配置选项、快速的性能和可靠的安全性,适用于个人用户、企业和数据中心。无论是开发测试、应用部署还是服务器管理,VMware 都是强大而可靠的工具,为用户提供了简单且可扩展的虚拟化解决方案。所以本书选用 VMware 介绍虚拟机的安装。

2.1.2 虚拟机的安装

2.1.2.1 安装工具准备

1) VMware 安装软件

VMware 虚拟机安装软件在 Windows 端的下载地址为:http://vmware.whswxkj.com/index.html? bd_vid = 8899204935209374782,点击"立即下载",即可下载 VMware,本书的配套资源提供一个免费版本 VMware10.7z,可下载使用。

2) WinSCP

WinSCP 是一个在 Windows 环境下使用 SSH 的开源图形化 SFTP 客户端,同时支持 SCP 协议。它的主要功能就是在本地与远程计算机之间安全地复制文件。用 WinSCP 在 Windows 和 Linux 中间传输信息及文件,特别的快捷与方便。WinSCP 的下载地址: https://winscp.net/eng/index.php。

3) CentOS 系统 iso 镜像

大数据平台一般安装在 Linux 操作系统中,最常用的 Linux 操作系统有 CentOS 和 Ubuntu,它们都是开源软件,并且都可以免费使用和下载,本书选用 CentOS 7。我们需要下载 CentOS 7 的 iso 文件 CentOS-7-x86_64-DVD-2009.iso,下载地址为:http://mirrors.cqu.edu.cn/CentOS/7.9.2009/isos/x86_64,将下载的镜像文件 CentOS-7-x86_64-DVD-2009.iso 放入 D:/tools。

2.1.2.2 安装步骤

（1）安装 VMware。找到 VMware 安装工具 VMware-workstation-full-10.0.1-1379776.exe，双击开始安装，如图 2.1.2、图 2.1.3 所示。

图 2.1.2　VMware 安装加载界面

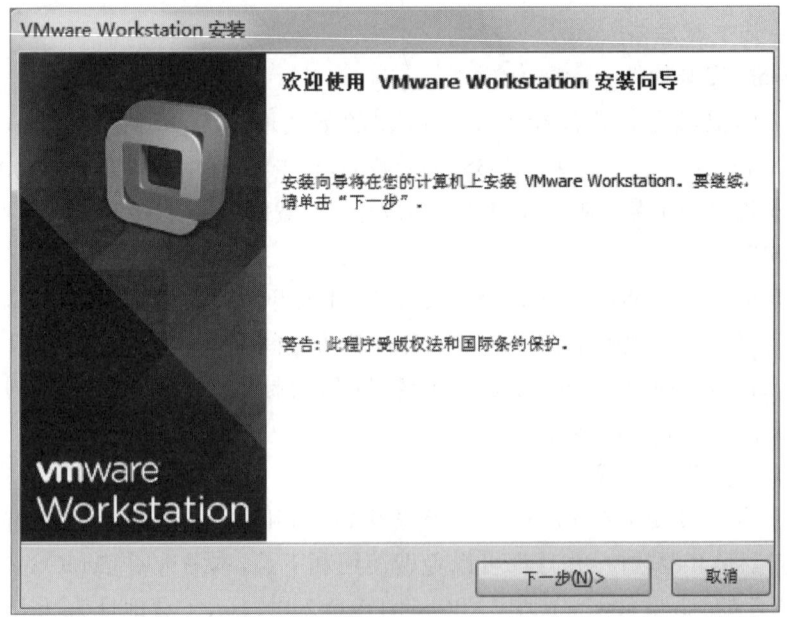

图 2.1.3　VMware 安装欢迎界面

(2)点击"下一步"按钮,出现许可协议窗口,选中"我接受许可协议中的条款"后,点击"下一步"按钮,如图2.1.4所示。

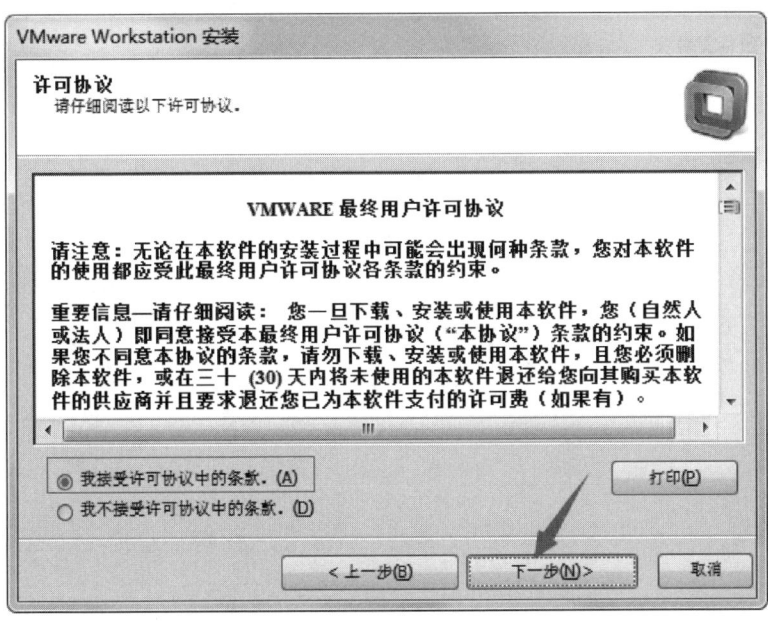

图 2.1.4　VMware 许可协议选择窗口

(3)选择接受许可协议条款后出现安装类型选择界面,如图 2.1.5 所示。

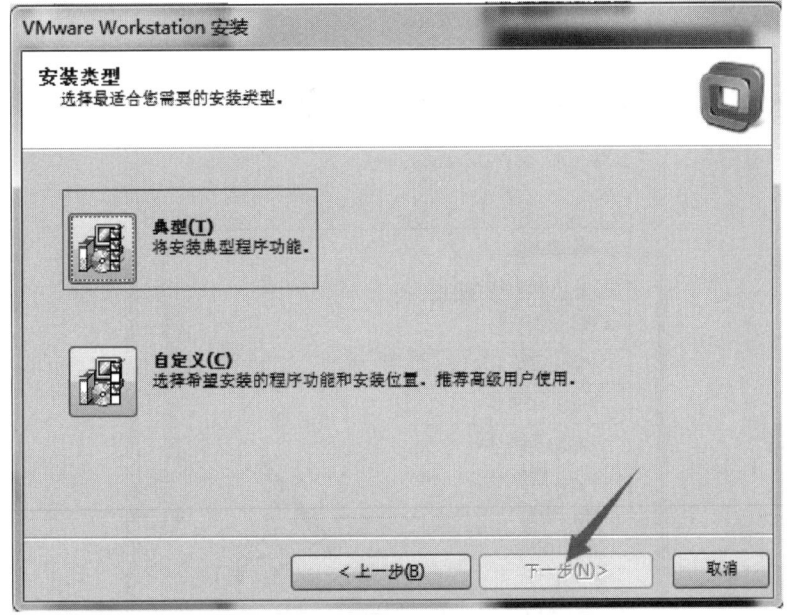

图 2.1.5　安装类型选择界面

（4）选择"典型"，点击"下一步"按钮，打开目标文件夹选择界面，如图 2.1.6 所示。

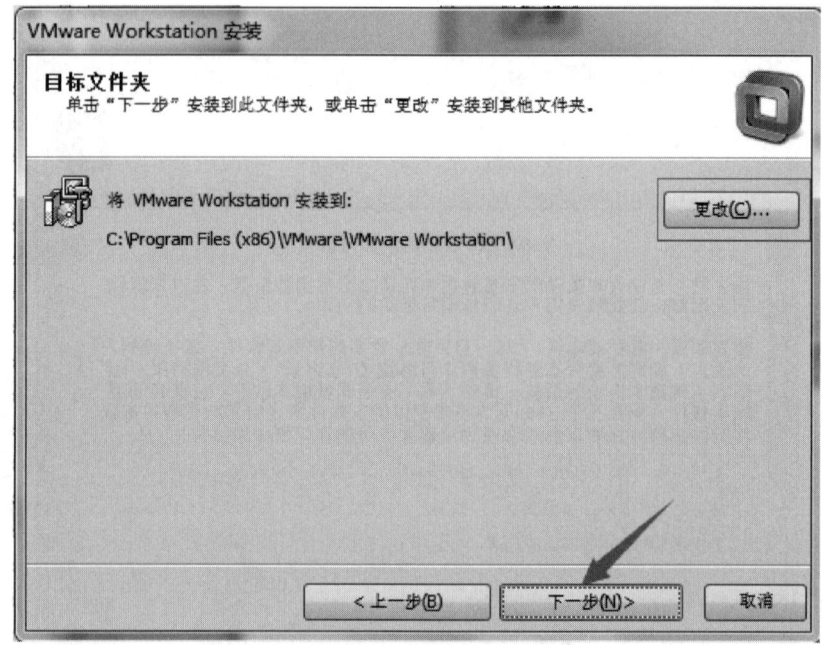

图 2.1.6　目标文件夹选择界面

（5）虚拟机 VMware Workstation 软件安装的默认文件夹为"C:\Program Files（x86）\WMware\VMware Workstation\"。如果要修改目标文件夹，则点击"更改"，点击"下一步"按钮，打开浏览文件夹界面，如图 2.1.7 所示。

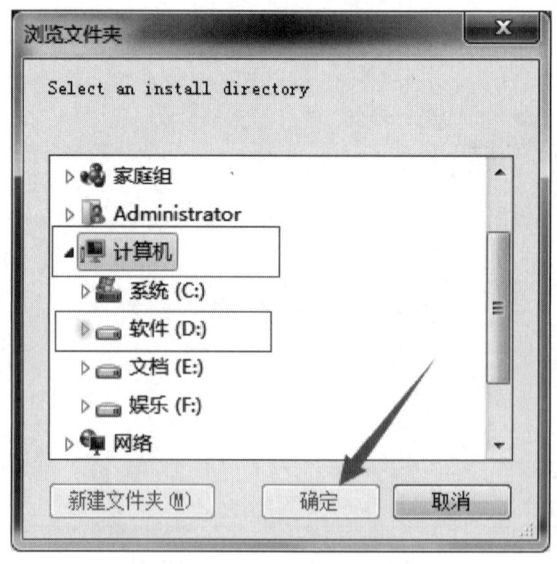

图 2.1.7　浏览文件夹界面

(6) 根据自己的需要,选择计算机磁盘,点击"计算机",选择"D:"后,点击"确定"按钮,如图 2.1.8 所示,打开选择安装文件夹界面。

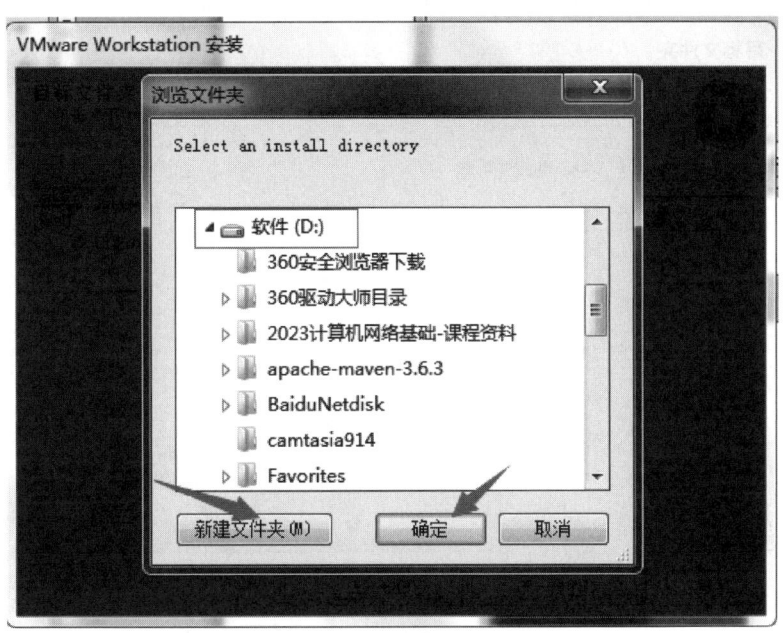

图 2.1.8 选择安装文件夹界面

(7) 因系统不允许安装在根目录上,此处需要选择或新建一个文件夹作为目标文件夹。点击"新建文件夹"按钮,点击"确定"按钮,输入文件夹名称"vmware",如图 2.1.9 所示。

图 2.1.9 新建目标文件夹"vmware"

(8) 点击"确定"按钮,目标文件夹更改完成,如图 2.1.10 所示。

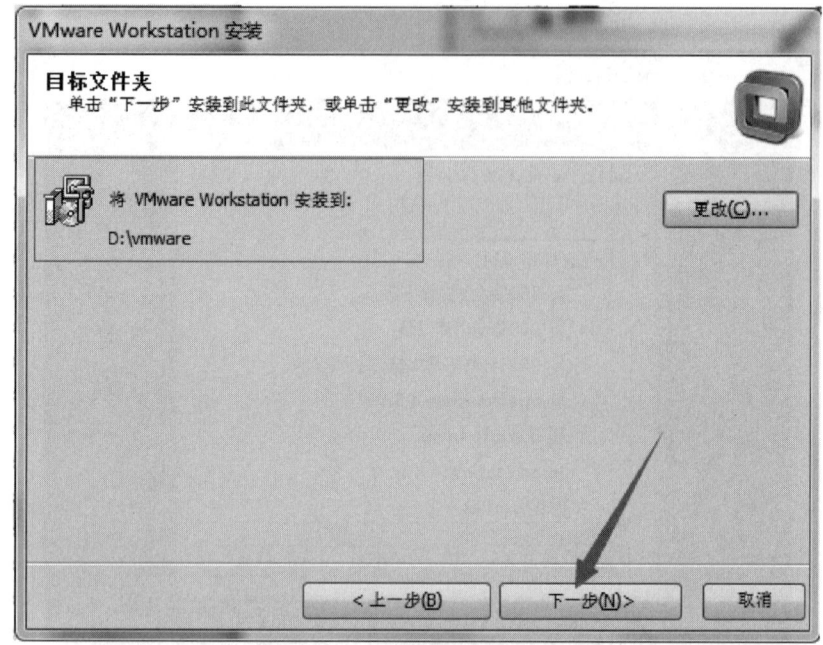

图 2.1.10　目标文件夹设置完成

(9) 点击"下一步"按钮,打开软件更新界面,如图 2.1.11 所示。

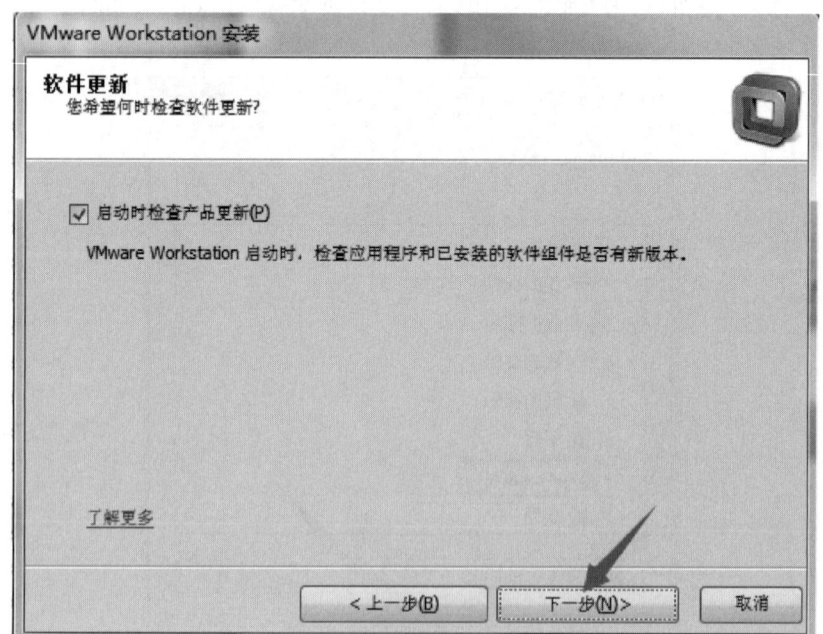

图 2.1.11　软件更新界面

(10)点击"下一步"按钮,打开用户体验改进计划界面,如图 2.1.12 所示。

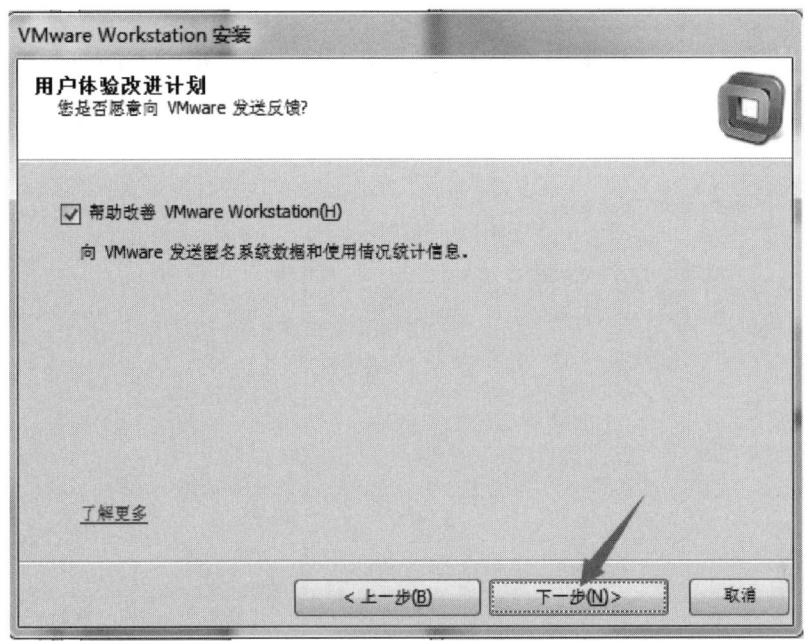

图 2.1.12　用户体验改进计划界面

(11)点击"下一步"按钮,打开创建快捷方式位置界面,这儿勾选"桌面"和"开始菜单程序文件夹",如图 2.1.13 所示。

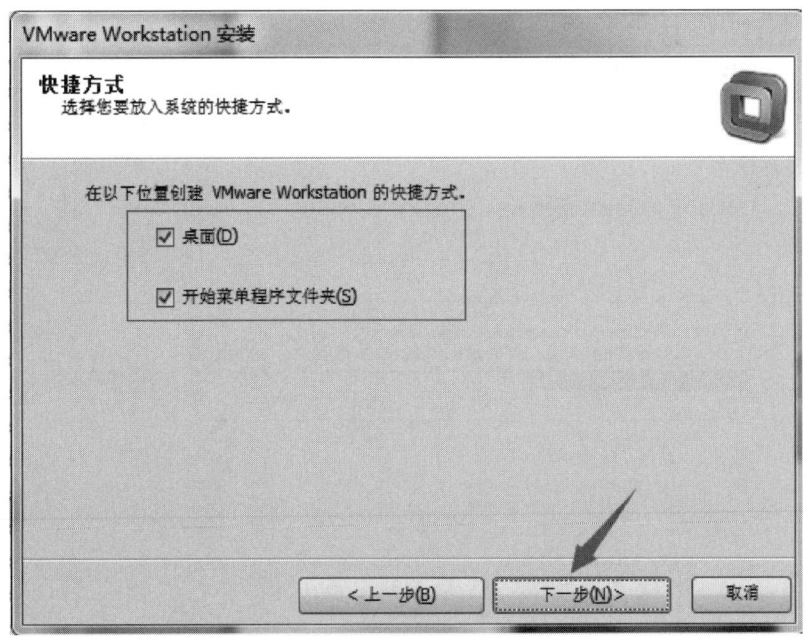

图 2.1.13　创建快捷方式位置界面

（12）点击"下一步"按钮，打开已准备好执行请求操作界面，如图 2.1.14 所示。

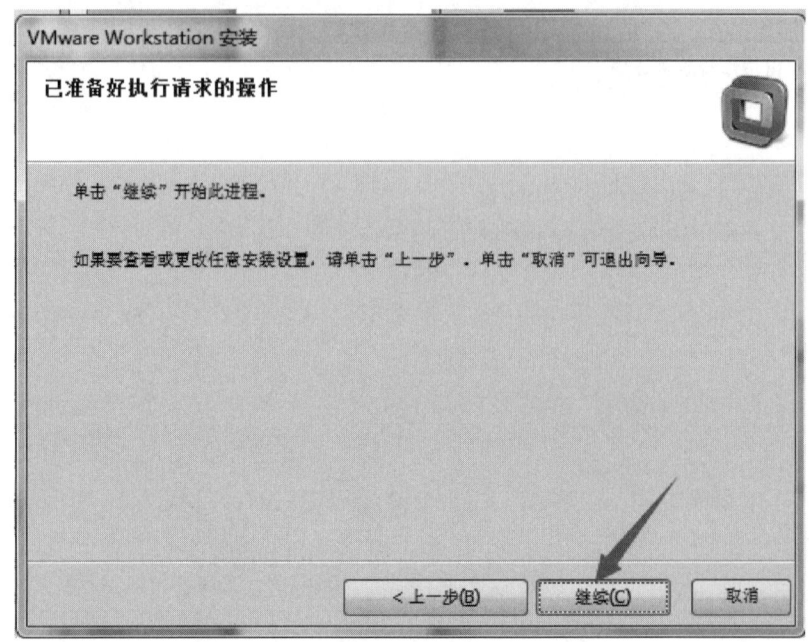

图 2.1.14　已准备好执行请求操作界面

（13）点击"继续"按钮，打开正在执行请求的操作界面，如图 2.1.15 所示。

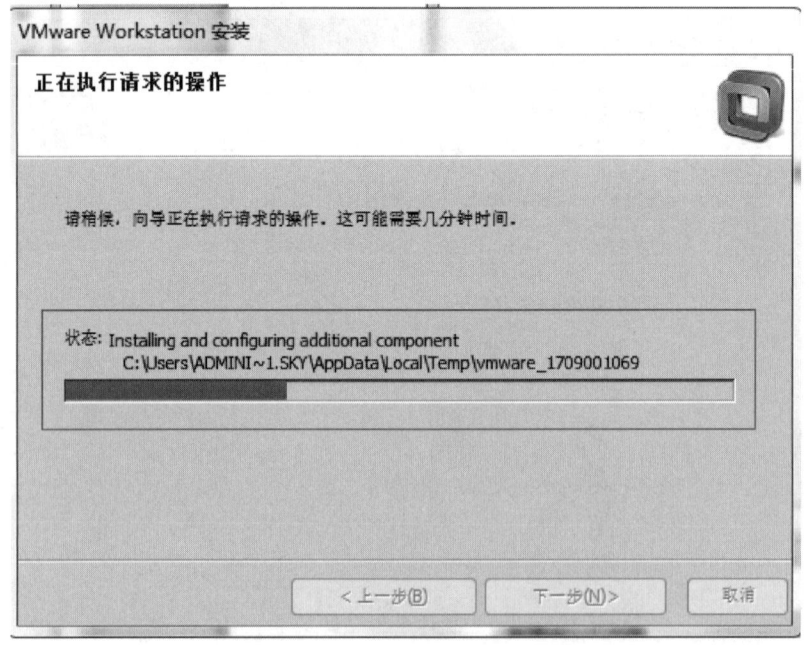

图 2.1.15　正在执行请求的操作界面

(14) 等待几分钟,当安装进度条满格后,安装向导完成,如图 2.1.16 所示。

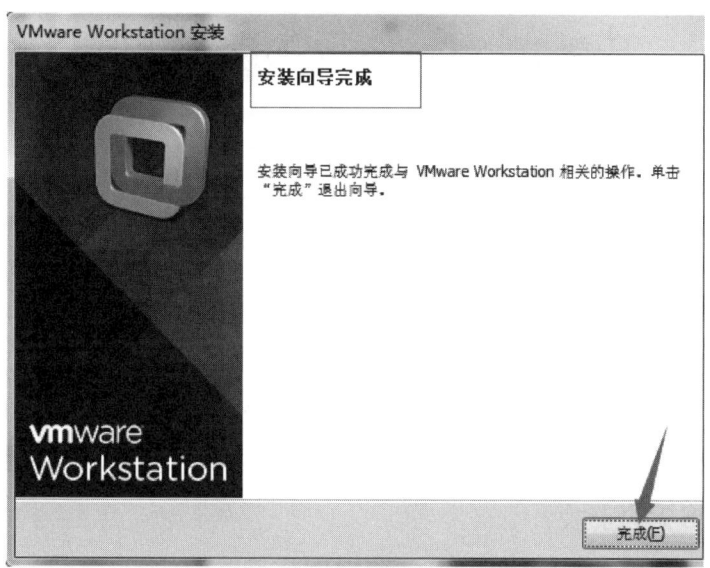

图 2.1.16　安装向导完成

(15) 点击"完成"按钮,完成 VMware Workstation 的安装。查看电脑桌面和开始菜单,出现了 VMware Workstation 图标和菜单项,如图 2.1.17 所示。

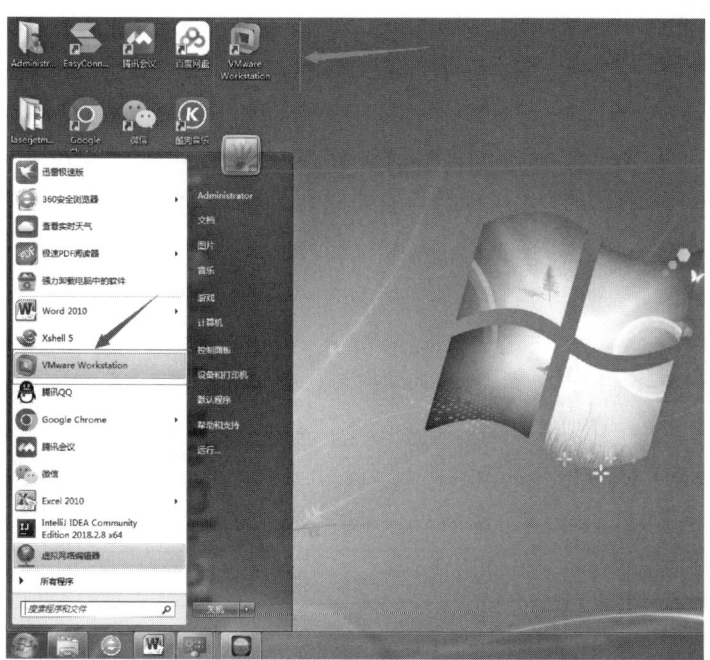

图 2.1.17　VMware Workstation 图标和菜单项

至此,完成了虚拟机软件 VMware Workstation 的安装。

任务 2.2　CentOS 7 的安装与配置

任务描述

本任务要在虚拟机 VMware 中安装 CentOS 7 系统,并学会 CentOS 7 命令的使用。

关键步骤

(1) 熟练掌握 CentOS 7 的安装流程。
(2) 熟练掌握 CentOS 7 的配置流程。
(3) 熟练掌握 CentOS 7 常用操作命令的使用。

2.2.1　CentOS 7 的安装

(1) 双击桌面上的 VMware Workstation 图标,打开虚拟机,如图 2.2.1 所示。

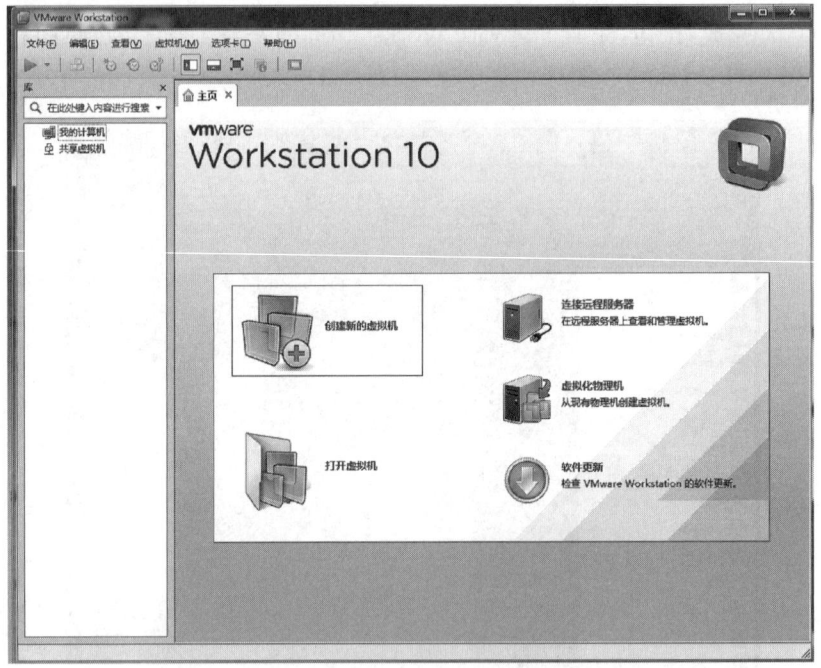

图 2.2.1　VMware 主界面

(2) 点击"创建新的虚拟机"图标,进入虚拟机设置向导界面,这里建议初学者选择"典型(推荐)"单选按钮,如图 2.2.2 所示。

(3) 点击"下一步"按钮,打开"新建虚拟机向导"界面,若初学者已准备好 Linux 系统的映像文件(.iso 文件),此处可选择"安装程序光盘映像文件(iso)"单选按钮,并通过"浏览"

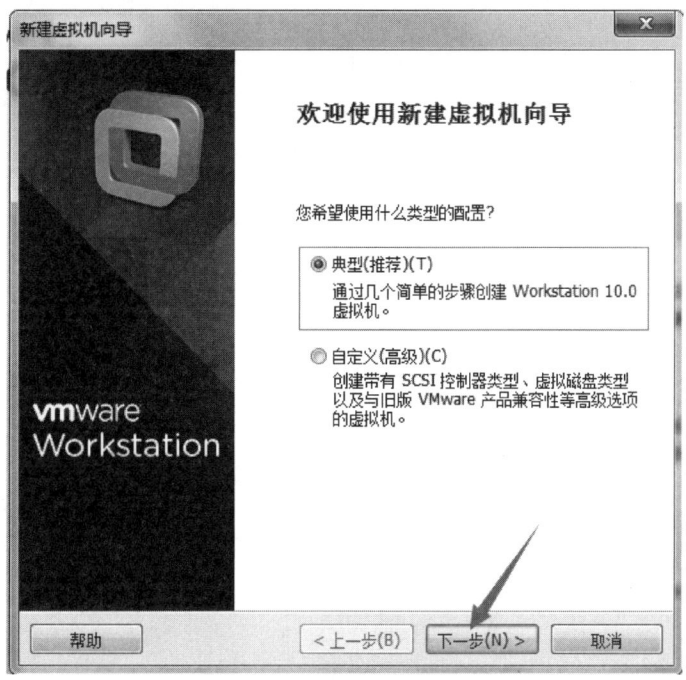

图 2.2.2 安装类型界面

按钮找到要安装 Linux 系统的 .iso 文件,这里找到 CentOS-7-x86_64-DVD-2009.iso,如图 2.2.3 至图 2.2.5 所示。

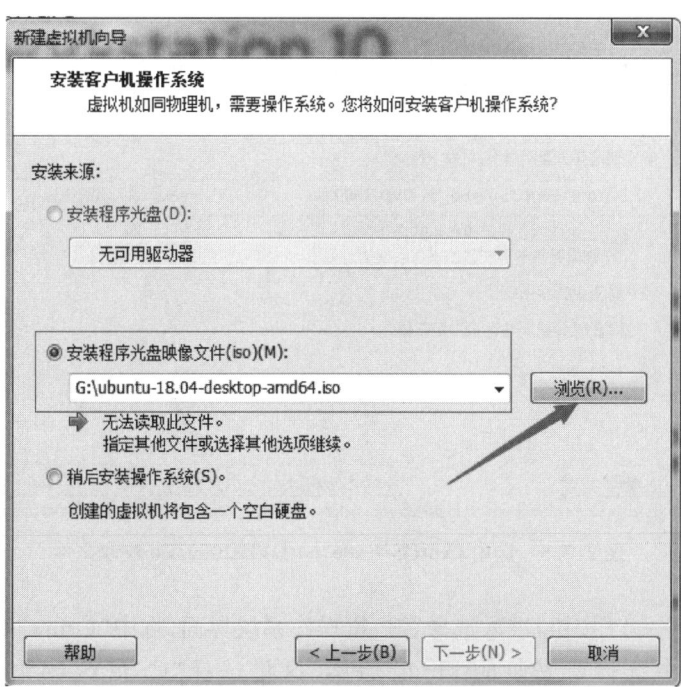

图 2.2.3 安装客户机操作系统界面

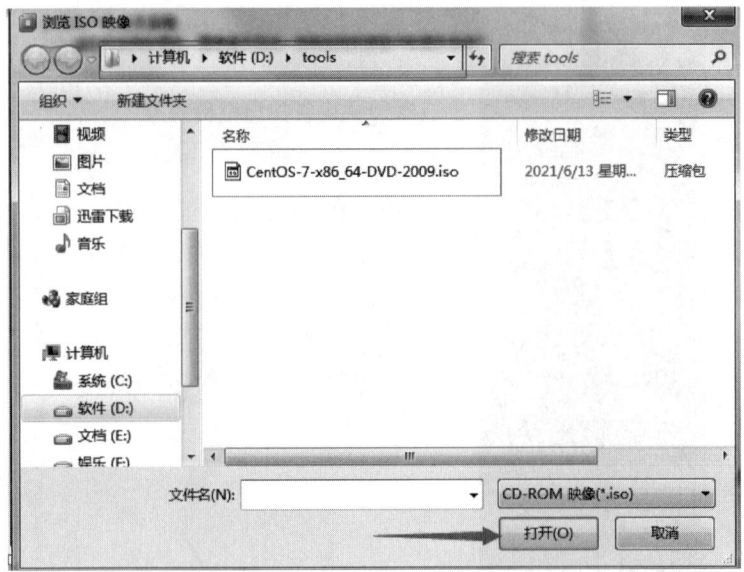

图 2.2.4 找到 CentOS-7-x86_64-DVD-2009.iso 映像文件

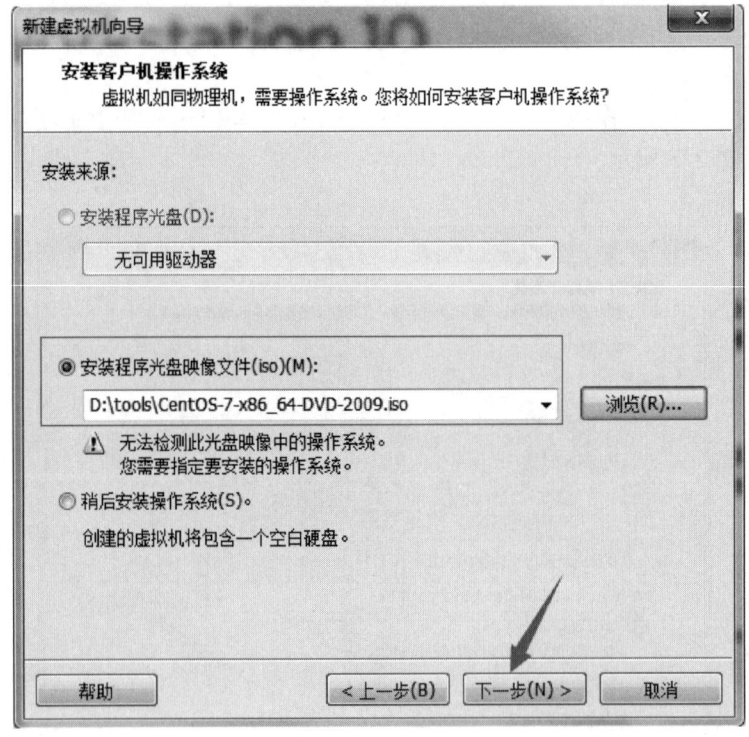

图 2.2.5 选中 CentOS-7-x86_64-DVD-2009.iso 映像文件

（4）点击"下一步"按钮，进入选择客户机操作系统界面，选中"Linux"单选按钮并在"版本"下拉列表框中选择要安装的 Linux 版本，这里选择"CentOS 64 位"，如图 2.2.6、图 2.2.7 所示。

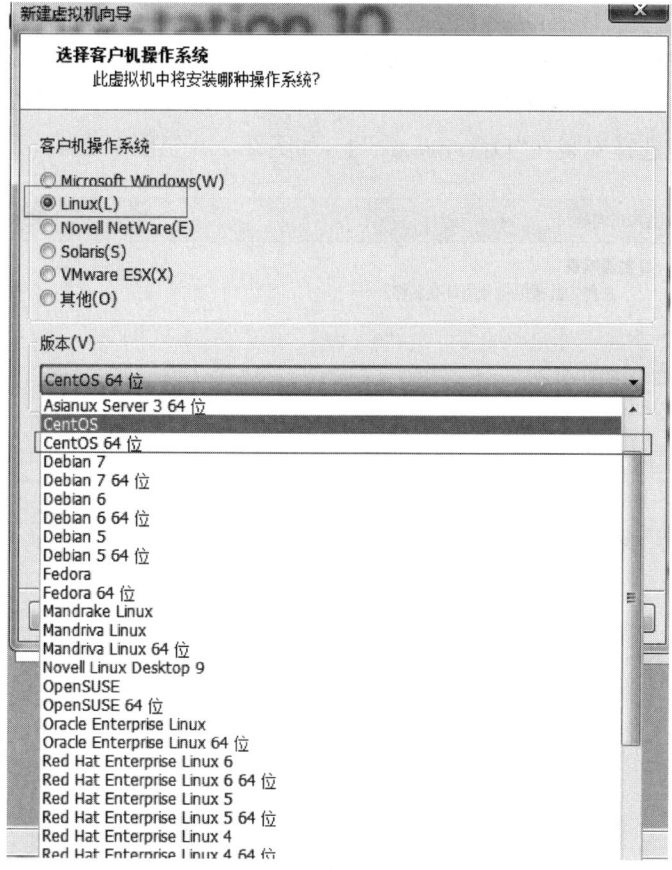

图 2.2.6 选择客户机操作系统界面

图 2.2.7 选中客户机操作系统界面

（5）点击"下一步"按钮，进入命名虚拟机界面，给虚拟机起一个名字，如选 CentOS，然后单击"浏览"按钮，选择虚拟机系统安装文件的保存位置，默认保存在"C:\Users\Administrator.SKY-20220811DYE\Documents\Virtual Machines"下，可以重新选择或新建一个文件夹，这里选择安装在"D:\vmware"上，如图 2.2.8 至图 2.2.10 所示。

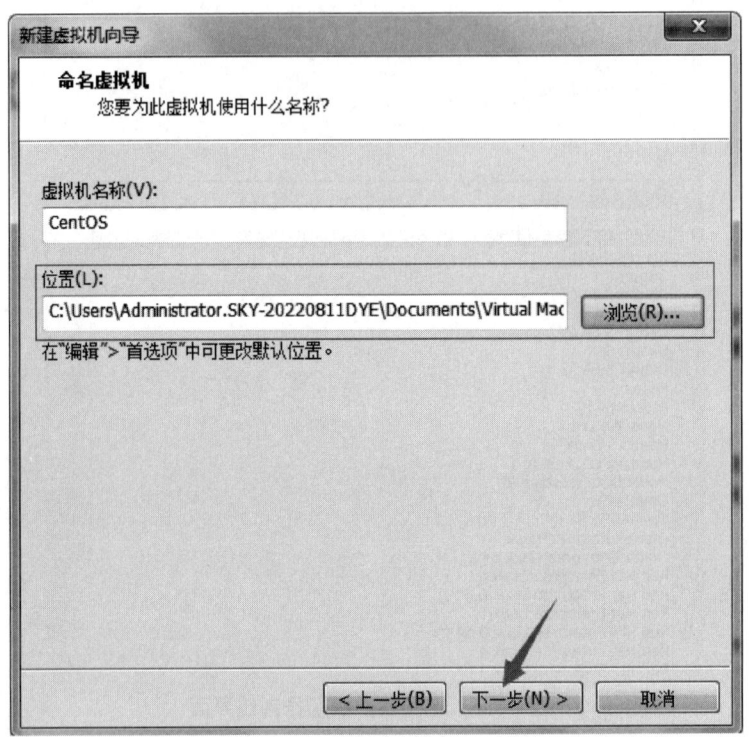

图 2.2.8　命名虚拟机界面

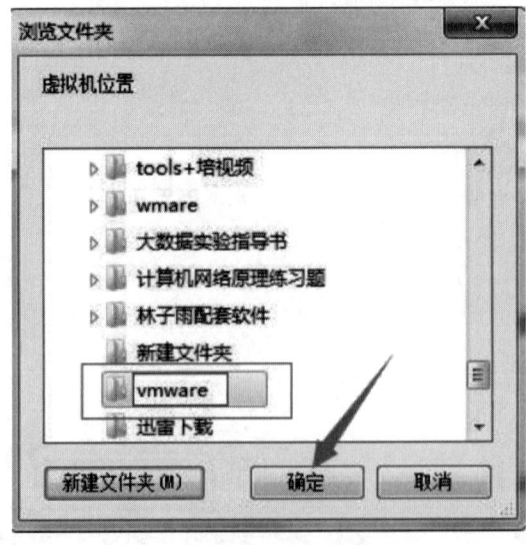

图 2.2.9　选择目标文件夹"vmware"

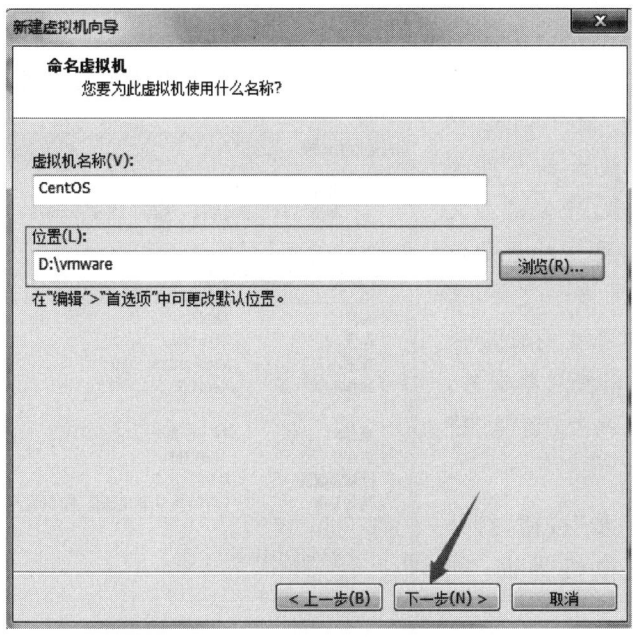

图 2.2.10　选中目标文件夹"D:\vmware"

（6）单击"下一步"按钮，进入指定磁盘容量界面。默认虚拟硬盘大小为 20GB（虚拟硬盘会以文件形式存放在虚拟机系统安装目录中）。虚拟硬盘的空间可以根据需要调整大小，但不用担心其占用的空间，因为实际占用的空间还是以安装的系统大小而非此处划分的硬盘大小为依据。此"指定磁盘容量"界面保持默认设置即可，如图 2.2.11 所示。

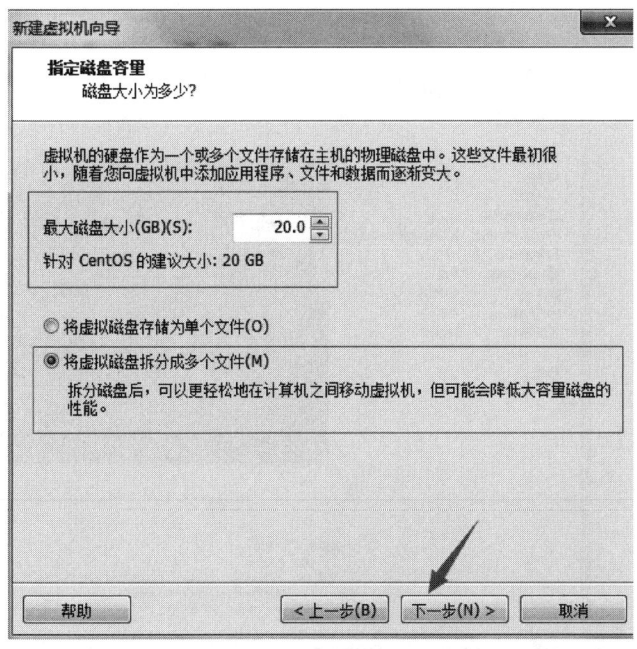

图 2.2.11　"指定磁盘容量"界面

注意

在 NTFS 格式的硬盘中,支持文件的大小为 2 TB,将虚拟磁盘文件存为单文件或者拆分为多个文件均可。而 FAT32 格式的硬盘,支持的最大单文件为 4 GB。从使用上考虑,虚拟磁盘文件必须拆分多个文件。对于是使用单文件还是拆分为多个文件,需要根据主机性能和硬盘的性能来决定。性能好的可以使用单文件,提升虚拟机性能。此处,选择"将虚拟磁盘拆分成多个文件"。

(7) 点击"下一步"按钮,打开已准备好创建虚拟机界面,如图 2.2.12 所示。

(8) 点击"完成"按钮,回到 VMware Workstation 界面,"我的计算机"下出现了"CentOS",如图 2.2.13 所示。

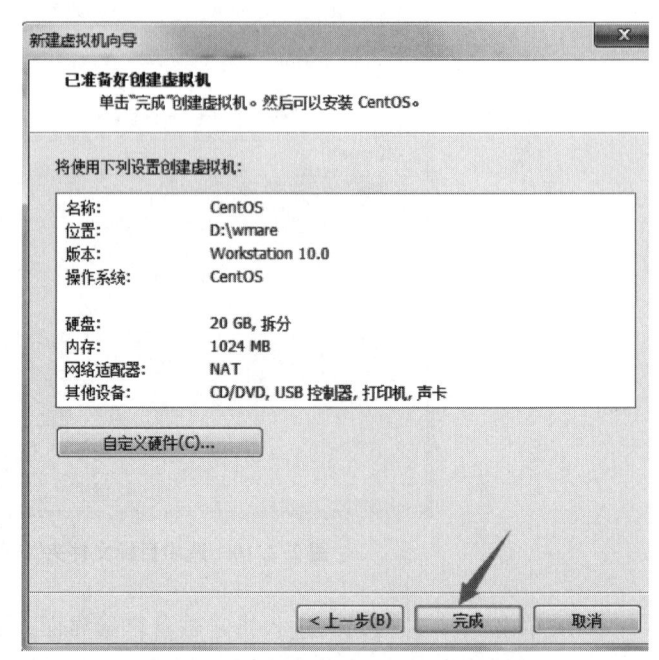

图 2.2.12　已准备好创建虚拟机界面

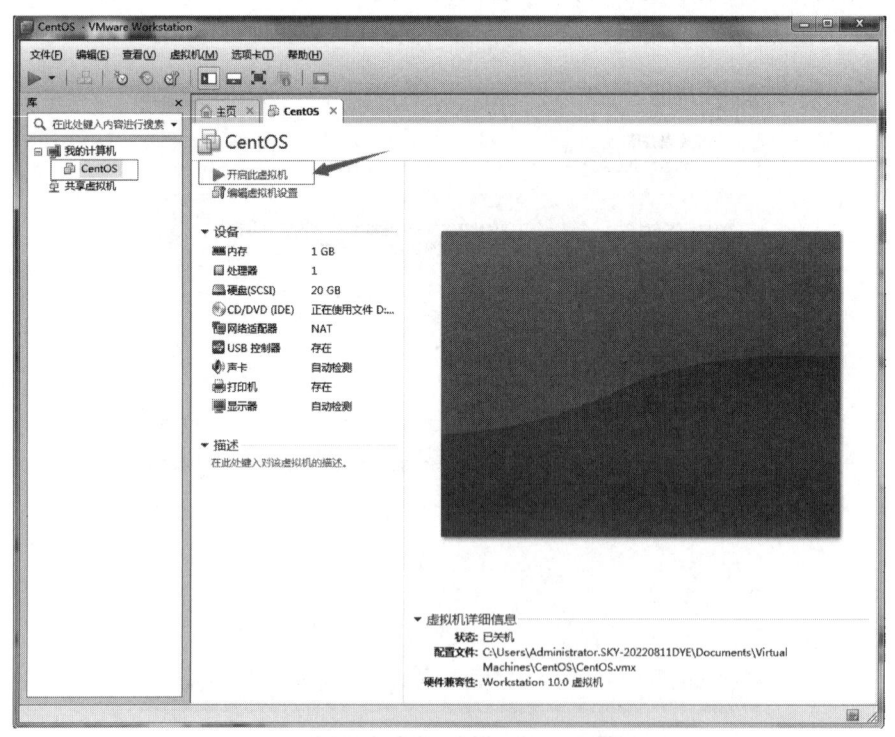

图 2.2.13　VMware Workstation 界面

(9) 点击"开启此虚拟机",开始安装 CentOS,安装界面及进程如图 2.2.14、图 2.2.15 所示。

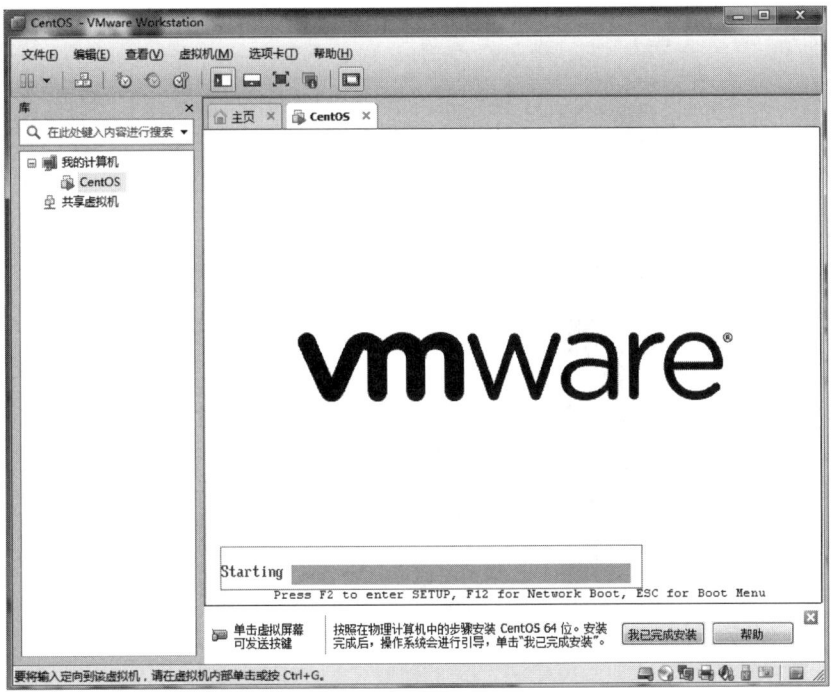

图 2.2.14　开始安装 CentOS 界面

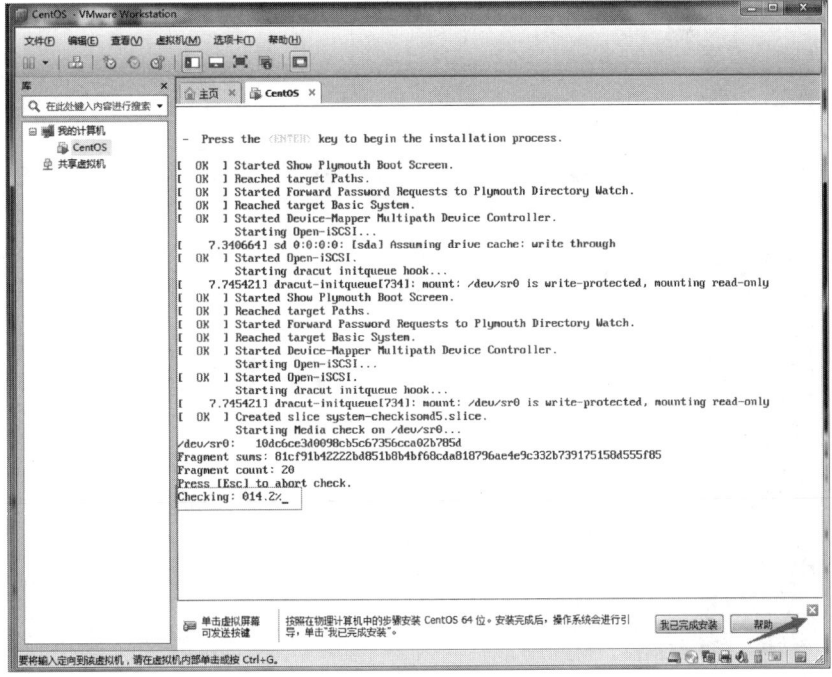

图 2.2.15　CentOS 安装进程

(10) 等待 Checking 进度达到 100% 后,进入 CentOS 7 安装欢迎界面,如图 2.2.16 所示。

图 2.2.16　CentOS 7 安装欢迎界面

(11) 选择"中文"语言,"简体中文(中国)"后,点击"继续"按钮,打开安装信息摘要界面,如图 2.2.17 所示。

图 2.2.17　安装信息摘要界面

（12）点击"系统"—"安装位置"，打开安装目标位置界面，如图 2.2.18 所示。

图 2.2.18　安装目标位置界面

（13）点击"完成"按钮，打开安装信息摘要界面，如图 2.2.19 所示。

图 2.2.19　安装信息摘要界面

（14）点击"开始安装"按钮，系统开始安装，出现安装进度条，如图 2.2.20 所示。

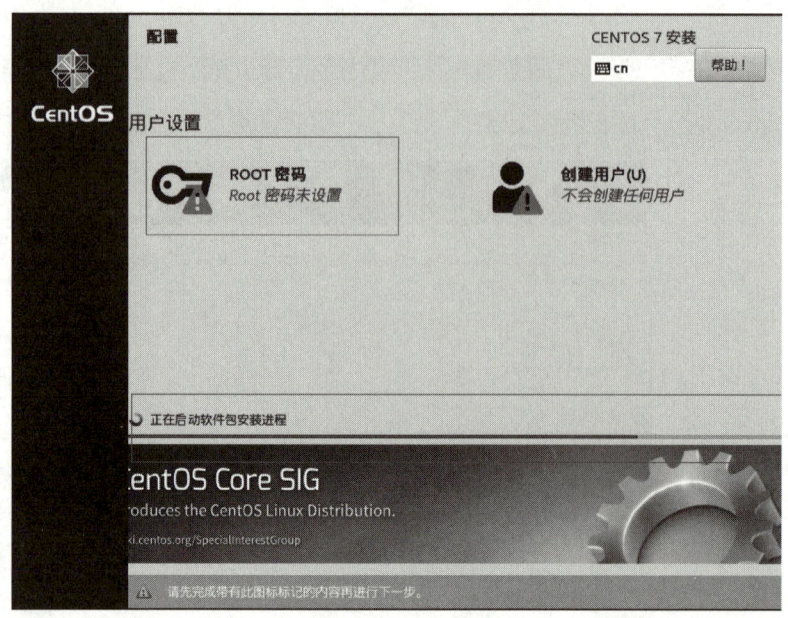

图 2.2.20 系统安装界面

（15）点击"用户设置"—"ROOT 密码"，设置 root 用户密码，为了便于记忆，这里将密码设置为"root123"，确认密码"root123"，如图 2.2.21 所示。

图 2.2.21 设置 root 用户密码

在进行用户信息设置的同时，系统仍然在进行装载与配置。

(16) 点击"完成"按钮，观察安装进度条，等待安装完成，如图 2.2.22 所示。

图 2.2.22　执行安装

(17) 等待几分钟后，安装进度条满格，CentOS 系统安装完成，如图 2.2.23 所示。

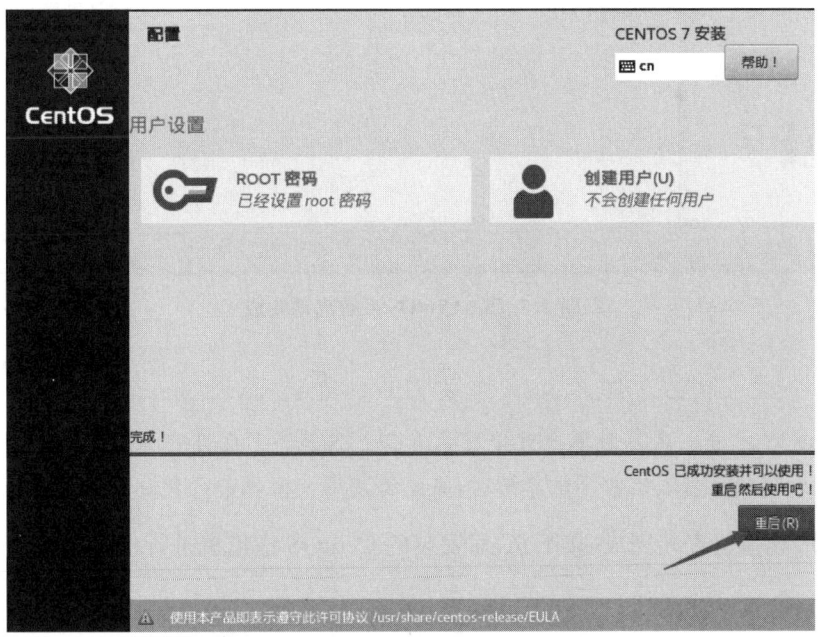

图 2.2.23　CentOS 系统安装完成

(18) 点击"重启"按钮，重启虚拟机，启动 CentOS 系统，如图 2.2.24 所示。

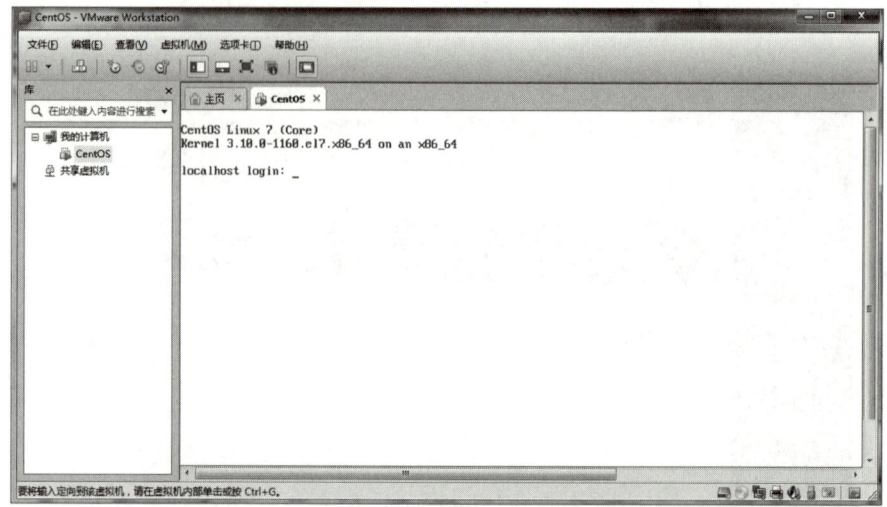

图 2.2.24　启动 CentOS 系统

（19）输入用户名：root，密码：root123，CentOS 系统启动完成，如图 2.2.25 所示。

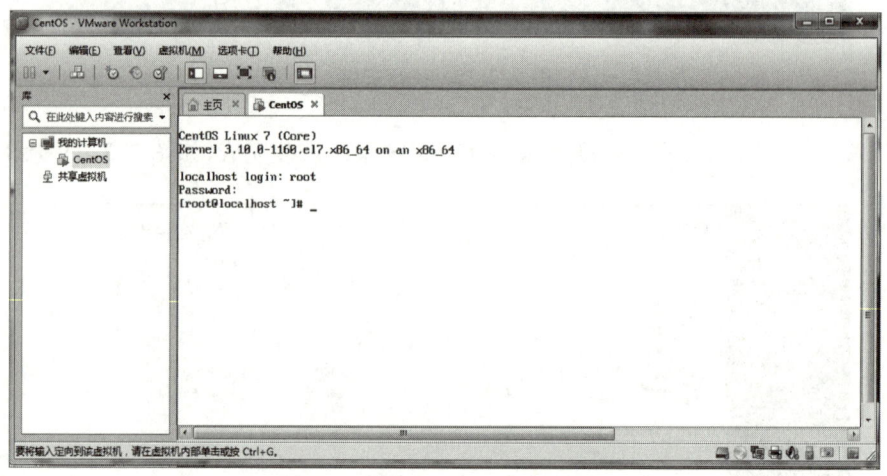

图 2.2.25　CentOS 系统启动完成

> **注意**
>
> 在 CentOS 中输入密码时不会直接显示字符。这是为了保证安全性，防止他人看到用户的密码。当我们输入密码后按下回车键时，系统将使用该密码进行身份验证或其他操作。

CentOS 虚拟机安装完成，接下来，对安装的 CentOS 虚拟机进行相应的配置。

2.2.2　CentOS 7 的配置

2.2.2.1　修改主机名

CentOS 7 自带 vi 编辑器，vim 是 vi 的升级版本，它不仅兼容 vi 的所有指令，而且还有一些新的特性，如多级撤消、易用性、语法加亮、可视化操作、对 vi 的完全兼容等，用户可以把 vim 当成 vi 来使用。所以编者推荐使用 vim 编辑器。vim 编辑器的下载、安装以及修改主机名的操作如下。

第 1 步：下载 vim 编辑器。

在 CentOS 7 命令行输入如下代码下载 vim 编辑器：

```
yum search vim
```

下载 vim 编辑器的过程如图 2.2.26 所示。

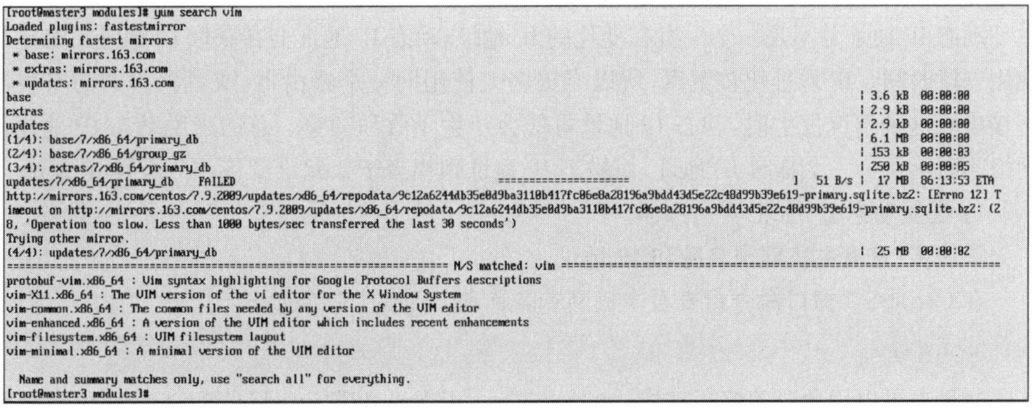

图 2.2.26　下载 vim 编辑器

第 2 步：安装 vim 编辑器。

在 CentOS 7 命令行安装 vim 编辑器，命令如下：

```
yum install -y vim*
```

安装 vim 编辑器的过程如图 2.2.27 所示。

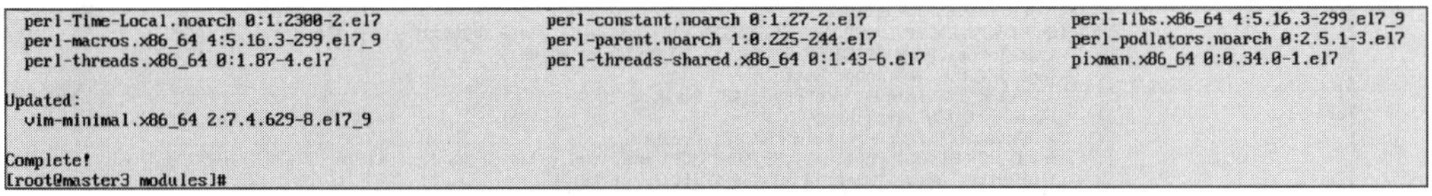

图 2.2.27　安装 vim 编辑器

第 3 步：修改主机名。

在 CentOS 7 中，修改主机名，立即生效，命令如下：

```
hostnamectl set-hostname master
bash
```

修改主机名运行结果如图 2.2.28 所示。

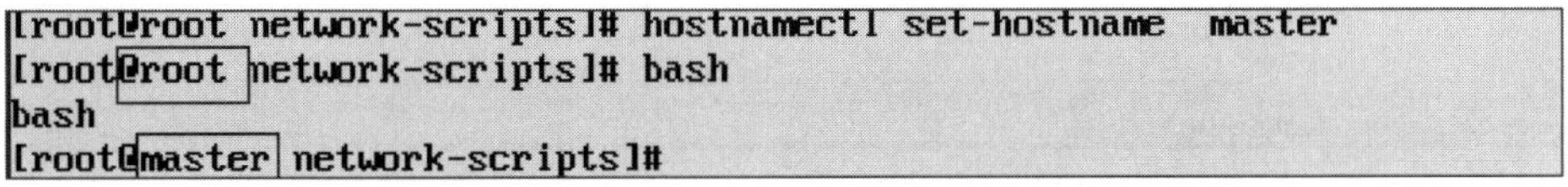

图 2.2.28　修改主机名运行结果

可以看到,输出的主机名由 root 已经修改为 master,说明已经正确修改了主机名。

2.2.2.2 配置 IP 地址

IP 地址有两种形式,即动态 IP 地址和静态 IP 地址。

动态 IP 地址和静态 IP 地址最大的区别是动态 IP 地址不需要用户记住 IP 地址,路由器等网络设备可以自动获取 IP 地址以供用户上网,而静态 IP 地址则是一个分配给用户固定的上网 IP 地址。大部分情况下两者基本没有区别,但是当动态 IP 地址与其他人的 IP 地址发生冲突时,就需要使用静态 IP 地址来维持网络的稳定性。

动态 IP 地址并不是一个一直在变化的 IP 地址,动态 IP 地址会在获取 IP 地址后稳定地使用一段时间。IP 地址比较宝贵,所以当很多人使用同一个路由器,或者路由器与路由器直接串联这种情况发生时,动态 IP 地址可能会产生矛盾和冲突。总的来说动态 IP 地址是网络不断给用户一个临时 IP 地址,而静态 IP 地址则相当于分配给设备一个永久 IP 地址。

1) 配置动态 IP 地址

第 1 步:查看主机网卡名称和 IP 地址。

在 CentOS 7 窗口命令行查看主机网卡名称和 IP 地址,命令如下:

```
ip address
```

这里也可以用命令的缩写格式,如"ip a""ip ad""ip add""ip addr"等,查看网卡名称及地址,运行结果如图 2.2.29 所示。

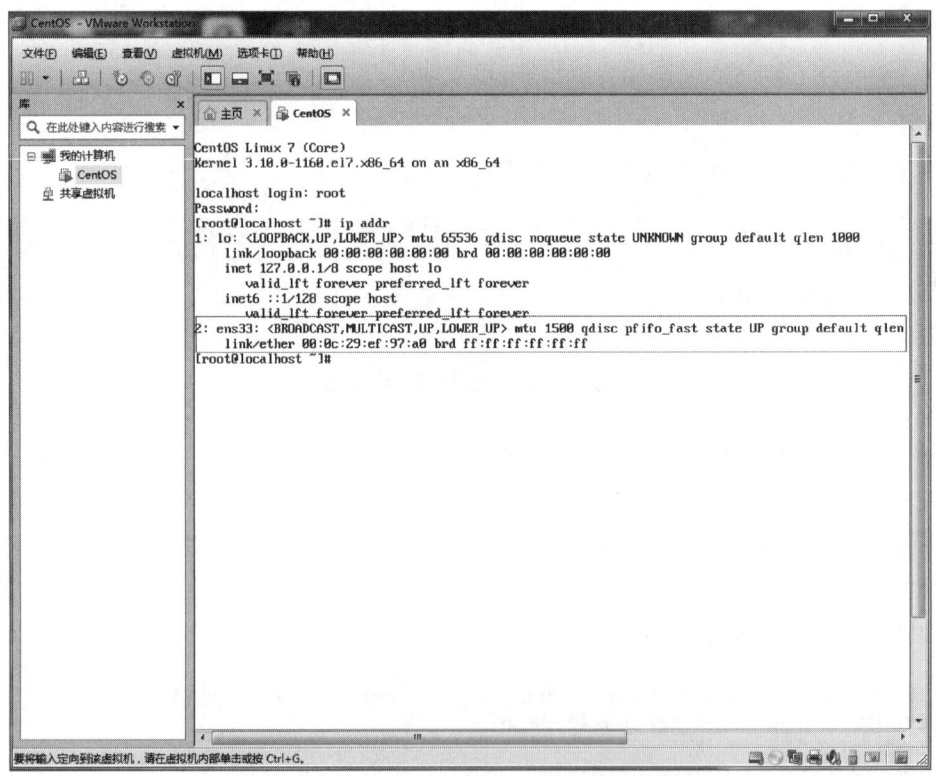

图 2.2.29　查看网卡名称及地址命令运行结果

可见网卡名称为 ens33,刚安装好的 CentOS 7 虚拟机未发现有 IP 地址。

第 2 步:配置主机动态 IP 地址。

给主机配置动态 IP 地址,找到网卡配置文件 ifcfg-ens33,修改相应代码,命令如下:

```
cd /etc/sysconfig/network-scripts    #设置当前目录
vi ifcfg-ens33                       #修改网卡配置文件
```

进入 ens33 的配置页面,如图 2.2.30 所示。

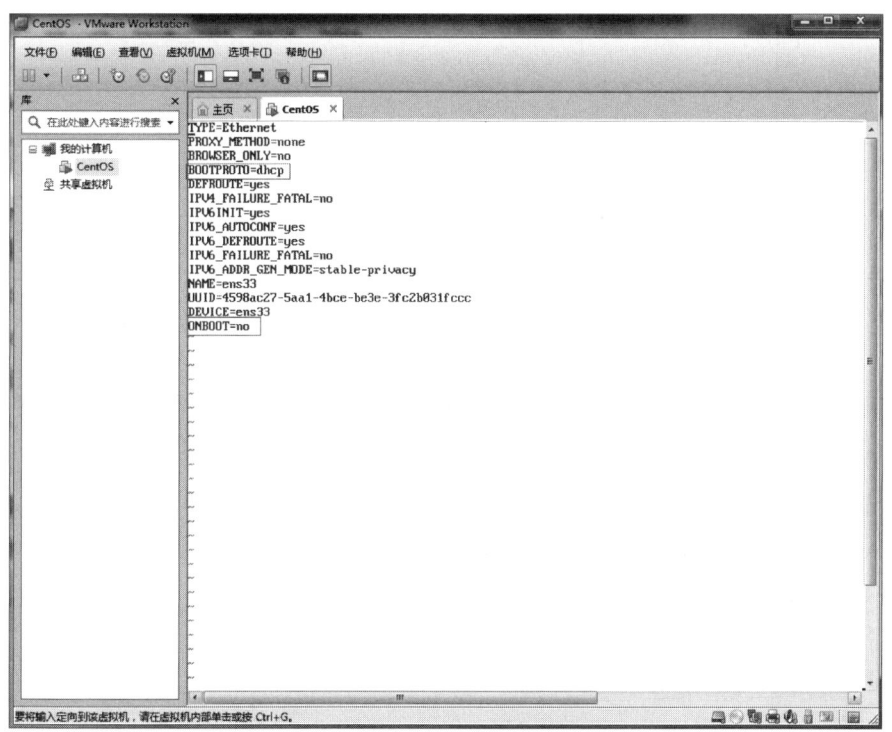

图 2.2.30　ens33 的配置界面

修改 ens33 的参数,将 BOOTPROTO 设置为动态主机配置协议"dhcp",ONBOOT 设置为"yes"。在插入"Insert"模式下,修改如下代码:

```
BOOTPROTO = dhcp
ONBOOT = yes
```

修改结束后,在 Insert 状态下,按 Esc 键,键入":wq!"就可以回到之前的命令行,如图 2.2.31、图 2.2.32 所示。

第 3 步:重启网络。

网卡地址参数修改好后,要重新启动网络,才可生效,动态获取 IP 地址,命令如下:

```
systemctl restart network
```

再次执行 ip addr 命令,发现网卡 ens33 已经获取到 IP 地址:192.168.204.128,如图 2.2.33 所示。

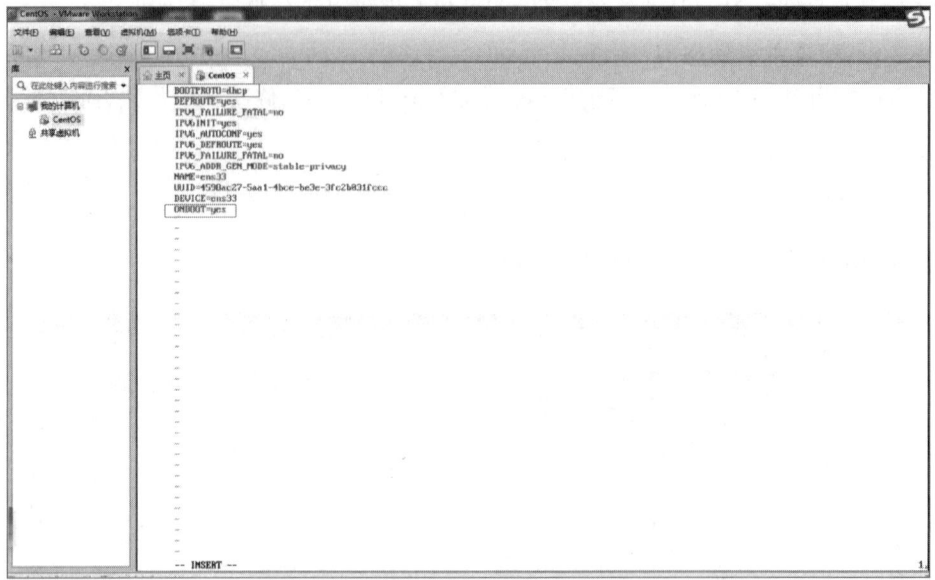

图 2.2.31　网卡 ens33 动态 IP 地址配置

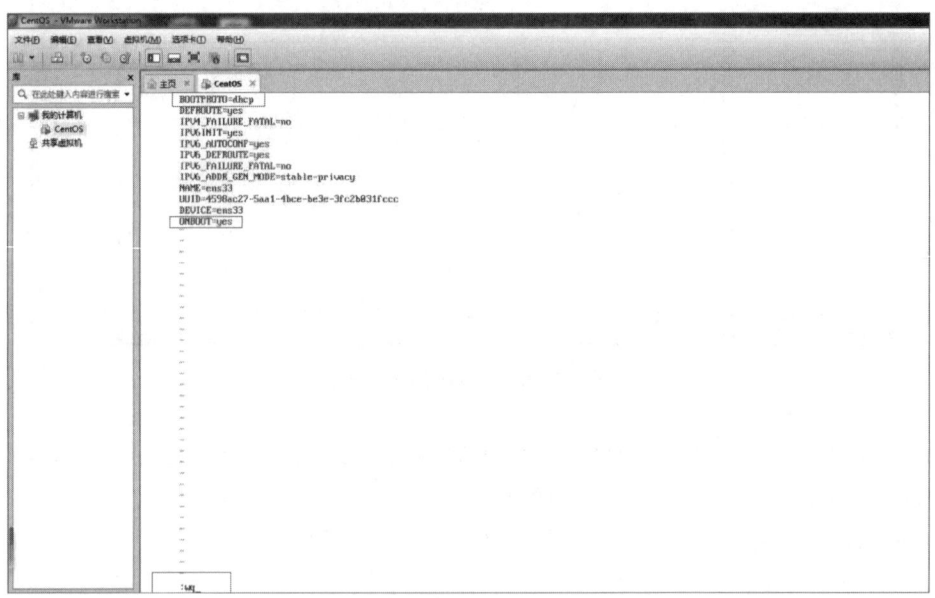

图 2.2.32　保存网卡 ens33 配置信息

第 4 步:联网测试。

网卡动态获取 IP 地址,需要测试网络连通性,看是否可以访问外网,如访问百度网站,在窗口命令行执行如下命令:

ping　www.baidu.com

可见网络设置成功,完成动态 IP 地址配置,如图 2.2.34 所示。

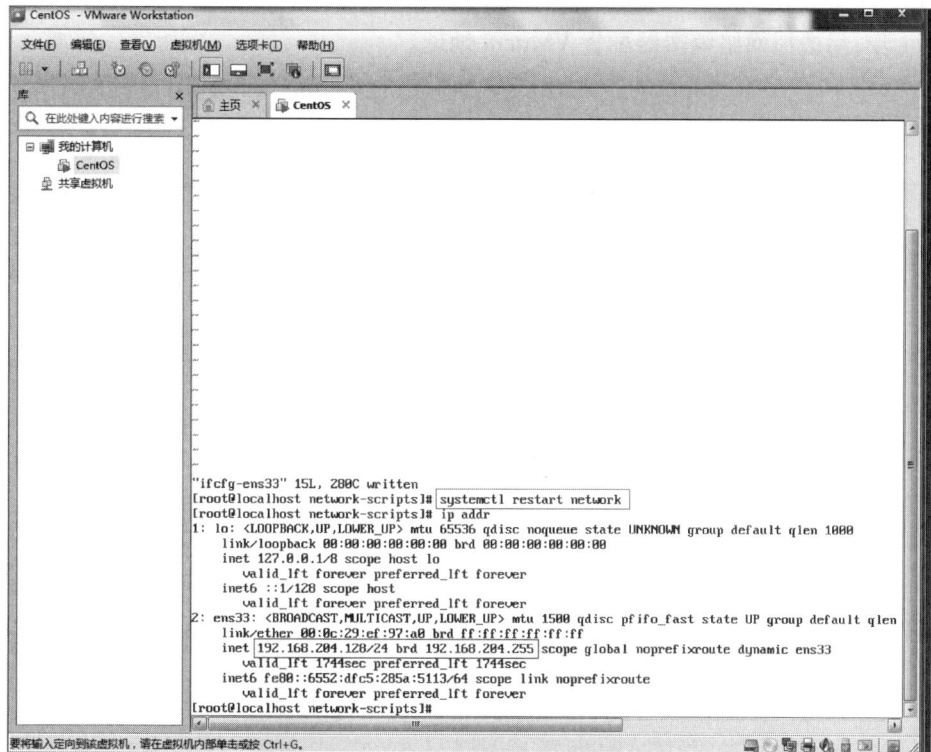

图 2.2.33　重启虚拟机网络查看已获取 IP 地址

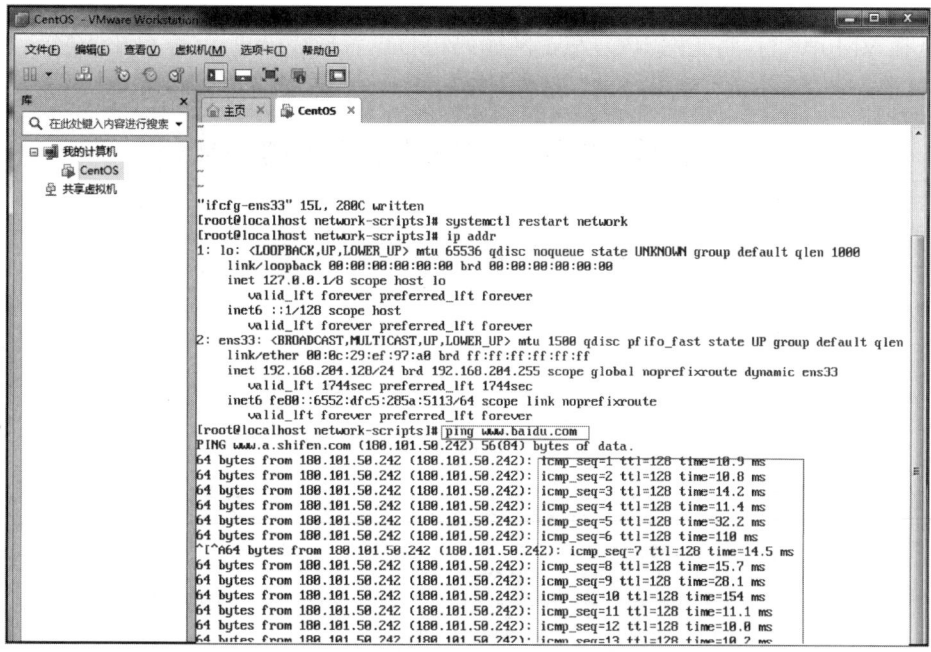

图 2.2.34　网络设置成功

2）配置静态 IP 地址

第 1 步：用虚拟网络编辑器配置 **VMnet8** 地址。

在 VMware Workstation 虚拟机顶端菜单栏选择"编辑"—"虚拟网络编辑器",如图 2.2.35 所示。

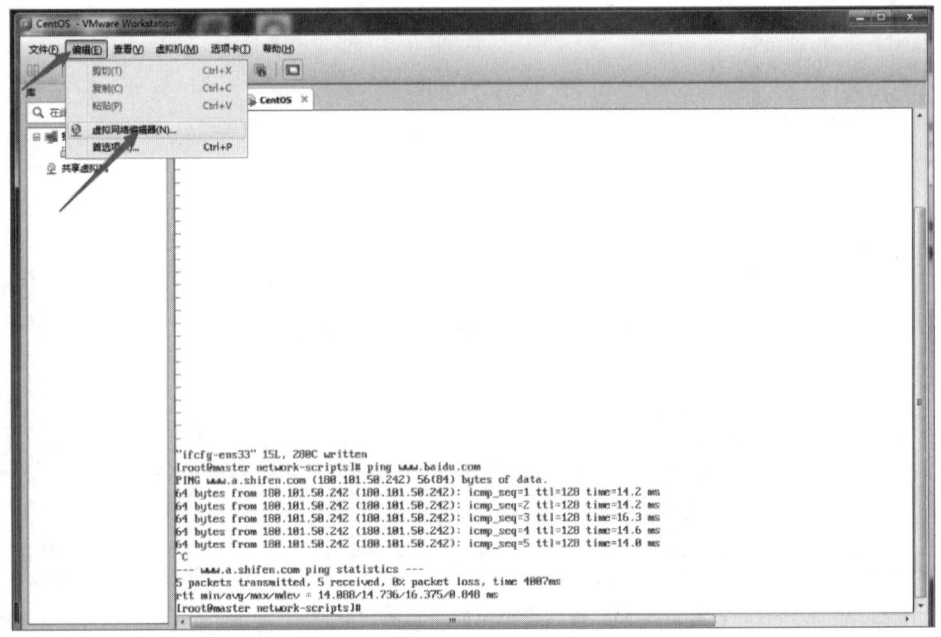

图 2.2.35　选择虚拟网络编辑器

选择 VMnet8 行,将子网 IP(I)和子网掩码(M)设置成 Windows 系统中 VMnet8 同一网段 IP 地址和子网掩码,点击"NAT 设置"按钮,再点击"确定"按钮,如图 2.2.36 所示。

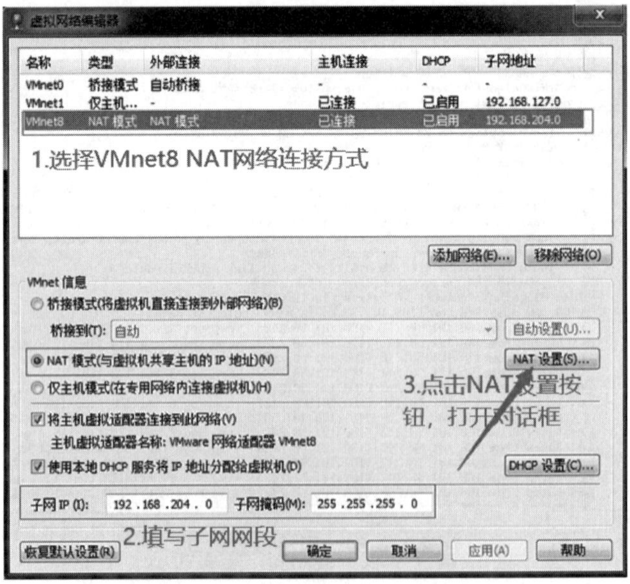

图 2.2.36　配置虚拟网络编辑器

打开 NAT 设置窗口后,设置网关 IP 地址,如图 2.2.37 所示。

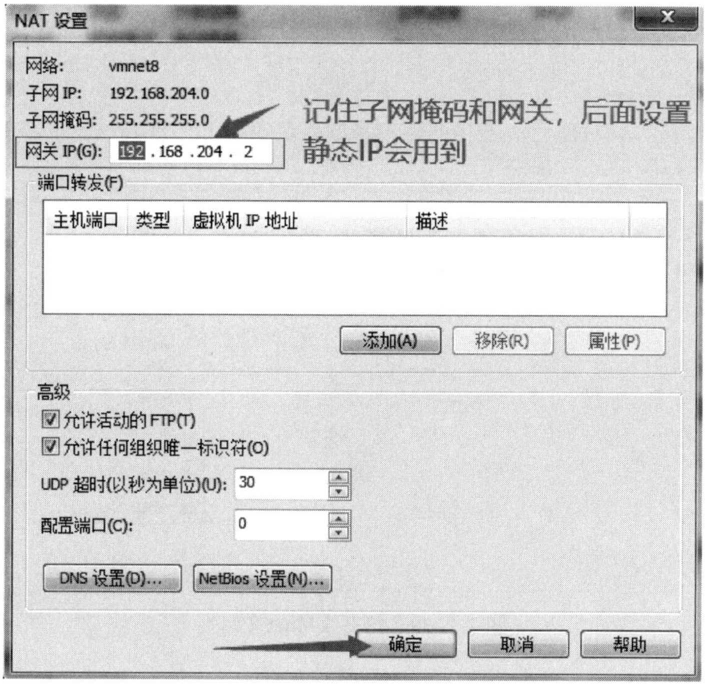

图 2.2.37　NAT 设置

点击"确定"按钮,完成虚拟网络编辑器配置。

第 2 步:配置 Windows 系统的 VMnet8 地址。

回到 Windows 系统,打开"开始"菜单—"控制面板"—"网络和 Internet"—"网络连接"—"网络和共享中心"—"更改适配器设置"窗口,如图 2.2.38 所示。

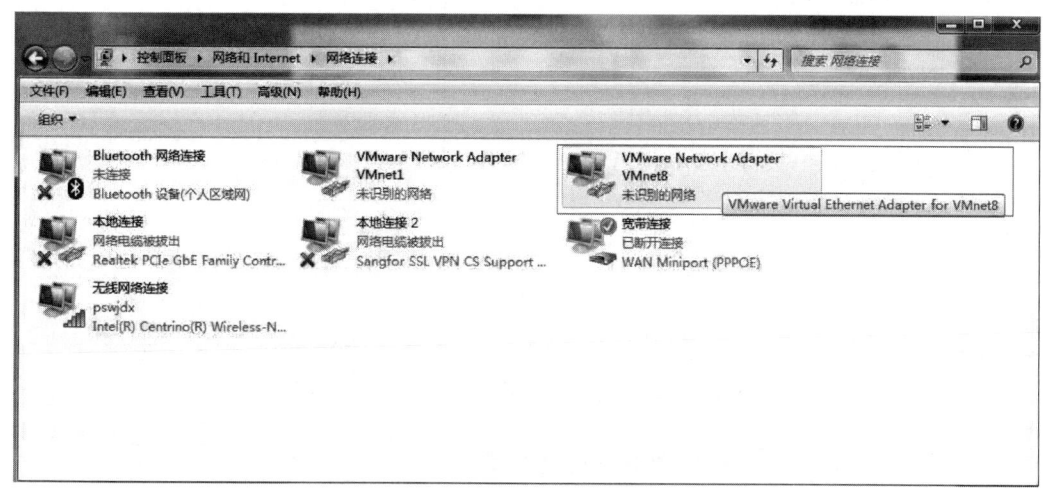

图 2.2.38　适配器设置窗口

用鼠标右击"VMware Network AdapterVMnet8"—"属性",打开"属性"设置窗口,查看"Internet 协议版本 4(TCP/IPv4)属性",查看 IP 地址,可见该 IP 地址和 IP 子网掩码与虚拟机中 VMnet8 同一网段,即"192.168.204.0"和"255.255.255.0",如图 2.2.39、图 2.2.40所示。

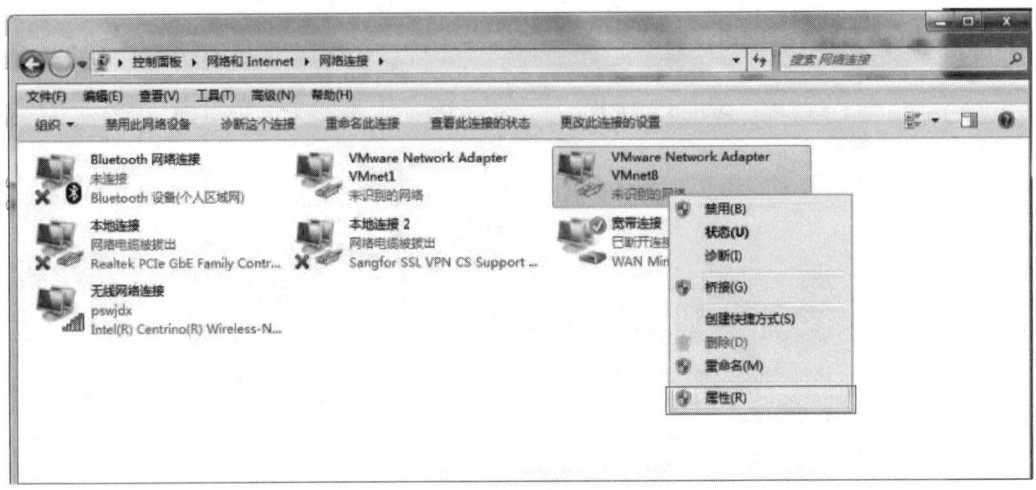

图 2.2.39　打开 VMnet 8 属性

图 2.2.40　查看 Windows 系统中 VMnet8 网段和子网掩码

第 3 步:查看 Windows 系统 DNS 服务器配置。

继续在 Windows 系统中查看 DNS 服务器,用鼠标右击"开始"—"运行",输入 cmd 命令,打开 Windows 的命令行窗口,如图 2.2.41 至图 2.2.43 所示。

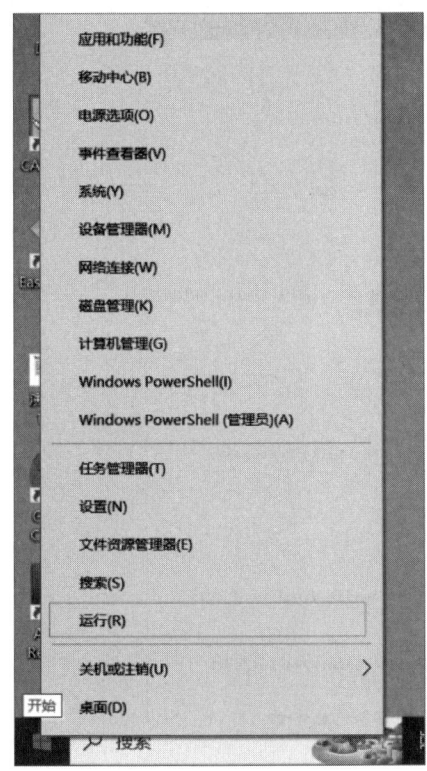

图 2.2.41　打开命令行窗口

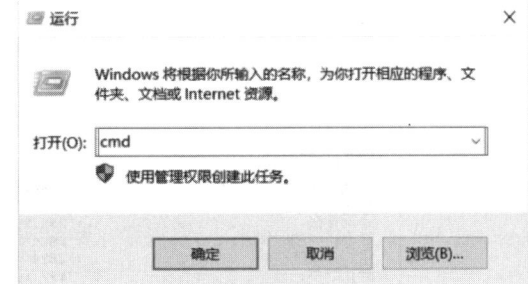

图 2.2.42　输入命令 cmd

图 2.2.43　命令行窗口

查看 Windows 系统网络配置信息，输入命令：

ipconfig /all

发现 DNS 服务器地址有两个，分别为"192.168.1.1""192.168.0.1"，如图 2.2.44 所示，该地址将被设置为虚拟机静态 IP 地址的域名服务器 DNS 地址。

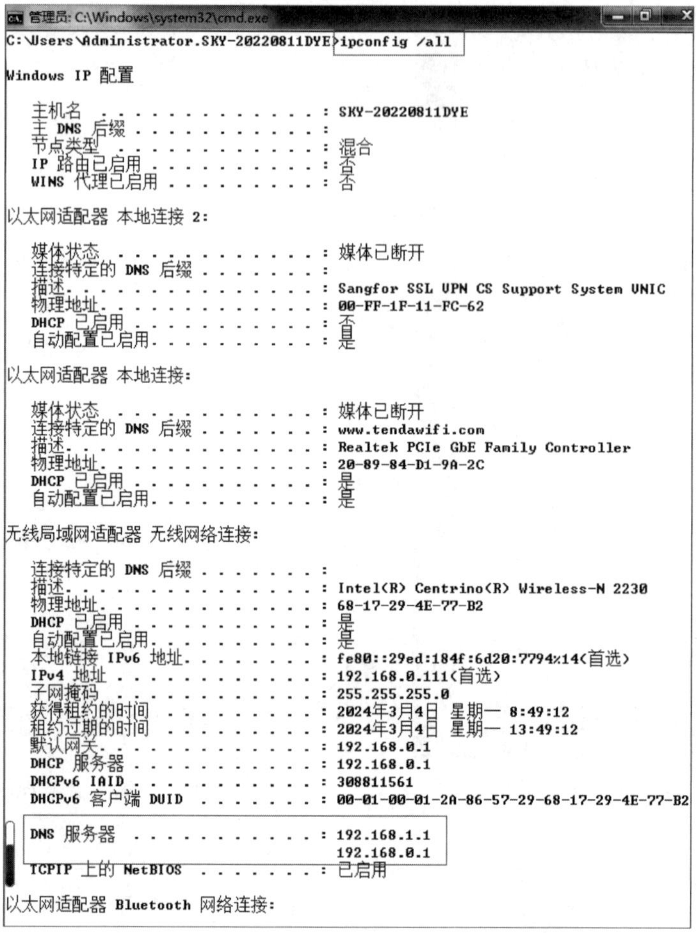

图 2.2.44　查看 Windows 系统网络配置信息

第 4 步：设置虚拟机静态 IP 地址。

再次打开虚拟机 CentOS 7，修改网卡参数，命令如下：

```
vi /etc/sysconfig/network-scripts/ifcfg-ens33
```

修改内容：

```
bootproto = static
onboot = yes
```

在最后添加 IP 地址、子网掩码、网关和 DNS 服务器，与上述查看的 VMnet 8 网段相同，域名服务器 DNS 与 Windows 系统中的 DNS 相同，具体设置根据自己的系统确定，此处设置的静态地址信息如下：

```
IPADDR = 192.168.204.129
NETWORK = 255.255.255.0
GATEWAY = 192.168.204.2
DNS1 = 192.168.1.1
DNS2 = 192.168.0.1
```

具体配置命令清单如图 2.2.45 所示。

```
主页 ×   CentOS ×
TYPE=Ethernet
PROXY_METHOD=none
BROWSER_ONLY=no
BOOTPROTO=static
DEFROUTE=yes
IPV4_FAILURE_FATAL=no
IPV6INIT=yes
IPV6_AUTOCONF=yes
IPV6_DEFROUTE=yes
IPV6_FAILURE_FATAL=no
IPV6_ADDR_GEN_MODE=stable-privacy
NAME=ens33
UUID=4598ac27-5aa1-4bce-be3e-3fc2b031fccc
DEVICE=ens33
ONBOOT=yes
IPADDR=192.168.204.129
NETWORK=255.255.255.0
GATEWAY=192.168.204.2
DNS1=192.168.1.1
DNS2=192.168.0.1
~
~
~
~
```

图 2.2.45　静态 IP 地址配置命令清单

按 Esc 键,输入":wq"保存退出编辑状态。

第 5 步:重启网络。

重启网络,再次查看地址,并测试网络连通情况,命令如下:

```
systemctl restart network
ip addr
ping  www.baidu.com
```

静态 IP 地址配置正确测试结果如图 2.2.46 所示。

```
[root@master network-scripts]# systemctl restart network
[root@master network-scripts]# ip addr
1: lo: <LOOPBACK,UP,LOWER_UP> mtu 65536 qdisc noqueue state UNKNOWN group default qlen 1000
    link/loopback 00:00:00:00:00:00 brd 00:00:00:00:00:00
    inet 127.0.0.1/8 scope host lo
       valid_lft forever preferred_lft forever
    inet6 ::1/128 scope host
       valid_lft forever preferred_lft forever
2: ens33: <BROADCAST,MULTICAST,UP,LOWER_UP> mtu 1500 qdisc pfifo_fast state UP group default qlen 1000
    link/ether 00:0c:29:ef:97:a0 brd ff:ff:ff:ff:ff:ff
    inet 192.168.204.129/24 brd 192.168.204.255 scope global noprefixroute ens33
       valid_lft forever preferred_lft forever
    inet6 fe80::6552:dfc5:285a:5113/64 scope link noprefixroute
       valid_lft forever preferred_lft forever
[root@master network-scripts]# ping www.baidu.com
PING www.a.shifen.com (180.101.50.188) 56(84) bytes of data.
64 bytes from 180.101.50.188 (180.101.50.188): icmp_seq=1 ttl=128 time=9.58 ms
64 bytes from 180.101.50.188 (180.101.50.188): icmp_seq=2 ttl=128 time=11.0 ms
^[[^A64 bytes from 180.101.50.188 (180.101.50.188): icmp_seq=3 ttl=128 time=7.61 ms
64 bytes from 180.101.50.188 (180.101.50.188): icmp_seq=4 ttl=128 time=7.53 ms
64 bytes from 180.101.50.188 (180.101.50.188): icmp_seq=5 ttl=128 time=17.8 ms
64 bytes from 180.101.50.188 (180.101.50.188): icmp_seq=6 ttl=128 time=9.72 ms
64 bytes from 180.101.50.188 (180.101.50.188): icmp_seq=7 ttl=128 time=7.22 ms
64 bytes from 180.101.50.188 (180.101.50.188): icmp_seq=8 ttl=128 time=14.9 ms
64 bytes from 180.101.50.188 (180.101.50.188): icmp_seq=9 ttl=128 time=10.5 ms
```

图 2.2.46　静态 IP 地址配置正确测试结果

可见静态地址已设置为 192.168.204.129,子网掩码为 255.255.255.0,能访问 www.baidu.com,这说明 DNS 设置正确。

2.2.2.3 配置主机名和 IP 地址的映射关系

第 1 步:修改主机名。

修改主机名的命令如下:

```
hostnamectl set-hostname [主机名]
```

将本主机名设为 master,并立即生效,命令如下:

```
hostnamectl set-hostname master
bash
```

第 2 步:配置主机名和 IP 地址的映射关系。

在 CentOS 7 中,主机名和 IP 地址的映射关系是在文件/etc/hosts 中配置的,可以通过如下代码打开/etc/hosts 文件:

```
vi /etc/hosts
```

添加主机名和 IP 地址的对应关系,以之前设置的主机名 master、IP 地址为 192.168.204.129 为例,在 hosts 文件末尾添加命令如下:

```
192.168.204.129    master
```

配置主机名和 IP 地址的映射如图 2.2.47 所示。

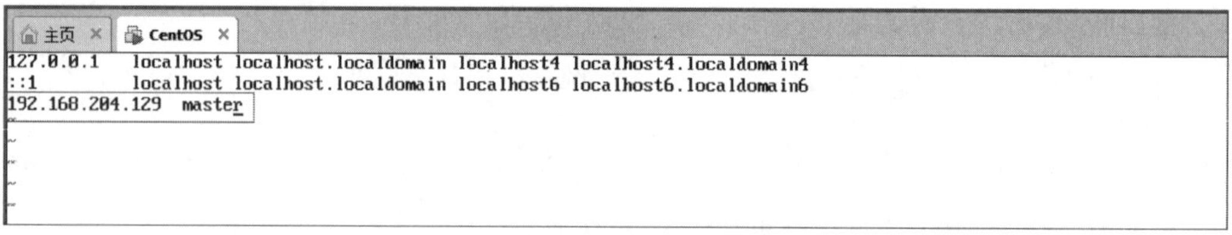

图 2.2.47　配置主机名和 IP 地址的映射

第 3 步:测试主机名和 IP 地址的映射关系。

接下来,通过 ping 主机名的形式来测试主机名和 IP 地址的映射关系是否已经配置好,命令如下:

```
ping master
```

正确 ping 通数据运行结果如图 2.2.48 所示。

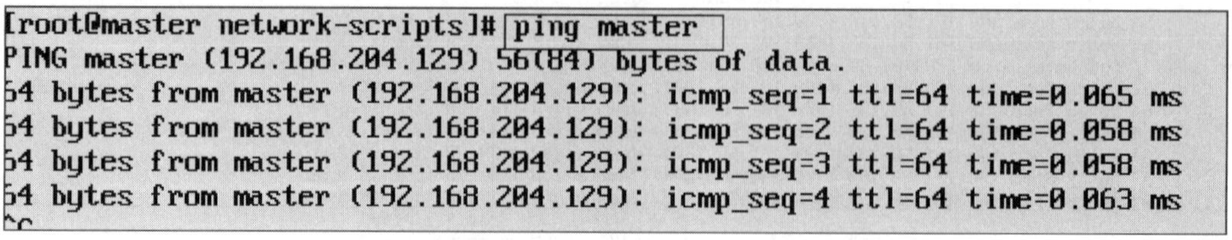

图 2.2.48　正确 ping 通数据运行结果

可以看到，通过 ping 主机名的形式能够正确 ping 通数据，说明主机名和 IP 地址映射关系已经配置好了。

2.2.2.4　关闭防火墙

防火墙开启后集群内部通信会出现各种问题。系统默认情况下，防火墙是关闭的，如果防火墙开启，则用 systemctl stop firewalld 语句关闭防火墙。在 CentOS 7 常用的防火墙操作命令如下：

```
#检查防火墙状态
systemctl status firewalld
#设置开机启用防火墙
systemctl enable firewalld.service
#设置开机禁用防火墙
systemctl disable firewalld.service
#启动防火墙
systemctl start firewalld
#关闭防火墙
systemctl stop firewalld
```

防火墙配置命令执行结果如图 2.2.49 所示。

```
[root@master network-scripts]# systemctl status firewalld
● firewalld.service - firewalld - dynamic firewall daemon
   Loaded: loaded (/usr/lib/systemd/system/firewalld.service; enabled; vendor preset: enabled)
   Active: active (running) since Mon 2024-03-04 09:22:15 CST; 12h ago
     Docs: man:firewalld(1)
 Main PID: 695 (firewalld)
   CGroup: /system.slice/firewalld.service
           └─695 /usr/bin/python2 -Es /usr/sbin/firewalld --nofork --nopid

Mar 04 09:15:58 localhost.localdomain systemd[1]: Starting firewalld - dynamic firewall daemon...
Mar 04 09:22:15 localhost.localdomain systemd[1]: Started firewalld - dynamic firewall daemon.
Mar 04 09:22:16 localhost.localdomain firewalld[695]: WARNING: AllowZoneDrifting is enabled. This is considered an insecure configuration option. It ... it now.
Hint: Some lines were ellipsized, use -l to show in full.
[root@master network-scripts]# systemctl enable firewalld
[root@master network-scripts]# systemctl disable firewalld
Removed symlink /etc/systemd/system/multi-user.target.wants/firewalld.service.
Removed symlink /etc/systemd/system/dbus-org.fedoraproject.FirewallD1.service.
[root@master network-scripts]# systemctl disable firewalld.service
[root@master network-scripts]# systemctl start firewalld
[root@master network-scripts]# systemctl stop firewalld
[root@master network-scripts]# systemctl status firewalld
● firewalld.service - firewalld - dynamic firewall daemon
   Loaded: loaded (/usr/lib/systemd/system/firewalld.service; disabled; vendor preset: enabled)
   Active: inactive (dead)
     Docs: man:firewalld(1)

Mar 04 09:15:58 localhost.localdomain systemd[1]: Starting firewalld - dynamic firewall daemon...
Mar 04 09:22:15 localhost.localdomain systemd[1]: Started firewalld - dynamic firewall daemon.
Mar 04 09:22:16 localhost.localdomain firewalld[695]: WARNING: AllowZoneDrifting is enabled. This is considered an insecure configuration option. It ... it now.
Mar 04 22:11:13 master systemd[1]: Stopping firewalld - dynamic firewall daemon...
Mar 04 22:11:14 master systemd[1]: Stopped firewalld - dynamic firewall daemon.
Hint: Some lines were ellipsized, use -l to show in full.
[root@master network-scripts]#
```

图 2.2.49　防火墙配置命令执行结果

可以看到，执行完这些命令之后，系统已经正确地关闭了防火墙。

2.2.2.5　配置 SSH 免密码登录

Hadoop 的启动和运行过程中涉及远程过程调用、登录远程服务器执行相关的命令和功能。为了使 Hadoop 能够自主完成启动并运行 MapReduce 等程序，需要配置服务器的 SSH 免密码登录。

在单台服务器上配置 SSH 免密码登录的过程比较简单，只需要在命令行执行如下命令：

```
ssh-keygen -t rsa    #生成密钥
```

输入"ssh-keygen -t rsa"后一直按回车键即可，执行结果如图 2.2.50 所示。

```
[root@master network-scripts]# ssh-keygen -t rsa
Generating public/private rsa key pair.
Enter file in which to save the key (/root/.ssh/id_rsa):
Created directory '/root/.ssh'.
Enter passphrase (empty for no passphrase):
Enter same passphrase again:
Your identification has been saved in /root/.ssh/id_rsa.
Your public key has been saved in /root/.ssh/id_rsa.pub.
The key fingerprint is:
SHA256:a4/KdBUsvQPfhvn967vQ65ALR2Ztfq9EjvvpHG3SDx0 root@master
The key's randomart image is:
+---[RSA 2048]----+
|                 |
|        o        |
|       o +       |
|      + * .      |
|     S B o+.E    |
|      o ++==+.   |
|     . + .o=Bo*  |
|      o o o o++B=|
|       o...  +OOB|
+----[SHA256]-----+
[root@master network-scripts]#
```

图 2.2.50 "ssh-keygen -t rsa"执行结果

在命令行中输入"ssh 主机名"，即可验证服务器的免密码登录，命令如下。此处不用输入密码就可以登录到 master 上，如图 2.2.51 所示。

```
cp ~/.ssh/id_rsa.pub  ~/.ssh/authorized_keys    #将生成的密钥复制到授权文件
ssh master    #登录测试
```

```
[root@master network-scripts]# ssh master
Last login: Mon Mar  4 22:31:49 2024 from master
[root@master ~]#
```

图 2.2.51 不用密码登录测试

> **注意**
>
> 首次配置好 SSH 免密码登录后，运行"ssh 主机名"登录服务器时，期间会提示"Are you sure you want to continue connecting（yes/no）？"，直接输入"yes"即可。以后再通过"ssh 主机名"登录服务器时，就没有这个提示了。退出通过 SSH 登录的服务器，执行命令"exit"，如图 2.2.52 所示。

可以看到，已经能够通过"ssh 主机名"正确登录服务器，说明 SSH 免密码登录配置成功了。至此，大数据平台 Hadoop 环境的准备工作就已经完成了。

```
[root@master network-scripts]# ssh-keygen -t rsa
Generating public/private rsa key pair.
Enter file in which to save the key (/root/.ssh/id_rsa):
Created directory '/root/.ssh'.
Enter passphrase (empty for no passphrase):
Enter same passphrase again:
Your identification has been saved in /root/.ssh/id_rsa.
Your public key has been saved in /root/.ssh/id_rsa.pub.
The key fingerprint is:
SHA256:a4/KdBUsvQPfhvn967vQ65ALR2Ztfq9EjvvpHG3SDx0 root@master
The key's randomart image is:
+---[RSA 2048]----+
|                 |
|       o         |
|      o +        |
|     + * .       |
|    S B o+.E     |
|     o ++==+.    |
|    . + .o=Bo*   |
|     o o o o++B=|
|      o....+OOB=|
+----[SHA256]-----+
[root@master network-scripts]# cp ~/.ssh/id_rsa.pub  ~/.ssh/authorized_keys
[root@master network-scripts]# ssh master
The authenticity of host 'master (192.168.204.129)' can't be established.
ECDSA key fingerprint is SHA256:r4AVgFSHY8fK1Sy4HpMZcj8GqCR0uZTAHZTmXb jCJhg.
ECDSA key fingerprint is MD5:ff:82:ef:fe:a0:a8:ae:d1:48:97:77:40:a5:e5:93:f8.
Are you sure you want to continue connecting (yes/no)? yes
Warning: Permanently added 'master,192.168.204.129' (ECDSA) to the list of known hosts.
Last login: Mon Mar  4 11:52:34 2024 from 192.168.204.1
[root@master ~]# exit
logout
Connection to master closed.
[root@master network-scripts]# ssh master
Last login: Mon Mar  4 22:31:49 2024 from master
[root@master ~]#
```

图 2.2.52　登录测试

2.2.3　CentOS 7 的常用操作命令

Linux Shell 是指一种程序,有了它,用户就能通过键盘输入指令来操作计算机。Linux Shell 会执行用户输入的命令,并且在显示器上显示执行结果。这种交互的全过程都是基于文本的,与 Windows 系统的图形化操作不同,这种面向命令行的用户界面被称为 CLI (command line interface)。在图形化用户界面 GUI(graphical user interface)出现之前,人们一直是通过命令行界面 CLI 来操作计算机的。现在,基于图形界面的工具越来越多,许多工作都不必使用 Shell 就可以完成了。然而,专业的 Linux 用户认为 Shell 是一个非常有用的工具,学习 Linux 时一定要学习 Shell,至少要掌握一些基础知识和基本的命令。

1) 文件与目录操作命令

文件与目录操作命令可以在 Linux 系统上创建文件和目录,并对文件和目录进行各种操作,常用的文件与目录操作命令及其功能如表 2.2.1 所示。

表 2.2.1　常见的文件与目录操作命令及其功能

命令	解析
cd /home	进入"/home"目录
cd ..	返回上一级目录

(续表)

命令	解析
cd ../..	返回上两级目录
cd -	返回上次所在目录
cp file1 file2	将 file1 复制为 file2
cp -a dir1 dir2	复制一个目录
cp -a /tmp/dir1 .	复制一个目录到当前工作目录（"."代表当前目录）
ls	查看目录中的文件
ls -a	显示隐藏文件
ls -l	显示详细信息
ls -lrt	按时间显示文件（l 表示详细列表，r 表示反向排序，t 表示按时间排序）
pwd	显示工作路径
mkdir dir1	创建"dir1"目录
mkdir dir1 dir2	同时创建两个目录
mkdir -p /tmp/dir1/dir2	创建一个目录树
mv dir1 dir2	移动/重命名一个目录
rm -f file1	删除"file1"
rm -rf dir1	删除"dir1"目录及其子目录内容

2）文件内容查看命令

文件内容查看命令可以用多种方式查看文件的内容，其命令及其功能如表 2.2.2 所示。

表 2.2.2 文件内容查看命令及其功能

命令	解析
cat file1	从第一个字节开始正向查看文件的内容
head -2 file1	查看一个文件的前两行
more file1	查看一个长文件的内容
tac file1	从最后一行开始反向查看一个文件的内容
tail -3 file1	查看一个文件的最后三行

3）文件内容处理命令

文件内容处理命令可以文件内容进行查找、比较、编辑等各种操作，其命令及其功能如表 2.2.3 所示。

表 2.2.3　文件内容处理命令及其功能

命令	解析	
grep str /tmp/test	在文件"/tmp/test"中查找"str"	
grep ^str /tmp/test	在文件"/tmp/test"中查找以"str"开始的行	
grep [0-9] /tmp/test	查找"/tmp/test"文件中所有包含数字的行	
grep str -r /tmp/*	在目录"/tmp"及其子目录中查找"str"	
diff file1 file2	找出两个文件的不同处	
sdiff file1 file2	以对比的方式显示两个文件的不同	
vi file 操作解析	i	进入编辑文本模式
	Esc	退出编辑文本模式
	:w	保存当前修改
	:q	不保存退出 vi
	:wq	保存当前修改并退出 vi

4）查询操作

查询操作命令可以用多种方式在系统中查找文件和目录，查询操作命令及其功能如表 2.2.4 所示。

表 2.2.4　查询操作命令及其功能

命令	解析
find / -name file1	从"/"开始进入根文件系统查找文件和目录
find / -user user1	查找属于用户"user1"的文件和目录
find /home/user1 -name *.bin	在目录"/home/user1"中查找以".bin"结尾的文件
find /usr/bin -type f -atime +100	查找在过去 100 天内未被使用过的执行文件
find /usr/bin -type f -mtime -10	查找在 10 天内被创建或者修改过的文件
locate *.ps	寻找以".ps"结尾的文件，先运行"updatedb"命令
find -name '*.[ch]' | xargs grep -E 'expr'	在当前目录及其子目录所有.c 和.h 文件中查找"'expr'"
find -type f -print0 | xargs -r0 grep -F 'expr'	在当前目录及其子目录的常规文件中查找"'expr'"
find -maxdepth 1 -type f | xargs grep -F 'expr'	在当前目录中查找"'expr'"

5）压缩、解压命令

压缩、解压命令可以对 Linux 中的文件进行压缩或解压，其命令及其功能如表 2.2.5 所示。

表 2.2.5 压缩、解压操作命令及其功能

命令	解析
bzip2 file1	压缩 file1
bunzip2 file1.bz2	解压 file1.bz2
gzip file1	压缩 file1
gzip -9 file1	最大程度压缩 file1
gunzip file1.gz	解压 file1.gz
tar -cvf archive.tar file1	把 file1 打包成 archive.tar(-c:建立压缩档案;-v:显示所有过程;-f:使用档案名字,是必需的,是最后一个参数)
tar -cvf archive.tar file1 dir1	把 file1,dir1 打包成 archive.tar
tar -tf archive.tar	显示一个包中的内容
tar -xvf archive.tar	释放一个包
tar -xvf archive.tar -C /tmp	把压缩包释放到"/tmp"目录下
zip file1.zip file1	创建一个 zip 格式的压缩包
zip -r file1.zip file1 dir1	把文件和目录压缩成一个 zip 格式的压缩包
unzip file1.zip	解压一个 zip 格式的压缩包到当前目录
unzip test.zip -d /tmp/	解压一个 zip 格式的压缩包到"/tmp"目录

6) 软件包管理

(1) rpm 命令使用。rpm 命令是 rpm 软件包的管理工具。rpm 原本是 Red Hat Linux 发行版专门用来管理 Linux 各项套件的程序,它遵循 GPL 规则且功能强大方便,因而广受欢迎,后来逐渐受到其他发行版的采用。rpm 套件管理方式的出现,让 Linux 易于安装、升级,间接提升了 Linux 的适用度。rpm 命令及其功能如表 2.2.6 所示。

表 2.2.6 rpm 命令及其功能

命令	解析
rpm [OPTIONS] PACHAGE_FILE	命令格式
rpm -ivh your-package	直接安装
rpmrpm -force -ivh your-package.rpm	忽略报错,强制安装
rpm -ql	查询出所有安装过的包
rpm -q 包名	获得某个软件包的全名
rpm -ql 包名	获得 rpm 包中文件安装的位置
rpm -e 包名	卸载

(2) yum 命令。yum(yellow dog updater modified)是一个在各种 Linux 系统中的 Shell 前端软件包管理器。基于 rpm 包管理,能够从指定的服务器自动下载 rpm 包并且安装,可以自动处理依赖性关系,并且一次安装所有依赖的软件包,无须烦琐地一次次下载、安装。yum 命令及其功能如表 2.2.7 所示。

表 2.2.7 yum 命令及其功能

命令	解析
yum -y install [package]	下载并安装一个 rpm 包
yum localinstall [package.rpm]	安装一个 rpm 包,使用你自己的软件仓库解决所有依赖关系
yum -y update	更新当前系统中安装的所有 rpm 包
yum update [package]	更新一个 rpm 包
yum remove [package]	删除一个 rpm 包
yum list	列出当前系统中安装的所有包
yum search [package]	在 rpm 仓库中搜寻软件包
yum clean [package]	清除缓存目录"/var/cache/yum"下的软件包
yum clean headers	删除所有头文件
yum clean all	删除所有缓存的包和头文件

7) 网络相关操作命令

网络操作命令可以在 Linux 系统中对联网信息进行配置,如网卡的 IP 地址、启用或关闭网络、网络配置信息查看等。网络相关操作命令及其功能如表 2.2.8 所示。

表 2.2.8 网络相关操作命令及其功能

命令	解析
ifconfig eth0	显示一个以太网卡的配置
ifconfig eth0 192.168.1.1 netmask 255.255.255.0	配置网卡的 IP 地址
ifdown eth0	禁用"eth0"网络设备
ifup eth0	启用"eth0"网络设备
iwconfig eth1	显示一个无线网卡的配置
iwlist scan	显示无线网络
ip addr show	显示网卡的 IP 地址

任务 2.3　WinSCP 的安装与使用

📋 任务描述

本任务要在 Windows 操作系统中安装 WinSCP,远程连接 Linux 服务器,实现 Windows 操作系统与 Linux 操作系统的文件上传与下载功能,为后续安装工具传递到 CentOS 7 做好准备。

📋 关键步骤

（1）下载 WinSCP 安装文件。

（2）安装 WinSCP。

（3）操作应用 WinSCP。

WinSCP 是一款安装在 Windows 操作系统中的软件,能够远程连接 Linux 服务器,并能够将本地 Windows 操作系统中的文件上传到远程 Linux 操作系统中,同时也能够将远程 Linux 操作系统中的文件下载到本地 Windows 操作系统中,使用起来非常方便。

WinSCP 是一个 Windows 环境下使用的 SSH 的开源图形化 SFTP 客户端,它的主要功能是在本地与远程计算机间安全地复制文件,并且可以直接编辑文件。

2.3.1　下载 WinSCP 安装文件

WinSCP 官网下载地址为:https://winscp.net/eng/docs/lang:chs,下载文件名为:WinSCP-6.3.1-Setup.exe。进入官网页面后,点击菜单栏的"Download"进入 WinSCP 下载页面,如图 2.3.1 所示。

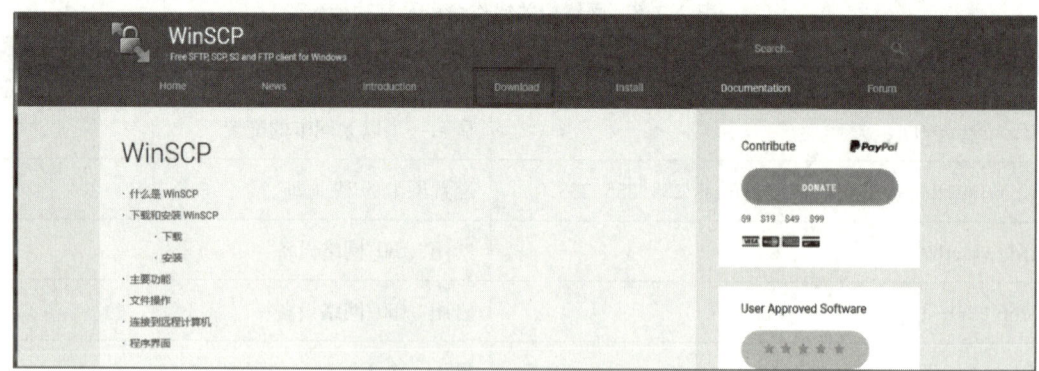

图 2.3.1　WinSCP 下载页面

点击左下方"DOWNLOAD WINSCP 6.3.1(11 MB)"选项,下载该软件(此版本为目前最新版),如图 2.3.2 所示。

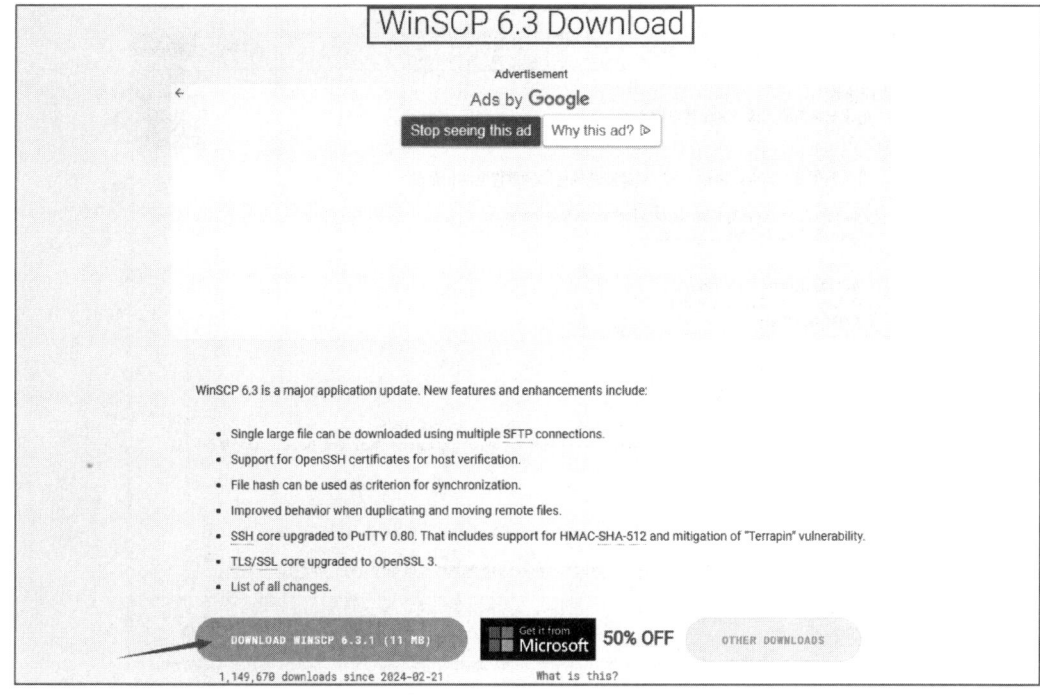

图 2.3.2　WinSCP 下载操作

2.3.2　WinSCP 安装

（1）将 WinSCP-6.3.1-Setup.exe 下载到磁盘后，双击安装文件，选择安装模式为"为所有用户安装"，如图 2.3.3 所示。

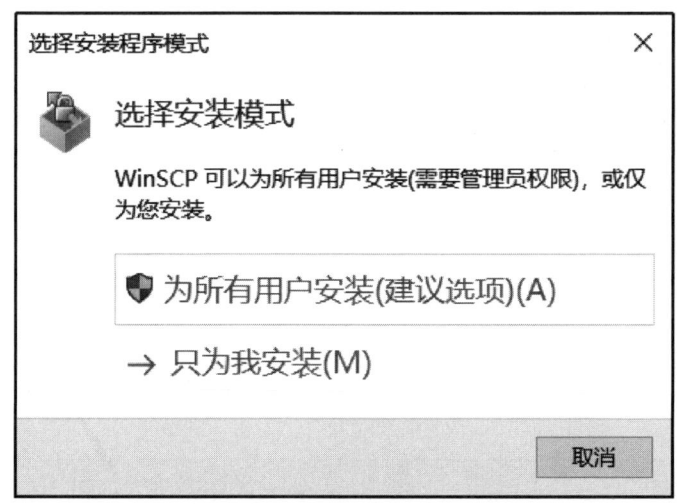

图 2.3.3　选择安装程序模式

(2) 开始安装 WinSCP,打开"许可协议"页面,点击"接受"按钮,如图 2.3.4 所示。

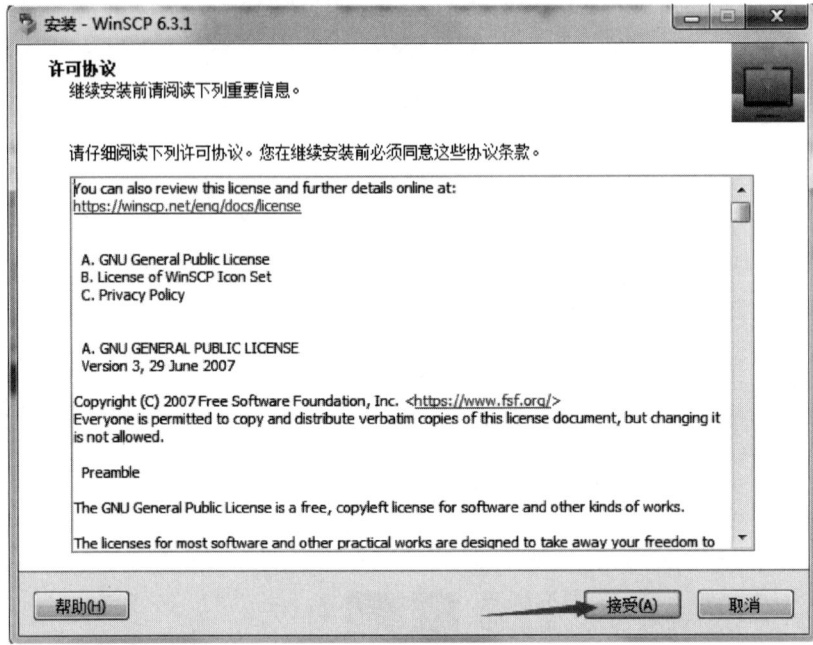

图 2.3.4 许可协议页面

(3) 打开"安装类型"页面,选择"典型安装",如图 2.3.5 所示。

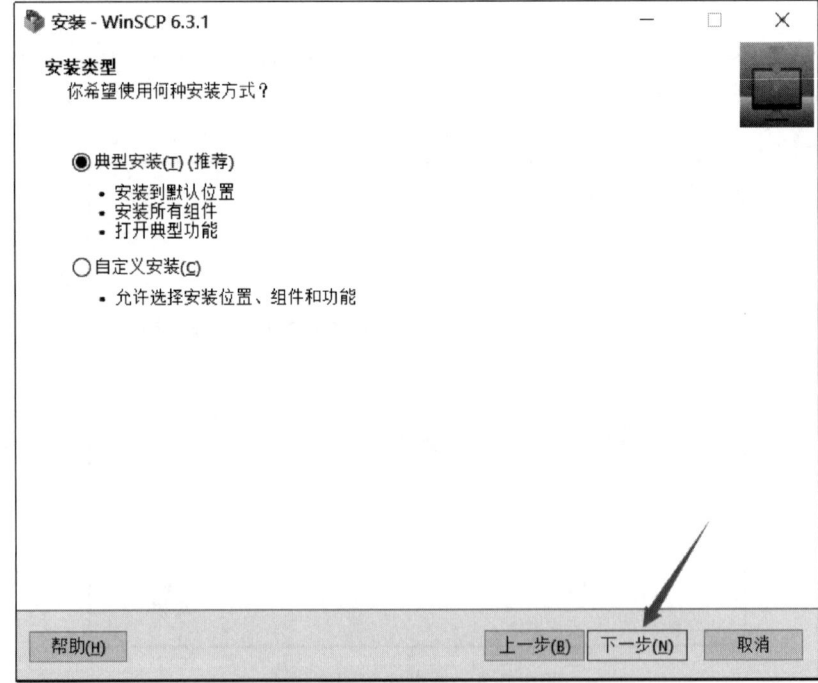

图 2.3.5 安装类型页面

（4）点击"下一步"按钮，打开"初始化用户设置"页面，如图 2.3.6 所示。

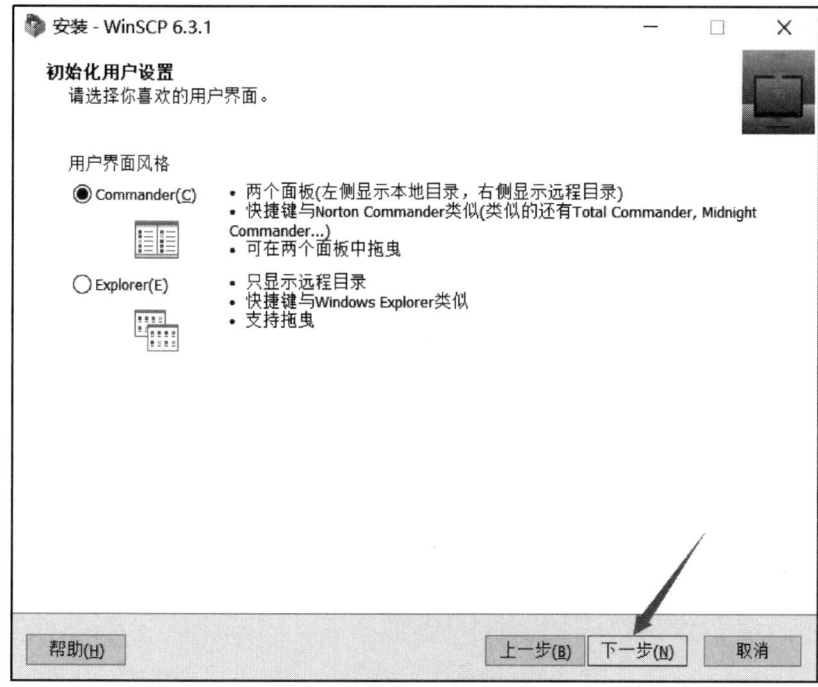

图 2.3.6　初始化用户设置页面

（5）点击"下一步"按钮，打开"准备安装"页面，如图 2.3.7 所示。

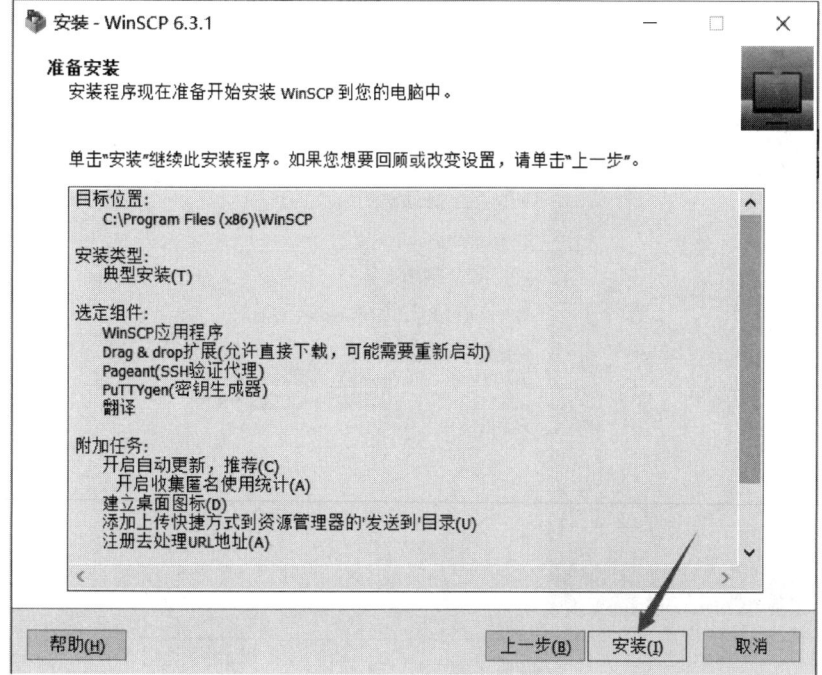

图 2.3.7　准备安装页面

(6) 点击"安装"按钮,打开"正在安装"页面,如图 2.3.8 所示。

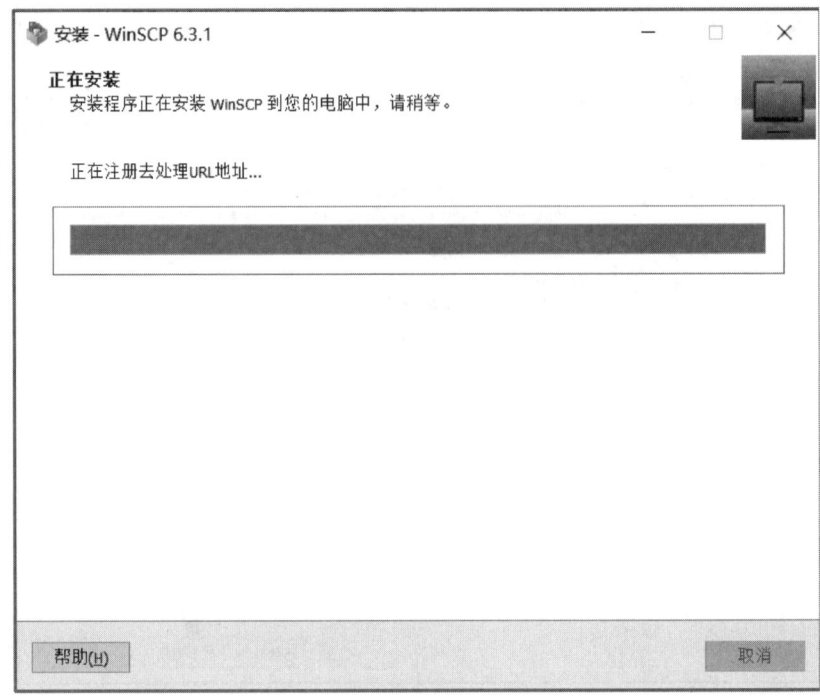

图 2.3.8　正在安装 WinSCP

(7) 等待安装进度条满格,打开"WinSCP 安装完成"页面,如图 2.3.9 所示。

图 2.3.9　WinSCP 安装完成

（8）点击"完成"按钮，完成 WinSCP 安装，桌面上出现 WinScp 图标，如图 2.3.10 所示。

图 2.3.10 桌面上的 WinSCP 图标

2.3.3 WinSCP 的应用

（1）双击 WinSCP 图标，开始使用 WinSCP，如图 2.3.11 所示。

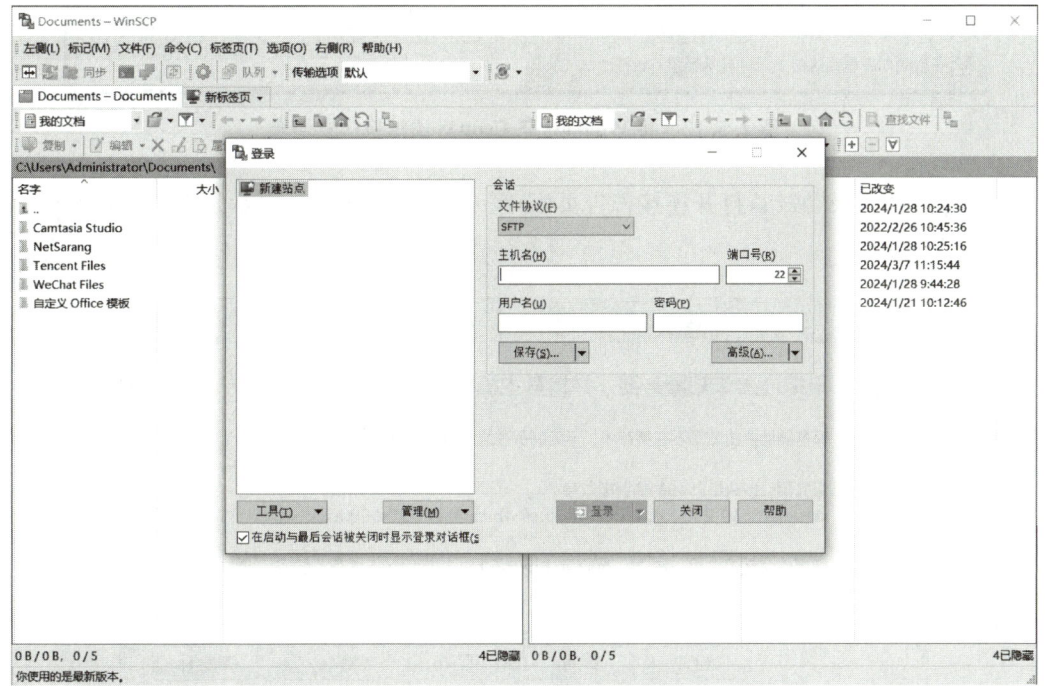

图 2.3.11 WinSCP 运行界面

（2）在"主机名""用户名"和"密码"标签下的文本框中录入已安装好的 CentOS 虚拟机的 IP 地址、用户名和密码。这里填入以下信息：

主机名(H)：192.168.204.129
用户名(U)：root
密码(P)：root123

Windows 与 CentOS 虚拟机建立连接如图 2.3.12 所示。

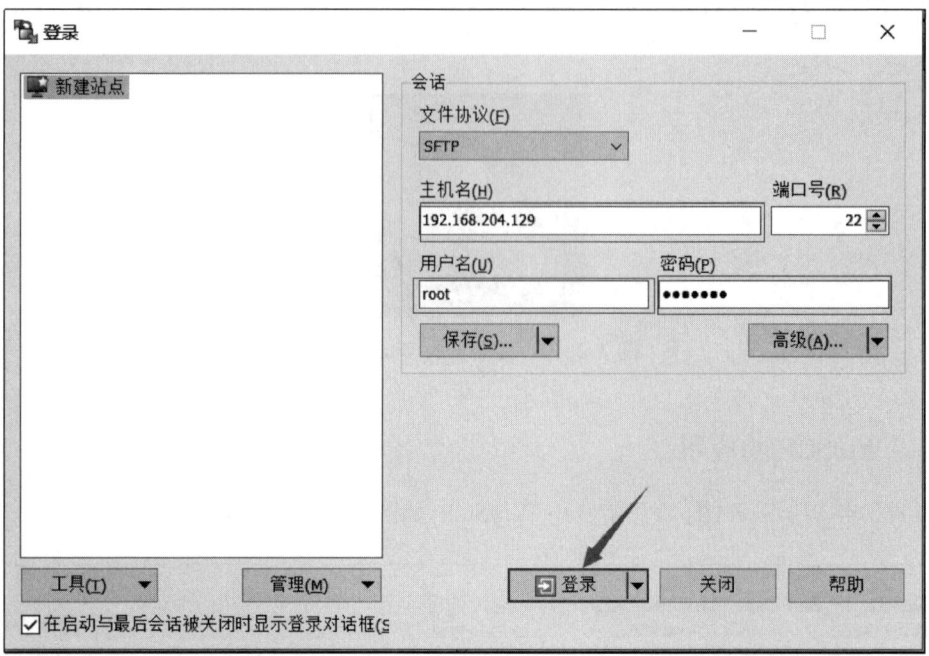

图 2.3.12　将 Windows 与 CentOS 虚拟机建立连接

（3）点击"登录"按钮，打开连接警告页面，第一次登录，会弹出提示是否缓存到本机，如图 2.3.13 所示。

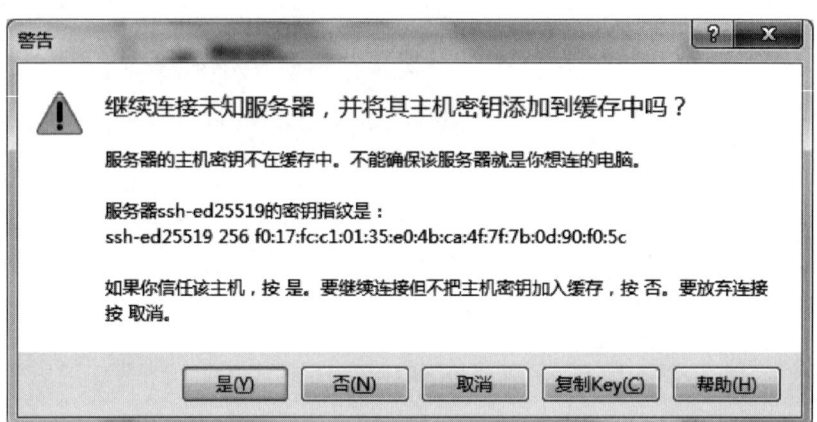

图 2.3.13　连接警告页面

（4）点击"是"按钮，连接建立成功窗口，左侧窗口显示 Windows 本地目录，右侧显示 CenstOS 虚拟机当前目录"/root"，如图 2.3.14 所示。我们将 Windows 中的 Hadoop 安装软件 hadoop-3.1.3.tar.gz 上传到 CentOS 虚拟机上，默认上传到"/root"中。

（5）点击页面左上方的"我的文档"右边的文件夹图标，打开"打开目录"窗口，可通过点击"浏览"按钮，选择要上传到虚拟机中的文件在 Windows 中的保存位置。这里找到 hadoop-2.7.7.tar.gz 安装软件的目录在"D:/tools"，如图 2.3.15 所示。

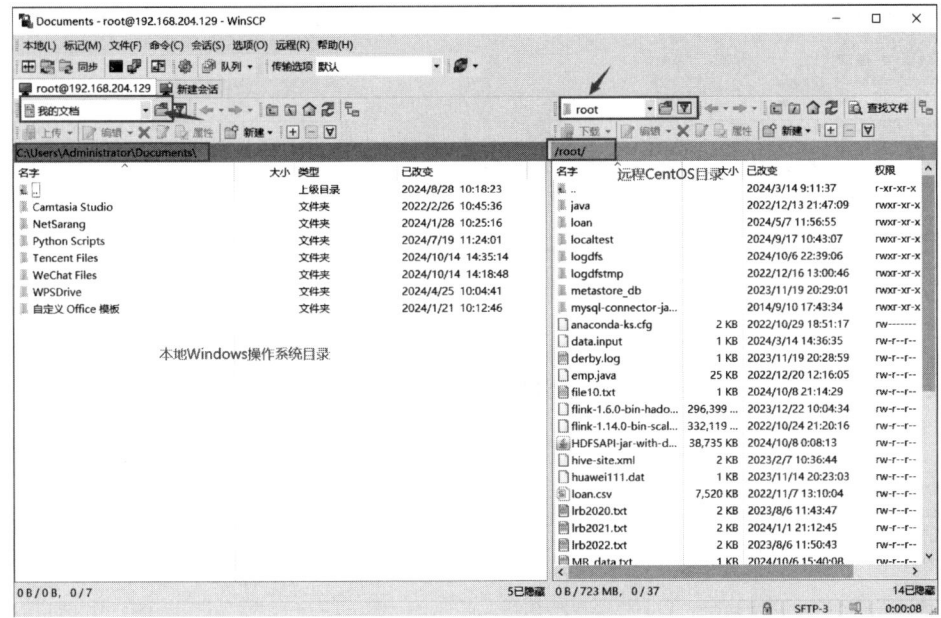

图 2.3.14　连接建立成功

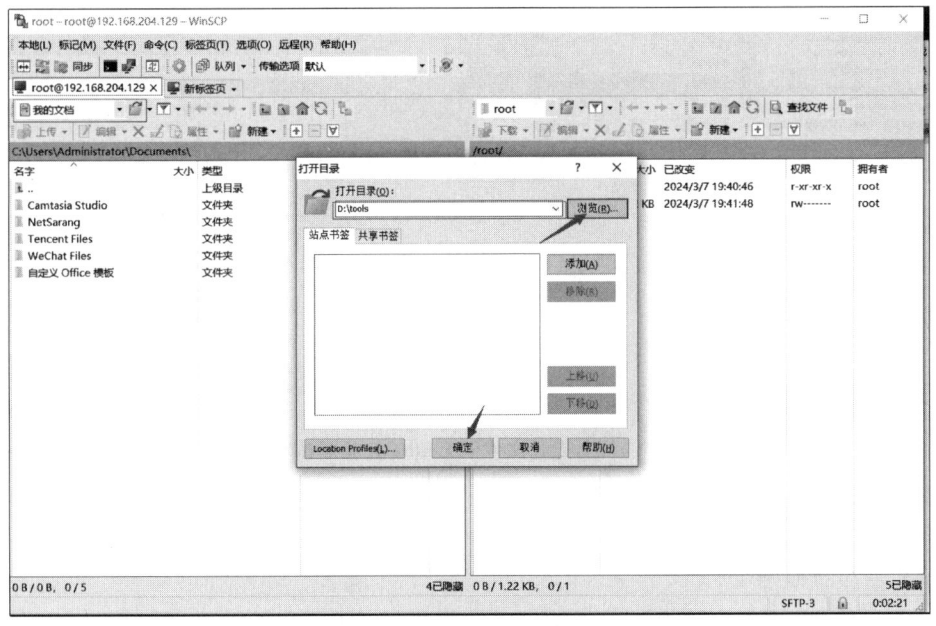

图 2.3.15　打开 Windows 中的源文件目录

（6）点击"确定"按钮，可以看见左侧窗口已切换到"D:/tools"，显示了该目录下的所有文件，找到 hadoop-2.7.7.tar.gz，如图 2.3.16 所示。

（7）用鼠标右键单击 hadoop-2.7.7.tar.gz，打开快捷菜单，选择"上传"，或直接选中 hadoop-2.7.7.tar.gz 拖到右侧窗口，将文件传输到 Centos 虚拟机的"/root"目录中，如图 2.3.17 所示。

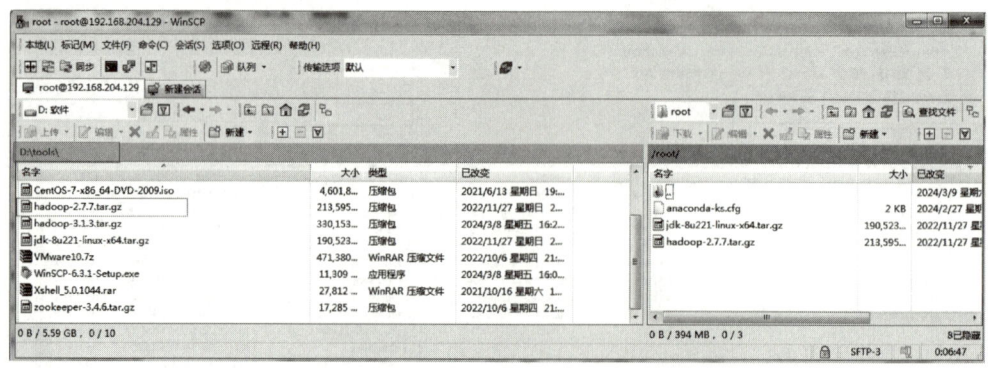

图 2.3.16　找到 Windows 中要上传的源文件

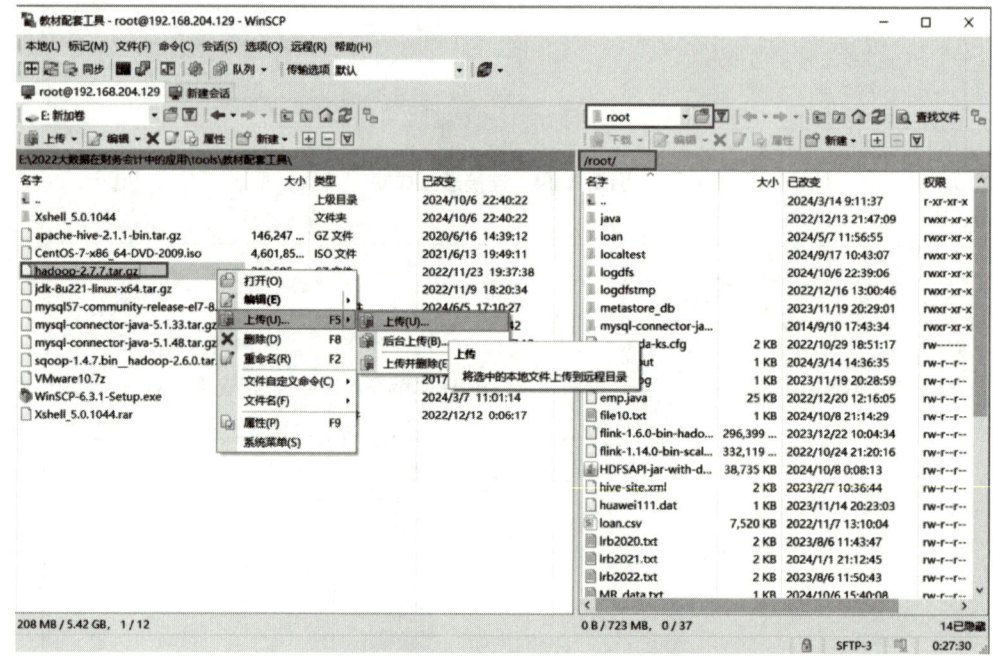

图 2.3.17　上传源文件到 Centos 虚拟机操作界面

相关操作说明如下：

右击文件，可以编辑、删除，赋予各种读写权限。当然也可以删除目录，给目录赋予各种权限，但是目录中有大量文件时，删除速度非常慢。

上传和下载，直接在你想要上传和下载的文件上右键，选择上传或下载就可以，也可以直接用鼠标拖动文件。

压缩文件，WinSCP 可以把文件或者目录打包。选中文件或目录后，右键自定义命令，选择 Tar/Gzip 格式，确定后会生成一个 archive.tgz 的压缩包。如果解压缩 .tgz 文件的话，可以用下边的 untar/gzip 的命令菜单。

任务2.4　Xshell 的安装与使用

任务描述

本任务要在 Windows 操作系统中安装 Xshell,对 Linux 主机进行远程管理,达到远程控制终端的目的,为后续方便操作 CentOS 7 系统做好准备。

关键步骤

(1) 下载 Xshell 安装包。
(2) 安装 Xshell 5。
(3) 使用 Xshell 5。

Xshell 是 Windows 旗下一款功能非常强大的安全终端模拟软件,它支持远程登录协议,可以非常方便地对 Linux 主机进行远程管理。Xshell 通过互联网到远程主机的安全连接,能帮助用户在复杂的网络环境中轻松完成网络配置和网络操作等工作。

Xshell 可以在 Windows 界面下用来访问远端不同系统下的服务器,从而比较好地达到远程控制终端的目的。此外,Xshell 还有丰富的外观配色方案以及样式选择。

2.4.1　Xshell 安装包的下载

XShell 在商业环境使用下是需要购买许可的。XShell 官网地址为:https://www.xshellcn.com。用户可以在课程资源中下载 Xshell 5 安装包 Xshell_5.0.1044.exe。

2.4.2　Xshell 5 的安装

(1) 下载 Xshell_5.0.1044.exe 后双击该文件,按照提示进行安装即可,如图 2.4.1、图 2.4.2 所示。

图 2.4.1　Xshell 5 安装界面

图 2.4.2　Xshell 5 安装欢迎界面

（2）点击"下一步"按钮，打开"安装类型"页面，如图 2.4.3 所示。

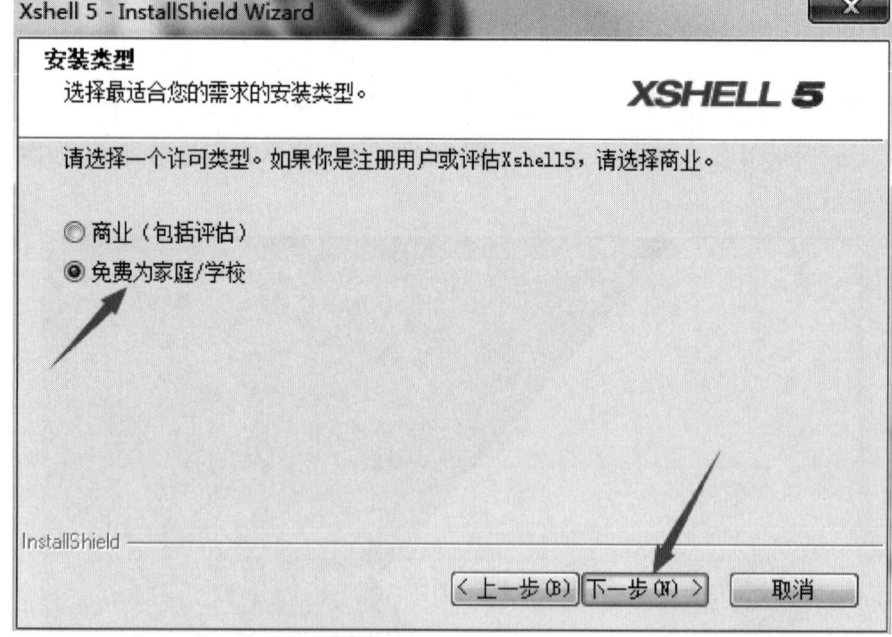

图 2.4.3　"安装类型"页面

(3) 选择"免费为家庭/学校",点击"下一步"按钮,打开如图 2.4.4 所示。

图 2.4.4 "许可证协议"页面

(4) 选择"我接受许可证协议中的条款",点击"下一步"按钮,打开"选择目的地位置"页面,如图 2.4.5 所示。

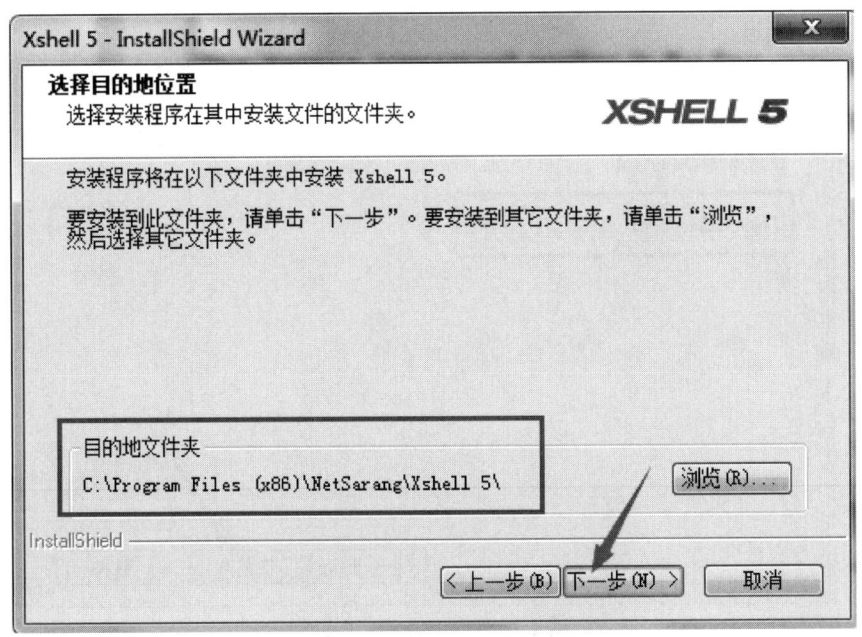

图 2.4.5 "选择目的地位置"页面

（5）选定"目的地文件夹"后，点击"下一步"按钮，打开"选择程序文件夹"页面，如图2.4.6所示。

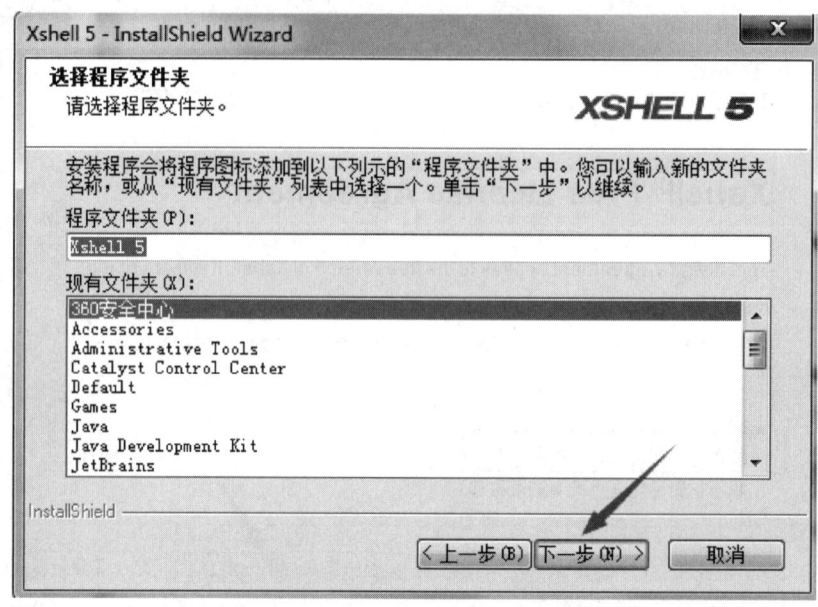

图2.4.6 "选择程序文件夹"页面

（6）在选择程序文件夹页面中默认现有选择，也可以重新修改新的文件名。此处直接点击"下一步"按钮，打开"选择语言"页面，如图2.4.7所示。

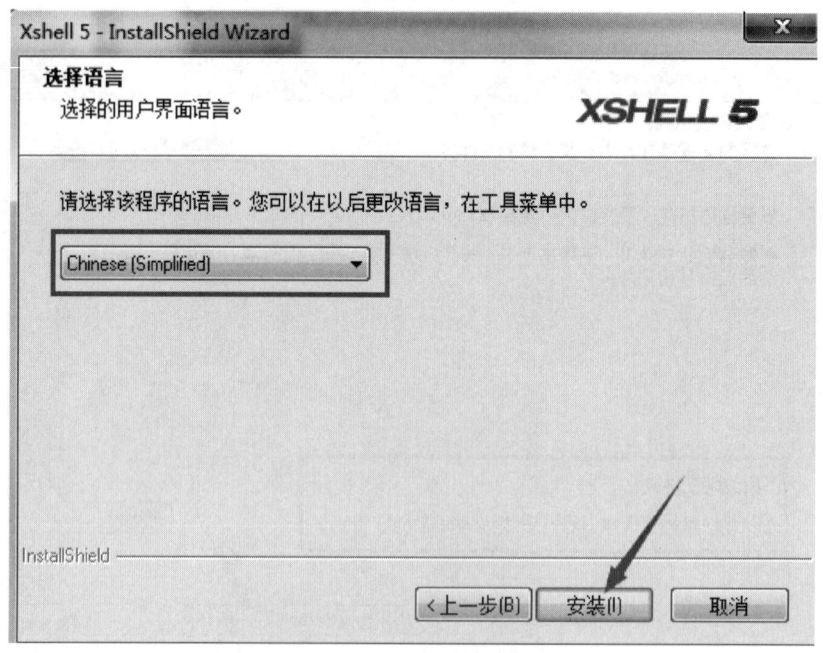

图2.4.7 "选择语言"页面

（7）选择"Chinese(Simplified)"点击"安装"按钮，打开"安装状态"页面，直到完成，如图 2.4.8、图 2.4.9 所示。

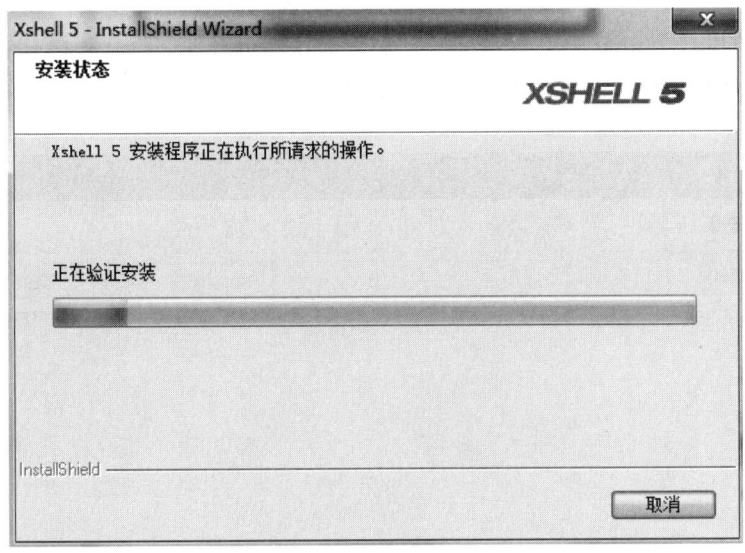

图 2.4.8 "安装状态"页面

图 2.4.9 Xshell 5 安装完成

Xshell 5 完成后桌面上会出现 Xshell 5 图标，如图 2.4.10 所示。

图 2.4.10 Xshell 5 图标

2.4.3　Xshell 5 的使用

用 Xshell 可以与 CentOS 虚拟机建立连接。连接建立后，对 CentOS 虚拟机在命令行中的操作，就可以在 Xshell 中进行，复制、粘贴等操作都很方便。操作方法如下。

（1）双击桌面上的 Xshell 5 图标，打开"会话"页面，如图 2.4.11 所示。

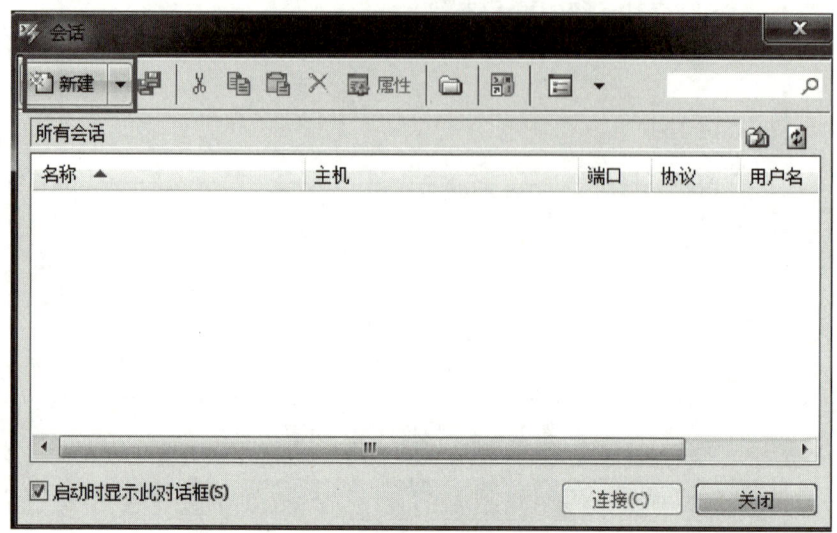

图 2.4.11　会话页面

（2）点击"新建"—"会话"，建立会话，如图 2.4.12 所示。

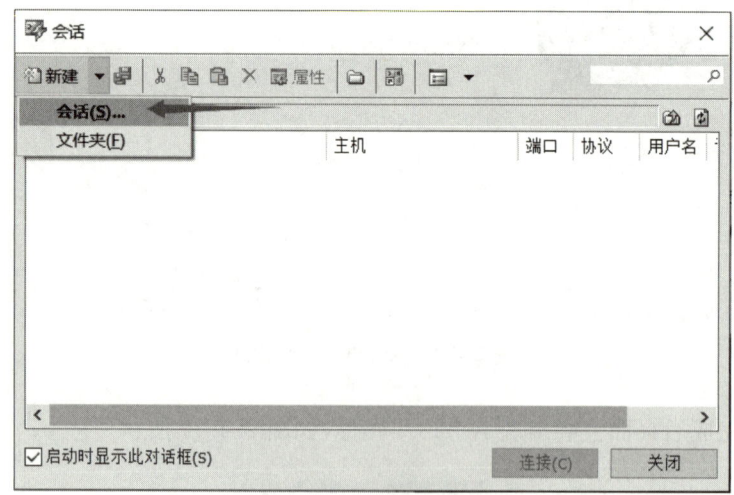

图 2.4.12　建立会话页面

（3）点击"连接"按钮，打开"新建会话属性"页面，录入常规名称、主机地址等信息。此处录入如下信息：

```
常规名称(N):master
主机(H):192.168.204.129
```

配置结果如图 2.4.13 所示。

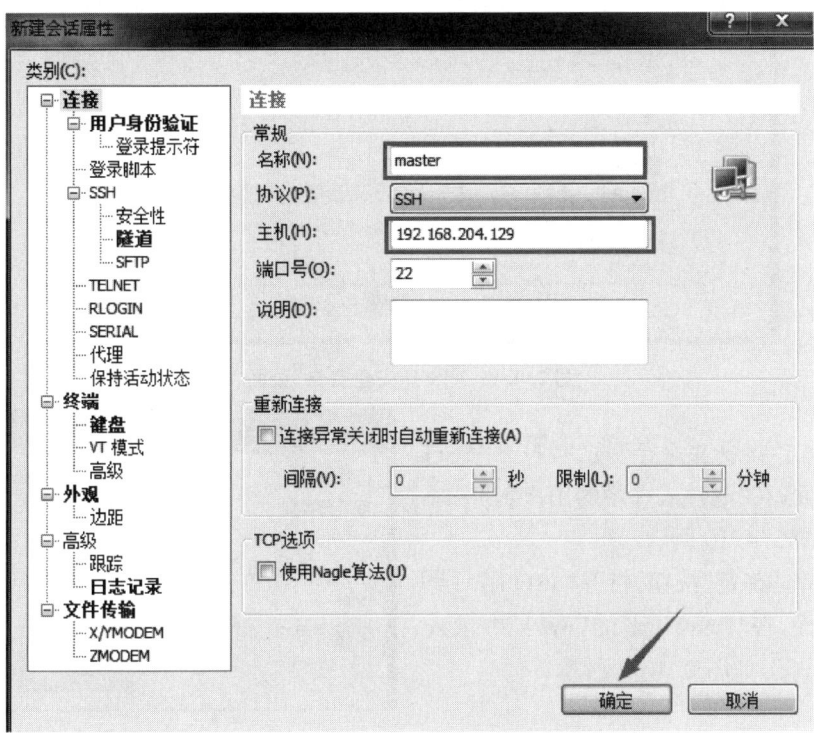

图 2.4.13 "新建会话属性"页面

(4) 点击"确定"按钮,打开"会话—所有会话"页面,如图 2.4.14 所示。

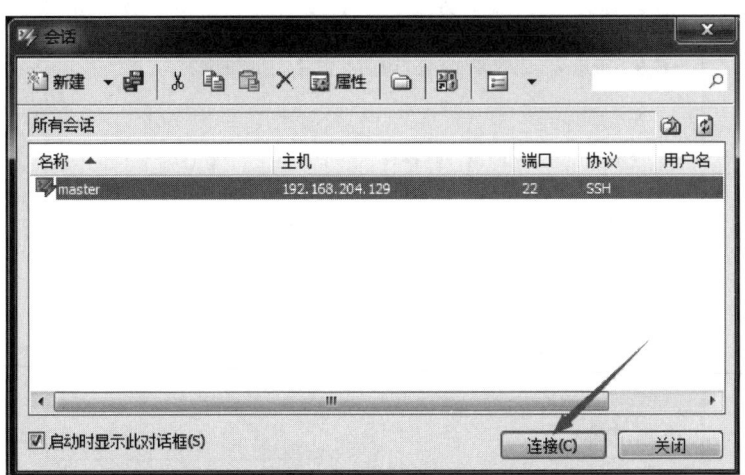

图 2.4.14 "会话—所有会话"页面

（5）点击"连接"按钮，打开"SSH 安全警告"页面，如图 2.4.15 所示。

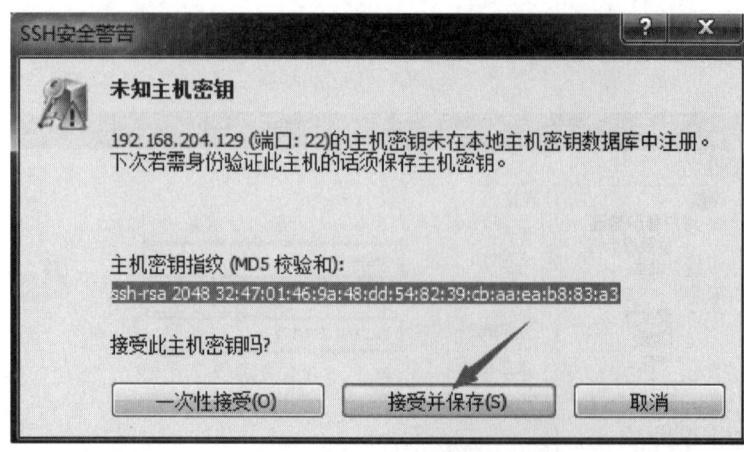

图 2.4.15 "SSH 安全警告"页面

（6）点击"接受并保存"按钮，打开"SSH 用户名"页面，在"请输入登录的用户名"中录入 root，如图 2.4.16 所示。

（7）点击"确定"按钮，打开"SSH 用户身份验证"页面，在"Password"的"密码"中录入密码"root123"，如图 2.4.17 所示。

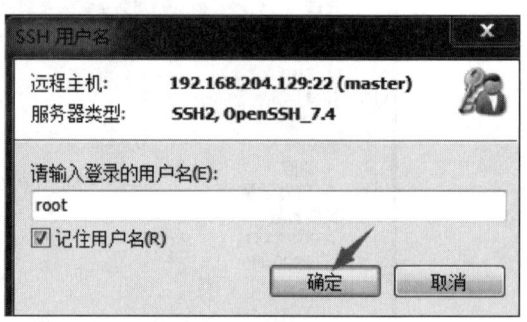

图 2.4.16 "SSH 用户名"页面

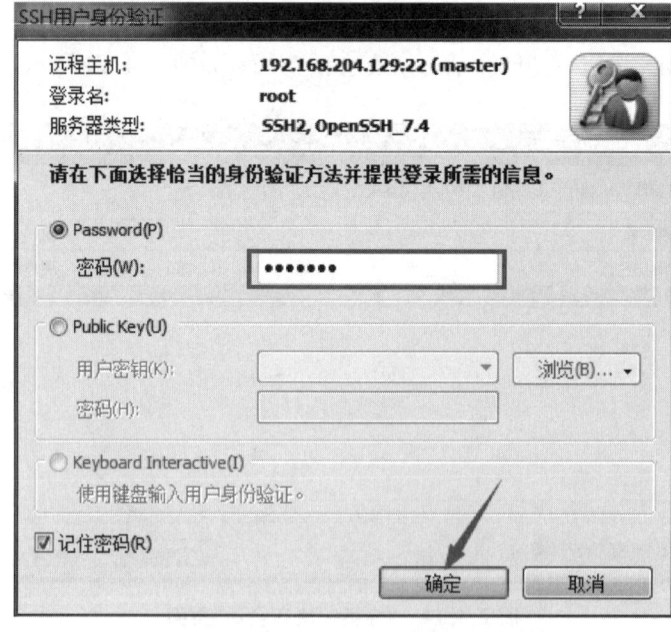

图 2.4.17 "SSH 用户身份验证"页面

（8）点击"确定"按钮，完成了 Xshell 会话连接建立工作，如图 2.4.18 所示。

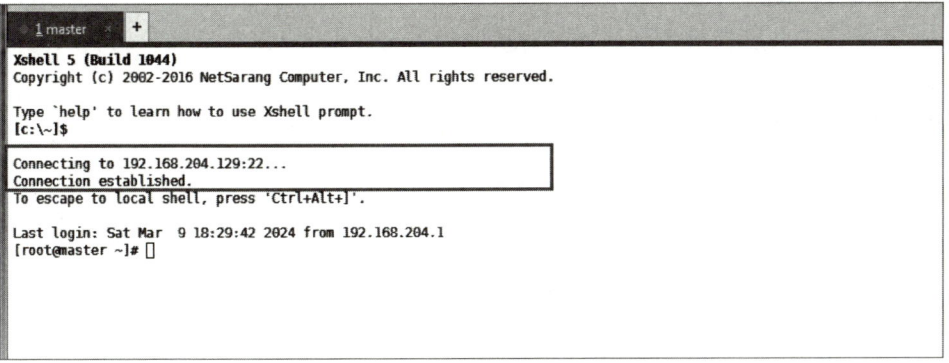

图 2.4.18　建立 Xshell 会话连接

至此，对 CentOS 虚拟机的操作就在 Xshell 会话窗口中进行。

 注意

图 2.4.13 中的【终端】【外观】【高级】和【文件传输】根据需求设置。

在 Xshell 会话窗口中，常用的快捷键如下：

```
Alt + N：新建会话
Alt + S：简单模式
Alt + R：透明模式
Alt + A：总在最前面
Alt + Enter：全屏
Alt + 1：切到第一个会话，2,3,4…类推
Ctrl + Alt + F：新建传输文件
Ctrl + Shift + L：清屏
```

单元总结

本单元为安装 Hadoop 大数据处理平台进行基础准备，即安装虚拟机 VMware、在 VMware 中安装 CentOS 7，为在不同系统中传递安装工具包安装了 WinSCP，为便于对 CentOS 进行操作又安装了 Xshell。本单元简单介绍了上述工具的功能，并通过实际操作详细介绍了各工具的下载、安装和配置全过程，最后在安装完成的 CentOS 7 系统上，对命令的使用格式进行了介绍。

单元习题

一、简答题

1. 虚拟机技术的作用是什么？

2. 使用哪些工具可以实现不同操作系统之间文件的相互传递?

二、技能训练题

1. 请独立完成虚拟机 VMware、CentOS 7 系统的安装,将虚拟机的地址设置为动态地址。

2. 在 CentOS 7 系统中练习文件与目录操作命令,完成下列任务:

(1) 在"/home"目录下,创建一个子目录"user"。

(2) 在"/home/user"目录下创建一个文本文件 mydata.txt,文件内容为"I love bigdata. I love Accounting!"。

(3) 查看"/home/user"目录下的文件,并查看一下 mydata.txt 文件内容。

(4) 将 mydata.txt 文件复制到"/root/"下,并改名为 mydata2.txt。

(5) 删除"/root/mydata2.txt"。

单元 3
Hadoop 大数据处理平台的安装与配置

单元 2 为搭建 Hadoop 环境作了相应的准备工作,本单元将深入讨论如何安装配置 Hadoop 环境。这里 Hadoop 的安装配置版本为 hadoop-2.7.7,并以 root 用户的身份安装配置 Hadoop 环境,读者也可以自行新建其他用户用于 Hadoop 的安装和配置。

学习目标

知识目标
1. 了解 Hadoop 的安装模式。
2. 掌握 Hadoop 的目录结构。
3. 掌握 Hadoop 命令的功能。

技能目标
1. 掌握 JDK 的安装和配置。
2. 掌握 Hadoop 的本地模式、伪分布模式和分布模式的安装与配置。
3. 掌握 Hadoop 命令的运用。

单元任务

任务 3.1 Hadoop 的安装模式。
任务 3.2 JDK 的安装和配置。
任务 3.3 Hadoop 的本地模式安装和配置。
任务 3.4 Hadoop 的伪分布模式安装和配置。
任务 3.5 Hadoop 的完全分布模式安装。

任务 3.1 Hadoop 的安装模式

任务描述

本任务学习 Hadoop 的 3 种安装模式:本地模式、伪分布模式和分布模式,为选择适合用户 PC 环境和工作特点的安装模式提供理论支撑。

关键步骤

(1) 了解本地模式功能特点。

(2) 了解伪分布模式功能特点。

(3) 了解分布模式功能特点。

为方便开发人员的开发和测试，Hadoop 提供了 3 种不同的安装模式，分别为本地模式、伪分布模式和分布模式。

3.1.1 本地模式

本地模式能够方便开发人员在开发 Hadoop 程序时进行调试、跟踪、排查问题，而且这种安装模式是 3 种安装模式中最简单的，用户只需要在 Hadoop 的 hadoop-env.sh 文件中配置 JAVA_HOME 即可。

本地模式以 Hadoop Jar 命令运行 Hadoop 程序，并将运行结果直接输出到本地磁盘。

3.1.2 伪分布模式

伪分布模式的大部分应用场景是测试环境，它能够在逻辑上提供与分布模式一样的运行环境（在物理上伪分布模式部署在单台服务器上；而分布模式需要部署在多台服务器上，以实现物理上的完全集群分布）。

伪分布模式能够模拟分布模式的环境，其优点在于节省服务器的部署成本，但是整个物理服务器只有一台，所有 Hadoop 都运行在这台物理服务器上，这就造成了单点故障问题。一旦某个进程"挂掉"，将导致整个 Hadoop 运行环境出现故障而不可用。这也是伪分布模式不能应用于生产环境的一个重要原因。

伪分布模式的安装和部署比本地安装模式复杂，除了需要在 Hadoop 的 hadoop-env.sh 文件中配置 JAVA_HOME，还要配置 Hadoop 所使用的文件系统、HDFS 的副本数量和 YARN 地址，以及服务器的 SSH 免密码登录等。

伪分布模式以 Hadoop Jar 命令运行 Hadoop 程序，并将运行结果输出到 HDFS 中。

3.1.3 分布模式

分布模式也称完全分布模式，它与伪分布模式有着本质的区别：分布模式是在物理服务器上实现的完全分布式集群，部署在多台物理服务器上；而伪分布模式在逻辑上是分布模式，但它是部署在单台物理服务器上的。

对于生产环境，要求 Hadoop 环境的高可靠性和高可用性，往往某个节点故障就会导致整个集群不可用；同时，要求生产环境的数据必须可靠，某个数据节点出现故障或者数据发生丢失后，数据必须可恢复。这就要求生产环境上必须部署 Hadoop 的分布模式，以应对生产环境的各种要求。

分布模式的部署是 3 种安装模式中最复杂的，它需要部署在多台物理服务器上，要提前将服务器环境规划好，除了要配置 Hadoop 所使用的文件系统、HDFS 的副本数量和 YARN 地址，还要配置各台服务器之间的 SSH 免密码登录、各 Hadoop 节点之间的 RPC 通信等。

分布模式以 Hadoop Jar 命令运行 Hadoop 程序，并将运行结果输出到 HDFS 中。

任务 3.2　JDK 的安装和配置

任务描述

Hadoop 是基于 Java 语言开发的,在安装 Hadoop 之前,用户要先安装 Java。本任务通过实际操作 JDK 的下载、安装和环境配置过程,训练读者的 JDK 安装与配置技能。

关键步骤

(1) 下载 JDK 安装包。
(2) 上传 JDK 安装包到 CentOS7 系统。
(3) 安装并配置 JDK。

Hadoop 是基于 Java 语言开发的,用户要想在服务器上安装、配置 Hadoop 环境,并运行 Hadoop MapReduce 应用程序,则要先在服务器上安装配置 Java JDK(Java JDK 是 Sun 公司开发的,2010 年 Oracle 公司收购了 Sun 公司)环境。

3.2.1　下载 JDK 安装包

从 Oracle 官网下载 JDK。本书中使用的 JDK 版本是 JDK 1.8。JDK 1.8 的下载地址为:https://www.oracle.com/technetwork/javase/downloads/jdk8-downloads-2133151.html。

注意

这里下载的 JDK 安装包版本为 jdk-8u221-linux-x64.tar.gz。

3.2.2　上传 JDK 安装包到 CentOS7 虚拟机

打开 WinSCP,使用 root 用户身份登录 CentOS 7 虚拟机,将下载的 JDK 安装文件 jdk-8u221-linux-x64.tar.gz 上传到 CentOS 7 虚拟机的"/root"目录下,如图 3.2.1 所示。

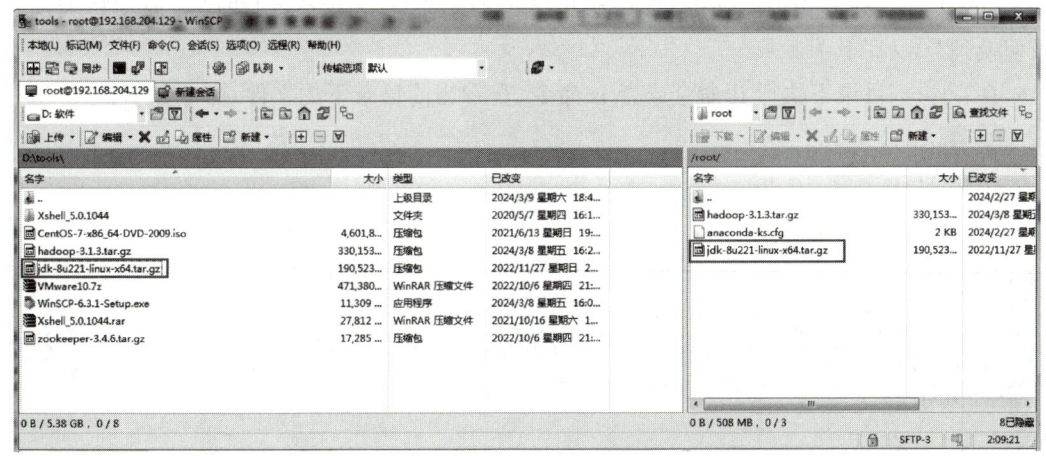

图 3.2.1　用 WinSCP 将 JDK 安装文件上传到 CentOS 7 虚拟机

打开 Xshell 连接登录到 CentOS 7 虚拟机,在命令行中将目录切换到"/root"下,命令如下:

```
[root@master ~]# cd /root
[root@master ~]# pwd
```

运行结果如图 3.2.2 所示。

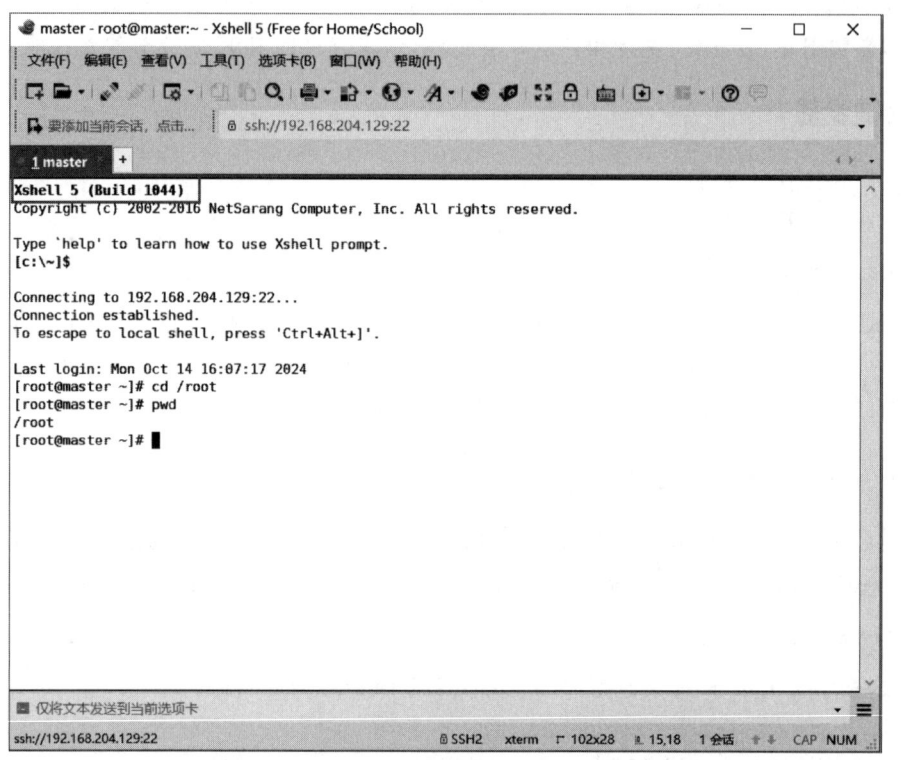

图 3.2.2　用 Xshell 连接登录到 CentOS 7 虚拟机

"cd /root"表示将目录切换到"/root"下,Linux 操作系统中的根目录为"/"。

"pwd"表示查看当前所在的目录,这里输出的结果为"/root",说明已经成功将当前目录切换到"/root"下了。

在"/root"目录下执行 ll 命令或者 ls 命令,查看当前目录下的文件,命令如下:

```
[root@master ~]# ll
[root@master ~]# ls
```

运行结果如图 3.2.3 所示。

```
[root@master ~]# ll
总用量 520684
-rw-------. 1 root root      1257 2月  27 22:41 anaconda-ks.cfg
-rw-r--r--. 1 root root 338075860 3月   8 16:27 hadoop-3.1.3.tar.gz
-rw-r--r--. 1 root root 195094741 11月 27 2022 jdk-8u221-linux-x64.tar.gz
[root@master ~]# ls
anaconda-ks.cfg  hadoop-3.1.3.tar.gz  jdk-8u221-linux-x64.tar.gz
[root@master ~]#
```

图 3.2.3　用 ls 命令查看 jdk 安装文件上传成功

可以看到，无论是 ll 命令还是 ls 命令，都输出了 jdk-8u221-linux-x64. tar. gz 文件（ll 命令比 ls 命令输出的信息要详细些），这说明 jdk-8u221-linux-x64. tar. gz 文件已经正确上传到了 CentOS 7 虚拟机中。接下来，安装并配置 JDK。

3. 2. 3　安装并配置 JDK

这里下载的 JDK 版本为 jdk-8u221-linux-x64. tar. gz，即以“. tar. gz”结尾的文件。这种文件不需要进行特别的安装，只需要解压并进行相应的配置即可。

3. 2. 3. 1　安装 JDK

安装 JDK 本质上就是解压 JDK。CentOS 的当前目录已切换到“/root”下，创建“/opt/modules”目录，解压 jdk-8u221-linux-x64. tar. gz 到“/opt/modules”目录，命令如下：

```
[root@master ~]#  mkdir  /opt/modules
[root@master ~]#  tar -zxvf jdk-8u221-linux-x64.tar.gz -C  /opt/modules
[root@master ~]#  ls  /opt/modules
```

运行结果如图 3.2.4 所示。

```
jdk1.8.0_221/man/man1/javapackager.1
jdk1.8.0_221/man/man1/orbd.1
jdk1.8.0_221/man/man1/jstack.1
jdk1.8.0_221/man/man1/policytool.1
jdk1.8.0_221/man/man1/jstat.1
jdk1.8.0_221/man/man1/tnameserv.1
jdk1.8.0_221/man/man1/javaws.1
jdk1.8.0_221/man/man1/jrunscript.1
jdk1.8.0_221/man/man1/javac.1
jdk1.8.0_221/man/man1/schemagen.1
jdk1.8.0_221/man/man1/jhat.1
jdk1.8.0_221/man/man1/java.1
jdk1.8.0_221/man/man1/jcmd.1
jdk1.8.0_221/man/man1/xjc.1
jdk1.8.0_221/man/man1/jarsigner.1
jdk1.8.0_221/man/man1/jmc.1
jdk1.8.0_221/man/man1/appletviewer.1
jdk1.8.0_221/man/man1/javafxpackager.1
jdk1.8.0_221/man/man1/pack200.1
jdk1.8.0_221/man/man1/keytool.1
jdk1.8.0_221/man/man1/extcheck.1
jdk1.8.0_221/man/man1/jmap.1
jdk1.8.0_221/man/man1/jstatd.1
jdk1.8.0_221/man/man1/javadoc.1
jdk1.8.0_221/THIRDPARTYLICENSEREADME.txt
jdk1.8.0_221/COPYRIGHT
[root@master ~]# ls  /opt/modules
jdk1.8.0_221
[root@master ~]#
```

图 3. 2. 4　安装 JDK

可以看到，“/opt/modules”目录下多了一个“jdk1.8.0_221”目录，说明解压成功。

接下来，将当前目录切换到“/opt/modules”目录下，同样可以执行如下命令：

```
[root@master ~]#  cd /opt/modules
[root@master modules]#  ls
```

运行结果如图 3.2.5 所示。

```
[root@master ~]# cd /opt/modules
[root@master modules]# ls
jdk1.8.0_221
[root@master modules]#
```

图 3. 2. 5　JDK 安装成功

可以看到,"/opt/modules"目录下存在"jdk1.8.0_221"目录,说明 JDK 安装成功。将"jdk1.8.0_221"改名为"jdk",便于后面操作,命令如下:

```
[root@master modules]#  mv jdk1.8.0_221  jdk
[root@master modules]#  ls
```

运行结果如图 3.2.6 所示。

```
[root@master3 modules]# ls
hadoop   jdk
[root@master3 modules]# _
```

图 3.2.6 将 jdk1.8.0_221 改名为 jdk

可见"jdk1.8.0_221"目录名已被改为"jdk"。接下来就要配置 JDK 环境变量了。

3.2.3.2 配置 JDK 环境变量

在 CentOS 7 操作系统中,系统环境变量是在/etc/profile 文件中配置的,所以配置 JDK 系统环境变量也需要在/etc/profile 配置文件中进行配置,具体步骤如下。

(1) 打开/etc/profile 文件,输入如下命令:

```
[root@master ~]#  vim  /etc/profile   #在 Vim 编辑器中打开/etc/profile 文件
```

(2) 配置 JDK 系统环境变量,在 Vim 编辑器中按 i 键进入编辑模式,并在/etc/profile 文件的最后追加如下内容:

```
export JAVA_HOME = /opt/modules/jdk
export PATH = $PATH:$JAVA_HOME/bin
```

修改结果如图 3.2.7 所示。

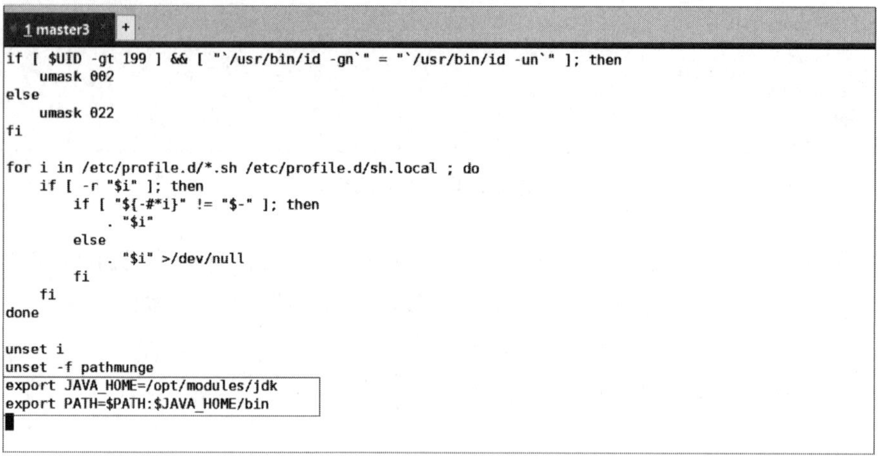

```
1 master3
if [ $UID -gt 199 ] && [ "`/usr/bin/id -gn`" = "`/usr/bin/id -un`" ]; then
    umask 002
else
    umask 022
fi

for i in /etc/profile.d/*.sh /etc/profile.d/sh.local ; do
    if [ -r "$i" ]; then
        if [ "${-#*i}" != "$-" ]; then
            . "$i"
        else
            . "$i" >/dev/null
        fi
    fi
done

unset i
unset -f pathmunge
export JAVA_HOME=/opt/modules/jdk
export PATH=$PATH:$JAVA_HOME/bin
```

图 3.2.7 配置 JDK 环境变量

(3) 按 Esc 键,录入":wq"回车后,保存并退出 vim 编辑状态,回到 CentOS 命令行状态。

3.2.3.3 使环境变量生效

使 JDK 系统环境变量生效有两种方式:一种是重启 CentOS 7 虚拟机;另一种就是通过

输入"source /etc/profile"命令。这里选择第二种方式,操作命令如下:

```
[root@master ~]# source /etc/profile
```

3.2.3.4 检验 JDK 是否安装并配置成功

在命令行输入如下命令验证 JDK 是否安装并配置成功:

```
[root@master ~]# java -version
```

运行结果如图 3.2.8 所示。

```
[root@master ~]# vi /etc/profile
[root@master ~]# java -version
java version "1.8.0_221"
Java(TM) SE Runtime Environment (build 1.8.0_221-b11)
Java HotSpot(TM) 64-Bit Server VM (build 25.221-b11, mixed mode)
[root@master ~]#
```

图 3.2.8 检验 JDK 是否安装并配置成功

可以看到,命令行输出了"java version 1.8.0_221"字样,说明 JDK 已安装并配置成功。下面就可以开始进行 Hadoop 的本地模式安装和配置。

任务 3.3 Hadoop 的本地模式安装和配置

任务描述

本任务通过实际操作 Hadoop 的下载、安装和环境配置过程,训练读者的 Hadoop 安装与配置技能,并能调用 Hadoop 自带的程序解决实际问题。

关键步骤

(1) 下载 Hadoop 安装包。
(2) 安装并配置 Hadoop 环境。
(3) 以本地模式配置 Hadoop。
(4) 验证 Hadoop 本地模式是否安装成功。

如前所述,Hadoop 的本地模式是 3 种安装模式中最简单的一种,只需要在 Hadoop 的 hadoop-env.sh 文件中配置 JAVA_HOME 即可。

3.3.1 下载 Hadoop 安装包

3.3.1.1 登录 Apache 官网下载 Hadoop 安装包

登录 Apache 官网下载 Hadoop 安装包,网址为:https://archive.apache.org/dist/hadoop/common/。本书中下载的 Apache Hadoop 版本为 hadoop-2.7.7,选择版本的界面如图 3.3.1 所示,下载界面如图 3.3.2 所示。

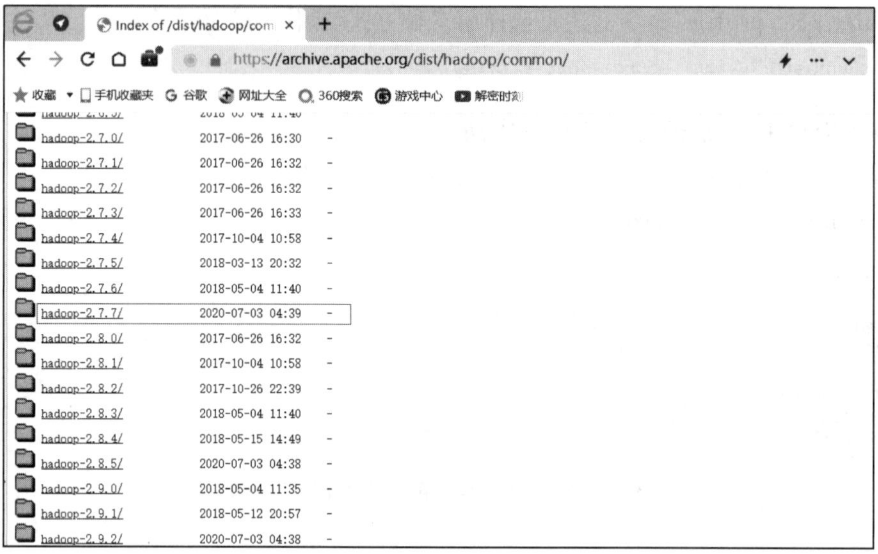

图 3.3.1　选择 hadoop-2.7.7 版本

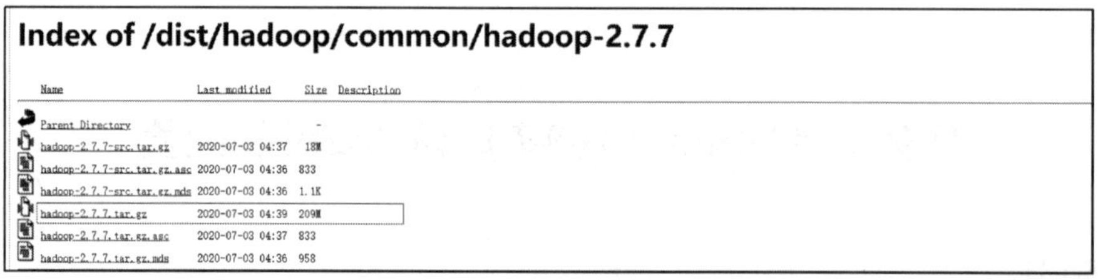

图 3.3.2　下载 hadoop-2.7.7 版本

3.3.1.2　用 WinSCP 上传 Hadoop 安装包到 CentOS 7

下载 Hadoop 的 binary 版本（编译好的二进制版本）到本地磁盘，然后利用 WinSCP 将下载的 Hadoop 安装包 hadoop-2.7.7.tar.gz 上传到 CentOS 7 虚拟机的"/root"目录下，如图 3.3.3 所示。

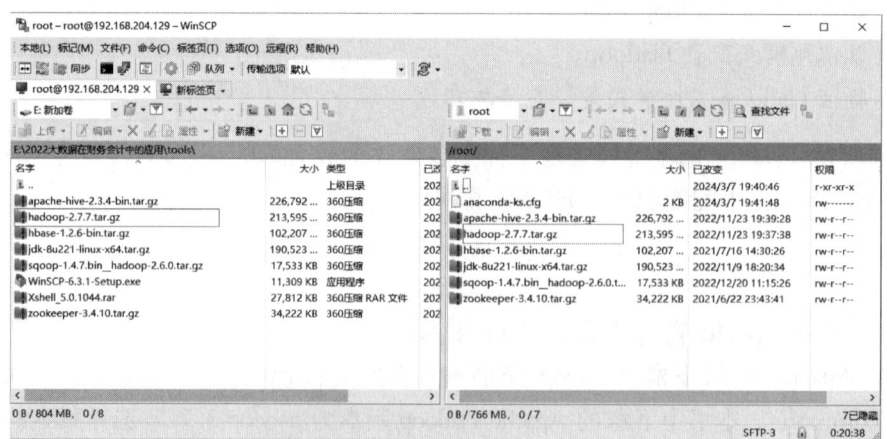

图 3.3.3　上传 hadoop-2.7.7.tar.gz 到 CentOS 7 虚拟机

3.3.2 安装并配置 Hadoop 环境

Hadoop 的安装和 JDK 一样，无须特殊的安装操作，只需要解压即可。

3.3.2.1 安装 Hadoop

登录 CentOS 7 虚拟机，将目录切换到"/root"，查看当前目录下的文件，命令操作如下：

```
cd /root
ls
```

查看到"/root"目录下的文件有 hadoop-2.7.7.tar.gz 安装包，如图 3.3.4 所示。

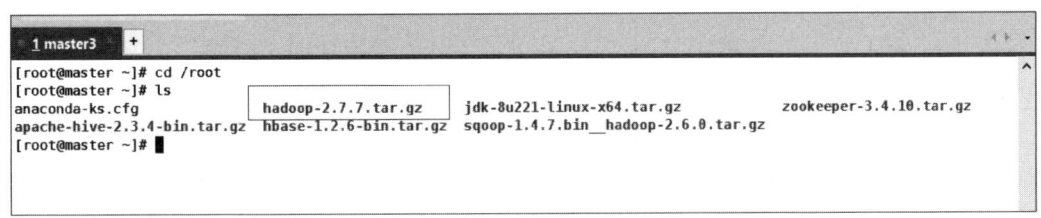

图 3.3.4　查看安装包

可以看到，当前目录下存在 hadoop-2.7.7.tar.gz 文件，说明 Hadoop 安装包成功上传到了 CentOS 7 虚拟机中。

接下来，输入如下命令解压 hadoop-2.7.7.tar.gz 文件：

```
tar -zxvf hadoop-2.7.7.tar.gz -C /opt/modules
```

查看文件是否解压成功，命令如下：

```
cd /opt/modules
ls
```

运行结果如图 3.3.5 所示。

```
[root@master modules]# cd /opt/modules/
[root@master modules]# ls
hadoop-2.7.7  jdk
[root@master modules]#
```

图 3.3.5　hadoop-2.7.7 安装成功

可以看到，当前目录多了一个 hadoop-2.7.7 文件夹，说明解压成功。

3.3.2.2 修改文件夹名

为便于后面配置方便，此处将 hadoop-2.7.7 文件夹名称修改为 hadoop，命令如下：

```
mv  hadoop-2.7.7  hadoop
ls
```

运行结果如图 3.3.6 所示。

接下来配置 Hadoop 系统环境变量。

```
[root@master modules]# mv hadoop-2.7.7/ hadoop
[root@master modules]# ls
hadoop   jdk
[root@master modules]#
```

图 3.3.6　修改文件夹名称为 hadoop

3.3.2.3　配置 Hadoop 系统环境变量

Hadoop 系统环境变量同样是在/etc/profile 文件中配置，命令如下：

```
vim  /etc/profile
```

在 vim 的插入"Insert"模式下，在/etc/profile 文件末尾追加如下内容：

```
export HADOOP_HOME=/opt/modules/hadoop
export HADOOP_CONF_DIR=$HADOOP_HOME/etc/hadoop
export ATH=$PATH:$HADOOP_HOME/bin:$HADOOP_HOME/sbin:$HADOOP_CONF_DIR
```

修改配置文件如图 3.3.7 所示。

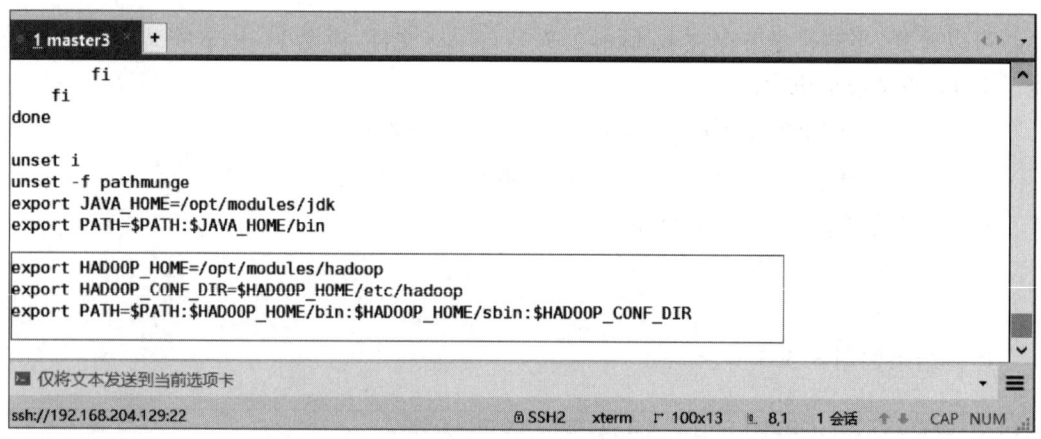

图 3.3.7　修改配置文件

修改结束后，按 Esc 键，录入":wq"保存退出。

3.3.2.4　使 Hadoop 系统环境变量生效

接着在命令行输入，使配置文件生效，命令如下：

```
source  /etc/profile
```

3.3.2.5　验证 Hadoop 是否安装成功

要验证 Hadoop 是否安装成功，只需要在命令行输入如下命令即可：

```
hadoop version
```

验证 Hadoop 是否安装成功的命令运行结果如图 3.3.8 所示。

可以看到，结果输出了"hadoop 2.7.7"，说明 Hadoop 安装并配置成功。

```
[root@master modules]# vi /etc/profile
[root@master modules]# source /etc/profile
[root@master modules]# hadoop version
Hadoop 2.7.7
Subversion Unknown -r c1aad84bd27cd79c3d1a7dd58202a8c3ee1ed3ac
Compiled by stevel on 2018-07-18T22:47Z
Compiled with protoc 2.5.0
From source with checksum 792e15d20b12c74bd6f19a1fb886490
This command was run using /opt/modules/hadoop/share/hadoop/common/hadoop-common-2.7.7.jar
[root@master modules]#
```

图 3.3.8　验证 Hadoop 是否安装成功

3.3.3　以本地模式配置 Hadoop

以本地模式配置 Hadoop，只需要在配置文件 hadoop-env.sh 中配置 JDK 安装目录即可。hadoop-env.sh 文件在"＄HADOOP_HOME/etc/hadoop"目录下，即 Hadoop 安装目录下的"etc/hadoop"目录下。这里将 Hadoop 安装在了目录"/opt/modules/hadoop-2.7.7"下，所以 hadoop-env.sh 文件在"/opt/modules/hadoop-2.7.7/etc/hadoop"目录下，命令如下：

```
cd /opt/modules/hadoop/etc/hadoop/
vim hadoop-env.sh
```

在 hadoop-env.sh 文件内容中找到 Java 路径设置代码，格式如下：

```
# export JAVA_HOME =
```

删除"＃"注释，将 Java JDK 的安装目录填写到"＝"后面，将该行修改为以下格式：

```
export JAVA_HOME = /opt/modules/jdk
```

修改配置文件 hadoop-env.sh 结果如图 3.3.9 所示。

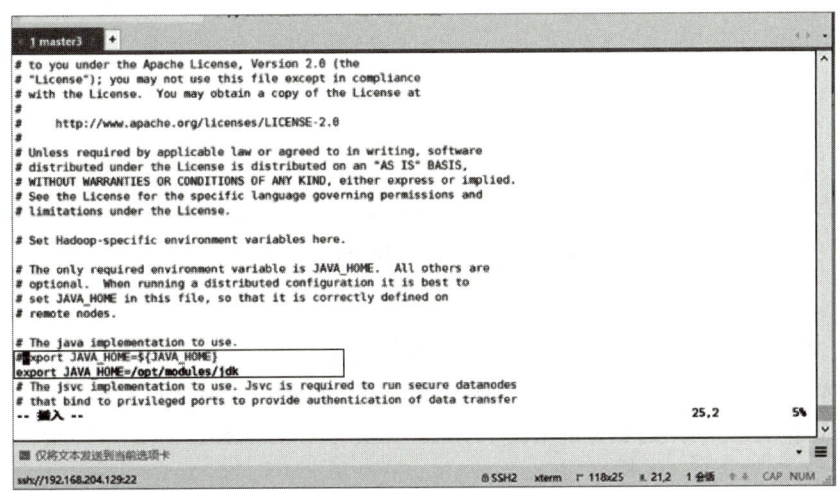

图 3.3.9　修改配置文件 hadoop-env.sh 结果

在插入模式下按 Esc 键，录入":wq"，按回车键，保存并退出 vim 编辑器。

3.3.4　验证 Hadoop 本地模式是否安装成功

验证本地模式是否安装成功的方式就是运行 Hadoop 自带的一个统计单词计数的

MapReduce 示例程序,将本地写有英文单词的数据文件输入 MapReduce 程序,经过 MapReduce 程序的处理,最终将结果文件输出到本地即可。

3.3.4.1 准备数据文件

创建目录"/home/hadoop/input",命令如下:

```
mkdir -p /home/hadoop/input
```

进入"/home/hadoop/input"目录,创建 data.input 文件,命令如下:

```
cd /home/hadoop/input/
vim data.input
```

data.input 文件的内容如下:

```
hadoop mapreduce hive flume
hbase spark storm flume sqoop hadoop hive kafka
spark hadoop storm
```

编辑 data.input 文件内容如图 3.3.10 所示。

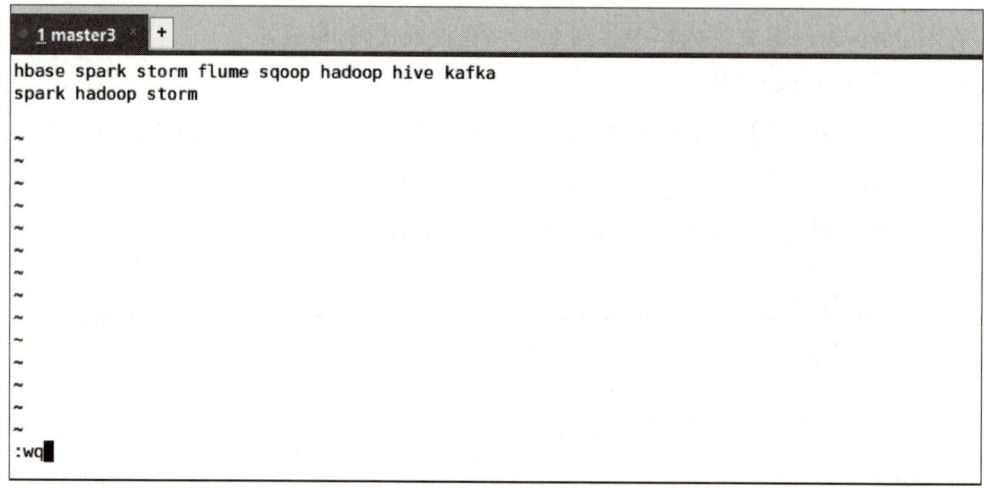

图 3.3.10 编辑 data.input 文件

3.3.4.2 运行 Hadoop 自带的 MapReduce 程序

Hadoop 自带的 MapReduce 程序在"$HADOOP_HOME/share/hadoop-2.7.7/mapreduce"目录下以 Jar 包的形式存在,具体的 Jar 包为 hadoop-mapreduce-examples-2.7.7.jar。

| 这里安装的 $HADOOP_HOME 目录为"/opt/modules/hadoop-2.7.7",所以 Hadoop 自带的 MapReduce 示例程序在"/opt/modules/hadoop-2.7.7/share/hadoop/mapreduce"目录的 hadoop-mapreduce-examples-2.7.7.jar 文件中。|

接下来运行 Hadoop 自带的 MapReduce 示例程序,统计 data.input 文件中的单词计数。执行如下命令:

```
hadoop jar /opt/modules/hadoop/share/hadoop/mapreduce/hadoop-mapreduce-examples-2.7.7.jar wordcount /home/hadoop/input/data.input /home/hadoop/output
```

通用格式说明如下：

(1) hadoop jar：以 Hadoop 命令行的形式运行 MapReduce 程序。

(2) /opt/modules/hadoop/share/hadoop/mapreduce/hadoop-mapreduce-examples-2.7.7.jar：Hadoop 自带的 MapReduce 程序所在 Jar 包的完整路径。

(3) wordcount：标识使用的是单词计数的 MapReducc 程序，因为 hadoop-mapreduce-examples-2.7.7.jar 文件中存在多个 MapReduce 程序。

参数说明如下：

(1) "/home/hadoop/input/data.input"是输入 data.input 文件所在的本地完整路径名称。

(2) "/home/hadoop/output"是本地结果数据输出目录。

若执行成功，输出信息如图 3.3.11 所示。

```
24/03/14 17:08:09 INFO mapred.LocalJobRunner: Finishing task: attempt_local1660035008_0001_r_000000_0
24/03/14 17:08:09 INFO mapred.LocalJobRunner: reduce task executor complete.
24/03/14 17:08:10 INFO mapreduce.Job:  map 100% reduce 100%
24/03/14 17:08:10 INFO mapreduce.Job: Job job_local1660035008_0001 completed successfully
24/03/14 17:08:10 INFO mapreduce.Job: Counters: 30
        File System Counters
                FILE: Number of bytes read=592854
                FILE: Number of bytes written=1179156
                FILE: Number of read operations=0
                FILE: Number of large read operations=0
                FILE: Number of write operations=0
        Map-Reduce Framework
                Map input records=4
                Map output records=15
                Map output bytes=155
                Map output materialized bytes=118
                Input split bytes=99
                Combine input records=15
                Combine output records=9
                Reduce input groups=9
                Reduce shuffle bytes=118
                Reduce input records=9
                Reduce output records=9
                Spilled Records=18
                Shuffled Maps =1
                Failed Shuffles=0
                Merged Map outputs=1
                GC time elapsed (ms)=25
                Total committed heap usage (bytes)=246767616
        Shuffle Errors
                BAD_ID=0
                CONNECTION=0
                IO_ERROR=0
                WRONG_LENGTH=0
                WRONG_MAP=0
                WRONG_REDUCE=0
        File Input Format Counters
                Bytes Read=96
        File Output Format Counters
                Bytes Written=88
[root@master input]#
```

图 3.3.11　运行 Hadoop 自带的 MapReduce 程序统计单词个数执行成功结果

3.3.4.3　查看执行结果

将 wordcount 执行结果输出到"/home/hadoop/output"目录下，因此需要先查看此目录下是否生成了结果文件，命令如下：

```
cd /home/hadoop/output/
ls
```

运行结果如图 3.3.12 所示。

```
[root@master input]# cd /home/hadoop/output/
[root@master output]# ls
part-r-00000  _SUCCESS
[root@master output]#
```

图 3.3.12　查看统计结果

可以看到,"/home/hadoop/output"目录下生成了 part-r-00000 和 _SUCCESS 文件。其中,执行结果存放在 part-r-00000 文件中。

接下来查看 part-r-00000 文件中的内容,命令如下:

```
cat  part-r-00000
```

运行结果如图 3.3.13 所示。

```
[root@master output]# cat part-r-00000
flume      2
hadoop     3
hbase      1
hive       2
kafka      1
mapreduce         1
spark      2
sqoop      1
```

图 3.3.13　查看 part-r-00000 文件内容

这里使用的命令是 cat part-r-00000。可以看到,part-r-00000 文件中存放了每个单词及该单词对应的数量,正确地输出了 MapReduce 执行结果。

至此,本地模式的 Hadoop 环境搭建完成并验证成功。

任务 3.4　Hadoop 的伪分布模式安装和配置

任务描述

本任务在完成 Hadoop 本地模式安装的基础上,对 Hadoop 的配置文件和环境变量进行配置,再格式化 NameNode、启动 Hadoop,达到理解原理、熟悉安装流程、掌握伪分布模式安装与配置 Hadoop 的目的,并能用伪分布模式调用 Hadoop 自带的程序解决实际问题。

关键步骤

(1) 以伪分布模式配置 Hadoop 的配置文件。
(2) 格式化 NameNode。
(3) 启动 Hadoop。
(4) 验证 Hadoop 伪分布模式是否安装并启动成功。

Hadoop 伪分布模式的安装和配置比本地模式要复杂些，除了需要在 Hadoop 的 hadoop-env.sh 文件中配置 JAVA_HOME，还要配置 Hadoop 所使用的文件系统、HDFS 的副本数量和 YARN 地址，以及服务器的 SSH 免密码登录等。

Hadoop 伪分布模式同样需要在 hadoop-env.sh 文件中配置 JAVA_HOME，因此本任务基于 JDK 和本地 Hadoop 完成成功的基础，继续进行 Hadoop 伪分布模式的配置。

3.4.1 以伪分布模式配置 Hadoop 的配置文件

对于 Hadoop 伪分布模式的配置，除了需要配置 hadoop-env.sh 文件，还需要配置以下 4 个文件：core-site.xml、hdfs-site.xml、mapred-site.xml 和 yarn-site.xml，每个文件都与 hadoop-env.sh 文件在同一目录下，即"/opt/modules/hadoop/etc/hadoop/"。各个文件的作用如下：

（1）core-site.xml：指定 NameNode 的位置。hadoop.tmp.dir 是 Hadoop 文件系统依赖的基础配置，很多路径都依赖它。如果 hdfs-site.xml 中不配置 NameNode 和 DataNode 的存放位置，则默认就放在这个路径中。

（2）hdfs-site.xml：配置 NameNode 和 DataNode 存放文件的具体路径；配置副本的数量。

（3）mapred-site.xml：在 hadoop-2.7.7 版本中是没有此文件的，需要将 mapred-site.xml.template 重命名；配置 MapReduce 作业是提交到 YARN 集群还是使用本地作业执行器在本地执行。

（4）yarn-site.xml：配置 ResourceManager 所在节点的主机名；配置辅助服务列表。这些服务由 NodeManager 执行。

1）配置 core-site.xml 文件

命令如下：

```
cd /opt/modules/hadoop/etc/hadoop/
vim core-site.xml
```

在其中添加以下代码：

```
<configuration>
    <property>
        <name>fs.defaultFS</name>
        <value>hdfs://master:9000</value>
    </property>
    <property>
        <name>hadoop.tmp.dir</name>
        <value>file:/opt/modules/hadoop/tmp</value>
    </property>
</configuraition>
```

2）配置 hdfs-site.xml 文件

命令如下：

```
cd /opt/modules/hadoop/etc/hadoop/
vim hdfs-site.xml
```

在其中添加以下代码:

```
<configuration>
    <property>
        <name>dfs.replication</name>
        <value>1</value>
    </property>
    <property>
        <name>dfs.namenode.name.dir</name>
        <value>file:/opt/modules/hadoop/tmp/dfs/name</value>
    </property>
    <property>
        <name>dfs.datanode.data.dir</name>
        <value>file:/opt/modules/hadoop/tmp/dfs/data</value>
    </property>
</configuration>
```

注意

由于配置的是 Hadoop 的伪分布模式,这里将文件的副本数量配置为 1。在分布模式下,此值至少需要配置为 3。

3) 配置 mapred-site.xml 文件

将 mapred-site.xml.template 复制为 mapred-site.xml,再编辑 mapred-site.xml,命令如下:

```
cd /opt/modules/hadoop/etc/hadoop/
cp  mapred-site.xml.template   mapred-site.xml
vim mapred-site.xml
```

在其中添加以下代码:

```
<configuration>
    <property>
        <name>mapreduce.framework.name</name>
        <value>yarn</value>
    </property>
</configuration>
```

4) 配置 yarn-site.xml 文件

命令如下:

```
cd /opt/modules/hadoop/etc/hadoop/
vim yarn-site.xml
```

在其中添加以下代码:

```
<configuration>
    <property>
        <name>yarn.resourcemanager.hostname</name>
        <value>master</value>
    </property>
    <property>
        <name>yarn.nodemanager.aux-services</name>
        <value>mapreduce_shuffle</value>
    </property>
</configuration>
```

注意

4个配置文件中的 master 是在安装配置 CentOS 7 虚拟机时配置的虚拟机主机名,之前配置了主机名和 IP 地址的映射关系,配置主机名后可通过主机名映射到 IP 地址进行通信。

至此,Hadoop 伪分布模式配置完成。接下来需要格式化 NameNode,启动 Hadoop,并验证 Hadoop 伪分布模式是否安装并启动成功。

3.4.2 格式化 NameNode

格式化 NameNode 的操作很简单,只需要在命令行执行如下命令即可:

```
hdfs namenode -format
```

格式化输出结果如图 3.4.1 所示。

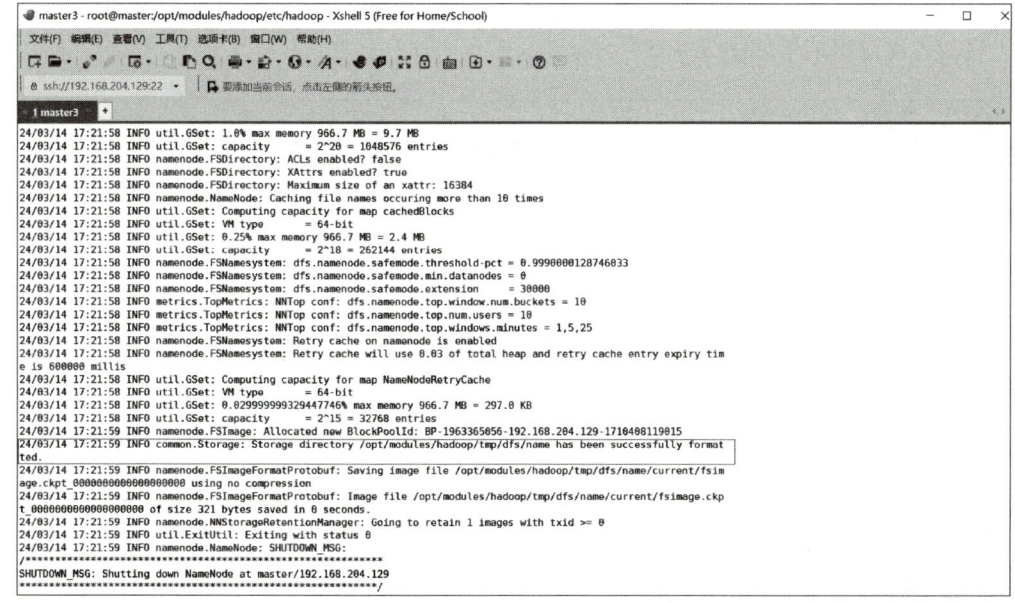

图 3.4.1 格式化输出结果

其中出现"24/03/14 17:21:59 INFO common.Storage:Storage directory /opt/

modules/hadoop/tmp/dfs/name has been successfully formatted."信息，说明格式化 NameNode 成功。

将虚拟机目录切换到 Hadoop 的安装目录"/opt/modules/hadoop"，查看当前目录下的信息，命令如下：

```
cd /opt/modules/hadoop/
ls
```

输出结果如图 3.4.2 所示。

```
[root@master hadoop]# cd /opt/modules/hadoop/
[root@master hadoop]# ls
bin  etc  include  lib  libexec  LICENSE.txt  logs  NOTICE.txt  README.txt  sbin  share  tmp
[root@master hadoop]#
```

图 3.4.2　格式化成功出现 tmp 文件夹

可以看到，Hadoop 的安装目录"/opt/modules/hadoop"下多了一个 tmp 文件夹，这也说明 NameNode 已格式化成功。

3.4.3　启动 Hadoop

格式化 NameNode 成功之后，就需要启动 Hadoop。启动 Hadoop 分为两步，即先启动 HDFS，再启动 YARN。

1) 启动 HDFS

在命令行输入如下命令启动 HDFS：

```
start-dfs.sh
```

启动过程输出结果如图 3.4.3 所示。

```
[root@master hadoop]# start-dfs.sh
Starting namenodes on [master]
master: starting namenode, logging to /opt/modules/hadoop/logs/hadoop-root-namenode-master.out
localhost: starting datanode, logging to /opt/modules/hadoop/logs/hadoop-root-datanode-master.out
Starting secondary namenodes [0.0.0.0]
0.0.0.0: starting secondarynamenode, logging to /opt/modules/hadoop/logs/hadoop-root-secondarynamenode-master.out
[root@master hadoop]#
```

图 3.4.3　HDFS 启动过程

根据输出信息，得知运行 start-dfs.sh 命令启动了 NameNode、DataNode 和 SecondaryNameNode 三个进程。用 jps 查看启动的进程，操作命令如下：

```
jps
```

输出结果如图 3.4.4 所示。

```
[root@master hadoop]# jps
5025 Jps
4755 DataNode
4916 SecondaryNameNode
4629 NameNode
[root@master hadoop]#
```

图 3.4.4　用 jps 查看启动的进程

可以看到，系统确实启动了 NameNode、DataNode 和 Secondary NameNode 这三个进程。

2）启动 YARN

在命令行输入如下命令启动 YARN：

```
start-yarn.sh
```

输出结果如图 3.4.5 所示。

```
[root@master hadoop]# start-yarn.sh
starting yarn daemons
starting resourcemanager, logging to /opt/modules/hadoop/logs/yarn-root-resourcemanager-master.out
localhost: starting nodemanager, logging to /opt/modules/hadoop/logs/yarn-root-nodemanager-master.out
[root@master hadoop]#
```

图 3.4.5 启动 YARN 过程

根据输出信息，得知启动了 NodeManager 和 ResourceManager 两个进程。

查看启动的进程，操作命令如下：

```
jps
```

输出结果如图 3.4.6 所示。

```
[root@master hadoop]# jps
5490 Jps
4755 DataNode
4916 SecondaryNameNode
4629 NameNode
5192 NodeManager
5081 ResourceManager
[root@master hadoop]#
```

图 3.4.6 用 jps 查看启动的进程

可以看到，通过 start-yarn.sh 命令启动 YARN 后，启动了 NodeManager 和 ResourceManager 两个进程。

3.4.4 验证 Hadoop 伪分布模式是否安装并启动成功

验证 Hadoop 伪分布模式是否安装并启动成功有两种方式：一种是以浏览器方式验证，即在浏览器中输入相应的地址查看 NameNode 的状态是否为"活跃"状态，另一种是运行 MapReduce 程序来验证是否安装并启动成功。

1）以浏览器方式验证环境搭建是否成功

在浏览器中查看 NameNode 的状态。在 Windows 浏览器中输入 Master 虚拟机的 IP 地址及端口号：

```
http://192.168.204.129:50070
```

登录界面如图 3.4.7 所示。

可以看到"Overview 'master:9000' (active)"，说明当前 NameNode 处于"活跃"状态。

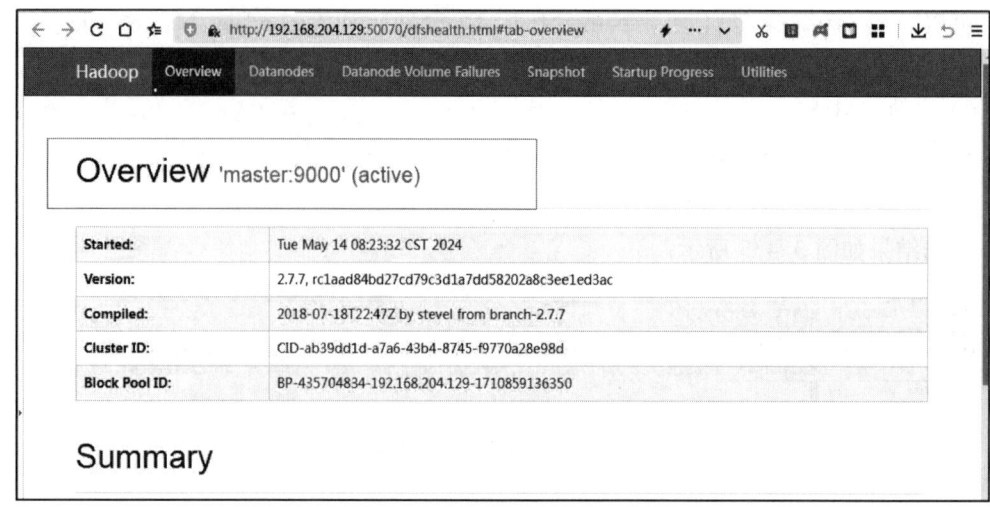

图 3.4.7　查看 NameNode 的"活跃"状态

2) 运行 MapReduce 程序验证环境搭建是否成功

验证思路为:在 CentOS 7 虚拟机上新建测试数据文件,并将文件上传到 Hadoop 的 HDFS 中,执行 Hadoop 自带的 MapReduce 程序,查看执行结果。其操作步骤如下。

第 1 步:准备数据文件。

此处准备数据文件的步骤与上个任务准备数据文件的步骤相同,仍然用 data.input 文件,内容如下:

```
hadoop mapreduce hive flume
hbase spark storm flume sqoop hadoop hive kafka
spark hadoop storm
```

在 HDFS 上创建输入文件目录。在 HDFS 上新建"/data/input"目录,具体操作命令如下:

```
hdfs dfs -mkdir /data
hdfs dfs -mkdir /data/input
```

查看"/data/input"目录是否创建成功,命令如下:

```
hdfs dfs -ls /data/
```

输出结果如图 3.4.8 所示。

```
[root@master hadoop]# hdfs dfs -ls /data/
Found 1 items
drwxr-xr-x   - root supergroup          0 2024-03-14 17:41 /data/input
[root@master hadoop]#
```

图 3.4.8　HDFS 上创建"/data/input"目录

可以看到,"/data/input"目录创建成功了。

第 2 步:上传数据文件到 HDFS。

上传数据到 HDFS 比较简单,只需要执行如下命令即可:

单元 3　Hadoop 大数据处理平台的安装与配置

```
hdfs dfs -put /home/hadoop/input/data.input /data/input
```

注意

Hadoop 的具体命令用法会在下一单元中详细讲解，这里先用该命令将文件上传到 HDFS 中。

接下来查看文件是否上传成功，输入如下命令：

```
hdfs dfs -ls /data/input
```

输出结果如图 3.4.9 所示。

```
[root@master hadoop]# hdfs dfs -ls /data/input
Found 1 items
-rw-r--r--   1 root supergroup         96 2024-03-14 17:41 /data/input/data.input
[root@master hadoop]#
```

图 3.4.9　查看上传是否成功

第 3 步：执行 MapReduce 程序。

这里同样运行 Hadoop 自带的 wordcount 计数程序，具体操作命令如下：

```
hadoop jar /opt/modules/hadoop/share/hadoop/mapreduce/hadoop-mapreduce-examples-2.7.7.jar wordcount /data/input/data.input /data/output
```

参数说明如下：

/data/input/data.input：输入 data.input 文件所在的 HDFS 上的完整路径名称。

/data/output：HDFS 结果数据输出目录。

执行成功后会输出如图 3.4.10 的信息。

```
24/03/14 17:44:10 INFO mapreduce.Job:  map 0% reduce 0%
24/03/14 17:44:19 INFO mapreduce.Job:  map 100% reduce 0%
24/03/14 17:44:27 INFO mapreduce.Job:  map 100% reduce 100%
24/03/14 17:44:28 INFO mapreduce.Job: Job job_1710409009490_0001 completed successfully
24/03/14 17:44:28 INFO mapreduce.Job: Counters: 49
        File System Counters
                FILE: Number of bytes read=118
                FILE: Number of bytes written=245641
                FILE: Number of read operations=0
                FILE: Number of large read operations=0
                FILE: Number of write operations=0
                HDFS: Number of bytes read=201
                HDFS: Number of bytes written=76
                HDFS: Number of read operations=6
                HDFS: Number of large read operations=0
                HDFS: Number of write operations=2
        Job Counters
                Launched map tasks=1
                Launched reduce tasks=1
                Data-local map tasks=1
                Total time spent by all maps in occupied slots (ms)=7057
                Total time spent by all reduces in occupied slots (ms)=4564
                Total time spent by all map tasks (ms)=7057
                Total time spent by all reduce tasks (ms)=4564
                Total vcore-milliseconds taken by all map tasks=7057
                Total vcore-milliseconds taken by all reduce tasks=4564
                Total megabyte-milliseconds taken by all map tasks=7226368
                Total megabyte-milliseconds taken by all reduce tasks=4673536
        Map-Reduce Framework
                Map input records=4
                Map output records=15
```

图 3.4.10　MapReduce 程序执行成功

第 4 步：查看执行结果。

查看执行结果也比较简单，先查看 HDFS 上是否创建了"/data/output"目录，命令如下：

```
hdfs dfs -ls /data
```

输出结果如图 3.4.11 所示。

```
[root@master hadoop]# hdfs dfs -ls /data
Found 2 items
drwxr-xr-x   - root supergroup          0 2024-03-14 17:41 /data/input
drwxr-xr-x   - root supergroup          0 2024-03-14 17:44 /data/output
```

图 3.4.11　查看执行结果

可以看到，在 wordcount 程序执行的过程中，自动创建了"/data/output"目录。
接下来查看"/data/output"目录下的信息，命令如下：

```
hdfs dfs -ls /data/output
```

输出结果如图 3.4.12 所示。

```
[root@master hadoop]# hdfs dfs -ls /data/output
Found 2 items
-rw-r--r--   1 root supergroup          0 2024-03-14 17:44 /data/output/_SUCCESS
-rw-r--r--   1 root supergroup         76 2024-03-14 17:44 /data/output/part-r-00000
[root@master hadoop]#
```

图 3.4.12　查看 wordcount 程序运行结果

可见 wordcount 运行结果存放到了 part-r-00000 文件中，输入如下命令查看文件中的内容：

```
hdfs dfs -cat /data/output/part-r-00000
```

输出结果如图 3.4.13 所示。

```
[root@master hadoop]# hdfs dfs -cat /data/output/part-r-00000
flume      2
hadoop     3
hbase      1
hive       2
kafka      1
mapreduce       1
spark      2
sqoop      1
storm      2
[root@master hadoop]#
```

图 3.4.13　查看 part-r-00000 文件内容

可见 wordcount 程序将 data.input 文件的单词个数全部统计出来了。

任务 3.5　Hadoop 的完全分布模式安装

任务描述

本任务在完成 Hadoop 本地模式安装的基础上，对 Hadoop 的配置文件和环境变量进行进一步配置，再格式化 NameNode、启动 Hadoop，达到理解原理、熟悉安装流程的目的。学生练习用 3 台虚拟主机进行 Hadoop 完全分布模式安装与配置，并能用完全分布模式调用 Hadoop 自带的程序解决实际问题。

关键步骤

（1）服务器规划。
（2）由 master 克隆出两台虚拟机 slave1 和 slave2。
（3）启动 3 台虚拟机，配置 slave1 和 slave2 的地址。
（4）设置主机名，将主机名与 IP 地址建立映射。
（5）配置关闭防火墙。
（6）配置免密码登录。
（7）搭建并测试 Hadoop 集群环境。

在实际工作中，可以将 Hadoop 集群搭建在物理机上，也可以搭建在虚拟机上，但是如果搭建在虚拟机上，需要保证虚拟机的可靠性和稳定性。需要搭建的计算机集群包含大量服务器，但考虑到读者搭建 Hadoop 集群的服务器数量有限，大部分读者的计算机性能也有限，无法安装更多台 CentOS 7 虚拟机，因此本任务给出一个基于 3 台虚拟机搭建 Hadoop 集群的示例。

3.5.1　服务器规划

本任务主要介绍基于 3 台 CentOS 7 服务器搭建的 Hadoop 集群，具体规划如表 3.5.1 所示。

表 3.5.1　Hadoop 集群搭建服务器规划

主机名	IP	安装的软件	运行的进程
master	192.168.204.129	JDK Hadoop YARN	NameNode DataNode NodeManager
slave1	192.168.204.130	JDK Hadoop YARN	DataNode SecondaryNameNode NodeManager
slave2	192.168.204.131	JDK Hadoop YARN	DataNode ResourceManager NodeManager

读者可按照表 3.5.1 安装相应的虚拟机环境,具体安装操作可以参见上一个任务。同样,在搭建 Hadoop 集群之前,先要做一些准备工作。

3.5.2 由 master 克隆出两台虚拟机 slave1 和 slave2

(1) 打开 VMware Workstation,右击 master 虚拟机,打开快捷菜单,选择"管理"—"克隆",执行虚拟机克隆功能,如图 3.5.1 所示。

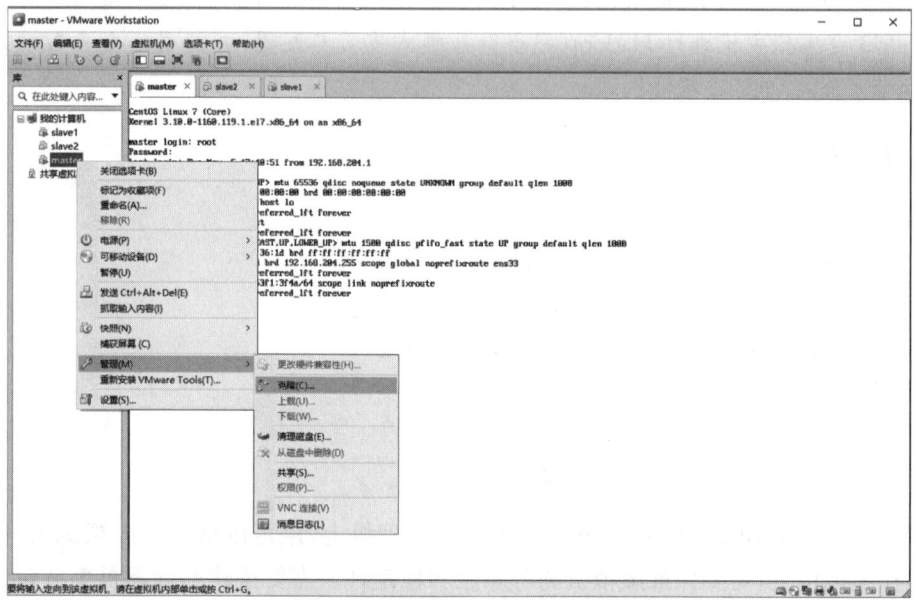

图 3.5.1　执行虚拟机克隆功能

(2) 打开"欢迎使用克隆虚拟机向导"页面,若此时 master 处于开机状态,则提示"无法为处于开启或挂起状态的虚拟机或快照创建克隆",如图 3.5.2 所示。

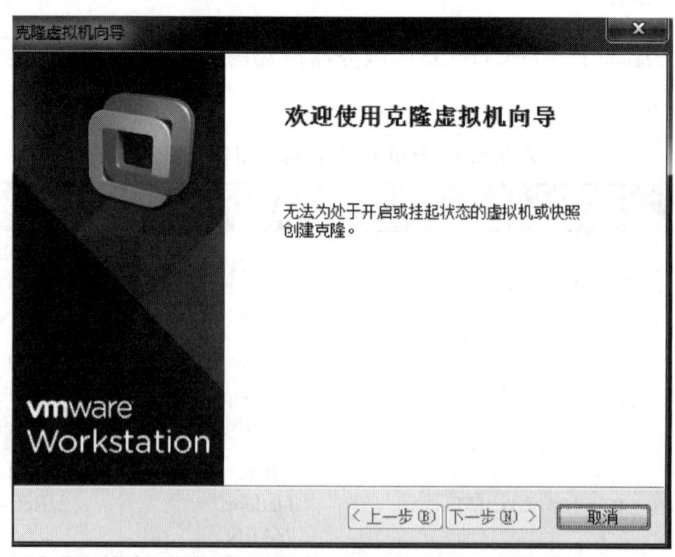

图 3.5.2　克隆虚拟机向导页面,无法克隆提示

（3）点击"取消"按钮，重新回到 VMware Workstation，准备关闭 master。

（4）用鼠标右击 master 虚拟机，打开快捷菜单，选择"电源"—"关机"，执行关闭虚拟机功能，如图 3.5.3 所示。

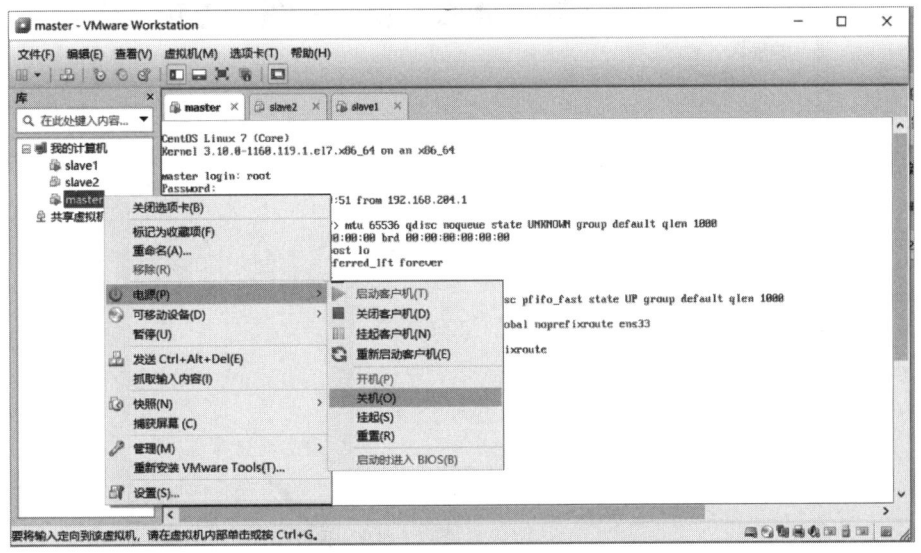

图 3.5.3　关闭虚拟机操作界面

提示检查客户机操作系统，确认关闭虚拟机 master，如图 3.5.4 所示。

（5）点击"关机"按钮，执行关闭虚拟机 master。

（6）再次执行虚拟机克隆功能。用鼠标右击 master 虚拟机，打开快捷菜单，选择"管理"—"克隆"，打开欢迎使用克隆虚拟机向导页面，如图 3.5.5 所示。

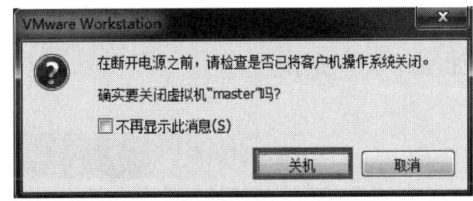

图 3.5.4　确认关闭虚拟机 master

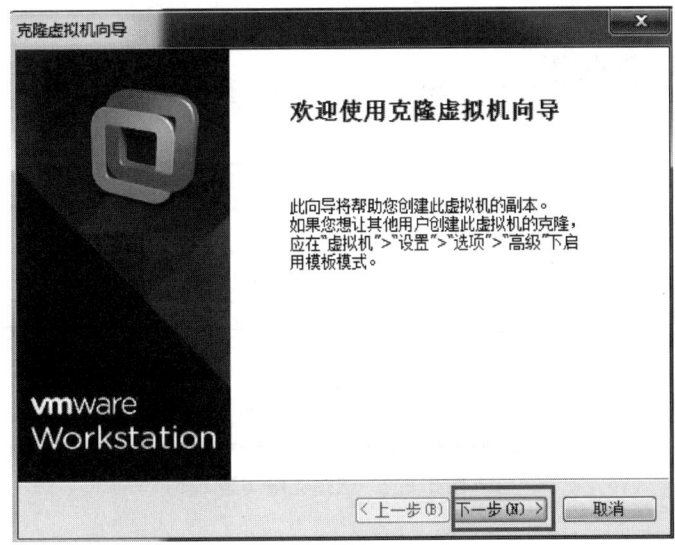

图 3.5.5　欢迎使用克隆虚拟机向导页面

(7) 点击"下一步"按钮,打开"克隆虚拟机向导",在"克隆源"中选中"虚拟机中的当前状态",如图 3.5.6 所示。

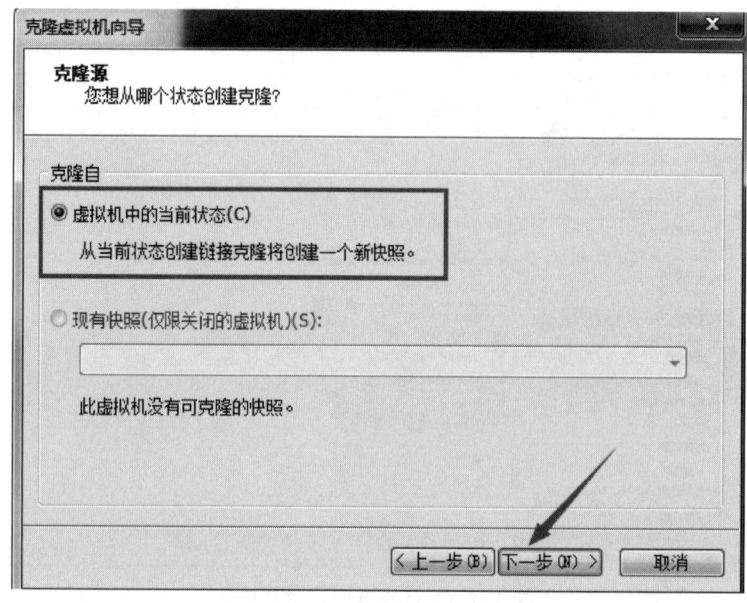

图 3.5.6 选择克隆

(8) 点击"下一步"按钮,打开"克隆类型"向导,在"克隆方法"中选中"创建完整克隆",如图 3.5.7 所示。

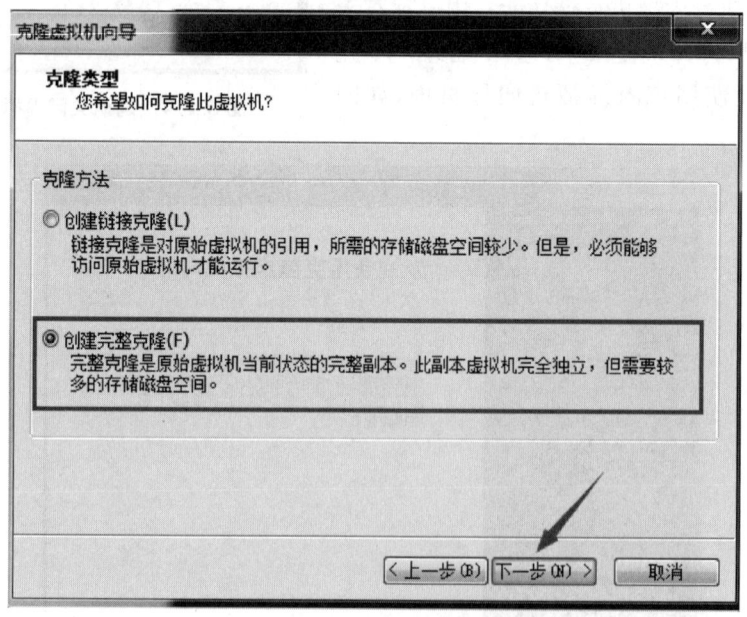

图 3.5.7 选择克隆类型

(9) 点击"下一步"按钮,打开"新虚拟机名称"向导,命名虚拟机名称和安装位置,可以对克隆后的虚拟机命名,并选择虚拟机的安装目录。此处暂时就选默认值,如图 3.5.8 所示。

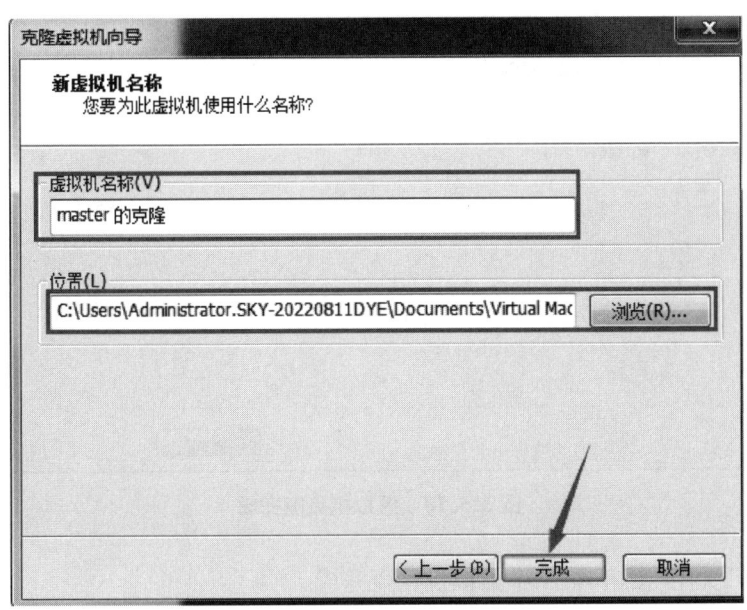

图 3.5.8　新虚拟机命名和存放位置选择

(10) 点击"完成"按钮,开始克隆虚拟机,如图 3.5.9 所示。

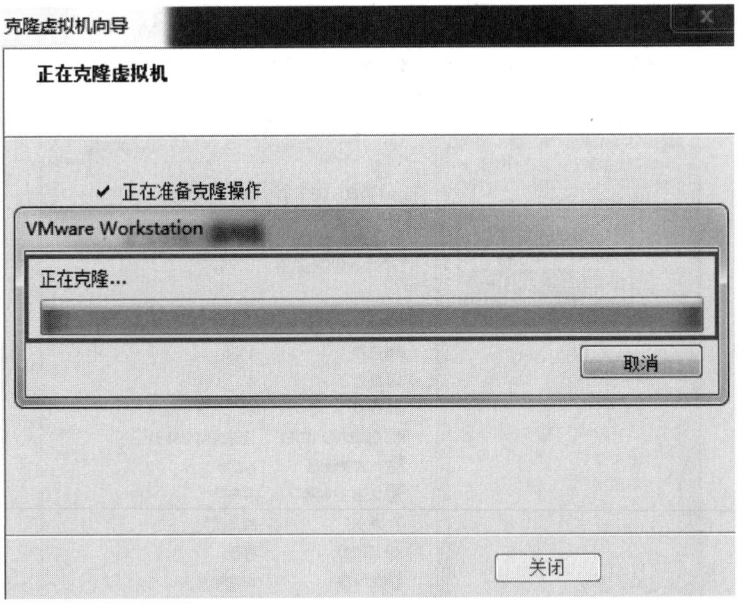

图 3.5.9　克隆虚拟机

(11) 等待克隆进度条满格后,完成虚拟机克隆工作,如图 3.5.10 所示。

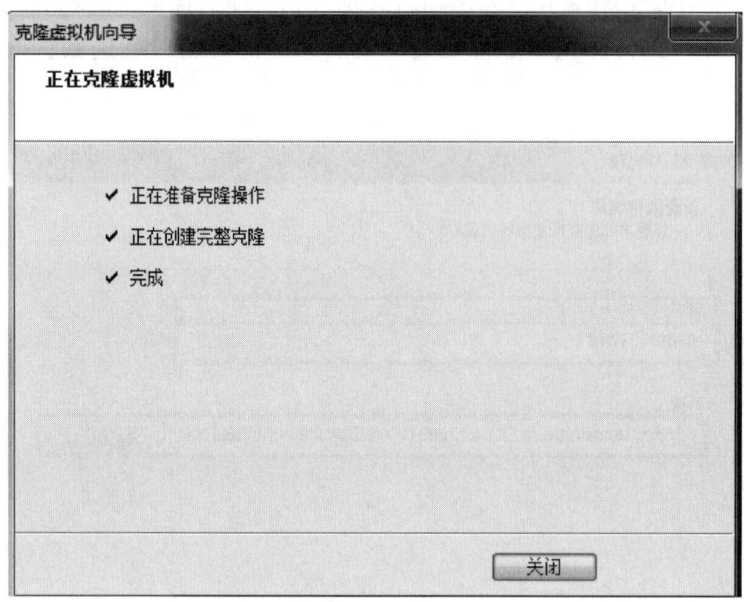

图 3.5.10 虚拟机克隆完成

(12) 点击"关闭"按钮,第二个虚拟机克隆完成。

用同样方法再克隆第三个虚拟机。

返回 VMware Workstation,可见新建了两个虚拟机"master 的克隆"和"master 的克隆(2)",如图 3.5.11 所示。

图 3.5.11 成功新建了两个虚拟机

将新克隆的虚拟机分别命名为 slave1 和 slave2,如图 3.5.12 所示。

图 3.5.12　将新建的虚拟机命名为 slave1 和 slave2

3.5.3　启动 3 台虚拟机,配置 slave1 和 slave2 的地址

(1) 启动 3 台虚拟机,查看 slave1 和 slave2 的地址,发现与 master 相同,都为 192.168. 204.129,如图 3.5.13 所示,需要重新设置静态 IP 地址。

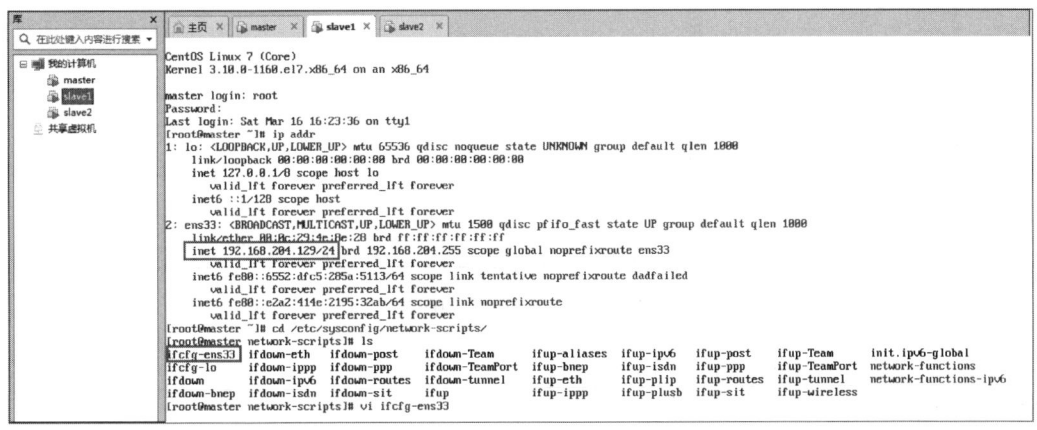

图 3.5.13　查看 slave1 的网卡地址

(2) 配置 slave1 和 slave2 的 IP 地址和主机名。

在 slave1 上执行以下命令:

```
cd /etc/sysconfig/network-scripts
vi  ifcfg-ens33
```

在 Insert 模式下,将文件中原来的"IPADDR = 192.168.204.129"修改为"IPADDR = 192.168.204.130"后,按 Esc 键,输入":wq"保存退出,如图 3.5.14 所示。

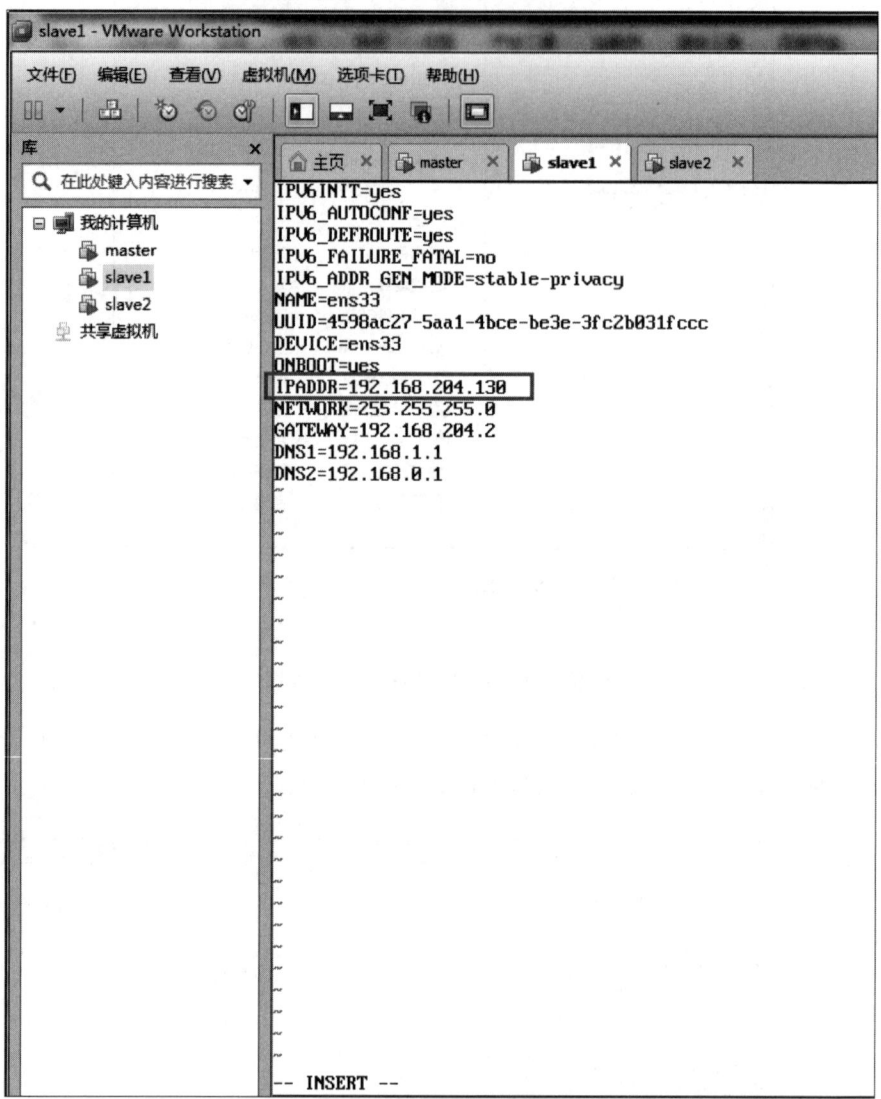

图 3.5.14　修改 slave1 的网卡地址

(3) 重启网络,再查看 slave1 的 IP 地址。
命令如下:

```
systemctl retart network
ip addr
```

执行结果如图 3.5.15 所示。

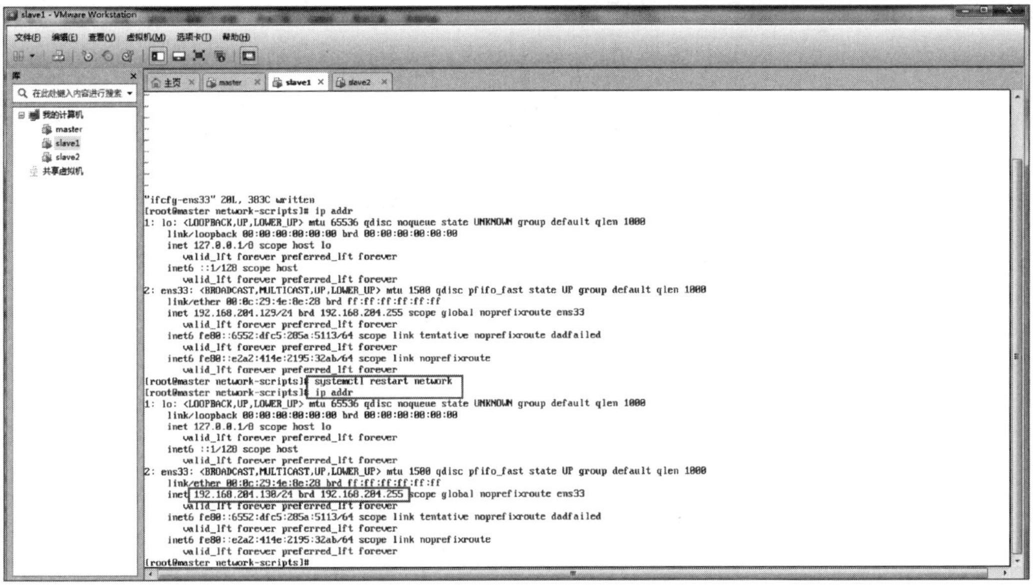

图 3.5.15 slave1 网卡地址修改成功

IP 地址设置成功，由 192.168.204.129 被修改为 192.168.204.130。

用同样方法，把 slave2 的 IP 地址修改为 192.168.204.131，如图 3.5.16 所示。

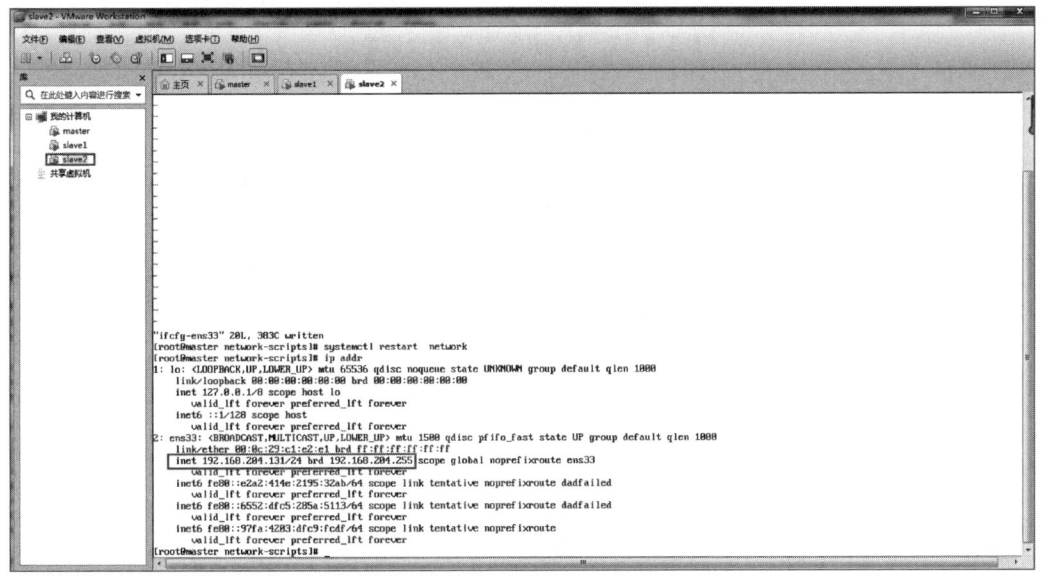

图 3.5.16 slave2 网卡地址修改成功

3.5.4 设置主机名，将主机名与 IP 地址建立映射

配置主机名和 IP 的映射关系，在配置文件中用主机名来代替烦琐的 IP 地址，在 IP 地址发生改变的情况下，也只需要修改 hosts 文件，而不需要去修改每一个配置文件里的 IP 地址。

3.5.4.1 用 Xshell 开启三个连接窗口

(1) 双击桌面上的 Xshell 图标,打开 Xshell 窗口新建会话窗口,如图 3.5.17 所示。

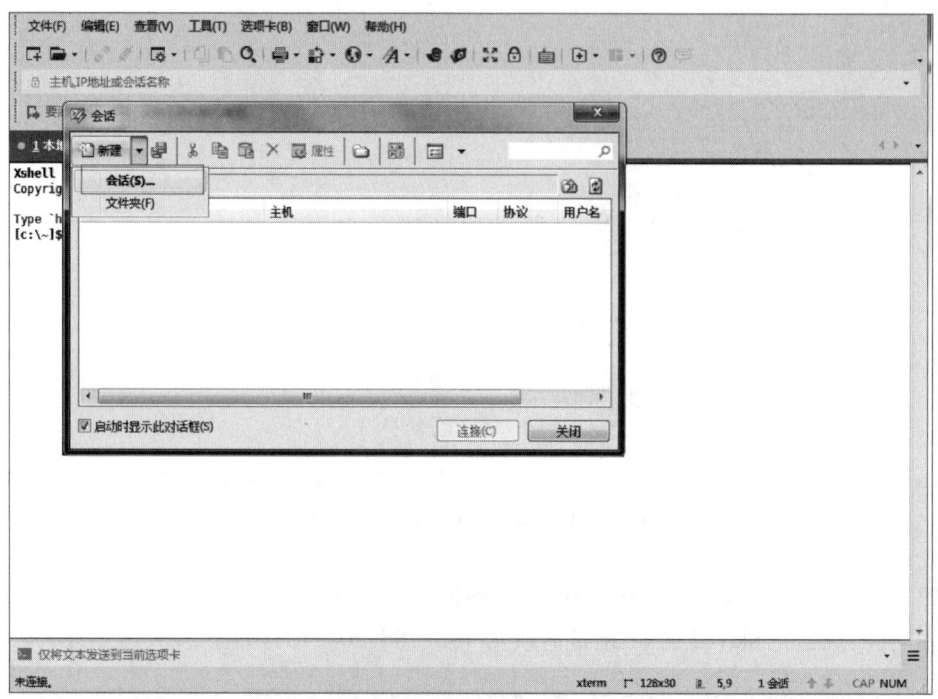

图 3.5.17　Xshell 窗口新建会话窗口

(2) 点击"新建"—"会话",打开新建会话属性页面,如图 3.5.18 所示。

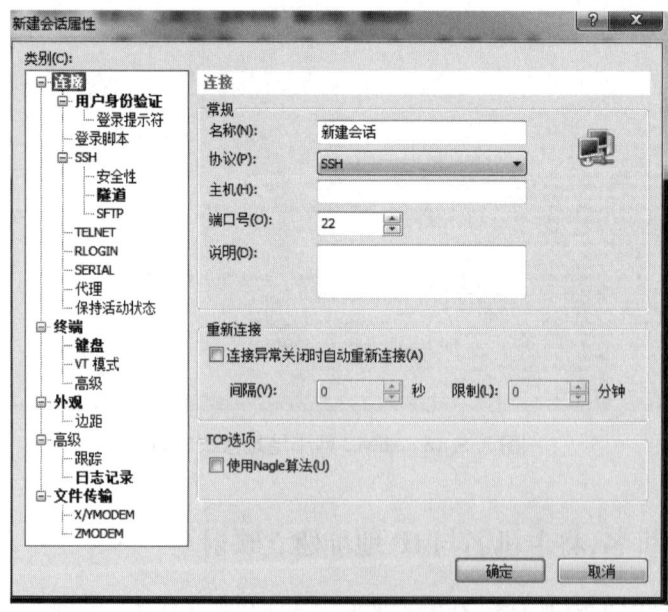

图 3.5.18　新建会话属性页面

(3) 在右侧文本框中录入信息如下：

名称：master

主机：192.168.204.129

新建会话页面设置如图 3.5.19 所示。

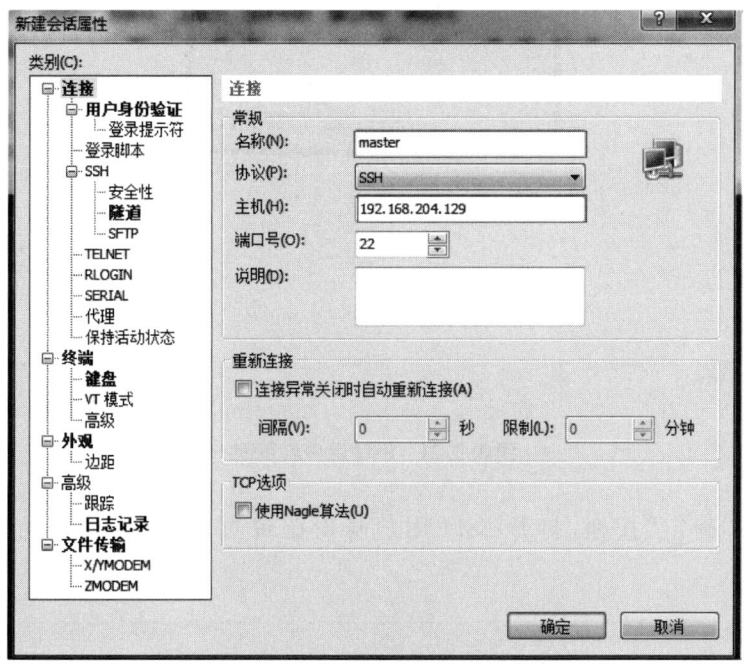

图 3.5.19　新建会话页面设置

(4) 点击"确定"按钮，建立 master 的会话，如图 3.5.20 所示。

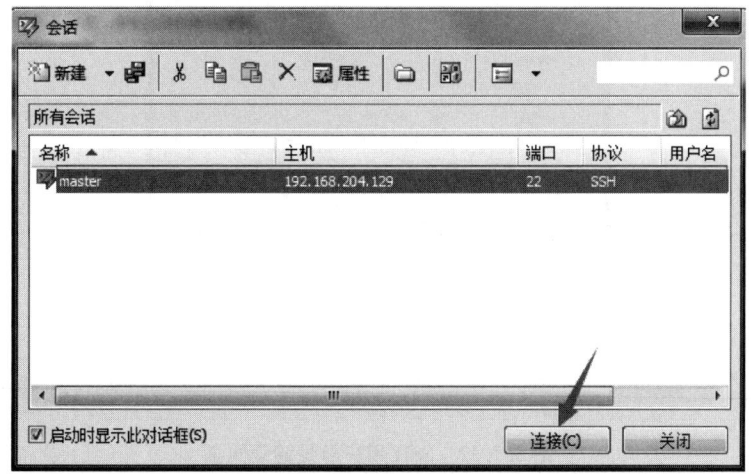

图 3.5.20　建立 master 的会话

(5) 点击"连接"按钮，打开 SSH 用户名页面，录入用户名为"root"，如图 3.5.21 所示。

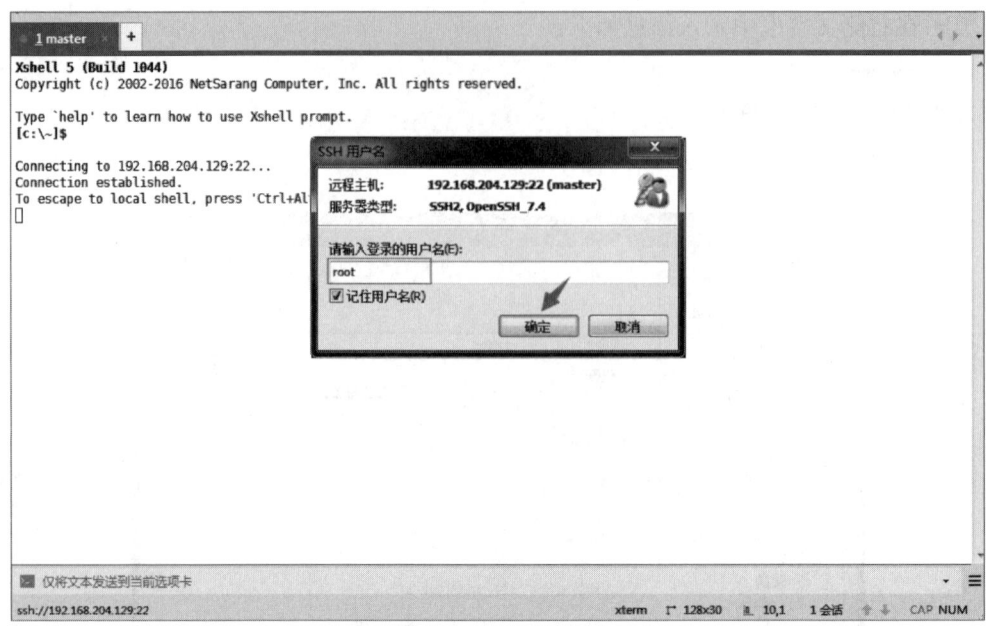

图 3.5.21　SSH 用户名页面

(6) 点击"确定"按钮，打开 SSH 用户身份验证页面，录入密码为"root123"，如图 3.5.22 所示。

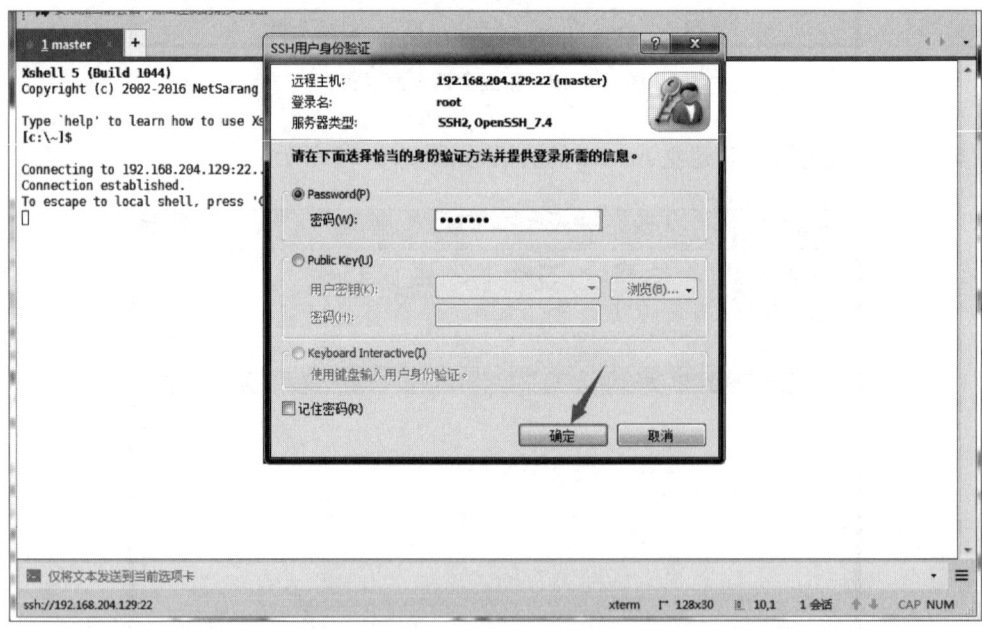

图 3.5.22　SSH 用户身份验证页面

(7) 点击"确定"按钮，在 Xshell 中连接 master 成功，以后就可以直接在 Xshell 中对 master 进行配置了，如图 3.5.23 所示。

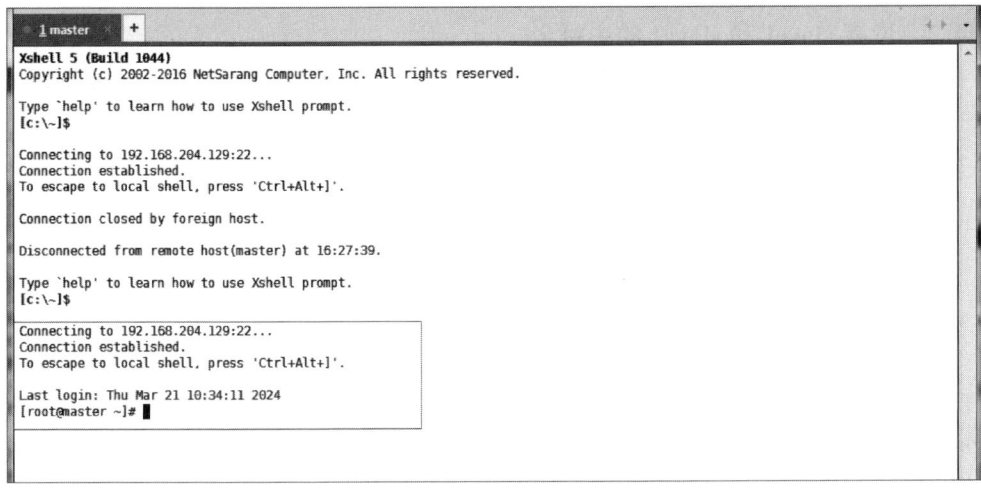

图 3.5.23 Xshell 连接 master 成功

用同样的方法,在 Xshell 中建立 slave1 和 slave2 的连接,如图 3.5.24 所示。

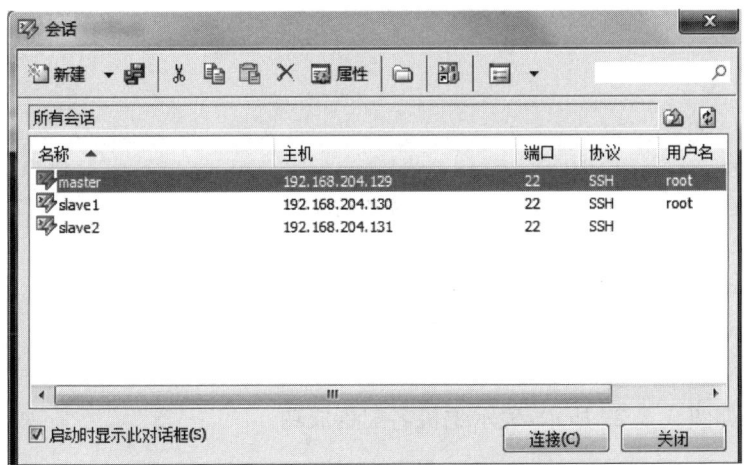

图 3.5.24 在 Xshell 中建成三个虚拟机的连接

分别打开 slave1、slave2 连接,在 Xshell 中启动 master、slave1、slave2 三个虚拟机,如图 3.5.25 所示。

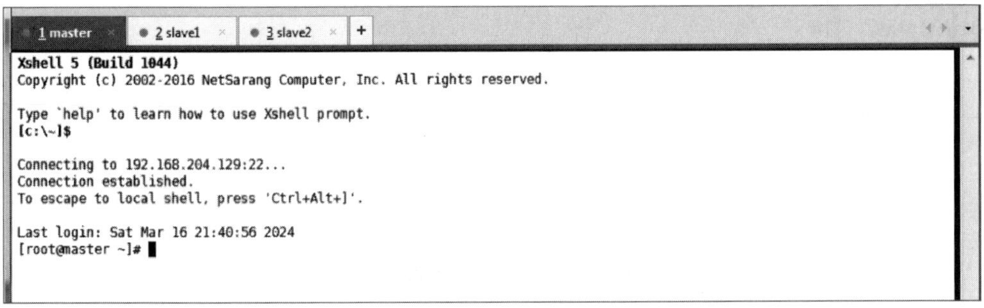

图 3.5.25 启动 master、slave1、slave2 三个虚拟机

3.5.4.2　设置 slave1 和 slave2 的主机名

在 slave1 和 slave2 上分别执行 hostnamectl set-hostname 命令，将主机名分别配置为 slave1 和 slave2。

在 slave1 上执行如下命令：

```
hostnamectl set-hostname slave1
bash
```

执行结果如图 3.5.26 所示，表示主机名配置成功。

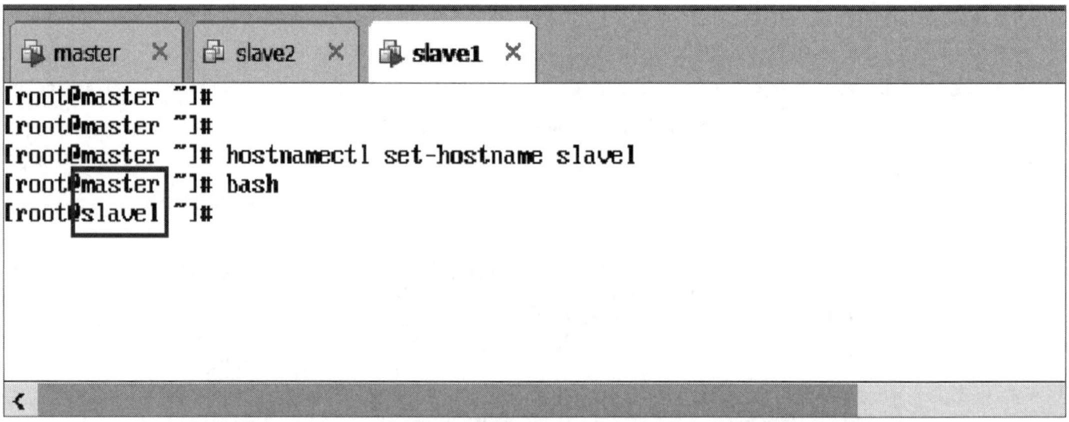

图 3.5.26　将主机名配置为 slave1

在 slave2 上执行如下命令：

```
hostnamectl set-hostname slave2
bash
```

执行结果如图 3.5.27 所示，表示主机名配置成功。

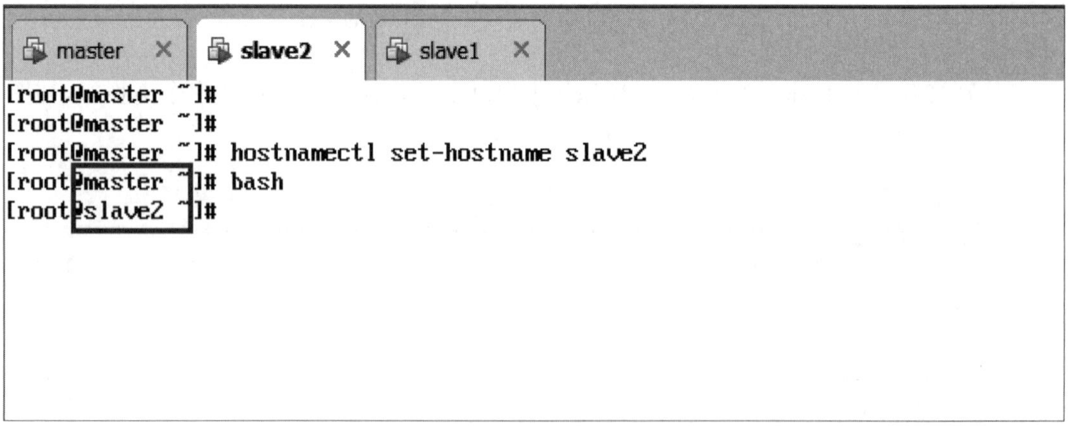

图 3.5.27　将主机名配置为 slave2

3.5.4.3　配置主机名与 IP 地址的映射

在 master、slave1、slave2 三台虚拟机上分别执行以下命令：

```
vim /etc/hosts
```

在插入模式下，在 hosts 文件末尾添加以下代码：

```
192.168.204.129   master
192.168.204.130 slave1
192.168.204.131 slave2
```

按 Esc 键，输入“:wq”保存退出，结果如图 3.5.28 所示。

```
128.0.0.1       localhost localhost.localdomain localhost4 localhost4.localdomain4
::1             localhost localhost.localdomain localhost6 localhost6.localdomain6

192.168.204.129 master
192.168.204.130 slave1
192.168.204.131 slave2
```

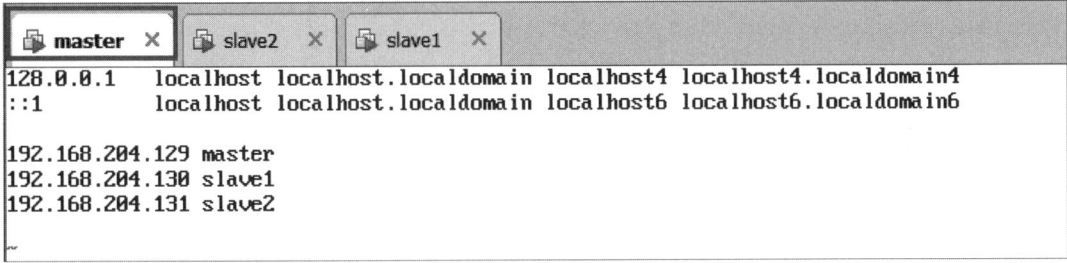

图 3.5.28　在 master 上建立 IP 地址与主机名映射

用同样方法，分别在 slave1、slave2 上执行 vim /etc/hosts 命令修改 IP 地址与主机名映射，如图 3.5.29、图 3.5.30 所示。

```
129.0.0.1       localhost localhost.localdomain localhost4 localhost4.localdomain4
::1             localhost localhost.localdomain localhost6 localhost6.localdomain6

192.168.204.129 master
192.168.204.130 slave1
192.168.204.131 slave2
```

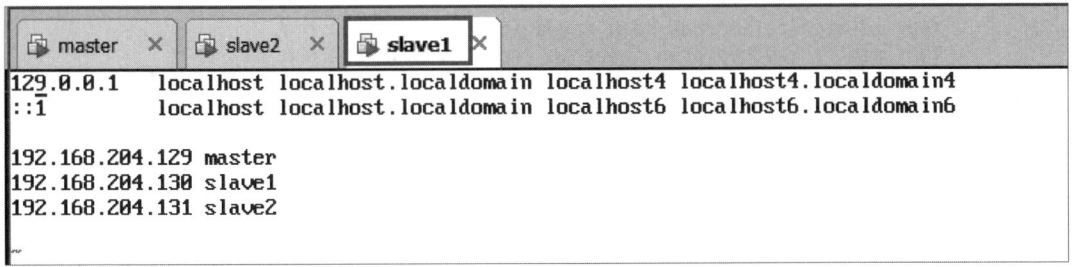

图 3.5.29　在 slave1 上建立 IP 地址与主机名映射

```
128.0.0.1       localhost localhost.localdomain localhost4 localhost4.localdomain4
::1             localhost localhost.localdomain localhost6 localhost6.localdomain6

192.168.204.129 master
192.168.204.130 slave1
192.168.204.131 slave2
```

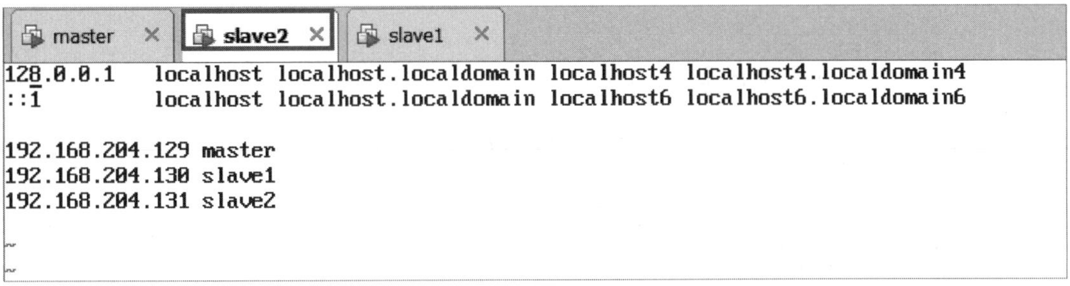

图 3.5.30　在 slave2 上建立 IP 地址与主机名映射

> |vi/vim 的命令在插入模式下按 Esc 键后，以下代码的功能：
> ":q"在 vim 中表示退出；
> ":wq"表示保存并退出；
> ":q!"表示强制不保存退出。|

3.5.5 配置关闭防火墙

内网环境下防火墙默认都是关闭的，防火墙开启后集群内部通信会出现各种问题。

在 master、slave1、slave2 三个节点都需要配置防火墙，常用命令如下：

```
systemctl stop firewalld        #临时关闭防火墙
systemctl disable firewalld     #开机自动关闭防火墙
```

3.5.6 配置免密码登录

配置 root 用户的免密码登录所有节点。在 master、slave1、slave2 节点上分别执行以下生成登录密钥命令。输入 ssh-keygen -t rsa 后按三次回车键即可。

在 master 上执行以下命令：

```
[root@master~]#  ssh-keygen -t rsa
```

执行结果如图 3.5.31 所示。

```
Enter passphrase (empty for no passphrase):
Enter same passphrase again:
Your identification has been saved in /root/.ssh/id_rsa.
Your public key has been saved in /root/.ssh/id_rsa.pub.
The key fingerprint is:
SHA256:Wr+yRLliLitHx6g9GAvdko6wEinW25LcvoGQjrLFlMM root@master
The key's randomart image is:
+---[RSA 2048]----+
|                 |
|                 |
|                 |
| .o    .         |
| =ooEo  S        |
|O+*.=.o+ o       |
|*B+X=o+ o .      |
|=o*==.o. .       |
|o  o+*o .o.      |
+----[SHA256]-----+
[root@master usr]#
```

图 3.5.31 生成密钥过程的信息

以上输出展示了生成密钥过程的信息。

执行以下命令查看密钥：

```
[root@master~]#  cd  /root/.ssh
[root@master.ssh]# ls
```

执行结果如图 3.5.32 所示。

```
[root@master /]# cd /root/.ssh
[root@master .ssh]# ls
id_rsa  id_rsa.pub
[root@master .ssh]#
```

图 3.5.32　查看密钥文件

查看 id_rsa.pub 的内容，命令如下：

[root@master~]#　cat id_rsa.pub

执行结果如图 3.5.33 所示。

```
[root@master .ssh]# cat id_rsa.pub
ssh-rsa AAAAB3NzaC1yc2EAAAADAQABAAABAQCzrjJejl1OJ7ueoMLMbvM9Z2kKosdSQ436joU8+4zyfIK6I9UphDjIZpYS83I5MeosFDaKS3VDXpKpJ3eULiflpOOl
UvNmIZXxxaa9yH9lZmenfVPAKhP3YK0BU4jXC66kwKjzRLAB0qsi9AvaotRsVzZP02m/TEm/GPMcP9QzrXqX2tGrGK5seMvMUXxlmeoth6fR6Zjaa05BPeiEiZOl2XdM
mEY+2WJF2kkxoP7aazWshi4pn/ADp/v9nL/jLtrL5naEZAD/WLjSFaT3JwSqqPDstm0TjZbGyzxPatd2uiSFmoSgwj9fmyrOGkXCCjulTJnFeA6LLd+KwPsJ8RkT roo
t@master
[root@master .ssh]#
```

图 3.5.33　查看密钥文件 id_rsa.pub 的内容

将密钥复制到 master、slave1、slave2 上，在 master 上执行如下命令：

[root@master ~]# ssh-copy-id master

[root@master ~]# ssh-copy-id slave1

[root@master ~]# ssh-copy-id slave2

执行结果如图 3.5.34 至图 3.5.36 所示。

```
[root@master .ssh]# ssh-copy-id master
/usr/bin/ssh-copy-id: INFO: Source of key(s) to be installed: "/root/.ssh/id_rsa.pub"
The authenticity of host 'master (192.168.204.129)' can't be established.
ECDSA key fingerprint is SHA256:r4AVgFSHY8fK1Sy4HpMZcj8GqCR0uZTAHZTmXbjCJhg.
ECDSA key fingerprint is MD5:ff:82:ef:fe:a0:a8:ae:d1:48:97:77:40:a5:e5:93:f8.
Are you sure you want to continue connecting (yes/no)? yes
/usr/bin/ssh-copy-id: INFO: attempting to log in with the new key(s), to filter out any that are already installed
/usr/bin/ssh-copy-id: INFO: 1 key(s) remain to be installed -- if you are prompted now it is to install the new keys
root@master's password:

Number of key(s) added: 1

Now try logging into the machine, with:   "ssh 'master'"
and check to make sure that only the key(s) you wanted were added.
```

图 3.5.34　传输密钥到 master 过程

```
[root@master .ssh]# ssh-copy-id slave1
/usr/bin/ssh-copy-id: INFO: Source of key(s) to be installed: "/root/.ssh/id_rsa.pub"
The authenticity of host 'slave1 (192.168.204.130)' can't be established.
ECDSA key fingerprint is SHA256:r4AVgFSHY8fK1Sy4HpMZcj8GqCR0uZTAHZTmXbjCJhg.
ECDSA key fingerprint is MD5:ff:82:ef:fe:a0:a8:ae:d1:48:97:77:40:a5:e5:93:f8.
Are you sure you want to continue connecting (yes/no)? yes
/usr/bin/ssh-copy-id: INFO: attempting to log in with the new key(s), to filter out any that are already installed
/usr/bin/ssh-copy-id: INFO: 1 key(s) remain to be installed -- if you are prompted now it is to install the new keys
root@slave1's password:

Number of key(s) added: 1

Now try logging into the machine, with:   "ssh 'slave1'"
and check to make sure that only the key(s) you wanted were added.
```

图 3.5.35　传输密钥到 slave1 过程

```
[root@master .ssh]# ssh-copy-id slave2
/usr/bin/ssh-copy-id: INFO: Source of key(s) to be installed: "/root/.ssh/id_rsa.pub"
The authenticity of host 'slave2 (192.168.204.131)' can't be established.
ECDSA key fingerprint is SHA256:r4AVgFSHY8fK1Sy4HpMZcj8GqCR0uZTAHZTmXbjCJhg.
ECDSA key fingerprint is MD5:ff:82:ef:fe:a0:a8:ae:d1:48:97:77:40:a5:e5:93:f8.
Are you sure you want to continue connecting (yes/no)? yes
/usr/bin/ssh-copy-id: INFO: attempting to log in with the new key(s), to filter out any that are already installed
/usr/bin/ssh-copy-id: INFO: 1 key(s) remain to be installed -- if you are prompted now it is to install the new keys
root@slave2's password:

Number of key(s) added: 1

Now try logging into the machine, with:   "ssh 'slave2'"
and check to make sure that only the key(s) you wanted were added.
```

图 3.5.36　传输密钥到 slave1 过程

上述输出展示了传输密钥过程的信息。在执行过程中，提示"Are you sure you want to continue connecting（yes/no）?"回答"yes"，提示"root@master's password："录入登录主机的密码，这里三台虚拟机都是"root123"。

查看密钥是否传输成功，执行如下命令：

```
[root@master ~]#   cd /root/.ssh
[root@master .ssh]#   ls
```

执行结果如图 3.5.37 所示。

```
[root@master .ssh]# cd /root/.ssh
[root@master .ssh]# ls
authorized_keys  id_rsa  id_rsa.pub  known_hosts
[root@master .ssh]#
```

图 3.5.37　再次查看密钥文件

与图 3.5.32 相比，多了两个文件，即 authorized_keys 和 known_hosts。

查看一下 authorized_keys 文件内容，命令如下：

```
[root@master .ssh]#   cat authorized_keys
```

执行结果如图 3.5.38 所示。

图 3.5.38　查看 authorized_keys 文件内容

可见图 3.5.33 密钥文件 id_rsa.pub 的内容已经复制到 authorized_keys 中。

下面来进行免密码登录验证。在 master 节点验证是否完成免密码登录 master、slave1、slave2 节点，命令如下：

```
[root@master~]# ssh master
[root@master~]# exit
```

执行结果如图 3.5.39 所示。

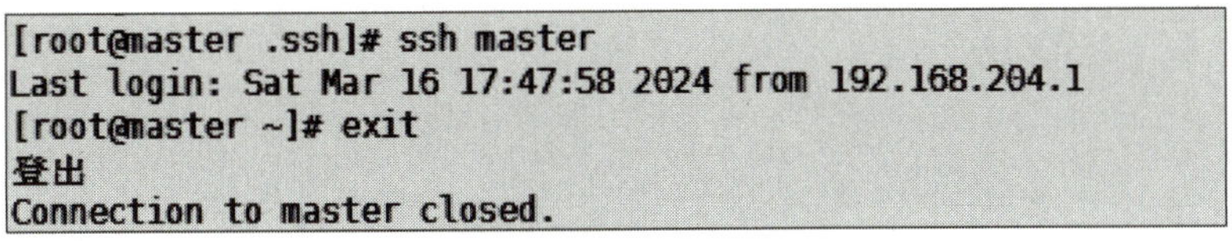

```
[root@master .ssh]# ssh master
Last login: Sat Mar 16 17:47:58 2024 from 192.168.204.1
[root@master ~]# exit
登出
Connection to master closed.
```

图 3.5.39　验证登录 master 不用密码

```
[root@master~]#　ssh slave1
[root@master~]#　exit
```

执行结果如图 3.5.40 所示。

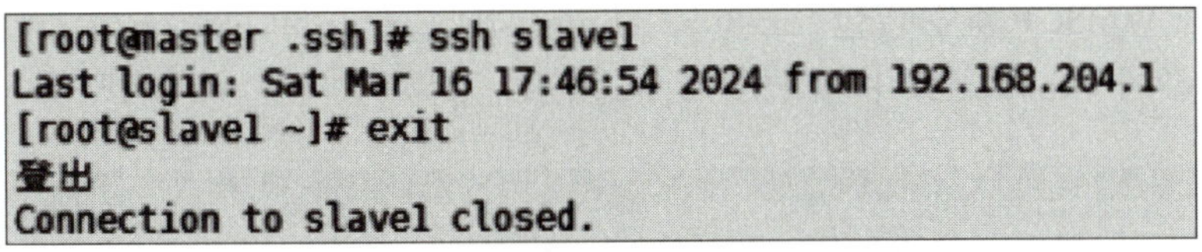

```
[root@master .ssh]# ssh slave1
Last login: Sat Mar 16 17:46:54 2024 from 192.168.204.1
[root@slave1 ~]# exit
登出
Connection to slave1 closed.
```

图 3.5.40　验证登录 slave1 不用密码

```
[root@master~]#　ssh slave2
[root@master~]#　exit
```

执行结果如图 3.5.41 所示。

```
[root@master .ssh]# ssh slave2
Last login: Sat Mar 16 17:47:33 2024 from 192.168.204.1
[root@slave2 ~]# exit
登出
Connection to slave2 closed.
```

图 3.5.41　验证登录 slave2 不用密码

上述输出展示了通过 SSH 远程登录和退出登录时的信息。

使用 Exit，可以退出登录，回到 master 节点。

执行过程中，不用输入密码，master 节点就可以远程登录到 master、slave1、slave2 节点。说明已经成功完成了 master 节点到各节点的免密登录。

注意

由于集群中有 3 个节点，如果两两之间都需要免密登录，其余节点都需要重复上述步骤。其余节点也执行完，可继续验证：slave1-master、slave1-slave1、slave1-slave2、slave2-master、slave2-slave1、slave2-slave2 之间的免密。

即在 slave1、slave2 分别执行以下代码序列：

```
ssh-keygen -t rsa
ssh-copy-id master
ssh-copy-id slave1
ssh-copy-id slave2
```

在 slave1、slave2 上分别验证免密登录三个节点：

```
ssh  master
exit
ssh slave1
exit
ssh  slave2
exit
```

验证过程使用 Exit 退出一次连接。

3.5.7　搭建并测试 Hadoop 集群环境

（1）打开 WinSCP 将安装包 jdk-8u221-linux-x64.tar.gz 和 hadoop-2.7.7.tar.gz 上传到 master 节点的"/root"目录中，如图 3.5.42 所示。

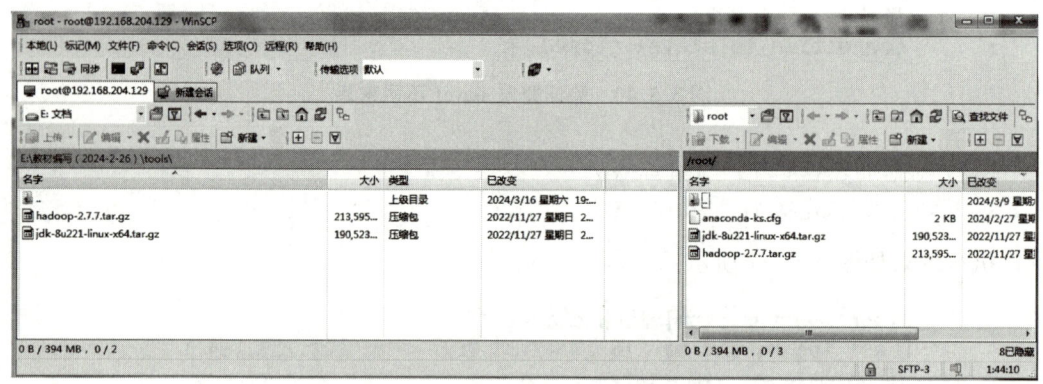

图 3.5.42　用 WinSCP 上传安装包

（2）在 master、slave1、slave2 三个节点上创建目录"/opt/modules"，以备将安装包解压到该目录，分别执行以下命令：

```
[root@master~]#  mkdir /opt/modules
```

（3）解压 jdk 软件包。在 master 节点执行以下命令序列：

```
[root@master ~]# cd /root
[root@master ~]# tar -zxvf   jdk-8u221-linux-x64.tar.gz -C /opt/modules
[root@master ~]# cd  /opt/modules
[root@master ~]# ls
[root@master ~]# mv  jdk1.8.0_221  jdk    #重命名为jdk
```

> **注意**
>
> 需要注意的是命令中的版本号需要根据实际版本号修改，如这里用的 8u221，也可以用其他 java8 的版本。

tar 解压文件参数如下：

-z：调用 gzip 程序来压缩文件，压缩后的文件名称以.gz 结尾。

-x：解压文件。
-v：显示详细的 tar 处理的文件信息。
-f：要操作的文件名。
-C：解压的目标位置。

（4）配置 JDK 环境变量。修改/etc/profile 文件，配置完毕后在 master 节点执行"java -version"，命令如下：

```
[root@master~]# vi /etc/profile
```

在 INSERT 模式下，在文件末尾添加 JAVA_HOME 信息，命令如下：

```
export JAVA_HOME=/opt/modules/jdk
export PATH=$PATH:$JAVA_HOME/bin
```

按 Esc 键，打":wq"保存退出。

使环境变量生效，命令如下：

```
[root@master~]# source /etc/profile
```

验证安装。验证 JDK 安装成功，命令如下：

```
[root@master~]# java -version
```

执行结果如图 3.5.43 所示。

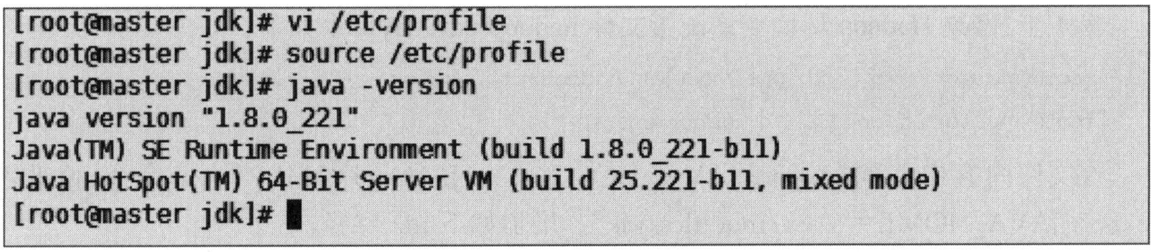

```
[root@master jdk]# vi /etc/profile
[root@master jdk]# source /etc/profile
[root@master jdk]# java -version
java version "1.8.0_221"
Java(TM) SE Runtime Environment (build 1.8.0_221-b11)
Java HotSpot(TM) 64-Bit Server VM (build 25.221-b11, mixed mode)
[root@master jdk]#
```

图 3.5.43　配置 JDK 环境变量

上述输出展示了 Java 版本的信息。

（5）分发 JDK 安装文件。分发安装目录到其余的两个节点上，命令如下：

```
[root@master ~]# scp -r /opt/modules/jdk root@slave1:/opt/modules/
[root@master ~]# scp -r /opt/modules/jdk root@slave2:/opt/modules/
```

执行结果如图 3.5.44 所示。

图 3.5.44　分发安装文件到 slave1、slave2

以上输出展示了 scp 传输文件夹过程的信息。

（6）分发环境变量到其余节点上，命令如下：

```
[root@master ~]# scp /etc/profile root@slave1:/etc/profile
[root@master ~]# scp /etc/profile root@slave2:/etc/profile
```

执行结果如图 3.5.45 所示。

```
[root@master /]# scp /etc/profile root@slave1:/etc/profile
profile                                          100% 2028    1.4MB/s   00:00
[root@master /]# scp /etc/profile root@slave2:/etc/profile
profile                                          100% 2028    798.4KB/s 00:00
[root@master /]#
```

图 3.5.45　分发环境变量到 slave1、slave2

以上输出展示了传输文件过程的信息。

(7) 使环境变量生效。在 slave1、slave2 节点上分别执行如下命令：

```
[root@slave1 ~] source /etc/profile
[root@slave2 ~] source /etc/profile
```

(8) 在主机 master 上将 Hadoop 安装包解压到 /opt/modules 文件夹下，命令如下：

```
[root@master ~]# cd /root
[root@master ~]# tar -zxvf hadoop-2.7.7.tar.gz -C /opt/modules
[root@master ~]# cd /opt/modules
[root@master ~]# mv hadoop-2.7.7 hadoop
```

(9) 修改 Hadoop 配置文件。

第 1 步：修改 Hadoop 环境变量配置文件 hadoop-env.sh，命令如下：

```
[root@master ~]# cd /opt/modules/hadoop/etc/hadoop
[root@master hadoop]# vi hadoop-env.sh
```

在文件内容中找到"export JAVA_HOME = ${JAVA_HOME}"这条命令，修改为 "export JAVA_HOME = /opt/modules/jdk"。增加如下 jdk 路径：

```
export JAVA_HOME = /opt/modules/jdk
```

按 Esc 键，按":wq"保存退出。

第 2 步：修改 Hadoop 核心配置文件 core-site.xml，命令如下：

```
root@master hadoop]# vi core-site.xml
```

添加以下代码：

```
configuration>
        <! -- 用于设置 Hadoop 的文件系统 -->
        <property>
                <name>fs.defaultFS</name>
                <value>hdfs://master:9000</value>
        </property>
        <! -- 配置 Hadoop 的临时目录 -->
        <property>
                <name>hadoop.tmp.dir</name>
                <value>/opt/modules/hadoop/tmp</value>
        </property>
</configuration>
```

第 3 步，修改 hdfs 核心配置文件 hdfs-site.xml，命令如下：

```
root@master hadoop]# vi hdfs-site.xml
```

添加以下代码：

```xml
<configuration>
    <!-- 指定 HDFS 副本的数量 -->
    <property>
        <name>dfs.replication</name>
        <value>3</value>
    </property>
    <!-- 指定 secondaryNamenode 节点 -->
    <property>
        <name>dfs.namenode.secondary.http-address</name>
        <value>slave1:50090</value>
    </property>
    <!-- 关闭文件的访问权限验证 -->
    <property>
        <name>dfs.permissions</name>
        <value>false</value>
    </property>
    <property>
        <name>dfs.webhdfs.enabled</name>
        <value>true</value>
    </property>
</configuration>
```

第 4 步：修改 mapreduce 的配置文件 mapred-site.xml。

将配置文件的模板文件 mapred-site.xml.template 重命名为 mapred-site.xml，并修改 mapred-site.xml 文件内容，命令如下：

```
root@master hadoop]# mv mapred-site.xml.template mapred-site.xml
root@master hadoop]# vi mapred-site.xml
```

在 mapred-site.xml 中添加以下代码：

```xml
<configuration>
    <!-- 指定 mr 运行时框架，这里指定在 yarn 上，默认是 local -->
    <property>
        <name>mapreduce.framework.name</name>
        <value>yarn</value>
    </property>
</configuration>
```

第 5 步：修改 YARN 的配置文件 yarn-site.xml，命令如下：

```
root@master hadoop]# vi yarn-site.xml
```

添加以下代码：

```xml
<configuration>
    <!-- 指定YARN的主节点(ResourceManager)的地址 -->
<property>
        <name>yarn.resourcemanager.hostname</name>
        <value>slave2</value>
</property>
<!-- NodeManager上运行的附属服务。需配置成mapreduce_shuffle,才可运行MapReduce程序默认值:"" -->
    <property>
        <name>yarn.nodemanager.aux-services</name>
        <value>mapreduce_shuffle</value>
    </property>
<!-- 是否启动一个线程检查每个任务正使用的物理内存量,如果任务超出分配值,则直接将其杀掉,默认是true -->
<property>
<name>yarn.nodemanager.pmem-check-enabled</name>
<value>false</value>
</property>
<!-- nm虚拟内存检查,默认为true,会导致任务被kill,设置为false关闭-->
<property>
<name>yarn.nodemanager.vmem-check-enabled</name>
<value>false</value>
</property>
</configuration>
```

第 6 步：修改 slaves 文件，命令如下：

```
root@master hadoop]# vi slaves
```

设置节点信息，删掉 localhost 所在行，输入以下代码：

```
master
slave1
slave2
```

第 7 步：配置环境变量。编辑环境变量的配置文件，命令如下：

```
vi /etc/profile
```

在最后添加环境代码：

```
export HADOOP_HOME=/opt/modules/hadoop
export PATH=$HADOOP_HOME/bin:$HADOOP_HOME/sbin:$PATH
```

按 Esc 键，输入":wq"保存文件并退出编辑状态。
使新的环境变量生效，命令如下：

```
source /etc/profile
```

第 8 步：分发系统环境变量配置文件到 slave1、slave2 两个节点，命令如下：

```
scp /etc/profile root@slave1:/etc/profile
scp /etc/profile root@slave2:/etc/profile
```

使 slave1、slave2 节点环境变量生效，在两节点上分别执行如下命令：

```
source /etc/profile
```

第 9 步：分发 Hadoop 安装文件到 slave1、slave2 两个节点。在 master 节点执行如下命令：

```
scp -r /opt/modules/hadoop root@slave1:/opt/modules/
scp -r /opt/modules/hadoop root@slave2:/opt/modules/
```

第 10 步：启动 HDFS 集群。初始化集群仅在主节点 master 执行如下命令：

```
hdfs namenode -format
```

执行结果如图 3.5.46 所示。

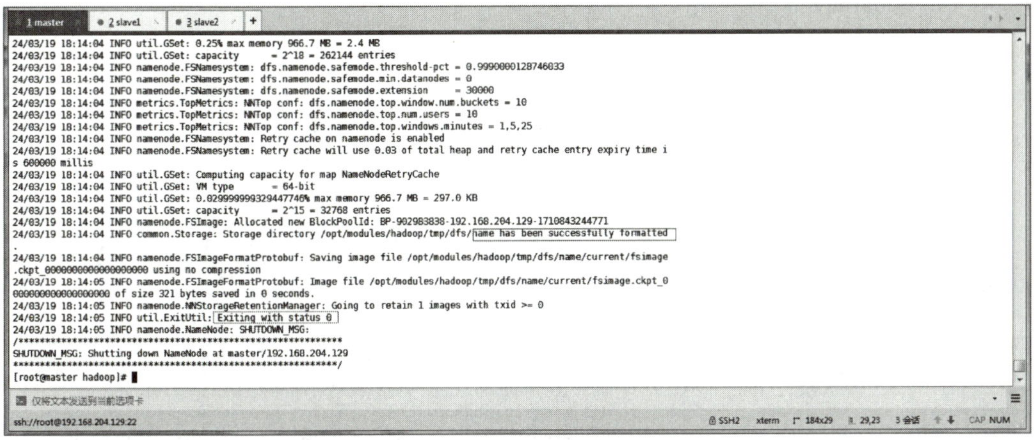

图 3.5.46　初始化 HDFS 集群

上述输出展示了 Hadoop Namanode 初始化过程的信息，其中有"name has been successfully formatted"，说明格式化成功。

第 11 步：启动 HDFS 集群并测试。在主节点 master 执行如下命令：

```
start-dfs.sh
```

执行结果如图 3.5.47 所示。

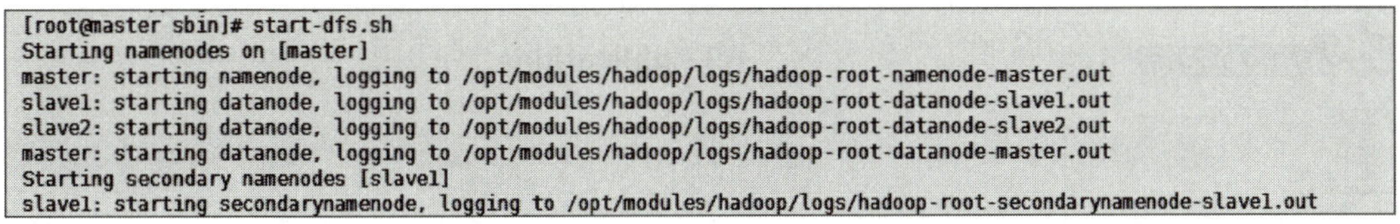

图 3.5.47　启动 HDFS 集群

上述输出展示了启动 HDFS 过程的信息。

在浏览器访问 master 集群，在地址栏用 IP:50070 可访问 HDFS WebUI 界面，这里访问 master 网址，如下所示：

```
http://192.168.204.129:50070
```

执行结果如图 3.5.48 所示。

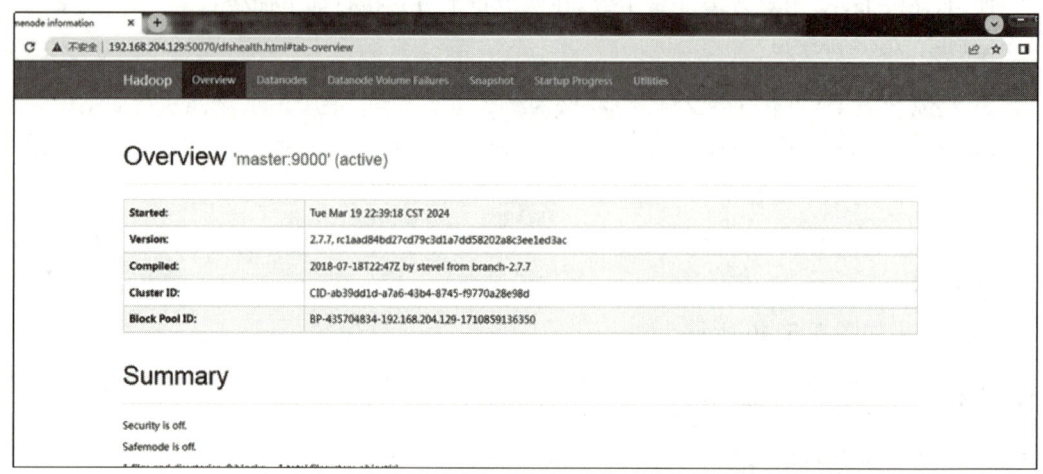

图 3.5.48　浏览器访问 master 集群界面

第 12 步：启动 YARN 集群，在 slave2 执行如下命令：

```
start-yarn.sh
```

执行结果如图 3.5.49 所示。

```
[root@slave2 modules]# start-yarn.sh
starting yarn daemons
starting resourcemanager, logging to /opt/modules/hadoop/logs/yarn-root-resourcemanager-slave2.out
master: starting nodemanager, logging to /opt/modules/hadoop/logs/yarn-root-nodemanager-master.out
slave1: starting nodemanager, logging to /opt/modules/hadoop/logs/yarn-root-nodemanager-slave1.out
slave2: starting nodemanager, logging to /opt/modules/hadoop/logs/yarn-root-nodemanager-slave2.out
```

图 3.5.49　启动 YARN 集群过程

在浏览器访问 slave2 节点 IP:8088 可访问 YARN WebUI 界面，这里在地址栏输入如下网址和端口号，如下所示：

```
http://192.168.204.131:8088
```

执行结果如图 3.5.50 所示。

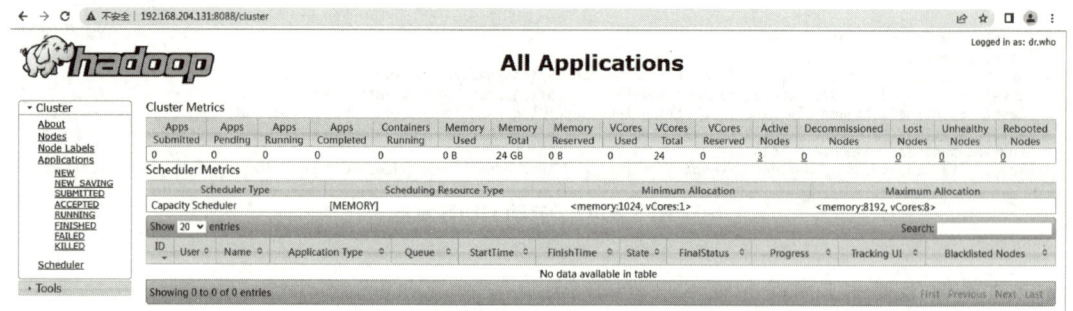

图 3.5.50　在浏览器访问 YARN 界面

第 13 步：测试并查看对应 Java 进程各角色进程情况。在 master 节点执行如下命令：

```
[root@master ~]#　jps
```

该命令查看系统中存在的 Java 进程,可见 master 节点信息有 NodeManager、NameNode、DataNode,如图 3.5.51 所示。

```
[root@master sbin]# jps
13300 NodeManager
12903 NameNode
13032 DataNode
13420 Jps
```

图 3.5.51　查看 master 中的 Java 进程

在 slave1 节点查看系统中存在的 Java 进程,执行如下命令:

`[root@slave1 ~]#　jps`

可见 slave1 节点有 SecondaryNameNode 进程,如图 3.5.52 所示。

```
[root@slave1 modules]# jps
6081 DataNode
6420 Jps
6181 SecondaryNameNode
6293 NodeManager
```

图 3.5.52　查看 slave1 中的 Java 进程

在 slave2 节点查看系统中存在的 Java 进程,执行以下命令:

`[root@slave2 ~]#　jps`

可见 slave2 节点有 ResourceManager 进程没有 NameNode 进程,如图 3.5.53 所示。

```
[root@slave2 modules]# jps
5285 DataNode
5639 NodeManager
5962 Jps
5534 ResourceManager
```

图 3.5.53　查看 slave2 中的 Java 进程

查看 HDFS 文件系统上主目录,命令如下:

`hdfs dfs -ls /`

至此,完成了 Hadoop 的完成分布式安装。

第 14 步:关闭 HDFS 集群命令。

如需关闭 HDFS 集群,需要在 master 主节点执行如下命令:

`[root@master ~]#　stop-dfs.sh`

如需关闭 YARN 集群,需要在 slave2 节点执行如下命令:

`[root@slave2 ~]#　stop-yarn.sh`

> **注意**
>
> (1) 启动 HDFS 集群和 YARN 集群,可以用 start-all.sh 一条命令代替 start-yarn.sh 和 start-dfs.sh 两条命令;

(2) 关闭 HDFS 集群和 YARN 集群，可以用 stop-all.sh 一条命令代替 stop-dfs.sh 和 stop-yarn.sh 两条命令。

单元总结

本单元主要学习了 Hadoop 的安装模式。通过实际操作，详细介绍了 JDK 的安装，Hadoop 本地安装、伪分布模式安装和分布模式安装的全过程，并在不同安装模式下，对 Hadoop 的典型命令和应用程序进行了操作体验。同时，在本地 CentOS 7 系统进行文件和文件夹操作，与 HDFS 系统之间实现文件上传、下载等。

单元习题

一、简答题

1. 简述 JDK 的安装过程。
2. Hadoop 有哪几种安装模式？请对这几种安装模式进行比较。
3. Hadoop 分布模式安装，需要修改哪些配置文件？

二、技能训练题

1. 独立完成 Hadoop 伪分布模式安装。
2. Hadoop 安装完成后，完成以下操作：

(1) 在本地 CentOS 7 系统新建一个文本文件 my_hadoop.txt，文件内容如下：

> In the era of big data, financial analysts will face problems such as large data volume, diverse types, and low value density.

(2) 在 HDFS 上新建"/data/input"目录，将 my_hadoop.txt 上传到"/data/input"目录，再执行 Hadoop 自带的 MapReduce 程序 wordcount，统计 my_hadoop.txt 中各单词个数。

单元 4

大数据存储技术 HDFS

完成了 Hadoop 的安装和配置,本单元将详细说明 Hadoop 的 HDFS。HDFS 是 Hadoop 中存储数据的基石,存储着所有的数据,具有高可靠性、高容错性、高可扩展性、高吞吐量等特征,能够部署在大规模廉价的服务器集群上,极大地降低部署成本。

学习目标

知识目标

1. 理解 HDFS 的块分布。
2. 理解 HDFS 数据读取与写入。
3. 理解 HDFS 中的数据完整性。
4. 掌握 HDFS 命令的功能。

技能目标

1. 掌握 Hadoop 的 HDFS 命令使用。
2. 能用 HDFS 解决会计数据的存储操作。

单元任务

任务 4.1　Hadoop HDFS 架构和容错。
任务 4.2　Hadoop HDFS 文件管理。
任务 4.3　Hadoop HDFS 命令。

任务 4.1　Hadoop HDFS 架构和容错

任务描述

在完成大数据平台 Hadoop 安装后,读者需要学会 Hadoop 核心组件的使用。本任务对 HDFS 架构模式和容错机制进行学习,了解 Hadoop 分布式文件系统 HDFS 的工作原理,有助于更好地掌握文件管理命令的操作使用。

关键步骤

(1) 了解 HDFS 架构模式。

(2) 了解 HDFS 容错机制。

HDFS 是 Hadoop 中的核心组件之一,是分布式计算中数据存储与管理的基础,其良好的架构特征使其能够存储海量的数据。本任务就系统介绍 Hadoop HDFS 的架构。

4.1.1 HDFS 架构

HDFS 采用 Master/Slave 架构存储数据,且支持 NameNode 的 HA。HDFS 架构主要有包含客户端(Client)、名称节点(NameNode)、次要名称节点(SecondaryNameNode)和数据节点(DataNode)四个重要组成部分,如图 4.1.1 所示。

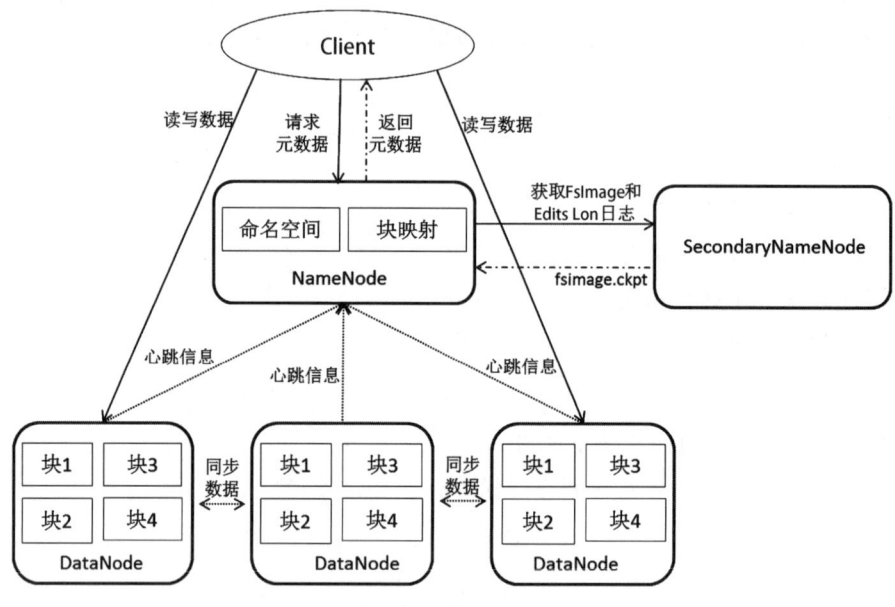

图 4.1.1 HDFS 架构

HDFS 架构中各组成部分的工作机制如下:

(1) 客户端向 NameNode 发起请求,获取元数据信息,这些元数据信息包括命名空间、块映射信息及 DataNode 的位置信息等。

(2) NameNode 将元数据信息返回给客户端。

(3) 客户端获取到元数据信息后,到相应的 DataNode 上读写数据。

(4) 相关联的 DataNode 之间会相互复制数据,以达到 DataNode 副本数的要求。

(5) DataNode 会定期向 NameNode 发送心跳信息,将自身节点的状态信息报告给 NameNode。

(6) SecondaryNameNode 并不是 NameNode 的备份。SecondaryNameNode 会定期获取 NameNode 上的 FsImage 和 EditLog 日志,并将两者进行合并,产生 fsimage.ckpt 推送给 NameNode。

4.1.1.1 NameNode

NameNode 是整个 Hadoop 集群中至关重要的组件,它维护着整个 HDFS 树,以及文件系统树中所有的文件和文件路径的元数据信息。这些元数据信息包括文件名、命名空间、文件属性(文件生成的时间、文件的副本数、文件的权限)、文件数据块、文件数据块与所在 DataNode 之间的映射关系等。

一旦 NameNode 宕机或 NameNode 上的元数据信息损坏或丢失,基本上就会丢失 Hadoop 集群中存储的所有数据,整个 Hadoop 集群也会随之瘫痪。

在 Hadoop 运行过程中,NameNode 的主要功能如下:

(1) NameNode 负责管理分布式文件系统的命名空间(namespace),保存了两个核心的数据结构,即 FsImage 和 EditLog。

(2) FsImage 用于维护文件系统树以及文件树中所有的文件和文件夹的元数据。

(3) 操作日志文件 EditLog 记录了所有针对文件的创建、删除、重命名等操作。

(4) NameNode 启动后加载 FsImage 和 EditLog 到内存中。

(5) NameNode 记录了每个文件中各个块所在的数据节点的位置信息,即文件、Block 与 DataNode 之间的映射关系。

NameNode 的数据结构如图 4.1.2 所示。

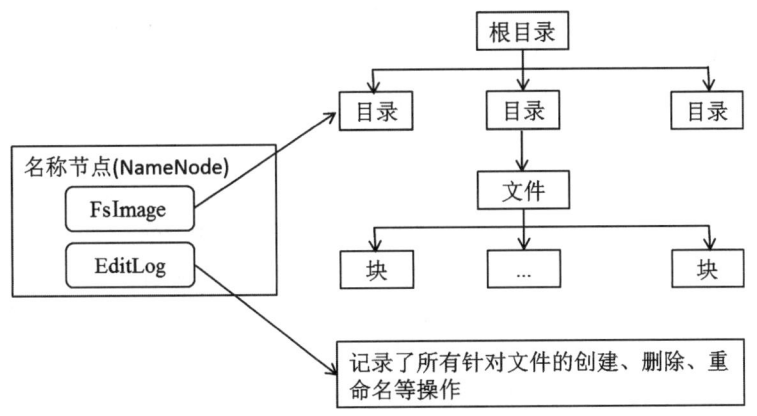

图 4.1.2　NameNode 的数据结构

4.1.1.2　SecondaryNameNode

SecondaryNameNode 并不是 NameNode 的备份,在 NameNode 发生故障时也不能立刻接管 NameNode 的工作。SecondaryNameNode 在 Hadoop 运行的过程中具有两个作用:一个是备份数据镜像,另一个是定期合并日志与镜像,因此可以称其为 Hadoop 的检查点 (checkpoint)。SecondaryNameNode 定期合并 NameNode 中的 FsImage 和 EditLog,能够防止 NameNode 故障重启时把整个 FsImage 镜像文件加载到内存中,耗费过长的启动时间。

SecondaryNameNode 的工作流程如图 4.1.3 所示。

由图 4.1.3 可见,SecondaryNameNode 的工作流程如下:

(1) SecondaryNameNode 会通知 NameNode 生成新的 EditLog 日志文件。

(2) NameNade 生成新的 EditLog 日志文件,然后将新的日志信息写到新生成的 EditLog 日志文件中。

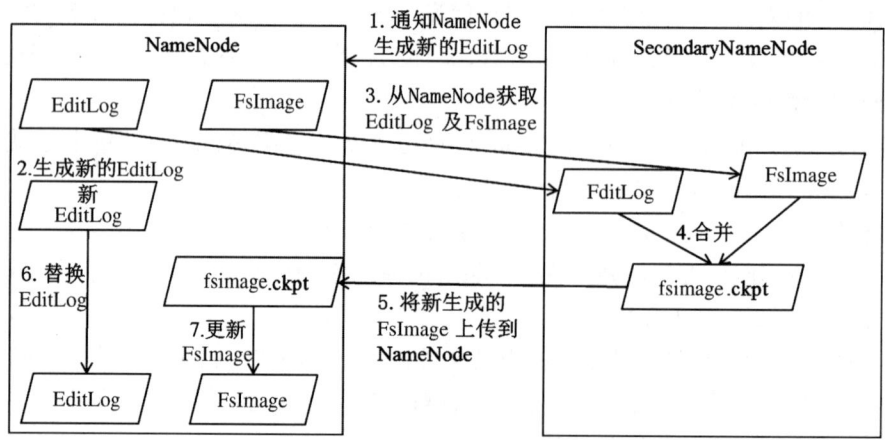

图 4.1.3　SecondaryNameNode 的工作流程

（3）SecondaryNameNode 复制 NameNode 上的 FsImage 镜像和 EditLog 日志文件，此时使用的是 http get 方式。

（4）SecondaryNameNode 将 FsImage 镜像文件加载到内存中，然后执行 EditLog 日志文件的操作，生成新的镜像文件 fsimage.ckpt。

（5）SecondaryNameNode 将新的镜像文件 fsimage.ckpt 文件发送给 NameNode，此时使用的是 http post 方式。

（6）NameNode 将 EdItLog 日志文件替换成新生成的 EditLog 日志文件，同时将 FsImage 文件替换成 ScondaryNameNode 发送过来的新的 FsImage 文件。

（7）NameNode 更新 FsImage 文件，将此次执行 checkpoint 的时间写入 FsImage 文件中。

经过 SecondaryNameNode 对 FsImage 镜像文件和 EditLog 日志文件的复制和合并操作之后，NameNode 中的 FsImage 镜像文件就保存了最新的 checkpoint 的元数据信息，EditLog 日志文件也会重新写入数据，两个文件中的数据不会变得很大。因此当重启 NameNode 时，不会耗费太长的启动时间。

SecondayNameNode 周期性地进行 checkpoint 操作需要满足一定的前提条件，这些条件如下：

（1）EditLog 日志文件的大小达到了一定的阈值，此时会对其进行合并操作。

（2）每隔一段时间进行 checkpoint 操作。

这些条件可以在 core-site.xml 文件中进行配置和调整，代码如下：

```
<property>
<name>fs.checkpoint.period</name>
<value>3600</value>
</property>
<property>
<name>fs.checkpoint.size</name>
<value>67108864</value>
</property>
```

上述代码配置了 checkpoint 发生的时间周期和 EditLog 日志文件的大小阈值,说明如下:

(1) fs.checkpoint.period 表示触发 checkpoint 发生的时间周期,这里配置的时间周期为 1 小时。

(2) fs.checkpoint.size 表示 EditLog 日志文件大小达到多大的阈值时会发生 checkpoint 操作,这里配置的 EditLog 大小阈值为 64MB。

上述代码中配置的 checkpoint 操作发生的情况如下:

(1) 如果 EditLog 日志文件经过 1 小时未能达到 64MB,但是满足了 checkpoint 发生的周期为 1 小时的条件,也会发生 checkpoint 操作。

(2) 如果 EditLog 日志文件大小在 1 小时之内达到了 64MB,满足了 checkpoint 发生的 EditLog 日志文件大小阈值的条件,则会发生 checkpoint 操作。

> **注意**
> 如果 NameNode 发生故障或 NameNode 上的元数据信息丢失或损坏导致 NameNode 无法启动,此时就需要人工干预,将 NameNode 中的元数据状态恢复到 SecondaryNameNode 中的元数据状态。此时,如果 SecondayNameNode 上的元数据信息与 NameNode 关机时的元数据信息不同步,则或多或少地会导致 Hadoop 集群中丢失一部分数据。由于此原因,应尽量避免将 NameNode 和 SecondaryNameNode 部署在同一台服务器上。

4.1.1.3 DataNode

DataNode 是真正存储数据的节点。这些数据以数据块的形式存储在 DataNode 上。一个数据块包含两个文件:一个是存储数据本身的文件,另一个是存储元数据的文件(这些元数据主要包括数据块长度、数据块的校验和时间戳)。

DataNode 运行时的工作机制如图 4.1.4 所示。

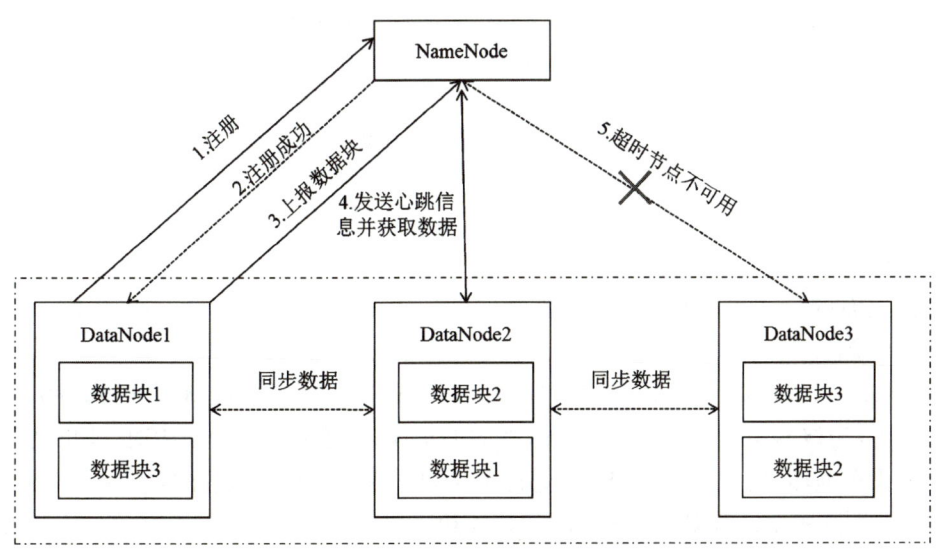

图 4.1.4　DataNode 运行时的工作机制

DataNode 运行时的工作机制如下：

（1）DataNode 启动之后，向 NameNode 注册。

（2）NameNode 返回注册成功的信息给 DataNode。

（3）DataNode 收到 NameNode 返回的注册成功的信息之后，会周期性地向 NameNode 上报当前 DataNode 的所有块信息，默认发送所有数据块的时间周期是 1 小时。

（4）DataNode 周期性地向 NameNode 发送心跳信息；NameNode 收到 DataNode 发来的心跳信息后，会将 DataNode 需要执行的命令放入心跳信息的返回数据中，返回给 DataNode。DataNode 向 NameNode 发送心跳信息的默认时间周期是 3 秒。

（5）若 NameNode 超过一定的时间没有收到 DataNode 发来的心跳信息，则 NameNode 会认为对应的 DataNode 不可用。默认的超时时间是 10 分钟。

（6）在存储上相互关联的 DataNode 会同步数据块，以达到数据副本数的要求。

当 DataNode 发生故障导致 DataNode 无法与 NameNode 通信时，NameNode 不会立即认为 DataNode 已经"死亡"，要经过一段短暂的超时时长后才会认为 DataNode 已经"死亡"。HDFS 中默认的超时时长为 10 min + 30 s，可以用如下公式来表示这个超时时长：

```
timeout = 2 × dfs.namenode.heartbeat.recheck-interval + 10 × dfs.heartbeat.interval
```

其中，各参数的含义如下：

（1）timeout 表示超时时长。

（2）dfs.namenode.hearbeat.recheck-interval 表示检查过期 DataNode 的时间间隔，与 dfs.hearbeat.interval 结合使用，默认的单位是毫秒，默认时间是 5 分钟。

（3）dfs.hearbeat.interval 表示检测数据节点的时间间隔，默认的单位为秒，默认的时间是 3 秒。

所以，可以得出 DataNode 的默认超时时长为 630 秒（即 2×5×60 + 10×3）。

DataNode 的超时时长也可以在 hdfs-site.xml 文件中进行配置，代码如下：

```
<property>
<name>dfs.namenode.heartbeat.recheck-interval</name>
<value>3000</value>
</property>
<property>
<name>dfs.hearbeat.interval</name>
<value>2</value>
</property>
```

根据上面的公式可以得出，在配置文件中配置的超时时长为 26 秒（即 2×3 000÷1 000 + 10×2）。

当 DataNode 被 NameNode 判定为"死亡"时，HDFS 就会马上自动进行数据块的容错复制。此时，当被 NameNode 判定为"死亡"的 DataNode 重新加入集群中时，如果其存储的数据块并没有损坏，就会造成 HDFS 上某些数据块的备份数超过系统配置的备份数目。

HDFS 删除多余的数据块需要的时间长短和数据块报告的时间间隔有关。该参数可以在 hdfs-site.xml 文件中进行配置，代码如下：

```
<property>
<name>dfs.blockreport.intervalMsec</name>
<value>21600000</value>
<description>Determines block reporting interval in milliseconds.</description>
</property>
```

数据块报告的时间间隔默认为 21 600 000 毫秒,即 6 小时,用户可通过调整此参数的大小来调整数据报告的时间间隔。

4.1.2 HDFS 容错机制

HDFS 的容错机制大体上可以分为两个方面:文件系统的容错和 Hadoop 自身的容错。

4.1.2.1 文件系统的容错

文件系统的容错可以通过 NameNode 高可用、SecondaryNameNode 机制、数据块副本机制和心跳机制来实现。这里重点说明分布模式下 HDFS 的容错。HDFS 的容错机制如图 4.1.5 所示。

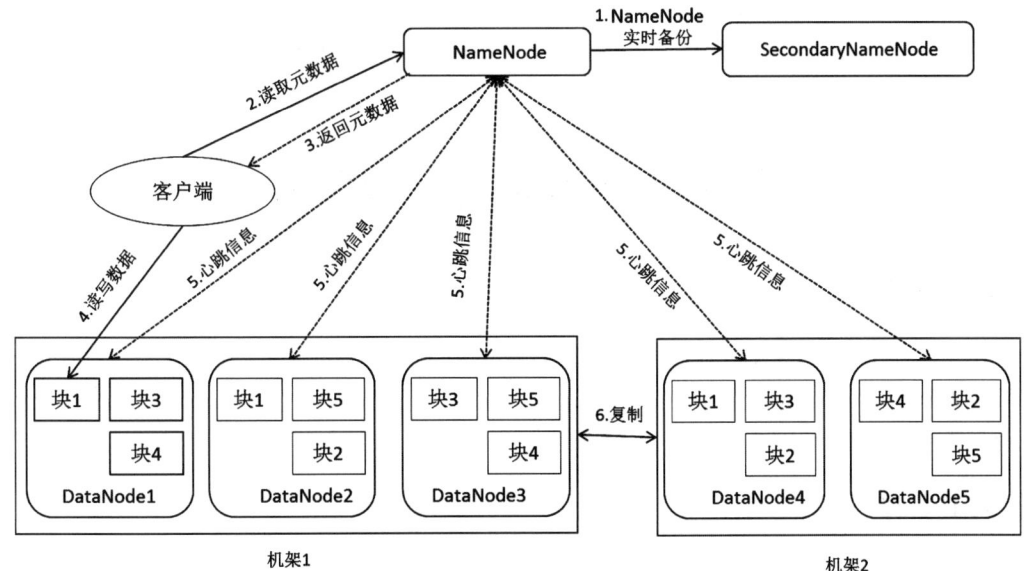

图 4.1.5　HDFS 的容错机制

(1) NameNode 实时备份主 NameNode 上的元数据信息,一旦主 NameNode 发生故障不可用,则备 NameNode 迅速接管主 NameNode 的工作。

(2) 客户端向 NameNode 读取元数据信息。

(3) NameNode 向客户端返回元数据信息。

(4) 客户端向 DataNode 读写数据,此时会分为读取数据和写入数据两种情况:①读取数据:HDFS 会检测文件块的完整性,确认文件块的校验和是否一致,如果不一致,则从其他的 DataNode 上获取相应的副本。②写入数据:HDFS 会检测文件块的完整性,同时记录新创建的文件的所有文件块的校验和。

（5）DataNode 会定期向 NameNode 发送心跳信息，将自身节点的状态告知 NameNode；NameNode 会将 DataNode 需要执行的命令放入心跳信息的返回结果中，返回给 DataNode 执行。当 DataNode 发生故障没有正常发送心跳信息时，NameNode 会检测文件块的副本数是否小于系统设置值，如果小于设置值，则自动复制新的副本并分发到其他的 DataNode 上。

（6）集群中有数据关联的 DataNode 之间会复制数据副本。

当集群中的 DataNode 发生故障而失效，或者在集群中添加新的 DataNode 时，可能会导致数据分布不均匀。当某个 DataNode 上的空闲空间资源大于系统设置的临界值时，HDFS 就会从其他的 DataNode 上将数据迁移过来。相对地，如果某个 DataNode 上的资源出现超负荷运载，HDFS 就会根据一定的规则寻找有空闲资源的 DataNode，将数据迁移过去。

还有一种从侧面说明 HDFS 支持容错的机制，即当从 HDFS 中删除数据时，数据并不是马上就会从 HDFS 中被删除，而是会将这些数据放到"回收站"目录中，随时可以恢复，直到超过了一定的时间才会真正删除这些数据。

4.1.2.2 Hadoop 自身的容错

Hadoop 自身的容错理解起来比较简单，当升级 Hadoop 系统时，如果出现 Hadoop 版本不兼容的问题，可以通过回滚 Hadoop 版本的方式来实现自身的容错。

任务 4.2 Hadoop HDFS 文件管理

任务描述

在完成大数据平台 Hadoop 安装后，需要学会 Hadoop 核心组件的使用。本任务对 HDFS 块分布、数据读取过程、数据写入过程和数据完整性原理进行学习，了解 Hadoop 分布式文件系统 HDFS 的工作原理，有助于更好地掌握文件管理命令的操作使用。

关键步骤

（1）了解 HDFS 的块分布。
（2）熟悉数据读取过程。
（3）熟悉数据写入过程。
（4）了解数据完整性。

在 HDFS 中，NameNode 作为整个集群的管理中心，保存着整个 HDFS 中的元数据信息，而真正保存数据的是 DataNode。

4.2.1 HDFS 的块分布

HDFS 会将数据文件切分成一个个小的数据块进行存储，同时会将这些数据块的副本保存多份，分别保存到不同的 DataNode 上。HDFS 中数据块的副本数由 hdfs-site.xml 文

件中的 dfs.replication 属性决定,配置代码如下:

```
<property>
<name>dfs.replication</name>
<value>3</value>
</property>
```

Hadoop 默认的副本数为3,并且在机架的存放上也有一定的策略。Hadoop 的默认布局策略,即默认的副本存放策略如下:

(1)第1个副本存放在 HDFS 客户端所在的节点上。
(2)第2个副本放在与第1个副本不同的机架上,并且是随机选择的节点。
(3)第3个副本放在与第2个副本相同的机架上,并且是不同的节点。

4.2.2 数据读取

HDFS 中的数据读取过程需要客户端先访问 NameNode,获取元数据信息,然后到具体的 DataNode 上读取数据,如图 4.2.1 所示。

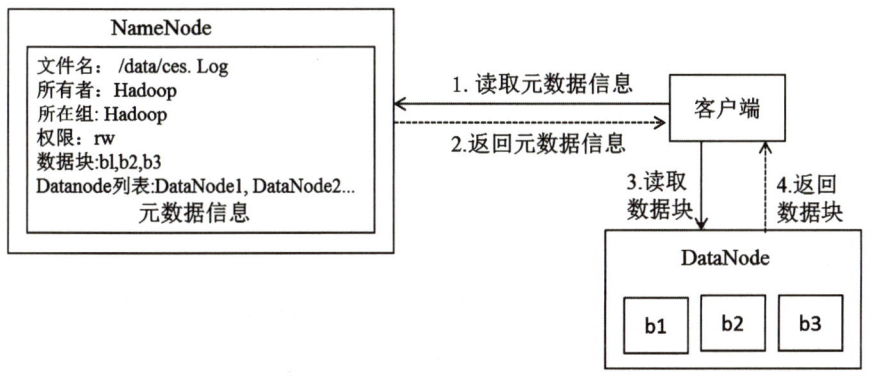

图 4.2.1　HDFS 读取数据流程

(1)客户端向 NameNode 发起请求,读取元数据信息。NameNode 上存储着整个 HDFS 集群的元数据信息,这些元数据信息包括文件名、所有者、所在组、权限、数据块和 DataNode 列表等。这个过程中还要对客户端的身份信息进行验证,同时检测是否存在要读取的文件,并且需要验证客户端的身份是否具有访问权限。
(2)NameNode 将相关的元数据信息返回给客户端。
(3)客户端到指定的 DataNode 上读取相应的数据块。
(4)DataNode 返回相应的数据块信息。

第(3)和第(4)步会持续进行,一直到文件的所有数据块都读取完毕或者 HDFS 客户端主动关闭了文件流为止。

4.2.3 数据写入

HDFS 中的数据写入过程同样需要客户端先访问 NameNode,获取元数据信息,然后到具体的 DataNode 上写入数据,步骤如下:

(1) 客户端请求 NameNode 读取元数据信息。这个过程中,NameNode 要对客户端的身份信息进行验证,同时需要验证客户端的身份是否具有写入权限。

(2) NameNode 返回相应的元数据信息给客户端。

(3) 客户端向第一个 DataNode 写入数据块。

(4) 第 1 个 DataNode 向第 2 个 DataNode 写入数据块。

(5) 第 2 个 DataNode 向第 3 个 DataNode 写入数据块。

(6) 第 3 个 DataNode 向第 2 个 DataNode 返回确认结果。

(7) 第 2 个 DataNode 向第 1 个 DataNode 返回确认结果。

(8) 第 1 个 DataNode 向客户端返回确认结果。

(9) 请求关闭文件流。

HDFS 写入数据流程如图 4.2.2 所示。

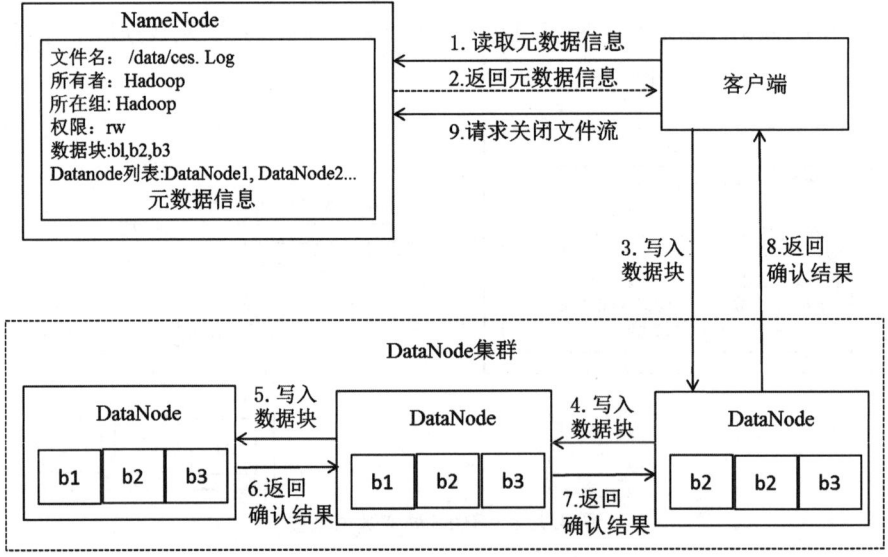

图 4.2.2　HDFS 写入数据流程

其中,第(4)和第(5)步是异步执行的,当 HDFS 中的多个 DataNode 发生故障或者发生错误时,只要正确写入了满足最少数目要求的数据副本数,HDFS 客户端就可以从数据块的副本中恢复数据。

最少数目要求的数据副本数由 hdfs-site.xml 文件中的 dfs.namenode.replication.min 属性决定,代码如下:

```
<property>
<name>dfs.namenode.replication.min</name>
<value>1</value>
</property>
```

最少数目要求的数据副本数默认为 1,即只要正确写入了数据的一个副本,客户端就可以从数据副本中恢复数据。

4.2.4 数据完整性

通常,在校验数据是否损坏时可以用如下方式:
(1) 当数据第一次引入时,计算校验和。
(2) 当数据经过一系列的传输或者复制时,再次计算校验和。
(3) 对比第(1)和第(2)步的校验和是否一致,如果两次数据的校验和不一致,则证明数据已经被损坏。

这种使用校验和来验证数据的技术只能检测数据是否被损坏,并不能修复数据。

HDFS 中校验数据是否损坏使用的也是校验和技术,无论是进行数据的写入还是进行数据的读取,都会验证数据的校验和。校验和的字节数由 core-site.xml 文件中的 io.bytes.per.checksum 属性指定,默认的字节长度为 512 B,代码如下:

```
<property>
<name>io.bytes.per.checksum</name>
<value>512</value>
</property>
```

当 HDFS 写入数据时,HDFS 客户端会将要写入的数据及对应数据的校验和发送到 DataNode 组成的复制管道中,其中最后一个 DataNode 负责验证数据的校验和是否一致。如果检测到校验和与 HDFS 客户端发送的校验和不一致,则 HDFS 客户端会收到校验和异常的信息,可以在程序中捕获到这个异常,进行相应的处理,如重新写入数据或者用其他方式处理。

HDFS 读取数据时也会验证校验和,此时会将它们与 DataNode 中存储的校验和进行比较。如果其与 DataNode 中存储的校验和不一致,则说明数据已经损坏,需要重新从其他 DataNode 读取数据。其中,每个 DataNode 都会保存一个校验和日志,客户端成功验证一个数据块之后,DataNode 会更新该校验和日志。

此外,每个 DataNode 也会在后台运行一个扫描器(data block scanner),定期验证存储在这个 DataNode 上的所有数据块。

HDFS 提供数据块副本机制。当一个数据块损坏时,HDFS 能够自动复制其他完好的数据块来修复损坏的数据块,得到一个新的、完好的数据块,以达到系统设置的副本数要求,因此 HDFS 在某些数据块出现损坏时,保证了数据的完整性。

任务 4.3 Hadoop HDFS 命令

任务描述

在完成大数据平台 Hadoop 安装后,需要学会 Hadoop 核心组件的使用。本任务对 HDFS 的常用命令进行学习,并结合具体案例,练习 HDFS 目录的创建与查看、本地计算机和 HDFS 文件相互复制、HDFS 文件的复制与删除、HDFS 文件内容的查看等操作,掌握 HDFS 文件管理命令的操作使用。

关键步骤

(1) HDFS 常用命令总览。
(2) HDFS 目录的创建与查看。
(3) 本地计算机和 HDFS 之间的文件复制。
(4) HDFS 文件的复制与删除。
(5) HDFS 文件内容的查看。

与 Linux 命令类似,Hadoop 集群中也有一些命令可便捷地操作文件或是目录,接下来将介绍这些 HDFS 命令。

4.3.1 HDFS 常用命令总览

用户可以利用 HDFS 命令对 HDFS 进行操作。HDFS 有很多用户接口,其中命令行是最基本的,也是所有开发者必须熟悉的。所有命令行均由 bin/hadoop 脚本引发,不指定参数,运行 Hadoop 脚本将显示所有命令的描述。若要完全了解 Hadoop 命令,可输入"hdfs dfs-help"查看所有命令的帮助文件。

HDFS 命令的格式如下:

```
hdfs dfs  -命令
```

> **注意**
> 在 Hadoop 中有三种使用命令的格式,hadoop fs、hadoop dfs 和 hdfs dfs,三者的区别如下:hadoop fs 是通用的文件系统命令,针对任何系统,如本地文件、HDFS 文件、HFTP 文件或其他系统。hadoop dfs 是特定针对 HDFS 的文件系统的相关操作,但是已经不推荐使用。hdfs dfs 与 hadoop dfs 类似,同样是针对 HDFS 文件系统的操作,替代 hadoop dfs。

以下是一些常用 HDFS 命令,如表 4.3.1 所示。

表 4.3.1 常用 HDFS 命令

命令	说明
hdfs dfs -mkdir	创建 HDFS 目录
hdfs dfs -ls	列出 HDFS 目录
hdfs dfs -copyFromLocal	复制本地(local)文件到 HDFS
hdfs dfs -put	复制本地(local)文件到 HDFS
hdfs dfs -cat	列出 HDFS 目录下的文件内容
hdfs dfs -copyToLocal	将 HDFS 上的文件复制到本地(local)
hdfs dfs -get	将 HDFS 上的文件复制到本地(local)
hdfs dfs -cp	复制 HDFS 文件
hdfs dfs -rm	删除 HDFS 文件

4.3.2 创建与查看 HDFS 目录

4.3.2.1 创建 HDFS 目录

1) 创建 HDFS 目录的一般方法

创建 HDFS 目录的命令如下：

```
hdfs dfs -mkdir
```

在 Hadoop 上创建目录与在 Linux 上创建目录类似，根目录用"/"表示。

例如，创建"test"目录，打开 Master 节点的终端，输入如下命令：

```
hdfs dfs -mkdir /test
```

例如，在 test 目录下创建"cwfx"子目录，命令如下：

```
hdfs dfs -mkdir /test/cwfx
```

例如，在 test 目录下创建"kuaiji"子目录，命令如下：

```
hdfs dfs -mkdir /test/cwfx/kuaiji
```

执行结果如图 4.3.1 所示。

```
[root@master ~]# hdfs dfs -mkdir /test
[root@master ~]# hdfs dfs -mkdir /test/cwfx
[root@master ~]# hdfs dfs -mkdir /test/cwfx/kuaiji
```

图 4.3.1 创建 HDFS 目录

说明：在使用 HDFS 命令之前，必须先启动 Hadoop 集群，且命令执行在 Master 节点的终端上。

在创建"/test/cwfx"目录之前，必须先创建"test"目录，不能直接使用 hdfs dfs -mkdir /test/cwfx/kuaiji 命令创建"kuaiji"目录。

2) 创建多级 HDFS 目录

当创建目录时，如果要逐级地创建也很麻烦，所以 HDFS 提供了-p 选项，可以帮助用户一次创建多级目录。例如，创建多级目录"/dir1/dir2/dir3"的命令如下：

```
hdfs dfs -mkdir -p /dir1/dir2/dir3
```

执行结果如图 4.3.2 所示。

```
[root@master ~]# hdfs dfs -mkdir -p /dir1/dir2/dir3
[root@master ~]#
```

图 4.3.2 创建多级 HDFS 目录

当在 hdfs dfs -mkdir 命令后使用-p 选项时，多级目录可以不事先创建。例如，hdfs dfs -mkdir -p /dir1/dir2/dir3，"dir1"目录可以不存在。

4.3.2.2 查看 HDFS 目录

与 Linux 的 ls 命令类似，Hadoop 也有查看文件列表的命令，命令如下：

```
hdfs dfs -ls <args>
```

其中，<args>为可选参数。下面介绍查看命令的常见用法。

1) 查看创建的目录

查看上面创建的"test"目录，命令如下：

```
hdfs dfs -ls /test
```

执行结果如图 4.3.3 所示。

```
[root@master ~]# hdfs dfs -ls /test
Found 1 items
drwxr-xr-x   - root supergroup          0 2024-05-16 22:21 /test/cwfx
[root@master ~]#
```

图 4.3.3　查看创建的目录

通过图 4.3.3 所示的执行结果可以看到"test"目录下的子目录和文件，如子目录"cwfx"。

2) 查看根目录

根目录是用"/"表示的，查看根目录的命令如下：

```
hdfs dfs -ls /
```

执行结果如图 4.3.4 所示。

```
drwxr-xr-x   - root supergroup          0 2024-05-16 22:23 /dir1     刚建的目录
drwxr-xr-x   - root supergroup          0 2024-04-30 22:36 /home
drwxr-xr-x   - root supergroup          0 2024-05-16 22:21 /test
drwxrwxrwx   - root supergroup          0 2024-04-30 22:22 /tmp
drwxr-xr-x   - root supergroup          0 2024-04-30 22:18 /usr
[root@master ~]#
```

图 4.3.4　查看根目录

上述命令用来显示根目录下的子目录和文件，如图 4.3.4 中已经创建的"dir1"和"test"目录。

3) 查看所有子目录

参数-R 可用于查看所有 HDFS 子目录，R 代表递归（recursive），命令如下：

```
hdfs dfs -ls -R /
```

执行结果如图 4.3.5 所示。

```
drwxr-xr-x   - root supergroup          0 2024-03-25 15:29 /dir1
drwxr-xr-x   - root supergroup          0 2024-03-25 15:29 /dir1/dir2
drwxr-xr-x   - root supergroup          0 2024-03-25 15:29 /dir1/dir2/dir3
drwxr-xr-x   - root supergroup          0 2024-03-25 15:25 /test
drwxr-xr-x   - root supergroup          0 2024-03-25 15:26 /test/cwfx
drwxr-xr-x   - root supergroup          0 2024-03-25 15:26 /test/cwfx/kuaiji
[root@master ~]#
```

图 4.3.5　查看所有子目录

使用参数-R 查看命令，可以一次性列出所有 HDFS 子目录。

4.3.3 本地计算机和 HDFS 之间的文件复制

4.3.3.1 从本地计算机复制文件到 HDFS

1）创建文件

【例 4-1】 现有江苏财源有限公司资产负债表如表 4.3.2 所示，要求建立一个文本文件，将该表中的数据保存到 HDFS 中。

表 4.3.2　江苏财源有限公司资产负债表　　　　　　　　　　单位：元

项目①	期末余额	期初余额②	项目③	期末余额	期初余额
流动资产：			流动负债：		
货币资金	18 821 947.13	24 883 922.02	短期借款	0.00	0.00
交易性金融资产	0.00	0.00	交易性金融负债	0.00	0.00
衍生金融资产	0.00	0.00	衍生金融负债	0.00	0.00
应收票据	0.00	0.00	应付票据	0.00	0.00
应收账款	5 993 145.62	5 896 411.62	应付账款	1 568 231.20	2 658 543.50
应收款项融资	0.00	0.00	预收款项	0.00	0.00
预付款项	0.00	0.00	合同负债	0.00	0.00
其他应收款	10 000.00	0.00	应付职工薪酬	125 986.00	120 000.00
应收利息	0.00	0.00	应交税费	325 862.30	305 866.50
应收股利	0.00	0.00	其他应付款	0.00	0.00
存货	9 561 823.55	10 237 715.94	应付利息	0.00	0.00
合同资产	0.00	0.00	应付股利	0.00	0.00
持有待售资产	0.00	0.00	持有待售负债	0.00	0.00
一年内到期的非流动资产	0.00	0.00	一年内到期的非流动负债	0.00	0.00
其他流动资产	0.00	0.00	其他流动负债	0.00	0.00
流动资产合计	34 386 916.30	41 018 049.58	流动负债合计	2 020 079.50	3 084 410.00
非流动资产：			非流动负债：		
债权投资	0.00	0.00	长期借款	3 725 700.00	3 725 700.00
其他债权投资	0.00	0.00	应付债券		
长期应收款	0.00	0.00	租赁负债	0.00	0.00
长期股权投资	17 551 162.00	10 551 162.00	长期应付款	0.00	0.00
其他权益工具投资	0.00	0.00	长期应付职工薪酬	0.00	0.00

---

① 财务报表中此处表头为"资产"，后同。
② 财务报表中此处表头为"上年年末余额"，后同。
③ 财务报表中此处表头为"负债和所有者权益（或股东权益）"，后同。

(续表)

项目	期末余额	期初余额	项目	期末余额	期初余额
其他非流动金融资产	0.00	0.00	预计负债	0.00	0.00
投资性房地产	0.00	0.00	递延收益	0.00	0.00
固定资产	3 356 982.50	3 689 521.60	递延所得税负债	0.00	0.00
在建工程	1 240 558.80	1 240 558.80	其他非流动负债	0.00	0.00
生产性生物资产	0.00	0.00	非流动负债合计	3 725 700.00	3 725 700.00
油气资产	0.00	0.00	负债合计	5 745 779.50	6 810 110.00
使用权资产	0.00	0.00	所有者权益:		
无形资产	143 925.00	156 952.00	实收资本	50 000 000.00	50 000 000.00
开发支出	0.00	0.00	其他权益工具	0.00	0.00
商誉	0.00	0.00	资本公积	0.00	0.00
长期待摊费用	0.00	0.00	其他综合收益	0.00	0.00
递延所得税资产	0.00	0.00	专项储备	0.00	0.00
其他非流动资产	0.00	0.00	盈余公积	273 192.39	164 429.28
			未分配利润	660 572.71	-318 295.30
非流动资产合计	22 292 628.30	15 638 194.40	所有者权益合计	50 933 765.10	49 846 133.98
资产总计	56 679 544.60	56 656 243.98	负债和所有者权益总计	56 679 544.60	56 656 243.98

操作方法如下:

第1步:将表4.3.2内容整理成文本文件,每行的数据之间用","号间隔,格式如下:

```
流动资产_货币资金,18821947.13,24883922.02
流动资产_交易性金融资产,0.00,0.00
流动资产_衍生金融资产,0.00,0.00
流动资产_应收票据,0.00,0.00
流动资产_应收账款,5993145.62 ,5896411.62
流动资产_应收款项融资,0.00,0.00
流动资产_预付款项,0.00,0.00
流动资产_其他应收款,10000.00 ,0.00
流动资产_应收利息,0.00,0.00
流动资产_应收股利,0.00,0.00
流动资产_存货,9561823.55,10237715.94
流动资产_合同资产,0.00 ,0.00
流动资产_持有待售资产,0.00,    0.00
流动资产_一年内到期的非流动资产,0.00,0.00
流动资产_其他流动资产,0.00,0.00
流动资产合计,34386916.30,41018049.58
非流动资产_债权投资,0.00,0.00
非流动资产_其他债权投资,0.00,0.00
非流动资产_长期应收款,0.00,0.00
```

非流动资产_长期股权投资,17551162.00,10551162.00
非流动资产_其他权益工具投资,0.00,0.00
非流动资产_其他非流动金融资产,0.00,0.00
非流动资产_投资性房地产,0.00,0.00
非流动资产_固定资产,3356982.50,3689521.60
非流动资产_在建工程,1240558.80,1240558.80
非流动资产_生产性生物资产,0.00,0.00
非流动资产_油气资产,0.00,0.00
非流动资产_使用权资产,0.00,0.00
非流动资产_无形资产,143925.00,156952.00
非流动资产_开发支出,0.00,0.00
非流动资产_商誉,0.00,0.00
非流动资产_长期待摊费用,0.00,0.00
非流动资产_递延所得税资产,0.00,0.00
非流动资产_其他非流动资产,0.00 ,0.00
非流动资产合计,22292628.30,15638194.40
资产总计,56679544.60,56656243.98
流动负债_短期借款,0.00,0.00
流动负债_交易性金融负债,0.00,0.00
流动负债_衍生金融负债,0.00,0.00
流动负债_应付票据,0.00 ,0.00
流动负债_应付账款,1568231.20,2658543.50
流动负债_预收款项,0.00,0.00
流动负债_合同负债,0.00 ,0.00
流动负债_应付职工薪酬,125986.00,120000.00
流动负债_应交税费,25862.30,305866.50
流动负债_其他应付款,0.00,0.00
流动负债_应付利息,0.00,0.00
流动负债_应付股利,0.00,0.00
流动负债_持有待售负债,0.00,0.00
流动负债_一年内到期的非流动负债,0.00,0.00
流动负债_其他流动负债,0.00,0.00
流动负债合计,2020079.50,3084410.00
非流动负债_长期借款,3725700.00,3725700.00
非流动负债_应付债券,0.00,0.00
非流动负债_租赁负债,0.00,0.00
非流动负债_长期应付款,0.00,0.00
非流动负债_长期应付职工薪酬,0.00,0.00
非流动负债_预计负债,0.00,0.00
非流动负债_递延收益,0.00,0.00
非流动负债_递延所得税负债,0.00,0.00
非流动负债_其他非流动负债,0.00,0.00
非流动负债合计,3725700.00,3725700.00
负债合计,5745779.50,6810110.00

所有者权益_实收资本,50000000.00,50000000.00

所有者权益_其他权益工具,0.00,0.00

所有者权益_资本公积,0.00,0.00

所有者权益_其他综合收益,0.00,0.00

所有者权益_专项储备,0.00,0.00

所有者权益_盈余公积,273192.39,164429.28

所有者权益_未分配利润,660572.71,-318295.30

所有者权益合计,50933765.10,49846133.98

负债和所有者权益总计,56679544.60,56656243.98

第 2 步：在 CentOS 7 的"/home"目录下再创建一个子目录"cwbb"，并在该目录下创建文本文件 zcfzb.txt。

命令如下：

```
mkdir /home/cwbb
cd /home/cwbb
vi zcfzb.txt
```

在插入模式下，将资产负债表的数据粘贴进来，按 Esc 键后录入":wq"保存退出。用 vi 创建文本文件 zcfzb.txt，如图 4.3.6 所示。

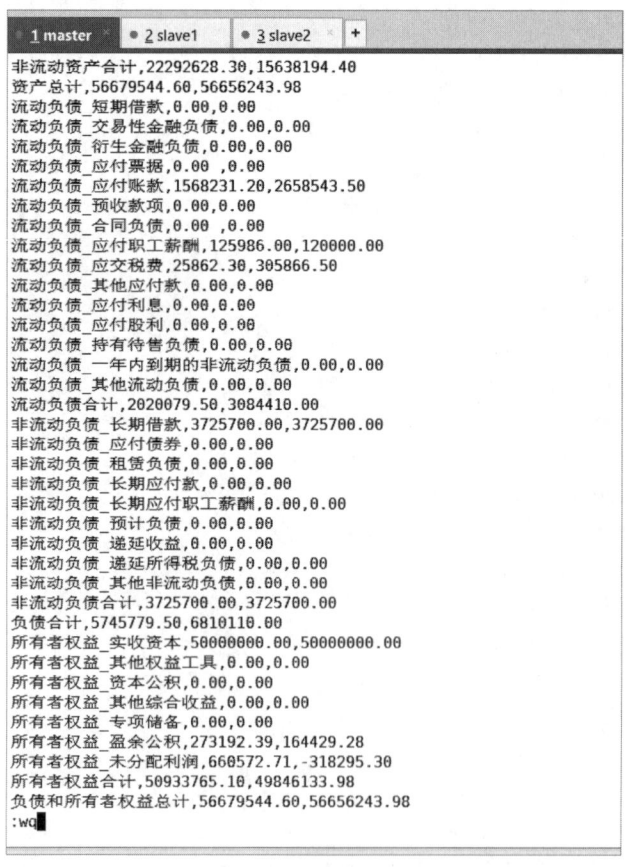

图 4.3.6　用 vi 创建文本文件 zcfzb.txt

查看"/home/cwbb"目录下的文件,命令如下,发现已创建了 zcfzb.txt,如图 4.3.7 所示。

```
ls  /home/cwbb
```

```
[root@master ~]# ls /home/cwbb
zcfzb.txt
[root@master ~]#
```

图 4.3.7　文本文件 zcfzb.txt 创建完成

第 3 步:复制文件。

从本地计算机(CentOS 7 虚拟机)复制文件到 HDFS,也被称为上传文件到 HDFS。有两种命令可以使用,一种是 hdfs dfs -put,另一种是 hdfs dfs -copyFromLocal。

在 Master 节点的终端输入如下命令:

```
hdfs  dfs  -put  zcfzb.txt  /test/zcfzb.txt
hdfs dfs -ls  /test
```

执行结果如图 4.3.8 所示。

```
[root@master cwbb]# hdfs  dfs  -put  zcfzb.txt  /test/zcfzb.txt
[root@master cwbb]# hdfs dfs -ls  /test
Found 2 items
drwxr-xr-x   - root supergroup          0 2024-05-16 22:21 /test/cwfx
-rw-r--r--   2 root supergroup       3244 2024-05-16 22:56 /test/zcfzb.txt
[root@master cwbb]#
```

图 4.3.8　本地 zcfzb.txt 文件已成功上传到 HDFS 上

本段代码可以实现将本地 zcfzb.txt 文件上传到 HDFS 的"/test"目录下,文件名保持为 zcfzb.txt,也可以在复制的时候重命名文件,或不写复制的文件名,直接写要复制到的路径。以下代码表示文件名保持不变:

```
hdfs  dfs  -put  zcfzb.txt  /test
```

|在上传文件时,当前目录下 zcfzb.txt 文件必须存在。|

使用 hdfs dfs -copyFromLocal[源文件][目标文件]也可实现上传文件的功能。例如,使用下面命令将本地 zcfzb.txt 上传到"/test"目录下,并重命名为 zcfzb1.txt:

```
hdfs  dfs  -copyFromLocal  zcfzb.txt  /test/zcfzb1.txt
hdfs  dfs  -ls /test
```

执行结果如图 4.3.9 所示。

```
[root@master cwbb]# hdfs  dfs -copyFromLocal  zcfzb.txt  /test/zcfzb1.txt
[root@master cwbb]# hdfs dfs -ls  /test
Found 3 items
drwxr-xr-x   - root supergroup          0 2024-05-16 22:21 /test/cwfx
-rw-r--r--   2 root supergroup       3244 2024-05-16 22:56 /test/zcfzb.txt
-rw-r--r--   2 root supergroup       3244 2024-05-16 22:58 /test/zcfzb1.txt
[root@master cwbb]#
```

图 4.3.9　本地 zcfzb.txt 文件上传到 HDFS 上重命名为 zcfzb1.txt

2) 强制复制文件

当复制本地文件至 HDFS 目录时,如果文件已经存在,系统会提示"File exists",即文件已经存在,将不会复制,再次执行以下命令:

```
hdfs dfs -put zcfzb.txt /test/zcfzb.txt
```

执行结果如图 4.3.10 所示。

```
[root@master cwbb]# hdfs dfs -put zcfzb.txt /test/zcfzb.txt
put: `/test/zcfzb.txt': File exists
[root@master cwbb]# t
```

图 4.3.10 文件已存在,不能复制

当文件已经存在时,可以使用-f(强制)选项,进行强制复制,命令如下:

```
hdfs dfs -put -f zcfzb.txt /test/zcfzb.txt
```

强制复制本地文件 zcfzb.txt 到 HDFS 目录"/test/zcfzb.txt",执行结果如图 4.3.11 所示。

```
[root@master cwbb]# hdfs dfs -put -f zcfzb.txt /test/zcfzb.txt
[root@master cwbb]# hdfs dfs -ls /test
Found 3 items
drwxr-xr-x   - root supergroup          0 2024-05-16 22:21 /test/cwfx
-rw-r--r--   2 root supergroup       3244 2024-05-16 23:14 /test/zcfzb.txt
-rw-r--r--   2 root supergroup       3244 2024-05-16 22:58 /test/zcfzb1.txt
[root@master cwbb]#
```

图 4.3.11 强制复制文件到 HDFS

3) 复制多个文件

用户可以一次复制多个本地文件到 HDFS 目录。

(1) 文件准备。现有江苏财源有限公司 2020 年度和 2021 年度利润表,分别如表 4.3.3 和表 4.3.4 所示。将这两个表的数据以文本文件形式存入本地目录,文件名分别为 lrb2020.txt 和 lrb2021.txt。

表 4.3.3 江苏财源有限公司 2020 年度利润表　　　　　　　　　　　　　单位:元

项目	本期金额	上期金额
一、营业收入	17 592 046.78	11 610 750.87
减:营业成本	13 047 503.39	8 611 352.24
税金及附加	105 552.28	69 664.50
销售费用	347 071.45	529 067.10
管理费用	2 588 741.69	2 008 569.52
研发费用	0.00	0.00
财务费用	310 252.27	104 766.50
其中:利息支出	45 500.00	

(续表)

项目	本期金额	上期金额
利息收入	0.00	0.00
加:其他收益	0.00	0.00
投资收益(损失以"－"号填列)	0.00	0.00
二、营业利润(亏损以"－"号填列)	1 192 925.70	287 331.01
加:营业外收入	0.00	10 000.00
减:营业外支出	420 000.00	
三、利润总额(亏损总额以"－"号填列)	772 925.70	297 331.01
减:所得税费用	89 336.75	
四、净利润(净亏损以"－"号填列)	683 588.95	297 331.01
(一)持续经营净利润		
(二)终止经营净利润		
五、其他综合收益的税后净额		
六、综合收益总额		
归属于母公司所有者的综合收益总额		
七、每股收益:		
基本每股收益(元/股)		
稀释每股收益(元/股)		

表 4.3.4　江苏财源有限公司 2021 年度利润表　　　　单位:元

项目	本期金额	上期金额
一、营业收入	20 559 863.00	17 592 046.78
减:营业成本	15 248 645.35	13 047 503.39
税金及附加	123 359.18	105 552.28
销售费用	405 623.15	347 071.45
管理费用	3 025 468.00	2 588 741.69
研发费用	0.00	0.00
财务费用	362 592.50	310 252.27
其中:利息支出	130 000.00	45 500.00
利息收入	0.00	0.00
加:其他收益	0.00	0.00
投资收益(损失以"－"号填列)	0.00	0.00
二、营业利润(亏损以"－"号填列)	1 394 174.82	1 192 925.70
加:营业外收入	56 000.00	0.00
减:营业外支出	0.00	420 000.00

(续表)

项目	本期金额	上期金额
三、利润总额（亏损总额以"－"号填列）	1 450 174.82	772 925.70
减：所得税费用	362 543.70	89 336.75
四、净利润（净亏损以"－"号填列）	1 087 631.12	683 588.95
（一）持续经营净利润	1 087 631.12	683 588.95
（二）终止经营净利润		
五、其他综合收益的税后净额		
六、综合收益总额	1 087 631.12	683 588.95
归属于母公司所有者的综合收益总额	1 087 631.12	683 588.95
七、每股收益：		
基本每股收益(元/股)		
稀释每股收益(元/股)		

① 创建 lrb2020.txt 文件，将上述 2020 年度利润表数据组织如下，作为其内容：

```
一、营业收入,17592046.78,11610750.87
减：营业成本,13047503.39,8611352.24
税金及附加,105552.28,69664.50
销售费用,347071.45,529067.10
管理费用,2588741.69,2008569.52
研发费用,0.00,0.00
财务费用,310252.27,104766.50
其中：利息支出,45500.00,0.00
    利息收入,0.00,0.00
加：其他收益,0.00,0.00
投资收益(损失以"－"号填列),0.00,0.00
二、营业利润(亏损以"－"号填列),1192925.70,287331.01
加：营业外收入,0.00,10,000.00
减：营业外支出,420,000.00,0
三、利润总额(亏损总额以"－"号填列),772925.70,297331.01
减：所得税费用,89336.75,0
四、净利润(净亏损以"－"号填列),683588.95,297331.01
(一)持续经营净利润,0,0
(二)终止经营净利润,0,0
五、其他综合收益的税后净额,0,0
六、综合收益总额,0,0
归属于母公司所有者的综合收益总额,0,0
七、每股收益,0,0
基本每股收益(元/股),0,0
稀释每股收益(元/股),0,0
```

执行创建文件命令如下：

```
cd /home/cwbb
vi lrb2020.txt
```

执行结果如图 4.3.12 所示。

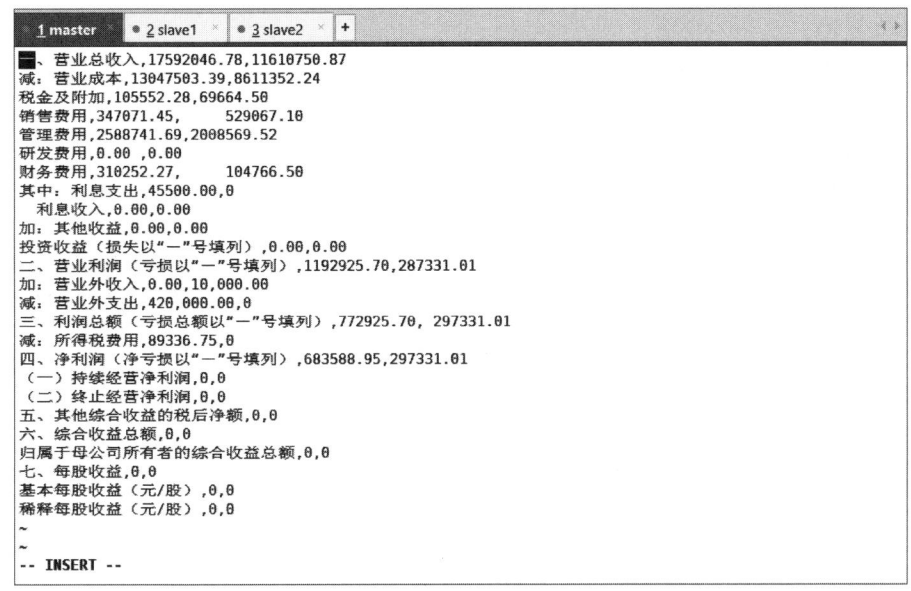

图 4.3.12　创建 2020 年度利润表数据文件 lrb2020.txt

② 创建 lrb2021.txt 文件，将上述 2021 年度利润表数据组织如下，作为其内容：

一、营业收入,20559863.00,17592046.78

减:营业成本,15248645.35,13047503.39

税金及附加,123359.18,105552.28

销售费用,405623.15 ,347071.45

管理费用,3025468.00,2588741.69

研发费用,0.00,0.00

财务费用,362592.50,310252.27

其中:利息支出,130000.00,45500.00

　利息收入,0.00,0

加:其他收益,0.00,0

投资收益(损失以"－"号填列),0.00,0

二、营业利润(亏损以"－"号填列),1394174.82,1192925.70

加:营业外收入,56000.00,0

减:营业外支出,0.00 ,420000.00

三、利润总额(亏损总额以"－"号填列),1450174.82,772925.70

减:所得税费用,362543.70,89336.75

四、净利润(净亏损以"－"号填列),1087631.12,683588.95

(一) 持续经营净利润,1087631.12,683588.95

(二)终止经营净利润,0,0

五、其他综合收益的税后净额,0,0

六、综合收益总额,1087631.12,　　683588.95

归属于母公司所有者的综合收益总额,1087631.12 ,683588.95

七、每股收益,0,0

基本每股收益(元/股),0,0

稀释每股收益(元/股),0,0

执行创建文件命令如下：

vi lrb2021.txt

执行结果如图 4.3.13 所示。

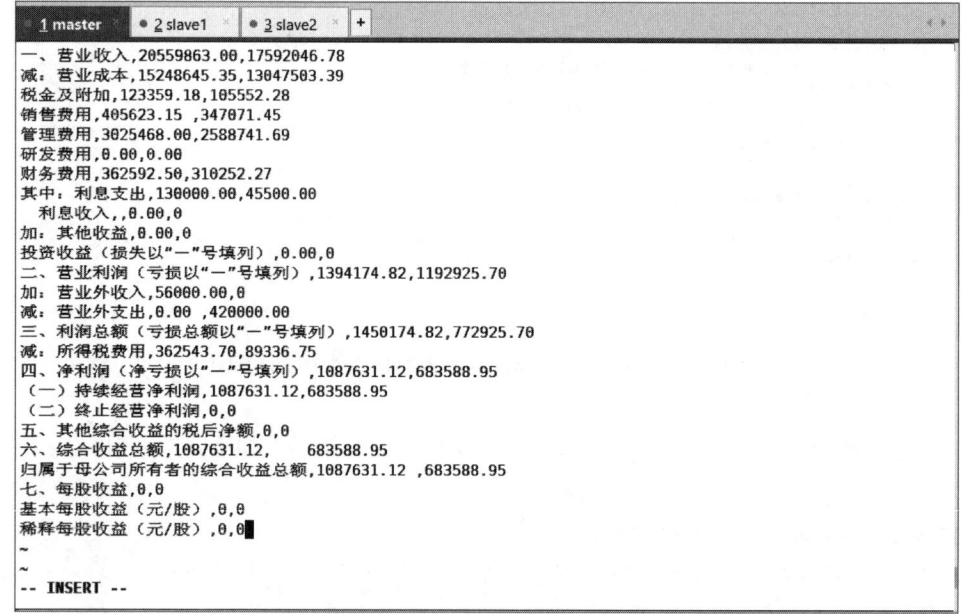

图 4.3.13　创建 2021 年度利润表数据文件 lrb2021.txt

(2) 用一条命令复制多个文件。将 lrb2020.txt 和 lrb2021.txt 这两个文件复制到"/test"目录下,命令如下：

hdfs dfs -put lrb2020.txt lrb2021.txt /test

执行结果如图 4.3.14 所示。

图 4.3.14　复制多个文件

从图 4.3.14 中可以看到,在"/test"目录中,多了已复制成功的 lrb2020.txt 和 lrb2021.txt 两个文件。

4) 复制目录

用"hdfs dfs -put"命令除了可以复制文件,还可以复制目录。例如,将本地的目录"/opt/modules/hadoop/etc"复制到 HDFS 目录"/test"下,命令如下:

```
hdfs dfs -put /opt/modules/hadoop/etc /test
hdfs dfs -ls /test
```

执行结果如图 4.3.15 所示。

```
Found 6 items
drwxr-xr-x   - root supergroup          0 2024-03-25 15:26 /test/cwfx
drwxr-xr-x   - root supergroup          0 2024-03-25 22:56 /test/etc
-rw-r--r--   3 root supergroup       1022 2024-03-25 22:22 /test/lrb2020.txt
-rw-r--r--   3 root supergroup       1079 2024-03-25 22:22 /test/lrb2021.txt
-rw-r--r--   3 root supergroup       3245 2024-03-25 16:42 /test/zcfzb.txt
-rw-r--r--   3 root supergroup       3245 2024-03-25 16:27 /test/zcfzb1.txt
[root@master ~]#
```

图 4.3.15　复制目录

从图 4.3.15 中,只看到了"etc"的目录名称,还可以使用以下命令,来列出 HDFS 目录"/test/etc"下的所有文件。

```
hdfs dfs -ls -R /test/etc
```

执行结果如图 4.3.16 所示。

```
drwxr-xr-x   - root supergroup          0 2024-05-16 23:27 /test/etc/hadoop
-rw-r--r--   2 root supergroup       4436 2024-05-16 23:27 /test/etc/hadoop/capacity-scheduler.xml
-rw-r--r--   2 root supergroup       1335 2024-05-16 23:27 /test/etc/hadoop/configuration.xsl
-rw-r--r--   2 root supergroup        318 2024-05-16 23:27 /test/etc/hadoop/container-executor.cfg
-rw-r--r--   2 root supergroup       1014 2024-05-16 23:27 /test/etc/hadoop/core-site.xml
-rw-r--r--   2 root supergroup       3670 2024-05-16 23:27 /test/etc/hadoop/hadoop-env.cmd
-rw-r--r--   2 root supergroup       4234 2024-05-16 23:27 /test/etc/hadoop/hadoop-env.sh
-rw-r--r--   2 root supergroup       2490 2024-05-16 23:27 /test/etc/hadoop/hadoop-metrics.properties
-rw-r--r--   2 root supergroup       2598 2024-05-16 23:27 /test/etc/hadoop/hadoop-metrics2.properties
-rw-r--r--   2 root supergroup       9683 2024-05-16 23:27 /test/etc/hadoop/hadoop-policy.xml
-rw-r--r--   2 root supergroup       1301 2024-05-16 23:27 /test/etc/hadoop/hdfs-site.xml
-rw-r--r--   2 root supergroup       1449 2024-05-16 23:27 /test/etc/hadoop/httpfs-env.sh
-rw-r--r--   2 root supergroup       1657 2024-05-16 23:27 /test/etc/hadoop/httpfs-log4j.properties
-rw-r--r--   2 root supergroup         21 2024-05-16 23:27 /test/etc/hadoop/httpfs-signature.secret
-rw-r--r--   2 root supergroup        620 2024-05-16 23:27 /test/etc/hadoop/httpfs-site.xml
-rw-r--r--   2 root supergroup       3518 2024-05-16 23:27 /test/etc/hadoop/kms-acls.xml
-rw-r--r--   2 root supergroup       1527 2024-05-16 23:27 /test/etc/hadoop/kms-env.sh
-rw-r--r--   2 root supergroup       1631 2024-05-16 23:27 /test/etc/hadoop/kms-log4j.properties
-rw-r--r--   2 root supergroup       5540 2024-05-16 23:27 /test/etc/hadoop/kms-site.xml
-rw-r--r--   2 root supergroup      11801 2024-05-16 23:27 /test/etc/hadoop/log4j.properties
-rw-r--r--   2 root supergroup        951 2024-05-16 23:27 /test/etc/hadoop/mapred-env.cmd
-rw-r--r--   2 root supergroup       1383 2024-05-16 23:27 /test/etc/hadoop/mapred-env.sh
```

图 4.3.16　查看"etc"目录下的所有文件

5) 复制并输入

在复制目录时使用的是-put 选项,还可以使用-copyFromLocal 选项。两者的不同之处是-put 选项接受标准输入(stdin),下面看两个使用-put 选项接受 stdin 的例子。

原本显示在屏幕上的内容存储到 HDFS 的文件中，命令如下：

```
echo abc | hdfs dfs -put - /test/echoin.txt
```

其中，echo abc 原本是要指定显示在屏幕上的内容 abc，现在通过符号"|"（pipe 管道）传递给 Hadoop 命令，并且存储到 HDFS 目录下的文件 echoin.txt 中。

列出 /test/echoin.txt 文件的内容，执行结果如图 4.3.17 所示。

```
[root@master hadoop-2.7.7]# echo  abc | hdfs dfs -put  -   /test/echoin.txt
[root@master hadoop-2.7.7]# hdfs dfs -cat /test/echoin.txt
abc
```

图 4.3.17　显示文件内容

本地目录的列表存储到 HDFS 的文件中，命令如下：

```
ls /opt/modules/hadoop/etc/hadoop | hdfs dfs -put - /test/hadoopetc.txt
```

其中，ls /opt/modules/hadoop/etc/hadoop 命令会把本地目录"/opt/modules/hadoop/etc/hadoop"的列表显示在屏幕上，但是通过后面的"|"传递给了 hadoop 命令，所以最后会存储到 HDFS 目录下的 hadoopetc.txt 文件中。

列出 /test/hadoopetc.txt 文件的内容，执行结果如图 4.3.18 所示。

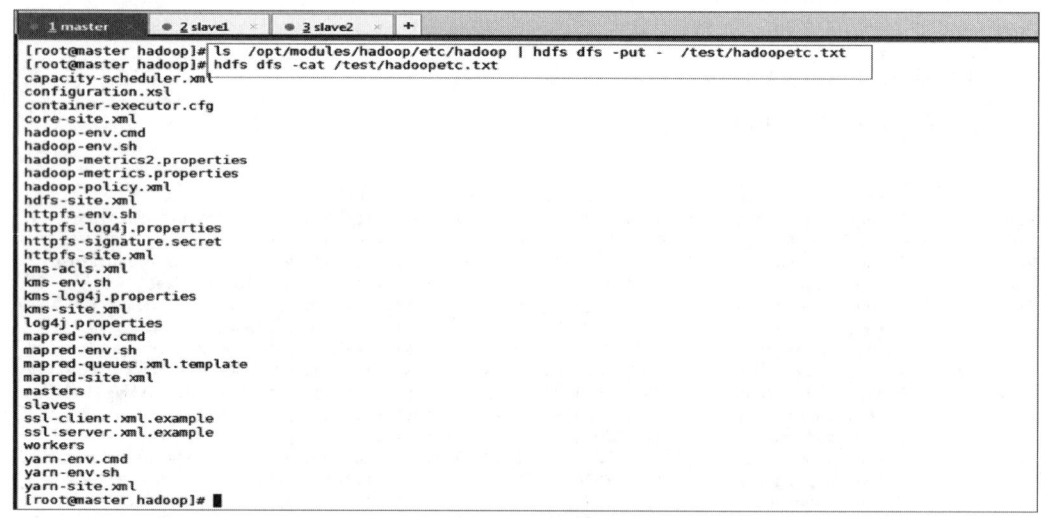

图 4.3.18　将本地目录的列表存储到 HDFS 的文件中

图 4.3.18 所示的文件内容是 ls　/opt/modules/hadoop/etc/hadoop 命令所产生的本地目录列表。

4.3.3.2　将 HDFS 上的文件复制到本地计算机

将 HDFS 上的文件复制到本地计算机也称为文件下载。

有两种命令可以实现，一种是"hdfs dfs -get"，另一种是"hdfs dfs -copyToLocal"，两种命令用法相同，以第一种为例，语法如下：

```
hdfs  dfs  -get  [HDFS 路径][本地路径]
```

使用此命令可以实现将 HDFS 的文件或者目录复制到本地计算机,下面分别介绍。

1) 将 HDFS 的文件复制到本地计算机

先在本地计算机上创建 localtest 测试目录,命令如下:

```
mkdir  localtest
```

然后将 HDFS 的文件/test/hadoopetc.txt 复制到本地计算机的测试目录,命令如下:

```
hdfs  dfs  -get  /test/hadoopetc.txt  ./localtest
```

最后查看本地 localtest 测试目录内文件,命令如下:

```
ls  ./localtest
```

执行结果如图 4.3.19 所示。

```
[root@master hadoop]# mkdir  localtest
[root@master hadoop]# hdfs  dfs  -get  /test/hadoopetc.txt  ./localtest
[root@master hadoop]# ls  ./localtest
hadoopetc.txt
[root@master hadoop]#
```

图 4.3.19　将 HDFS 的文件复制到本地计算机

注意

在复制 HDFS 上的文件到本地的时候,此文件必须存在,否则会出现"No Such File or Derectory"的错误提示。例如,将 HDFS 上的/test/hadoop.txt 下载到本地,命令如下:

```
hadoop  fs -get  /test/hadoop.txt  ./localtest
```

执行结果如图 4.3.20 所示。

```
[root@master ~]# hadoop  fs -get /test/hadoop.txt  ./localtest
get: `/test/hadoop.txt': No such file or directory
[root@master ~]#
```

图 4.3.20　命令出错

另外,可以在复制文件的时候,重命名文件。例如,将 HDFS 的文件/test/hadoopetc.txt,复制到本地的./localtest,同时将文件名修改为 mrkj.txt,命令如下:

```
hadoop  fs  -get  /test/hadoopetc.txt  ./localtest/mrkj.txt
ls  ./localtest
```

执行结果如图 4.3.21 所示。

```
[root@master ~]# hadoop fs -get /test/hadoopetc.txt  ./localtest/mrkj.txt
[root@master ~]# ls ./localtest/
hadoopetc.txt  mrkj.txt
[root@master ~]#
```

图 4.3.21　复制文件的同时重命名文件

2) 将 HDFS 的目录复制到本地计算机

用"-get"选项除了可以复制 HDFS 的文件到本地计算机，还可以复制目录。例如，将 HDFS 上的目录"/test/etc"，复制到本地目录"/localtest"中，命令如下：

```
hadoop fs -get /test/etc ./localtest/
```

然后查看"./localtest"目录中的文件和目录，执行结果如图 4.3.22 所示。

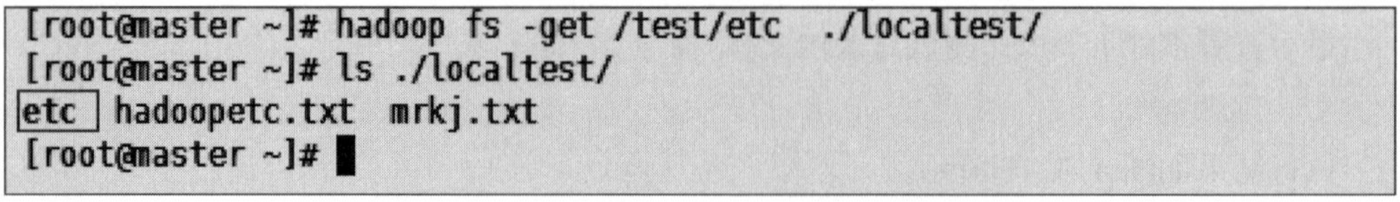

```
[root@master ~]# hadoop fs -get /test/etc ./localtest/
[root@master ~]# ls ./localtest/
etc  hadoopetc.txt  mrkj.txt
[root@master ~]#
```

图 4.3.22　将 HDFS 的目录复制到本地计算机

hadoop fs -copyToLocal 命令的用法与 hdfs dfs -get 一致，命令如下：

```
hadoop fs -copyToLocal /test/zcfzb.txt ./localtest/
hadoop fs -ls ./localtest/
```

然后查看"./localtest"目录中的文件和目录，执行结果如图 4.3.23 所示。

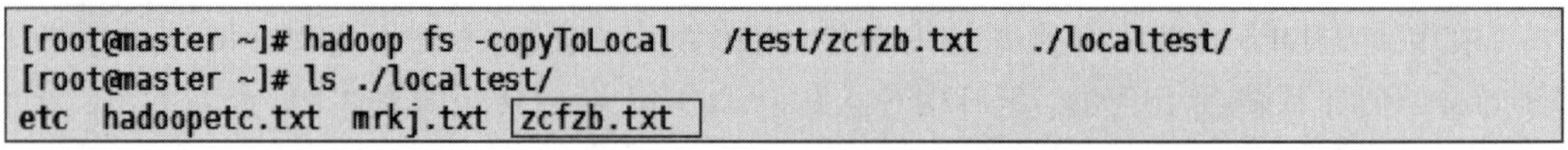

```
[root@master ~]# hadoop fs -copyToLocal /test/zcfzb.txt ./localtest/
[root@master ~]# ls ./localtest/
etc  hadoopetc.txt  mrkj.txt  zcfzb.txt
```

图 4.3.23　使用 -copyToLocal 选项复制文件到本地计算机

可见 zcfzb.txt 文件已复制到本地目录"./localtest"中。

4.3.4　复制与删除 HDFS 文件

4.3.4.1　复制 HDFS 文件

复制 HDFS 文件是指在 HDFS 中复制文件或目录到另一个 HDFS 目录。复制文件的命令为"hadoo fs -cp"，下面介绍此命令的具体使用方法。首先，在 HDFS 上创建测试目录，命令如下：

```
hadoop fs -mkdir /test/temp
```

其次，复制 HDFS 文件到测试目录，命令如下：

```
hadoop fs -cp /test/zcfzb1.txt /test/temp
```

将 HDFS 文件 /test/zcfzb1.txt 复制到 HDFS 测试目录"/test/temp"下。

最后，查看测试目录中是否有复制的文件，命令如下：

```
hadoop fs -ls /test/temp
```

执行结果如图 4.3.24 所示。

4.3.4.2　删除 HDFS 文件

删除文件的命令为 hadoop fs -rm。例如，删除 /test/temp/zcfzb1.txt 文件的命令如下：

```
[root@master ~]# hadoop fs -mkdir /test/temp
[root@master ~]# hadoop fs -cp /test/zcfzbl.txt  /test/temp
[root@master ~]# hadoop fs -ls /test/temp
Found 1 items
-rw-r--r--   3 root supergroup       3245 2024-03-25 23:53 /test/temp/zcfzbl.txt
[root@master ~]#
```

图 4.3.24　复制 HDFS 文件

```
hadoop fs -rm /test/temp/zcfzbl.txt
```

执行结果如图 4.3.25 所示。

```
[root@master ~]# hadoop fs -rm /test/temp/zcfzbl.txt
24/03/25 23:57:16 INFO fs.TrashPolicyDefault: Namenode trash configuration: Deletion interval = 0 minutes, Emptier interval = 0 minutes.
Deleted /test/temp/zcfzbl.txt
[root@master ~]#
[root@master ~]# hadoop fs -ls /test/temp/
[root@master ~]#
```

图 4.3.25　删除 HDFS 文件

可见 HDFS 上的"/test/temp"目录下的 zcfzbl.txt 文件已被删除。

删除 HDFS 目录的命令为 hdfs　fs　-rm　-R,如果没有-R,则不能删除目录。例如,删除 HDFS 目录"/test/temp"的命令如下:

```
hadoop fs -rm -R /test/temp
```

执行结果如图 4.3.26 所示。

```
[root@master ~]# hadoop fs -rm /test/temp
rm: '/test/temp': Is a directory
[root@master ~]# hadoop fs -rm -R /test/temp
24/03/26 00:02:07 INFO fs.TrashPolicyDefault: Namenode trash configuration: Deletion interval = 0 minutes, Emptier interval = 0 minutes.
Deleted /test/temp
[root@master ~]# hadoop fs -ls /test
Found 8 items
drwxr-xr-x   - root supergroup          0 2024-03-25 15:26 /test/cwfx
-rw-r--r--   3 root supergroup          4 2024-03-25 23:06 /test/echoin.txt
drwxr-xr-x   - root supergroup          0 2024-03-25 22:56 /test/etc
-rw-r--r--   3 root supergroup        509 2024-03-25 23:12 /test/hadoopetc.txt
-rw-r--r--   3 root supergroup       1022 2024-03-25 22:22 /test/lrb2020.txt
-rw-r--r--   3 root supergroup       1079 2024-03-25 22:22 /test/lrb2021.txt
-rw-r--r--   3 root supergroup       3245 2024-03-25 16:42 /test/zcfzb.txt
-rw-r--r--   3 root supergroup       3245 2024-03-25 16:27 /test/zcfzbl.txt
[root@master ~]#
```

图 4.3.26　删除 HDFS 目录

从图 4.3.26 中可以看到,通过删除目录命令,删除了目录"/test/temp"。

4.3.5　查看 HDFS 文件内容

用户可以使用 hdfs dfs -test、hdfs dfs -cat、hdfs dfs -tail 等含不同参数的命令查看 HDFS 集群中的文件内容。但是,只有文本文件的内容可以查看,其他类型的文件则显示乱码。例如,查看/test/zcfzbl.txt 文件,命令如下:

```
hadoop fs -cat /test/lrb2020.txt
```

执行结果如图 4.3.27 所示。

```
[root@master ~]# hadoop fs -cat /test/lrb2020.txt
一、营业收入,17592046.78,11610750.87
减：营业成本,13047503.39,8611352.24
税金及附加,105552.28,69664.50
销售费用,347071.45,        529067.10
管理费用,2588741.69,2008569.52
研发费用,0.00 ,0.00
财务费用,310252.27,         104766.50
其中：利息支出,45500.00,0
    利息收入,0.00,0.00
加：其他收益,0.00,0.00
投资收益（损失以"一"号填列）,0.00,0.00
二、营业利润（亏损以"一"号填列）,1192925.70,287331.01
加：营业外收入,0.00,10,000.00
减：营业外支出,420,000.00,0
三、利润总额（亏损总额以"一"号填列）,772925.70, 297331.01
减：所得税费用,89336.75,0
四、净利润（净亏损以"一"号填列）,683588.95,297331.01
（一）持续经营净利润,0,0
（二）终止经营净利润,0,0
五、其他综合收益的税后净额,0,0
六、综合收益总额,0,0
归属于母公司所有者的综合收益总额,0,0
七、每股收益,0,0
基本每股收益（元/股）,0,0
稀释每股收益（元/股）,0,0
[root@master ~]#
```

图 4.3.27　查看 HDFS 文件内容

单元总结

　　本单元先对 Hadoop 的 HDFS 进行了相关的介绍，如 HDFS 的架构和容错机制，Hadoop HDFS 的文件管理，包括 HDFS 的块分布、数据读取和写入，HDFS 如何保证数据的完整性。随后以实际案例的形式介绍了 HDFS 文件管理命令的使用，如创建与查看 HDFS 目录、本地计算机与 HDFS 之间的交互、复制与删除 HDFS 文件、查看 HDFS 文件内容等。

单元习题

一、简答题

1. HDFS 的架构主要包含哪些组成部分？请画出 HDFS 架构图。

2. 简述 SecondaryNameNode 的工作流程，并画出 SecondaryNameNode 的工作流程图。

3. 简述 HDFS 读取数据的流程。

4. 简述 HDFS 写入数据的流程。

二、技能训练题

1. 在 HDFS 上创建目录"/demo/test01"。
2. 在本地"/home/cwbb"目录下的文件 lrb2020.txt 上传到 HDFS 的"/demo/test01"目录中,文件名改名为 lrb.txt。
3. 将"apple"输入 HDFS 的/demo/test01/lrb.txt 文件。
4. 将 HDFS 文件/demo/test01/lrb.txt 复制到 HDFS 目录"/demo"。

单元 5

大数据并行计算技术 MapReduce

Hadoop 中最核心的两大组件就是 HDFS 和 MapReduce，HDFS 提供了承载海量数据存储的能力，而 MapRecuce 则提供了承载海量数据高度并行计算的能力。前面已对 HDFS 进行了简单介绍，本单元将对 MapReduce 进行简单说明。

学习目标

知识目标

1. 了解 MapReduce 的原理和部署结构。
2. 了解 MapReduce 的运行流程。
3. 了解 MapReduce 的容错机制。

技能目标

1. 掌握 MapReduce 程序运行流程。
2. 能用 MapReduce 解决实际问题。

单元任务

任务 5.1 MapReducc 的原理和部署结构。
任务 5.2 MapReduce 的工作机制。

任务 5.1　MapReduce 的原理和部署结构

任务描述

在完成大数据平台 Hadoop 安装后，需要学会 Hadoop 核心组件的使用。本任务介绍 MapReduce 原理和 MapReduce 的部署结构，掌握 MapReduce 关键技术。

关键步骤

（1）了解 MapReduce 的原理。
（2）了解 MapReduce 的部署结构。

MapReduce 是 Hadoop 框架的核心组件之一，它将大型的、复杂的计算任务抽象成 Map

阶段和 Reduce 阶段。理解 MapReduce 执行的原理有助于更好地进行会计业务分析。本任务将对 MapReduce 的原理进行简要介绍。

5.1.1 MapReduce 的原理

Hadoop 中 MapReduce 最核心的思想就是分而治之，通过 MapReduce 这个名字就可以看出，MapReduce 包含 Map 和 Reduce 两部分。它将一个大型的计算问题分解为一个个小的、简单的计算任务，交由 MapReduce 中的 Map 部分执行，随后 Reduce 部分会对 Map 部分输出的中间结果进行聚合统计，输出最终的计算结果。MapReduce 的工作原理如图 5.1.1 所示。

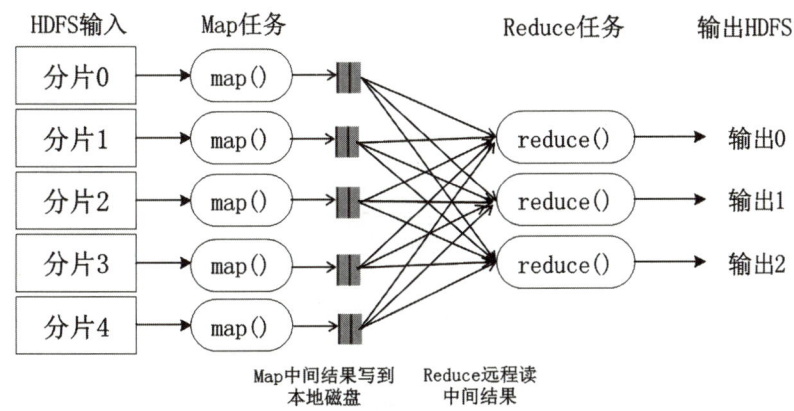

图 5.1.1 MapReduce 的工作原理

由图 5.1.1 可知，每个任务在框架中都是高度并行计算的，然后 MapReduce 框架将各个计算子任务的计算结果进行合并，得出最终的计算结果。任务的高度并行化极大地提高了 Hadoop 处理海量数据的性能。MapReduce 框架将一个大型的计算任务拆分为多个简单的计算任务，交由多个 Map 并行计算，每个 Map 的计算结果经过中间结果处理阶段的处理后输入 Reduce 阶段，Reduce 阶段将输入的数据进行合并处理，输出最终的计算结果。

同时，用户无须关心 MapReduce 底层各节点之间的通信机制与通信过程，只需简单地编写 map() 函数和 reduce() 函数即可开发 Hadoop MapReduce 程序。

5.1.2 MapReduce 的部署结构

MapReduce 框架由一个主节点（ResourceManager）、多个子节点（NodeManager）和每个执行任务的 AppMaster 共同组成。一般 MapReduce 的计算节点和存储节点部署在同一台服务器上。MapReduce 的部署结构如图 5.1.2 所示。

这种部署结构可以使 MapReduce 框架在已经存储好数据的节点上快速、高效地调度任务，尽可能地不用通过 RPC 从其他服务器上获取数据来执行任务，使整个集群的网络带宽被高效利用，极大地提升了处理任务的效率。

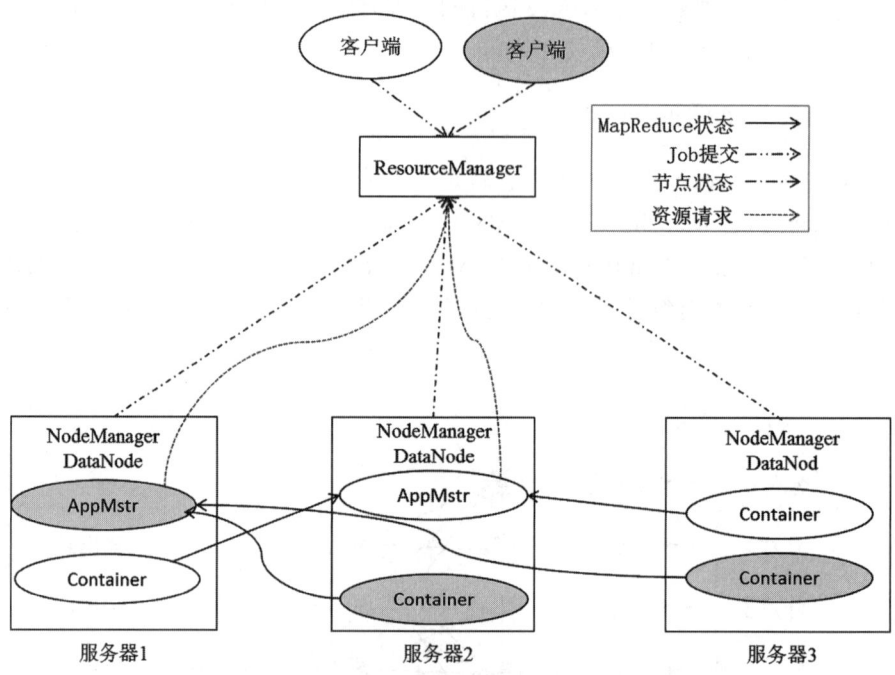

图 5.1.2　MapReduce 的部署结构

任务 5.2　MapReduce 的工作机制

任务描述

在完成大数据平台 Hadoop 安装后,需要学会 Hadoop 核心组件的使用。本任务介绍 MapReduce 的运行流程和 MapReduce 的容错机制,掌握 MapReduce 关键技术。

关键步骤

(1) 熟悉 MapReduce 的运行流程。

(2) 了解 MapReduce 的容错机制。

MapReduce 编程模型简化了分布式系统中并行计算的复杂度,开发人员能够不必关心 MapReduce 程序的底层实现细节,只专注于解决业务需求。本任务简单介绍 MapReduce 的工作机制。

5.2.1　MapReduce 的运行流程

在 MapReduce 框架内部,整个运行流程可以分为原始数据阶段、Map 阶段、中间结果处理阶段、Reduce 阶段和结果数据阶段,而每个阶段中的数据传输格式是不一样的。
MapReduce 的简单运行流程如图 5.2.1 所示。

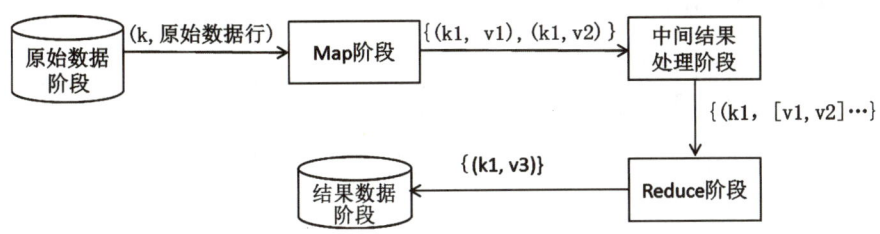

图 5.2.1　MapReduce 的简单运行流程

(1) 原始数据阶段,即 Map 阶段接收经过 Hadoop 框架的处理,将"(k,原始数据行)"格式的数据输入 Map 阶段,即 Map 阶段接收到的数据都是"(k,原始数据行)"格式。

(2) 数据经过 Map 阶段的处理之后,输出"{(k1, v1),(k1,v2)}格式的中间结果。

(3) Map 阶段输出的中间结果经由 Hadoop 的中间结果处理阶段的处理(如聚合、排序等)之后,会形成"{(k1,[v1,v2]…}"格式的数据。

(4) 中间结果处理阶段形成的"(k1,[v1,v2])…}"格式的数据会输入 Reduce 阶段进行处理。此时,key 相同的数据会被输入同一个 Reduce 函数进行处理。

(5) 数据经过 Reduce 阶段的处理之后,最终会形成"{(k1, v3)}"格式的数据存入 HDFS 中,即结果数据阶段。

下面通过一个 wordcount 执行过程的实例,来理解 MapReduce 的运行流程。

wordcount 程序任务是:输入一个包含大量单词的文本文件,输出文件中每个单词及其出现频数,并按照单词字母顺序排序,每个单词和其频数占一行,单词和频数之间有间隔。wordcount 程序任务如表 5.2.1 所示,其执行结果实例如图 5.2.2 所示。

表 5.2.1　wordcount 程序任务

程序	wordcount
输入	一个包含大量单词的文本文件
输出	文件中每个单词及其出现次数(频数),并按照单词字母顺序排序,每个单词和其频数占一行,单词和频数之间有间隔

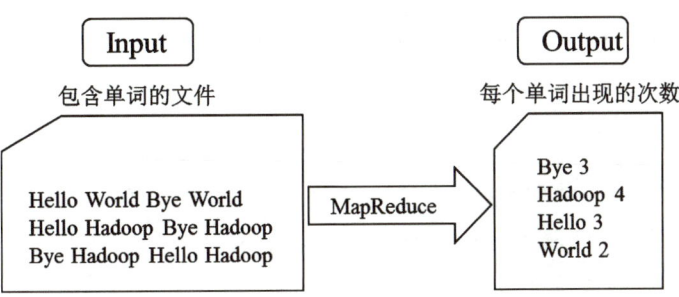

图 5.2.2　wordcount 的执行结果实例

wordcount 程序的 MapReduce 执行过程如图 5.2.3 所示。

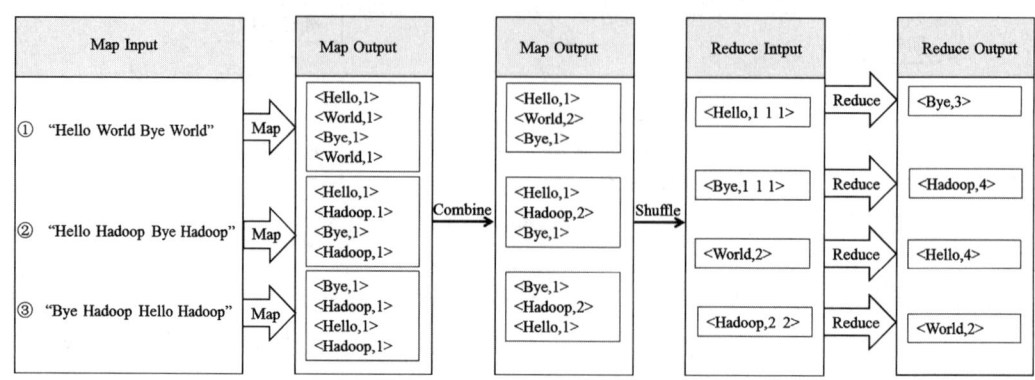

图 5.2.3 MapReduce 执行过程

5.2.2 MapReduce 的容错机制

MapReduce 的容错机制包括 Task 容错、AppMaster 容错、NodeManager 容错和 ResourceManager 容错等。

5.2.2.1 Task 容错

AppMaster 一段时间没有收到任务进度的更新，就会将任务标记为失败，但是不会立刻"杀死"执行任务的进程，而是等待一定的超时时间。该超时时间可以在 mapred-site.xml 文件中进行配置，具体的属性为 mapreduce.task.timeout，代码如下：

```
<property>
    <name>mapreduce.task.timeout</name>
    <value>600000</value>
</property>
```

超时时间默认值为 10 min，即在任务被标记为失败的 10 分钟之后才会将任务失败的进程"杀死"。

MapReduce 提供了重试机制，重试的次数主要由 mapred-site.xml 文件中的 mapreduce.map.maxattempts 属性和 mapreduce.reduce.maxattempts 属性配置，代码如下：

```
<property>
    <name>mapreduce.map.maxattempts</name>
    <value>4</value>
</property>
<property>
    <name>mapreduce.reduce.maxattempts</name>
    <value>4</value>
</property>
```

默认重试次数为 4，即任务失败后，MapReduce 框架会重试 4 次，如果任务依然失败，MapReduce 才会认为任务彻底失败了。

用户也可以配置允许任务失败的最大百分比,可以在属性 mapreduce. map. failures. maxpercent 和 mapreduce. reduce. failures. maxpercent 中配置。

5.2.2.2 AppMaster 容错

AppMaster 提供了重传机制,YARN 中的应用程序失败后,最多尝试次数在 Mapred-site.xml 文件中的 mapreduce.am.max-attempts 属性中配置,代码如下:

```
<property>
    <name>mapreduce.am.max-attempts</name>
    <value>2</value>
</property>
```

尝试次数默认值为 2,即当 AppMaster 失败 2 次后,运行的任务将会失败。

在 MapReduce 内部,YARN 框架对 AppMaster 的最大尝试次数做了限制。其中,每个在 YARN 中运行的应用程序不能超过这个数量限制,具体限制由 yarn-site.xml 文件中的 yarn.resourcemanager.am.max-attempts 属性控制,配置信息如下:

```
<property>
    <name>yarn.resourcemanager.am.max-attempts</name>
    <value>2</value>
</property>
```

5.2.2.3 NodeManager 容错

当 NodeManager 发生故障,停止向 ResourceManager 节点发送心跳信息时,ResourceManager 节点并不会立即移除 NodeManager,而是要等待一段时间。该时间可以由 yarn.resourcemanager.nm.liveness-monitor.expiry-interval-ms 属性设置,代码如下:

```
<property>
    <name>yarn.resourcemanager.nm.liveness-monitor.expiry-interval-ms</name>
    <value>600000</value>
</property>
```

等待时间默认值为 10 min,即 NodeManager 发生故障后,ResourceManager 节点接收不到 NodeManager 发送过来的心跳信息,过 10 min 之后才会将 NodeManager 移除。

当 NodeManager 上运行的失败任务数量达到一定的值时,AppMaster 就会将该节点上的任务调度到其他节点上。任务失败的阈值由 mapred-site.xml 文件中的 mapreduce.job.maxtaskfailures.per.tracker 属性设置,代码如下:

```
<property>
    <name>mapreduce.job.maxtaskfailures.per.tracker</name>
    <value>3</value>
</property>
```

此默认值为 3,即当一个 NodeManager 上有超过 3 个任务失败,AppMaster 就会将该节点上的任务调度到其他节点上。

5.2.2.4 ResourceManager 容错

新版本的 Hadoop 中提供了 ResourceManager 节点的 HA 机制，如果主 ResourceManager 失败，备 ResourceManager 会迅速接管工作。

Hadoop 中对 ResourceManager 节点提供了检查点机制，当所有的 ResourceManager 节点失败后，重启 ResourceManager 节点，可以从上一个失败的 ResourceManager 节点保存的检查点进行状态恢复。

这些检查点的存储是由 yarn-site.xml 文件中的 yarn.resourcemanager.store.class 属性设置的，代码如下：

```
<property>
    <name>yarn.resourcemanager.store.class</name>
    <value>org.apache.hadoop.yarn.server.resourcemanager.recovery.
    FileSystemRMStateStore
    </value>
</property>
```

检查点的存储默认保存到文件中。

单元总结

本单元简单介绍了 MapReduce 的原理和部署结构，并且对 MapReduce 的运行流程和容错机制作了进一步说明。

单元习题

简答题

1. 请简述 MapReduce 的工作原理。
2. 在 MapReduce 框架内部，整个运行流程分为哪几个阶段？
3. MapReduce 的容错机制有哪些？

单元 6

数据仓库 Hive 的安装部署

Hive 是基于 Hadoop 的数据仓库工具,可以将结构化的数据文件映射为一张数据库表。Hadoop MapReduce 编程需要使用者掌握一门 Hadoop 支持的开发语言。在 Hadoop 出现之前,大部分的数据分析人员,包括财务分析人员,基本都用 SQL 语句分析数据库中的数据,如果让这些数据分析人员重新学习一门 Hadoop 支持的开发语言,将会耗费巨大的人力成本和学习成本。Hive 能提供简单的 SQL 查询功能,可以将 SQL 语句转换为 MapReduce 任务运行,可以让财务数据分析人员能够使用 Hadoop 强大的 MapReduce 编程模型进行数据分析。

学习目标

知识目标

1. 了解 Hive 的架构。
2. 了解 Hive 的 3 种部署模式。

技能目标

1. 掌握 MySQL 的安装和配置。
2. 掌握 Hive 的环境部署。
3. 掌握 MySQL 和 Hive 的基本应用。

单元任务

任务 6.1　Hive 的架构和部署模式。
任务 6.2　安装并配置 MySQL 数据库。
任务 6.3　Hive 的环境安装与配置。

任务 6.1　Hive 的架构和部署模式

任务描述

要用大数据技术对会计数据进行分析,需要使用数据仓库 Hive,而 Hive 必须安装在 Hadoop 大数据平台上。本任务将介绍 Hive 的架构模式、Hive 的 3 种安装模式、Hive 和传统数据库的区别,使读者在简单了解 Hive 工作原理的基础上,走进下一个任务 Hive 的安装。

关键步骤

（1）熟悉 Hive 的架构。
（2）熟悉内嵌模式。
（3）熟悉本地模式。
（4）熟悉远程模式。
（5）熟悉 Hive 和传统数据库的区别。

Hive 的出现使得传统数据分析人员能够快速上手使用 Hadoop 进行数据的分析和处理。这得益于 Hive 优良的架构特征。除此之外，Hive 提供了 3 种不同的安装模式，分别是内嵌模式、本地模式和远程模式。

6.1.1 Hive 的架构

Hive 在架构上并不是分布式的，它被设计成独立于 Hadoop 集群之外，可以将它看成 Hadoop 的客户端，它能够将 HiveQL 转化成 MapReduce 作业在 Hadoop 中执行。

> 注意
>
> 有些 HiveQL 语句不能转化成 MapReduce 作业，如下面的查询语句：
>
> select * from user；
>
> 这种 HiveQL 语句不会被 Hive 转化成 MapRedure 作业，Hive 只会从 DataNode 将数据获取到之后，按照顺序依次输出。

Hive 的架构如图 6.1.1 所示。

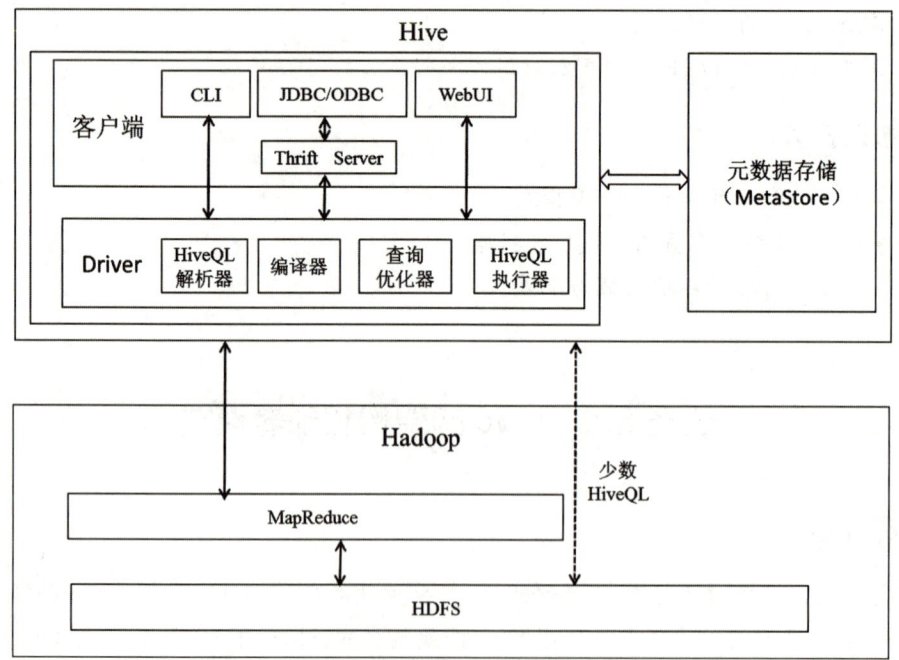

图 6.1.1　Hive 的架构

由图 6.1.1 可以看出以下信息：

(1) Hive 的客户端可以通过 CLI、JDBC 和 ODBC 等客户端进行访问。除此之外，Hive 还支持 WebUI(Web user interface)访问。CLI 是 Hive 自带的一个命令行界面，提供在 Hive Shell 下执行类似 SQL 命令的相关 HiveQL 操作，也是 Hive 提供的标准接口，可以使用一条 HiveQL 命令返回存储在 Hadoop 上的数据；JDBC、ODBC 以及 Thrift Server 可以向用户提供进行编程访问的接口；WebUI，通过浏览器访问和操作 Hive 服务端，可以查看 Hive 数据库模式，执行 HiveQL 相关操作命令。

(2) Hive 的核心组件 Driver 包括 HiveQL 解析器、编译器、查询优化器和 HiveQL 执行器。它们完成 HiveQL 查询语句从词法分析、语法分析、编译、优化到查询计划的生成。

(3) 元数据存储(MetaStore)模块是一个独立的关系型数据库，通常是与 MySQL 数据库连接后创建的一个 MySQL 实例，也可以是 Hive 自带的 Derby 数据库实例。Hive 采用类 SQL 语法模式的 HiveQL 操作存储在 Hadoop 分布式环境上的数据。因此需要在 Hive 与 Hadoop 之间提供一层抽象接口，实现 Hive 与 Hadoop 之间不同数据格式的转换。接口属性包括表名、列名、表分区名以及数据在 HDFS 上的存储位置。接口属性内容被称为 Hive 表元数据，它以元数据内容形式存储在数据库中，用来限定 Hive 进行格式化操作的方式，也能从 Hadoop 中获取任何非结构化数据。

(4) Hive 将大部分 HiveQL 语句转化为 MapReduce 作业提交到 Hadoop 执行；少数 HiveQL 语句不会转化为 MapReduce 作业，直接从 HDFS 上获取数据后按照顺序输出。

6.1.2 内嵌模式

内嵌模式是 Hive 安装部署中最简单的一种模式。这种模式中，Hive 的元数据信息和 Hive 服务运行在同一个 JVM 实例中，此时，Hive 存储元数据信息使用的是内嵌的 Deby 数据库。另外，这种模式只能支持最多一个用户打开 Hive 会话进行数据操作。Hive 的内嵌模式如图 6.1.2 所示。

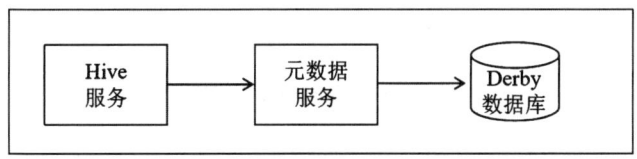

图 6.1.2　Hive 的内嵌模式

由图 6.1.2 可以看出，Hive 服务和元数据服务运行在同一个 JVM 实例中，Hive 服务通过元数据服务向 Derby 数据库存储元数据信息。

6.1.3 本地模式

在 Hive 的本地模式中，Hive 服务和元数据服务运行在同一个 JVM 实例中，同时使用外置的数据库如 MySQL 或 PostgreSQL 等数据库作为存储元数据的数据库。Hive 的本地模式如图 6.1.3 所示。

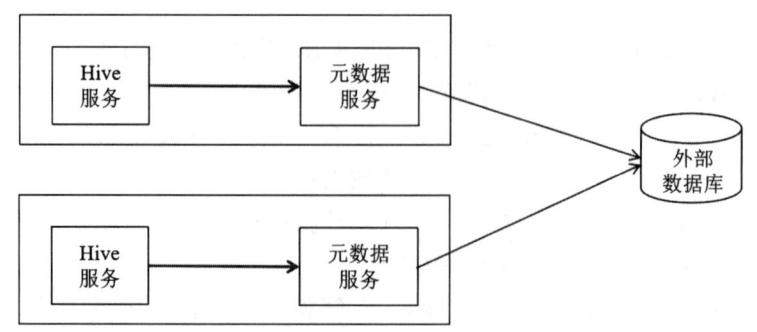

图 6.1.3　Hive 的本地模式

由图 6.1.3 可以看出,本地模式下,Hive 服务和元数据服务运行在同一个 JVM 实例中,但是存储元数据的数据库被独立出来。图 6.1.3 中的外部数据库可以是 MySQL、PostgreSQL、Oracle 数据库等。同时,多个 JVM 实例中运行的多个 Hive 服务和元数据服务可以连接同一个存储元数据信息的外部数据库。

6.1.4　远程模式

在远程模式下,Hive 服务和元数据服务运行在不同的进程内。此时,数据库服务可以放置到远程的某台服务器上,同时可以将数据库放置在防火墙等安全隔离服务的背后,增强了数据库服务的安全性。Hive 的远程模式如图 6.1.4 所示。

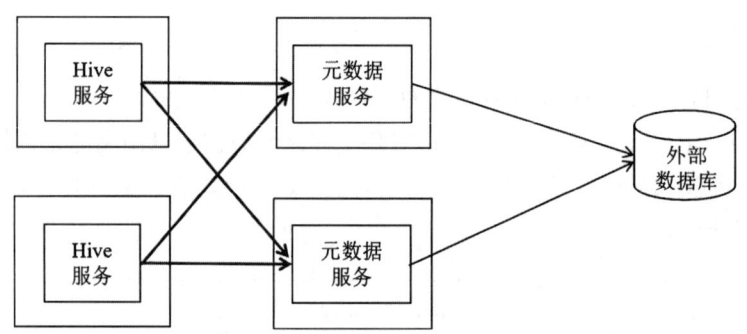

图 6.1.4　Hive 的远程模式

由图 6.1.4 可以看出,在 Hive 的远程模式中,Hive 服务和元数据服务分别运行在不同的 JVM 实例中,多个 Hive 服务和元数据服务之间可以交叉访问。同时,存储元数据的外部数据库可以部署到远程服务器上,由防火墙等安全防护进程提供安全保障。

综上所述,在生产环境下,推荐使用本地模式和远程模式安装和部署 Hive。

6.1.5　Hive 和传统数据库的区别

Hive 的底层逻辑依赖的是 HDFS 和 MapReduce,在很多方面有别于传统数据库。Hive 采用了 SQL 的查询语言 HiveQL,因此很容易将 Hive 理解为数据库。其实从结构上来看,Hive 和传统数据库除了拥有类似的查询语言,再无类似之处。两者的区别如表 6.1.1 所示。

表 6.1.1　Hive 和传统数据库的区别

比较项目	Hive	传统数据库
查询语言	HiveQL	SQL
数据存储位置	HDFS	Raw Device 或者 Local FS
数据格式	用户定义	系统决定
数据更新	不支持	支持
索引	无	有
执行	MapRedcue	Executor
执行延迟	高	低
可扩展性	高	低
数据规模	大	小

两者的区别对比如下：

（1）查询语言。SQL 被广泛地应用在数据仓库中，因此，开发者专门针对 Hive 的特性设计了类 SQL 的查询语言 HiveQL。熟悉 SQL 开发的开发者可以很方便地使用 Hive 进行开发。

（2）数据存储位置。Hive 是建立在 Hadoop 之上的，所有 Hive 的数据都是存储在 HDFS 中的。而数据库则可以将数据保存在块设备或者本地文件系统中。

（3）数据格式。Hive 中没有定义专门的数据格式，数据格式可以由用户指定，用户定义数据格式需要指定三个属性：列分隔符（通常为空格、"\t"、"\x001"）、行分隔符（"\n"）以及读取文件数据的方法（Hive 中默认有 TextFile、SequenceFile 以及 RCFile 三个文件格式）。在加载数据的过程中，不需要从用户数据格式到 Hive 定义的数据格式的转换，因此，Hive 在加载的过程中不会对数据本身进行任何修改，而只是将数据内容复制或者移动到相应的 HDFS 目录中。而在数据库中，不同的数据库有不同的存储引擎，定义了自己的数据格式。所有数据都会按照一定的组织存储，因此，数据库加载数据的过程会比较耗时。

（4）数据更新。Hive 是针对数据仓库应用设计的，而数据仓库的内容是读多写少的，因此，Hive 中不支持对数据的改写和添加，所有的数据都是在加载的时候确定好的。而数据库中的数据通常是需要经常修改的，因此可以使用 INSERT INTO ... VALUES 添加数据，使用 UPDATE ... SET 修改数据。

（5）索引。Hive 在加载数据的过程中不会对数据进行任何处理，甚至不会对数据进行扫描，因此也没有对数据中的某些 Key 建立索引。Hive 要访问数据中满足条件的特定值时，需要暴力扫描整个数据，因此访问延迟较高。由于 MapReduce 的引入，Hive 可以并行访问数据，即使没有索引，对于大数据量的访问，Hive 仍然可以体现出优势。数据库中，通常会针对一个或者几个列建立索引，因此对于少量的特定条件的数据的访问，数据库可以有很高的效率，较低的延迟。由于数据的访问延迟较高，决定了 Hive 不适合在线数据查询。

（6）执行。Hive 中大多数查询的执行是通过 Hadoop 提供的 MapReduce 来实现的（类似 select * from tbl 的查询不需要 MapReduce)。而数据库通常有自己的执行引擎。

（7）执行延迟。Hive 在查询数据的时候，没有索引，需要扫描整个表，因此延迟较高。另外一个导致 Hive 执行延迟高的因素是 MapReduce 框架。MapReduce 本身具有较高的延迟，因此在利用 MapReduce 执行 Hive 查询时，也会有较高的延迟。相对的，数据库的执行延迟较低。当然，这个低是有条件的，即数据规模较小，当数据规模大到超过数据库的处理能力时，Hive 的并行计算将体现出优势。

（8）可扩展性。Hive 是建立在 Hadoop 之上的，因此 Hive 的可扩展性和 Hadoop 的可扩展性是一致的。而数据库由于 ACID 语义的严格限制，扩展行非常有限。目前最先进的并行数据库 Oracle 在理论上的扩展能力也只有 100 台左右。

（9）数据规模。Hive 建立在集群上并可以利用 MapReduce 进行并行计算，因此可以支持很大规模的数据。对应的，数据库可以支持的数据规模较小。

任务 6.2 安装并配置 MySQL 数据库

任务描述

Hive 中的元数据通常存储在关系型数据库中。本任务详细介绍 MySQL 的安装和配置过程，并通过获取临时密码登录 MySQL，再重新设置新密码和用户 root 的权限，创建数据库，为与 Hive 建立连接做好准备工作。

关键步骤

（1）查看系统已安装的 MySQL。
（2）卸载之前已安装的 MySQL 版本。
（3）安装自动下载工具 wget。
（4）下载 MySQL 安装包。
（5）安装 MySQL。
（6）安装 MySQL 服务。
（7）启动 MySQL。
（8）修改 MySQL 临时密码。
（9）配置允许远程访问。
（10）修改 MySQL 允许任何人连接。

6.2.1 查看系统已安装的 MySQL

Linux 系统默认安装了 Mariadb 数据库，用户可以使用以下命令来检查系统是否已安装 MariaDB 或 MySQL。如果系统安装了 MySQL 或 MariaDB，这些命令将列出相关的软件包；如果没有列出任何内容，表示系统上没有安装 MySQL 或 MariaDB。

```
rpm -qa  | grep  mariadb    #检查系统是否已安装 MariaDB
rpm -qa  | grep  mysql      #检查系统是否已安装 MySQL
```

执行结果如图 6.2.1 所示。

```
[root@slave1 ~]# rpm -qa  | grep  mariadb    #检查系统是否已安装MariaDB
mariadb-libs-5.5.68-1.el7.x86_64
[root@slave1 ~]# rpm -qa  | grep  mysql    #检查系统是否已安装mysql
[root@slave1 ~]#
```

图 6.2.1　查看系统是否安装 Mariadb 和 MySQL

由图 6.2.1 可见，系统中已安装了 MariaDB，没有安装 MySQL。

若之前已安装过 MySQL，执行以下命令：

```
rpm -qa  | grep  mysql
```

显示的结果如图 6.2.2 所示。

```
[root@master ~]# rpm -qa  | grep  mysql
mysql-community-client-5.7.44-1.el7.x86_64
mysql57-community-release-el7-8.noarch
mysql-community-libs-5.7.44-1.el7.x86_64
mysql-community-common-5.7.44-1.el7.x86_64
mysql-community-server-5.7.44-1.el7.x86_64
[root@master ~]#
```

图 6.2.2　查询之前已安装过的 MySQL

从图 6.2.2 可见，系统中若已安装了 MySQL，安装的软件包有以下几个：

（1）mysql-community-client-5.7.44-1.el7.x86_64。

（2）mysql57-community-release-el7-8.noarch。

（3）mysql-community-libs-5.7.44-1.el7.x86_64。

（4）mysql-community-common-5.7.44-1.el7.x86_64。

（5）mysql-community-server-5.7.44-1.el7.x86_64。

用户若要重新安装数据库，则要删除已安装的所有数据库软件包。

6.2.2　卸载之前已安装的 MySQL 版本

如果之前安装过 MySQL，就要卸载已安装的 MySQL 版本；如果之前没安装过 MySQL，可省略这一步。

若已安装了图 6.2.2 所示的所有软件包，则要逐条删除，命令如下：

```
rpm -e --nodeps   mysql-community-client-5.7.44-1.el7.x86_64
rpm -e --nodeps   mysql57-community-release-el7-8.noarch
rpm -e --nodeps   mysql-community-libs-5.7.44-1.el7.x86_64
rpm -e --nodeps   mysql-community-common-5.7.44-1.el7.x86_64
rpm -e --nodeps   mysql-community-server-5.7.44-1.el7.x86_64
```

运行结果如图 6.2.3 所示。

```
[root@master ~]# rpm -e --nodeps mysql-community-client-5.7.44-1.el7.x86_64
[root@master ~]# rpm -e --nodeps mysql57-community-release-el7-8.noarch
[root@master ~]# rpm -e --nodeps mysql-community-libs-5.7.44-1.el7.x86_64
[root@master ~]# rpm -e --nodeps mysql-community-common-5.7.44-1.el7.x86_64
[root@master ~]# rpm -e --nodeps mysql-community-server-5.7.44-1.el7.x86_64
[root@master ~]#
```

图 6.2.3 卸载之前的版本的 MySQL

6.2.3 安装自动下载工具 wget

wget 是一个能从网络上自动下载文件的自由工具,支持通过 HTTP、HTTPS、FTP 三个最常见的 TCP/IP 协议下载。"wget"这个名称来源于"World Wide Web"与"get"的结合。所谓自动下载,是指 wget 可以在用户退出系统之后在后台继续执行,直到下载任务完成。安装 wget 的命令如下:

```
yum -y install wget
```

运行结果如图 6.2.4 所示。

```
[root@master conf]# yum -y install wget
已加载插件: fastestmirror
Loading mirror speeds from cached hostfile
base                                                        | 3.6 kB
docker-ce-stable                                            | 3.5 kB
extras                                                      | 2.9 kB
updates                                                     | 2.9 kB
软件包 wget-1.14-18.el7_6.1.x86_64 已安装并且是最新版本
无须任何处理
```

图 6.2.4 下载并安装 wget

6.2.4 下载 MySQL 安装包

下载 MySQL 安装包的代码如下:

```
wget https://dev.mysql.com/get/mysql57-community-release-el7-8.noarch.rpm
```

运行结果如图 6.2.5 所示。

```
[root@master ~]# wget https://dev.mysql.com/get/mysql57-community-release-el7-8.noarch.rpm
--2024-04-10 17:21:23--  https://dev.mysql.com/get/mysql57-community-release-el7-8.noarch.rpm
正在解析主机 dev.mysql.com (dev.mysql.com)... 23.66.135.36, 2600:1406:3c:481::2e31, 2600:1406:3c:4a2::2e31
正在连接 dev.mysql.com (dev.mysql.com)|23.66.135.36|:443... 已连接。
已发出 HTTP 请求,正在等待回应... 302 Moved Temporarily
位置: https://repo.mysql.com/mysql57-community-release-el7-8.noarch.rpm [跟随至新的 URL]
--2024-04-10 17:21:31--  https://repo.mysql.com/mysql57-community-release-el7-8.noarch.rpm
正在解析主机 repo.mysql.com (repo.mysql.com)... 23.42.93.135, 2600:1406:2e00:880::1d68, 2600:1406:2e00:89c::1d68
正在连接 repo.mysql.com (repo.mysql.com)|23.42.93.135|:443... 已连接。
已发出 HTTP 请求,正在等待回应... 200 OK
长度: 9116 (8.9K) [application/x-redhat-package-manager]
正在保存至: "mysql57-community-release-el7-8.noarch.rpm"

100%[======================================================================>] 9,116       --.-K/s 用时 0s

2024-04-10 17:21:31 (102 MB/s) - 已保存 "mysql57-community-release-el7-8.noarch.rpm" [9116/9116])

[root@master ~]#
```

图 6.2.5 下载 MySQL 安装包

6.2.5 安装 MySQL

用 rpm 下载并安装 MySQL,命令如下:

```
rpm -ivh mysql57-community-release-el7-8.noarch.rpm
```

运行结果如图 6.2.6 所示。

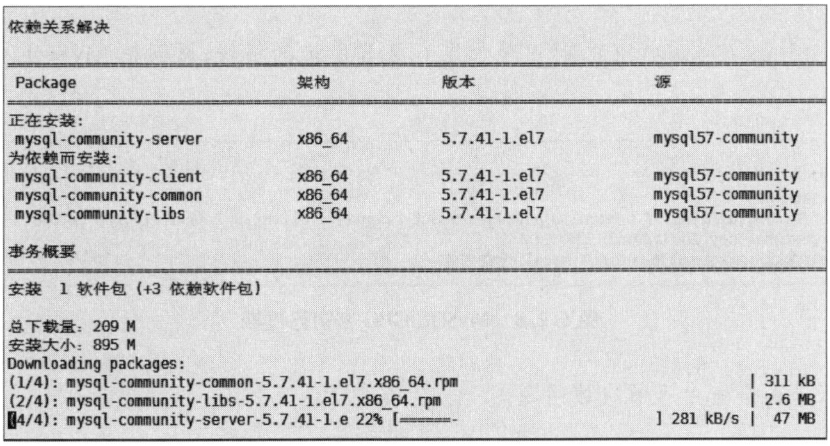

图 6.2.6　安装 MySQL

6.2.6　安装 MySQL 服务

Linux 服务器安装成功后,经常使用 yum 安装 rpm 包以满足使用的需要。安装完 Linux 服务器后,默认"/etc/yum.repos.d/"目录下已经有 *.repo 文件,只要 Linux 服务器可以联网,就可以使用它进行 rpm 包的安装。

首先,进入"/etc/yum.repos.d/"目录,命令如下:

```
cd /etc/yum.repos.d/
```

其次,运行以下代码安装 MySQL 服务(这个过程可能有点慢),命令如下:

```
yum -y install mysql-server
```

运行结果如图 6.2.7 所示。

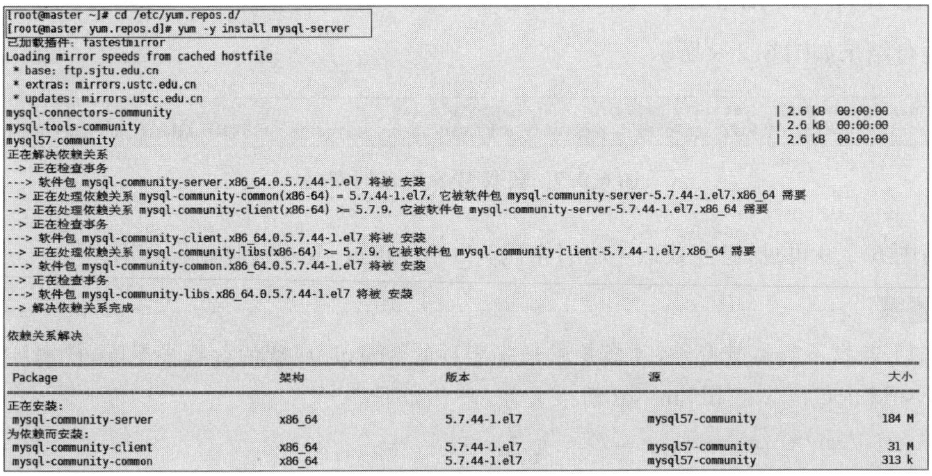

图 6.2.7　安装 MySQL 服务

注意

(1) 如果配置过本地源了，则安装 MySQL Server，命令如下：

```
yum -y install mysql-community-server
```

(2) 若 Linux 安装 MySQL 时出现如图 6.2.8 所示的报错，原因是 MySQL GPG 密钥已过期。

```
总计：221 M
安装大小：932 M
Downloading packages:
warning: /var/cache/yum/mysql57-community/packages/mysql-community-client-5.7.41-1.el7.x86_64.rpm: Header V4 R
SA/SHA256 Signature, key ID 3a79bd29: NOKEY
从 file:///etc/pki/rpm-gpg/RPM-GPG-KEY-mysql 检索密钥
```

图 6.2.8　MySQL GPG 密钥已过期

执行以下两个命令可解决该问题：

```
rpm --import https://repo.mysql.com/RPM-GPG-KEY-mysql-2022
```

【参考网址：https://www.cnblogs.com/leecy/p/16328065.html】

6.2.7　启动 MySQL

启动 MySQL，命令如下：

```
systemctl start mysqld
```

6.2.8　修改 MySQL 临时密码

MySQL 安装成功后会有一个临时密码，用户可以使用 grep 命令查看临时密码先登录 MySQL，然后修改 MySQL 密码。

6.2.8.1　获取 MySQL 临时密码

用 grep 获取 MySQL 临时密码，命令如下：

```
grep 'temporary password' /var/log/mysqld.log
```

运行结果如图 6.2.9 所示。

```
[root@master ~]# grep 'temporary password' /var/log/mysqld.log
2024-04-12T06:44:18.045812Z 1 [Note] A temporary password is generated for root@localhost: 0DPQYni:dPau
```

图 6.2.9　获取 MySQL 临时密码

由图 6.2.9 可见，已经获取了临时密码为"0DPQYni:dPau"，复制好备用。

注意

(1) 若找不到临时密码，可能是原来安装过的 Mysql 残留的数据未删除，就删除 /var/log/mysqld.log 和 /var/lib/mysql 两个文件，命令如下：

```
rm -rf /var/log/mysqld.log
rm -rf /var/lib/mysql
```

(2) 再重启 MySQL 服务：

```
systemctl restart mysqld
```

(3) 再获取 MySQL 临时密码：

```
grep 'temporary password' /var/log/mysqld.log
```

6.2.8.2 使用临时密码登录

登录 MySQL，用户名 root，密码用刚获取的临时密码为"0DPQYni;dPau"，命令如下：

```
mysql -uroot -p
```

输入临时密码"0DPQYni;dPau"，即可登录 MySQL，如图 6.2.10 所示。

图 6.2.10 用临时密码登录 MySQL

> **注意**
>
> 若在执行 mysql -uroot -p 时，输入临时密码后出现"ERROR 1045（28000）：Access denied for user 'root'@'localhost' (using password：YES)"错误提示，执行以下命令查询到临时密码后，再次启动 MySQL。

```
cat /var/log/mysqld.log | grep  password
```

运行结果如图 6.2.11 所示。

图 6.2.11 查询临时密码重新登录

6.2.8.3 把 MySQL 的密码校验强度改为低风险

设置密码校验强度为低风险的命令如下：

```
set global validate_password_policy=LOW;
```

运行结果如图 6.2.12 所示。

```
mysql> set global validate_password_policy=LOW;
Query OK, 0 rows affected (0.00 sec)

mysql>
```

图 6.2.12　设置密码校验强度为低风险

6.2.8.4 修改 MySQL 的密码长度

设置 MySQL 密码长度的命令如下：

```
set global validate_password_length=6;
```

运行结果如图 6.2.13 所示。

```
mysql> set global validate_password_length=6;
Query OK, 0 rows affected (0.00 sec)

mysql>
```

图 6.2.13　设置密码长度

6.2.8.5 修改 MySQL 密码

重新设置一个 MySQL 的新密码"123456"，命令如下：

```
ALTER USER 'root'@'localhost' IDENTIFIED BY '123456';
```

运行结果如图 6.2.14 所示。

```
mysql> ALTER USER 'root'@'localhost' IDENTIFIED BY '123456';
Query OK, 0 rows affected (0.01 sec)

mysql>
```

图 6.2.14　修改 MySQL 密码为"123456"

6.2.8.6 退出 MySQL

完成密码设置后，退出 MySQL，准备安装 Hive，命令如下：

```
exit;
```

运行结果如图 6.2.15 所示。

```
mysql> exit;
Bye
[root@master ~]#
```

图 6.2.15　退出 MySQL 回到 CentOS 命令行

6.2.9 允许远程访问

若要允许远程访问,需要先关闭 CentOS 的防火墙,命令如下:

```
systemctl disable firewalld
```

6.2.10 修改 MySQL 允许任何人连接

6.2.10.1 登录 MySQL

登录 MySQL,用户名为 root,命令如下:

```
mysql -uroot -p
```

输入刚设置的密码"123456",运行结果如图 6.2.16 所示。

```
[root@master ~]# mysql -uroot -p
Enter password:
Welcome to the MySQL monitor.  Commands end with ; or \g.
Your MySQL connection id is 5
Server version: 5.7.44 MySQL Community Server (GPL)

Copyright (c) 2000, 2023, Oracle and/or its affiliates.

Oracle is a registered trademark of Oracle Corporation and/or its
affiliates. Other names may be trademarks of their respective
owners.

Type 'help;' or '\h' for help. Type '\c' to clear the current input statement.

mysql>
```

图 6.2.16 用新设置的密码登录 MySQL

6.2.10.2 切换到 MySQL 数据库

切换到 MySQL 数据库,命令如下:

```
use mysql;
```

运行结果如图 6.2.17 所示。

```
mysql> use mysql
Reading table information for completion of table and column names
You can turn off this feature to get a quicker startup with -A

Database changed
mysql>
```

图 6.2.17 切换到 MySQL 数据库

6.2.10.3 查看 user 表

用 select 语句查看 MySQL 数据库的表的 user,命令如下:

```
select Host,User from user;
```

运行结果如图 6.2.18 所示。

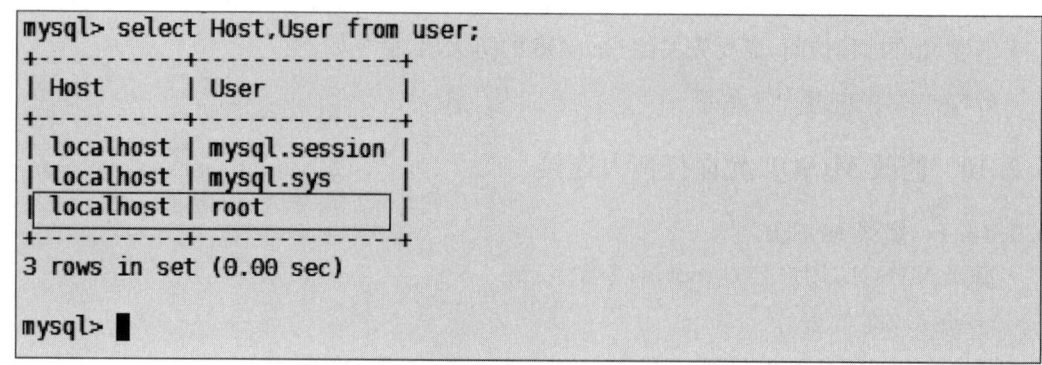

图 6.2.18　查看 user 表

从运行结果可以看出 root 用户只允许登录 localhost 主机,需要修改为允许 root 用户访问任何主机。

6.2.10.4　修改权限为允许 root 用户访问任何主机

修改 user 表中 root 用户权限,允许 root 用户访问任何主机,命令如下:

```
update user set Host='%' where User='root';
select Host,User from user;
```

运行结果如图 6.2.19 所示。

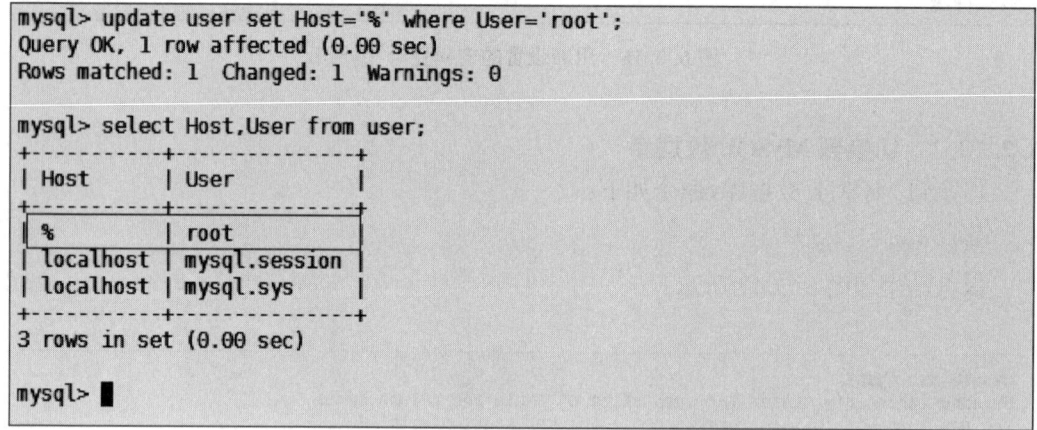

图 6.2.19　允许 root 用户访问任何主机

6.2.10.5　刷新权限

修改 user 表中 root 用户权限后,需要刷新权限,并新建数据库 Hive,命令如下:

```
flush privileges;
create database hive;
```

运行结果如图 6.2.20 所示。

```
mysql> flush privileges;
Query OK, 0 rows affected (0.00 sec)

mysql> create database hive;
Query OK, 1 row affected (0.01 sec)

mysql>
```

图 6.2.20　刷新权限并新建数据库 Hive

6.2.10.6　退出 MySQL 回到 CentOS 命令行

退出 MySQL 回到 CentOS 命令行,命令如下:

```
exit;
```

任务 6.3　Hive 的环境安装与配置

任务描述

本任务详细介绍 Hive 的安装和配置过程,包括 Hive 安装包下载与安装、Hive 环境变量设置、添加依赖包、与 MySQL 建立连接、启动 Hive 并测试安装成功等,为用 Hive 进行数据分析作准备。

关键步骤

(1) Hive 安装包准备。
(2) 解压 Hive 安装包。
(3) 设置 Hive 环境变量。
(4) 完成相关配置并添加依赖包。
(5) 初始化 MySQL 元数据库。
(6) 启动 Hive 并测试是否安装成功。

Hive 的安装模式有内嵌模式、本地模式和远程模式三种,本书的重点是学会用 HiveQL 语句进行数据分析,因此本任务只介绍 Hive 的本地模式。

6.3.1　Hive 安装包准备

6.3.1.1　下载 Hive 安装包

下载 Hive 安装包的网址如下:

```
http://archive.apache.org/dist/hive/hive-2.1.1/apache-hive-2.1.1-bin.tar.gz
```

打开的下载页面如图 6.3.1 所示。

图 6.3.1 Hive 安装包下载页面

6.3.1.2 用 WinSCP 将 Hive 安装包上传到 CentOS 系统

用 WinSCP 将 Hive 安装包 apache-hive-2.1.1-bin.tar.gz 上传到 CentOS 的"/root"目录下,如图 6.3.2、图 6.3.3 所示。

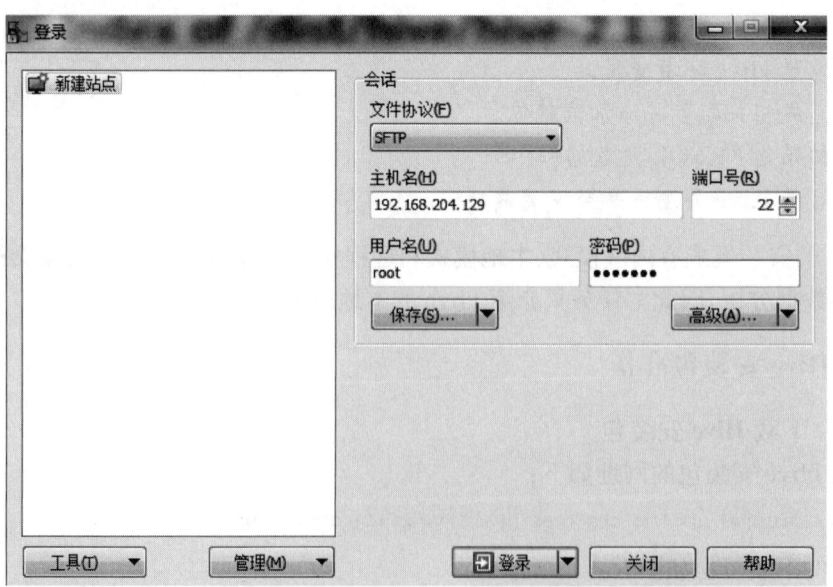

图 6.3.2 用 WinSCP 连接 Windows 与虚拟机 master

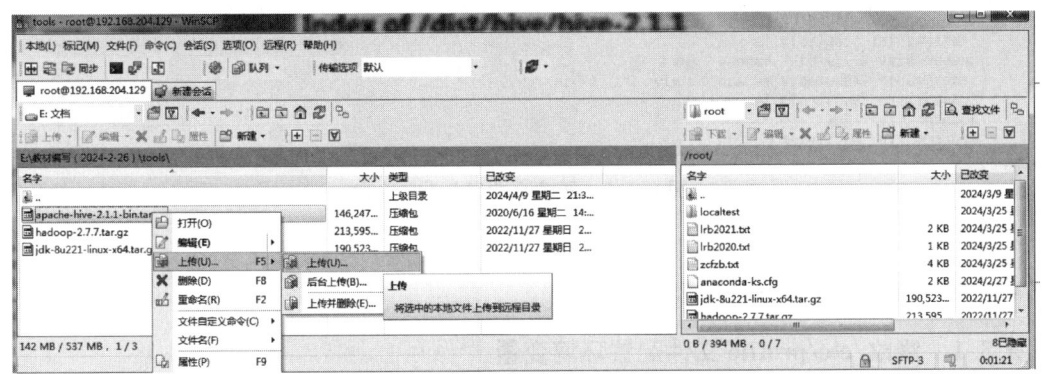

图 6.3.3 将 Hive 安装包上传到虚拟机

6.3.2 解压 Hive 安装包

6.3.2.1 将 Hive 安装包解压到指定目录

将 master 节点"/root"的 Hive 安装包解压到"/opt/modules"目录下，操作命令如下：

```
cd /root
tar -zxvf apache-hive-2.1.1-bin.tar.gz  -C  /opt/modules
```

运行结果如图 6.3.4 所示。

```
[root@master ~]# cd /root
[root@master ~]# tar -zxvf apache-hive-2.1.1-bin.tar.gz  -C  /opt/modules
apache-hive-2.1.1-bin/LICENSE
apache-hive-2.1.1-bin/NOTICE
apache-hive-2.1.1-bin/README.txt
apache-hive-2.1.1-bin/RELEASE_NOTES.txt
apache-hive-2.1.1-bin/examples/files/2000_cols_data.csv
apache-hive-2.1.1-bin/examples/files/agg_01-p1.txt
apache-hive-2.1.1-bin/examples/files/agg_01-p2.txt
apache-hive-2.1.1-bin/examples/files/agg_01-p3.txt
apache-hive-2.1.1-bin/examples/files/alltypes.txt
apache-hive-2.1.1-bin/examples/files/alltypes2.txt
apache-hive-2.1.1-bin/examples/files/apache.access.2.log
apache-hive-2.1.1-bin/examples/files/apache.access.log
apache-hive-2.1.1-bin/examples/files/archive_corrupt.rc
apache-hive-2.1.1-bin/examples/files/array_table.txt
apache-hive-2.1.1-bin/examples/files/avro_charvarchar.txt
apache-hive-2.1.1-bin/examples/files/avro_date.txt
apache-hive-2.1.1-bin/examples/files/avro_timestamp.txt
apache-hive-2.1.1-bin/examples/files/AvroPrimitiveInList.parquet
apache-hive-2.1.1-bin/examples/files/AvroSingleFieldGroupInList.parquet
```

图 6.3.4 解压 Hive 安装包

6.3.2.2 重命名解压后的文件夹

重命名解压后的文件夹用到的命令如下：

```
cd  /opt/modules
mv apache-hive-2.1.1-bin/  hive
```

运行结果如图 6.3.5 所示。

```
[root@master ~]# cd  /opt/modules
[root@master modules]# ls
apache-hive-2.1.1-bin  hadoop  jdk
[root@master modules]# mv apache-hive-2.1.1-bin/  hive
[root@master modules]# ls
hadoop  hive  jdk
[root@master modules]# 
```

图 6.3.5　重命名为“hive”文件夹

6.3.3　设置 Hive 环境变量

6.3.3.1　修改/etc/profile 文件配置环境变量

修改/etc/profile 文件配置环境变量，末尾添加环境变量，命令如下：

```
vi  /etc/profile
```

命令末尾添加：

```
export HIVE_HOME=/opt/modules/hive
export PATH=$HIVE_HOME/bin:$PATH
```

运行结果如图 6.3.6 所示。

```
1 master
if [ "$HISTCONTROL" = "ignorespace" ] ; then
    export HISTCONTROL=ignoreboth
else
    export HISTCONTROL=ignoredups
fi

export PATH USER LOGNAME MAIL HOSTNAME HISTSIZE HISTCONTROL

# By default, we want umask to get set. This sets it for login shell
# Current threshold for system reserved uid/gids is 200
# You could check uidgid reservation validity in
# /usr/share/doc/setup-*/uidgid file
if [ $UID -gt 199 ] && [ "`/usr/bin/id -gn`" = "`/usr/bin/id -un`" ]; then
    umask 002
else
    umask 022
fi

for i in /etc/profile.d/*.sh /etc/profile.d/sh.local ; do
    if [ -r "$i" ]; then
        if [ "${-#*i}" != "$-" ]; then
            . "$i"
        else
            . "$i" >/dev/null
        fi
    fi
done

unset i
unset -f pathmunge

export JAVA_HOME=/opt/modules/jdk
export PATH=$PATH:$JAVA_HOME/bin

export HADOOP_HOME=/opt/modules/hadoop

export PATH=$PATH:$HADOOP_HOME/bin:$HADOOP_HOME/sbin

export HIVE_HOME=/opt/modules/hive
export PATH=$HIVE_HOME/bin:$PATH

-- INSERT --
```

图 6.3.6　配置环境变量

6.3.3.2　使环境变量生效

使环境变量生效的命令如下：

```
source  /etc/profile
```

运行结果如图 6.3.7 所示。

```
[root@master modules]# vi  /etc/profile
[root@master modules]# source  /etc/profile
[root@master modules]#
```

图 6.3.7　使环境变量生效

6.3.3.3　修改配置文件 hive-env.sh

先进入配置文件目录,再将配置文件 hive-env.sh.template 重命名为 hive-env.sh,命令如下:

```
cd  /opt/modules/hive/conf/
mv hive-env.sh.template   hive-env.sh
```

运行结果如图 6.3.8 所示。

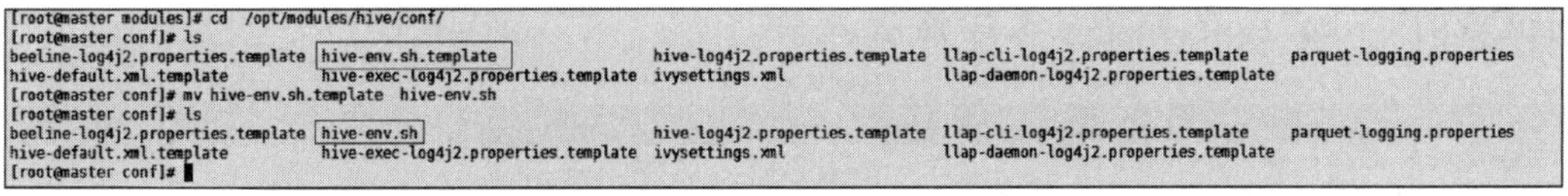

```
[root@master modules]# cd /opt/modules/hive/conf/
[root@master conf]# ls
beeline-log4j2.properties.template  hive-env.sh.template       hive-log4j2.properties.template  llap-cli-log4j2.properties.template  parquet-logging.properties
hive-default.xml.template           hive-exec-log4j2.properties.template  ivysettings.xml            llap-daemon-log4j2.properties.template
[root@master conf]# mv hive-env.sh.template  hive-env.sh
[root@master conf]# ls
beeline-log4j2.properties.template  hive-env.sh                hive-log4j2.properties.template  llap-cli-log4j2.properties.template  parquet-logging.properties
hive-default.xml.template           hive-exec-log4j2.properties.template  ivysettings.xml            llap-daemon-log4j2.properties.template
[root@master conf]#
```

图 6.3.8　重命名配置文件 hive-env.sh

修改 hive-env.sh,命令如下:

```
vi hive-env.sh
```

在末尾添加以下代码:

```
export JAVA_HOME=/opt/modules/jdk
export HADOOP_HOME=/opt/modules/hadoop
export HIVE_HOME=/opt/modules/hive
```

运行结果如图 6.3.9 所示。

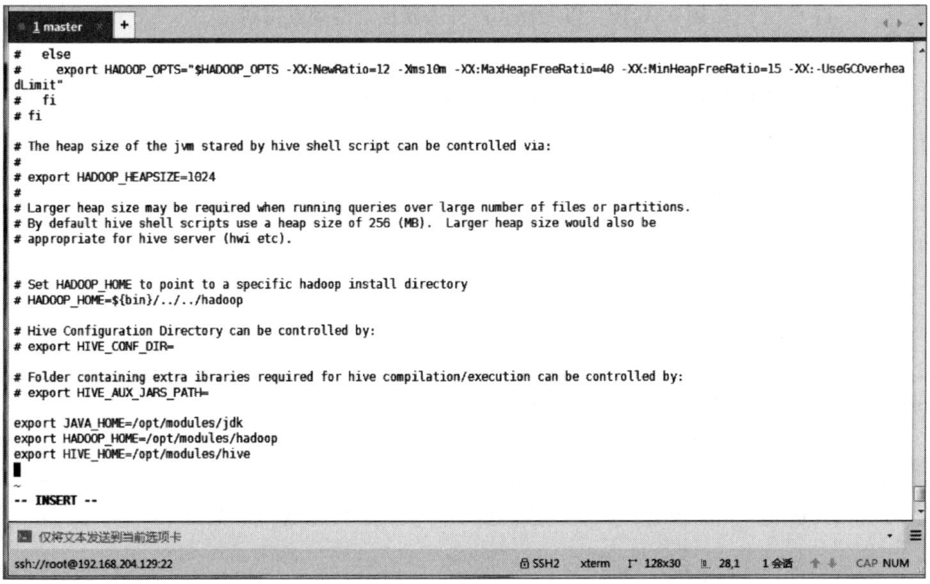

图 6.3.9　修改配置文件 hive-env.sh

6.3.3.4 jline 版本冲突问题

客户端需要和 Hadoop 通信,所以需要更改 Hadoop 中 jline 的版本,即保留一个高版本的 jline-jar 包,命令如下:

```
cp $HIVE_HOME/lib/jline-2.12.jar  $HADOOP_HOME/share/hadoop/yarn/lib/
```

6.3.4 完成相关配置并添加依赖包

6.3.4.1 驱动拷贝

因为服务端需要和 MySQL 通信,所以服务端需要将 MySQL 的依赖包放在 Hive 的 "lib" 目录下。mysql-connector-java 是 MySQL 的 JDBC 驱动包,用 JDBC 连接 MySQL 数据库时必须使用该 jar 包,用 WinSCP 将 mysql-connector-java-5.1.48-bin.jar 上传到 CentOS 的"/root"目录,如图 6.3.10 所示。

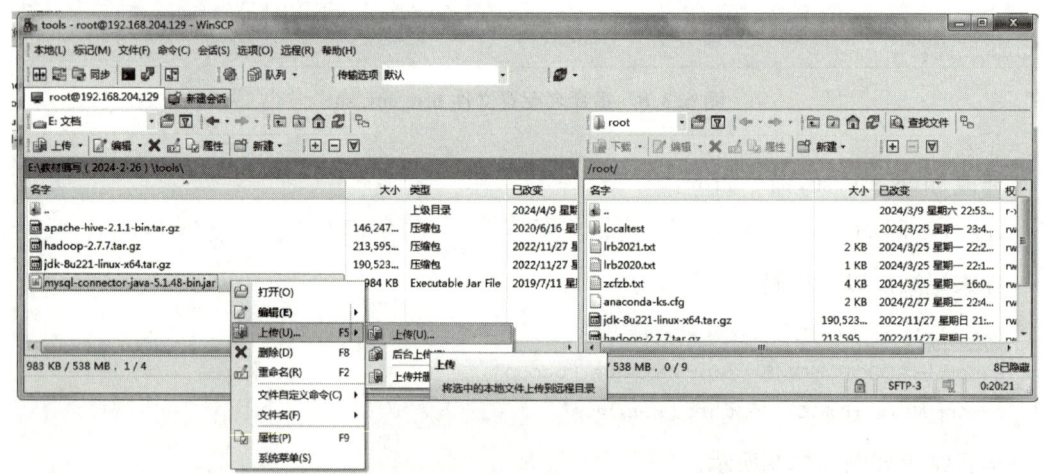

图 6.3.10　用 WinSCP 将依赖包上传到虚拟机

将 MySQL 的依赖包复制到 Hive 的"lib"目录下,命令如下:

```
cp /root/mysql-connector-java-5.1.48-bin.jar  $HIVE_HOME/lib
```

6.3.4.2 修改配置文件 hive-site.xml

如果 $HIVE_HOME/conf 下没有 hive-site.xml 文件,就将 hive-default.xml.template 复制并改名为 hive-site.xml,命令如下:

```
cd  $HIVE_HOME/conf
cp hive-default.xml.template hive-site.xml
vi hive-site.xml    #:3,$d(删除第三行(包含)以后所有代码)
```

> **注意**
>
> 此处操作是在插入模式下,按 Esc 键,输入":3,$d"按回车键后,运行结果如图 6.3.11 所示,再把第二行末尾的"<!—"删除。

```
<?xml version="1.0" encoding="UTF-8" standalone="no"?>
<?xml-stylesheet type="text/xsl" href="configuration.xsl"?><!--
~
~
```

图 6.3.11　将 hive-site.xml 第 3 行后所有代码删除

添加以下代码：

```xml
<configuration>
<!-- Hive 产生的元数据存放位置-->
    <property>
        <name>hive.metastore.warehouse.dir</name>
        <value>/usr/hive_remote/warehouse</value>
    </property>
    <!--需要登录 MySQL 数据库,创建一个 hive 数据库备用-->
    <property>
        <name>javax.jdo.option.ConnectionURL</name>
        <value>jdbc:mysql://master:3306/hive?createDatabaseIfNotExist=true&amp;useSSL=false</value>
    </property>
    <!--安装 MySQL 数据库的驱动类-->
    <property>
        <name>javax.jdo.option.ConnectionDriverName</name>
        <value>com.mysql.jdbc.Driver</value>
    </property>
    <!--安装 MySQL 数据库用户名称-->
    <property>
        <name>javax.jdo.option.ConnectionUserName</name>
        <value>root</value>
    </property>
    <!--安装 MySQL 数据库的密码-->
    <property>
        <name>javax.jdo.option.ConnectionPassword</name>
        <value>123456</value>
    </property>
    <!--cli 显示表头和列名-->
    <property>
        <name>hive.cli.print.header</name>
        <value>true</value>
    </property>
    <property>
```

```xml
        <name>hive.cli.print.current.db</name>
        <value>true</value>
    </property>
</configuration>
```

修改完成后,在"INSERT"模式下按 Esc 键,输入":wq"保存退出,运行结果如图 6.3.12 所示。

```
[root@master conf]# vi hive-site.xml
<?xml version="1.0" encoding="UTF-8" standalone="no"?>
<?xml-stylesheet type="text/xsl" href="configuration.xsl"?>
<configuration>
<!-- Hive 产生的元数据存放位置-->
<property>
<name>hive.metastore.warehouse.dir</name>
<value>/usr/hive_remote/warehouse</value> #若/usr/hive_remote/warehouse路径没有,则自行创建
</property>
<!--需要登录MySQL数据库,创建一个hive 数据库备用-->
<property>
<name>javax.jdo.option.ConnectionURL</name>
<value>jdbc:mysql://master:3306/hive?
createDatabaseIfNotExist=true&amp;useSSL=false</value>
</property>
<!--安装MySQL数据库的驱动类-->
<property>
<name>javax.jdo.option.ConnectionDriverName</name>
<value>com.mysql.jdbc.Driver</value>
</property>
<!--安装MySQL数据库用户名称-->
<property>
<name>javax.jdo.option.ConnectionUserName</name>
<value>root</value>
</property>
<!--安装MySQL数据库的密码-->
<property>
<name>javax.jdo.option.ConnectionPassword</name>
<value>123456</value>
```

图 6.3.12　修改配置文件 hive-site.xml

6.3.5　初始化 MySQL 元数据库

将 MySQL 数据库作为 Hive 元数据库,初始化 Hive 元数据,并通过以下 schematool 命令执行初始化:

```
cd $HIVE_HOME/bin
schematool -dbType mysql -initSchema
```

运行结果如图 6.3.13 所示。

```
[root@master ~]# cd $HIVE_HOME/bin
[root@master bin]# schematool -dbType mysql -initSchema
which: no hbase in (/opt/modules/hive/bin:/usr/local/sbin:/usr/local/bin:/usr/sbin:/usr/bin:/opt/modules/jdk/bin:/opt/modules/hadoop/bin:/opt/modules/hadoop/sbin:/root/bin)
SLF4J: Class path contains multiple SLF4J bindings.
SLF4J: Found binding in [jar:file:/opt/modules/hive/lib/log4j-slf4j-impl-2.4.1.jar!/org/slf4j/impl/StaticLoggerBinder.class]
SLF4J: Found binding in [jar:file:/opt/modules/hadoop/share/hadoop/common/lib/slf4j-log4j12-1.7.10.jar!/org/slf4j/impl/StaticLoggerBinder.class]
SLF4J: See http://www.slf4j.org/codes.html#multiple_bindings for an explanation.
SLF4J: Actual binding is of type [org.apache.logging.slf4j.Log4jLoggerFactory]
Metastore connection URL:        jdbc:mysql://master:3306/hive?createDatabaseIfNotExist=true&useSSL=false
Metastore Connection Driver :    com.mysql.jdbc.Driver
Metastore connection User:       root
Starting metastore schema initialization to 2.1.0
Initialization script hive-schema-2.1.0.mysql.sql
Initialization script completed
schemaTool completed
[root@master bin]#
```

图 6.3.13 初始化 MySQL 元数据库

6.3.6 启动 Hive 并测试是否安装成功

6.3.6.1 启动 Hadoop 集群

启动 Hive 之前,请先启动 Hadoop 集群,命令如下:

```
start-all.sh
```

运行结果如图 6.3.14 所示。

```
[root@localhost bin]# jps
2558 QuorumPeerMain
3405 Jps
2248 ResourceManager
1921 DataNode
2105 SecondaryNameNode
1825 NameNode
```

图 6.3.14 启动 Hadoop 集群

这里已经配置了 PATH,所以,不要把 start-all.sh 和 hive 命令的路径加上。

6.3.6.2 启动 Hive

启动 Hive,命令如下:

```
hive
```

运行结果如图 6.3.15 所示。

```
[root@master bin]# hive
which: no hbase in (/opt/modules/hive/bin:/usr/local/sbin:/usr/local/bin:/usr/sbin:/usr/bin:/opt/modules/jdk/bin:/opt/modules/hadoop/bin:/opt/modules/hadoop/sbin:/root/bin)
SLF4J: Class path contains multiple SLF4J bindings.
SLF4J: Found binding in [jar:file:/opt/modules/hive/lib/log4j-slf4j-impl-2.4.1.jar!/org/slf4j/impl/StaticLoggerBinder.class]
SLF4J: Found binding in [jar:file:/opt/modules/hadoop/share/hadoop/common/lib/slf4j-log4j12-1.7.10.jar!/org/slf4j/impl/StaticLoggerBinder.class]
SLF4J: See http://www.slf4j.org/codes.html#multiple_bindings for an explanation.
SLF4J: Actual binding is of type [org.apache.logging.slf4j.Log4jLoggerFactory]
Logging initialized using configuration in jar:file:/opt/modules/hive/lib/hive-common-2.1.1.jar!/hive-log4j2.properties Async: true
Hive-on-MR is deprecated in Hive 2 and may not be available in the future versions. Consider using a different execution engine (i.e. spark, tez) or using Hive 1.X releases.
hive (default)>
```

图 6.3.15 启动 Hive

由图 6.3.15 可见,Hive 启动成功,出现提示符"hive(default)>",代表可以使用 HQL 命令了。

6.3.6.3 测试 Hive 是否安装成功

查看数据库,测试启动是否成功,命令如下:

```
hive (default)> show databases;
```

运行结果如图 6.3.16 所示。

```
hive (default)> show databases;
OK
database_name
default
Time taken: 1.509 seconds, Fetched: 1 row(s)
hive (default)>
```

图 6.3.16　用 Hive 查看数据库

由图 6.3.16 可见,Hive 中默认存在 database_name 和 default 两个数据库。

至此,完成了 Hive 本地模式的安装与配置。

> **注意**
>
> 如果无法启动 Hive,可能是 Hadoop 还处在安全模式中,可以使用以下命令查看和设置 Hive 的安装模式:
>
> ```
> hdfs dfsadmin -safemode get          #查看安全模式
> hdfs dfsadmin -safemode leave        #离开安全模式
> hdfs dfsadmin -safemode forceExit    #强制退出安全模式
> ```

单元总结

本单元主要学习了 Hive 的环境搭建,对 Hive 的架构、Hive 的 3 种部署模式进行了介绍,对 MySQL 安装和配置的详细过程进行了操作,并选择 Hive 的本地模式进行安装和配置,最后通过数据库和数据表的创建,验证了 Hive 安装与配置结果正确。

单元习题

一、简答题

1. 请简述 Hive 工具的功能和特点。
2. Hive 的部署模式有哪几种?
3. Hive 和传统数据库的区别有哪些?

二、技能训练题

1. 独立完成 Hive 的安装与配置。
2. 分别在 MySQL 和 Hive 中创建数据库 bigdata_db。

单元 7

数据仓库 Hive 在数据处理中的应用

Haoop 出现之前,人们更多地是基于关系型数据库进行数据分析。随着 Hadoop 的出现及大数据的发展,人们开始意识到使用 Hadoop 分析海量数据的优势。但是,这也产生了一个问题:用户如何将数据从现有的关系型数据库架构转移到 Hadoop 上? Hive 的出现就是为了解决这个问题,它能够使精通 SQL 但编程能力较弱的数据分析人员利用 Hadoop 进行各种数据分析。本单元就 Hive 在数据处理中的应用进行简单介绍。

教学目标

知识目标

1. 了解 Hive 命令使用规范。
2. 了解 Hive 中的数据类型。
3. 了解 Hive 数据定义规范。
4. 了解 Hive 数据操作规范。
5. 了解 Hive 数据查询的各种运用。
6. 了解 Hive 视图与查询的区别。
7. 了解 Hive 索引的功能。
8. 了解常用 Hive 函数的功能。

技能目标

1. 掌握 Hive 数据操作命令的使用。
2. 学会用 Hive 数据查询的各种命令解决实际问题。
3. 掌握 Hive 视图的灵活运用。
4. 学会用 Hive 函数进行数据分析。

单元任务

任务 7.1　Hive 命令说明。
任务 7.2　Hive 数据定义。
任务 7.3　Hive 数据操作。
任务 7.4　Hive 数据查询。
任务 7.5　Hive 视图。
任务 7.6　Hive 函数。

任务 7.1 Hive 命令说明

🔹 任务描述

前面的学习中已经安装好了 Hive,为了熟练运用 Hive 进行大数据分析,用户需要熟悉 HiveQL 语句。本任务先启动 Hadoop,再启动 Hive,然后运行查看 Hive 命令选项,了解 Hive 命令的用法和功能,为掌握 HiveQL 语句的使用打好基础。

🔹 关键步骤

(1) 学会查看 Hive 命令选项,了解 Hive 命令的用法。

(2) Hive 命令的使用前提是先启动 Hadoop 再启动 Hive。

在 Hive 提供的所有连接方式中,命令行界面是最常用的一种方式。用户可以使用 Hive 的命令行对 Hive 中数据库、数据表和数据进行各种操作。

7.1.1 Hive 命令选项

在服务器上启动 Hadoop 之后,输入"hive"命令就能够进入 Hive 的命令行。

7.1.1.1 启动 Hadoop

启动 Hadoop,命令如下:

```
[root@master ~]# start-all.sh
[root@master ~]# jps
```

运行结果如图 7.1.1 所示。

```
[root@master ~]# start-all.sh
This script is Deprecated. Instead use start-dfs.sh and start-yarn.sh
Starting namenodes on [master]
master: starting namenode, logging to /opt/modules/hadoop/logs/hadoop-root-namenode-master.out
slave1: starting datanode, logging to /opt/modules/hadoop/logs/hadoop-root-datanode-slave1.out
master: starting datanode, logging to /opt/modules/hadoop/logs/hadoop-root-datanode-master.out
slave2: starting datanode, logging to /opt/modules/hadoop/logs/hadoop-root-datanode-slave2.out
Starting secondary namenodes [slave1]
slave1: starting secondarynamenode, logging to /opt/modules/hadoop/logs/hadoop-root-secondarynamenode-slave1.out
starting yarn daemons
starting resourcemanager, logging to /opt/modules/hadoop/logs/yarn-root-resourcemanager-master.out
slave1: starting nodemanager, logging to /opt/modules/hadoop/logs/yarn-root-nodemanager-slave1.out
slave2: starting nodemanager, logging to /opt/modules/hadoop/logs/yarn-root-nodemanager-slave2.out
master: starting nodemanager, logging to /opt/modules/hadoop/logs/yarn-root-nodemanager-master.out
[root@master ~]# jps
2468 DataNode
2885 NodeManager
2364 NameNode
3038 Jps
```

图 7.1.1 启动 Hadoop

由图 7.1.1 可见,执行 start-all.sh 命令后,再用 jps 查看到了 DataNode、NodeManager、NameNode 和 Jps 进程,说明 Hadoop 启动成功。

7.1.1.2 查看 Hive 的命令选项

查看 Hive 的命令选项,命令如下:

```
[root@master ~]# hive --help
```

运行结果如图 7.1.2 所示。

```
[root@master ~]# hive --help
which: no hbase in (/opt/modules/hive/bin:/usr/local/sbin:/usr/local/bin:/usr/sbin:/usr/bin:/opt/modules/jdk/bin:/opt/modules/hadoop/bin:/opt/m
odules/hadoop/sbin:/root/bin)
Usage ./hive <parameters> --service serviceName <service parameters>
Service List: beeline cleardanglingscratchdir cli hbaseimport hbaseschematool help hiveburninclient hiveserver2 hplsql hwi jar lineage llapdump
 lap llapstatus metastore metatool orcfiledump rcfilecat schemaTool version
Parameters parsed:
  --auxpath : Auxillary jars
  --config : Hive configuration directory
  --service : Starts specific service/component. cli is default
Parameters used:
  HADOOP_HOME or HADOOP_PREFIX : Hadoop install directory
  HIVE_OPT : Hive options
For help on a particular service:
  ./hive --service serviceName --help
Debug help: ./hive --debug --help
```

图 7.1.2 查看 Hive 的命令选项

由图 7.1.2 可以看到,输出了 Hive 的一些命令选项,说明用户可以通过"--service serviceName"的方式启动某个服务。以下信息列出了 Hive 主要的命令行选项:

Service List: beeline cleardanglingscratchdir cli hbaseimport hbaseschematool help hiveburninclient hiveserver2 hplsql hwi jar lineage llapdump lap llapstatus metastore metatool orcfiledump rcfilecat schemaTool version

部分重要选项的说明如下:
(1) cli:命令行界面。
(2) hiveserver2:启动 Hive 远程模式时需要启动的服务,其可以监听来自其他进程的连接。
(3) jar:扩展自 Hadoop jar 命令,可以执行需要 Hive 环境的应用程序。
(4) metastore:启动整个 Hive 元数据服务。

接下来,在 CentOS 7 服务器的命令行输入如下命令,查看 Hive 的 CLI 选项:

```
[root@master ~]# hive --help --service cli
```

运行结果如图 7.1.3 所示。

```
[root@master ~]# hive --help --service cli
which: no hbase in (/opt/modules/hive/bin:/usr/local/sbin:/usr/local/bin:/usr/sbin:/usr/bin:/opt/modules/jdk/bin:/opt/modules/hadoop/bin:/opt/m
odules/hadoop/sbin:/root/bin)
SLF4J: Class path contains multiple SLF4J bindings.
SLF4J: Found binding in [jar:file:/opt/modules/hive/lib/log4j-slf4j-impl-2.4.1.jar!/org/slf4j/impl/StaticLoggerBinder.class]
SLF4J: Found binding in [jar:file:/opt/modules/hadoop/share/hadoop/common/lib/slf4j-log4j12-1.7.10.jar!/org/slf4j/impl/StaticLoggerBinder.class]
SLF4J: See http://www.slf4j.org/codes.html#multiple_bindings for an explanation.
SLF4J: Actual binding is of type [org.apache.logging.slf4j.Log4jLoggerFactory]
usage: hive
 -d,--define <key=value>          Variable substitution to apply to hive
                                  commands. e.g. -d A=B or --define A=B
    --database <databasename>     Specify the database to use
 -e <quoted-query-string>         SQL from command line
 -f <filename>                    SQL from files
 -H,--help                        Print help information
    --hiveconf <property=value>   Use value for given property
    --hivevar <key=value>         Variable substitution to apply to hive
                                  commands. e.g. --hivevar A=B
 -i <filename>                    Initialization SQL file
 -S,--silent                      Silent mode in interactive shell
 -v,--verbose                     Verbose mode (echo executed SQL to the
                                  console)
[root@master ~]#
```

图 7.1.3 查看 Hive 的 CLI 选项

选项说明如下：

(1) -d,--define <key = value>：主要用来定义变量，如-d A = B 或者--define A = B。

(2) --database <databasename>：指定使用的数据库名称。

(3) -e <quoted-query-string>：从服务器命令行执行 SQL 语句。

(4) -f <filename>：从文件中执行 SQL 语句。

(5) -H,--help：输出帮助信息。

(6) --hiveconf <property = value>：设置 Hive 的属性值，能够覆盖 hive-site.xml 文件中配置的属性值。

(7) --hivevar <key = value>：在 Hive 命令中替换参数。

(8) -i <filename>：初始化 SQL 文件。

(9) -S,--silent：集成模式下开启静默模式。

(10) -v,--verbose：输出详细信息。

7.1.2　Hive 命令的使用

在命令行输入"hive"命令，即可进入 Hive 命令行终端，命令如下：

```
[root@master ~]# hive
```

运行结果如图 7.1.4 所示。

```
[root@master ~]# hive
which: no hbase in (/opt/modules/hive/bin:/usr/local/sbin:/usr/local/bin:/usr/sbin:/usr/bin:/opt/modules/jdk/bin:/opt/modules/hadoop/bin:/opt/modules/hadoop/sbin:/root/bin)
SLF4J: Class path contains multiple SLF4J bindings.
SLF4J: Found binding in [jar:file:/opt/modules/hive/lib/log4j-slf4j-impl-2.4.1.jar!/org/slf4j/impl/StaticLoggerBinder.class]
SLF4J: Found binding in [jar:file:/opt/modules/hadoop/share/hadoop/common/lib/slf4j-log4j12-1.7.10.jar!/org/slf4j/impl/StaticLoggerBinder.class]
SLF4J: See http://www.slf4j.org/codes.html#multiple_bindings for an explanation.
SLF4J: Actual binding is of type [org.apache.logging.slf4j.Log4jLoggerFactory]
Logging initialized using configuration in jar:file:/opt/modules/hive/lib/hive-common-2.1.1.jar!/hive-log4j2.properties Async: true
Hive-on-MR is deprecated in Hive 2 and may not be available in the future versions. Consider using a different execution engine (i.e. spark, tez) or using Hive 1.X releases.
hive (default)>
```

图 7.1.4　进入 Hive 命令行终端

任务 7.2　Hive 数据定义

任务描述

Hive 的查询语言 HiveQL 接近 MySQL 的 SQL，熟悉 SQL 的数据分析人员能够很容易使用 HiveQL 进行数据分析。本任务学习 Hive 的数据定义 DDL 语言，包括对 Hive 数据库的创建、修改和删除，数据表的创建、修改和删除等，这些是 HiveQL 的重要内容。通过查看数据库和数据表存放在 HDFS 上的位置和格式，理解 Hive 与 HDFS 的关系。

关键步骤

(1) 掌握 Hive 数据库的基本操作。

(2) 掌握 Hive 中创建表的基本操作。
(3) 理解管理表和外部表的概念和区别。
(4) 掌握外部表和分区表的创建、删除和修改。

Hive 的查询语言 HiveQL 接近 MySQL 的 SQL,熟悉 SQL 的数据分析人员能够很容易使用 HiveQL 进行数据分析。本任务将对 Hive 的数据定义,即 SQL 中的数据定义语言(data definition language,DDL)作出简要介绍。

7.2.1　Hive 操作数据库

Hive 中的数据库是组织表的目录,也称命名空间。在生产环境下,Hive 往往会用数据库将表组织起来。

Hive 中默认的数据库为 default,如果用户没有指定数据库,则会使用 Hive 的默认数据库。当在 Hive 中没有创建其他的数据库时,查看 Hive 中数据库的命令如下:

```
hive (default)> SHOW DATABASES;
```

运行结果如图 7.2.1 所示。

```
hive (default)> SHOW DATABASES;
OK
database_name
default
Time taken: 1.369 seconds, Fetched: 1 row(s)
hive (default)>
```

图 7.2.1　查看数据库

可以看到,此时 Hive 中只有一个默认的 default 数据库。使用如下语句在 Hive 中创建一个数据库:

```
hive (default)> CREATE DATABASE db_jscy;
```

运行结果如图 7.2.2 所示。

```
hive (default)> CREATE DATABASE db_jscy;
OK
Time taken: 0.525 seconds
hive (default)>
```

图 7.2.2　创建数据库

> **注意**
>
> HiveQL 命令不区分大小写,本单元统一将关键字用大写字母表示,用户命名的数据库名、表名和字段名用小写字母表示。

此时,如果 db_jscy 数据库存在,将会抛出一个异常。可以使用如下命令避免抛出异常:

```
hive (default)> CREATE DATABASE IF NOT EXISTS db_jscy;
```

运行结果如图 7.2.3 所示。

```
hive (default)> CREATE DATABASE IF NOT EXISTS db_jscy;
OK
Time taken: 0.039 seconds
hive (default)>
```

图 7.2.3　避免抛出异常创建数据库

此时，再次查看 Hive 中存在的数据库，命令如下：

```
hive (default)> SHOW DATABASES;
```

运行结果如图 7.2.4 所示。

```
hive (default)> SHOW DATABASES;
OK
database_name
db_jscy
default
Time taken: 0.026 seconds, Fetched: 2 row(s)
hive (default)>
```

图 7.2.4　再次查看 Hive 中的数据库

从图 7.2.4 可以看到，多了一个 db_jscy 数据库。

Hive 中的每个数据库都会以一个目录的形式保存在 Hadoop 的 HDFS 上，数据库中的表以子目录的形式存放，数据库中的数据则是在表目录下以文件的形式存储。如果创建数据库时用户没有指定数据库的存放位置，则默认存放在 HDFS 的 "/usr/hive_remote/warehouse" 目录下，存放位置由 hive-site.xml 文件中的 hive.metastore.warehouse.dir 属性配置，命令如下：

```
<property>
    <name>hive.metastore.warehouse.dir</name>
    <value>/user/hive_remote/warehouse</value>
</property>
```

查看 HDFS 中 "/user/hive/warehouse" 目录下的内容，命令如下：

```
[root@master ~]# hadoop fs -ls /usr/hive_remote/warehouse
```

运行结果如图 7.2.5 所示。

```
[root@master conf]# hadoop fs -ls /usr/hive_remote/warehouse
Found 4 items
drwxr-xr-x   - root supergroup          0 2024-04-25 10:34 /usr/hive_remote/warehouse/db_jscy.db
drwxr-xr-x   - root supergroup          0 2024-04-24 22:17 /usr/hive_remote/warehouse/gzb
drwxr-xr-x   - root supergroup          0 2024-04-25 09:50 /usr/hive_remote/warehouse/ygxxb
drwxr-xr-x   - root supergroup          0 2024-04-18 17:07 /usr/hive_remote/warehouse/zcfzb
[root@master conf]#
```

图 7.2.5　Hive 中数据库在 HDFS 上的存放位置

可以看到，创建的 db_jscy 数据库在 HDFS 中的 "/usr/hive_remote/warehouse" 目录下

以 db 的子目录形式存在,也可以在 Hive 命令行输入如下命令,查看 db_jscy 数据库的存放位置:

```
hive (default)> DESCRIBE DATABASE db_jscy;
```

运行结果如图 7.2.6 所示。

```
hive (default)> DESCRIBE DATABASE db_jscy;
OK
db_name comment location            owner_name    owner_type    parameters
db_jscy            hdfs://master:9000/usr/hive_remote/warehouse/db_jscy.db root        USER
Time taken: 1.251 seconds, Fetched: 1 row(s)
hive (default)>
```

图 7.2.6　查看 db_jscy 数据库的存放位置

数据库目录的名字都是以 .db 结尾的。

用户可以通过修改 hive-site.xml 文件中的配置来修改 Hive 数据库的存放位置,但是更多的是在创建数据库时指定数据库的存放位置。创建数据库并指定数据库在 HDFS 上的存放位置的命令如下:

```
hive (default)> exit;
[root@master /]# hdfs dfs -mkdir -p /usr/hadoop/hive
hive (default)> CREATE DATABASE IF NOT EXISTS db_jscy2 LOCATION '/usr/hadoop/hive';
```

运行结果如图 7.2.7 所示。

```
hive (default)> CREATE DATABASE IF NOT EXISTS db_jscy2 LOCATION '/usr/hadoop/hive';
OK
Time taken: 0.494 seconds
hive (default)>
```

图 7.2.7　创建数据库并指定在 HDFS 上的存放位置

查看 db_jscy2 的存放位置,命令如下:

```
hive (default)>  DESCRIBE DATABASE db_jscy2;
```

运行结果如图 7.2.8 所示。

```
hive (default)> DESCRIBE DATABASE db_jscy2;
OK
db_name comment location            owner_name    owner_type    parameters
db_jscy2            hdfs://master:9000/usr/hadoop/hive         root        USER
Time taken: 0.236 seconds, Fetched: 1 row(s)
hive (default)>
```

图 7.2.8　查看 db_jscy2 的存放位置

用户可以使用 USE 命令切换数据库,命令如下:

```
hive (default)> USE db_jscy;
```

运行结果如图 7.2.9 所示。

```
hive (default)> USE db_jscy;
OK
Time taken: 0.049 seconds
hive (db_jscy)>
```

图 7.2.9　用 USE 命令切换数据库

可见命令提示符由"hive (default)>"切换为"hive (db_jscy)>",说明当前数据库已经切换到"db_jscy"。

在当前数据库中,可以用"SHOW TABLES;"查看数据库中的表,命令如下:

  hive (db_jscy)>　SHOW TABLES;

运行结果如图 7.2.10 所示。

```
hive (db_jscy)> SHOW TABLES;
OK
tab_name
Time taken: 0.104 seconds
hive (db_jscy)>
```

图 7.2.10　查看数据库中的表

由图 7.2.10 可见此时 db_jscy 数据库还没有表。

数据库可以创建,也可以删除。删除 Hive 中的数据库的命令如下:

  hive (db_jscy)>　DROP DATABASE db_jscy;
  hive (db_jscy)>　SHOW DATABASES;

运行结果如图 7.2.11 所示。

```
hive (db_jscy)> DROP DATABASE db_jscy;
OK
Time taken: 0.652 seconds
hive (db_jscy)> SHOW DATABASES;
OK
database_name
db_jscy2
default
Time taken: 0.04 seconds, Fetched: 2 row(s)
hive (db_jscy)>
```

图 7.2.11　删除 Hive 中的数据库

由图 7.2.11 可见 db_jscy 已不存在。

当数据库不存在或者删除一个非空数据库时,将抛出异常。可以输入如下语句避免异常:

  hive (default)>　DROP DATABASE db_jscy;　＃删除不存在的数据库会抛出异常
  hive (default)>　DROP DATABASE IF EXISTS db_jscy CASCADE;　＃不会抛出异常

运行结果如图 7.2.12 所示。

```
hive (default)> DROP DATABASE db_jscy;
FAILED: SemanticException [Error 10072]: Database does not exist: db_jscy
hive (default)> DROP DATABASE IF EXISTS db_jscy CASCADE;
OK
Time taken: 0.039 seconds
hive (default)>
```

图 7.2.12　删除非空或不存在数据库避免异常命令

可以使用 ALTER DATABASE 命令修改数据库的 DBPROPERTIES 属性,命令如下:

hive (default)> ALTER DATABASE db_jscy2 SET DBPROPERTIES('author'='suchang');

运行结果如图 7.2.13 所示。

```
hive (default)> ALTER DATABASE db_jscy2 SET DBPROPERTIES('author'='suchang');
OK
Time taken: 0.348 seconds
hive (default)>
```

图 7.2.13　修改数据库属性

注意

|数据库名和数据库所在位置等其他元数据信息不可更改。|

7.2.2　创建表

Hive 中创建表的语句参数如下:

```
CREATE [EXTERNAL] TABLE [IF NOT EXISTS] 表名
[(列名 数据类型[COMMENT 列注释],…)]
[COMMENT 表注释]
[PARTITIONED BY (列名 数据类型[COMMENT 列注释],…)]
[CLUSTERED BY (列名,列名,…)]
[SORTED BY (列名[ASC|DESC],…)] INTO 桶名 BUCKETS]
[ROW FORMAT 列格式]
[STORED AS 文件格式]
[LOCATION  存放在 hdfs 上的路径]
```

说明:在 Hive 中创建数据表的完整语句包括以下部分:

(1) CREATE TABLE:关键字,用于指示 Hive 创建一个新的表。
(2) 表名:在数据库中必须是唯一的,并且遵循 Hive 的命名约定。
(3) 列定义:列出表中的所有列及其数据类型。
(4) 可选参数:可以指定分区列、桶列以及存储属性,如文件格式、存储位置等。

以下通过一个具体案例来熟悉用建表语句创建一个表的过程。

【例 7-1】　江苏财源有限公司员工基本信息表(部分)数据如表 7.2.1 所示,针对该基本信息表,创建一个数据库 jscy,其中再创建一个表 ygxxb。

表 7.2.1　江苏财源有限公司员工基本信息表(部分)

职工编号	姓名	性别	部门	职务类别	基本工资(元)
001	王柏宇	男	办公室	公司经理	3 200.00
002	齐敏	女	办公室	行政助理	2 500.00
003	李红梅	女	财务部	财务部经理	3 000.00
004	王向东	男	财务部	会计人员	2 000.00
005	陈艳丽	女	财务部	出纳	1 800.00
006	龚文娟	女	人事处	人事处处长	3 000.00
007	林大维	男	研发部	研发部经理	2 200.00
008	朱韩斌	男	研发部	研发人员	2 000.00
009	赵齐伟	男	研发部	研发人员	2 000.00
010	张小英	女	研发部	研发人员	2 000.00

第 1 步:创建数据库 jscy,命令如下:

```
hive (default)> CREATE DATABASE jscy;
hive (default)> USE jscy;
```

运行结果如图 7.2.14 所示。

```
hive (default)> CREATE DATABASE jscy;
OK
Time taken: 2.955 seconds
hive (default)> USE jscy;
OK
Time taken: 0.139 seconds
hive (jscy)>
```

图 7.2.14　创建并切换数据库

第 2 步:用 CREATE TABLE 命令创建表 ygxxb,命令如下:

```
CREATE TABLE IF NOT EXISTS  jscy.ygxxb(
zgbh STRING COMMENT '职工编号',
xm STRING COMMENT '姓名',
xb STRING COMMENT '性别',
bm STRING COMMENT  '部门',
zwlb STRING COMMENT '职务类别',
jbgz FLOAT COMMENT '基本工资'
)
COMMENT  '江苏财源公司员工基本信息表'
ROW FORMAT   DELIMITED
FIELDS TERMINATED BY  ','
LINES TERMINATED BY  '\n'
STORED AS TEXTFILE
LOCATION  '/usr/hive_remote/warehouse/jscy.db/ygxxb';
```

在[例 7-1]中有几个需要关注的点:

(1) IF NOT EXISTS:说明创建是可选的,用于避免在表已经存在的情况下重复创建。

(2) jscy.ygxxb:指定了数据库名 jscy、表名 ygxxb。建表时,可以在表名前面加上数据库名,这样,在当前所在的数据库并非目标数据库 jscy 时,也能将表建在目标数据库 jscy 中。用户也可以使用 USE 语句,先将当前所在的数据库切换到目标数据库 jscy。

(3) 表 ygxxb 有六个列:zgbh、xm、xb、bm、zwlb、jbgz,数据类型分别为 STRING、STRING、STRING、STRING、STRING、FLOAT。

(4) COMMENT:关键字用于添加列和表的注释信息。

(5) ROW FORMAT DELIMITED:定义了行的分隔符是换行 '\n' 和字段的分隔符是 ','。

(6) STORED AS TEXTFILE:指定了文件存储格式是文本文件 TEXTFILE。

(7) LOCATION 指定表存在的位置,省略不写时,将表存储在当前所在的数据库目录中。

(8) Hive 数据类型。Hive 中提供了多种数据类型,其中基本数据类型和复合数据类型分别如表 7.2.2、表 7.2.3 所示。

表 7.2.2 Hive 中的基本数据类型

数据类型	长度(字节)	范围	示例
TINYINT	1	$-128 \sim 127$	100Y
SMALLINT	2	$-32\,768 \sim 32\,767$	100S
INT	4	$-2^{32} \sim 2^{32}-1$	100
BIGINT	8	$-2^{64} \sim 2^{64}-1$	100L
FLOAT	4	单精度浮点数	5.21
DOUBLE	8	双精度浮点数	5.21
DECIMAL	—	高精度浮点数	DECIMAL(9, 8)
BOOLEAN	—	布尔类型	TRUE/FALSE
STRING	—	字符串	'hive'

表 7.2.3 Hive 中的复合数据类型

数据类型	描述	示例
STRUCT	结构体,可以通过"字段名.属性名"的方式访问	STRUCT('xm', 'suchang')
MAP	key-value 对。可以通过"字段名[属性名]"的方式访问	MAP('a',1,'b',2)
ARRAY	一组具有相同类型的变量的集合,可以通过"字段名[下标]"的方式访问,下标从 0 开始	ARRAY(1,2,3)

运行结果如图 7.2.15 所示。

```
hive (jscy)> CREATE TABLE IF NOT EXISTS  jscy.ygxxb(
        > zgbh STRING COMMENT '职工编号',
        > xm STRING COMMENT '姓名',
        > xb STRING COMMENT '性别',
        > bm STRING COMMENT '部门',
        > zwlb STRING COMMENT '职务类别',
        > jbgz FLOAT COMMENT '基本工资'
        > COMMENT  '江苏财源公司员工基本信息表'
        > ROW FORMAT  DELIMITED
        > FIELDS TERMINATED BY  ','
        > LINES TERMINATED BY  '\n'
        > STORED AS TEXTFILE
        > LOCATION  '/usr/hive_remote/warehouse/jscy.db/ygxxb';
OK
Time taken: 0.435 seconds
hive (jscy)>
```

图 7.2.15　用 CREATE TABLE 命令创建 ygxxb 表

在服务器 master 上的"/root/"目录下创建 ygxxb.txt，将表 7.2.1 的数据组织成文本文档，字段数据之间用","间隔，文件内容如下：

```
001,王柏宇,男,办公室,公司经理,3200.00
002,齐  敏,女,办公室,行政助理,2500.00
003,李红梅,女,财务部,财务部经理,3000.00
004,王向东,男,财务部,会计人员,2000.00
005,陈艳丽,女,财务部,出纳,1800.00
006,龚文娟,女,人事处,人事处处长,3000.00
007,林大维,男,研发部,研发部经理,2200.00
008,朱韩斌,男,研发部,研发人员,2000.00
009,赵齐伟,男,研发部,研发人员,2000.00
010,张小英,女,研发部,研发人员,2000.00
```

命令如下：

```
hive (default)> exit;
[root@master ~]# cd /root
[root@master ~]# vim ygxxb.txt
```

运行结果如图 7.2.16 所示。

```
1 master      2 slave1     3 slave2    +
001,王柏宇,男,办公室,公司经理,3200.00
002,齐  敏,女,办公室,行政助理,2500.00
003,李红梅,女,财务部,财务部经理,3000.00
004,王向东,男,财务部,会计人员,2000.00
005,陈艳丽,女,财务部,出纳,1800.00
006,龚文娟,女,人事处,人事处处长,3000.00
007,林大维,男,研发部,研发部经理,2200.00
008,朱韩斌,男,研发部,研发人员,2000.00
009,赵齐伟,男,研发部,研发人员,2000.00
010,张小英,女,研发部,研发人员,2000.00
~
~
:wq
```

图 7.2.16　将表 7.2.1 的数据创建为 ygxxb.txt

单元 7　数据仓库 Hive 在数据处理中的应用 | 197

LOAD DATA 命令加载数据，命令如下：

```
[root@master ~]# hive
hive (jscy)>  LOAD DATA LOCAL INPATH '/root/ygxxb.txt'  INTO TABLE ygxxb;
```

运行结果如图 7.2.17 所示。

```
hive (jscy)> LOAD DATA LOCAL INPATH '/root/ygxxb.txt'  INTO TABLE ygxxb;
Loading data to table jscy.ygxxb
OK
Time taken: 1.102 seconds
hive (jscy)>
```

图 7.2.17　加载数据成功

加载数据成功后，现在用 SELECT 命令查询表 ygxxb 的记录数据，命令如下：

```
hive (jscy)> SELECT * FROM ygxxb;
```

运行结果如图 7.2.18 所示。

```
hive (jscy)> SELECT * FROM ygxxb;
OK
ygxxb.zgbh      ygxxb.xm        ygxxb.xb        ygxxb.bm        ygxxb.zwlb      ygxxb.jbgz
001     王柏宇  男      办公室  公司经理 3200.0
002     齐 敏   女      办公室  行政助理 2500.0
003     李红梅  女      财务部  财务部经理       3000.0
004     王向东  男      财务部  会计人员 2000.0
005     陈艳丽  女      财务部  出纳    1800.0
006     蔡文娟  女      人事处  人事处处长       3000.0
007     林大雄  男      研发部  研发部经理       2200.0
008     朱韩斌  男      研发部  研发人员 2000.0
009     赵齐伟  男      研发部  研发人员 2000.0
010     张小英  女      研发部  研发人员 2000.0
Time taken: 1.173 seconds, Fetched: 10 row(s)
hive (jscy)>
```

图 7.2.18　查询表数据

用户可以使用如下命令查看表信息：

```
hive (jscy)>  DESC ygxxb;
```

运行结果如图 7.2.19 所示。

```
hive (jscy)> DESC ygxxb;
OK
col_name        data_type       comment
zgbh                    string                  ????
xm                      string                  ??
xb                      string                  ??
bm                      string                  ??
zwlb                    string                  ????
jbgz                    float                   ????
Time taken: 0.129 seconds, Fetched: 6 row(s)
hive (jscy)>
```

图 7.2.19　查看表信息

用户如果想查看更详细的信息，则使用如下命令：

```
hive (jscy)>  DESC EXTENDED  ygxxb;
```

运行结果如图 7.2.20 所示。

```
hive (jscy)> DESC EXTENDED ygxxb;
OK
col_name        data_type       comment
zgbh            string          ????
xm              string          ??
xb              string          ??
bm              string          ??
zwlb            string          ????
jbgz            float           ????

Detailed Table Information      Table(tableName:ygxxb, dbName:jscy, owner:root, createTime:1714055502, lastAccessTime:0, retenti
on:0, sd:StorageDescriptor(cols:[FieldSchema(name:zgbh, type:string, comment:????), FieldSchema(name:xm, type:string, comment:??
), FieldSchema(name:xb, type:string, comment:??), FieldSchema(name:bm, type:string, comment:??), FieldSchema(name:zwlb, type:str
ing, comment:????), FieldSchema(name:jbgz, type:float, comment:????)], location:hdfs://master:9000/usr/hive_remote/warehouse/jsc
y.db/ygxxb, inputFormat:org.apache.hadoop.mapred.TextInputFormat, outputFormat:org.apache.hadoop.hive.ql.io.HiveIgnoreKeyTextOut
putFormat, compressed:false, numBuckets:-1, serdeInfo:SerDeInfo(name:null, serializationLib:org.apache.hadoop.hive.serde2.lazy.L
azySimpleSerDe, parameters:{serialization.format=,, line.delim=
, field.delim=,}), bucketCols:[], sortCols:[], parameters:{}, skewedInfo:SkewedInfo(skewedColNames:[], skewedColValues:[], skewe
dColValueLocationMaps:{}), storedAsSubDirectories:false), partitionKeys:[], parameters:{transient_lastDdlTime=1714055632, commen
t=?????????????, totalSize=492, numFiles=1}, viewOriginalText:null, viewExpandedText:null, tableType:MANAGED_TABLE)
Time taken: 0.142 seconds, Fetched: 9 row(s)
hive (jscy)>
```

图 7.2.20　用 DESC EXTENDED 查看表的更详细信息

或者使用如下命令：

```
hive (jscy)> DESC FORMATTED ygxxb;
```

运行结果如图 7.2.21 所示。

```
hive (jscy)> DESC FORMATTED ygxxb;
OK
col_name        data_type       comment
# col_name              data_type               comment

zgbh                    string                  ????
xm                      string                  ??
xb                      string                  ??
bm                      string                  ??
zwlb                    string                  ????
jbgz                    float                   ????

# Detailed Table Information
Database:               jscy
Owner:                  root
CreateTime:             Thu Apr 25 22:31:42 CST 2024
LastAccessTime:         UNKNOWN
Retention:              0
Location:               hdfs://master:9000/usr/hive_remote/warehouse/jscy.db/ygxxb
Table Type:             MANAGED_TABLE
Table Parameters:
        comment                 ?????????????
        numFiles                1
        totalSize               492
        transient_lastDdlTime   1714055632

# Storage Information
SerDe Library:          org.apache.hadoop.hive.serde2.lazy.LazySimpleSerDe
InputFormat:            org.apache.hadoop.mapred.TextInputFormat
OutputFormat:           org.apache.hadoop.hive.ql.io.HiveIgnoreKeyTextOutputFormat
Compressed:             No
Num Buckets:            -1
Bucket Columns:         []
Sort Columns:           []
Storage Desc Params:
        field.delim             ,
        line.delim              \n
        serialization.format    ,
Time taken: 0.18 seconds, Fetched: 35 row(s)
hive (jscy)>
```

图 7.2.21　用 DESC FORMATTED 查看表的更详细信息

创建表之后,可以输入如下语句查看已存在的表:

```
hive (jscy)>  SHOW TABLES;
```

运行结果如图 7.2.22 所示。

```
hive (jscy)> SHOW TABLES;
OK
tab_name
ygxxb
Time taken: 0.103 seconds, Fetched: 1 row(s)
hive (jscy)>
```

图 7.2.22　查看已存在的表

也可以输入如下语句查看指定数据库中已存在的表:

```
hive (jscy)>  SHOW TABLES IN jscy;
```

运行结果如图 7.2.23 所示。

```
hive (jscy)> SHOW TABLES IN jscy;
OK
tab_name
ygxxb
Time taken: 0.08 seconds, Fetched: 1 row(s)
hive (jscy)>
```

图 7.2.23　查看指定数据库中已存在的表

还可以通过复制一张已存在的表来创建表(只复制表结构,不复制数据),命令如下:

```
hive> CREATE TABLE IF NOT EXISTS jscy.ygxxb2   LIKE jscy.ygxxb;
```

运行结果如图 7.2.24 所示。

```
hive (jscy)>  CREATE TABLE IF NOT EXISTS jscy.ygxxb2   LIKE jscy.ygxxb;
OK
Time taken: 0.605 seconds
hive (jscy)>
```

图 7.2.24　通过复制一张已存在的表来创建表

此时,查看 jscy 数据库中已存在的表,命令如下:

```
hive>   SHOW TABLES IN jscy;
```

运行结果如图 7.2.25 所示。

```
hive (jscy)>  SHOW TABLES IN jscy;
OK
tab_name
ygxxb
ygxxb2
Time taken: 0.044 seconds, Fetched: 2 row(s)
hive (jscy)>
```

图 7.2.25　查看 jscy 数据库中已存在的表

可以发现,多了一张 ygxxb2 表。

7.2.3 管理表

如果 Hive 中没有特别指定,则默认创建的表都是管理表,也称内部表,由 Hive 负责管理表中的数据,管理表不共享数据。删除管理表时,会删除管理表中的数据和元数据信息。

7.2.4 外部表

当一份数据需要被共享时,可以创建一个外部表指向这份数据。创建外部表时,需要在创建表语句中加入 EXTERNAL 关键字。建表语句如下:

```
CREATE EXTERNAL TABLE IF NOT EXISTS  jscy.ygxxb_external(
zgbh STRING COMMENT '职工编号',
xm STRING COMMENT '姓名',
xb STRING COMMENT '性别',
bm STRING COMMENT  '部门',
zwlb STRING COMMENT '职务类别',
jbgz FLOAT COMMENT '基本工资')
ROW FORMAT  DELIMITED
FIELDS TERMINATED BY  ','
LINES TERMINATED BY  '\n'
STORED AS TEXTFILE
LOCATION  '/usr/hive_remote/warehouse/ygxxb_external';
```

运行结果如图 7.2.26 所示。

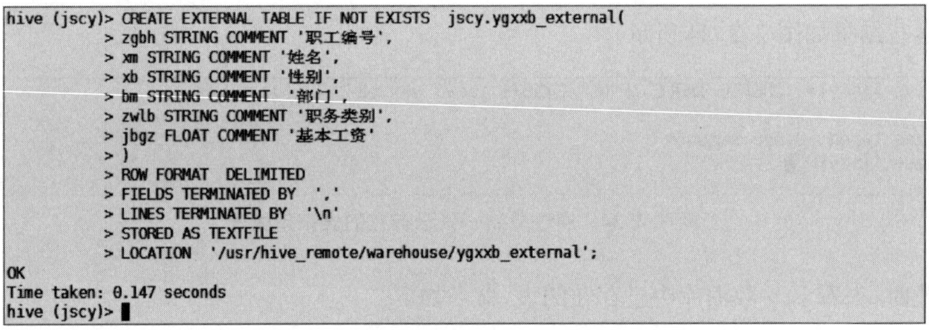

```
hive (jscy)> CREATE EXTERNAL TABLE IF NOT EXISTS  jscy.ygxxb_external(
           > zgbh STRING COMMENT '职工编号',
           > xm STRING COMMENT '姓名',
           > xb STRING COMMENT '性别',
           > bm STRING COMMENT  '部门',
           > zwlb STRING COMMENT '职务类别',
           > jbgz FLOAT COMMENT '基本工资'
           > )
           > ROW FORMAT  DELIMITED
           > FIELDS TERMINATED BY  ','
           > LINES TERMINATED BY  '\n'
           > STORED AS TEXTFILE
           > LOCATION  '/usr/hive_remote/warehouse/ygxxb_external';
OK
Time taken: 0.147 seconds
hive (jscy)>
```

图 7.2.26 创建外部表用关键字 EXTERNAL

可以看到,创建外部表时只需要在创建语句中加入 EXTERNAL 关键字。删除外部表时,只会删除外部表的元数据信息,不会删除数据。

用户可以使用 DESC FORMATTED tablename 语句查看当前表是管理表还是外部表。

如果是管理表,会看到"Table Type: MANAGED_TABLE"信息,命令如下:

```
DESC FORMATTED ygxxb;
```

运行结果如图 7.2.27 所示。

如果是外部表,则会看到"Table Type: EXTERNAL_TABLE"信息,命令如下:

```
DESC FORMATTED ygxxb_external;
```

```
hive (jscy)> DESC FORMATTED ygxxb;
OK
col_name            data_type          comment
# col_name          data_type          comment

zgbh                string             ????
xm                  string             ??
xb                  string             ??
bm                  string             ??
zwlb                string             ????
jbgz                float              ????

# Detailed Table Information
Database:           jscy
Owner:              root
CreateTime:         Thu Apr 25 22:31:42 CST 2024
LastAccessTime:     UNKNOWN
Retention:          0
Location:           hdfs://master:9000/usr/hive_remote/warehouse/jscy.db/ygxxb
Table Type:         MANAGED_TABLE
Table Parameters:
        comment                 ?????????????
        numFiles                1
        totalSize               492
        transient_lastDdlTime   1714055632

# Storage Information
SerDe Library:      org.apache.hadoop.hive.serde2.lazy.LazySimpleSerDe
InputFormat:        org.apache.hadoop.mapred.TextInputFormat
OutputFormat:       org.apache.hadoop.hive.ql.io.HiveIgnoreKeyTextOutputFormat
Compressed:         No
Num Buckets:        -1
Bucket Columns:     []
Sort Columns:       []
Storage Desc Params:
        field.delim             ,
        line.delim              \n
        serialization.format    ,
Time taken: 0.23 seconds, Fetched: 35 row(s)
hive (jscy)>
```

图 7.2.27　查看当前表属性是管理表

运行结果如图 7.2.28 所示。

```
hive (jscy)> DESC FORMATTED ygxxb_external;
OK
col_name            data_type          comment
# col_name          data_type          comment

zgbh                string             ????
xm                  string             ??
xb                  string             ??
bm                  string             ??
zwlb                string             ????
jbgz                float              ????

# Detailed Table Information
Database:           jscy
Owner:              root
CreateTime:         Sun Apr 28 16:05:50 CST 2024
LastAccessTime:     UNKNOWN
Retention:          0
Location:           hdfs://master:9000/usr/hive_remote/warehouse/ygxxb_external
Table Type:         EXTERNAL_TABLE
Table Parameters:
        EXTERNAL                TRUE
        transient_lastDdlTime   1714291550

# Storage Information
SerDe Library:      org.apache.hadoop.hive.serde2.lazy.LazySimpleSerDe
InputFormat:        org.apache.hadoop.mapred.TextInputFormat
OutputFormat:       org.apache.hadoop.hive.ql.io.HiveIgnoreKeyTextOutputFormat
Compressed:         No
Num Buckets:        -1
Bucket Columns:     []
Sort Columns:       []
Storage Desc Params:
        field.delim             ,
        line.delim              \n
        serialization.format    ,
Time taken: 0.142 seconds, Fetched: 33 row(s)
hive (jscy)>
```

图 7.2.28　查看当前表属性是外部表

也可以通过复制一张表来创建外部表(只复制表结构,不复制数据),命令如下:

```
CREATE EXTERNAL TABLE IF NOT EXISTS jscy.ygxxb3 LIKE jscy.ygxxb;
```

运行结果如图 7.2.29 所示。

```
hive (jscy)> CREATE EXTERNAL TABLE IF NOT EXISTS jscy.ygxxb3 LIKE jscy.ygxxb;
OK
Time taken: 0.217 seconds
hive (jscy)>
```

图 7.2.29　通过复制一张表来创建外部表

管理表和外部表可以互相转化。将 ygxxb 表转化为外部表,命令如下:

```
ALTER TABLE ygxxb set TBLPROPERTIES ('EXTERNAL' = 'TRUE');
```

运行结果如图 7.2.30 所示。

```
hive (jscy)> ALTER TABLE ygxxb set TBLPROPERTIES ('EXTERNAL' = 'TRUE');
OK
Time taken: 0.186 seconds
hive (jscy)>
```

图 7.2.30　将管理表转化为外部表

再用"DESC FORMATTED ygxxb;"命令查看表属性,从运行结果中发现"Table Type：EXTERNAL_TABLE"信息,说明表属性已修改为外部表。运行结果如图 7.2.31 所示。

```
hive (default)> DESC FORMATTED ygxxb;
OK
col_name              data_type              comment
# col_name            data_type              comment

zgbh                  string
xm                    string
xb                    string
bm                    string
zwlb                  string
jbgz                  float

# Detailed Table Information
Database:             default
Owner:                root
CreateTime:           Thu Apr 25 09:49:58 CST 2024
LastAccessTime:       UNKNOWN
Retention:            0
Location:             hdfs://master:9000/usr/hive_remote/warehouse/ygxxb
Table Type:           EXTERNAL_TABLE
Table Parameters:
        EXTERNAL              TRUE
        last_modified_by      root
        last_modified_time    1714292562
        numFiles              1
        numRows               0
        rawDataSize           0
        totalSize             492
        transient_lastDdlTime 1714292562
```

图 7.2.31　查看 ygxxb 表属性被修改为外部表

将 ygxxb 表转化为管理表,命令如下:

```
ALTER TABLE ygxxb set TBLPROPERTIES ('EXTERNAL' = 'FALSE');
```

运行结果如图 7.2.32 所示。

```
hive (default)> ALTER TABLE ygxxb set TBLPROPERTIES ('EXTERNAL' = 'FALSE');
OK
Time taken: 0.236 seconds
hive (default)>
```

图 7.2.32　将 ygxxb 由外部表转化为管理表

再用"DESC FORMATTED ygxxb;"命令查看表属性,从运行结果中发现"Table Type:MANAGED_TABLE"信息,说明表属性又被改回为管理表。运行结果如图 7.2.33 所示。

```
hive (default)> DESC FORMATTED ygxxb;
OK
col_name            data_type           comment
# col_name          data_type           comment

zgbh                string
xm                  string
xb                  string
bm                  string
zwlb                string
jbgz                float

# Detailed Table Information
Database:           default
Owner:              root
CreateTime:         Thu Apr 25 09:49:58 CST 2024
LastAccessTime:     UNKNOWN
Retention:          0
Location:           hdfs://master:9000/usr/hive_remote/warehouse/ygxxb
Table Type:         MANAGED_TABLE
Table Parameters:
    EXTERNAL                FALSE
    last_modified_by        root
    last_modified_time      1714292708
    numFiles                1
    numRows                 0
    rawDataSize             0
    totalSize               492
    transient_lastDdlTime   1714292708
```

图 7.2.33　查看表 ygxxb 属性被修改为管理表

7.2.5　分区表

Hive 支持表分区,分区可以将一个表中的数据进行水平切分,在性能上有着显著的优势。分区表在生产环境中使用的比较多。

7.2.5.1　分区管理表

在 Hive 中创建一个分区管理表,命令如下:

```
CREATE TABLE ygxxb_info(
zgbh STRING,
xm STRING,
xb STRING,
```

```
bm STRING,
zwlb STRING,
jbgz FLOAT
)
PARTITIONED BY (province STRING, city STRING);
```

运行结果如图 7.2.34 所示。

```
hive (jscy)> CREATE TABLE ygxxb_info(
            > zgbh STRING,
            > xm STRING,
            > xb STRING,
            > bm STRING,
            > zwlb STRING,
            > jbgz FLOAT
            > )
            > PARTITIONED BY (province STRING, city STRING);
OK
Time taken: 0.929 seconds
```

图 7.2.34　创建分区表

可以看到,创建分区表时,需要使用 PATITIONED BY 自定义分区字段。

需要注意的是,分区字段不能和表字段重名,否则将会抛出"FAILED: SemanticException [Error 10035]:Column repeated in partitioning columns"错误。下面是创建分区管理表的语句:

```
CREATE TABLE ygxxb_info2(
zgbh STRING,
xm STRING,
xb STRING,
bm STRING,
zwlb STRING,
jbgz FLOAT
)
PARTITIONED BY (bm STRING, city STRING);
```

运行结果如图 7.2.35 所示。

```
hive (jscy)> CREATE TABLE ygxxb_info2(
            > zgbh STRING,
            > xm STRING,
            > xb STRING,
            > bm STRING,
            > zwlb STRING,
            > jbgz FLOAT
            > )
            > PARTITIONED BY (bm STRING, city STRING);
FAILED: SemanticException [Error 10035]: Column repeated in partitioning columns
hive (jscy)>
```

图 7.2.35　创建分区表时分区字段和表字段可能重名

此时,bm 字段既是表字段又是分区字段,就会抛出"FAILED：SemanticException

[Error 10035]:Column repeated in partitioning columns"错误。

Hive 中的表以目录形式存在于 HDFS 中的数据库目录下,而表的分区则是以表的子目录的形式存在,子目录如下:

```
/usr/hive_remote/warehouse/ygxxb_info/province=jiangsu/city=nanjing
```

可以使用如下语句查询分区管理表中的数据:

```
SELECT * FROM ygxxb_info WHERE province= 'jiangsu' AND city = 'nanjing';
```

运行结果如图 7.2.36 所示。

```
hive (jscy)> SELECT * FROM ygxxb_info WHERE province= 'jiangsu' AND city = 'nanjing';
OK
ygxxb_info.zgbh ygxxb_info.xm    ygxxb_info.xb    ygxxb_info.bm    ygxxb_info.zwlb ygxxb_info.jbgz ygxxb_info.province      ygxxb_in
fo.city
Time taken: 2.797 seconds
hive (jscy)>
```

图 7.2.36　查询分区管理表中的数据

Hive 也会将分区字段的数据输出,因此时 ygxxb_info 表中没有数据,查询结果没有记录。上述语句查询的是 province = 'jiangsu' 和 city = 'nanjing' 下的数据,Hive 只会扫描 HDFS 上"/usr/hive_remote/warehouse/ygxxb_info/province=jiangsu/city=nanjing"目录下的数据,这对于数据量非常巨大的 Hive 表来说,性能提升是非常明显的,也可以查询所有分区下的数据,命令如下:

```
SELECT * FROM ygxxb_info ;
```

运行结果如图 7.2.37 所示。

```
hive (jscy)> SELECT * FROM ygxxb_info ;
OK
ygxxb_info.zgbh ygxxb_info.xm    ygxxb_info.xb    ygxxb_info.bm    ygxxb_info.zwlb ygxxb_info.jbgz ygxxb_info.province      ygxxb_info.city
Time taken: 0.298 seconds
hive (jscy)>
```

图 7.2.37　查询所有分区下的数据

命令执行成功,如果 ygxxb_info 表中有数据,就会查询出所有省份所有城市的数据。

在生产环境下,最常使用的就是按照时间对 Hive 中的表数据分区。如果数据表中的数据和分区个数都非常大,则查询所有分区的数据会触发一个巨大的 MapReduce 任务。可以将 Hive 的安全措施设置为 strict 模式,设置为 strict 模式后,如果一个针对分区表的查询没有加上分区条件,此查询作业就会禁止提交。可以在 hive_site.xml 文件中配置 hive.mapred.mode 属性,代码如下:

```
<property>
    <name>hive.mapred.mode</name>
    <value>strict</value>
</property>
```

也可以在 Hive 命令行输入如下命令设置 strict 模式:

```
hive> set hive.mapred.mode= strict;
```

前者对 Hive 所有会话生效,后者仅对本次会话生效。

将安全模式设置为 strict 后,若查询分区表时没有添加分区条件,则会抛出"FAILED:

SemanticException Queries against partitioned tables without a partition filter are disabled for safety reasons."错误,命令如下:

```
hive (jscy)>   set hive.mapred.mode= strict;
hive (jscy)>   SELECT * FROM ygxxb_info ;
```

运行结果如图 7.2.38 所示。

```
hive (jscy)> set hive.mapred.mode= strict;
hive (jscy)> SELECT * FROM ygxxb_info ;
FAILED: SemanticException Queries against partitioned tables without a partition filter are disabled for safety reasons. If you know what
d that hive.mapred.mode is not set to 'strict' to enable them. No partition predicate for Alias "ygxxb_info" Table "ygxxb_info"
hive (jscy)>
```

图 7.2.38　安全模式设置为 strict 时查询分区数据出错

将安装模式设置为 nonstrict 时,即使没有添加分区条件,也可以正常查询数据,命令如下:

```
hive (jscy)>   set hive.mapred.mode= nonstrict;
hive (jscy)>   SELECT * FROM ygxxb_info ;
```

运行结果如图 7.2.39 所示。

```
hive (jscy)> set hive.mapred.mode= nonstrict;
hive (jscy)> SELECT * FROM ygxxb_info ;
OK
ygxxb_info.zgbh  ygxxb_info.xm   ygxxb_info.xb   ygxxb_info.bm   ygxxb_info.zwlb  ygxxb_info.jbgz  ygxxb_info.province   ygxxb_info.city
Time taken: 0.303 seconds
hive (jscy)>
```

图 7.2.39　安全模式设置为 nonstrict 时可查询所有数据

用户可以使用 SHOW PARTITIONS 命令查看表中的分区情况,命令如下:

```
hive> SHOW PARTITIONS ygxxb_info;
```

运行结果如图 7.2.40 所示。

```
hive (jscy)> SHOW PARTITIONS ygxxb_info;
OK
partition
Time taken: 0.694 seconds
hive (jscy)>
```

图 7.2.40　查看表中分区命令运行成功

如果表中存在非常多的分区,用户可以指定一个或者多个特定分区字段值的分区子句,进行过滤查询,命令如下:

```
Hive(jscy)>   SHOW PARTITIONS ygxxb_info PARTITION(province='jiangsu' );
```

运行结果如图 7.2.41 所示。

```
hive (jscy)> SHOW PARTITIONS ygxxb_info PARTITION(province='jiangsu' );
OK
partition
Time taken: 0.6 seconds
hive (jscy)>
```

图 7.2.41　指定特定分区过滤查询

使用 DESC EXTENDED tablename 语句也可以显示分区键,命令如下:

```
Hive(jscy)> DESC EXTENDED ygxxb_info;
```

运行结果如图 7.2.42 所示。

图 7.2.42 用 DESC EXTENDED 显示分区键

同样地,使用 DESC FORMATTED tablename 语句也能显示分区键,命令如下:

```
hive> DESC FORMATTED ygxxb_info;
```

运行结果如图 7.2.43 所示。

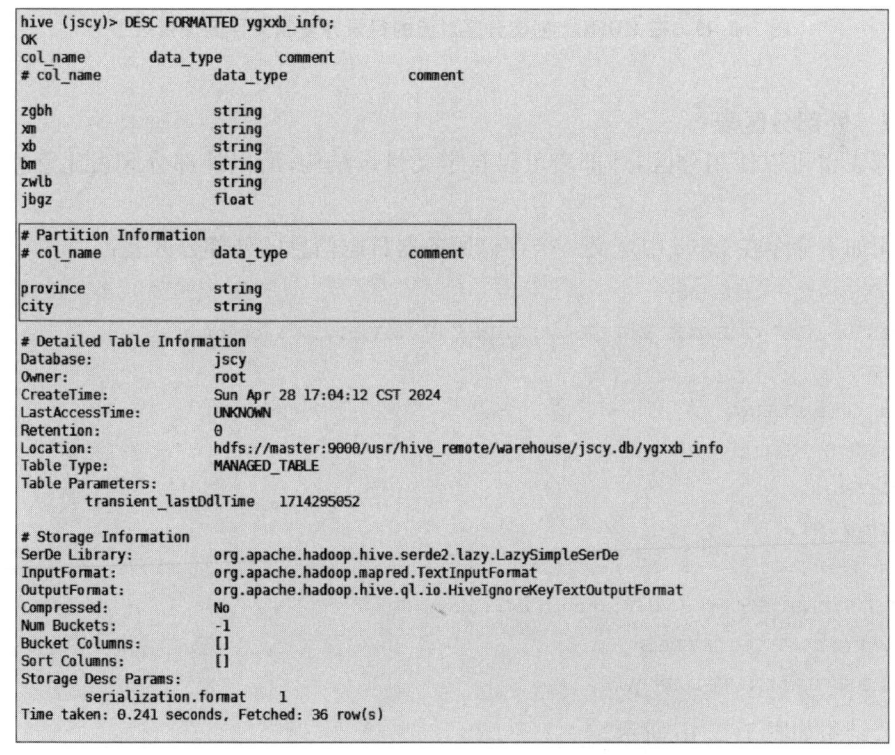

图 7.2.43 用 DESC FORMATTED 显示分区键

在管理表中,可以通过载入数据的方式创建分区,命令如下:

```
hive (jscy)>  LOAD DATA LOCAL INPATH '/root/ygxxb.txt'  INTO TABLE ygxxb_info
PARTITION(province='jiangsu', city= 'nanjing');
hive (jscy)>  SELECT * FROM ygxxb_info ;
```

运行结果如图 7.2.44 所示。

```
hive (jscy)> LOAD DATA LOCAL INPATH '/root/ygxxb.txt'  INTO TABLE ygxxb_info PARTITION(province='jiangsu', city= 'nanjing');
Loading data to table jscy.ygxxb_info partition (province=jiangsu, city=nanjing)
OK
Time taken: 3.221 seconds
hive (jscy)> SELECT * FROM ygxxb_info ;
OK
ygxxb_info.zgbh ygxxb_info.xm   ygxxb_info.xb   ygxxb_info.bm   ygxxb_info.zwlb ygxxb_info.jbgz ygxxb_info.province      ygxxb_info.city
001,王柏宇,男,办公室,公司经理,3200.00   NULL    NULL    NULL    NULL    NULL    jiangsu nanjing
002,齐  敏,女,办公室,行政助理,2500.00   NULL    NULL    NULL    NULL    NULL    jiangsu nanjing
003,李红梅,女,财务部,财务部经理,3000.00 NULL    NULL    NULL    NULL    NULL    jiangsu nanjing
004,王向东,男,财务部,会计人员,2000.00   NULL    NULL    NULL    NULL    NULL    jiangsu nanjing
005,陈艳丽,女,财务部,出纳,1800.00       NULL    NULL    NULL    NULL    NULL    jiangsu nanjing
006,龚文娟,女,人事处,人事处处长,3000.00 NULL    NULL    NULL    NULL    NULL    jiangsu nanjing
007,林大维,男,研发部,研发部经理,2200.00 NULL    NULL    NULL    NULL    NULL    jiangsu nanjing
008,朱韩斌,男,研发部,研发人员,2000.00   NULL    NULL    NULL    NULL    NULL    jiangsu nanjing
009,赵齐伟,男,研发部,研发人员,2000.00   NULL    NULL    NULL    NULL    NULL    jiangsu nanjing
010,张小英,女,研发部,研发人员,2000.00   NULL    NULL    NULL    NULL    NULL    jiangsu nanjing
Time taken: 1.357 seconds, Fetched: 10 row(s)
hive (jscy)>
```

图 7.2.44　载入数据创建分区

Hive 将在 HDFS 上创建分区对应的目录"/usr/hive_remote/warehouse/ygxxb_info/province=jiangsu/city=nanjing",同时会将本地"/root"目录下的 ygxxb.txt 文件复制到创建的分区目录下,如图 7.2.45 所示。

```
[root@master ~]# hadoop fs -ls  /usr/hive_remote/warehouse/ygxxb_info/province=jiangsu/city=nanjing
Found 1 items
-rwxr-xr-x   3 root supergroup        492 2024-04-28 18:03 /usr/hive_remote/warehouse/ygxxb_info/province=jiangsu/city=nanjing/ygxxb.txt
[root@master ~]#
```

图 7.2.45　在 HDFS 上创建分区对应的目录并复制文件到该目录下

7.2.5.2　外部分区表

外部表也可以使用分区,外部表可以自定义目录结构,所以外部分区表比管理分区表更加灵活。

采用如下命令在 Hive 中定义一个存储服务器日志信息的外部分区表:

```
hive (jscy)>  USE jscy;
hive (jscy)>  CREATE EXTERNAL TABLE IF NOT EXISTS log_msg(
id INT,
visit_time STRING,
ip_addr STRING,
api STRING,
up_flow INT,
down_flow INT)
PARTITIONED BY (year INT, month INT, day INT)
ROW FORMAT DELIMITED
FIELDS TERMINATED BY '\t' ;
```

运行结果如图 7.2.46 所示。

```
hive (default)> USE    jscy;
OK
Time taken: 0.079 seconds
hive (jscy)> CREATE EXTERNAL TABLE IF NOT EXISTS log_msg(
           > id int,
           > visit_time STRING,
           > ip_addr STRING,
           > api STRING,
           > up_flow int,
           > down_flow int)
           > PARTITIONED BY (year INT, month INT, day INT)
           > ROW FORMAT DELIMITED
           > FIELDS TERMINATED BY '\t' ;
OK
Time taken: 0.131 seconds
hive (jscy)>
```

图 7.2.46　创建外部表 log_msg

在创建表时没有指定表的存储路径,所以创建外部分区表之后,查询语句查不到任何数据,需要单独为外部表分区键指定值和存储位置,命令如下:

hive (jscy)>　ALTER TABLE log_msg ADD PARTITION(year=2024, month=4, day=28) LOCATION '/hadoop/test/log_msg/2024/4/28';

运行结果如图 7.2.47 所示。

```
hive (jscy)> ALTER TABLE log_msg ADD PARTITION(year=2024, month=4, day=28) LOCATION   '/hadoop/test/log_msg/2024/4/28';
OK
Time taken: 0.413 seconds
hive (jscy)>
```

图 7.2.47　修改外部表分区键指定值和存储位置

删除外部分区表和删除外部表一样,不会删除数据。
使用 SHOW PARTTIONS 命令也可以查看一个外部表的分区,命令如下:

hive (jscy)>　SHOW PARTITIONS log_msg;

运行结果如图 7.2.48 所示。

```
hive (jscy)> SHOW PARTITIONS log_msg;
OK
partition
year=2024/month=4/day=28
Time taken: 0.266 seconds, Fetched: 1 row(s)
hive (jscy)>
```

图 7.2.48　查看外部表 log_msg 分区

使用 DESC EXTENDED tablename 命令和 DESC FORMATTED tablename 命令可以查看外部分区表的分区信息。
用 DESC EXTENDED 查看分区信息,命令如下:

hive (jscy)>　DESC EXTENDED log_msg;

运行结果如图 7.2.49 所示。

```
hive (jscy)> SHOW PARTITIONS log_msg;
OK
partition
year=2024/month=4/day=28
Time taken: 0.266 seconds, Fetched: 1 row(s)
hive (jscy)> DESC EXTENDED log_msg;
OK
col_name            data_type           comment
id                  int
visit_time          string
ip_addr             string
api                 string
up_flow             int
down_flow           int
year                int
month               int
day                 int

# Partition Information
# col_name          data_type           comment

year                int
month               int
day                 int

Detailed Table Information    Table(tableName:log_msg, dbName:jscy, owner:root, createTime:1714299136, lastAccessTime:0, retention:0, sd
:StorageDescriptor(cols:[FieldSchema(name:id, type:int, comment:null), FieldSchema(name:visit_time, type:string, comment:null), FieldSchem
a(name:ip_addr, type:string, comment:null), FieldSchema(name:api, type:string, comment:null), FieldSchema(name:up_flow, type:int, comment:
null), FieldSchema(name:down_flow, type:int, comment:null), FieldSchema(name:year, type:int, comment:null), FieldSchema(name:month, type:i
nt, comment:null), FieldSchema(name:day, type:int, comment:null)], location:hdfs://master:9000/usr/hive_remote/warehouse/jscy.db/log_msg,
inputFormat:org.apache.hadoop.mapred.TextInputFormat, outputFormat:org.apache.hadoop.hive.ql.io.HiveIgnoreKeyTextOutputFormat, compressed:
false, numBuckets:-1, serdeInfo:SerDeInfo(name:null, serializationLib:org.apache.hadoop.hive.serde2.lazy.LazySimpleSerDe, parameters:{seri
alization.format=     , field.delim=
Time taken: 0.132 seconds, Fetched: 18 row(s)
hive (jscy)>
```

图 7.2.49　用 DESC EXTENDED 查看外部表分区

用 DESC FORMATTED 查看分区信息，命令如下：

```
hive (jscy)>  DESC FORMATTED log_msg;
```

运行结果如图 7.2.50 所示。

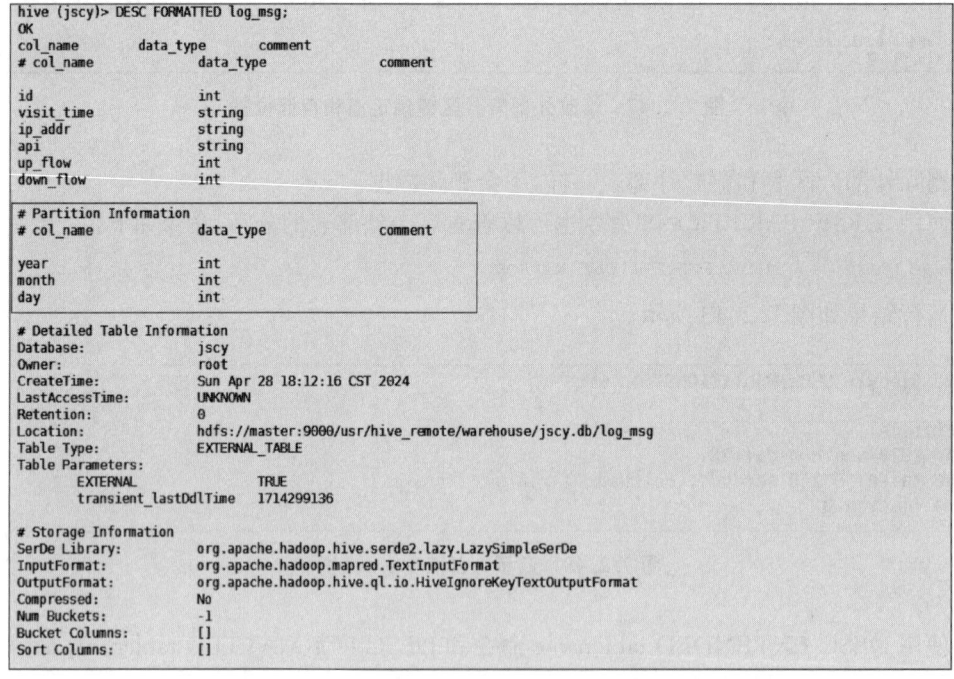

图 7.2.50　用 DESC FORMATTED 查看外部表分区

无论是管理表还是外部表，如果存在分区，加载数据时就需要加载进入指定的分区，下面通过一个实例来熟悉分区表的创建和载入过程。

在本地目录"/var/log/"下有许多系统日志文件，可以通过以下命令查看日志文件名，命令如下：

```
[root@master /]#  cd /var/log
[root@master log]#  ls
```

查询结果如图 7.2.51 所示。

```
[root@master log]# cd /
[root@master /]# cd /var/log
[root@master log]# ls
anaconda            boot.log-20240428  dmesg               maillog-20240428   secure-20240407   tallylog               vmware-network.8.log
audit               btmp               dmesg.old           messages           secure-20240418   tuned                  vmware-network.9.log
boot.log            btmp-20240407      firewalld           messages-20240407  secure-20240425   vmware-network.1.log   vmware-network.log
boot.log-20240311   chrony             grubby_prune_debug  messages-20240418  secure-20240428   vmware-network.2.log   vmware-vgauthsvc.log.0
boot.log-20240316   cron               lastlog             messages-20240425  spooler           vmware-network.3.log   vmware-vmsvc-root.1.log
boot.log-20240319   cron-20240407      maillog             messages-20240428  spooler-20240407  vmware-network.4.log   vmware-vmsvc-root.log
boot.log-20240321   cron-20240418      maillog-20240407    mysqld.log         spooler-20240418  vmware-network.5.log   vmware-vmtoolsd-root.log
boot.log-20240330   cron-20240425      maillog-20240418    rhsm               spooler-20240425  vmware-network.6.log   wtmp
boot.log-20240425   cron-20240428      maillog-20240425    secure             spooler-20240428  vmware-network.7.log   yum.log
[root@master log]#
```

图 7.2.51　查看本地日志文件

查看其中的 cron-20240428 文件内容，命令如下：

```
[root@master log]# cat cron-20240428
```

查询到 cron-20240428 文件部分内容结果如图 7.2.52 所示。

```
[root@master log]# cat cron-20240428
Apr 25 10:27:07 master run-parts(/etc/cron.daily)[2574]: finished man-db.cron
Apr 25 10:27:07 master anacron[2493]: Job `cron.daily' terminated
Apr 25 10:47:03 master anacron[2493]: Job `cron.weekly' started
Apr 25 10:47:03 master anacron[2493]: Job `cron.weekly' terminated
Apr 25 10:47:03 master anacron[2493]: Normal exit (2 jobs run)
Apr 25 11:01:01 master CROND[3108]: (root) CMD (run-parts /etc/cron.hourly)
Apr 25 11:01:01 master run-parts(/etc/cron.hourly)[3108]: starting 0anacron
Apr 25 11:01:01 master run-parts(/etc/cron.hourly)[3117]: finished 0anacron
Apr 25 12:01:01 master CROND[3792]: (root) CMD (run-parts /etc/cron.hourly)
Apr 25 12:01:01 master run-parts(/etc/cron.hourly)[3792]: starting 0anacron
Apr 25 12:01:01 master run-parts(/etc/cron.hourly)[3801]: finished 0anacron
Apr 25 13:01:01 master CROND[3839]: (root) CMD (run-parts /etc/cron.hourly)
Apr 25 13:01:01 master run-parts(/etc/cron.hourly)[3839]: starting 0anacron
Apr 25 13:01:01 master run-parts(/etc/cron.hourly)[3848]: finished 0anacron
Apr 25 14:01:01 master CROND[3885]: (root) CMD (run-parts /etc/cron.hourly)
Apr 25 14:01:01 master run-parts(/etc/cron.hourly)[3885]: starting 0anacron
Apr 25 14:01:01 master run-parts(/etc/cron.hourly)[3894]: finished 0anacron
Apr 25 15:01:01 master CROND[3931]: (root) CMD (run-parts /etc/cron.hourly)
Apr 25 15:01:01 master run-parts(/etc/cron.hourly)[3931]: starting 0anacron
Apr 25 15:01:01 master run-parts(/etc/cron.hourly)[3940]: finished 0anacron
Apr 25 16:01:01 master CROND[3977]: (root) CMD (run-parts /etc/cron.hourly)
Apr 25 16:01:01 master run-parts(/etc/cron.hourly)[3977]: starting 0anacron
Apr 25 16:01:01 master run-parts(/etc/cron.hourly)[3986]: finished 0anacron
Apr 25 17:01:02 master CROND[4027]: (root) CMD (run-parts /etc/cron.hourly)
Apr 25 17:01:02 master run-parts(/etc/cron.hourly)[4027]: starting 0anacron
Apr 25 17:01:02 master run-parts(/etc/cron.hourly)[4036]: finished 0anacron
Apr 25 18:01:01 master CROND[4313]: (root) CMD (run-parts /etc/cron.hourly)
Apr 25 18:01:01 master run-parts(/etc/cron.hourly)[4313]: starting 0anacron
Apr 25 18:01:01 master run-parts(/etc/cron.hourly)[4322]: finished 0anacron
Apr 25 19:01:01 master CROND[4360]: (root) CMD (run-parts /etc/cron.hourly)
Apr 25 19:01:01 master run-parts(/etc/cron.hourly)[4360]: starting 0anacron
Apr 25 19:01:01 master run-parts(/etc/cron.hourly)[4369]: finished 0anacron
Apr 25 20:01:01 master CROND[4405]: (root) CMD (run-parts /etc/cron.hourly)
Apr 25 20:01:01 master run-parts(/etc/cron.hourly)[4405]: starting 0anacron
Apr 25 20:01:01 master run-parts(/etc/cron.hourly)[4414]: finished 0anacron
Apr 25 21:01:01 master CROND[4452]: (root) CMD (run-parts /etc/cron.hourly)
Apr 25 21:01:01 master run-parts(/etc/cron.hourly)[4452]: starting 0anacron
```

图 7.2.52　cron-20240428 文件部分内容

现在创建一个数据表 log_msg_cron，将日志文件 cron-20240428 内容导入到表 log_msg_cron 中，命令序列如下：

```
[root@master log]#   hive
hive (default)>  USE jscy;
hive (jscy)>  CREATE EXTERNAL TABLE log_msg_cron(
mm      STRING  COMMENT  'month',
dy      INT     COMMENT  'day',
tm      STRING  COMMENT  'time',
ht      STRING COMMENT   'hostname',
run_pt  STRING COMMENT   'run parts'
)
PARTITIONED BY(year INT, month INT, day INT)
ROW FORMAT DELIMITED FIELDS TERMINATED BY  ' ';
hive (jscy)> ALTER TABLE log_msg_cron ADD PARTITION(year=2024, month=04, day=
28)
LOCATION  '/hadoop/test/1og_msg_cron/2024/04/28';
hive (jscy)> LOAD DATA LOCAL INPATH  '/var/log/cron-20240428'
INTO TABLE log_msg_cron PARTITION(year=2024,month=04, day=28);
```

运行结果如图 7.2.53 所示。

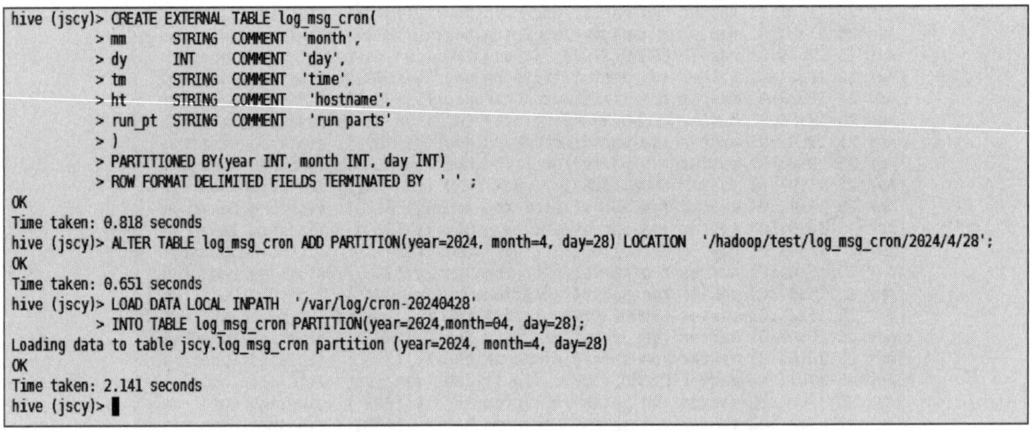

```
hive (jscy)> CREATE EXTERNAL TABLE log_msg_cron(
           > mm      STRING  COMMENT  'month',
           > dy      INT     COMMENT  'day',
           > tm      STRING  COMMENT  'time',
           > ht      STRING  COMMENT   'hostname',
           > run_pt  STRING  COMMENT   'run parts'
           > )
           > PARTITIONED BY(year INT, month INT, day INT)
           > ROW FORMAT DELIMITED FIELDS TERMINATED BY  ' ' ;
OK
Time taken: 0.818 seconds
hive (jscy)> ALTER TABLE log_msg_cron ADD PARTITION(year=2024, month=4, day=28) LOCATION  '/hadoop/test/log_msg_cron/2024/4/28';
OK
Time taken: 0.651 seconds
hive (jscy)> LOAD DATA LOCAL INPATH  '/var/log/cron-20240428'
           > INTO TABLE log_msg_cron PARTITION(year=2024,month=04, day=28);
Loading data to table jscy.log_msg_cron partition (year=2024, month=4, day=28)
OK
Time taken: 2.141 seconds
hive (jscy)>
```

图 7.2.53　创建分区表 log_msg_cron 并导入日志数据

查询 log_msg_cron 表数据，验证数据导入是否成功，命令如下：

```
hive (jscy)>  SELECT * FROM log_msg_cron;
```

运行结果如图 7.2.54 所示。

可见数据导入成功，查看 HDFS 上的文件夹，新建了"/hadoop/test/1og_msg_cron/2024/04/28"目录，该目录下有日志文件 cron-20240428，如图 7.2.55 所示。

```
hive (jscy)> SELECT * FROM log_msg_cron;
OK
log_msg_cron.mm  log_msg_cron.dy  log_msg_cron.tm  log_msg_cron.ht  log_msg_cron.run_pt        log_msg_cron.year  log_msg_cron.month  log_msg_cr
on.day
Apr    25    10:27:07    master    run-parts(/etc/cron.daily)[2574]:         2024    4    28
Apr    25    10:27:07    master    anacron[2493]:    2024    4    28
Apr    25    10:47:03    master    anacron[2493]:    2024    4    28
Apr    25    10:47:03    master    anacron[2493]:    2024    4    28
Apr    25    11:01:01    master    CROND[3108]:    2024    4    28
Apr    25    11:01:01    master    run-parts(/etc/cron.hourly)[3108]:    2024    4    28
Apr    25    11:01:01    master    run-parts(/etc/cron.hourly)[3117]:    2024    4    28
Apr    25    12:01:01    master    CROND[3792]:    2024    4    28
Apr    25    12:01:01    master    run-parts(/etc/cron.hourly)[3792]:    2024    4    28
Apr    25    12:01:01    master    run-parts(/etc/cron.hourly)[3801]:    2024    4    28
Apr    25    13:01:01    master    CROND[3839]:    2024    4    28
Apr    25    13:01:01    master    run-parts(/etc/cron.hourly)[3839]:    2024    4    28
Apr    25    13:01:01    master    run-parts(/etc/cron.hourly)[3848]:    2024    4    28
Apr    25    14:01:01    master    CROND[3885]:    2024    4    28
Apr    25    14:01:01    master    run-parts(/etc/cron.hourly)[3885]:    2024    4    28
Apr    25    14:01:01    master    run-parts(/etc/cron.hourly)[3894]:    2024    4    28
Apr    25    15:01:01    master    CROND[3931]:    2024    4    28
Apr    25    15:01:01    master    run-parts(/etc/cron.hourly)[3931]:    2024    4    28
Apr    25    15:01:01    master    run-parts(/etc/cron.hourly)[3940]:    2024    4    28
Apr    25    16:01:01    master    CROND[3977]:    2024    4    28
Apr    25    16:01:01    master    run-parts(/etc/cron.hourly)[3977]:    2024    4    28
Apr    25    16:01:01    master    run-parts(/etc/cron.hourly)[3986]:    2024    4    28
Apr    25    17:01:02    master    CROND[4027]:    2024    4    28
Apr    25    17:01:02    master    run-parts(/etc/cron.hourly)[4027]:    2024    4    28
Apr    25    17:01:02    master    run-parts(/etc/cron.hourly)[4036]:    2024    4    28
Apr    25    18:01:01    master    CROND[4313]:    2024    4    28
Apr    25    18:01:01    master    run-parts(/etc/cron.hourly)[4313]:    2024    4    28
Apr    25    18:01:01    master    run-parts(/etc/cron.hourly)[4322]:    2024    4    28
Apr    25    19:01:01    master    CROND[4360]:    2024    4    28
Apr    25    19:01:01    master    run-parts(/etc/cron.hourly)[4360]:    2024    4    28
Apr    25    19:01:01    master    run-parts(/etc/cron.hourly)[4369]:    2024    4    28
Apr    25    20:01:01    master    CROND[4405]:    2024    4    28
Apr    25    20:01:01    master    run-parts(/etc/cron.hourly)[4405]:    2024    4    28
Apr    25    20:01:01    master    run-parts(/etc/cron.hourly)[4414]:    2024    4    28
Apr    25    21:01:01    master    CROND[4452]:    2024    4    28
Apr    28    16:01:01    master    run-parts(/etc/cron.hourly)[2313]:    2024    4    28
Apr    28    16:01:02    master    anacron[2322]:    2024    4    28
Apr    28    16:01:02    master    run-parts(/etc/cron.hourly)[2324]:    2024    4    28
Apr    28    16:01:02    master    anacron[2322]:    2024    4    28
Apr    28    16:50:02    master    anacron[2322]:    2024    4    28
Apr    28    16:50:02    master    run-parts(/etc/cron.daily)[2702]:    2024    4    28
Apr    28    16:50:02    master    run-parts(/etc/cron.daily)[2714]:    2024    4    28
Apr    28    16:50:02    master    run-parts(/etc/cron.daily)[2702]:    2024    4    28
Time taken: 2.673 seconds, Fetched: 56 row(s)
hive (jscy)>
```

图 7.2.54　查询 log_msg_cron 表数据导入成功

```
[root@master log]# hadoop fs -ls /hadoop/test/log_msg_cron/2024/4/28
Found 1 items
-rwxr-xr-x   3 root supergroup       4219 2024-04-28 23:12 /hadoop/test/log_msg_cron/2024/4/28/cron-20240428
[root@master log]#
```

图 7.2.55　外部表分区目录和数据

7.2.6　删除表

用户可以使用如下语句删除表：

```
hive (jscy)> DROP TABLE ygxxb;
```

运行结果如图 7.2.56 所示。

```
hive (default)> use jscy;
OK
Time taken: 1.008 seconds
hive (jscy)> DROP TABLE ygxxb;
OK
Time taken: 2.285 seconds
hive (jscy)>
```

图 7.2.56　删除表 ygxxb

或者采用如下命令：

```
hive (jscy)> DROP TABLE IF EXISTS ygxxb;
```

该命令即使数据表不存在，也不会出现错误提示，运行结果如图 7.2.57 所示。

```
hive (jscy)> DROP TABLE IF EXISTS ygxxb;
OK
Time taken: 0.048 seconds
hive (jscy)>
```

图 7.2.57　如果表 ygxxb 存在就会被删除

7.2.7　修改表

用户可以通过 ALTER TABLE 语句修改表，这种操作会修改元数据，但不会修改数据。

7.2.7.1　修改表名称

将名称为 log_msg 的表重命名为 log_message，命令如下：

```
hive (jscy)> SHOW TABLES ;
hive (jscy)> ALTER TABLE log_msg RENAME TO log_message;
hive (jscy)> SHOW TABLES ;
```

运行结果如图 7.2.58 所示。

```
hive (jscy)> show tables;
OK
tab_name
log_msg
log_msg_cron
ygxxb2
ygxxb3
ygxxb_external
ygxxb_info
Time taken: 0.218 seconds, Fetched: 6 row(s)
hive (jscy)> ALTER TABLE log_msg RENAME TO log_message;
OK
Time taken: 0.406 seconds
hive (jscy)> show tables;
OK
tab_name
log_message
log_msg_cron
ygxxb2
ygxxb3
ygxxb_external
ygxxb_info
Time taken: 0.043 seconds, Fetched: 6 row(s)
hive (jscy)> [root@master log]#
```

图 7.2.58　将名称为 log_msg 的表重命名为 log_message

7.2.7.2　增加表分区

使用 ALTER TABLE tablename ADD PARTITION 语句为外部表增加一个新的分区，

命令如下:

```
hive (jscy)> ALTER TABLE  log_msg_cron ADD IF NOT EXISTS PARTITION (year=2024,month=4,day=29) LOCATION  '/hadoop/test/log_msg_cron/2024/04/29';
```

运行结果如图 7.2.59 所示。

```
hive (jscy)> ALTER TABLE  log_msg_cron ADD IF NOT EXISTS PARTITION (year=2024, month=4,day=29) LOCATION  '/hadoop/test/log_msg_c
ron/2024/04/29';
OK
Time taken: 2.532 seconds
hive (jscy)>
```

图 7.2.59 增加表分区

查看 log_msg_cron 表的分区信息,命令如下:

```
hive (jscy)> SHOW PARTITIONS log_msg_cron;
```

运行结果如图 7.2.60 所示。

```
hive (jscy)> SHOW PARTITIONS log_msg_cron;
OK
partition
year=2024/month=4/day=28
year=2024/month=4/day=29
Time taken: 0.252 seconds, Fetched: 2 row(s)
hive (jscy)>
```

图 7.2.60 查看表分区

从图 7.2.60 可以看到,log_msg_cron 表中多了一个"year = 2024/month = 4/day = 29"分区。

7.2.7.3 修改表分区

用户可以修改表的分区,命令如下:

```
hive (jscy)> ALTER TABLE  log_msg_cron PARTITION (year=2024, month=4,day=29) RENAME TO PARTITION (year=2024, month=4,day=27);
hive (jscy)> SHOW PARTITIONS log_msg_cron;
```

运行结果如图 7.2.61 所示。

```
hive (jscy)> ALTER TABLE  log_msg_cron PARTITION (year=2024, month=4,day=29) RENAME TO PARTITION (year=2024, month=4,day=27);
OK
Time taken: 1.217 seconds
hive (jscy)> SHOW PARTITIONS log_msg_cron;
OK
partition
year=2024/month=4/day=27
year=2024/month=4/day=28
Time taken: 0.216 seconds, Fetched: 2 row(s)
hive (jscy)>
```

图 7.2.61 修改并查看表分区

从图 7.2.61 可以看到,log_msg_cron 的分区 year = 2024/month = 4/day = 29 已被修改为 year = 2024/month = 4/day = 27 分区。

也可以对表的分区路径进行修改,命令如下:

ALTER TABLE log_msg_cron PARTITION (year=2024,month=4,day=27)
SET LOCATION '/hadoop/hive/log_msg_cron/2024/04/27';

运行结果如图 7.2.62 所示。

```
hive (jscy)> ALTER TABLE log_msg_cron  PARTITION (year=2024,month=4,day=27)
        > SET LOCATION '/hadoop/hive/log_msg_cron/2024/04/27';
OK
Time taken: 0.724 seconds
hive (jscy)>
```

图 7.2.62　修改分区路径

7.2.7.4　删除表分区

表分区也可以被删除,命令如下:

ALTER TABLE log_msg_cron DROP IF EXISTS PARTITION (year=2024,month=4,day=27);

运行结果如图 7.2.63 所示。

```
hive (jscy)> ALTER TABLE log_msg_cron DROP IF EXISTS  PARTITION (year=2024,month=4,day=27);
Dropped the partition year=2024/month=4/day=27
OK
Time taken: 1.454 seconds
```

图 7.2.63　删除表分区

再次查看 log_msg_cron 表的分区信息,命令如下:

hive (jscy)>　SHOW PARTITIONS log_msg;

运行结果如图 7.2.64 所示。

```
hive (jscy)> SHOW PARTITIONS log_msg_cron;
OK
partition
year=2024/month=4/day=28
Time taken: 0.574 seconds, Fetched: 1 row(s)
hive (jscy)>
```

图 7.2.64　再次查看表分区

从图 7.2.64 可以看到,year = 2024/month = 4/day = 27 分区已经被删除。

7.2.7.5　修改列信息

用户可以使用如下语句修改表中的列信息:

hive (jscy)>　ALTER TABLE log_msg_cron
CHANGE COLUMN ht host STRING COMMENT 'master'
AFTER run_pt;
hive (jscy)>　DESC log_msg_cron ;

运行结果如图 7.2.65 所示。

```
hive (jscy)> ALTER TABLE log_msg_cron
            > CHANGE COLUMN ht host STRING
            > COMMENT 'master'
            > AFTER  run_pt;
OK
Time taken: 0.478 seconds
hive (jscy)> DESC log_msg_cron ;
OK
col_name        data_type       comment
mm              string          month
dy              int             day
tm              string          time
run_pt          string          run parts
host            string          master
year            int
month           int
day             int

# Partition Information
# col_name      data_type       comment

year            int
month           int
day             int
Time taken: 0.165 seconds, Fetched: 15 row(s)
hive (jscy)>
```

图 7.2.65　修改列信息

上述语句的作用是将 log_msg_cron 中的 ht 字段修改为 host，修改注释为"master"，同时将 host 字段放到 run_pt 字段后面。用"DESC log_msg_cron；"命令查询修改后的表结构，由图 7.2.65 可见已经成功。

如果希望将 ht 字段移动到表中的第一个位置，则只需要将 AFTER 关键字修改为 FIRST。

修改列信息一般只会修改元数据信息，不会修改数据。如果对表中的字段进行了位置移动，则需要将数据匹配最新的表字段顺序。

7.2.7.6　增加列

用户可以使用如下语句在 log_msg_cron 表中添加字段：

```
hive (jscy)>  ALTER TABLE log_msg_cron ADD COLUMNS(
app_name STRING,
app_version STRING);
hive (jscy)>  DESC log_msg_cron ;
```

运行结果如图 7.2.66 所示。

从图 7.2.66 可以看到，log_msg_cron 表中增加了 app_name 和 app_version 两个列。如果新增的字段在表中的顺序有误，可以使用 ALTER TABLE tablename CHANGE COLUMN 语句修改表中字段的顺序。

```
hive (jscy)> ALTER TABLE log_msg_cron ADD COLUMNS(
            > app_name STRING,
            > app_version STRING);
OK
Time taken: 0.332 seconds
hive (jscy)> DESC log_msg_cron ;
OK
col_name            data_type           comment
mm                  string                          month
dy                  int                             day
tm                  string                          time
run_pt              string                          run parts
host                string                          master
app_name            string
app_version         string
year                int
month               int
day                 int

# Partition Information
# col_name          data_type                       comment

year                int
month               int
day                 int
Time taken: 0.109 seconds, Fetched: 17 row(s)
hive (jscy)> [root@master ~]#
```

图 7.2.66　增加列

7.2.7.7　删除或修改列

下面的语句将会移除 log_msg_cron 表中的所有表字段,并指定新的表字段:

```
hive (jscy)>  ALTER TABLE log_msg_cron REPLACE COLUMNS(
app_name STRING,
app_version STRING);
hive (jscy)>  DESC log_msg_cron;
```

运行结果如图 7.2.67 所示。

```
hive (jscy)> ALTER TABLE log_msg_cron REPLACE COLUMNS(
            > app_name STRING,
            > app_version STRING);
OK
Time taken: 0.866 seconds
hive (jscy)> DESC log_msg_cron;
OK
col_name            data_type           comment
app_name            string
app_version         string
year                int
month               int
day                 int

# Partition Information
# col_name          data_type                       comment

year                int
month               int
day                 int
Time taken: 0.21 seconds, Fetched: 12 row(s)
hive (jscy)>
```

图 7.2.67　删除原有列用新列代替

从"DESC log_msg_cron；"命令的运行结果可以看到，log_msg_cron 表中的表字段被移除并重新指定为 app_name 和 app_version 两个新字段。

7.2.7.8　修改表属性

用户可以通过 ALTER TABLE tablename　SET TBLPROPERTIES 语句修改表属性，命令如下：

> hive (jscy)＞ ALTER TABLE log_msg_cron SET TBLPROPERTIES('author'='suchang');

该命令修改表属性，将表的作者修改为 'suchang'。运行结果如图 7.2.68 所示。

```
hive (jscy)> ALTER TABLE log_msg_cron SET TBLPROPERTIES('author '='suchang');
OK
Time taken: 0.206 seconds
hive (jscy)>
```

图 7.2.68　修改表属性

 注意

|只能增加或修改表的属性，无法删除表的属性。|

7.2.7.9　修改存储属性

将 log_msg_cron 表的存储格式修改为 SEQUENCEFILE，命令如下：

> hive (jscy)＞ ALTER TABLE log_msg_cron PARTITION(year=2024,month=4,day=28)
> SET FILEFORMAT SEQUENCEFILE;

运行结果如图 7.2.69 所示。

```
hive (jscy)> ALTER TABLE log_msg_cron PARTITION(year=2024,month=4,day=28)
          > SET FILEFORMAT SEQUENCEFILE;
OK
Time taken: 0.69 seconds
hive (jscy)>
```

图 7.2.69　修改存储属性为 SEQUENCEFILE

也可以将 log_msg_cron 表的存储格式修改为 TEXTFILE，命令如下：

> hive (jscy)＞ ALTER TABLE log_msg_cron PARTITION(year=2024,month=4,day=28)
> SET FILEFORMAT TEXTFILE;

运行结果如图 7.2.70 所示。

```
hive (jscy)> ALTER TABLE  log_msg_cron PARTITION(year=2024,month=4,day=28) SET FILEFORMAT textfile;
OK
Time taken: 0.359 seconds
```

图 7.2.70　修改存储属性为 TEXTFILE

任务 7.3 Hive 数据操作

任务描述

本任务学习 Hive 数据操作命令,主要是为数据表添加数据,用户可以将本地或 HDFS 上的文件内容导入表,也可以通过单个语句或查询语句插入数据,运用在实际工作中,表现为将要进行分析的原始数据导入数据表中,为大数据分析作好数据准备。

关键步骤

(1) 向 Hive 表中导入数据。
(2) 通过查询语句插入数据。
(3) 通过单个语句创建并加载数据。
(4) 从 Hive 中导出数据。

本任务主要介绍在 Hive 数据库中如何实现数据的导入和导出。在 Hive 中创建了数据库和数据表后,用户只有将数据正确地导入 Hive 数据表,同时能够将数据正确地从 Hive 数据表导出,才能基于 Hive 分析存储在 HDFS 中的数据。

7.3.1 向 Hive 表中导入数据

Hive 支持向数据表中一次导入大量的数据。

7.3.1.1 向 Hive 表中导入数据的一般操作

以下通过一个具体案例来演示向 Hive 表中导入数据的一般操作。

【例 7-2】 江苏财源有限公司员工基本信息表数据如表 7.3.1 所示,将该基本信息表中的数据导入 Hive 表,下面来练习操作过程。

表 7.3.1 江苏财源有限公司员工基本信息表

职工编号	姓名	性别	部门	职务类别	基本工资(元)
001	王柏宇	男	办公室	公司经理	3 200.00
002	齐 敏	女	办公室	行政助理	2 500.00
003	李红梅	女	财务部	财务部经理	3 000.00
004	王向东	男	财务部	会计人员	2 000.00
005	陈艳丽	女	财务部	出纳	1 800.00
006	龚文娟	女	人事处	人事处处长	3 000.00
007	林大维	男	研发部	研发部经理	2 200.00
008	朱韩斌	男	研发部	研发人员	2 000.00

(续表)

职工编号	姓名	性别	部门	职务类别	基本工资(元)
009	赵齐伟	男	研发部	研发人员	2 000.00
010	张小英	女	研发部	研发人员	2 000.00
011	王伟亮	男	生产部	车间主任	2 800.00
012	孙松涛	男	生产部	生产工人	1 600.00
013	张金平	男	生产部	生产工人	1 600.00
014	耿小龙	男	生产部	生产工人	1 600.00
015	李杰民	男	生产部	生产工人	1 600.00
016	杜昱明	男	生产部	生产工人	1 600.00
017	陈祥俊	男	生产部	生产工人	1 600.00
018	王晓西	女	生产部	生产工人	1 600.00
019	任 可	女	销售部	销售部经理	2 100.00
020	潘 涛	男	销售部	销售人员	1 800.00
021	邹燕燕	女	销售部	销售人员	1 800.00
022	孙小凡	女	销售部	销售人员	1 800.00
023	赵文彬	男	销售部	供应部经理	2 100.00
024	邱秀丽	女	供应部	采购人员	1 800.00
025	王心萍	女	供应部	采购人员	1 800.00
026	宋 辉	男	供应部	采购人员	1 800.00
027	高 明	女	仓管部	仓管部经理	2 000.00
028	张瑞峰	男	仓管部	仓库管理人员	1 600.00
029	马一鸣	男	仓管部	仓库管理人员	1 600.00
030	崔 静	男	仓管部	仓库管理人员	1 600.00

在任务 7.2 中,我们已经将前 10 条数据放在一个文本文件/root/ygxxb.txt 中,现将 ygxxb.txt 改名为 ygxxb1.txt,再将表中第 11~20 行数据放在 ygxxb2.txt 中,第 21~30 行数据放在 ygxxb3.txt 中,另创建一个独立的目录单独存放这些数据,操作如下。

第 1 步:在本地"/home/hadoop"目录下再创建"data"子目录,将/root/ygxxb.txt 复制到该目录下,并改名为 ygxxb1.txt,命令如下:

```
[root@master ~]# mkdir /home/hadoop/data
[root@master ~]# cp /root/ygxxb.txt /home/hadoop/data/ygxxb1.txt
```

运行结果如图 7.3.1 所示。

```
[root@master ~]# mkdir /home/hadoop/data
[root@master ~]# cp /root/ygxxb.txt /home/hadoop/data/ygxxb1.txt
[root@master ~]#
```

图 7.3.1 创建子目录存放原始数据

第 2 步：在服务器 master 的"/home/hadoop/data"目录下创建 ygxxb2.txt 文件,将表 7.3.1 中第 11~20 行数据组织成文本文档,字段数据之间用","间隔,内容如下：

```
011,王伟亮,男,生产部,车间主任,2800.00
012,孙松涛,男,生产部,生产工人,1600.00
013,张金平,男,生产部,生产工人,1600.00
014,耿小龙,男,生产部,生产工人,1600.00
015,李杰民,男,生产部,生产工人,1600.00
016,杜昱明,男,生产部,生产工人,1600.00
017,陈祥俊,男,生产部,生产工人,1600.00
018,王晓西,女,生产部,生产工人,1600.00
019,任  可,女,销售部,销售部经理,2100.00
020,潘  涛,男,销售部,销售人员,1800.00
```

命令如下：

```
[root@master ~]# cd /home/hadoop/data
[root@master ~]# vim ygxxb2.txt
```

在"INSERT"模式下,将上述 11~20 行数据复制,再粘贴到 vim 编辑器,按 Esc 键,输入":wq"保存退出,运行结果如图 7.3.2 所示。

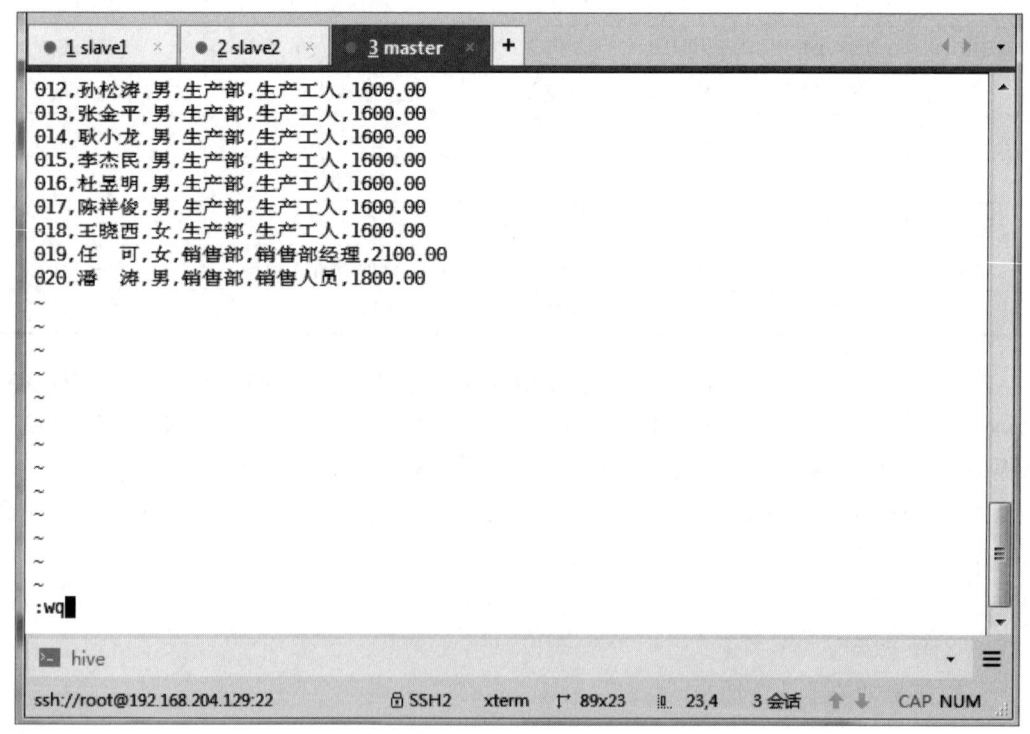

图 7.3.2　创建文本文件 ygxxb2.txt

第 3 步：在服务器 master 的"/home/hadoop/data"目录下创建 ygxxb3.txt 文件,将表 7.3.1 中第 21~30 行数据组织成文本文档,字段数据之间用","间隔,内容如下：

```
021,邹燕燕,女,销售部,销售人员,1800.00
022,孙小凡,女,销售部,销售人员,1800.00
023,赵文彬,男,销售部,供应部经理,2100.00
024,邱秀丽,女,供应部,采购人员,1800.00
025,王心萍,女,供应部,采购人员,1800.00
026,宋  辉,男,供应部,采购人员,1800.00
027,高  明,女,仓管部,仓管部经理,2000.00
028,张瑞峰,男,仓管部,仓库管理人员,1600.00
029,马一鸣,男,仓管部,仓库管理人员,1600.00
030,崔  静,男,仓管部,仓库管理人员,1600.00
```

命令如下：

```
[root@master ~]#  cd /home/hadoop/data
[root@master ~]#  vim ygxxb3.txt
```

在"INSERT"模式下，将上述第 21～30 行数据复制，再粘贴到 vim 编辑器，按 Esc 键，输入":wq"保存退出，运行结果如图 7.3.3 所示。

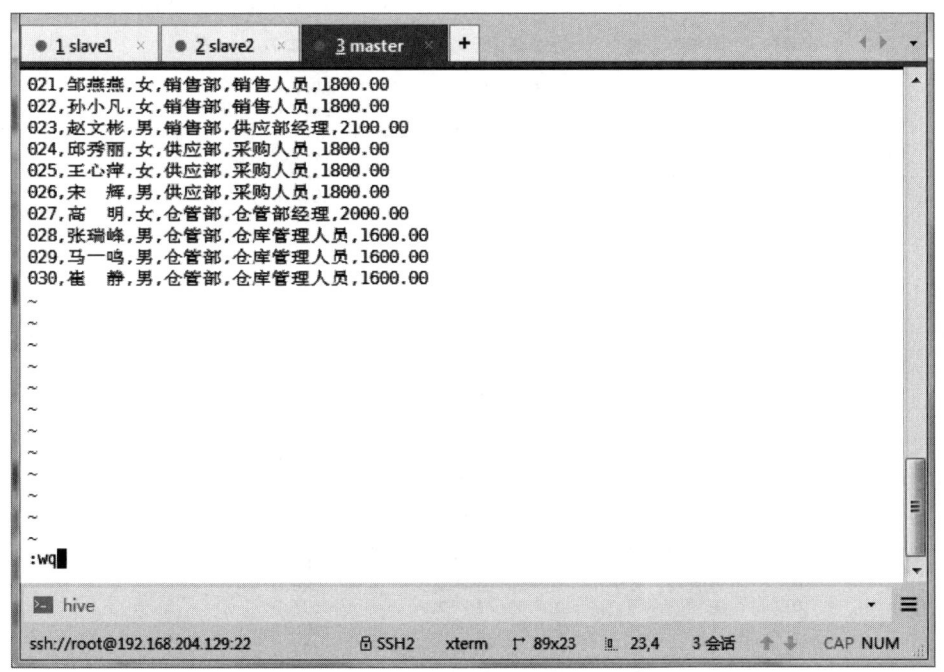

图 7.3.3 创建文本文件 ygxxb3.txt

在上一任务中，已创建了空表 ygxxb2，现向该表导入数据，可以使用如下语句：

```
[root@master ~]#  hive
[root@master ~]#  USE jscy;
hive (jscy)>         LOAD DATA LOCAL INPATH  '/home/hadoop/data'  INTO TABLE
ygxxb2;
```

运行结果如图 7.3.4 所示。

```
hive (default)> USE jscy;
OK
Time taken: 1.045 seconds
hive (jscy)> LOAD DATA LOCAL INPATH '/home/hadoop/data' INTO TABLE ygxxb2;
Loading data to table jscy.ygxxb2
OK
Time taken: 1.614 seconds
hive (jscy)>
```

图 7.3.4　向 Hive 表中导入数据

上述语句表示将本地目录"/home/hadoop/data"下的所有文件中的数据导入 ygxxb2 表中。用 SELECT 语句查询一下表 ygxxb2，命令如下：

hive (jscy)＞ SELECT ＊ FROM ygxxb2;

运行结果如图 7.3.5 所示。

```
hive (jscy)> SELECT * FROM ygxxb2;
OK
ygxxb2.zgbh    ygxxb2.xm    ygxxb2.xb    ygxxb2.bm    ygxx
gz
001    王柏宇    男    办公室    公司经理    3200.0
002    齐 敏    女    办公室    行政助理    2500.0
003    李红梅    女    财务部    财务部经理    3000.0
004    王向东    男    财务部    会计人员    2000.0
005    陈艳丽    女    财务部    出纳    1800.0
006    龚文娟    女    人事处    人事处处长    3000.0
007    林大维    男    研发部    研发部经理    2200.0
008    朱韩斌    男    研发部    研发人员    2000.0
009    赵齐伟    男    研发部    研发人员    2000.0
010    张小英    女    研发部    研发人员    2000.0
001    王柏宇    男    办公室    公司经理    3200.0
002    齐 敏    女    办公室    行政助理    2500.0
003    李红梅    女    财务部    财务部经理    3000.0
004    王向东    男    财务部    会计人员    2000.0
005    陈艳丽    女    财务部    出纳    1800.0
006    龚文娟    女    人事处    人事处处长    3000.0
007    林大维    男    研发部    研发部经理    2200.0
008    朱韩斌    男    研发部    研发人员    2000.0
009    赵齐伟    男    研发部    研发人员    2000.0
010    张小英    女    研发部    研发人员    2000.0
011    王伟亮    男    生产部    车间主任    2800.0
012    孙松涛    男    生产部    生产工人    1600.0
013    张金平    男    生产部    生产工人    1600.0
014    耿小龙    男    生产部    生产工人    1600.0
015    李杰民    男    生产部    生产工人    1600.0
016    杜昱明    男    生产部    生产工人    1600.0
017    陈祥俊    男    生产部    生产工人    1600.0
018    王晓西    女    生产部    生产工人    1600.0
019    任 可    女    销售部    销售部经理    2100.0
020    潘 涛    男    销售部    销售人员    1800.0
021    邹燕燕    女    销售部    销售人员    1800.0
022    孙小凡    女    销售部    销售人员    1800.0
023    赵文彬    男    销售部    供应部经理    2100.0
024    邱秀丽    女    供应部    采购人员    1800.0
025    王心萍    女    供应部    采购人员    1800.0
026    宋 辉    男    供应部    采购人员    1800.0
027    高 明    女    仓管部    仓管部经理    2000.0
028    张瑞峰    男    仓管部    仓库管理人员    1600.0
029    马一鸣    男    仓管部    仓库管理人员    1600.0
030    崔 静    男    仓管部    仓库管理人员    1600.0
Time taken: 2.338 seconds, Fetched: 40 row(s)
hive (jscy)>
```

图 7.3.5　数据导入成功

7.3.1.2 覆盖形式导入数据

如果需要覆盖 ygxxb2 表中的数据,需要加上 OVERWRITE 关键字,命令如下:

```
hive (jscy)> LOAD DATA LOCAL INPATH '/home/hadoop/data' OVERWRITE INTO TABLE ygxxb2;
```

运行结果如图 7.3.6 所示。

```
hive (jscy)> LOAD DATA LOCAL INPATH '/home/hadoop/data' OVERWRITE INTO TABLE ygxxb2;
Loading data to table jscy.ygxxb2
OK
Time taken: 1.103 seconds
hive (jscy)>
```

图 7.3.6　覆盖表中原有数据再导入指定数据

上述命令执行后,会清空 ygxxb2 表中原有的数据,然后将本地"/home/hadoop/data"目录下文件中的所有数据添加到 ygxxb2 表中。

7.3.1.3　将 HDFS 上的数据导入到 Hive 数据表

Hive 支持将 HDFS 上的数据导入到 HIVE 数据表中,此时需要去掉 LOCAL 关键字。

先进行数据准备,将本地"/home/hadoop/data"目录下所有文件上传到 HDFS 的"/usr/hadoop/data"目录下,命令如下:

```
[root@master]# hadoop fs -put /home/hadoop/data /usr/hadoop/
[root@master]# hadoop fs -ls /usr/hadoop/data
```

运行结果如图 7.3.7 所示。

```
[root@master data]# hadoop fs -put /home/hadoop/data /usr/hadoop/
[root@master data]# hadoop fs -ls /usr/hadoop/data
Found 3 items
-rw-r--r--   3 root supergroup        492 2024-04-29 13:28 /usr/hadoop/data/ygxxb1.txt
-rw-r--r--   3 root supergroup        491 2024-04-29 13:28 /usr/hadoop/data/ygxxb2.txt
-rw-r--r--   3 root supergroup        520 2024-04-29 13:28 /usr/hadoop/data/ygxxb3.txt
[root@master data]#
```

图 7.3.7　将本地数据上传到 HDFS

将 HDFS 上的"/usr/hadoop/data"目录下所有文件以覆盖方式导入 ygxxb2 中,去掉 LOCAL 关键字,加上"OVERWRITE",命令如下:

```
[root@master]# hive
hive (default)> use jscy;
hive (jscy)> LOAD DATA INPATH '/usr/hadoop/data' OVERWRITE INTO TABLE ygxxb2;
```

运行结果如图 7.3.8 所示。

```
hive (jscy)> LOAD DATA INPATH '/usr/hadoop/data' OVERWRITE INTO TABLE ygxxb2;
Loading data to table jscy.ygxxb2
OK
Time taken: 1.272 seconds
hive (jscy)>
```

图 7.3.8　将 HDFS 文件数据导入到 HIVE 数据表

7.3.1.4 导入数据到一个分区表

如果要导入数据的目标表是一个分区表,则导入数据时必须指定分区。以下用一个案例说明。

【例 7-3】 将本地的日志目录"/var/log/"下的两个文件 cron-20240425 和 cron-20240428(读者可以查询选择自己主机上的日志文件)上传到 HDFS,再导入 Hive 表中。

第 1 步:将文件上传到 HDFS 上,命令如下:

```
[root@master /]# hadoop fs -mkdir -p /usr/hadoop/log
[root@master /]# hadoop fs -put /var/log/cron-20240425 /usr/hadoop/log
[root@master /]# hadoop fs -put /var/log/cron-20240428 /usr/hadoop/log
[root@master /]# hadoop fs -ls /usr/hadoop/log
```

运行结果如图 7.3.9 所示。

```
[root@master /]# hadoop fs -mkdir -p /usr/hadoop/log
[root@master /]# hadoop fs -put /var/log/cron-20240425 /usr/hadoop/log
[root@master /]# hadoop fs -put /var/log/cron-20240428 /usr/hadoop/log
[root@master /]# hadoop fs -ls /usr/hadoop/log
Found 2 items
-rw-r--r--   2 root supergroup       3309 2024-04-30 10:59 /usr/hadoop/log/cron-20240425
-rw-r--r--   2 root supergroup       4219 2024-04-30 10:59 /usr/hadoop/log/cron-20240428
[root@master /]#
```

图 7.3.9 把本日志文件上传到 HDFS 上

第 2 步:重新创建 log_msg_cron 表。

任务 7.2 中已创建好 log_msg_cron 表,但表结构已被修改,此处先执行删除操作,再重新创建。启动 Hive,切换到 jscy 数据库,删除原来的 log_msg_cron 表,执行创建带分区的外部表 log_msg_cron,命令如下:

```
[root@master log]# hive
hive (default)> USE jscy;
hive (jscy)> DROP TABLE IF EXISTS log_msg_cron;
hive (jscy)> CREATE EXTERNAL TABLE log_msg_cron(
    mm      STRING  COMMENT  'month',
    dy      INT     COMMENT  'day',
    tm      STRING  COMMENT  'time',
    ht      STRING  COMMENT  'hostname',
    run_pt  STRING  COMMENT  'run parts'
    )
    PARTITIONED BY(year INT, month INT, day INT)
    ROW FORMAT DELIMITED FIELDS TERMINATED BY ' ';
```

运行结果如图 7.3.10 所示。

```
hive (default)> USE jscy;
OK
Time taken: 5.564 seconds
hive (jscy)> DROP TABLE IF EXISTS log_msg_cron;
OK
Time taken: 0.132 seconds
hive (jscy)> CREATE EXTERNAL TABLE log_msg_cron(
    > mm      STRING  COMMENT  'month',
    > dy      INT     COMMENT  'day',
    > tm      STRING  COMMENT  'time',
    > ht      STRING  COMMENT  'hostname',
    > run_pt  STRING  COMMENT  'run parts'
    > )
    > PARTITIONED BY(year INT, month INT, day INT)
    > ROW FORMAT DELIMITED FIELDS TERMINATED BY ' ';
OK
Time taken: 0.474 seconds
hive (jscy)>
```

图 7.3.10　外部分区表 log_msg_cron 创建成功

第 3 步：向分区表中导入数据。

先为分区表 log_msg_cron 增加一个分区，再向分区导入数据，命令如下：

```
hive (jscy)> ALTER TABLE log_msg_cron ADD PARTITION(year=2024, month=04, day=28)
LOCATION '/hadoop/test/log_msg_cron/2024/04/28';
hive (jscy)> LOAD DATA INPATH '/usr/hadoop/log/cron-20240428' INTO TABLE log_msg_cron PARTITION(year=2024,month=04, day=28);
```

运行结果如图 7.3.11 所示。

```
hive (jscy)> ALTER TABLE log_msg_cron ADD PARTITION(year=2024, month=04, day=28)
    > LOCATION '/hadoop/test/log_msg_cron/2024/04/28';
OK
Time taken: 0.67 seconds
hive (jscy)> LOAD DATA INPATH '/usr/hadoop/log/cron-20240428' INTO TABLE log_msg_cron PARTITION(year=2024,month=04, day=28);
Loading data to table jscy.log_msg_cron partition (year=2024, month=4, day=28)
OK
Time taken: 2.149 seconds
hive (jscy)>
```

图 7.3.11　指定分区向分区表中导入数据

注意

加上 LOCAL 关键字，Hive 会将本地文件上传一份到 HDFS 指定的目录下；如果不加 LOCAL 关键字，Hive 会将 HDFS 上的文件移动到指定的目录下。

7.3.2　通过查询语句插入数据

7.3.2.1　将查询表的查询结果插入到另一个表中

用户可以使用如下语句从 ygxxb2 表中查询数据并向 ygxxb 表中插入数据，命令如下：

```
hive (jscy)> INSERT OVERWRITE TABLE ygxxb SELECT * FROM ygxxb2;
```

运行结果如图 7.3.12 所示。

```
hive (jscy)> INSERT OVERWRITE TABLE ygxxb SELECT * FROM ygxxb2;
WARNING: Hive-on-MR is deprecated in Hive 2 and may not be available in the future versions. Consider using a different
ve 1.X releases.
Query ID = root_20240430101828_870354bd-5b77-4660-83c7-3fd3192051d5
Total jobs = 3
Launching Job 1 out of 3
Number of reduce tasks is set to 0 since there's no reduce operator
Starting Job = job_1714441198855_0001, Tracking URL = http://master:8088/proxy/application_1714441198855_0001/
Kill Command = /opt/hadoop-2.7.7/bin/hadoop job  -kill job_1714441198855_0001
Hadoop job information for Stage-1: number of mappers: 1; number of reducers: 0
2024-04-30 10:18:52,334 Stage-1 map = 0%,  reduce = 0%
2024-04-30 10:19:02,433 Stage-1 map = 100%,  reduce = 0%, Cumulative CPU 1.32 sec
MapReduce Total cumulative CPU time: 1 seconds 320 msec
Ended Job = job_1714441198855_0001
Stage-4 is selected by condition resolver.
Stage-3 is filtered out by condition resolver.
Stage-5 is filtered out by condition resolver.
Moving data to directory hdfs://master:9000/usr/hive_remote/warehouse/jscy.db/ygxxb/.hive-staging_hive_2024-04-30_10-18
-28_306_6856924330183828579-1/-ext-10000
Loading data to table jscy.ygxxb
MapReduce Jobs Launched:
Stage-Stage-1: Map: 1   Cumulative CPU: 1.32 sec   HDFS Read: 6071 HDFS Write: 1532 SUCCESS
Total MapReduce CPU Time Spent: 1 seconds 320 msec
OK
ygxxb2.zgbh      ygxxb2.xm       ygxxb2.xb       ygxxb2.bm       ygxxb2.zwlb     ygxxb2.jbgz
Time taken: 37.274 seconds
hive (jscy)>
```

图 7.3.12　通过查询语句插入数据

7.3.2.2　查询分区表的一个分区，将查询结果插入另一个表的分区中

用户向分区表中插入数据时必须指定分区，以下通过一个案例说明。

【例 7-4】　查询分区表 log_msg_cron 的分区 PARTITION(year = 2024, month = 4, day = 28)，并将查询到的数据插入 log_msg_cron2 的相应分区中。

第 1 步：创建 log_msg_cron2 分区表。用户可以通过复制 log_msg_cron 结构创建外部分区表 log_msg_cron2，命令如下：

```
hive (jscy)>  DROP TABLE IF EXISTS log_msg_cron2;
hive (jscy)>  CREATE EXTERNAL TABLE log_msg_cron2 LIKE log_msg_cron;
```

运行结果如图 7.3.13 所示。

```
hive (jscy)> DROP TABLE IF EXISTS log_msg_cron2;
OK
Time taken: 0.2 seconds
hive (jscy)>  CREATE EXTERNAL TABLE log_msg_cron2 LIKE log_msg_cron;
OK
Time taken: 0.311 seconds
hive (jscy)> ALTER TABLE log_msg_cron2 ADD PARTITION(year=2024, month=04, day=28)
            > LOCATION   '/hadoop/test/log_msg_cron2/2024/04/28';
OK
```

图 7.3.13　创建 log_msg_cron2 分区表

第 2 步：为外部表 log_msg_cron2 添加两个分区 PARTITION(year＝2024, month＝04, day＝25) 和 PARTITION(year = 2024, month = 4, day = 28)，用 HDFS 上的数据"/usr/hadoop/log/cron-20240425"导入第一个分区，用查询 log_msg_cron 分区的数据导入第二个分区，命令如下：

hive (jscy)> ALTER TABLE log_msg_cron2 ADD PARTITION(year=2024, month=04, day=25)
LOCATION '/hadoop/test/log_msg_cron2/2024/04/25';
hive (jscy)> ALTER TABLE log_msg_cron2 ADD PARTITION(year=2024, month=04, day=28)
LOCATION '/hadoop/test/log_msg_cron2/2024/04/28';
hive (jscy)> LOAD DATA INPATH '/usr/hadoop/log/cron-20240425' INTO TABLE log_msg_cron2 PARTITION(year=2024,month=04, day=25);
hive (jscy)> INSERT OVERWRITE TABLE log_msg_cron2 PARTITION(year=2024,month=4,day=28)
SELECT mm,dy,tm,ht,run_pt FROM log_msg_cron
WHERE year=2024 AND month=4 AND day=28;

运行结果如图 7.3.14 所示。

图 7.3.14　向分区表中插入数据指定分区

> 注意

此时的 OVERWRITE 关键字可以去掉。如果使用 OVERWRITE 关键字,则会替换原有数据表或分区中的内容;如果不使用 OVERWRITE 关键字,则只会在原有数据表或分区中追加数据。

7.3.2.3　一次性向数据表中的多个分区导入数据

Hive 支持一次性向数据表中的多个分区导入数据。复制分区表 log_msg_cron2 的结构创建表 log_msg_cron3,并给表 log_msg_cron3 添加两个分区 PARTITION(year=2024, month=04, day=25)和 PARTITION(year=2024, month=04, day=28),命令如下:

```
hive (jscy)> CREATE EXTERNAL TABLE log_msg_cron3 LIKE log_msg_cron2;
hive (jscy)> ALTER TABLE log_msg_cron3 ADD PARTITION(year=2024, month=04, day=25)
LOCATION  '/hadoop/test/log_msg_cron3/2024/04/25';
hive (jscy)> ALTER TABLE log_msg_cron3 ADD PARTITION(year=2024, month=04, day=28)
LOCATION  '/hadoop/test/log_msg_cron3/2024/04/28';
```

运行结果如图 7.3.15 所示。

```
hive (jscy)> CREATE EXTERNAL TABLE log_msg_cron3 LIKE log_msg_cron2;
OK
hive (jscy)>  ALTER TABLE log_msg_cron3 ADD PARTITION(year=2024, month=04, day=25)
            > LOCATION   '/hadoop/test/log_msg_cron3/2024/04/25';
OK
Time taken: 0.338 seconds
hive (jscy)> ALTER TABLE log_msg_cron3 ADD PARTITION(year=2024, month=04, day=28)
            > LOCATION   '/hadoop/test/log_msg_cron3/2024/04/28';
OK
Time taken: 0.253 seconds
hive (jscy)>
```

图 7.3.15 创建表 log_msg_cron3 和两个表分区

```
FROM log_msg_cron2
INSERT OVERWRITE TABLE log_msg_cron3   PARTITION(year=2024,month=04,day=25)
SELECT mm,dy,tm,ht,run_pt   WHERE year=2024 AND month=04   AND day=25
INSERT OVERWRITE TABLE log_msg_cron3   PARTITION(year=2024,month=04,day=28)
SELECT mm,dy,tm,ht,run_pt   WHERE year=2024 AND month=04 AND day=28;
```

运行结果如图 7.3.16 所示。

```
hive (jscy)> FROM log_msg_cron2
           > INSERT OVERWRITE TABLE log_msg_cron3  PARTITION(year=2024,month=04,day=25)
           > SELECT mm,dy,tm,ht,run_pt  WHERE year=2024 AND month=04  AND day=25
           > INSERT OVERWRITE TABLE log_msg_cron3  PARTITION(year=2024,month=04,day=28)
           > SELECT mm,dy,tm,ht,run_pt  WHERE year=2024 AND month=04 AND day=28;
WARNING: Hive-on-MR is deprecated in Hive 2 and may not be available in the future versions. Consider using a different
 execution engine (i.e. spark, tez) or using Hive 1.X releases.
Query ID = root_20240430134119_3880b768-8928-492a-a203-c32f9689cf6c
Total jobs = 5
Launching Job 1 out of 5
Number of reduce tasks is set to 0 since there's no reduce operator
Starting Job = job_1714441198855_0003, Tracking URL = http://master:8088/proxy/application_1714441198855_0003/
Kill Command = /opt/hadoop-2.7.7/bin/hadoop job  -kill job_1714441198855_0003
Hadoop job information for Stage-2: number of mappers: 1; number of reducers: 0
2024-04-30 13:42:00,349 Stage-2 map = 0%,  reduce = 0%
2024-04-30 13:42:06,363 Stage-2 map = 100%,  reduce = 0%, Cumulative CPU 2.26 sec
MapReduce Total cumulative CPU time: 2 seconds 260 msec
Ended Job = job_1714441198855_0003
Stage-5 is selected by condition resolver.
Stage-4 is filtered out by condition resolver.
Stage-6 is filtered out by condition resolver.
Stage-11 is selected by condition resolver.
Stage-10 is filtered out by condition resolver.
Stage-12 is filtered out by condition resolver.
Moving data to directory hdfs://master:9000/hadoop/test/log_msg_cron3/2024/04/25/.hive-staging_hive_2024-04-30_13-41-19
_745_2090939846432456576-1/-ext-10000
Moving data to directory hdfs://master:9000/hadoop/test/log_msg_cron3/2024/04/28/.hive-staging_hive_2024-04-30_13-41-19
_745_2090939846432456576-1/-ext-10002
Loading data to table jscy.log_msg_cron3 partition (year=2024, month=4, day=25)
Loading data to table jscy.log_msg_cron3 partition (year=2024, month=4, day=28)
MapReduce Jobs Launched:
Stage-Stage-2: Map: 1   Cumulative CPU: 2.26 sec   HDFS Read: 12670 HDFS Write: 5039 SUCCESS
Total MapReduce CPU Time Spent: 2 seconds 260 msec
OK
mm      dy      tm      ht      run_pt
Time taken: 52.454 seconds
hive (jscy)>
```

图 7.3.16 一次性向数据表中的多个分区导入数据

上述语句可以实现一次查询，将符合条件的数据插入 log_msg_cron3 表的指定分区中，需要注意的是，必须将 FROM 语句写在前面。

7.3.3 通过单个语句创建并加载数据

Hive 支持在一个语句中创建表并向表中加载数据，命令如下：

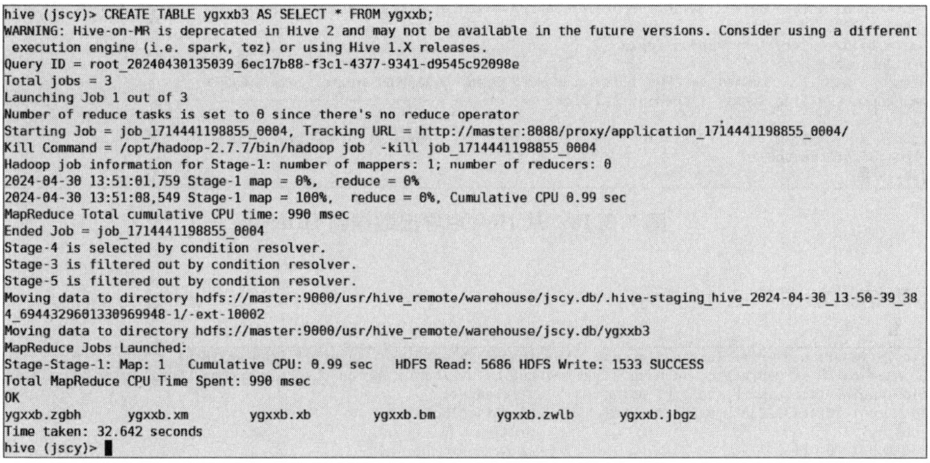

```
hive (jscy)> CREATE TABLE ygxxb3 AS SELECT * FROM ygxxb;
```

运行结果如图 7.3.17 所示。

图 7.3.17 通过单个语句创建并加载数据

7.3.4 从 Hive 中导出数据

7.3.4.1 从 Hive 中导出数据到 HDFS

Hive 支持数据导出，需要使用 DIRECTORY 关键字。将 Hive 中的数据导出到 HDFS，命令如下：

```
[root@master]# hdfs dfs -mkdir -p /usr/hadoop/ygxxb
[root@master]# hive
hive (default)> USE jscy;
hive (jscy)> INSERT OVERWRITE DIRECTORY '/usr/hadoop/ygxxb' SELECT * FROM ygxxb;
```

运行结果如图 7.3.18 所示。

7.3.4.2 将 Hive 中的数据导出到本地

用户也可将 Hive 中的数据导出到本地，需要在本地目录前加上 LOCAL 关键字，命令如下：

```
[root@master]# mkdir -p /home/hadoop/hive/ygxxb
[root@master]# hive
hive (default)> USE jscy;
hive (jscy)> INSERT OVERWRITE LOCAL DIRECTORY '/home/hadoop/hive/ygxxb'
             SELECT * FROM ygxxb;
```

```
hive (jscy)> insert overwrite directory '/usr/hadoop/ygxxb' select * from ygxxb;
WARNING: Hive-on-MR is deprecated in Hive 2 and may not be available in the future versions. Consider using a different
execution engine (i.e. spark, tez) or using Hive 1.X releases.
Query ID = root_20240430222159_1710e3c5-5972-4cf6-97a7-01c5c45d93cd
Total jobs = 3
Launching Job 1 out of 3
Number of reduce tasks is set to 0 since there's no reduce operator
Starting Job = job_1714486305503_0001, Tracking URL = http://master:8088/proxy/application_1714486305503_0001/
Kill Command = /opt/hadoop-2.7.7/bin/hadoop job  -kill job_1714486305503_0001
Hadoop job information for Stage-1: number of mappers: 1; number of reducers: 0
2024-04-30 22:22:23,199 Stage-1 map = 0%,  reduce = 0%
2024-04-30 22:22:31,365 Stage-1 map = 100%,  reduce = 0%, Cumulative CPU 1.73 sec
MapReduce Total cumulative CPU time: 1 seconds 730 msec
Ended Job = job_1714486305503_0001
Stage-3 is selected by condition resolver.
Stage-2 is filtered out by condition resolver.
Stage-4 is filtered out by condition resolver.
Moving data to directory hdfs://master:9000/usr/hadoop/ygxxb/.hive-staging_hive_2024-04-30_22-21-59_440_867285667950708
2981-1/-ext-10000
Moving data to directory /usr/hadoop/ygxxb
MapReduce Jobs Launched:
Stage-Stage-1: Map: 1   Cumulative CPU: 1.73 sec   HDFS Read: 5666 HDFS Write: 1464 SUCCESS
Total MapReduce CPU Time Spent: 1 seconds 730 msec
OK
ygxxb.zgbh         ygxxb.xm         ygxxb.xb         ygxxb.bm         ygxxb.zwlb         ygxxb.jbgz
Time taken: 34.658 seconds
hive (jscy)>
```

图 7.3.18　从 Hive 中导出数据到 HDFS

运行结果如图 7.3.19 所示。

```
hive (jscy)> insert overwrite local directory '/home/hadoop/hive/ygxxb' select * from ygxxb;
WARNING: Hive-on-MR is deprecated in Hive 2 and may not be available in the future versions. Consider using a different
execution engine (i.e. spark, tez) or using Hive 1.X releases.
Query ID = root_20240430223655_ba0db70f-25aa-4d66-8996-d6f4ea18c4ae
Total jobs = 1
Launching Job 1 out of 1
Number of reduce tasks is set to 0 since there's no reduce operator
Starting Job = job_1714486305503_0002, Tracking URL = http://master:8088/proxy/application_1714486305503_0002/
Kill Command = /opt/hadoop-2.7.7/bin/hadoop job  -kill job_1714486305503_0002
Hadoop job information for Stage-1: number of mappers: 1; number of reducers: 0
2024-04-30 22:37:25,394 Stage-1 map = 0%,  reduce = 0%
2024-04-30 22:37:31,346 Stage-1 map = 100%,  reduce = 0%, Cumulative CPU 1.71 sec
MapReduce Total cumulative CPU time: 1 seconds 710 msec
Ended Job = job_1714486305503_0002
Moving data to local directory /home/hadoop/hive/ygxxb
MapReduce Jobs Launched:
Stage-Stage-1: Map: 1   Cumulative CPU: 1.71 sec   HDFS Read: 5716 HDFS Write: 1464 SUCCESS
Total MapReduce CPU Time Spent: 1 seconds 710 msec
OK
ygxxb.zgbh         ygxxb.xm         ygxxb.xb         ygxxb.bm         ygxxb.zwlb         ygxxb.jbgz
Time taken: 38.383 seconds
hive (jscy)>
```

图 7.3.19　从 Hive 中导出数据到本地

如果 Hive 表中的数据满足用户需要的数据格式,可以直接复制文件以达到导出数据的目的。例如,导出数据到 HDFS,命令如下:

```
[root@master /]# hdfs dfs -mkdir -p /home/hadoop
[root@master /]# hdfs dfs -cp /usr/hive_remote/warehouse/jscy.db/ygxxb /home/hadoop/
[root@master /]# hdfs dfs -ls /home/hadoop/
```

运行结果如图 7.3.20 所示。

用户可以使用如下命令直接将数据导出到本地:

```
[root@master /]# hadoop fs -get /usr/hive_remote/warehouse/jscy.db/ygxxb /home/hadoop/hive/
[root@master /]# ls /home/hadoop/hive/
```

```
[root@master /]# hdfs dfs  -ls  /home/hadoop/
Found 3 items
drwxr-xr-x   - root supergroup          0 2024-04-30 22:36 /home/hadoop/hive
drwxr-xr-x   - root supergroup          0 2024-05-08 23:49 /home/hadoop/loan
drwxr-xr-x   - root supergroup          0 2024-04-30 22:46 /home/hadoop/ygxxb
[root@master /]#
```

图 7.3.20　直接复制 Hive 表到 HDFS

运行结果如图 7.3.21 所示。

```
[root@master hadoop-2.7.7]# hadoop fs -get /usr/hive_remote/warehouse/jscy.db/ygxxb  /home/hadoop/hive/
[root@master hadoop-2.7.7]# ls /home/hadoop/hive
ygxxb
[root@master hadoop-2.7.7]#
```

图 7.3.21　直接复制 Hive 表到本地

任务 7.4　Hive 数据查询

任务描述

本任务学习 Hive 数据查询命令，即 SELECT 查询语句的灵活运用，并介绍该命令的各种子句、子查询、连接和合并等操作，这些是大数据分析的重要命令，用大数据技术进行数据分析主要体现在用 Hive 数据查询命令实现大数据分析。

关键步骤

(1) 掌握 SELECT 查询语句的使用。
(2) 掌握 WHERE 条件语句的使用。
(3) 掌握 GROUP BY 语句的使用。
(4) 掌握 HAVING 语句的使用。
(5) 掌握 JOIN 语句的使用。
(6) 掌握 ORDER BY 和 SORT BY 语句的使用。
(7) 掌握类型转换命令的使用。
(8) 掌握 UNION ALL 语句的使用。

7.4.1　SELECT 查询语句

Hive 中的数据查询基本与 MySQL 相同，这里就系统地介绍 Hive 中的数据查询功能。SELECT 查询语句比较简单，SELECT 后面跟要查询的字段，命令如下：

```
hive (jscy)>   SELECT zgbh, xm, xb FROM ygxxb;
```

运行结果如图 7.4.1 所示。

```
hive (jscy)> SELECT zgbh, xm, xb FROM ygxxb;
OK
zgbh    xm      xb
001     王柏宇   男
002     齐  敏   女
003     李红梅   女
004     王向东   男
005     陈艳丽   女
006     龚文娟   女
007     林大维   男
008     朱韩斌   男
009     赵齐伟   男
010     张小英   女
011     王伟亮   男
012     孙松涛   男
013     张金平   男
014     耿小龙   男
015     李杰民   男
016     杜昱明   男
017     陈祥俊   男
018     王晓西   女
019     任  可   女
020     潘  涛   男
021     邹燕燕   女
022     孙小凡   女
023     赵文彬   男
024     邱秀丽   女
025     王心萍   女
026     宋  辉   男
027     高  明   女
028     张瑞峰   男
029     马一鸣   男
030     崔  静   男
Time taken: 3.651 seconds, Fetched: 30 row(s)
hive (jscy)>
```

图 7.4.1　SELECT 查询语句的使用

7.4.2　WHERE 条件语句

WHERE 条件语句主要是对查询进行条件限制，命令如下：

```
hive (jscy)>  SELECT  *  FROM ygxxb  WHERE zgbh='023';
```

运行结果如图 7.4.2 所示。

```
hive (jscy)> SELECT * FROM ygxxb  WHERE zgbh='023';
OK
ygxxb.zgbh     ygxxb.xm       ygxxb.xb      ygxxb.bm        ygxxb.zwlb      ygxxb.jbgz
023            赵文彬          男            销售部          供应部经理       2100.0
Time taken: 0.936 seconds, Fetched: 1 row(s)
hive (jscy)>
```

图 7.4.2　WHERE 条件语句的使用

WHERE 条件语句常用的操作符如表 7.4.1 所示。

表 7.4.1　WHERE 条件语句常用的操作符

操作符	支持的数据类型	说明
A = B	基本数据类型	如果 A 等于 B,则返回 true,否则返回 false
A<=>B	基本数据类型	如果 A 和 B 都为 NULL,则返回 true,其他情况和 A=B 相同
A<>B,A!=B	基本数据类型	如果 A 或者 B 为 NULL,则返回 NULL;如果 A 不等于 B 返回 true,否则返回 false
A<B	基本数据类型	如果 A 或者 B 为 NULL,则返回 NULL;如果 A 小于 B 返回 true,否则返回 false
A<=B	基本数据类型	如果 A 或者 B 为 NULL,则返回 NULL;如果 A 小于或者等于 B 返回 true,否则返回 false
A>B	基本数据类型	如果 A 或者 B 为 NULL,则返回 NULL;如果 A 大于 B 返回 true,否则返回 false
A>=B	基本数据类型	如果 A 或者 B 为 NULL,则返回 NULL;如果 A 大于或者等于 B 返回 true,否则返回 false
A IS NULL	所有数据类型	如果 A 为 NULL 返回 true,否则返回 false
A IS NOT NULL	所有数据类型	如果 A 不为 NULL 返回 true,否则返回 false
A BETWEEN B AND C	基本数据类型	如果 A、B、C 任一为 NULL,则返回 NULL;如果 A 大于或等于 B 并且 A 小于或等于 C,返回 true,否则返回 false
A NOT BETWEEN B AND C	基本数据类型	如果 A、B、C 任一为 NULL,则返回 NULL;如果小于 B 或者 A 大于 C,则返回 tue,否则返回 false
A LIKE B	STRING 类型	如果 A 模糊匹配 B,则返回 true,否则返回 false
A NOT LIKE B	STRING 类型	如果 A 不模糊匹配 B,则返回 true,否则返回 false
A RLIKE B,A REGEXP B	STRING 类型	B 是一个正则表达式;如果 A 匹配正则表达式,返回 true,否则返回 false

7.4.3　GROUP BY 语句

GROUP BY 语句主要是对查询的数据进行分组,通常会和聚合函数一起使用,命令如下:

```
hive (jscy)> SELECT bm,avg(jbgz) FROM ygxxb GROUP BY bm;
```

运行结果如图 7.4.3 所示。

```
hive (jscy)> SELECT bm,avg(jbgz) FROM ygxxb GROUP BY bm;
WARNING: Hive-on-MR is deprecated in Hive 2 and may not be available in the future versions. Consider using a different
    execution engine (i.e. spark, tez) or using Hive 1.X releases.
Query ID = root_20240430232612_459f9193-3a90-4e8a-adb4-cf5dc3486cc6
Total jobs = 1
Launching Job 1 out of 1
Number of reduce tasks not specified. Estimated from input data size: 1
In order to change the average load for a reducer (in bytes):
  set hive.exec.reducers.bytes.per.reducer=<number>
In order to limit the maximum number of reducers:
  set hive.exec.reducers.max=<number>
In order to set a constant number of reducers:
  set mapreduce.job.reduces=<number>
Starting Job = job_1714486305503_0003, Tracking URL = http://master:8088/proxy/application_1714486305503_0003/
Kill Command = /opt/hadoop-2.7.7/bin/hadoop job  -kill job_1714486305503_0003
Hadoop job information for Stage-1: number of mappers: 1; number of reducers: 1
2024-04-30 23:26:51,246 Stage-1 map = 0%,  reduce = 0%
2024-04-30 23:26:57,878 Stage-1 map = 100%,  reduce = 0%, Cumulative CPU 2.39 sec
2024-04-30 23:27:16,836 Stage-1 map = 100%,  reduce = 100%, Cumulative CPU 6.18 sec
MapReduce Total cumulative CPU time: 6 seconds 180 msec
Ended Job = job_1714486305503_0003
MapReduce Jobs Launched:
Stage-Stage-1: Map: 1  Reduce: 1   Cumulative CPU: 6.18 sec   HDFS Read: 10876 HDFS Write: 403 SUCCESS
Total MapReduce CPU Time Spent: 6 seconds 180 msec
OK
bm      _c1
人事处   3000.0
仓管部   1700.0
供应部   1800.0
办公室   2850.0
生产部   1750.0
研发部   2050.0
财务部   2266.6666666666665
销售部   1920.0
Time taken: 68.301 seconds, Fetched: 8 row(s)
hive (jscy)>
```

图 7.4.3　GROUP BY 语句的使用

7.4.4　HAVING 语句

HAVING 语句主要用来对 GROUP BY 语句的结果进行条件限制,命令如下:

```
hive (jscy)>  SELECT bm,avg(jbgz) FROM  ygxxb  GROUP BY bm HAVING avg(jbgz)>2000;
```

运行结果如图 7.4.4 所示。

```
hive (jscy)> SELECT bm,avg(jbgz) FROM ygxxb GROUP BY bm HAVING avg(jbgz)>2000;
WARNING: Hive-on-MR is deprecated in Hive 2 and may not be available in the future versions. Consider using a different
    execution engine (i.e. spark, tez) or using Hive 1.X releases.
Query ID = root_20240430233032_741d0298-0db1-4101-b79d-29c64202f108
Total jobs = 1
Launching Job 1 out of 1
Number of reduce tasks not specified. Estimated from input data size: 1
In order to change the average load for a reducer (in bytes):
  set hive.exec.reducers.bytes.per.reducer=<number>
In order to limit the maximum number of reducers:
  set hive.exec.reducers.max=<number>
In order to set a constant number of reducers:
  set mapreduce.job.reduces=<number>
Starting Job = job_1714486305503_0004, Tracking URL = http://master:8088/proxy/application_1714486305503_0004/
Kill Command = /opt/hadoop-2.7.7/bin/hadoop job  -kill job_1714486305503_0004
Hadoop job information for Stage-1: number of mappers: 1; number of reducers: 1
2024-04-30 23:30:48,799 Stage-1 map = 0%,  reduce = 0%
2024-04-30 23:31:03,488 Stage-1 map = 100%,  reduce = 0%, Cumulative CPU 3.22 sec
2024-04-30 23:31:18,963 Stage-1 map = 100%,  reduce = 100%, Cumulative CPU 6.11 sec
MapReduce Total cumulative CPU time: 6 seconds 110 msec
Ended Job = job_1714486305503_0004
MapReduce Jobs Launched:
Stage-Stage-1: Map: 1  Reduce: 1   Cumulative CPU: 6.11 sec   HDFS Read: 11322 HDFS Write: 251 SUCCESS
Total MapReduce CPU Time Spent: 6 seconds 110 msec
OK
bm      _c1
人事处   3000.0
办公室   2850.0
研发部   2050.0
财务部   2266.6666666666665
Time taken: 47.953 seconds, Fetched: 4 row(s)
hive (jscy)>
```

图 7.4.4　HAVING 语句的使用

7.4.5 JOIN 语句

JOIN 语句可实现将两个表或多个表横向连接,连接方式有 INNER JOIN、LEFT OUTER JOIN、RIGHT OUTER JOIN、FULL OUTER JOIN、LEFT SEMI JOIN、笛卡尔积 JOIN、map-side JOIN、多表 JOIN 等多种形式。下面通过一个具体案例分别介绍几种 JOIN 语句的使用方法。

【例 7-5】 仍以江苏财源公司员工基本信息表为例,为便于阅读,这里将表 7.3.1 江苏财源公司员工基本信息表重新整理为表 7.4.2,岗位工资标准如表 7.4.3 所示,奖金标准如表 7.4.4 所示,下面练习连接操作。

表 7.4.2 江苏财源公司员工基本信息表

职工编号	姓名	性别	部门	职务类别	基本工资(元)
001	王柏宇	男	办公室	公司经理	3 200.00
002	齐 敏	女	办公室	行政助理	2 500.00
003	李红梅	女	财务部	部门经理	3 000.00
004	王向东	男	财务部	会计人员	2 000.00
005	陈艳丽	女	财务部	出纳	1 800.00
006	林大维	男	研发部	部门经理	2 200.00
007	朱韩斌	男	研发部	研发人员	2 000.00
008	张小英	女	研发部	研发人员	2 000.00
009	王伟亮	男	生产部	车间主任	2 800.00
010	孙松涛	男	生产部	生产工人	1 600.00
010	张金平	男	生产部	生产工人	1 600.00
012	任 可	女	销售部	部门经理	2 100.00
013	潘 涛	男	销售部	销售人员	1 800.00
014	邱秀丽	女	供应部	采购人员	1 800.00
015	王心萍	女	供应部	采购人员	1 800.00
016	高 明	女	仓管部	部门经理	2 000.00
017	张瑞峰	男	仓管部	仓管人员	1 600.00

表 7.4.3 岗位工资标准

职务类别	岗位工资(元)	职务类别	岗位工资(元)
公司经理	2 000.00	研发人员	1 200.00
行政助理	1 600.00	生产工人	1 100.00
部门经理	1 600.00	销售人员	1 200.00
会计人员	1 200.00	采购人员	1 200.00
出纳	1 200.00	仓管人员	1 200.00

表 7.4.4　奖金标准

部门	奖金(元)	部门	奖金(元)
办公室	800.00	销售部	650.00
财务部	700.00	供应部	650.00
研发部	700.00	仓管部	650.00
生产部	700.00		

（1）对表 7.4.2 至表 7.4.4 创建本地的 3 个文本文件，即员工信息表 ygxxb_j.txt、岗位工资标准 gwgzbz.txt、奖金标准 jjbz.txt，存放在"/home/hadoop/data"目录下。各字段数据之间以","间隔，数据格式如下：

员工信息表 ygxxb_j.txt 数据：

```
001,王柏宇,男,办公室,公司经理,3200.00
002,齐  敏,女,办公室,行政助理,2500.00
003,李红梅,女,财务部,部门经理,3000.00
004,王向东,男,财务部,会计人员,2000.00
005,陈艳丽,女,财务部,出纳,1800.00
006,林大维,男,研发部,部门经理,2200.00
007,朱韩斌,男,研发部,研发人员,2000.00
008,张小英,女,研发部,研发人员,2000.00
009,王伟亮,男,生产部,车间主任,2800.00
010,孙松涛,男,生产部,生产工人,1600.00
011,张金平,男,生产部,生产工人,1600.00
012,任  可,女,销售部,部门经理,2100.00
013,潘  涛,男,销售部,销售人员,1800.00
014,邱秀丽,女,供应部,采购人员,1800.00
015,王心萍,女,供应部,采购人员,1800.00
016,高  明,女,仓管部,部门经理,2000.00
017,张瑞峰,男,仓管部,仓管人员,1600.00
```

岗位工资标准 gwgzbz.txt 数据：

```
公司经理,2000.00
行政助理,1600.00
部门经理,1600.00
会计人员,1200.00,
出纳,1200.00
研发人员,1200.00
生产工人,1100.00
销售人员,1200.00
采购人员,1200.00
```

奖金标准 jjbz.txt 数据：

办公室,800.00
财务部,700.00
研发部,700.00
生产部,700.00
销售部,650.00
供应部,650.00
仓管部,650.00

（2）将本地目录切换到"/home/hadoop/data"，用 vim 创建文件，命令如下：

```
[root@master /]# cd /home/hadoop/data
[root@master data]# vi ygxxb_j.txt
[root@master data]# vi gwgzbz.txt
[root@master data]# vi jjbz.txt
```

运行结果分别如图 7.4.5、图 7.4.6、图 7.4.7 所示。

图 7.4.5　创建员工信息 ygxxb_j.txt

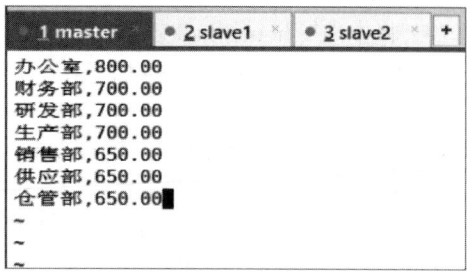

图 7.4.6　创建岗位工资标准 gwgzbz.txt　　　图 7.4.7　创建奖金标准 jjbz.txt

（3）启动 Hive，分别创建员工信息表 ygxxb_j、岗位工资标准表 gwgzbz、奖金标准表

jjbz，命令如下：

```
[root@master /]# hive
hive (default)> USE jscy;
hive (jscy)> CREATE TABLE IF NOT EXISTS ygxxb_j (
zgbh STRING COMMENT '职工编号',
xm STRING COMMENT '姓名',
xb STRING COMMENT '性别',
bm STRING COMMENT '部门',
zwlb STRING COMMENT '职务类别',
jbgz FLOAT COMMENT '基本工资'
)
ROW FORMAT DELIMITED
FIELDS TERMINATED BY ','
LINES TERMINATED BY '\n'
STORED AS TEXTFILE ;

hive (jscy)> CREATE TABLE IF NOT EXISTS gwgzbz (
zwlb STRING COMMENT '职务类别',
gwgz FLOAT COMMENT '岗位工资'
)
ROW FORMAT DELIMITED
FIELDS TERMINATED BY ','
LINES TERMINATED BY '\n'
STORED AS TEXTFILE ;

hive (jscy)> CREATE TABLE IF NOT EXISTS jjbz (
bm STRING COMMENT '部门',
jj FLOAT COMMENT '奖金'
)
ROW FORMAT DELIMITED
FIELDS TERMINATED BY ','
LINES TERMINATED BY '\n'
STORED AS TEXTFILE ;
```

运行结果如图7.4.8所示。

（4）将本地"/home/hadoop/data"目录下的ygxxb_j.txt、gwgzbz.txt和jjbz.txt数据分别导入到3个Hive表中。命令如下：

```
hive (jscy)>  LOAD DATA LOCAL INPATH '/home/hadoop/data/ygxxb_j.txt' INTO TABLE ygxxb_j;
hive (jscy)>  LOAD DATA LOCAL INPATH '/home/hadoop/data/gwgzbz.txt' INTO TABLE gwgzbz;
hive (jscy)>  LOAD DATA LOCAL INPATH '/home/hadoop/data/jjbz.txt' INTO TABLE  jjbz;
```

运行结果如图7.4.9所示。

```
hive (jscy)>  CREATE TABLE IF NOT EXISTS ygxxb_j (
            > zgbh STRING COMMENT '职工编号',
            > xm STRING COMMENT '姓名',
            > xb STRING COMMENT '性别',
            > bm STRING COMMENT '部门',
            > zwlb STRING COMMENT '职务类别',
            > jbgz FLOAT COMMENT '基本工资'
            > )
            > ROW FORMAT  DELIMITED
            > FIELDS TERMINATED BY  ','
            > LINES TERMINATED BY  '\n'
            > STORED AS TEXTFILE ;
OK
Time taken: 0.851 seconds
hive (jscy)> CREATE TABLE IF NOT EXISTS  gwgzbz (
            > zwlb STRING COMMENT '职务类别',
            > gwgz FLOAT COMMENT '岗位工资'
            > )
            > ROW FORMAT  DELIMITED
            > FIELDS TERMINATED BY  ','
            > LINES TERMINATED BY  '\n'
            > STORED AS TEXTFILE ;
OK
Time taken: 0.107 seconds
hive (jscy)> CREATE TABLE IF NOT EXISTS  jjbz (
            > bm STRING COMMENT '部门',
            > jj FLOAT COMMENT '奖金'
            > )
            > ROW FORMAT  DELIMITED
            > FIELDS TERMINATED BY  ','
            > LINES TERMINATED BY  '\n'
            > STORED AS TEXTFILE ;
OK
Time taken: 0.146 seconds
hive (jscy)>
```

图 7.4.8 创建三个 Hive 表

```
hive (jscy)> LOAD DATA LOCAL INPATH '/home/hadoop/data/ygxxb_j.txt' INTO TABLE  ygxxb_j;
Loading data to table jscy.ygxxb_j
OK
Time taken: 2.01 seconds
hive (jscy)> LOAD DATA LOCAL INPATH  '/home/hadoop/data/gwgzbz.txt' INTO TABLE  gwgzbz;
Loading data to table jscy.gwgzbz
OK
Time taken: 0.83 seconds
hive (jscy)> LOAD DATA LOCAL INPATH  '/home/hadoop/data/jjbz.txt' INTO TABLE  jjbz;
Loading data to table jscy.jjbz
OK
Time taken: 0.646 seconds
hive (jscy)>
```

图 7.4.9 从本地导入数据到三个 Hive 表

(5) 查询 3 个 Hive 表的数据,看是否导入成功,命令如下:

```
hive (jscy)>  SELECT * FROM  ygxxb_j;
hive (jscy)>  SELECT * FROM  gwgzbz;
hive (jscy)>  SELECT * FROM  jjbz;
```

运行结果如图 7.4.10、图 7.4.11 所示。

```
hive (jscy)> select * from ygxxb_j;
OK
ygxxb_j.zgbh    ygxxb_j.xm    ygxxb_j.xb    ygxxb_j.bm    ygxxb_j.zwlb    ygxxb_j.jbgz
001    王柏宇    男    办公室    公司经理    3200.0
002    齐敏     女    办公室    行政助理    2500.0
003    李红梅    女    财务部    部门经理    3000.0
004    王向东    男    财务部    会计人员    2000.0
005    陈艳丽    女    财务部    出纳    1800.0
006    林大维    男    研发部    部门经理    2200.0
007    朱韩斌    男    研发部    研发人员    2000.0
008    张小英    女    研发部    研发人员    2000.0
009    王伟亮    男    生产部    车间主任    2800.0
010    孙松涛    男    生产部    生产工人    1600.0
011    张金平    男    生产部    生产工人    1600.0
012    任可     女    销售部    部门经理    2100.0
013    潘涛     男    销售部    销售人员    1800.0
014    邱秀丽    女    供应部    采购人员    1800.0
015    王心萍    女    供应部    采购人员    1800.0
016    高明     女    仓管部    部门经理    2000.0
017    张瑞峰    男    仓管部    仓管人员    1600.0
Time taken: 1.975 seconds, Fetched: 17 row(s)
```

图 7.4.10 ygxxb_j 表数据导入成功

```
hive (jscy)> select * from gwgzbz;
OK
gwgzbz.zwlb    gwgzbz.gwgz
公司经理    2000.0
行政助理    1600.0
部门经理    1600.0
会计人员    1200.0
出纳    1200.0
研发人员    1200.0
生产工人    1100.0
销售人员    1200.0
采购人员    1200.0
Time taken: 0.174 seconds, Fetched: 9 row(s)
hive (jscy)> select * from jjbz;
OK
jjbz.bm    jjbz.jj
办公室    800.0
财务部    700.0
研发部    700.0
生产部    700.0
销售部    650.0
供应部    650.0
仓管部    650.0
Time taken: 0.153 seconds, Fetched: 7 row(s)
hive (jscy)>
```

图 7.4.11 gwgzbz 表和 jjbz 表数据导入成功

7.4.5.1 INNER JOIN 语句

在 INNER JOIN 语句中,只有进行连接的两个表中都存在与连接条件相匹配的数据时才会被显示在结果数据中。根据[例 7-5],将 ygxxb_j 表和 gwgzbz 表按 zwlb 相等的条件进行连接。命令如下:

```
hive (jscy)>  SELECT y.*, g.zwlb,g.gwgz FROM ygxxb_j  y  INNER JOIN gwgzbz   g
              ON y.zwlb = g.zwlb ;
```

运行结果如图 7.4.12 所示。

```
MapReduce Jobs Launched:
Stage-Stage-3: Map: 1   Cumulative CPU: 2.64 sec   HDFS Read: 8002 HDFS Write: 1922 SUCCESS
Total MapReduce CPU Time Spent: 2 seconds 640 msec
OK
y.zgbh   y.xm   y.xb   y.bm    y.zwlb   y.jbgz   g.zwlb    g.gwgz
001      王柏宇  男     办公室   公司经理  3200.0   公司经理   2000.0
002      齐 敏  女     办公室   行政助理  2500.0   行政助理   1600.0
003      李红梅  女     财务部   部门经理  3000.0   部门经理   1600.0
004      王向东  男     财务部   会计人员  2000.0   会计人员   1200.0
005      陈艳丽  女     财务部   出纳 1800.0  出纳     1200.0
006      林大维  男     研发部   部门经理  2200.0   部门经理   1600.0
007      朱韩斌  男     研发部   研发人员  2000.0   研发人员   1200.0
008      张小英  女     研发部   研发人员  2000.0   研发人员   1200.0
010      孙松涛  男     生产部   生产工人  1600.0   生产工人   1100.0
011      张金平  男     生产部   生产工人  1600.0   生产工人   1100.0
012      任 可  女     销售部   部门经理  2100.0   部门经理   1600.0
013      潘 涛  男     销售部   销售人员  1800.0   销售人员   1200.0
014      邱秀丽  女     供应部   采购人员  1800.0   采购人员   1200.0
015      王心萍  女     供应部   采购人员  1800.0   采购人员   1200.0
016      高 明  女     仓管部   部门经理  2000.0   部门经理   1600.0
Time taken: 79.789 seconds, Fetched: 15 row(s)
```

图 7.4.12 INNER JOIN 执行成功

7.4.5.2 LEFT OUTER JOIN 语句

LEFT OUTER JOIN 语句表示左外连接,左外连接查询数据会包含左表中的全部记录,而右表中不符合条件的结果将以 NULL 的形式出现。

重新创建一个表 ygxxb_j2,内容是 ygxxb_j 表的第 2~10 条记录,命令如下：

```
hive (jscy)> CREATE TABLE IF NOT EXISTS ygxxb_j2 AS
             SELECT * FROM ygxxb_j  WHERE zgbh>=002 AND  zgbh<=010;
hive (jscy)> SELECT * FROM ygxxb_j2;
```

运行结果如图 7.4.13 所示。

```
hive (jscy)> CREATE TABLE IF NOT EXISTS ygxxb_j2 AS SELECT * FROM ygxxb_j WHERE zgbh>=002 AND  zgbh<=010;
WARNING: Hive-on-MR is deprecated in Hive 2 and may not be available in the future versions. Consider using a different
  execution engine (i.e. spark, tez) or using Hive 1.X releases.
Query ID = root_20240501135437_88706d7b-4648-457b-9473-cd1a7f97d17e
Total jobs = 3
Launching Job 1 out of 3
Number of reduce tasks is set to 0 since there's no reduce operator
Starting Job = job_1714486305503_0006, Tracking URL = http://master:8088/proxy/application_1714486305503_0006/
Kill Command = /opt/hadoop-2.7.7/bin/hadoop job  -kill job_1714486305503_0006
Hadoop job information for Stage-1: number of mappers: 1; number of reducers: 0
2024-05-01 13:55:10,771 Stage-1 map = 0%,  reduce = 0%
2024-05-01 13:55:20,519 Stage-1 map = 100%,  reduce = 0%, Cumulative CPU 2.17 sec
MapReduce Total cumulative CPU time: 2 seconds 170 msec
Ended Job = job_1714486305503_0006
Stage-4 is selected by condition resolver.
Stage-3 is filtered out by condition resolver.
Stage-5 is filtered out by condition resolver.
Moving data to directory hdfs://master:9000/usr/hive_remote/warehouse/jscy.db/.hive-staging_hive_2024-05-01_13-54-37_88
1_5892142841791716861-1/-ext-10002
Moving data to directory hdfs://master:9000/usr/hive_remote/warehouse/jscy.db/ygxxb_j2
MapReduce Jobs Launched:
Stage-Stage-1: Map: 1   Cumulative CPU: 2.17 sec   HDFS Read: 5758 HDFS Write: 495 SUCCESS
Total MapReduce CPU Time Spent: 2 seconds 170 msec
OK
ygxxb_j.zgbh   ygxxb_j.xm   ygxxb_j.xb   ygxxb_j.bm   ygxxb_j.zwlb   ygxxb_j.jbgz
Time taken: 47.036 seconds
hive (jscy)> SELECT * FROM ygxxb_j2;
OK
ygxxb_j2.zgbh   ygxxb_j2.xm   ygxxb_j2.xb   ygxxb_j2.bm   ygxxb_j2.zwlb   ygxxb_j2.jbgz
002    齐 敏   女    办公室   行政助理   2500.0
003    李红梅   女    财务部   部门经理   3000.0
004    王向东   男    财务部   会计人员   2000.0
005    陈艳丽   女    财务部   出纳 1800.0
006    林大维   男    研发部   部门经理   2200.0
007    朱韩斌   男    研发部   研发人员   2000.0
008    张小英   女    研发部   研发人员   2000.0
009    王伟亮   男    生产部   车间主任   2800.0
010    孙松涛   男    生产部   生产工人   1600.0
Time taken: 0.331 seconds, Fetched: 9 row(s)
```

图 7.4.13 创建一个表 ygxxb_j2

左表 ygxxb_j，右表 ygxxb_j2，现在用 LEFT OUTER JOIN 语句创建左外连接，命令如下：

```
SELECT y1.zgbh, y1.xm, y2.xm FROM ygxxb_j y1  LEFT OUTER JOIN ygxxb_j2
y2  ON y1.zgbh= y2.zgbh;
```

运行结果如图 7.4.14 所示。

```
MapReduce Jobs Launched:
Stage-Stage-3: Map: 1   Cumulative CPU: 1.85 sec   HDFS Read: 7235 HDFS Write: 857 SUCCESS
Total MapReduce CPU Time Spent: 1 seconds 850 msec
OK
y1.zgbh  y1.xm    y2.xm
001      王柏宇    NULL
002      齐 敏    齐 敏
003      李红梅    李红梅
004      王向东    王向东
005      陈艳丽    陈艳丽
006      林大维    林大维
007      朱韩斌    朱韩斌
008      张小英    张小英
009      王伟亮    王伟亮
010      孙松涛    孙松涛
011      张金平    NULL
012      任 可    NULL
013      潘 涛    NULL
014      邱秀丽    NULL
015      王心萍    NULL
016      高 明    NULL
017      张瑞峰    NULL
Time taken: 72.83 seconds, Fetched: 17 row(s)
hive (jscy)>
```

图 7.4.14　LEFT OUTER JOIN 语句执行结果

由图 7.4.14 可见，查询结果中包含左表中的全部记录，而右表中不符合条件的结果以 NULL 的形式出现。

7.4.5.3　RIGHT OUTER JOIN 语句

RIGHT OUTER JOIN 表示右外连接，右外连接查询数据会包含右表中的全部记录，而左表中不符合条件的结果将以 NULL 的形式出现，命令如下：

```
SELECT y1.zgbh, y1.xm, y2.xm FROM ygxxb_j y1  RIGHT OUTER JOIN ygxxb_j2
y2  ON y1.zgbh= y2.zgbh;
```

运行结果如图 7.4.15 所示。

7.4.5.4　FULL OUTER JOIN 语句

FULL OUTER JOIN 语句表示全外连接，结果数据会包含左表和右表的全部数据，不符合条件的用 NULL 表示，命令如下：

```
SELECT y1.zgbh, y1.xm, y2.xm FROM ygxxb_j y1 FULL OUTER JOIN ygxxb_j2
y2  ON y1.zgbh= y2.zgbh;
```

运行结果如图 7.4.16 所示。

```
2024-05-01 14:12:18    End of local task; Time Taken: 5.672 sec.
Execution completed successfully
MapredLocal task succeeded
Launching Job 1 out of 1
Number of reduce tasks is set to 0 since there's no reduce operator
Starting Job = job_1714486305503_0008, Tracking URL = http://master:8088/proxy/application_1714486305503_0008/
Kill Command = /opt/hadoop-2.7.7/bin/hadoop job  -kill job_1714486305503_0008
Hadoop job information for Stage-3: number of mappers: 1; number of reducers: 0
2024-05-01 14:12:44,761 Stage-3 map = 0%,  reduce = 0%
2024-05-01 14:13:04,908 Stage-3 map = 100%,  reduce = 0%, Cumulative CPU 3.26 sec
MapReduce Total cumulative CPU time: 3 seconds 260 msec
Ended Job = job_1714486305503_0008
MapReduce Jobs Launched:
Stage-Stage-3: Map: 1   Cumulative CPU: 3.26 sec   HDFS Read: 6844 HDFS Write: 565 SUCCESS
Total MapReduce CPU Time Spent: 3 seconds 260 msec
OK
y1.zgbh  y1.xm    y2.xm
002      齐  敏   齐  敏
003      李红梅    李红梅
004      王向东    王向东
005      陈艳丽    陈艳丽
006      林大维    林大维
007      朱韩斌    朱韩斌
008      张小英    张小英
009      王伟亮    王伟亮
010      孙松涛    孙松涛
Time taken: 83.03 seconds, Fetched: 9 row(s)
hive (jscy)>
```

图 7.4.15 RIGHT OUTER JOIN 语句执行结果

```
2024-05-01 14:16:18,265 Stage-1 map = 0%,  reduce = 0%
2024-05-01 14:16:41,326 Stage-1 map = 100%,  reduce = 0%, Cumulative CPU 7.74 sec
2024-05-01 14:16:52,777 Stage-1 map = 100%,  reduce = 100%, Cumulative CPU 9.86 sec
MapReduce Total cumulative CPU time: 9 seconds 860 msec
Ended Job = job_1714486305503_0009
MapReduce Jobs Launched:
Stage-Stage-1: Map: 2  Reduce: 1   Cumulative CPU: 9.86 sec   HDFS Read: 16710 HDFS Write: 857 SUCCESS
Total MapReduce CPU Time Spent: 9 seconds 860 msec
OK
y1.zgbh  y1.xm    y2.xm
001      王柏宇    NULL
002      齐  敏   齐  敏
003      李红梅    李红梅
004      王向东    王向东
005      陈艳丽    陈艳丽
006      林大维    林大维
007      朱韩斌    朱韩斌
008      张小英    张小英
009      王伟亮    王伟亮
010      孙松涛    孙松涛
011      张金平    NULL
012      任  可   NULL
013      潘  涛   NULL
014      邱秀丽    NULL
015      王心萍    NULL
016      高  明   NULL
017      张瑞峰    NULL
Time taken: 53.001 seconds, Fetched: 17 row(s)
hive (jscy)>
```

图 7.4.16 FULL OUTER JOIN 语句执行结果

7.4.5.5 LEFT SEMI JOIN 语句

LEFT SEMI JOIN 语句表示左半连接,其结果数据对应右表满足 ON 语句中的条件的左表中的数据,命令如下:

```
SELECT y1.zgbh,y1.xm  FROM ygxxb_j  y1  LEFT SEMI JOIN ygxxb_j2 y2
    ON y1.zgbh = y2.zgbh;
```

运行结果如图 7.4.17 所示。

图 7.4.17　LEFT SEMI JOIN 语句执行结果

注意

在 LEFT SEMI JOIN 语句中，SELECT 和 WHERE 子句不能引用右表中的字段。

7.4.5.6　笛卡尔积 JOIN 语句

笛卡尔积 JOIN 语句表示左表的每一行分别与右表的所有行连接，JOIN 结果表的总行数是左表行数乘以右表行数，命令如下：

```
SELECT  *  FROM  ygxxb_j  y1 JOIN  ygxxb_j2 y2;
```

注意

如果将 HIVE 的属性 hive.mapred.mode 设置为 strict，则会阻止执行笛卡尔积查询。

当左表和右表分别只有一行时，用笛卡尔积查询可以实现重要的数据分析，如对于会计报表的分析，从同一张表中取不同字段的值进行运算，可以用多个子查询，再将各子查询用笛卡尔积 JOIN 语句后进行运算，该使用将在任务 9.1 中展示。

7.4.5.7　map-side JOIN 语句

map-side JOIN 语句会在 Map 阶段将小表读到内存中，直接在 Map 端进行连接，这种连接需要在查询语句中显式说明，命令如下：

```
SELECT / * + MAPJOIN(y2) * / y1.zgbh, y2.zgbh,y2.jbgz FROM ygxxb_j y1
    JOIN ygxxb_j2 y2   ON y1.zgbh = y2.zgbh;
```

运行结果如图 7.4.18 所示。

由图 7.4.18 可见，运行结果中出现"Stage-3 map = 100%，reduce = 0%，Cumulative CPU 1.89 sec"信息，说明本次查询只在 Map 端执行。

```
2024-05-01 14:51:13      End of local task; Time Taken: 4.774 sec.
Execution completed successfully
MapredLocal task succeeded
Launching Job 1 out of 1
Number of reduce tasks is set to 0 since there's no reduce operator
Starting Job = job_1714486305503_0013, Tracking URL = http://master:8088/proxy/application_1714486305503_0013/
Kill Command = /opt/hadoop-2.7.7/bin/hadoop job  -kill job_1714486305503_0013
Hadoop job information for Stage-3: number of mappers: 1; number of reducers: 0
2024-05-01 14:51:36,046 Stage-3 map = 0%,  reduce = 0%
2024-05-01 14:51:44,998 Stage-3 map = 100%,  reduce = 0%, Cumulative CPU 1.89 sec
MapReduce Total cumulative CPU time: 1 seconds 890 msec
Ended Job = job_1714486305503_0013
MapReduce Jobs Launched:
Stage-Stage-3: Map: 1   Cumulative CPU: 1.89 sec   HDFS Read: 7310 HDFS Write: 330 SUCCESS
Total MapReduce CPU Time Spent: 1 seconds 890 msec
OK
y1.zgbh  y2.zgbh  y2.jbgz
002      002      2500.0
003      003      3000.0
004      004      2000.0
005      005      1800.0
006      006      2200.0
007      007      2000.0
008      008      2000.0
009      009      2800.0
010      010      1600.0
Time taken: 58.225 seconds, Fetched: 9 row(s)
hive (jscy)>
```

图 7.4.18　map-side JOIN 语句执行结果

可以通过设置 Hive 的属性 hive.auto.convert.join = true 自动开启 map-side JOIN；也可以设置 Hive 的属性 hive.mapjoin.smalltable.filesize 定义表的大小，默认为 25 000 000B。

7.4.5.8　多表 JOIN 语句

Hive 支持多张表进行连接，命令如下：

```
SELECT *
FROM ygxxb_j y
JOIN gwgzbz g   ON y.zwlb  = g.zwlb
JOIN jjbz   j   ON y.bm = j.bm;
```

运行结果如图 7.4.19 所示。

```
MapReduce Jobs Launched:
Stage-Stage-5: Map: 1   Cumulative CPU: 1.92 sec   HDFS Read: 9871 HDFS Write: 2331 SUCCESS
Total MapReduce CPU Time Spent: 1 seconds 920 msec
OK
y.zgbh  y.xm    y.xb  y.bm    y.zwlb    y.jbgz   g.zwlb    g.gwgz   j.bm     j.jj
001     王柏宇   男    办公室   公司经理           3200.0   公司经理   2000.0   办公室   800.0
002     齐 敏    女    办公室   行政助理           2500.0   行政助理   1600.0   办公室   800.0
003     李红梅   女    财务部   部门经理           3000.0   部门经理   1600.0   财务部   700.0
004     王向东   男    财务部   会计人员           2000.0   会计人员   1200.0   财务部   700.0
005     陈艳丽   女    财务部   出纳      1800.0   出纳       1200.0   财务部   700.0
006     林大维   男    研发部   部门经理           2200.0   部门经理   1600.0   研发部   700.0
007     朱韩斌   男    研发部   研发人员           2000.0   研发人员   1200.0   研发部   700.0
008     张小英   女    研发部   研发人员           2000.0   研发人员   1200.0   研发部   700.0
010     孙松涛   男    生产部   生产工人           1600.0   生产工人   1100.0   生产部   700.0
011     张金平   男    生产部   生产工人           1600.0   生产工人   1100.0   生产部   700.0
012     任 可    女    销售部   部门经理           2100.0   部门经理   1600.0   销售部   650.0
013     潘 涛    男    销售部   销售人员           1800.0   销售人员   1200.0   销售部   650.0
014     邱秀丽   女    供应部   采购人员           1800.0   采购人员   1200.0   供应部   650.0
015     王心萍   女    供应部   采购人员           1800.0   采购人员   1200.0   供应部   650.0
016     高 明    女    仓管部   部门经理           2000.0   部门经理   1600.0   仓管部   650.0
Time taken: 48.338 seconds, Fetched: 15 row(s)
hive (jscy)>
```

图 7.4.19　多表 JOIN 语句执行结果

每个表连接都会启动一个 MapReduce 作业。第一个 MapReduce 作业连接 ygxxb_j 表和 gwgzbz 表,第二个 MapReduce 作业连接第一个 MapReduce 作业的输出结果和 jjbz 表。由图 7.4.19 可见,3 个原始表横向连成了一个宽表。

7.4.6 ORDER BY 和 SORT BY 语句

Hive 中的 ORDER BY 语句和 SQL 语句一样,可以实现对结果集的排序。ORDER BY 语句命令如下:

```
hive (jscy)> SELECT * FROM ygxxb_j ORDER BY xb ASC,jbgz DESC;
```

运行结果如图 7.4.20 所示。

```
2024-05-01 15:15:08,949 Stage-1 map = 0%, reduce = 0%
2024-05-01 15:15:16,786 Stage-1 map = 100%, reduce = 0%, Cumulative CPU 1.9 sec
2024-05-01 15:15:25,585 Stage-1 map = 100%, reduce = 100%, Cumulative CPU 3.62 sec
MapReduce Total cumulative CPU time: 3 seconds 620 msec
Ended Job = job_1714486305503_0017
MapReduce Jobs Launched:
Stage-Stage-1: Map: 1  Reduce: 1   Cumulative CPU: 3.62 sec   HDFS Read: 9823 HDFS Write: 1640 SUCCESS
Total MapReduce CPU Time Spent: 3 seconds 620 msec
OK
ygxxb_j.zgbh    ygxxb_j.xm   ygxxb_j.xb   ygxxb_j.bm   ygxxb_j.zwlb   ygxxb_j.jbgz
003     李红梅   女    财务部    部门经理    3000.0
002     齐  敏   女    办公室    行政助理    2500.0
012     任  可   女    销售部    部门经理    2100.0
008     张小英   女    研发部    研发人员    2000.0
016     高  明   女    仓管部    部门经理    2000.0
015     王心萍   女    供应部    采购人员    1800.0
014     邱秀丽   女    供应部    采购人员    1800.0
005     陈艳丽   女    财务部    出纳       1800.0
001     王柏宇   男    办公室    公司经理    3200.0
009     王伟亮   男    生产部    车间主任    2800.0
006     林大维   男    研发部    部门经理    2200.0
007     朱韩斌   男    研发部    研发人员    2000.0
004     王向东   男    财务部    会计人员    2000.0
013     潘  涛   男    销售部    销售人员    1800.0
010     孙松涛   男    生产部    生产工人    1600.0
011     张金平   男    生产部    生产工人    1600.0
017     张瑞峰   男    仓管部    仓管人员    1600.0
Time taken: 37.148 seconds, Fetched: 17 row(s)
```

图 7.4.20 ORDER BY 排序语句使用

上述语句表示按照 xb 字段升序排序,在 xb 相同的情况下,再按 jbgz 字段降序排序。

如果 Hive 表中的数据非常多,使用 ORDER BY 排序可能会导致执行的时间过长,此时可以设置 Hive 的属性 hive.mapred.mode 为 strict,则排序语句后面必须加上 LIMIT 限制查询的结果条数,以避免数据量太多造成的执行时间过长问题,命令如下:

```
hive> SET hive.mapred.mode=strict;
hive> SELECT * FROM ygxxb_j ORDER BY xb ASC,jbgz DESC LIMIT 10;
```

运行结果如图 7.4.21 所示。

SORT BY 语句会在每个 Reduce 中对数据进行排序,可以保证每个 Reduce 输出的数据是有序的(全局不一定有序),并可以提高全局排序的性能,命令如下:

```
hive (jscy)> SELECT * FROM ygxxb_j SORT BY xb ASC,jbgz DESC;
```

运行结果如图 7.4.22 所示。

```
Stage-Stage-1: Map: 1  Reduce: 1   Cumulative CPU: 2.91 sec   HDFS Read: 9978 HDFS Write: 993 SUCCESS
Total MapReduce CPU Time Spent: 2 seconds 910 msec
OK
ygxxb_j.zgbh   ygxxb_j.xm   ygxxb_j.xb   ygxxb_j.bm       ygxxb_j.zwlb   ygxxb_j.jbgz
003            李红梅       女           财务部  部门经理     3000.0
002            齐  敏       女           办公室  行政助理     2500.0
012            任  可       女           销售部  部门经理     2100.0
008            张小英       女           研发部  研发人员     2000.0
016            高  明       女           仓管部  部门经理     2000.0
005            陈艳丽       女           财务部  出纳         1800.0
014            邱秀丽       女           供应部  采购人员     1800.0
015            王心萍       女           供应部  采购人员     1800.0
001            王柏宇       男           办公室  公司经理     3200.0
009            王伟尧       男           生产部  车间主任     2800.0
Time taken: 39.911 seconds, Fetched: 10 row(s)
hive (jscy)>
```

图 7.4.21　用 LIMIT 限制查询结果条数

```
Hadoop job information for Stage-1: number of mappers: 1; number of reducers: 1
2024-05-01 15:27:05,109 Stage-1 map = 0%,  reduce = 0%
2024-05-01 15:27:22,361 Stage-1 map = 100%, reduce = 0%, Cumulative CPU 3.3 sec
2024-05-01 15:27:35,843 Stage-1 map = 100%, reduce = 100%, Cumulative CPU 5.75 sec
MapReduce Total cumulative CPU time: 5 seconds 750 msec
Ended Job = job_1714486305503_0019
MapReduce Jobs Launched:
Stage-Stage-1: Map: 1 Reduce: 1  Cumulative CPU: 5.75 sec  HDFS Read: 9681 HDFS Write: 1640 SUCCESS
Total MapReduce CPU Time Spent: 5 seconds 750 msec
OK
ygxxb_j.zgbh   ygxxb_j.xm   ygxxb_j.xb   ygxxb_j.bm       ygxxb_j.zwlb   ygxxb_j.jbgz
003            李红梅       女           财务部  部门经理     3000.0
002            齐  敏       女           办公室  行政助理     2500.0
012            任  可       女           销售部  部门经理     2100.0
008            张小英       女           研发部  研发人员     2000.0
016            高  明       女           仓管部  部门经理     2000.0
015            王心萍       女           供应部  采购人员     1800.0
014            邱秀丽       女           供应部  采购人员     1800.0
005            陈艳丽       女           财务部  出纳         1800.0
001            王柏宇       男           办公室  公司经理     3200.0
009            王伟尧       男           生产部  车间主任     2800.0
006            林大维       男           研发部  部门经理     2200.0
007            朱韩斌       男           研发部  研发人员     2000.0
004            王向东       男           财务部  会计人员     2000.0
013            潘  涛       男           销售部  销售人员     1800.0
010            孙松涛       男           生产部  生产工人     1600.0
011            张金平       男           生产部  生产工人     1600.0
017            张瑞峰       男           仓管部  仓管人员     1600.0
Time taken: 49.526 seconds, Fetched: 17 row(s)
```

图 7.4.22　SORT BY 排序语句使用

上述语句会在每个 Reduce 中对 xb 字段进行升序排序,在 xb 相同的情况下,再按 jbgz 字段降序排序。

如果 Reduce 个数为 1,则 ORDER BY 和 SORT BY 语句的查询结果相同;如果 Reduce 个数大于 1,则 SORT BY 语句输出的结果为局部有序。

7.4.7　类型转换

类型转换可以使用 cast(value As TYPE)语法,命令如下:

```
hive> SELECT xm ,jbgz FROM ygxxb WHERE cast(zgbh AS INT) >=20;
```

运行结果如图 7.4.23 所示。

上述语句表示将 zgbh 转化为 INT 类型,原来为 STRING 类型。

```
hive (jscy)> SELECT xm ,jbgz FROM ygxxb WHERE cast(zgbh AS INT) >=20;
OK
xm      jbgz
潘  涛    1800.0
邹燕燕    1800.0
孙小凡    1800.0
赵文彬    2100.0
邱秀丽    1800.0
王心萍    1800.0
宋  辉    1800.0
高  明    2000.0
张瑞峰    1600.0
马一鸣    1600.0
崔  静    1600.0
Time taken: 5.981 seconds, Fetched: 11 row(s)
```

图 7.4.23　类型转换 cast(value As TYPE)语句使用

7.4.8　UNION ALL 语句

Hive 支持 UNION ALL 语句查询，其主要用于多表数据合并的场景。使用 UNION ALL 语句要求各表查询出的字段类型必须完全匹配。

首先，创建三张表，从 ygxxb 中选取数据，生成研发部 ygyfb、销售部 ygxsb 和仓管部 ygcgb 三张 Hive 表，命令如下：

```
CREATE TABLE ygyfb AS SELECT * FROM ygxxb WHERE bm='研发部';
CREATE TABLE ygxsb AS SELECT * FROM ygxxb WHERE bm='销售部';
CREATE TABLE ygcgb AS SELECT * FROM ygxxb WHERE bm='仓管部';
```

运行结果如图 7.4.24、图 7.4.25、图 7.4.26 所示。

```
hive (jscy)> CREATE TABLE ygyfb AS SELECT * FROM ygxxb WHERE bm='研发部';
WARNING: Hive-on-MR is deprecated in Hive 2 and may not be available in the future versions. Consider using a different
execution engine (i.e. spark, tez) or using Hive 1.X releases.
Query ID = root_20240501160538_a9e5d420-9c48-4a9f-a4b2-b0b2b04cbe53
Total jobs = 3
Launching Job 1 out of 3
Number of reduce tasks is set to 0 since there's no reduce operator
Starting Job = job_1714486305503_0020, Tracking URL = http://master:8088/proxy/application_1714486305503_0020/
Kill Command = /opt/hadoop-2.7.7/bin/hadoop job  -kill job_1714486305503_0020
Hadoop job information for Stage-1: number of mappers: 1; number of reducers: 0
2024-05-01 16:05:53,985 Stage-1 map = 0%,  reduce = 0%
2024-05-01 16:06:00,542 Stage-1 map = 100%,  reduce = 0%, Cumulative CPU 1.9 sec
MapReduce Total cumulative CPU time: 1 seconds 900 msec
Ended Job = job_1714486305503_0020
Stage-4 is selected by condition resolver.
Stage-3 is filtered out by condition resolver.
Stage-5 is filtered out by condition resolver.
Moving data to directory hdfs://master:9000/usr/hive_remote/warehouse/jscy.db/.hive-staging_hive_2024-05-01_16-05-38_30
1_4091137872879899559-1/-ext-10002
Moving data to directory hdfs://master:9000/usr/hive_remote/warehouse/jscy.db/ygyfb
MapReduce Jobs Launched:
Stage-Stage-1: Map: 1   Cumulative CPU: 1.9 sec   HDFS Read: 6371 HDFS Write: 262 SUCCESS
Total MapReduce CPU Time Spent: 1 seconds 900 msec
OK
ygxxb.zgbh     ygxxb.xm      ygxxb.xb      ygxxb.bm       ygxxb.zwlb      ygxxb.jbgz
Time taken: 26.938 seconds
```

图 7.4.24　创建研发部 ygyfb 表

```
hive (jscy)> CREATE TABLE ygxsb AS SELECT * FROM ygxxb WHERE bm='销售部';
WARNING: Hive-on-MR is deprecated in Hive 2 and may not be available in the future versions. Consider using a different
 execution engine (i.e. spark, tez) or using Hive 1.X releases.
Query ID = root_20240501160621_c87e48b2-7d59-4efc-945b-b19acf04c426
Total jobs = 3
Launching Job 1 out of 3
Number of reduce tasks is set to 0 since there's no reduce operator
Starting Job = job_1714486305503_0021, Tracking URL = http://master:8088/proxy/application_1714486305503_0021/
Kill Command = /opt/hadoop-2.7.7/bin/hadoop job  -kill job_1714486305503_0021
Hadoop job information for Stage-1: number of mappers: 1; number of reducers: 0
2024-05-01 16:06:32,742 Stage-1 map = 0%,  reduce = 0%
2024-05-01 16:06:39,227 Stage-1 map = 100%,  reduce = 0%, Cumulative CPU 1.59 sec
MapReduce Total cumulative CPU time: 1 seconds 590 msec
Ended Job = job_1714486305503_0021
Stage-4 is selected by condition resolver.
Stage-3 is filtered out by condition resolver.
Stage-5 is filtered out by condition resolver.
Moving data to directory hdfs://master:9000/usr/hive_remote/warehouse/jscy.db/.hive-staging_hive_2024-05-01_16-06-21_61
2_4678080199614538442-1/-ext-10002
Moving data to directory hdfs://master:9000/usr/hive_remote/warehouse/jscy.db/ygxsb
MapReduce Jobs Launched:
Stage-Stage-1: Map: 1   Cumulative CPU: 1.59 sec   HDFS Read: 6371 HDFS Write: 311 SUCCESS
Total MapReduce CPU Time Spent: 1 seconds 590 msec
OK
ygxxb.zgbh      ygxxb.xm       ygxxb.xb       ygxxb.bm      ygxxb.zwlb      ygxxb.jbgz
Time taken: 20.279 seconds
```

图 7.4.25　创建销售部 ygxsb 表

```
hive (jscy)> CREATE TABLE ygcgb AS SELECT * FROM ygxxb WHERE bm='仓管部';
WARNING: Hive-on-MR is deprecated in Hive 2 and may not be available in the future versions. Consider using a different
 execution engine (i.e. spark, tez) or using Hive 1.X releases.
Query ID = root_20240501160715_8bbe2ec8-2eaa-4211-8d30-0056d00f9cf0
Total jobs = 3
Launching Job 1 out of 3
Number of reduce tasks is set to 0 since there's no reduce operator
Starting Job = job_1714486305503_0022, Tracking URL = http://master:8088/proxy/application_1714486305503_0022/
Kill Command = /opt/hadoop-2.7.7/bin/hadoop job  -kill job_1714486305503_0022
Hadoop job information for Stage-1: number of mappers: 1; number of reducers: 0
2024-05-01 16:07:30,245 Stage-1 map = 0%,  reduce = 0%
2024-05-01 16:07:37,795 Stage-1 map = 100%,  reduce = 0%, Cumulative CPU 1.98 sec
MapReduce Total cumulative CPU time: 1 seconds 980 msec
Ended Job = job_1714486305503_0022
Stage-4 is selected by condition resolver.
Stage-3 is filtered out by condition resolver.
Stage-5 is filtered out by condition resolver.
Moving data to directory hdfs://master:9000/usr/hive_remote/warehouse/jscy.db/.hive-staging_hive_2024-05-01_16-07-15_69
9_4290794525338558242-1/-ext-10002
Moving data to directory hdfs://master:9000/usr/hive_remote/warehouse/jscy.db/ygcgb
MapReduce Jobs Launched:
Stage-Stage-1: Map: 1   Cumulative CPU: 1.98 sec   HDFS Read: 6371 HDFS Write: 278 SUCCESS
Total MapReduce CPU Time Spent: 1 seconds 980 msec
OK
ygxxb.zgbh      ygxxb.xm       ygxxb.xb       ygxxb.bm      ygxxb.zwlb      ygxxb.jbgz
Time taken: 23.807 seconds
```

图 7.4.26　创建仓管部 ygcgb 表

其次,用 UNION ALL 语句,实现将上述三张表数据合并的操作,命令如下:

```
SELECT y.zgbh,y.xm,y.bm
FROM (
SELECT y1.zgbh, y1.xm, y1.bm FROM   ygyfb y1
UNION ALL
SELECT y2.zgbh, y2.xm, y2.bm FROM ygxsb y2
UNION ALL
SELECT y3.zgbh, y3.xm, y3.bm FROM ygcgb y3) y;
```

运行结果如图 7.4.27 所示。

```
hive (jscy)> SELECT y.zgbh,y.xm,y.bm
           > FROM (
           > SELECT y1.zgbh, y1.xm, y1.bm FROM  ygyfb y1
           > UNION ALL
           > SELECT y2.zgbh, y2.xm,y2.bm FROM ygxsb y2
           > UNION ALL
           > SELECT y3.zgbh, y3.xm,y3.bm FROM ygcgb y3) y;
WARNING: Hive-on-MR is deprecated in Hive 2 and may not be available in the future versions. Consider using a different
 execution engine (i.e. spark, tez) or using Hive 1.X releases.
Query ID = root_20240501161705_65bfdbc5-438e-4b4a-ae53-d6ae79c23541
Total jobs = 1
Launching Job 1 out of 1
Number of reduce tasks is set to 0 since there's no reduce operator
Starting Job = job_1714486305503_0023, Tracking URL = http://master:8088/proxy/application_1714486305503_0023/
Kill Command = /opt/hadoop-2.7.7/bin/hadoop job  -kill job_1714486305503_0023
Hadoop job information for Stage-1: number of mappers: 3; number of reducers: 0
2024-05-01 16:17:41,020 Stage-1 map = 0%,  reduce = 0%
2024-05-01 16:17:58,891 Stage-1 map = 100%,  reduce = 0%, Cumulative CPU 6.68 sec
MapReduce Total cumulative CPU time: 6 seconds 680 msec
Ended Job = job_1714486305503_0023
MapReduce Jobs Launched:
Stage-Stage-1: Map: 3   Cumulative CPU: 6.68 sec   HDFS Read: 20969 HDFS Write: 947 SUCCESS
Total MapReduce CPU Time Spent: 6 seconds 680 msec
OK
y.zgbh    y.xm      y.bm
019       任 可      销售部
020       潘 涛      销售部
021       邹燕燕     销售部
022       孙小凡     销售部
023       赵文彬     销售部
027       高 明      仓管部
028       张瑞峰     仓管部
029       马一鸣     仓管部
030       崔 静      仓管部
007       林大维     研发部
008       朱韩斌     研发部
009       赵齐伟     研发部
010       张小英     研发部
Time taken: 57.077 seconds, Fetched: 13 row(s)
```

图 7.4.27　UNION ALL 语句的使用

注意

在 Hive 中使用 UNION　ALL 语句,必须使用嵌套查询。

任务 7.5　Hive 视图

任务描述

视图是一种使用查询语句定义的虚拟表,是数据的一种逻辑结构,创建视图时不会把视图存储到磁盘上,定义视图的查询语句只是在执行视图的语句时才会被执行。本任务将简单介绍 Hive 中视图的创建与使用。

关键步骤

(1) 使用视图简化查询逻辑。

(2) 使用视图限制查询数据。

(3) 以 map 类型的字段生成视图。

(4) 删除视图命令的使用。

(5) 查看视图信息命令的使用。

7.5.1 使用视图简化查询逻辑

在实际工作过程中,使用 Hive 难免会遇到复杂的嵌套查询,如下面的查询语句:

```
FROM
(SELECT * FROM ygxxb_j y JOIN gwgzbz  g ON  y.zwlb= g.zwlb)  t
SELECT t.xm,t.zwlb,t.jbgz   WHERE   t.xm='李红梅';
```

运行结果如图 7.5.1 所示。

```
hive (jscy)>
         > FROM
         > (SELECT * FROM ygxxb_j y JOIN gwgzbz  g ON  y.zwlb= g.zwlb)  t
         > SELECT t.xm,t.zwlb,t.jbgz   WHERE   t.xm='李红梅';
WARNING: Hive-on-MR is deprecated in Hive 2 and may not be available in the future versions. Consider using a different
 execution engine (i.e. spark, tez) or using Hive 1.X releases.
Query ID = root_20240502221343_508c4049-e552-42d2-bf58-48437599290b
Total jobs = 1
SLF4J: Class path contains multiple SLF4J bindings.
SLF4J: Found binding in [jar:file:/opt/hive/lib/log4j-slf4j-impl-2.6.2.jar!/org/slf4j/impl/StaticLoggerBinder.class]
SLF4J: Found binding in [jar:file:/opt/hadoop-2.7.7/share/hadoop/common/lib/slf4j-log4j12-1.7.10.jar!/org/slf4j/impl/St
aticLoggerBinder.class]
SLF4J: See http://www.slf4j.org/codes.html#multiple_bindings for an explanation.
SLF4J: Actual binding is of type [org.apache.logging.slf4j.Log4jLoggerFactory]
2024-05-02 22:14:01     Starting to launch local task to process map join;      maximum memory = 518979584
2024-05-02 22:14:04     Dump the side-table for tag: 1 with group count: 9 into file: file:/tmp/root/0f1a49e3-35ae-463a
-8166-28ae45f8e9cb/hive_2024-05-02_22-13-43_979_8424938790576404089-1/-local-10004/HashTable-Stage-3/MapJoin-mapfile11-
-.hashtable
2024-05-02 22:14:04     Uploaded 1 File to: file:/tmp/root/0f1a49e3-35ae-463a-8166-28ae45f8e9cb/hive_2024-05-02_22-13-4
3_979_8424938790576404089-1/-local-10004/HashTable-Stage-3/MapJoin-mapfile11--.hashtable (527 bytes)
2024-05-02 22:14:04     End of local task; Time Taken: 3.214 sec.
Execution completed successfully
MapredLocal task succeeded
Launching Job 1 out of 1
Number of reduce tasks is set to 0 since there's no reduce operator
Starting Job = job_1714657474346_0002, Tracking URL = http://master:8088/proxy/application_1714657474346_0002/
Kill Command = /opt/hadoop-2.7.7/bin/hadoop job  -kill job_1714657474346_0002
Hadoop job information for Stage-3: number of mappers: 1; number of reducers: 0
2024-05-02 22:14:27,581 Stage-3 map = 0%,  reduce = 0%
2024-05-02 22:14:36,346 Stage-3 map = 100%,  reduce = 0%, Cumulative CPU 1.99 sec
MapReduce Total cumulative CPU time: 1 seconds 990 msec
Ended Job = job_1714657474346_0002
MapReduce Jobs Launched:
Stage-Stage-3: Map: 1   Cumulative CPU: 1.99 sec   HDFS Read: 7845 HDFS Write: 150 SUCCESS
Total MapReduce CPU Time Spent: 1 seconds 990 msec
OK
t.xm    t.zwlb   t.jbgz
李红梅   部门经理    3000.0
Time taken: 54.648 seconds, Fetched: 1 row(s)
```

图 7.5.1 嵌套查询运行结果

这里可以将嵌套查询的语句创建一个视图,命令如下:

```
CREATE VIEW IF NOT EXISTS ygxxb_view AS
SELECT  y.*, g.gwgz FROM ygxxb_j y JOIN gwgzbz  g ON  y.zwlb = g.zwlb;
```

这里的 zwlb 字段只能出现一次,否则会出现字段重复错误提示。运行结果如图 7.5.2 所示。

```
hive (jscy)> CREATE VIEW IF NOT EXISTS ygxxb_view AS
          > SELECT  y.*, g.gwgz FROM ygxxb_j y JOIN gwgzbz  g ON  y.zwlb = g.zwlb;
OK
zgbh      xm       xb       bm       zwlb       jbgz       gwgz
Time taken: 0.711 seconds
hive (jscy)>
```

图 7.5.2 创建视图时不执行查询

此时,查询语句就可以写成如下简单语句:

```
SELECT xm,zwlb,jbgz FROM ygxxb_view  WHERE   xm='李红梅';
```

运行结果如图 7.5.3 所示。

```
hive (jscy)> SELECT xm,zwlb,jbgz FROM ygxxb_view  WHERE   xm='李红梅';
WARNING: Hive-on-MR is deprecated in Hive 2 and may not be available in the future versions. Consider
using a different execution engine (i.e. spark, tez) or using Hive 1.X releases.
Query ID = root_20240502222836_f6df6b45-af97-40bb-9025-8234d6174808
Total jobs = 1
SLF4J: Class path contains multiple SLF4J bindings.
SLF4J: Found binding in [jar:file:/opt/hive/lib/log4j-slf4j-impl-2.6.2.jar!/org/slf4j/impl/StaticLogge
rBinder.class]
SLF4J: Found binding in [jar:file:/opt/hadoop-2.7.7/share/hadoop/common/lib/slf4j-log4j12-1.7.10.jar!/
org/slf4j/impl/StaticLoggerBinder.class]
SLF4J: See http://www.slf4j.org/codes.html#multiple_bindings for an explanation.
SLF4J: Actual binding is of type [org.apache.logging.slf4j.Log4jLoggerFactory]
2024-05-02 22:28:49     Starting to launch local task to process map join;       maximum memory = 51897
9584
2024-05-02 22:28:51     Dump the side-table for tag: 1 with group count: 9 into file: file:/tmp/root/0
f1a49e3-35ae-463a-8166-28ae45f8e9cb/hive_2024-05-02_22-28-36_787_4261413184772284214-1/-local-10004/Ha
shTable-Stage-3/MapJoin-mapfile31--.hashtable
2024-05-02 22:28:52     Uploaded 1 File to: file:/tmp/root/0f1a49e3-35ae-463a-8166-28ae45f8e9cb/hive_2
024-05-02_22-28-36_787_4261413184772284214-1/-local-10004/HashTable-Stage-3/MapJoin-mapfile31--.hashta
ble (527 bytes)
2024-05-02 22:28:52     End of local task; Time Taken: 2.887 sec.
Execution completed successfully
MapredLocal task succeeded
Launching Job 1 out of 1
Number of reduce tasks is set to 0 since there's no reduce operator
Starting Job = job_1714657474346_0004, Tracking URL = http://master:8088/proxy/application_17146574743
46_0004/
Kill Command = /opt/hadoop-2.7.7/bin/hadoop job  -kill job_1714657474346_0004
Hadoop job information for Stage-3: number of mappers: 1; number of reducers: 0
2024-05-02 22:29:08,455 Stage-3 map = 0%,   reduce = 0%
2024-05-02 22:29:17,319 Stage-3 map = 100%,  reduce = 0%, Cumulative CPU 1.92 sec
MapReduce Total cumulative CPU time: 1 seconds 920 msec
Ended Job = job_1714657474346_0004
MapReduce Jobs Launched:
Stage-Stage-3: Map: 1   Cumulative CPU: 1.92 sec   HDFS Read: 8074 HDFS Write: 150 SUCCESS
Total MapReduce CPU Time Spent: 1 seconds 920 msec
OK
xm      zwlb    jbgz
李红梅   部门经理        3000.0
Time taken: 41.643 seconds, Fetched: 1 row(s)
```

图 7.5.3　查询视图结果

可以看到,在查询视图时执行了查询,使用视图大大地简化了查询逻辑。

7.5.2　使用视图限制查询数据

Hive 中使用视图可以限制查询指定字段的数据和特定条件的数据,如以下语句:

```
CREATE TABLE ygxx_tab(zgbh STRING,xm STRING,xb STRING,bm STRING,zwlb STRING,jbgz FLOAT);
CREATE VIEW  ygxx_info AS SELECT zgbh,xm FROM ygxx_tab;
```

运行结果如图 7.5.4 所示。

```
hive (jscy)> CREATE TABLE ygxx_tab(zgbh STRING,xm STRING,xb STRING,bm STRING,zwlb STRING,jbgz FLOAT);
OK
Time taken: 0.185 seconds
hive (jscy)> CREATE VIEW  ygxx_info AS SELECT zgbh,xm FROM ygxx_tab;
OK
zgbh    xm
Time taken: 0.207 seconds
```

图 7.5.4　用视图限制查询字段

上述创建视图的语句限制只查询 ygxx_tab 表的 zgbh 和 xm 两个字段,对查询的字段做了限制。再看下面的语句:

```
CREATE VIEW IF NOT EXISTS ygxx_info2 AS SELECT zgbh,xm FROM ygxx_tab WHERE xm='李红梅';
```

运行结果如图 7.5.5 所示。

```
hive (jscy)> CREATE VIEW IF NOT EXISTS ygxx_info2 AS SELECT zgbh,xm FROM ygxx_tab WHERE xm='李红梅'
;
OK
zgbh    xm
Time taken: 0.546 seconds
```

图 7.5.5　用视图限制查询的行

这里创建视图的语句限制了只查询 xm 为"李红梅"的数据。

7.5.3　以 map 类型的字段生成视图

map 类型的数据访问格式为"字段名[属性名]",所以以 map 类型的字段生成视图也比较简单,命令如下:

```
CREATE EXTERNAL TABLE person (body map<STRING, STRING>)
ROW FORMAT DELIMITED
FIELDS TERMINATED BY '\001'
COLLECTION ITEMS TERMINATED BY '\002'
MAP KEYS TERMINATED BY '\003'
STORED AS TEXTFILE;
```

运行结果如图 7.5.6 所示。

```
hive (jscy)> CREATE EXTERNAL TABLE person (body map <STRING, STRING>)
            > ROW FORMAT DELIMITED
            > FIELDS TERMINATED BY '\001'
            > COLLECTION ITEMS TERMINATED BY '\002'
            > MAP KEYS TERMINATED BY '\003'
            > STORED AS TEXTFILE;
OK
Time taken: 0.383 seconds
```

图 7.5.6　以 map 类型的字段生成视图

可以创建一个视图,包含 height(身高)和 weight(体重)字段,命令如下:

```
hive (jscy)>  CREATE VIEW IF NOT EXISTS body_info(height,weight) AS
              SELECT body['height'],body['weight'] FROM person WHERE body['type']=
              'basic';
```

运行结果如图 7.5.7 所示。

```
hive (jscy)> CREATE VIEW IF NOT EXISTS body_info(height,weight)  AS SELECT body['height'],body['weight
'] FROM person WHERE body['type']='basic';
OK
_c0      _c1
Time taken: 0.659 seconds
```

图 7.5.7　创建 height 和 weight 字段的视图

上述语句表示将 person 表中的基础身体数据（身高和体重）单独抽象成一个视图，方便查询。

7.5.4　删除视图

删除视图非常简单，只需要执行如下语句即可：

```
DROP VIEW IF EXISTS person_body;
```

运行结果如图 7.5.8 所示。

```
hive (jscy)> DROP VIEW IF EXISTS person_body;
OK
Time taken: 0.185 seconds
```

图 7.5.8　删除视图

7.5.5　查看视图信息

Hive 可以通过 DESC EXTENDED viewname 和 DESC FORMATTED viewname 语句查看视图信息，命令如下：

```
DESC EXTENDED body_info;
```

运行结果如图 7.5.9 所示。

```
hive (jscy)> DESC EXTENDED body_info;
OK
col_name      data_type       comment
height                        string
weight                        string

Detailed Table Information    Table(tableName:body_info, dbName:jscy, owner:root, createTime:1714662
769, lastAccessTime:0, retention:0, sd:StorageDescriptor(cols:[FieldSchema(name:height, type:string, c
omment:null), FieldSchema(name:weight, type:string, comment:null)], location:null, inputFormat:org.apa
che.hadoop.mapred.TextInputFormat, outputFormat:org.apache.hadoop.hive.ql.io.HiveIgnoreKeyTextOutputFo
rmat, compressed:false, numBuckets:-1, serdeInfo:SerDeInfo(name:null, serializationLib:null, parameter
s:{}), bucketCols:[], sortCols:[], parameters:{}, skewedInfo:SkewedInfo(skewedColNames:[], skewedColVa
lues:[], skewedColValueLocationMaps:{}), storedAsSubDirectories:false), partitionKeys:[], parameters:{
transient_lastDdlTime=1714662769}, viewOriginalText:SELECT body['height'],body['weight'] FROM person W
HERE body['type']='basic', viewExpandedText:SELECT `_c0` AS `height`, `_c1` AS `weight` FROM (SELECT `
person`.`body`['height'], `person`.`body`['weight'] FROM `jscy`.`person` WHERE `person`.`body`['type']=
'basic') `jscy.body_info`, tableType:VIRTUAL_VIEW, rewriteEnabled:false)
Time taken: 0.332 seconds, Fetched: 4 row(s)
```

图 7.5.9　DESC EXTENDED 查看视图信息

```
DESC FORMATTED body_info;
```

运行结果如图 7.5.10 所示。

```
hive (jscy)> DESC FORMATTED body_info;
OK
col_name            data_type           comment
# col_name              data_type               comment

height                  string
weight                  string

# Detailed Table Information
Database:               jscy
Owner:                  root
CreateTime:             Thu May 02 23:12:49 CST 2024
LastAccessTime:         UNKNOWN
Retention:              0
Table Type:             VIRTUAL_VIEW
Table Parameters:
        transient_lastDdlTime   1714662769

# Storage Information
SerDe Library:          null
InputFormat:            org.apache.hadoop.mapred.TextInputFormat
OutputFormat:           org.apache.hadoop.hive.ql.io.HiveIgnoreKeyTextOutputFormat
Compressed:             No
Num Buckets:            -1
Bucket Columns:         []
Sort Columns:           []

# View Information
View Original Text:     SELECT body['height'],body['weight'] FROM person WHERE body['type']='basic'
View Expanded Text:     SELECT `_c0` AS `height`, `_c1` AS `weight` FROM (SELECT `person`.`body`[`heig
ht'],`person`.`body`['weight'] FROM `jscy`.`person` WHERE `person`.`body`['type']='basic') `jscy.body_
info`
View Rewrite Enabled:   No
Time taken: 0.165 seconds, Fetched: 28 row(s)
```

图 7.5.10　DESC FORMATTED 查看视图信息

注意

视图是只读的,用户不能插入或下载数据到视图中。视图只允许修改元数据中的 TBLPROPERTIES 属性。

任务 7.6　Hive 函数

任务描述

Hive 内部支持大量的函数,用户可以通过 SHOW FUNCTIONS 查看 Hive 内置的函数。灵活运用 Hive 提供的函数能极大节省数据分析成本。本任务学习 Hive 函数,主要包含数学函数、复合函数、类型转换函数、日期函数、条件函数、字符串函数、聚合函数和表生成函数等。

> **关键步骤**

(1) 数学函数的应用。
(2) 集合函数的应用。
(3) 类型转换函数的应用。
(4) 日期函数的应用。
(5) 条件函数的应用。
(6) 字符串函数的应用。
(7) 聚合函数的应用。
(8) 表生成函数的应用。

7.6.1 数学函数

数学函数是 Hive 内部提供的专门用于数学运算的函数,如 ROUND()函数和 SQRT()函数等。ROUND()函数主要用来对给定的数字进行四舍五入取近似值,命令如下:

```
hive> SELECT ROUND(5.5);
```

运行结果如图 7.6.1 所示。

```
hive (jscy)> SELECT ROUND(5.5);
OK
_c0
6
Time taken: 2.527 seconds, Fetched: 1 row(s)
```

图 7.6.1　ROUND()函数使用

SQRT()函数表示对给定的数字取平方根,命令如下:

```
hive> SELECT SQRT(5);
```

运行结果如图 7.6.2 所示。

```
hive (jscy)> SELECT SQRT(5);
OK
_c0
2.23606797749979
Time taken: 0.406 seconds, Fetched: 1 row(s)
```

图 7.6.2　SQRT()函数使用

7.6.2 集合函数

集合函数是 Hive 内部处理集合数据的函数,如 SIZE()函数和 MAP_KEYS()函数。

SIZE()函数主要用来获取 MAP 或者数组的长度,命令如下:

```
hive> SELECT SIZE(MAP("name", "suchang"));
```

运行结果如图 7.6.3 所示。

```
hive (jscy)> SELECT SIZE(MAP("name", "suchang"));
OK
_c0
1
Time taken: 0.481 seconds, Fetched: 1 row(s)
```

图 7.6.3　SIZE()函数使用

MAP_KEYS()函数主要用来获取 MAP 集合中所有的 KEYS 函数,命令如下:

```
hive> SELECT MAP_KEYS(MAP("name", "suchang"));
```

运行结果如图 7.6.4 所示。

```
hive (jscy)> SELECT MAP_KEYS(MAP("name", "suchang"));
OK
_c0
["name"]
Time taken: 0.206 seconds, Fetched: 1 row(s)
```

图 7.6.4　MAP_KEYS()函数使用

7.6.3　类型转换函数

Hive 内部提供了一些可以将数据类型进行转换的函数,这些函数能够将某些数据类型转换为便于查询或者计算统计的数据类型。例如,CAST()函数,其基本格式为 CAST(value as TYPE),能够将给定的数据 value 转化成 TYPE 类型,命令如下:

```
hive> SELECT CAST("5" AS INT);
```

运行结果如图 7.6.5 所示。

```
hive (jscy)> SELECT CAST("5" AS INT);
OK
_c0
5
Time taken: 0.161 seconds, Fetched: 1 row(s)
```

图 7.6.5　CAST()函数使用

7.6.4　日期函数

日期函数是一类专门处理日期数据的函数,能够方便地对日期数据进行转换和处理。

例如，UNIX_TIMESTAMP()函数，其能够方便地获取服务器的时间戳，命令如下：

```
hive> SELECT UNIX_TIMESTAMP();
```

运行结果如图 7.6.6 所示。

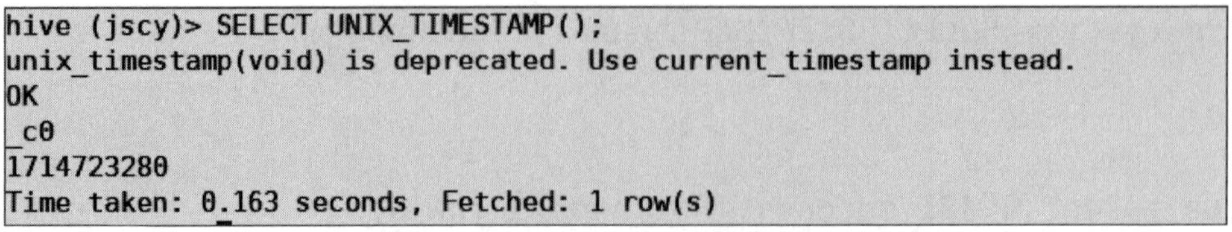

```
hive (jscy)> SELECT UNIX_TIMESTAMP();
unix_timestamp(void) is deprecated. Use current_timestamp instead.
OK
_c0
1714723280
Time taken: 0.163 seconds, Fetched: 1 row(s)
```

图 7.6.6　UNIX_TIMESTAMP()函数使用

7.6.5　条件函数

条件函数是一类进行条件判断的函数，通常会用于 WHERE 语句，如 ISNULL()函数和 NVL()函数。ISNULL()函数表示如果给定的数据为 NULL，则返回 true，否则返回 false，命令如下：

```
hive> SELECT ISNULL(NULL);
hive> SELECT ISNULL(1);
```

运行结果如图 7.6.7 所示。

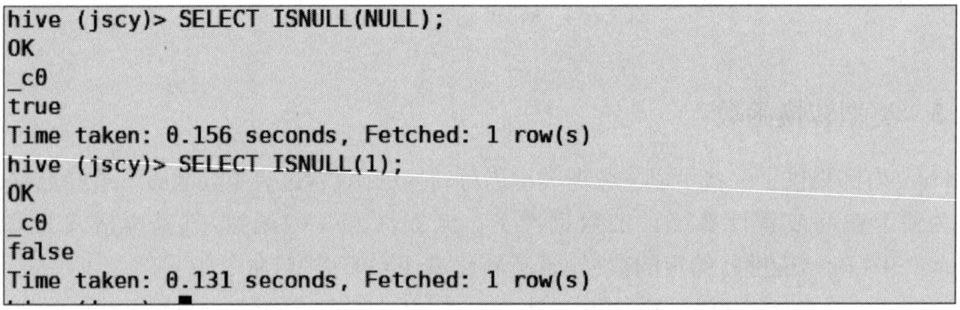

```
hive (jscy)> SELECT ISNULL(NULL);
OK
_c0
true
Time taken: 0.156 seconds, Fetched: 1 row(s)
hive (jscy)> SELECT ISNULL(1);
OK
_c0
false
Time taken: 0.131 seconds, Fetched: 1 row(s)
```

图 7.6.7　ISNULL()函数使用

NVL()函数的格式为 NVL(T value，T default_value)，表示如果 value 值为 NULL，则返回 default_value，否则返回 value，命令如下：

```
hive> SELECT NVL(1, 2);
hive> SELECT NVL(NULL, 2);
```

运行结果如图 7.6.8 所示。

7.6.6　字符串函数

字符串函数是一类处理字符串数据的函数，可以对字符串进行拼接、转换等操作，如 LENGTH()函数和 CONCAT()函数。LENGTH()函数用于获取给定字符串的长度，命令如下：

```
hive (jscy)> SELECT NVL(1, 2);
OK
_c0
1
Time taken: 0.169 seconds, Fetched: 1 row(s)
hive (jscy)> SELECT NVL(NULL, 2);
OK
_c0
2
Time taken: 0.102 seconds, Fetched: 1 row(s)
```

图 7.6.8　NVL( )函数使用

```
hive> SELECT LENGTH('abc');
```

运行结果如图 7.6.9 所示。

```
hive (jscy)> SELECT LENGTH( 'abc');
OK
_c0
3
Time taken: 0.208 seconds, Fetched: 1 row(s)
```

图 7.6.9　LENGTH( )函数使用

CONCAT( )函数能够对给定的字符串进行依次拼接操作,语句如下:

```
hive> SELECT CONCAT("abc", "def");
```

运行结果如图 7.6.10 所示。

```
hive (jscy)> SELECT CONCAT("abc", "def");
OK
_c0
abcdef
Time taken: 0.166 seconds, Fetched: 1 row(s)
```

图 7.6.10　CONCAT( )函数使用

7.6.7　聚合函数

聚合函数是一类对数据进行统计计算的函数,能够方便地对 Hive 中的数据进行统计处理,如 COUNT( )函数和 SUM( )函数。COUNT( )函数能够获取 Hive 数据表中的数据条数,命令如下:

```
hive> SELECT COUNT(*) FROM jscy.ygxxb;
```

运行结果如图 7.6.11 所示。

```
hive (jscy)> SELECT COUNT(*) FROM jscy.ygxxb;
WARNING: Hive-on-MR is deprecated in Hive 2 and may not be available in the future versions. Consider
using a different execution engine (i.e. spark, tez) or using Hive 1.X releases.
Query ID = root_20240503161136_699f6bff-e83b-4e31-bc73-cad16699ba77
Total jobs = 1
Launching Job 1 out of 1
Number of reduce tasks determined at compile time: 1
In order to change the average load for a reducer (in bytes):
  set hive.exec.reducers.bytes.per.reducer=<number>
In order to limit the maximum number of reducers:
  set hive.exec.reducers.max=<number>
In order to set a constant number of reducers:
  set mapreduce.job.reduces=<number>
Starting Job = job_1714719406883_0001, Tracking URL = http://master:8088/proxy/application_17147194068
83_0001/
Kill Command = /opt/hadoop-2.7.7/bin/hadoop job  -kill job_1714719406883_0001
Hadoop job information for Stage-1: number of mappers: 1; number of reducers: 1
2024-05-03 16:12:13,726 Stage-1 map = 0%,  reduce = 0%
2024-05-03 16:12:26,294 Stage-1 map = 100%,  reduce = 0%, Cumulative CPU 2.34 sec
2024-05-03 16:12:34,216 Stage-1 map = 100%,  reduce = 100%, Cumulative CPU 2.34 sec
MapReduce Total cumulative CPU time: 4 seconds 720 msec
Ended Job = job_1714719406883_0001
MapReduce Jobs Launched:
Stage-Stage-1: Map: 1  Reduce: 1   Cumulative CPU: 4.72 sec   HDFS Read: 9973 HDFS Write: 102 SUCCESS
Total MapReduce CPU Time Spent: 4 seconds 720 msec
OK
_c0
30
Time taken: 59.816 seconds, Fetched: 1 row(s)
```

图 7.6.11　COUNT()函数使用

由图 7.6.11 可见,Hive 调用 MapReduce 组件对数据库 jscy 中表 ygxxb 统计行数,统计结果是 30 条数据。

SUM()函数主要用来对数据表中的某一列数据进行求和统计,命令如下:

```
hive> SELECT SUM(jbgz) FROM jscy.ygxxb;
```

运行结果如图 7.6.12 所示。

```
hive (jscy)> SELECT SUM(jbgz) FROM jscy.ygxxb;
WARNING: Hive-on-MR is deprecated in Hive 2 and may not be available in the future versions. Consider
using a different execution engine (i.e. spark, tez) or using Hive 1.X releases.
Query ID = root_20240503161510_6530263e-3e42-4ea7-b999-9972d45864d0
Total jobs = 1
Launching Job 1 out of 1
Number of reduce tasks determined at compile time: 1
In order to change the average load for a reducer (in bytes):
  set hive.exec.reducers.bytes.per.reducer=<number>
In order to limit the maximum number of reducers:
  set hive.exec.reducers.max=<number>
In order to set a constant number of reducers:
  set mapreduce.job.reduces=<number>
Starting Job = job_1714719406883_0002, Tracking URL = http://master:8088/proxy/application_17147194068
83_0002/
Kill Command = /opt/hadoop-2.7.7/bin/hadoop job  -kill job_1714719406883_0002
Hadoop job information for Stage-1: number of mappers: 1; number of reducers: 1
2024-05-03 16:15:25,195 Stage-1 map = 0%,  reduce = 0%
2024-05-03 16:15:51,231 Stage-1 map = 100%,  reduce = 0%, Cumulative CPU 3.11 sec
2024-05-03 16:16:01,178 Stage-1 map = 100%,  reduce = 100%, Cumulative CPU 5.42 sec
MapReduce Total cumulative CPU time: 5 seconds 420 msec
Ended Job = job_1714719406883_0002
MapReduce Jobs Launched:
Stage-Stage-1: Map: 1  Reduce: 1   Cumulative CPU: 5.42 sec   HDFS Read: 10286 HDFS Write: 107 SUCCESS
Total MapReduce CPU Time Spent: 5 seconds 420 msec
OK
_c0
59500.0
Time taken: 52.973 seconds, Fetched: 1 row(s)
```

图 7.6.12　SUM()函数使用

由图 7.6.12 可见，Hive 调用 MapReduce 组件对数据库 jscy 中表 ygxxb 所有员工基本工资进行求和操作，计算出所有员工的基本工资总额是"59500.0"元。

7.6.8 表生成函数

表生成函数接收 0 个或者多个输入参数，产生多列或多行输出，如 EXPLODE()函数，命令如下：

```
hive>    SELECT EXPLODE(ARRAY("a","b","c"));
```

运行结果如图 7.6.13 所示。

```
hive (jscy)> SELECT EXPLODE(ARRAY("a","b","c"));
OK
col
a
b
c
Time taken: 0.299 seconds, Fetched: 3 row(s)
```

图 7.6.13　EXPLODE()函数使用

> **注意**
>
> Hive 内部提供了大量的内置函数供开发人员或数据分析人员使用，限于篇幅，这里不再一一赘述，读者可参见 Hive 官方文档来了解更多的 Hive 内置函数的用法。Hive 内置函数的官方文档链接地址为 https://cwiki.apache.org/confluence/display/Hive/LanguageManual+UDF。

单元总结

本单元主要介绍了 Hive 数据处理，对 Hive 的命令、数据类型进行了简要介绍，通过具体案例操作，练习了 Hive 的数据定义、数据操作和数据查询，另外对 Hive 的视图进行了应用说明，最后介绍了 Hive 的内置函数的使用方法。

单元习题

一、简答题

1. Hive 的集合数据类型有哪些？
2. Hive 的内部表和外部表的区别是什么？

二、技能训练题

请写出实现以下功能的 HiveQL 语句。

(1) 在 Hive 数据库中，创建 usr 表，含 3 个属性 id、name 和 age。

(2) 在 Hive 数据库中，创建 usr 表，含 3 个属性 id、name 和 age，存储路径为"/usr/local/hive/warehouse/hive/usr"。

(3) 在 Hive 数据库中，创建外部 usr 表，含 3 个属性 id、name 和 age，可以读取路径"/usr/local/data"下以","分隔的数据。

(4) 在 Hive 数据库中，创建分区 usr 表，含 3 个属性 id、name 和 age，还存在分区字段 sex。

(5) 在 Hive 数据库中，创建分区 usr1 表，它通过复制 usr 表得到。

单元 8
Hive 在财务报表分析和贷款数据分析中应用的综合案例

前面单元详细介绍了传统的关系型数据库 MySQL 和基于大数据平台 Hadoop 的数据仓库技术 Hive 的操作命令。本单元选用两个典型案例,将大数据技术和 Hive 技术运用于解决实际数据分析问题。

教学目标

知识目标
1. 了解财务报表分析的概念和目的。
2. 掌握财务比率分析方法。
3. 掌握财务综合分析方法。
4. 了解 Apriori 关联规则算法的原理及支持度与置信度的计算方法。

技能目标
1. 能根据实际需要,运用 Hive 的 SQL 命令构建数据查询语句对财务报表进行分析。
2. 能根据实际需要,运用 Hive 的 SQL 命令构建数据查询语句对贷款数据进行分析。

单元任务

任务 8.1 Hive 在财务报表分析中的应用。
任务 8.2 Hive 在贷款数据分析中的应用。

任务 8.1 Hive 在财务报表分析中的应用

任务描述

本任务对财务报表提供的数据进行系统和深入的分析研究,揭示有关指标之间的关系、变动情况及其形成原因,从而向使用者提供相关和全面的信息,也就是将财务报表及相关数据转换为对特定决策有用的信息,对企业过去的财务状况和经营成果以及未来前景作出评价,属于 Hive 在会计分析中的应用。

关键步骤

(1) 财务报表分析案例的方法。

(2) 财务报表分析指标的选择。

(3) 用 Hive 实施财务报表数据分析。

8.1.1 财务报表分析案例的方法

江苏财源有限公司实施了大数据财务管理,前期已搭建了大数据平台,财务数据也都存放在大数据平台上。年末,公司管理者想了解企业的偿债能力、营运能力和盈利能力,以评判企业现状,预测企业未来,为决策提供有力依据。这就需要财务人员能利用掌握的财务分析知识,整理财务数据,为进行财务分析做好准备。

财务报表分析又称财务分析,是指在财务报表及其相关资料的基础上,通过一定的方法和手段,对财务报表提供的数据进行系统和深入的分析研究,揭示有关指标之间的关系、变动情况及其形成原因,从而向使用者提供相关和全面的信息,也就是将财务报表及相关数据转换为对特定决策有用的信息,对企业过去的财务状况、经营成果以及未来前景作出评价。

财务分析的主要方法有财务比率分析法、财务图表分析法和财务综合分析法。

1) 财务比率分析法

财务比率分析法是解释财务报表的一种基本分析工具,是将财务报表中的相关项目进行比较,将分析对比的绝对数变成相对数,以说明财务报表上所列项目之间的相互关系,并作出某些解释和评价的一种方法。

2) 财务图表分析法

财务图表分析法是将企业连续几个会计期间的财务数据或财务指标绘制成图表,并根据图形走势来判断企业财务状况、经营成果的变化趋势的一种方法。这种方法能比较简单、直观的反映出企业财务状况的发展趋势,使分析者能够发现一些通过比较法所不易发现的问题。

3) 财务综合分析法

财务综合分析法是将各项财务指标作为一个整体,系统、全面、综合地对企业财务状况和经营成果进行剖析和评价,说明企业整体财务状况和效益的好坏的一种方法。财务综合分析法的实质是以上几种方法的综合运用。

8.1.2 财务报表分析指标的选择

要对公司进行财务分析,首先应该选定财务分析的指标。财务分析是以本单位资产负债表和利润表为基础,通过提取、加工和整理会计核算数据生成所需的数据报表,然后再对其进行加工处理,便可以得到一系列的财务指标。

根据管理者的要求,江苏财源有限公司计划用 Hive 进行财务分析,用 Hive 可以完成财务比率分析和财务综合分析。

其中,财务比率分析是对财务报表中的有关项目进行对比而得出的一系列的财务比率,从中发现数据以评价企业的财务状况和经营中存在的问题。常见的财务比率可分为变现能力比率、资产管理比率、长期负债比率、盈利能力比率、市价比率等几大类。下面来认识这些财务比率分析指标。

8.1.2.1 变现能力比率

变现能力比率又称偿债能力比率,是衡量企业资产产生现金能力大小的比率,它取决于在近期转变为现金的流动资产的多少,反映变现能力的财务比率主要有流动比率和速动比率两种。

1) 流动比率

流动比率是企业流动资产与流动负债之比。其计算公式为:

$$流动比率 = 流动资产 \div 流动负债$$

流动比率是衡量企业短期偿债能力的一个重要财务指标。流动比率越高,说明企业短期偿债能力越强,偿债越有保证。该指标过低,说明企业资金紧张,难以如期偿还到期债务。

过高的流动比率并非好现象,因为资产的获利能力与资产的流动性成反比,过高的流动比率说明企业存在闲置的流动资产,会导致企业的获利能力下降。根据行业经验,制造业企业合理的流动比率在 2 左右比较合适。

2) 速动比率

速动比率也称酸性测试比率,是流动资产扣除存货等资产后形成的速动资产与流动负债之比。其计算公式为:

$$速动比率 = 速动资产 \div 流动负债$$
$$= \left(流动资产 - 存货 - 预付账款 - 一年内到期的非流动资产 - 其他流动资产 \right) \div 流动负债$$

速动比率也是反映企业短期偿债能力的一个指标。速动比率越高,说明企业偿还流动负债的能力越强。但速动比率过高则表示企业会因现金及应收账款占用过多而增加企业的机会成本。根据经验,速动比率一般以等于 1 为宜,并非绝对以 1 为标准,还要结合其他因素考虑。若企业没有应收账款,速动比率低于 1 是很正常的。有时速动比率大于或等于 1,如果企业有对外担保或者存在或有负债,则会降低企业的偿债能力。因此,短期偿债能力分析要考虑各方因素,才能作出正确判断。

8.1.2.2 资产管理比率

资产管理比率又称运营效率比率,是用来衡量企业在资产管理方面效率高低的财务比率。资产管理比率包括存货周转率、应收账款周转率、流动资产周转率、固定资产周转率、总资产周转率等。

1) 存货周转率

存货周转率是衡量和评价企业购入存货、投入生产、销售收回等各环节管理状况的综合性指标。它是销售成本与平均存货余额的比值,也称为存货的周转次数。用时间表示的存货周转率就是存货周转天数。其计算公式为:

$$存货周转率 = 销售成本 \div 平均存货$$
$$存货周转天数 = 360 \div 存货周转率$$
$$平均存货 = (期初存货余额 + 期末存货余额) \div 2$$

2)应收账款周转率

应收账款周转率是反映年度内应收账款转换为现金的平均次数的指标。用时间表示的应收账款周转速度是应收账款周转天数,也称平均应收款回收期。它表示企业从取得应收账款的权利到收回款项所需要的时间。其计算公式为:

$$应收账款周转率 = 销售收入 \div 平均应收账款$$

$$应收账款周转天数 = 360 \div 应收账款周转率$$

$$平均应收账款 = (期初应收账款余额 + 期末应收账款余额) \div 2$$

3)流动资产周转率

流动资产周转率是销售收入与流动资产平均余额之比,它反映的是全部流动资产的利用效率。其计算公式为:

$$流动资产周转率 = 销售收入 \div 流动资产平均余额$$

$$流动资产平均余额 = (期初流动资产 + 期末流动资产) \div 2$$

4)固定资产周转率

固定资产周转率是企业销售收入与固定资产平均净值之比。该比率越高,说明固定资产的利用率越高,管理水平越好。其计算公式为:

$$固定资产周转率 = 销售收入 \div 固定资产平均净值$$

$$固定资产平均净值 = (期初固定资产净值 + 期末固定资产净值) \div 2$$

5)总资产周转率

总资产周转率是企业销售收入与资产平均总额之比,可以用来分析企业全部资产的使用效率。如果该比率较低,企业应采取措施提高销售收入或处置资产,以提高总资产利用率。其计算公式为:

$$总资产周转率 = 销售收入 \div 资产平均总额$$

$$资产平均总额 = (期初资产总额 + 期末资产总额) \div 2$$

8.1.2.3 长期负债比率

长期负债比率是说明债务和资产、净资产间关系的比率。它反映企业偿付到期长期债务的能力。企业的长期债务主要有长期借款、应付长期债券和长期应付款等。分析一个企业长期债务偿还能力,主要是为了确定该企业偿还债务本金与债务利息的能力。反映长期偿债能力的负债比率主要有资产负债率、产权比率、股东权益比率和利息保障倍数。

1)资产负债率

资产负债率是企业负债总额与资产总额之比,又称举债经营比率,它反映企业的资产总额中有多少是通过举债得到的。资产负债率反映企业偿还债务的综合能力,该比率越高,企业偿还债务的能力越差。反之,偿还债务的能力越强。其计算公式为:

$$资产负债率 = (负债总额 \div 资产总额) \times 100\%$$

2) 产权比率

产权比率又称负债权益比率,是负债总额与股东权益总额之比,也是衡量企业长期偿债能力的指标之一。其计算公式为:

$$产权比率 = 负债总额 \div 股东权益总额 \times 100\%$$

3) 股东权益比率

股东权益比率(又称自有资本比率或净资产比率)是股东权益与资产总额的比率,该比率反映企业资产中有多少是所有者投入的。企业的股东权益比率应当适中,如果权益比率过小,表明企业过度负债,容易削弱公司抵御外部冲击的能力;而权益比率过大,意味着企业没有积极地利用财务杠杆作用来扩大经营规模。

4) 利息保障倍数

利息保障倍数是税前利润加利息支出之和,即息税前利润与利息支出的比值,反映了企业用经营所得支付债务利息的能力。该比率越高,说明企业用经营所得支付债务利息的能力越强,它会增强贷款人对公司支付能力的信任程度。其计算公式为:

$$利息保障倍数 = (税前利润 + 利息支出) \div 利息支出 = 息税前利润 \div 利息支出$$

8.1.2.4 盈利能力比率

盈利能力比率是考查企业赚取利润能力高低的比率。反映企业盈利能力的主要指标有资产报酬率、股东权益报酬率和营业利润率等。

1) 资产报酬率

资产报酬率也称资产利润率或总资产收益率,是企业在一定时期内的净利润与资产平均总额之比。其计算公式为:

$$资产报酬率 = (净利润 \div 资产平均总额) \times 100\%$$

2) 股东权益报酬率

股东权益报酬率也称净资产收益率,是在一定时期内企业的净利润与股东权益平均总额之比。其计算公式为:

$$股东权益报酬率 = (净利润 \div 股东权益平均总额) \times 100\%$$

$$股东权益平均总额 = (期初股东权益总额 + 期末股东权益总额) \div 2$$

3) 营业利润率

营业利润率反映了企业的营业利润与营业收入的比例关系。其计算公式为:

$$营业利润率 = (营业利润 \div 营业收入) \times 100\%$$

8.1.2.5 市价比率

市价比率又称市场价值比率,实质上是反映每股市价和企业盈余、每股账面价值关系的比率,它是上述四类指标的综合反映。管理者可根据该比率了解投资人对企业的评价。市价比率包括每股盈余、市盈率、每股股利、股利支付比率和每股账面价值等指标。本书案例不涉及这类指标的分析,因此不详细展开。

8.1.3 用 Hive 实施财务报表数据分析

江苏财源有限公司执行《企业会计准则》,该公司 2020 年、2021 年、2022 年的资产负债表和利润表分别如表 8.1.1 至表 8.1.6 所示。根据这些资料,建立 Hive 表,并在 Hive 表中建立财务比率分析模型,进行偿债能力比率、资产管理比率和长期负债比率分析。

表 8.1.1 江苏财源有限公司 2020 年资产负债表　　　　　　　　　　单位:元

项目	期末余额	期初余额	项目	期末余额	期初余额
流动资产:			流动负债:		
货币资金	18 821 947.13	24 883 922.02	短期借款	0.00	0.00
交易性金融资产	0.00	0.00	交易性金融负债	0.00	0.00
衍生金融资产	0.00	0.00	衍生金融负债	0.00	0.00
应收票据	0.00	0.00	应付票据	0.00	0.00
应收账款	5 993 145.62	5 896 411.62	应付账款	1 568 231.20	2 658 543.50
应收款项融资	0.00	0.00	预收款项	0.00	0.00
预付款项	0.00	0.00	合同负债	0.00	0.00
其他应收款	10 000.00	0.00	应付职工薪酬	125 986.00	120 000.00
应收利息	0.00	0.00	应交税费	325 862.30	305 866.50
应收股利	0.00	0.00	其他应付款	0.00	0.00
存货	9 561 823.55	10 237 715.94	应付利息	0.00	0.00
合同资产	0.00	0.00	应付股利	0.00	0.00
持有待售资产	0.00	0.00	持有待售负债	0.00	0.00
一年内到期的非流动资产	0.00	0.00	一年内到期的非流动负债	0.00	0.00
其他流动资产	0.00	0.00	其他流动负债	0.00	0.00
流动资产合计	34 386 916.30	41 018 049.58	流动负债合计	2 020 079.50	3 084 410.00
非流动资产:			非流动负债:		
债权投资	0.00	0.00	长期借款	3 725 700.00	3 725 700.00
其他债权投资	0.00	0.00	应付债券	0.00	0.00
长期应收款	0.00	0.00	租赁负债	0.00	0.00
长期股权投资	17 551 162.00	10 551 162.00	长期应付款	0.00	0.00
其他权益工具投资	0.00	0.00	长期应付职工薪酬	0.00	0.00
其他非流动金融资产	0.00	0.00	预计负债	0.00	0.00
投资性房地产	0.00	0.00	递延收益	0.00	0.00
固定资产	3 356 982.50	3 689 521.60	递延所得税负债	0.00	0.00

（续表）

项目	期末余额	期初余额	项目	期末余额	期初余额
在建工程	1 240 558.80	1 240 558.80	其他非流动负债	0.00	0.00
生产性生物资产	0.00	0.00	非流动负债合计	3 725 700.00	3 725 700.00
油气资产	0.00	0.00	负债合计	5 745 779.50	6 810 110.00
使用权资产	0.00	0.00	所有者权益：		
无形资产	143 925.00	156 952.00	实收资本	50 000 000.00	50 000 000.00
开发支出	0.00	0.00	其他权益工具	0.00	0.00
商誉	0.00	0.00	资本公积	0.00	0.00
长期待摊费用	0.00	0.00	其他综合收益	0.00	0.00
递延所得税资产	0.00	0.00	专项储备	0.00	0.00
其他非流动资产	0.00	0.00	盈余公积	273 192.39	164 429.28
非流动资产合计	22 292 628.30	15 638 194.40	未分配利润	660 572.71	-318 295.30
			所有者权益合计	50 933 765.10	49 846 133.98
资产总计	56 679 544.60	56 656 243.98	负债和所有者权益总计	56 679 544.60	56 656 243.98

表 8.1.2　江苏财源有限公司 2020 年度利润表　　　　　　　　　　　　　　　　　单位：元

项目	本期金额	上期金额
一、营业收入	17 592 046.78	11 610 750.87
减：营业成本	13 047 503.39	8 611 352.24
税金及附加	105 552.28	69 664.50
销售费用	347 071.45	529 067.10
管理费用	2 588 741.69	2 008 569.52
研发费用	0.00	0.00
财务费用	310 252.27	104 766.50
其中：利息支出	45 500.00	
利息收入	0.00	0.00
加：其他收益	0.00	0.00
投资收益（损失以"-"号填列）	0.00	0.00
二、营业利润（亏损以"-"号填列）	1 192 925.70	287 331.01
加：营业外收入	0.00	10 000.00
减：营业外支出	420 000.00	
三、利润总额（亏损总额以"-"号填列）	772 925.70	297 331.01
减：所得税费用	89 336.75	

(续表)

项目	本期金额	上期金额
四、净利润(净亏损以"－"号填列)	683 588.95	297 331.01
(一) 持续经营净利润		
(二) 终止经营净利润		
五、其他综合收益的税后净额		
六、综合收益总额		
归属于母公司所有者的综合收益总额		
七、每股收益:		
(一) 基本每股收益(元/股)		
(二) 稀释每股收益(元/股)		

表 8.1.3　江苏财源有限公司 2021 年资产负债表　　　　单位：元

项目	期末余额	期初余额	项目	期末余额	期初余额
流动资产：			流动负债：		
货币资金	21 390 970.84	18 821 947.13	短期借款	0.00	
交易性金融资产	0.00		交易性金融负债	0.00	
衍生金融资产	0.00		衍生金融负债	0.00	
应收票据	0.00		应付票据	0.00	
应收账款	5 192 319.79	5 993 145.62	应付账款	1 295 287.80	1 568 231.20
应收款项融资	0.00		预收款项	0.00	
预付款项	0.00		合同负债	0.00	
其他应收款	10 000.00	10 000.00	应付职工薪酬	2 520.00	125 986.00
应收利息	0.00		应交税费	475 213.51	325 862.30
应收股利	0.00		其他应付款	0.00	
存货	8 468 074.50	9 561 823.55	应付利息	0.00	
合同资产	0.00		应付股利	0.00	
持有待售资产	0.00		持有待售负债	0.00	
一年内到期的非流动资产	0.00		一年内到期的非流动负债	0.00	
其他流动资产	0.00		其他流动负债	0.00	
流动资产合计	35 061 365.13	34 386 916.30	流动负债合计	1 773 021.31	2 020 079.50
非流动资产：			非流动负债：		
债权投资	0.00		长期借款	3 725 700.00	3 725 700.00
其他债权投资	0.00		应付债券	0.00	

(续表)

项目	期末余额	期初余额	项目	期末余额	期初余额
长期应收款	0.00		租赁负债	0.00	
长期股权投资	17 551 162.00	17 551 162.00	长期应付款	0.00	
其他权益工具投资	0.00		长期应付职工薪酬	0.00	
其他非流动金融资产	0.00		预计负债	0.00	
投资性房地产	0.00		递延收益	0.00	
固定资产	3 006 554.50	3 356 982.50	递延所得税负债	0.00	
在建工程	1 740 558.80	1 240 558.80	其他非流动负债	0.00	
生产性生物资产	0.00		非流动负债合计	3 725 700.00	3 725 700.00
油气资产	0.00		负债合计	5 498 721.31	5 745 779.50
使用权资产	0.00		所有者权益:		
无形资产	133 875.00	143 925.00	实收资本	50 000 000.00	50 000 000.00
开发支出	0.00		其他权益工具	0.00	
商誉	0.00		资本公积	0.00	
长期待摊费用	0.00		其他综合收益	0.00	
递延所得税资产	26 602.10	0.00	专项储备	0.00	
其他非流动资产	0.00	0.00	盈余公积	381 955.50	273 192.39
非流动资产合计	22 458 752.40	22 292 628.30	未分配利润	1 639 440.72	660 572.71
			所有者权益合计	52 021 396.22	50 933 765.10
资产总计	57 520 117.53	56 679 544.60	负债和所有者权益总计	57 520 117.53	56 679 544.60

表 8.1.4　江苏财源有限公司 2021 年度利润表　　　　　　　　　　单位：元

项目	本期金额	上期金额
一、营业收入	20 559 863.00	17 592 046.78
减：营业成本	15 248 645.35	13 047 503.39
税金及附加	123 359.18	105 552.28
销售费用	405 623.15	347 071.45
管理费用	3 025 468.00	2 588 741.69
研发费用	0.00	0.00
财务费用	362 592.50	310 252.27
其中：利息支出	130 000.00	45 500.00

（续表）

项目	本期金额	上期金额
利息收入	0.00	
加：其他收益	0.00	
投资收益（损失以"－"号填列）	0.00	
二、营业利润（亏损以"－"号填列）	1 394 174.82	1 192 925.70
加：营业外收入	56 000.00	
减：营业外支出	0.00	420 000.00
三、利润总额（亏损总额以"－"号填列）	1 450 174.82	772 925.70
减：所得税费用	362 543.70	89 336.75
四、净利润（净亏损以"－"号填列）	1 087 631.12	683 588.95
（一）持续经营净利润	1 087 631.12	683 588.95
（二）终止经营净利润		
五、其他综合收益的税后净额		
六、综合收益总额	1 087 631.12	683 588.95
归属于母公司所有者的综合收益总额	1 087 631.12	683 588.95
七、每股收益：		
基本每股收益（元/股）		
稀释每股收益（元/股）		

表 8.1.5　江苏财源有限公司 2022 年资产负债表　　　　　单位：元

项目	期末余额	期初余额	项目	期末余额	期初余额
流动资产：			流动负债：		
货币资金	20 935 895.98	21 390 970.84	短期借款		
交易性金融资产			交易性金融负债		
衍生金融资产			衍生金融负债		
应收票据	375 000.00	0.00	应付票据		
应收账款	2 508 806.80	5 192 319.79	应付账款	1 254 352.80	1 295 287.80
应收款项融资			预收款项		
预付款项			合同负债		
其他应收款	10 009.47	10 000.00	应付职工薪酬	31 422.00	2 520.00
应收利息			应交税费	156 878.14	475 213.51
应收股利			其他应付款	160.00	
存货	8 784 315.50	8 468 074.50	应付利息		

(续表)

项目	期末余额	期初余额	项目	期末余额	期初余额
合同资产			应付股利		
持有待售资产			持有待售负债		
一年内到期的非流动资产			一年内到期的非流动负债		
其他流动资产			其他流动负债		
流动资产合计	32 614 027.75	35 061 365.13	流动负债合计	1 442 812.94	1 773 021.31
非流动资产：			非流动负债：		
债权投资			长期借款	0.00	3 725 700.00
其他债权投资			应付债券		
长期应收款			租赁负债		
长期股权投资	17 551 162.00	17 551 162.00	长期应付款		
其他权益工具投资			长期应付职工薪酬		
其他非流动金融资产			预计负债		
投资性房地产			递延收益		
固定资产	3 245 753.50	3 006 554.50	递延所得税负债		
在建工程	3 178 458.72	1 740 558.80	其他非流动负债		
生产性生物资产			非流动负债合计	0.00	3 725 700.00
油气资产			负债合计	1 442 812.94	5 498 721.31
使用权资产			所有者权益：		
无形资产	120 150.00	133 875.00	实收资本	50 000 000.00	50 000 000.00
开发支出			其他权益工具		
商誉			资本公积		
长期待摊费用			其他综合收益		
递延所得税资产	26 602.10	26 602.10	专项储备		
其他非流动资产			盈余公积	873 094.06	381 955.50
非流动资产合计	24 122 126.32	22 458 752.40	未分配利润	4 420 247.07	1 639 440.72
			所有者权益合计	55 293 341.13	52 021 396.22
资产总计	56 736 154.07	57 520 117.53	负债和所有者权益总计	56 736 154.07	57 520 117.53

表 8.1.6　江苏财源有限公司 2022 年度利润表　　　　　　单位：元

项目	本期金额	上期金额
一、营业收入	25 419 020.00	20 559 863.00
减：营业成本	16 819 017.50	15 248 645.35
税金及附加	80 715.58	123 359.18
销售费用	313 827.50	405 623.15
管理费用	3 649 975.50	3 025 468.00
研发费用		
财务费用	236 355.51	362 592.50
其中：利息支出	50 000.00	130 000.00
利息收入		
加：其他收益		
投资收益（损失以"-"号填列）		
二、营业利润（亏损以"-"号填列）	4 319 128.41	1 394 174.82
加：营业外收入	82 500.00	56 000.00
减：营业外支出	50 000.00	
三、利润总额（亏损总额以"-"号填列）	4 351 628.41	1 450 174.82
减：所得税费用	1 079 683.50	362 543.70
四、净利润（净亏损以"-"号填列）	3 271 944.91	1 087 631.12
（一）持续经营净利润	3 271 944.91	1 087 631.12
（二）终止经营净利润		
五、其他综合收益的税后净额		
六、综合收益总额	3 271 944.91	1 087 631.12
归属于母公司所有者的综合收益总额	3 271 944.91	1 087 631.12
七、每股收益：		
基本每股收益(元/股)		
稀释每股收益(元/股)		

8.1.3.1　数据准备

接下来将完成以下操作：建立 2020 年、2021 年资产负债表数据，分别创建成文本文件 zcfzb2020.txt，zcfzb2021.txt；建立 2020 年、2021 年的利润表数据，分别创建成文本文件 lrb2020.txt，lrb2021.txt。所有数据之间用","间隔。

1) 创建 2020 年资产负债表数据文件 zcfzb2020.txt

将 2020 年资产负债表数据重新整理，数据之间用逗号","间隔，整理后的数据如下：

流动资产_货币资金,18821947.13,24883922.02
流动资产_交易性金融资产,0.00,0.00
流动资产_衍生金融资产,0.00,0.00
流动资产_应收票据,0.00,0.00
流动资产_应收账款,5993145.62,5896411.62
流动资产_应收款项融资,0.00,0.00
流动资产_预付款项,0.00,0.00
流动资产_其他应收款,10000.00 ,0.00
流动资产_应收利息,0.00,0.00
流动资产_应收股利,0.00,0.00
流动资产_存货,9561823.55,10237715.94
流动资产_合同资产,0.00 ,0.00
流动资产_持有待售资产,0.00,0.00
流动资产_一年内到期的非流动资产,0.00,0.00
流动资产_其他流动资产,0.00,0.00
流动资产合计,34386916.30,41018049.58
非流动资产_债权投资,0.00,0.00
非流动资产_其他债权投资,0.00,0.00
非流动资产_长期应收款,0.00,0.00
非流动资产_长期股权投资,17551162.00,10551162.00
非流动资产_其他权益工具投资,0.00,0.00
非流动资产_其他非流动金融资产,0.00,0.00
非流动资产_投资性房地产,0.00,0.00
非流动资产_固定资产,3356982.50,3689521.60
非流动资产_在建工程,1240558.80,1240558.80
非流动资产_生产性生物资产,0.00,0.00
非流动资产_油气资产,0.00,0.00
非流动资产_使用权资产,0.00,0.00
非流动资产_无形资产,143925.00,156952.00
非流动资产_开发支出,0.00,0.00
非流动资产_商誉,0.00,0.00
非流动资产_长期待摊费用,0.00,0.00
非流动资产_递延所得税资产,0.00,0.00
非流动资产_其他非流动资产,0.00 ,0.00
非流动资产合计,22292628.30,15638194.40
资产总计,56679544.60,56656243.98
流动负债_短期借款,0.00,0.00
流动负债_交易性金融负债,0.00,0.00
流动负债_衍生金融负债,0.00,0.00
流动负债_应付票据,0.00 ,0.00
流动负债_应付账款,1568231.20,2658543.50

流动负债_预收款项,0.00,0.00
流动负债_合同负债,0.00 ,0.00
流动负债_应付职工薪酬,125986.00,120000.00
流动负债_应交税费,25862.30,305866.50
流动负债_其他应付款,0.00,0.00
流动负债_应付利息,0.00,0.00
流动负债_应付股利,0.00,0.00
流动负债_持有待售负债,0.00,0.00
流动负债_一年内到期的非流动负债,0.00,0.00
流动负债_其他流动负债,0.00,0.00
流动负债合计,2020079.50,3084410.00
非流动负债_长期借款,3725700.00,3725700.00
非流动负债_应付债券,0.00,0.00
非流动负债_租赁负债,0.00,0.00
非流动负债_长期应付款,0.00,0.00
非流动负债_长期应付职工薪酬,0.00,0.00
非流动负债_预计负债,0.00,0.00
非流动负债_递延收益,0.00,0.00
非流动负债_递延所得税负债,0.00,0.00
非流动负债_其他非流动负债,0.00,0.00
非流动负债合计,3725700.00,3725700.00
负债合计,5745779.50,6810110.00
所有者权益_实收资本,50000000.00,50000000.00
所有者权益_其他权益工具,0.00,0.00
所有者权益_资本公积,0.00,0.00
所有者权益_其他综合收益,0.00,0.00
所有者权益_专项储备,0.00,0.00
所有者权益_盈余公积,273192.39,164429.28
所有者权益_未分配利润,660572.71,-318295.30
所有者权益合计,50933765.10,49846133.98
负债和所有者权益总计,56679544.60,56656243.98

在本地 CentOS 7 上,创建"/home/hadoop/cwbb"目录,切换该目录为当前目录,再用 vi 或 vim 编辑器创建文本文件 zcfzb2020.txt,命令如下:

```
[root@master /]#    mkdir -p /home/hadoop/cwbb
[root@master /]#    cd /home/hadoop/cwbb
[root@master cwbb]# vi zcfzb2020.txt
```

在 vi 编辑器中,切换到 INSERT 模式,将上述数据粘贴进去,按 Esc 键,输入":wq"保存退出。运行结果如图 8.1.1 所示。

单元 8　Hive 在财务报表分析和贷款数据分析中应用的综合案例 | 279

图 8.1.1　创建 2020 年资产负债表数据文件 zcfzb2020.txt

2) 创建 2021 年资产负债表数据文件 zcfzb2021.txt

将 2021 年资产负债表数据重新整理，数据之间用逗号","间隔，整理后的数据如下：

流动资产_货币资金,21390970.84,18821947.13
流动资产_交易性金融资产,0.00,0.00
流动资产_衍生金融资产,0.00,0.00
流动资产_应收票据,0.00,0.00
流动资产_应收账款,5192319.79,5993145.62
流动资产_应收款项融资,0.00,0.00
流动资产_预付款项,0.00,0.00
流动资产_其他应收款,10000.00,10000.00
流动资产_应收利息,0.00,0.00
流动资产_应收股利,0.00,0.00
流动资产_存货,8468074.50,9561823.55
流动资产_合同资产,0.00,0.00
流动资产_持有待售资产,0.00,0.00
流动资产_一年内到期的非流动资产,0.00,0.00
流动资产_其他流动资产,0.00,0.00

流动资产合计,35061365.13,34386916.30
非流动资产_债权投资,0.00,0.00
非流动资产_其他债权投资,0.00,0.00
非流动资产_长期应收款,0.00,0.00
非流动资产_长期股权投资,17551162.00,17551162.00
非流动资产_其他权益工具投资,0.00,0.00
非流动资产_其他非流动金融资产,0.00,0.00
非流动资产_投资性房地产,0.00,0.00
非流动资产_固定资产,3006554.50,3356982.50
非流动资产_在建工程,1740558.80,1240558.80
非流动资产_生产性生物资产,0.00,0.00
非流动资产_油气资产,0.00,0.00
非流动资产_使用权资产,0.00,0.00
非流动资产_无形资产,133875.00,143925.00
非流动资产_开发支出,0.00 ,0.00
非流动资产_商誉,0.00,0.00
非流动资产_长期待摊费用,0.00,0.00
非流动资产_递延所得税资产,26,602.10,0.00
非流动资产_其他非流动资产,0.00,0.00
非流动资产合计,22458752.40,22292628.30
资产总计,57520117.53,56679544.60
流动负债_短期借款,0.00 ,0.00
流动负债_交易性金融负债,0.00,0.00
流动负债_衍生金融负债,0.00,0.00
流动负债_应付票据,0.00 ,0.00
流动负债_应付账款,1295287.80,1568231.20
流动负债_预收款项,0.00,0.00
流动负债_合同负债,0.00,0.00
流动负债_应付职工薪酬,2520.00,125986.00
流动负债_应交税费,475213.51,325862.30
流动负债_其他应付款,0.00,0.00
流动负债_应付利息,0.00,0.00
流动负债_应付股利,0.00,0.00
流动负债_持有待售负债,0.00,0.00
流动负债_一年内到期的非流动负债,0.00,0.00
流动负债_其他流动负债,0.00,0.00
流动负债合计,1773021.31,2020079.50
非流动负债_长期借款,3725700.00,3725700.00
非流动负债_应付债券,0.00,0.00
非流动负债_租赁负债,0.00,0.00
非流动负债_长期应付款,0.00,0.00
非流动负债_长期应付职工薪酬,0.00,0.00
非流动负债_预计负债,0.00,0.00
非流动负债_递延收益,0.00,0.00
非流动负债_递延所得税负债,0.00,0

非流动负债_其他非流动负债,0,0.00
非流动负债合计,3725700.00,3725700.00
负债合计,5498721.31,5745779.50
所有者权益_实收资本,50000000.00,50000000.00
所有者权益_其他权益工具,0.00,0.00
所有者权益_资本公积,0.00,0.00
所有者权益_其他综合收益,0.00,0.00
所有者权益_专项储备,0.00,0.00
所有者权益_盈余公积,381955.50,273192.39
所有者权益_未分配利润,1639440.72,660572.71
所有者权益合计,52021396.22,50933765.10
负债和所有者权益总计,57520117.53,56679544.60

在本地 CentOS 7 系统上的"/home/hadoop/cwbb"目录下,用 vi 或 vim 编辑器创建文本文件 zcfzb2021.txt,命令如下:

```
[root@master /]#        cd /home/hadoop/cwbb
[root@master cwbb]#     vi zcfzb2021.txt
```

在 vi 编辑器中,切换到 INSERT 模式,将上述数据粘贴进去,按 Esc 键,输入":wq"保存退出。运行结果如图 8.1.2 所示。

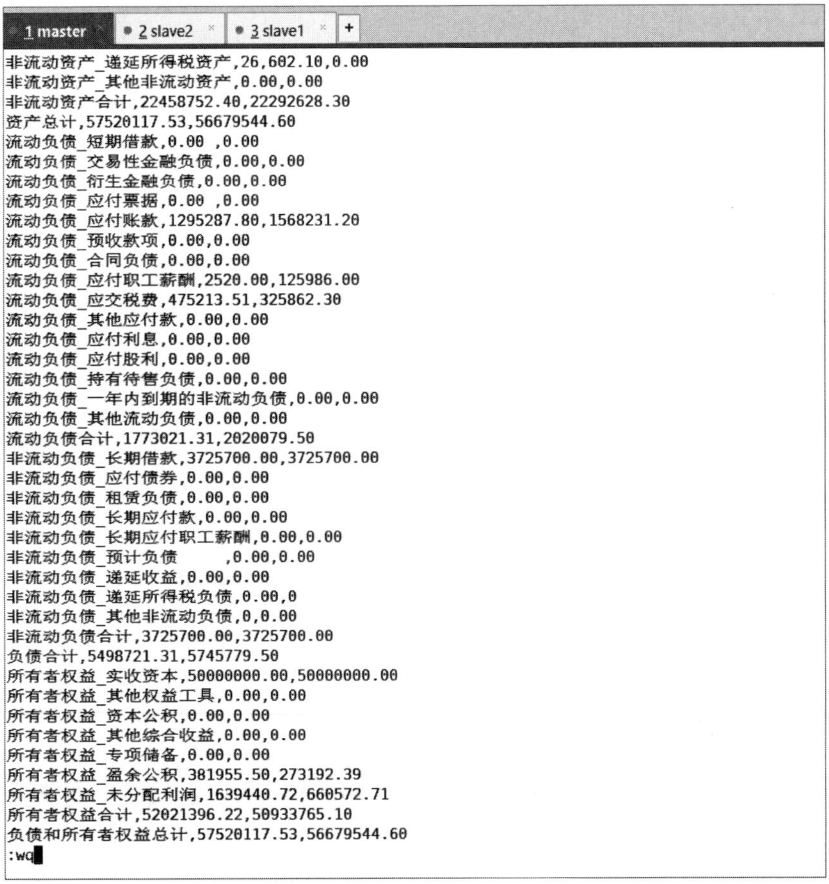

图 8.1.2 创建 2021 年资产负债表数据文件 zcfzb2021.txt

3) 创建 2020 年利润表数据文件 lrb2020.txt

将 2020 年利润表数据重新整理,数据之间用逗号","间隔,整理后的数据如下:

```
一、营业收入,17592046.78,11610750.87
减:营业成本,13047503.39,8611352.24
税金及附加,105552.28,69664.50
销售费用,347071.45,529067.10
管理费用,2588741.69,2008569.52
研发费用,0.00,0.00
财务费用,310252.27,104766.50
其中:利息支出,45500.00,0
    利息收入,0.00,0.00
加:其他收益,0.00,0.00
   投资收益,0.00,0.00
二、营业利润,1192925.70,287331.01
加:营业外收入,0.00,10000.00
减:营业外支出,420000.00,0.00
三、利润总额,772925.70,297331.01
减:所得税费用,89336.75,0.00
四、净利润,683588.95,297331.01
(一)持续经营净利润,0.00,0.00
(二)终止经营净利润,0.00,0.00
五、其他综合收益的税后净额,0.00,0.00
六、综合收益总额,0.00,0.00
归属于母公司所有者的综合收益总额,0.00,0.00
七、每股收益,0.00,0.00
基本每股收益(元/股),0.00,0.00
稀释每股收益(元/股),0.00,0.00
```

在本地 CentOS 7 上指定目录下,用 vi 或 vim 编辑器创建文本文件 lrb2020.txt,命令如下:

```
[root@master ~]#  vi lrb2020.txt
```

在 vi 编辑器中,切换到 INSERT 模式,将上述数据粘贴进去,按 Esc 键,输入":wq"保存退出。运行结果如图 8.1.4 所示。

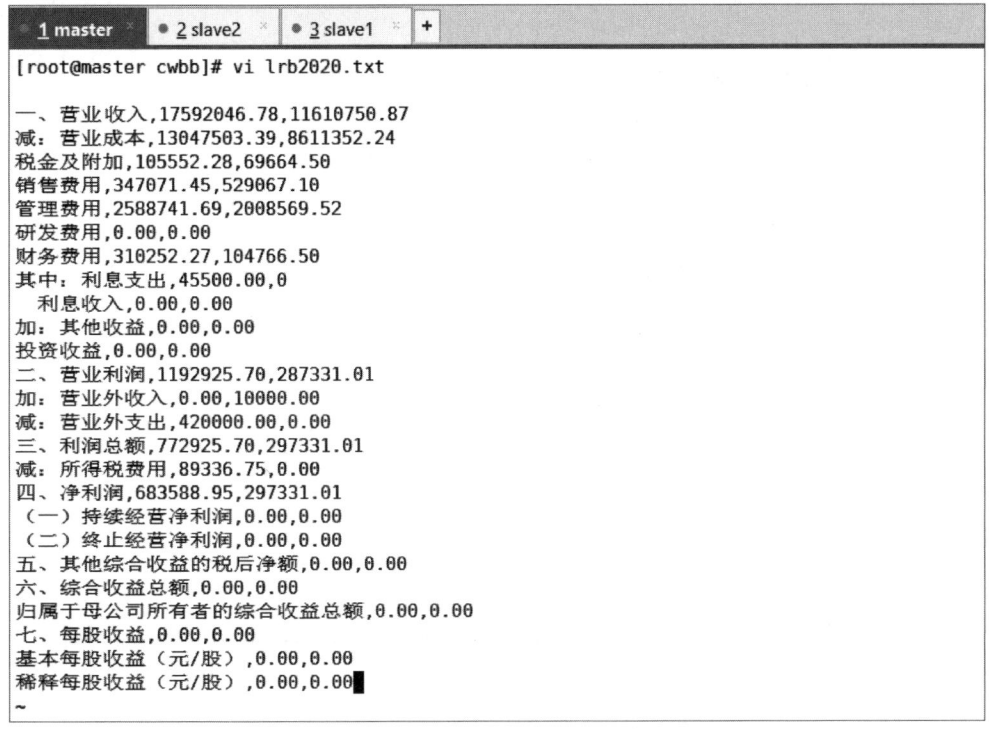

图 8.1.3　创建 2020 年利润表数据文件 lrb2020.txt

4）创建 2021 年利润表数据文件 lrb2021.txt

将 2021 年利润表数据重新整理，数据之间用逗号","间隔，整理后的数据如下：

一、营业收入,20559863.00,17592046.78

减:营业成本,15248645.35,13047503.39

税金及附加,123359.18,105552.28

销售费用,405623.15,347071.45

管理费用,3025468.00,2588741.69

研发费用,0.00,0.00

财务费用,362592.50,310252.27

　其中:利息支出,130000.00,45500.00

　　　利息收入,0.00,0.00

加:其他收益,0.00,0.00

　　投资收益,0.00,0.00

二、营业利润,1394174.82,1192925.70

加:营业外收入,56000.00,0.00

减:营业外支出,0.00,420000.00

三、利润总额,1450174.82,772925.70

减:所得税费用,362543.70,89336.75

四、净利润,1087631.12,683588.95

（一）持续经营净利润,1087631.12,683588.95
（二）终止经营净利润,0.00,0.00
五、其他综合收益的税后净额,0.00,0.00
六、综合收益总额,1087631.12,683588.95
归属于母公司所有者的综合收益总额,1087631.12,683588.95
七、每股收益,0.00,0.00
基本每股收益(元/股),0.00,0.00
稀释每股收益(元/股),0.00,0.00

在本地 CentOS 7 上指定目录下，用 vi 或 vim 编辑器创建文本文件 lrb2021.txt，命令如下：

```
[root@master ~]# vi lrb2021.txt
```

在 vi 编辑器中，切换到 INSERT 模式，将上述数据粘贴进去，按 Esc 键，输入":wq"保存退出。运行结果如图 8.1.4 所示。

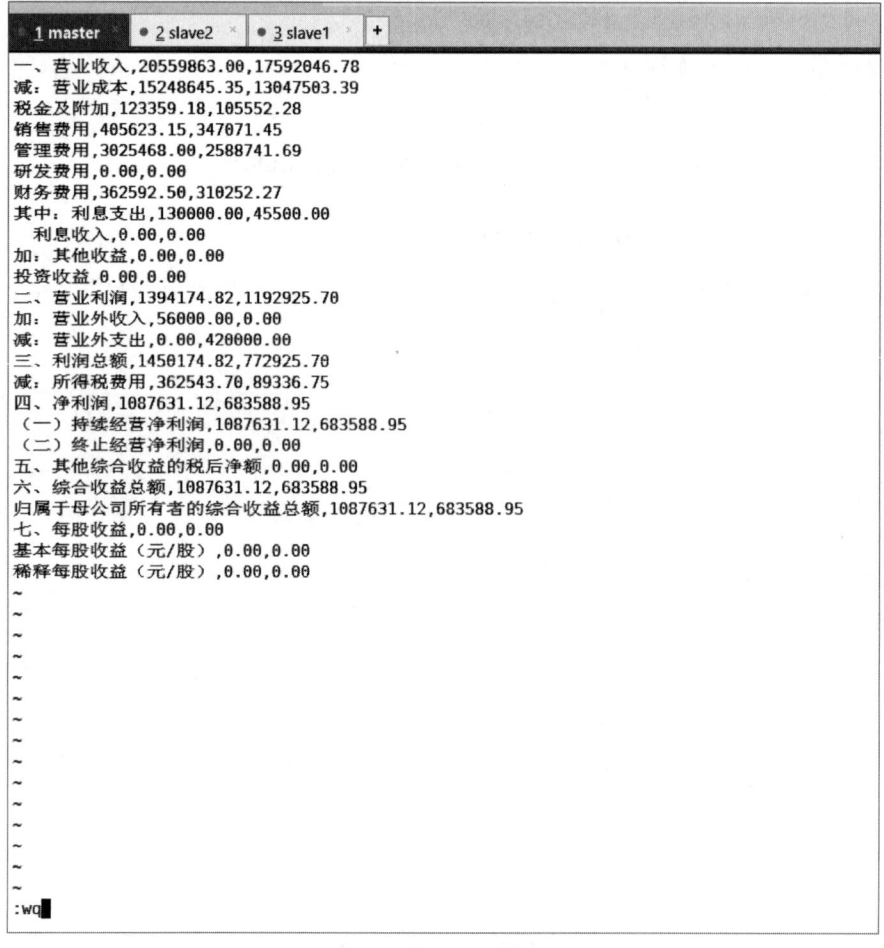

图 8.1.4　创建 2021 年利润表数据文件 lrb2021.txt

8.1.3.2 创建 Hive 数据库 cwbb

启动 Hive,在 Hive 中创建数据库 cwbb,并切换到该数据库,命令如下:

```
[root@master ~]# hive
hive (default)> CREATE DATABASE IF NOT EXISTS cwbb;
hive (default)> USE cwbb;
hive (cwbb)>
```

运行结果如图 8.1.5 所示。

```
hive (default)> CREATE DATABASE IF NOT EXISTS cwbb;
OK
Time taken: 0.037 seconds
hive (default)> USE cwbb;
OK
Time taken: 0.049 seconds
hive (cwbb)>
```

图 8.1.5 创建 Hive 数据库 cwbb 并切换

8.1.3.3 创建 4 个 Hive 数据表

在 Hive 上创建 2020 年和 2021 年资产负债表即 zcfzb2020、zcfzb2021,包含的字段名为 xm(项目)、qmye(期末余额)、qcye(期初余额)三列,命令如下:

```
hive (cwbb)> CREATE TABLE zcfzb2020(
xm STRING ,
qmye DOUBLE,
qcye DOUBLE
)
ROW FORMAT DELIMITED FIELDS TERMINATED BY ','
STORED AS TEXTFILE;

hive (cwbb)> CREATE TABLE zcfzb2021(
xm STRING ,
qmye DOUBLE,
qcye DOUBLE
)
ROW FORMAT DELIMITED FIELDS TERMINATED BY ','
STORED AS TEXTFILE;
```

其中,ROW FORMAT DELIMITED FIELDS TERMINATED BY ',' 表示数据字段之间以逗号","间隔,如果不设置则使用默认分隔符。Hive 的 HiveQL 语句最后以";"结束。运行结果如图 8.1.6 所示。

```
hive (cwbb)> CREATE TABLE zcfzb2020(
            > xm STRING ,
            > qmye DOUBLE,
            > qcye DOUBLE
            > )
            > ROW FORMAT DELIMITED FIELDS TERMINATED BY ','
            > STORED AS TEXTFILE;
OK
Time taken: 0.381 seconds
hive (cwbb)> CREATE TABLE zcfzb2021(
            > xm STRING ,
            > qmye DOUBLE,
            > qcye DOUBLE
            > )
            > ROW FORMAT DELIMITED FIELDS TERMINATED BY ','
            > STORED AS TEXTFILE;
OK
Time taken: 0.12 seconds
```

图 8.1.6　创建 Hive 表 zcfzb2020、zcfzb2021

在 Hive 上创建 2020 年和 2021 年利润表即 lrb2020、lrb2021,包含的字段名为 xm(项目)、bqje(本期金额)、sqje(上期金额)三列。命令如下：

```
hive (cwbb)>   CREATE TABLE lrb2020(xm STRING,bqje DOUBLE,sqje DOUBLE)
        ROW FORMAT DELIMITED FIELDS TERMINATED BY ','
STORED AS TEXTFILE;
hive (cwbb)>   CREATE TABLE lrb2021(xm STRING,bqje DOUBLE,sqje DOUBLE)
        ROW FORMAT DELIMITED FIELDS TERMINATED BY ','
STORED AS TEXTFILE;
```

同样,ROW FORMAT DELIMITED FIELDS TERMINATED BY',' 表示数据字段之间以逗号","间隔,如果不设置则使用默认分隔符。Hive 的 HiveQL 语句最后以";"结束。运行结果如图 8.1.7 所示。

```
hive (cwbb)> CREATE TABLE lrb2020(xm STRING,bqje DOUBLE,sqje DOUBLE)
           >        ROW FORMAT DELIMITED FIELDS TERMINATED BY ','
           > STORED AS TEXTFILE;
OK
Time taken: 0.116 seconds
hive (cwbb)> CREATE TABLE lrb2021(xm STRING,bqje DOUBLE,sqje DOUBLE)
           >        ROW FORMAT DELIMITED FIELDS TERMINATED BY ','
           > STORED AS TEXTFILE;
OK
Time taken: 0.19 seconds
```

图 8.1.7　创建 Hive 表 lrb2020、lrb2021

8.1.3.4　向 Hive 表中导入数据

将 8.1.3.1 中建立的文本文件 zcfzb2020.txt、zcfzb2021.txt 数据分别导入 Hive 表

zcfzb2020、zcfzb2021 中,命令如下:

```
hive (cwbb)> LOAD DATA LOCAL INPATH '/home/hadoop/cwbb/zcfzb2020.txt'
INTO TABLE zcfzb2020;

hive (cwbb)> LOAD DATA LOCAL INPATH '/home/hadoop/cwbb/zcfzb2021.txt'
INTO TABLE zcfzb2021;
```

运行结果如图 8.1.8 所示。

```
hive (cwbb)> LOAD DATA LOCAL INPATH '/home/hadoop/cwbb/zcfzb2020.txt' INTO TABLE zcfzb2020;
Loading data to table cwbb.zcfzb2020
OK
Time taken: 6.198 seconds
hive (cwbb)>  LOAD DATA LOCAL INPATH '/home/hadoop/cwbb/zcfzb2021.txt'
            > INTO TABLE zcfzb2021;
Loading data to table cwbb.zcfzb2021
OK
Time taken: 1.36 seconds
```

图 8.1.8　分别向 zcfzb2020、zcfzb2021 表导入数据

将 8.1.3.1 中建立的文本文件 lrb2020.txt、lrb2021.txt 数据分别导入 Hive 表 lrb2020、lrb2021 中,命令如下:

```
hive (cwbb)> LOAD DATA LOCAL INPATH '/home/hadoop/cwbb/lrb2020.txt'
INTO TABLE lrb2020;

hive (cwbb)> LOAD DATA LOCAL INPATH '/home/hadoop/cwbb/lrb2021.txt'
INTO TABLE lrb2021;
```

运行结果如图 8.1.9 所示。

```
hive (cwbb)> LOAD DATA LOCAL INPATH '/home/hadoop/cwbb/lrb2020.txt'
           > INTO TABLE lrb2020;
Loading data to table cwbb.lrb2020
OK
Time taken: 1.435 seconds
hive (cwbb)> LOAD DATA LOCAL INPATH '/home/hadoop/cwbb/lrb2021.txt'
           > INTO TABLE lrb2021;
Loading data to table cwbb.lrb2021
OK
Time taken: 0.804 seconds
```

图 8.1.9　分别向 lrb2020、lrb2021 表导入数据

至此,2020 年、2021 年的资产负债表和利润表的数据已经全部导入 Hive 表中,接下来可以利用 SELECT 查看各表数据。具体步骤如下。

(1) 查看 zcfzb2020 表中所有流动资产,命令如下:

```
hive (cwbb)> SELECT * FROM zcfzb2020 WHERE xm LIKE '流动资产%';
```

这里用通配符"%"代表所有字符,"xm LIKE' 流动资产%'"表示 xm 值中以"流动资产"开头的所有行数据,查询结果如图 8.1.10 所示。

```
hive (cwbb)> SELECT * FROM zcfzb2020 WHERE xm LIKE '流动资产%';
OK
zcfzb2020.xm        zcfzb2020.qmye      zcfzb2020.qcye
流动资产_货币资金         1.882194713E7       2.488392202E7
流动资产_交易性金融资产 0.0          0.0
流动资产_衍生金融资产     0.0          0.0
流动资产_应收票据         0.0          0.0
流动资产_应收账款         5993145.62           5896411.62
流动资产_应收款项融资     0.0          0.0
流动资产_预付款项         0.0          0.0
流动资产_其他应收款                    10000.0 0.0
流动资产_应收利息         0.0          0.0
流动资产_应收股利         0.0          0.0
流动资产_存货    9561823.55           1.023771594E7
流动资产_合同资产         0.0          0.0
流动资产_持有待售资产 0.0         0.0
流动资产_一年内到期的非流动资产 0.0     0.0
流动资产_其他流动资产     0.0          0.0
流动资产合计    3.43869163E7         4.101804958E7
Time taken: 2.93 seconds, Fetched: 16 row(s)
hive (cwbb)>
```

图 8.1.10 查询 zcfzb2020 表中数据

(2) 查看 zcfzb2021 表中所有非流动资产,命令如下:

```
hive (cwbb)> SELECT * FROM zcfzb2021 WHERE xm LIKE '非流动资产%';
```

这里仍用 WHERE 实现条件查询,"xm LIKE' 非流动资产%'"表示 xm 值中以"非流动资产"开头的所有行数据,查询结果如图 8.1.11 所示。

```
zcfzb2021.xm        zcfzb2021.qmye      zcfzb2021.qcye
非流动资产_债权投资       0.0          0.0
非流动资产_其他债权投资 0.0         0.0
非流动资产_长期应收款     0.0          0.0
非流动资产_长期股权投资 1.7551162E7          1.7551162E7
非流动资产_其他权益工具投资            0.0          0.0
非流动资产_其他非流动金融资产          0.0          0.0
非流动资产_投资性房地产 0.0          0.0
非流动资产_固定资产                    3006554.5            3356982.5
非流动资产_在建工程        1740558.8            1240558.8
非流动资产_生产性生物资产              0.0          0.0
非流动资产_油气资产         0.0          0.0
非流动资产_使用权资产     0.0          0.0
非流动资产_无形资产        133875.0             143925.0
非流动资产_开发支出                    0.0          0.0
非流动资产_商誉 0.0         0.0
非流动资产_长期待摊费用 0.0         0.0
非流动资产_递延所得税资产              26.0         602.1
非流动资产_其他非流动资产              0.0          0.0
非流动资产合计    2.24587524E7         2.22926283E7
Time taken: 0.334 seconds, Fetched: 19 row(s)
hive (cwbb)>
```

图 8.1.11 查询 zcfzb2021 表中数据

（3）查看利润表 lrb2020 表中所有数据，命令如下：

```
hive (cwbb)> SELECT * FROM lrb2020;
```

查询结果如图 8.1.12 所示。

```
hive (cwbb)> SELECT * FROM lrb2020;
OK
lrb2020.xm          lrb2020.bqje         lrb2020.sqje
一、营业收入          1.759204678E7        1.161075087E7
减：营业成本          1.304750339E7        8611352.24
税金及附加           105552.28            69664.5
销售费用             347071.45            529067.1
管理费用             2588741.69           2008569.52
研发费用             0.0        0.0
财务费用             310252.27            104766.5
  其中：利息支出      45500.0    0.0
     利息收入         0.0        0.0
加：其他收益          0.0        0.0
投资收益             0.0        0.0
二、营业利润          1192925.7            287331.01
加：营业外收入        0.0        10000.0
减：营业外支出        420000.0             0.0
三、利润总额          772925.7             297331.01
减：所得税费用        89336.75             0.0
四、净利润            683588.95            297331.01
  （一）持续经营净利润      0.0        0.0
  （二）终止经营净利润      0.0        0.0
五、其他综合收益的税后净额      0.0        0.0
六、综合收益总额              0.0        0.0
归属于母公司所有者的综合收益总额      0.0        0.0
七、每股收益          0.0        0.0
基本每股收益（元/股）        0.0        0.0
稀释每股收益（元/股）        0.0        0.0
Time taken: 0.204 seconds, Fetched: 25 row(s)
hive (cwbb)>
```

图 8.1.12　查询 lrb2020 表中数据

（4）查看利润表 lrb2021 表中所有数据，命令如下：

```
hive (cwbb)> SELECT * FROM lrb2021;
```

查询结果如图 8.1.13 所示。

可见，已经成功将资产负债表数据加载进 zcfzb2020 表、zcfzb2021 表中，也成功将利润表数据加载进 lrb2020 表、lrb2021 表中。

8.1.3.5　用 Hive 对财务数据进行分析

用 Hive 对该公司进行财务比率分析，即变现能力比率、长期负债比率、资产管理比率分析，具体的财务比率分析公式如表 8.1.7 所示。

```
hive (cwbb)> SELECT * FROM lrb2021;
OK
lrb2021.xm              lrb2021.bqje        lrb2021.sqje
一、营业收入             2.0559863E7         1.759204678E7
减：营业成本             1.524864535E7       1.304750339E7
税金及附加               123359.18           105552.28
销售费用                 405623.15           347071.45
管理费用                 3025468.0           2588741.69
研发费用                 0.0                 0.0
财务费用                 362592.5            310252.27
  其中：利息支出         130000.0            45500.0
    利息收入             0.0                 0.0
加：其他收益             0.0                 0.0
  投资收益               0.0                 0.0
二、营业利润             1394174.82          1192925.7
加：营业外收入           56000.0             0.0
减：营业外支出           0.0                 420000.0
三、利润总额             1450174.82          772925.7
减：所得税费用           362543.7            89336.75
四、净利润               1087631.12          683588.95
  （一）持续经营净利润   1087631.12          683588.95
  （二）终止经营净利润   0.0                 0.0
五、其他综合收益的税后净额  0.0               0.0
六、综合收益总额         1087631.12          683588.95
  归属于母公司所有者的综合收益总额    1087631.12    683588.95
七、每股收益             0.0                 0.0
  基本每股收益（元/股）  0.0                 0.0
  稀释每股收益（元/股）  0.0                 0.0
Time taken: 0.45 seconds, Fetched: 25 row(s)
hive (cwbb)>
```

图 8.1.13　查询 lrb2021 表中数据

表 8.1.7　财务比率分析公式一览表

财务指标		计算公式	操作表
变现能力比率	流动比率	流动资产合计.期末余额/流动负债合计.期末余额	资产负债表
	速动比率	(流动资产合计.期末余额-存货.期末余额-预付账款.期末余额)/流动负债合计.期末余额	资产负债表
长期负债比率	资产负债率	负债合计.期末余额/资产总计.期末余额	资产负债表
	股东权益比率	所有者权益合计.期末余额/资产总计.期末余额	资产负债表
	产权比率	负债合计.期末余额/所有者权益合计.期末余额	资产负债表
	利息保障倍数	三、利润总额.本期金额/(((应收账款.期末余额＋应收账款.期初余额＋应收票据.期末余额＋应收票据.期初余额)/2)	利润表 资产负债表
资产管理比率	应收账款周转率	一、营业收入.本期金额/((资产负债表:应收账款.期末余额＋应收账款.期初余额＋应收票据.期末余额＋应收票据.期初余额)/2)	利润表 资产负债表
	存货周转率	减:营业成本.本期金额/((资产负债表:存货.期末余额＋存货.期初余额)/2)	利润表 资产负债表

(续表)

财务指标		计算公式	操作表
资产管理比率	固定资产周转率	一、营业收入.本期金额/((固定资产.期末余额+固定资产.期初余额)/2)	利润表 资产负债表
	流动资产周转率	一、营业收入.本期金额/((流动资产合计.期末余额+流动资产合计.期初余额)/2)	利润表 资产负债表
	总资产周转率	一、营业收入.本期金额/((资产总计.期末余额+资产总计.期初余额)/2)	利润表 资产负债表

1) 变现能力比率

（1）流动比率计算。

在资产负债表中取出数据流动资产合计的期末余额和流动负债合计的期末余额，进行相除运算，求出流动比率，公式如下：

流动比率 = 流动资产合计.期末余额/流动负债合计.期末余额

在 Hive 中分别对 zcfzb2020 表、zcfzb2021 表进行操作，从表中查询"流动资产合计"的"期末余额"，再查询"流动负债合计"的"期末余额"，再将两个查询结果做 JOIN 连接操作，从连接结果取出 2 个值进行除运算，结果用 ROUND() 函数四舍五入保留 2 位小数。这里要注意，要实现 JOIN 操作，需要设置 hive.mapred.mode 为 unstrict。

对 2020 年资产负债表 zcfzb2020 计算流动比率，命令如下：

```
hive (cwbb)> SET hive.mapred.mode=unstrict;
hive (cwbb)> SELECT round(qmye1/qmye2,2)  ldbl2020  FROM
((SELECT  qmye qmye1  from zcfzb2020  where xm='流动资产合计') z1
JOIN (SELECT  qmye  qmye2  from zcfzb2020  where xm='流动负债合计') z2);
```

流动比率计算结果为 17.02，运行结果如图 8.1.14 所示。

```
2024-05-06 17:07:10     End of local task; Time Taken: 3.849 sec.
Execution completed successfully
MapredLocal task succeeded
Launching Job 1 out of 1
Number of reduce tasks is set to 0 since there's no reduce operator
Starting Job = job_1714976504535_0018, Tracking URL = http://master:8088/proxy/application_17149765045
35_0018/
Kill Command = /opt/hadoop-2.7.7/bin/hadoop job  -kill job_1714976504535_0018
Hadoop job information for Stage-3: number of mappers: 1; number of reducers: 0
2024-05-06 17:07:29,566 Stage-3 map = 0%,  reduce = 0%
2024-05-06 17:07:48,191 Stage-3 map = 100%,  reduce = 0%, Cumulative CPU 3.53 sec
MapReduce Total cumulative CPU time: 3 seconds 530 msec
Ended Job = job_1714976504535_0018
MapReduce Jobs Launched:
Stage-Stage-3: Map: 1   Cumulative CPU: 3.53 sec   HDFS Read: 9566 HDFS Write: 105 SUCCESS
Total MapReduce CPU Time Spent: 3 seconds 530 msec
OK
ldbl2020
17.02
Time taken: 62.455 seconds, Fetched: 1 row(s)
hive (cwbb)>
```

图 8.1.14 2020 年流动比率计算结果为 17.02

对 2021 年资产负债表 zcfzb2021 计算流动比率,命令如下:

```
hive (cwbb)> SELECT round(qmye1/qmye2,2)  ldbl2021  FROM
((SELECT  qmye qmye1  from zcfzb2021  where xm='流动资产合计') z1
   JOIN (SELECT  qmye  qmye2  from zcfzb2021  where xm='流动负债合计') z2);
```

流动比率计算结果为 19.77,运行结果如图 8.1.15 所示。

```
2024-05-06 17:09:06    End of local task; Time Taken: 2.356 sec.
Execution completed successfully
MapredLocal task succeeded
Launching Job 1 out of 1
Number of reduce tasks is set to 0 since there's no reduce operator
Starting Job = job_1714976504535_0019, Tracking URL = http://master:8088/proxy/application_17149765045
35_0019/
Kill Command = /opt/hadoop-2.7.7/bin/hadoop job  -kill job_1714976504535_0019
Hadoop job information for Stage-3: number of mappers: 1; number of reducers: 0
2024-05-06 17:09:18,446 Stage-3 map = 0%,  reduce = 0%
2024-05-06 17:09:26,796 Stage-3 map = 100%,  reduce = 0%, Cumulative CPU 2.05 sec
MapReduce Total cumulative CPU time: 2 seconds 50 msec
Ended Job = job_1714976504535_0019
MapReduce Jobs Launched:
Stage-Stage-3: Map: 1   Cumulative CPU: 2.05 sec   HDFS Read: 9582 HDFS Write: 105 SUCCESS
Total MapReduce CPU Time Spent: 2 seconds 50 msec
OK
ldbl2021
19.77
Time taken: 43.386 seconds, Fetched: 1 row(s)
hive (cwbb)>
```

图 8.1.15　2021 年流动比率计算结果为 19.77

(2) 速动比率计算。

在资产负债表中取出"流动资产合计"的"期末余额"、"存货"的"期末余额"、"预付账款"的"期末余额"和"流动负债合计"的"期末余额",再进行运算,求出速动比率,公式如下:

速动比率=(流动资产合计.期末余额-存货.期末余额-预付款项.期末余额)
/流动负债合计.期末余额

在 Hive 中对 zcfzb2020 表、zcfzb2021 表进行操作,用 4 个子查询分别取出公式中的数据,再将 4 个子查询进行 JOIN 连接操作,形成宽表,从连接结果取出 4 个值进行运算。这里要注意,要实现 JOIN 操作,需要设置 hive.mapred.mode 为 unstrict。

对 2020 年资产负债表 zcfzb2020 计算速动比率,命令如下:

```
hive (cwbb)> SET hive.mapred.mode=unstrict;
hive (cwbb)> SELECT  round((qmye1-qmye2-qmye3)/qmye4,2)  sdbl2020  FROM
(
(SELECT qmye qmye1  from zcfzb2020  where xm='流动资产合计') t1
JOIN (SELECT qmye qmye2  from zcfzb2020  where xm='流动资产_存货') t2
JOIN (SELECT qmye qmye3  from zcfzb2020  where xm='流动资产_预付款项') t3
JOIN (SELECT qmye qmye4  from zcfzb2020  where xm='流动负债合计') t4
);
```

2020 年速动比率计算结果为 12.29,运行结果如图 8.1.16 所示。

```
2024-05-06 17:12:12    End of local task; Time Taken: 7.318 sec.
Execution completed successfully
MapredLocal task succeeded
Launching Job 1 out of 1
Number of reduce tasks is set to 0 since there's no reduce operator
Starting Job = job_1714976504535_0021, Tracking URL = http://master:8088/proxy/application_17149765045
35_0021/
Kill Command = /opt/hadoop-2.7.7/bin/hadoop job  -kill job_1714976504535_0021
Hadoop job information for Stage-5: number of mappers: 1; number of reducers: 0
2024-05-06 17:12:26,000 Stage-5 map = 0%,  reduce = 0%
2024-05-06 17:12:35,766 Stage-5 map = 100%,  reduce = 0%, Cumulative CPU 2.15 sec
MapReduce Total cumulative CPU time: 2 seconds 150 msec
Ended Job = job_1714976504535_0021
MapReduce Jobs Launched:
Stage-Stage-5: Map: 1   Cumulative CPU: 2.15 sec   HDFS Read: 10594 HDFS Write: 105 SUCCESS
Total MapReduce CPU Time Spent: 2 seconds 150 msec
OK
sdbl2020
12.29
Time taken: 52.679 seconds, Fetched: 1 row(s)
hive (cwbb)>
```

图 8.1.16　2020 年速动比率计算结果结果为 12.29

对 2021 年资产负债表 zcfzb2021 计算速动比率，命令如下：

```
hive (cwbb)> SELECT   round((qmye1-qmye2-qmye3)/qmye4,2)   sdbl2021   FROM
(
(SELECT qmye qmye1    from zcfzb2021    where xm='流动资产合计') t1
JOIN (SELECT qmye qmye2    from zcfzb2021    where xm='流动资产_存货') t2
JOIN (SELECT qmye qmye3    from zcfzb2021    where xm='流动资产_预付款项') t3
JOIN (SELECT qmye qmye4    from zcfzb2021    where xm='流动负债合计') t4
);
```

2021 年速动比率计算结果为 15.0，运行结果如图 8.1.17 所示。

```
2024-05-06 17:14:02    End of local task; Time Taken: 3.955 sec.
Execution completed successfully
MapredLocal task succeeded
Launching Job 1 out of 1
Number of reduce tasks is set to 0 since there's no reduce operator
Starting Job = job_1714976504535_0022, Tracking URL = http://master:8088/proxy/application_17149765045
35_0022/
Kill Command = /opt/hadoop-2.7.7/bin/hadoop job  -kill job_1714976504535_0022
Hadoop job information for Stage-5: number of mappers: 1; number of reducers: 0
2024-05-06 17:14:13,719 Stage-5 map = 0%,  reduce = 0%
2024-05-06 17:14:23,483 Stage-5 map = 100%,  reduce = 0%, Cumulative CPU 2.2 sec
MapReduce Total cumulative CPU time: 2 seconds 200 msec
Ended Job = job_1714976504535_0022
MapReduce Jobs Launched:
Stage-Stage-5: Map: 1   Cumulative CPU: 2.2 sec   HDFS Read: 10610 HDFS Write: 104 SUCCESS
Total MapReduce CPU Time Spent: 2 seconds 200 msec
OK
sdbl2021
15.0
Time taken: 45.661 seconds, Fetched: 1 row(s)
hive (cwbb)>
```

图 8.1.17　2021 年速动比率计算结果结果为 15.0

2) 长期负债比率

(1) 资产负债率。

在资产负债表中取出"负债合计"的"期末余额"和"资产总计"的"期末余额"，再进行相

除运算,求出资产负债率,公式如下:

> 资产负债率=负债合计.期末余额/资产总计.期末余额

在 Hive 中对 zcfzb2020 表、zcfzb2021 表进行操作,用 2 个子查询分别取出公式中的数据,再将 2 个子查询进行 JOIN 连接操作,从连接结果取出 2 个值进行运算。这里要注意,要实现 JOIN 操作,需要设置 hive.mapred.mode 为 unstrict。

对 2020 年资产负债表 zcfzb2020 计算资产负债率,命令如下:

```
hive (cwbb)> set hive.mapred.mode=unstrict
hive (cwbb)> SELECT round(qmye1/qmye2,2)   zcfzl2020   FROM
((SELECT   qmye qmye1 from zcfzb2020   where xm='负债合计') z1
JOIN (SELECT   qmye   qmye2   from zcfzb2020   where xm='资产总计') z2);
```

2020 年资产负债率计算结果为 0.1,运行结果如图 8.1.18 所示。

```
2024-05-06 17:17:31     End of local task; Time Taken: 2.081 sec.
Execution completed successfully
MapredLocal task succeeded
Launching Job 1 out of 1
Number of reduce tasks is set to 0 since there's no reduce operator
Starting Job = job_1714976504535_0024, Tracking URL = http://master:8088/proxy/application_17149765045
35_0024/
Kill Command = /opt/hadoop-2.7.7/bin/hadoop job  -kill job_1714976504535_0024
Hadoop job information for Stage-3: number of mappers: 1; number of reducers: 0
2024-05-06 17:17:45,044 Stage-3 map = 0%,  reduce = 0%
2024-05-06 17:17:52,635 Stage-3 map = 100%,  reduce = 0%, Cumulative CPU 2.02 sec
MapReduce Total cumulative CPU time: 2 seconds 20 msec
Ended Job = job_1714976504535_0024
MapReduce Jobs Launched:
Stage-Stage-3: Map: 1   Cumulative CPU: 2.02 sec   HDFS Read: 9561 HDFS Write: 103 SUCCESS
Total MapReduce CPU Time Spent: 2 seconds 20 msec
OK
zcfzl2020
0.1
Time taken: 44.827 seconds, Fetched: 1 row(s)
hive (cwbb)>
```

图 8.1.18   2020 年资产负债率计算结果为 0.1

对 2021 年资产负债表 zcfzb2021 计算资产负债率,命令如下:

```
hive (cwbb)> hive.mapred.mode 为 unstrict
hive (cwbb)> SELECT round(qmye1/qmye2,2)   zcfzl2021   FROM
((SELECT   qmye qmye1 from zcfzb2021   where xm='负债合计') z1
JOIN (SELECT   qmye   qmye2   from zcfzb2021   where xm='资产总计') z2);
```

2021 年资产负债率计算结果为 0.1,运行结果如图 8.1.19 所示。

(2) 股东权益比率。

从资产负债表中取出"所有者权益合计"的"期末余额"和"资产总计"的"期末余额",再进行相除运算,求出股东权益比率,公式如下:

> 股东权益比率=所有者权益合计.期末余额/资产总计.期末余额

在 Hive 中对 zcfzb2020 表、zcfzb2021 表进行操作,用 2 个子查询分别取出公式中的数据,再将 2 个子查询进行 JOIN 连接操作,从连接结果取出 2 个值进行运算。这里要注意,要实现 JOIN 操作,需要设置 hive.mapred.mode 为 unstrict。

```
2024-05-06 17:19:30    End of local task; Time Taken: 3.701 sec.
Execution completed successfully
MapredLocal task succeeded
Launching Job 1 out of 1
Number of reduce tasks is set to 0 since there's no reduce operator
Starting Job = job_1714976504535_0025, Tracking URL = http://master:8088/proxy/application_17149765045
35_0025/
Kill Command = /opt/hadoop-2.7.7/bin/hadoop job  -kill job_1714976504535_0025
Hadoop job information for Stage-3: number of mappers: 1; number of reducers: 0
2024-05-06 17:19:41,707 Stage-3 map = 0%,  reduce = 0%
2024-05-06 17:19:49,093 Stage-3 map = 100%,  reduce = 0%, Cumulative CPU 1.96 sec
MapReduce Total cumulative CPU time: 1 seconds 960 msec
Ended Job = job_1714976504535_0025
MapReduce Jobs Launched:
Stage-Stage-3: Map: 1   Cumulative CPU: 1.96 sec   HDFS Read: 9568 HDFS Write: 103 SUCCESS
Total MapReduce CPU Time Spent: 1 seconds 960 msec
OK
zcfzl2021
0.1
Time taken: 44.092 seconds, Fetched: 1 row(s)
hive (cwbb)>
```

图 8.1.19　2021 年资产负债率计算结果为 0.1

对 2020 年资产负债表 zcfzb2020 计算股东权益比率,命令如下:

```
hive (cwbb)> hive.mapred.mode 为 unstrict
hive (cwbb)> SELECT round(qmye1/qmye2,2)  gdqybl2020  FROM
((SELECT  qmye qmye1 from zcfzb2020  where xm='所有者权益合计') z1
JOIN (SELECT  qmye  qmye2  from zcfzb2020  where xm='资产总计') z2);
```

2020 年股东权益比率计算结果为 0.9,运行结果如图 8.1.20 所示。

```
2024-05-06 16:56:50    End of local task; Time Taken: 4.103 sec.
Execution completed successfully
MapredLocal task succeeded
Launching Job 1 out of 1
Number of reduce tasks is set to 0 since there's no reduce operator
Starting Job = job_1714976504535_0015, Tracking URL = http://master:8088/proxy/application_17149765045
35_0015/
Kill Command = /opt/hadoop-2.7.7/bin/hadoop job  -kill job_1714976504535_0015
Hadoop job information for Stage-3: number of mappers: 1; number of reducers: 0
2024-05-06 16:57:07,467 Stage-3 map = 0%,  reduce = 0%
2024-05-06 16:57:17,418 Stage-3 map = 100%,  reduce = 0%, Cumulative CPU 2.19 sec
MapReduce Total cumulative CPU time: 2 seconds 190 msec
Ended Job = job_1714976504535_0015
MapReduce Jobs Launched:
Stage-Stage-3: Map: 1   Cumulative CPU: 2.19 sec   HDFS Read: 9561 HDFS Write: 103 SUCCESS
Total MapReduce CPU Time Spent: 2 seconds 190 msec
OK
gdqybl2020
0.9
Time taken: 52.719 seconds, Fetched: 1 row(s)
hive (cwbb)>
```

图 8.1.20　2020 年股东权益比率计算结果为 0.9

对 2021 年资产负债表 zcfzb2021 计算股东权益比率,命令如下:

```
hive (cwbb)> SELECT round(qmye1/qmye2,2)  gdqybl2021  FROM
((SELECT  qmye qmye1 from zcfzb2021  where xm='所有者权益合计') z1
JOIN (SELECT  qmye  qmye2  from zcfzb2021  where xm='资产总计') z2);
```

2021 年股东权益比率计算结果为 0.9,运行结果如图 8.1.21 所示。

```
2024-05-06 17:01:51    End of local task; Time Taken: 3.874 sec.
Execution completed successfully
MapredLocal task succeeded
Launching Job 1 out of 1
Number of reduce tasks is set to 0 since there's no reduce operator
Starting Job = job_1714976504535_0016, Tracking URL = http://master:8088/proxy/application_17149765045
35_0016/
Kill Command = /opt/hadoop-2.7.7/bin/hadoop job  -kill job_1714976504535_0016
Hadoop job information for Stage-3: number of mappers: 1; number of reducers: 0
2024-05-06 17:02:08,057 Stage-3 map = 0%,  reduce = 0%
2024-05-06 17:02:18,088 Stage-3 map = 100%,  reduce = 0%, Cumulative CPU 2.15 sec
MapReduce Total cumulative CPU time: 2 seconds 150 msec
Ended Job = job_1714976504535_0016
MapReduce Jobs Launched:
Stage-Stage-3: Map: 1   Cumulative CPU: 2.15 sec   HDFS Read: 9577 HDFS Write: 103 SUCCESS
Total MapReduce CPU Time Spent: 2 seconds 150 msec
OK
gdqybl2021
0.9
Time taken: 49.786 seconds, Fetched: 1 row(s)
hive (cwbb)>
```

图 8.1.21　2021 年股东权益比率计算结果为 0.9

（3）产权比率。

从资产负债表中取出"负债合计"的"期末余额"和"所有者权益合计"的"期末余额"，再进行相除运算，求出股东权益比率，公式如下：

产权比率＝负债合计·期末余额/所有者权益合计·期末余额

在 Hive 中对 zcfzb2020 表、zcfzb2021 表进行操作，用 2 个子查询分别取出公式中的数据，再将 2 个子查询进行 JOIN 连接操作，从连接结果取出 2 个值进行运算。这里要注意，要实现 JOIN 操作，需要设置 hive.mapred.mode 为 unstrict。

对 2020 年资产负债表 zcfzb2020 计算产权比率，命令如下：

```
hive (cwbb)> hive.mapred.mode 为 unstrict
hive (cwbb)> SELECT round(qmye1/qmye2,2) cqbl2020   FROM
((SELECT   qmye qmye1 from zcfzb2020   where xm='负债合计') z1
JOIN (SELECT   qmye qmye2  from zcfzb2020  where xm='所有者权益合计') z2);
```

2020 年产权比率计算结果为 0.11，运行结果如图 8.1.22 所示。

```
2024-05-06 17:27:30    End of local task; Time Taken: 4.665 sec.
Execution completed successfully
MapredLocal task succeeded
Launching Job 1 out of 1
Number of reduce tasks is set to 0 since there's no reduce operator
Starting Job = job_1714976504535_0027, Tracking URL = http://master:8088/proxy/application_17149765045
35_0027/
Kill Command = /opt/hadoop-2.7.7/bin/hadoop job  -kill job_1714976504535_0027
Hadoop job information for Stage-3: number of mappers: 1; number of reducers: 0
2024-05-06 17:27:43,463 Stage-3 map = 0%,  reduce = 0%
2024-05-06 17:27:53,223 Stage-3 map = 100%,  reduce = 0%, Cumulative CPU 2.05 sec
MapReduce Total cumulative CPU time: 2 seconds 50 msec
Ended Job = job_1714976504535_0027
MapReduce Jobs Launched:
Stage-Stage-3: Map: 1   Cumulative CPU: 2.05 sec   HDFS Read: 9569 HDFS Write: 104 SUCCESS
Total MapReduce CPU Time Spent: 2 seconds 50 msec
OK
cqbl2020
0.11
Time taken: 52.576 seconds, Fetched: 1 row(s)
hive (cwbb)>
```

图 8.1.22　2020 年产权比率计算结果为 0.11

对 2021 年资产负债表 zcfzb2021 计算产权比率，命令如下：

```
hive (cwbb)> hive.mapred.mode 为 unstrict
hive (cwbb)> SELECT round(qmye1/qmye2,2) cqbl2021 FROM
((SELECT  qmye qmye1 from zcfzb2021 where xm='负债合计') z1
JOIN (SELECT  qmye  qmye2  from zcfzb2021 where xm='所有者权益合计') z2);
```

2021 年产权比率计算结果为 0.11，运行结果如图 8.1.23 所示。

```
2024-05-06 17:30:40     End of local task; Time Taken: 4.692 sec.
Execution completed successfully
MapredLocal task succeeded
Launching Job 1 out of 1
Number of reduce tasks is set to 0 since there's no reduce operator
Starting Job = job_1714976504535_0028, Tracking URL = http://master:8088/proxy/application_17149765045
35_0028/
Kill Command = /opt/hadoop-2.7.7/bin/hadoop job  -kill job_1714976504535_0028
Hadoop job information for Stage-3: number of mappers: 1; number of reducers: 0
2024-05-06 17:31:01,461 Stage-3 map = 0%,  reduce = 0%
2024-05-06 17:31:09,076 Stage-3 map = 100%,  reduce = 0%, Cumulative CPU 2.24 sec
MapReduce Total cumulative CPU time: 2 seconds 240 msec
Ended Job = job_1714976504535_0028
MapReduce Jobs Launched:
Stage-Stage-3: Map: 1   Cumulative CPU: 2.24 sec   HDFS Read: 9585 HDFS Write: 104 SUCCESS
Total MapReduce CPU Time Spent: 2 seconds 240 msec
OK
cqbl2021
0.11
Time taken: 54.193 seconds, Fetched: 1 row(s)
hive (cwbb)>
```

图 8.1.23　2021 年产权比率计算结果为 0.11

（4）利息保障倍数。

从利润表中取出"三、利润总额"的"本期金额"，从资产负债表中取出"应收款项"的"期末余额"和"期初余额"、"应收票据"的"期末余额"和"期初余额"，再进行运算，求出利息保障倍数，公式如下：

利息保障倍数 = 三、利润总额.本期金额/((应收款项.期末余额 + 应收款项.期初余额 + 应收票据.期末余额 + 应收票据.期初余额)/2)

在 Hive 中对 lrb2020 表、lrb2021 表、zcfzb2020 表、zcfzb2021 表进行操作，用子查询分别取出公式中的数据，再将子查询进行 JOIN 连接操作，从连接结果取出值进行运算。这里要注意，要实现 JOIN 操作，需要设置 hive.mapred.mode 为 unstrict。

对 2020 年利润表 lrb2020 和资产负债表 zcfzb2020 计算利息保障倍数，命令如下：

```
SELECT round(bqje1/((qmye1+qcye1+qmye2+qcye2)/2),2) lxbzbs2020   FROM
(
(SELECT bqje bqje1  from  lrb2020   where xm='三、利润总额')   t1
JOIN (SELECT qmye qmye1,qcye qcye1 from zcfzb2020 where xm='流动负债_应付账款') t2
JOIN (SELECT qmye qmye2,qcye qcye2 from zcfzb2020 where xm='流动负债_应付票据') t3
);
```

2020 年利息保障倍数计算结果为 0.37，运行结果如图 8.1.24 所示。

```
2024-05-06 17:49:53     End of local task; Time Taken: 4.022 sec.
Execution completed successfully
MapredLocal task succeeded
Launching Job 1 out of 1
Number of reduce tasks is set to 0 since there's no reduce operator
Starting Job = job_1714976504535_0030, Tracking URL = http://master:8088/proxy/application_17149765045
35_0030/
Kill Command = /opt/hadoop-2.7.7/bin/hadoop job  -kill job_1714976504535_0030
Hadoop job information for Stage-4: number of mappers: 1; number of reducers: 0
2024-05-06 17:50:15,511 Stage-4 map = 0%,  reduce = 0%
2024-05-06 17:50:23,189 Stage-4 map = 100%,  reduce = 0%, Cumulative CPU 1.82 sec
MapReduce Total cumulative CPU time: 1 seconds 820 msec
Ended Job = job_1714976504535_0030
MapReduce Jobs Launched:
Stage-Stage-4: Map: 1   Cumulative CPU: 1.82 sec   HDFS Read: 11124 HDFS Write: 104 SUCCESS
Total MapReduce CPU Time Spent: 1 seconds 820 msec
OK
lxbzbs2020
0.37
Time taken: 58.844 seconds, Fetched: 1 row(s)
hive (cwbb)>
```

图 8.1.24　2020 年利息保障倍数计算结果为 0.37

对 2021 年利润表 lrb2021 和资产负债表 zcfzb2021 计算利息保障倍数,命令如下:

```
SELECT round(bqje1/((qmye1+qcye1+qmye2+qcye2)/2),2) lxbzbs2021   FROM
(
(SELECT bqje bqje1 from lrb2021   where xm='三、利润总额')   t1
JOIN (SELECT qmye qmye1,qcye qcye1 from zcfzb2021 where xm='流动负债_应付账款') t2
JOIN (SELECT qmye qmye2,qcye qcye2 from zcfzb2021 where xm='流动负债_应付票据') t3
);
```

2021 年利息保障倍数计算结果为 1.01,运行结果如图 8.1.25 所示。

```
2024-05-06 17:59:14     End of local task; Time Taken: 4.676 sec.
Execution completed successfully
MapredLocal task succeeded
Launching Job 1 out of 1
Number of reduce tasks is set to 0 since there's no reduce operator
Starting Job = job_1714976504535_0031, Tracking URL = http://master:8088/proxy/application_17149765045
35_0031/
Kill Command = /opt/hadoop-2.7.7/bin/hadoop job  -kill job_1714976504535_0031
Hadoop job information for Stage-4: number of mappers: 1; number of reducers: 0
2024-05-06 17:59:31,184 Stage-4 map = 0%,  reduce = 0%
2024-05-06 17:59:40,083 Stage-4 map = 100%,  reduce = 0%, Cumulative CPU 2.8 sec
MapReduce Total cumulative CPU time: 2 seconds 800 msec
Ended Job = job_1714976504535_0031
MapReduce Jobs Launched:
Stage-Stage-4: Map: 1   Cumulative CPU: 2.8 sec   HDFS Read: 11131 HDFS Write: 104 SUCCESS
Total MapReduce CPU Time Spent: 2 seconds 800 msec
OK
lxbzbs2021
1.01
Time taken: 55.6 seconds, Fetched: 1 row(s)
hive (cwbb)>
```

图 8.1.25　2021 年利息保障倍数计算结果为 1.01

3) 资产管理比率

(1) 应收账款周转率。

从利润表中取出"一、营业收入"的"本期金额",从资产负债表中取出"应收款项"的"期末余额"和"期初余额"、"应收票据"的"期末余额"和"期初余额",再进行运算,求出应收账款周转率,公式如下:

应收账款周转率＝一、营业收入.本期金额/((应收账款.期末余额＋应收账款.期初余额＋应收票据.期末余额＋应收票据.期初余额)/2)

在 Hive 中对 lrb2020 表、lrb2021 表、zcfzb2020 表、zcfzb2021 表进行操作，用子查询分别取出公式中的数据，再将子查询进行 JOIN 连接操作，从连接结果取出值进行运算。这里要注意，要实现 JOIN 操作，需要设置 hive.mapred.mode 为 unstrict。

对 2020 年利润表 lrb2020 和资产负债表 zcfzb2020 计算应收账款周转率，命令如下：

```
hive(cwbb)> SET hive.mapred.mode=unstrict;
hive(cwbb)> SELECT round(bqje1/((qmye1+qcye1+qmye2+qcye2)/2),2) yszkzzcs2020 FROM
(
(SELECT bqje bqje1 from lrb2020 where xm='一、营业收入') t1
JOIN (SELECT qmye qmye1,qcye qcye1 from zcfzb2020 where xm='流动资产_应收账款') t2
JOIN (SELECT qmye qmye2,qcye qcye2 from zcfzb2020 where xm='流动资产_应收票据') t3
);
```

2020 年应收账款周转率计算结果为 2.96，运行结果如图 8.1.26 所示。

```
2024-05-06 21:30:05     End of local task; Time Taken: 4.864 sec.
Execution completed successfully
MapredLocal task succeeded
Launching Job 1 out of 1
Number of reduce tasks is set to 0 since there's no reduce operator
Starting Job = job_1714998796246_0012, Tracking URL = http://master:8088/proxy/application_1714998796246_0012/
Kill Command = /opt/hadoop-2.7.7/bin/hadoop job  -kill job_1714998796246_0012
Hadoop job information for Stage-4: number of mappers: 1; number of reducers: 0
2024-05-06 21:30:20,383 Stage-4 map = 0%,  reduce = 0%
2024-05-06 21:30:30,201 Stage-4 map = 100%,  reduce = 0%, Cumulative CPU 1.88 sec
MapReduce Total cumulative CPU time: 1 seconds 880 msec
Ended Job = job_1714998796246_0012
MapReduce Jobs Launched:
Stage-Stage-4: Map: 1   Cumulative CPU: 1.88 sec   HDFS Read: 11126 HDFS Write: 104 SUCCESS
Total MapReduce CPU Time Spent: 1 seconds 880 msec
OK
yszkzzcs2020
2.96
Time taken: 50.952 seconds, Fetched: 1 row(s)
```

图 8.1.26　2020 年应收账款周转率计算结果为 2.96

对 2021 年利润表 lrb2021 和资产负债表 zcfzb2021 计算应收账款周转率，命令如下：

```
hive(cwbb)> SET hive.mapred.mode=unstrict;
hive(cwbb)> SELECT round(bqje1/((qmye1+qcye1+qmye2+qcye2)/2),2) yszkzzcs2021 FROM
(
(SELECT bqje bqje1 from lrb2021 where xm='一、营业收入') t1
JOIN (SELECT qmye qmye1,qcye qcye1 from zcfzb2021 where xm='流动资产_应收账款') t2
JOIN (SELECT qmye qmye2,qcye qcye2 from zcfzb2021 where xm='流动资产_应收票据') t3
);
```

2021 年应收账款周转率计算结果为 3.68，运行结果如图 8.1.27 所示。

```
2024-05-06 21:31:43    End of local task; Time Taken: 4.34 sec.
Execution completed successfully
MapredLocal task succeeded
Launching Job 1 out of 1
Number of reduce tasks is set to 0 since there's no reduce operator
Starting Job = job_1714998796246_0013, Tracking URL = http://master:8088/proxy/application_17149987962
46_0013/
Kill Command = /opt/hadoop-2.7.7/bin/hadoop job  -kill job_1714998796246_0013
Hadoop job information for Stage-4: number of mappers: 1; number of reducers: 0
2024-05-06 21:31:55,715 Stage-4 map = 0%,  reduce = 0%
2024-05-06 21:32:05,602 Stage-4 map = 100%,  reduce = 0%, Cumulative CPU 2.06 sec
MapReduce Total cumulative CPU time: 2 seconds 60 msec
Ended Job = job_1714998796246_0013
MapReduce Jobs Launched:
Stage-Stage-4: Map: 1   Cumulative CPU: 2.06 sec   HDFS Read: 11142 HDFS Write: 104 SUCCESS
Total MapReduce CPU Time Spent: 2 seconds 60 msec
OK
yszkzzcs2021
3.68
Time taken: 46.915 seconds, Fetched: 1 row(s)
```

图 8.1.27　2021 年应收账款周转率计算结果为 3.68

（2）存货周转率。

从利润表中取出"减：营业成本"的"本期金额"，从资产负债表中取出"存货"的"期末余额"和"期初余额"，再进行运算，求出存货周转次数，公式如下：

存货周转率＝减：营业成本.本期金额/((资产负债表：存货.期末余额＋存货.期初余额)/2)

在 Hive 中对 lrb2020 表、lrb2021 表、zcfzb2020 表、zcfzb2021 表进行操作，用子查询分别取出公式中的数据，再将子查询进行 JOIN 连接操作，从连接结果取出值进行运算。这里要注意，要实现 JOIN 操作，需要设置 hive.mapred.mode 为 unstrict。

对 2020 年利润表 lrb2020 和资产负债表 zcfzb2020 计算存货周转率，命令如下：

```
hive (cwbb)> SET hive.mapred.mode=unstrict;
hive (cwbb)> SELECT round(bqje1/((qmye1+qcye1)/2),2) chzzcs2020   FROM
(
(SELECT bqje bqje1 from  lrb2020  where xm='减：营业成本')  t1
JOIN (SELECT qmye qmye1,qcye qcye1 from zcfzb2020 where xm='流动资产_存货') t2
);
```

2020 年存货周转率计算结果为 1.32，运行结果如图 8.1.28 所示。

```
2024-05-06 21:34:47    End of local task; Time Taken: 3.363 sec.
Execution completed successfully
MapredLocal task succeeded
Launching Job 1 out of 1
Number of reduce tasks is set to 0 since there's no reduce operator
Starting Job = job_1714998796246_0015, Tracking URL = http://master:8088/proxy/application_17149987962
46_0015/
Kill Command = /opt/hadoop-2.7.7/bin/hadoop job  -kill job_1714998796246_0015
Hadoop job information for Stage-3: number of mappers: 1; number of reducers: 0
2024-05-06 21:35:00,322 Stage-3 map = 0%,  reduce = 0%
2024-05-06 21:35:12,243 Stage-3 map = 100%,  reduce = 0%, Cumulative CPU 1.81 sec
MapReduce Total cumulative CPU time: 1 seconds 810 msec
Ended Job = job_1714998796246_0015
MapReduce Jobs Launched:
Stage-Stage-3: Map: 1   Cumulative CPU: 1.81 sec   HDFS Read: 10482 HDFS Write: 104 SUCCESS
Total MapReduce CPU Time Spent: 1 seconds 810 msec
OK
chzzcs2020
1.32
Time taken: 50.774 seconds, Fetched: 1 row(s)
```

图 8.1.28　2022 年存货周转率计算结果为 1.32

对 2021 年利润表 lrb2021 和资产负债表 zcfzb2021 计算存货周转率，命令如下：

```
hive (cwbb)> SET hive.mapred.mode=unstrict;
hive (cwbb)> SELECT round(bqje1/((qmye1+qcye1)/2),2) chzzcs2021  FROM
(
(SELECT bqje bqje1 from lrb2021 where xm='减:营业成本') t1
JOIN (SELECT qmye qmye1,qcye qcye1 from zcfzb2021 where xm='流动资产_存货') t2
);
```

2021 年存货周转率计算结果为 1.69，运行结果如图 8.1.29 所示。

```
2024-05-06 21:36:14    End of local task; Time Taken: 4.979 sec.
Execution completed successfully
MapredLocal task succeeded
Launching Job 1 out of 1
Number of reduce tasks is set to 0 since there's no reduce operator
Starting Job = job_1714998796246_0016, Tracking URL = http://master:8088/proxy/application_17149987962
46_0016/
Kill Command = /opt/hadoop-2.7.7/bin/hadoop job  -kill job_1714998796246_0016
Hadoop job information for Stage-3: number of mappers: 1; number of reducers: 0
2024-05-06 21:36:25,665 Stage-3 map = 0%,  reduce = 0%
2024-05-06 21:36:33,044 Stage-3 map = 100%,  reduce = 0%, Cumulative CPU 1.77 sec
MapReduce Total cumulative CPU time: 1 seconds 770 msec
Ended Job = job_1714998796246_0016
MapReduce Jobs Launched:
Stage-Stage-3: Map: 1   Cumulative CPU: 1.77 sec   HDFS Read: 10498 HDFS Write: 104 SUCCESS
Total MapReduce CPU Time Spent: 1 seconds 770 msec
OK
chzzcs2021
1.69
Time taken: 45.431 seconds, Fetched: 1 row(s)
```

图 8.1.29 2021 年存货周转率计算结果为 1.69

（3）固定资产周转率。

从利润表中取出"一、营业收入"的"本期金额"，从资产负债表中取出"固定资产"的"期末余额"和"期初余额"，再进行运算，求出固定资产周转率，公式如下：

固定资产周转次数＝ 一、营业收入.本期金额/((固定资产.期末余额＋固定资产.期初余额)/2)

在 Hive 中对 lrb2020 表、lrb2021 表、zcfzb2020 表、zcfzb2021 表进行操作，用子查询分别取出公式中的数据，再将子查询进行 JOIN 连接操作，从连接结果取出值进行运算。这里要注意，要实现 JOIN 操作，需要设置 hive.mapred.mode 为 unstrict。

对 2020 年利润表 lrb2020 和资产负债表 zcfzb2020 计算固定资产周转率，命令如下：

```
hive (cwbb)> SET hive.mapred.mode=unstrict;
hive (cwbb)> SELECT round(bqje1/((qmye1+qcye1)/2),2) gdzczzcs2020  FROM
(
(SELECT bqje bqje1 from lrb2020 where xm='一、营业收入') t1
JOIN (SELECT qmye qmye1,qcye qcye1 from zcfzb2020 where xm='非流动资产合计') t2
);
```

2020 年固定资产周转率计算结果为 0.93，运行结果如图 8.1.30 所示。

```
2024-05-06 21:20:39      End of local task; Time Taken: 3.496 sec.
Execution completed successfully
MapredLocal task succeeded
Launching Job 1 out of 1
Number of reduce tasks is set to 0 since there's no reduce operator
Starting Job = job_1714998796246_0009, Tracking URL = http://master:8088/proxy/application_17149987962
46_0009/
Kill Command = /opt/hadoop-2.7.7/bin/hadoop job  -kill job_1714998796246_0009
Hadoop job information for Stage-3: number of mappers: 1; number of reducers: 0
2024-05-06 21:20:55,243 Stage-3 map = 0%,  reduce = 0%
2024-05-06 21:21:03,945 Stage-3 map = 100%,  reduce = 0%, Cumulative CPU 2.42 sec
MapReduce Total cumulative CPU time: 2 seconds 420 msec
Ended Job = job_1714998796246_0009
MapReduce Jobs Launched:
Stage-Stage-3: Map: 1   Cumulative CPU: 2.42 sec   HDFS Read: 10486 HDFS Write: 104 SUCCESS
Total MapReduce CPU Time Spent: 2 seconds 420 msec
OK
gdzczzcs2020
0.93
Time taken: 50.889 seconds, Fetched: 1 row(s)
```

图 8.1.30　2020 年固定资产周转率计算结果为 0.93

对 2021 年利润表 lrb2021 和资产负债表 zcfzb2021 计算固定资产周转率，命令如下：

```
hive (cwbb)> SET hive.mapred.mode=unstrict;
hive (cwbb)> SELECT round(bqje1/((qmye1+qcye1)/2),2) gdzczzcs2021    FROM
(
(SELECT bqje bqje1  from   lrb2021 where xm='一、营业收入')  t1
JOIN (SELECT qmye qmye1,qcye qcye1 from zcfzb2021 where xm='非流动资产合计')  t2
);
```

2021 年固定资产周转率计算结果为 0.92，运行结果如图 8.1.31 所示。

```
2024-05-06 21:22:42      End of local task; Time Taken: 4.198 sec.
Execution completed successfully
MapredLocal task succeeded
Launching Job 1 out of 1
Number of reduce tasks is set to 0 since there's no reduce operator
Starting Job = job_1714998796246_0010, Tracking URL = http://master:8088/proxy/application_17149987962
46_0010/
Kill Command = /opt/hadoop-2.7.7/bin/hadoop job  -kill job_1714998796246_0010
Hadoop job information for Stage-3: number of mappers: 1; number of reducers: 0
2024-05-06 21:22:55,056 Stage-3 map = 0%,  reduce = 0%
2024-05-06 21:23:01,722 Stage-3 map = 100%,  reduce = 0%, Cumulative CPU 2.16 sec
MapReduce Total cumulative CPU time: 2 seconds 160 msec
Ended Job = job_1714998796246_0010
MapReduce Jobs Launched:
Stage-Stage-3: Map: 1   Cumulative CPU: 2.16 sec   HDFS Read: 10477 HDFS Write: 104 SUCCESS
Total MapReduce CPU Time Spent: 2 seconds 160 msec
OK
gdzczzcs2021
0.92
Time taken: 45.978 seconds, Fetched: 1 row(s)
```

图 8.1.31　2021 年固定资产周转率计算结果为 0.92

（4）流动资产周转率。

从利润表中取出"一、营业收入"的"本期金额"，从资产负债表中取出"固定资产"的"期末余额"和"期初余额"，再进行运算，求出流动资产周转率，公式如下：

流动资产周转率＝一、营业收入.本期金额/((流动资产合计.期末余额＋流动资产合计.期初余额)/2)

在 Hive 中对 lrb2020 表、lrb2021 表、zcfzb2020 表、zcfzb2021 表进行操作,用子查询分别取出公式中的数据,再将子查询进行 JOIN 连接操作,从连接结果取出值进行运算。这里要注意,要实现 JOIN 操作,需要设置 hive.mapred.mode 为 unstrict。

对 2020 年利润表 lrb2020 和资产负债表 zcfzb2020 计算流动资产周转率,命令如下:

```
hive (cwbb)> SET hive.mapred.mode=unstrict;
hive (cwbb)> SELECT round(bqje1/((qmye1+qcye1)/2),2) ldzczzcx2020  FROM
(
(SELECT bqje bqje1  from  lrb2020  where xm='一、营业收入')  t1
JOIN (SELECT qmye qmye1,qcye qcye1 from zcfzb2020 where xm='流动资产合计') t2
);
```

2020 年流动资产周转率计算结果为 0.47,运行结果如图 8.1.32 所示。

```
2024-05-06 21:41:58     End of local task; Time Taken: 3.768 sec.
Execution completed successfully
MapredLocal task succeeded
Launching Job 1 out of 1
Number of reduce tasks is set to 0 since there's no reduce operator
Starting Job = job_1714998796246_0018, Tracking URL = http://master:8088/proxy/application_17149987962
46_0018/
Kill Command = /opt/hadoop-2.7.7/bin/hadoop job  -kill job_1714998796246_0018
Hadoop job information for Stage-3: number of mappers: 1; number of reducers: 0
2024-05-06 21:42:16,982 Stage-3 map = 0%,  reduce = 0%
2024-05-06 21:42:24,339 Stage-3 map = 100%,  reduce = 0%, Cumulative CPU 1.57 sec
MapReduce Total cumulative CPU time: 1 seconds 570 msec
Ended Job = job_1714998796246_0018
MapReduce Jobs Launched:
Stage-Stage-3: Map: 1  Cumulative CPU: 1.57 sec   HDFS Read: 10484 HDFS Write: 104 SUCCESS
Total MapReduce CPU Time Spent: 1 seconds 570 msec
OK
ldzczzcx2020
0.47
Time taken: 50.604 seconds, Fetched: 1 row(s)
```

图 8.1.32　2020 年流动资产周转率计算结果为 0.47

对 2021 年利润表 lrb2021 和资产负债表 zcfzb2021 计算流动资产周转率,命令如下:

```
hive (cwbb)> SET hive.mapred.mode=unstrict;
hive (cwbb)> SELECT round(bqje1/((qmye1+qcye1)/2),2) ldzczzcx2021  FROM
(
(SELECT bqje bqje1  from  lrb2021  where xm='一、营业收入')  t1
JOIN (SELECT qmye qmye1,qcye qcye1 from zcfzb2021 where xm='流动资产合计') t2
);
```

2021 年流动资产周转率计算结果为 0.59,运行结果如图 8.1.33 所示。

(5) 总资产周转率。

从利润表中取出"一、营业收入"的"本期金额",从资产负债表中取出"资产总计"的"期末余额"和"期初余额",再进行运算,求出固定资产周转率,公式如下:

总资产周转率＝一、营业收入.本期金额/((资产总计.期末余额＋资产总计.期初余额)/2)

```
2024-05-06 21:44:44    End of local task; Time Taken: 4.06 sec.
Execution completed successfully
MapredLocal task succeeded
Launching Job 1 out of 1
Number of reduce tasks is set to 0 since there's no reduce operator
Starting Job = job_1714998796246_0019, Tracking URL = http://master:8088/proxy/application_17149987962
46_0019/
Kill Command = /opt/hadoop-2.7.7/bin/hadoop job  -kill job_1714998796246_0019
Hadoop job information for Stage-3: number of mappers: 1; number of reducers: 0
2024-05-06 21:44:58,476 Stage-3 map = 0%,  reduce = 0%
2024-05-06 21:45:05,822 Stage-3 map = 100%,  reduce = 0%, Cumulative CPU 1.96 sec
MapReduce Total cumulative CPU time: 1 seconds 960 msec
Ended Job = job_1714998796246_0019
MapReduce Jobs Launched:
Stage-Stage-3: Map: 1   Cumulative CPU: 1.96 sec   HDFS Read: 10500 HDFS Write: 104 SUCCESS
Total MapReduce CPU Time Spent: 1 seconds 960 msec
OK
ldzczzcx2021
0.59
Time taken: 45.606 seconds, Fetched: 1 row(s)
```

图 8.1.33　2021 年流动资产周转率计算结果为 0.59

在 Hive 中对 lrb2020 表、lrb2021 表、zcfzb2020 表、zcfzb2021 表进行操作,用子查询分别取出公式中的数据,再将子查询进行 JOIN 连接操作,从连接结果取出值进行运算。这里要注意,要实现 JOIN 操作,需要设置 hive.mapred.mode 为 unstrict。

对 2020 年利润表 lrb2020 和资产负债表 zcfzb2020 计算总资产周转率,命令如下：

```
hive (cwbb)> SET hive.mapred.mode=unstrict;
hive (cwbb)> SELECT round(bqje1/((qmye1+qcye1)/2),2) zzczzcs2020   FROM
(
(SELECT bqje bqje1  from   lrb2020   where xm='一、营业收入')   t1
JOIN (SELECT qmye qmye1,qcye qcye1 from zcfzb2020 where xm='资产总计') t2
);
```

2020 年总资产周转率计算结果为 0.31,运行结果如图 8.1.34 所示。

```
2024-05-06 21:51:51    End of local task; Time Taken: 2.805 sec.
Execution completed successfully
MapredLocal task succeeded
Launching Job 1 out of 1
Number of reduce tasks is set to 0 since there's no reduce operator
Starting Job = job_1714998796246_0021, Tracking URL = http://master:8088/proxy/application_17149987962
46_0021/
Kill Command = /opt/hadoop-2.7.7/bin/hadoop job  -kill job_1714998796246_0021
Hadoop job information for Stage-3: number of mappers: 1; number of reducers: 0
2024-05-06 21:52:01,954 Stage-3 map = 0%,  reduce = 0%
2024-05-06 21:52:11,718 Stage-3 map = 100%,  reduce = 0%, Cumulative CPU 2.19 sec
MapReduce Total cumulative CPU time: 2 seconds 190 msec
Ended Job = job_1714998796246_0021
MapReduce Jobs Launched:
Stage-Stage-3: Map: 1   Cumulative CPU: 2.19 sec   HDFS Read: 10477 HDFS Write: 104 SUCCESS
Total MapReduce CPU Time Spent: 2 seconds 190 msec
OK
zzczzcs2020
0.31
Time taken: 41.908 seconds, Fetched: 1 row(s)
```

图 8.1.34　2020 年总资产周转率计算结果为 0.31

对 2021 年利润表 lrb2021 和资产负债表 zcfzb2021 计算总资产周转率,命令如下：

```
hive (cwbb)> SET hive.mapred.mode=unstrict;
hive (cwbb)> SELECT round(bqje1/((qmye1+qcye1)/2),2) zzczzcs2021  FROM
(
(SELECT bqje bqje1  from  lrb2021  where xm='一、营业收入')  t1
JOIN (SELECT qmye qmye1,qcye qcye1 from zcfzb2021 where xm='资产总计') t2
);
```

2021年总资产周转率计算结果为0.36,运行结果如图8.1.35所示。

```
2024-05-06 21:54:07     End of local task; Time Taken: 3.911 sec.
Execution completed successfully
MapredLocal task succeeded
Launching Job 1 out of 1
Number of reduce tasks is set to 0 since there's no reduce operator
Starting Job = job_1714998796246_0022, Tracking URL = http://master:8088/proxy/application_17149987962
46_0022/
Kill Command = /opt/hadoop-2.7.7/bin/hadoop job  -kill job_1714998796246_0022
Hadoop job information for Stage-3: number of mappers: 1; number of reducers: 0
2024-05-06 21:54:22,607 Stage-3 map = 0%,  reduce = 0%
2024-05-06 21:54:32,398 Stage-3 map = 100%,  reduce = 0%, Cumulative CPU 1.97 sec
MapReduce Total cumulative CPU time: 1 seconds 970 msec
Ended Job = job_1714998796246_0022
MapReduce Jobs Launched:
Stage-Stage-3: Map: 1   Cumulative CPU: 1.97 sec   HDFS Read: 10493 HDFS Write: 104 SUCCESS
Total MapReduce CPU Time Spent: 1 seconds 970 msec
OK
zzczzcs2021
0.36
Time taken: 47.517 seconds, Fetched: 1 row(s)
```

图 8.1.35　2020 年总资产周转率计算结果为 0.36

任务 8.2　Hive 在贷款数据分析中的应用

任务描述

本任务以美国的一家 P2P 在线借贷平台——Prosper 的贷款业务数据处理为例[1],属于 Hive 在金融数据分析中的应用。

该网站以类似拍卖的模式,撮合一些有闲钱的人和一些急于用钱的人。用户若有贷款需求,可在网站上列出期望数额和可承受的最大利率。潜在贷方则为数额和利率展开竞价。

关键步骤

(1) 贷款数据分析任务要求。
(2) 贷款数据分析任务实施。

---

[1]　本任务使用的案例业务及数据仅做教学使用,不涉及业务推介,请读者谨慎投资。

8.2.1 贷款数据分析任务要求

贷款数据 loan.csv(随本书配套资源数据,下载到本地 Windows 系统中,再用 WinSCP 上传到 CentOS 系统即可使用),有 113 937 条记录,文件内容(部分)如图 8.2.1 所示。

	A	B	C	D	E	F	G	H	I	J
1	Completed	0.158		Other	Self-emplo	TRUE	640	659	$25.000-49.999	
2	Current	0.092	7	Profession	Employed	FALSE	680	699	$50.000-74.999	
3	Completed	0.275		Other	Not availa	FALSE	480	499	Not displayed	
4	Current	0.0974	9	Skilled La	Employed	TRUE	800	819	$25.000-49.999	
5	Current	0.2085	4	Executive	Employed	TRUE	680	699	$100.000+	
6	Current	0.1314	10	Profession	Employed	TRUE	740	759	$100.000+	
7	Current	0.2712	2	Sales - Re	Employed	FALSE	680	699	$25.000-49.999	
8	Current	0.2019	4	Laborer	Employed	FALSE	700	719	$25.000-49.999	
9	Current	0.0629	9	Food Servi	Employed	TRUE	820	839	$25.000-49.999	
10	Current	0.0629	11	Food Servi	Employed	TRUE	820	839	$25.000-49.999	
11	Current	0.2489	7	Fireman	Employed	FALSE	640	659	$75.000-99.999	
12	Completed	0.1325		Waiter/Wai	Full-time	FALSE	640	659	$1-24.999	
13	Past Due (	0.1435	4	Sales - Re	Employed	FALSE	680	699	$25.000-49.999	
14	Current	0.1034	8	Constructi	Employed	TRUE	740	759	$50.000-74.999	
15	Current	0.0949	8	Computer P	Employed	FALSE	740	759	$100.000+	
16	Defaulted	0.3177	5	Other	Other	TRUE	700	719	$50.000-74.999	
17	Current	0.2809	4	Profession	Full-time	TRUE	640	659	$75.000-99.999	
18	Chargedoff	0.125		Profession	Not availa	TRUE	760	779	Not displayed	

图 8.2.1 贷款数据 loan.csv 文件内容(部分)

loan.csv 数据文件中字段对应的含义如表 8.2.1 所示。

表 8.2.1 loan.csv 数据文件中字段含义

序号	字段	含义	取值举例
1	LoanStatus	贷款状态	Completed
2	BorrowerRate	贷款率	0.158
3	ProsperScore	信用得分	5~10
4	Occupation	职业	Other
5	EmploymentStatus	就业状态	Self-employed
6	IsBorrowerHomeowner	是否有房	TRUE
7	CreditScoreRangeLower	信用评分下限	640
8	CreditScoreRangeUpper	信用得分上限	659
9	IncomeRange	收入范围	$ 25.000~49.999

数据分析要求如下:

(1) 在整体借款数据中,计算信用得分 ProsperScore 对于借款的影响。以信用得分为变量,统计借款次数,即以信用得分 ProsperScore 为变量,对借款进行计数统计,按降序排列,结果写入 HDFS 的"/home/hadoop/loan/loan_anas001/"文件夹中,即了解大多数借款人的信用得分。

(2) 找出借款较容易的行业前 5 及对应借款次数;给出借款较多的行业前 5,结果写入

HDFS 的"/home/hadoop/loan/loan_anase002/"文件夹中。

（3）分析贷款状态为违约（defaulted）的贷款人就业信息，将结果前 3 写入 HDFS 的"/home/hadoop/loan/loan_anas003/"文件夹中。

（4）对数据中收入范围进行分组统计，以降序排列，查看贷款人收入情况，结果写入 HDFS 的"/home/hadoop/loan/loan_anas004/"文件夹中。

（5）对信用得分上限及下限进行中间数求值，以此作为信用得分，计算各职业中的信用得分最高分。按照信用的得分降序，职业升序，将结果前 5 写入 HDFS 的"/home/hadoop/loan/loan_anas005/"文件夹中。

（6）分析职业对于贷款违约的影响。

请根据 Apriori 关联规则算法的原理找出与违约最多的贷款（借款状态，后项）之间的关联度最强的职业（前项），并计算出其支持度与置信度。要求如下：

支持度写到 HDFS 的"/home/hadoop/loan/loan_anas006/"文件夹中（保留五位小数）；

置信度写到 HDFS 的"/home/hadoop/loan/loan_anas007/"文件夹中（保留五位小数）。

注意

若前项为 A，后项为 B，支持度和置信度的计算公式如下：

支持度：表示同时包含 A 和 B 的事务占所有事务的比例，用 A&B 表示同时包含 A 和 B 的事务，Support = P(A&B)。

置信度：表示使用包含 A 的事务中同时包含 B 事务的比例，即同时包含 A 和 B 的事务占包含 A 事务的比例，用 P(A) 表示使用 A 事务的比例，Confidence = P(A&B)/P(A)。

8.2.2 贷款数据分析任务实施

8.2.2.1 原始数据上传到 CentOS 7 系统

打开 WinSCP，将 Windows 系统上的 loan.csv 上传到 CentOS 7 系统的"/root"文件夹下，如图 8.2.2 所示。

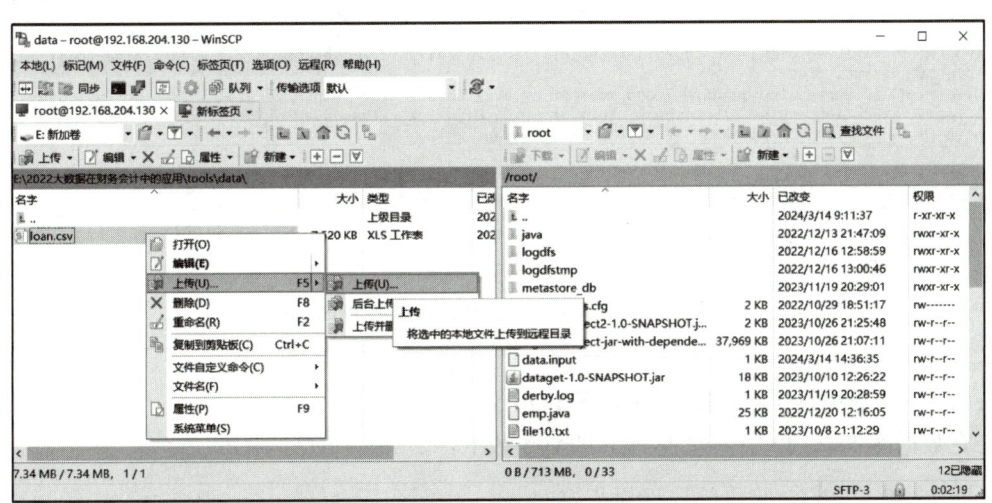

图 8.2.2　将贷款数据上传到 CentOS 7 系统

8.2.2.2 在 HDFS 上创建文件夹，将 loan.csv 上传至 HDFS 对应文件夹

启动 HDFS，在 HDFS 上创建"/usr/hadoop/loan_anas"文件夹，将 loan.csv 上传至该文件夹下，命令如下：

```
[root@master ~]# start_all.sh
[root@master ~]# hdfs dfs -mkdir -p /usr/hadoop/loan_anas
[root@master ~]# hdfs dfs -put /root/loan.csv /usr/hadoop/loan_anas
[root@master ~]# hdfs dfs -ls /usr/hadoop/loan_anas
```

运行结果如图 8.2.3 所示。

```
[root@master ~]# hdfs dfs -mkdir -p /usr/hadoop/loan_anas
[root@master ~]# hdfs dfs -put /root/loan.csv /usr/hadoop/loan_anas
[root@master ~]# hdfs dfs -ls /usr/hadoop/loan_anas
Found 1 items
-rw-r--r--   2 root supergroup    7699787 2024-05-07 12:00 /usr/hadoop/loan_anas/loan.csv
```

图 8.2.3　上传 loan.csv 到 HDFS 上

8.2.2.3 启动 Hive 并创建数据库 loan_db

启动 Hive 并创建数据库 loan_db 的命令如下：

```
[root@master ~]# hive
hive (default)> CREATE DATABASE IF NOT EXISTS loan_db;
hive (default)> USE loan_db;
hive (loan_db)>
```

运行结果如图 8.2.4 所示。

```
[root@master ~]# hive
SLF4J: Class path contains multiple SLF4J bindings.
SLF4J: Found binding in [jar:file:/opt/hive/lib/log4j-slf4j-impl-2.6.2.jar!/org/slf4j/impl/StaticLoggerBinder.class]
SLF4J: Found binding in [jar:file:/opt/hadoop-2.7.7/share/hadoop/common/lib/slf4j-log4j12-1.7.10.jar!/org/slf4j/impl/StaticLoggerBinder.class]
SLF4J: See http://www.slf4j.org/codes.html#multiple_bindings for an explanation.
SLF4J: Actual binding is of type [org.apache.logging.slf4j.Log4jLoggerFactory]

Logging initialized using configuration in jar:file:/opt/hive/lib/hive-common-2.3.4.jar!/hive-log4j2.properties Async: true
Hive-on-MR is deprecated in Hive 2 and may not be available in the future versions. Consider using a different execution engine (i.e. spark, tez) or using Hive 1.X releases.
hive (default)> CREATE DATABASE IF NOT EXISTS loan_db;
OK
Time taken: 6.044 seconds
hive (default)> USE loan_db;
OK
Time taken: 0.02 seconds
hive (loan_db)>
```

图 8.2.4　启动 Hive 并创建数据库 loan_db

8.2.2.4 在数据库 loan_db 中创建表 loan

在数据库 loan_db 中创建表 loan 的命令如下：

```
hive (loan_db)> CREATE TABLE loan(
LoanStatus STRING,
```

```
    BorrowerRate DECIMAL(10,5),
    ProsperScore   INT,
    Occupation STRING,
    EmploymentStatus STRING ,
    IsBorrowerHomeowner STRING,
    CreditScoreRangeLower INT ,
    CreditScoreRangeUpper INT ,
    IncomeRange STRING)
    ROW FORMAT DELIMITED FIELDS TERMINATED BY ',';
```

运行结果如图 8.2.5 所示。

```
hive (loan_db)> CREATE TABLE loan(
    > LoanStatus   STRING,
    > BorrowerRate DECIMAL(10,5),
    > ProsperScore   INT,
    > Occupation STRING,
    > EmploymentStatus STRING ,
    > IsBorrowerHomeowner STRING,
    > CreditScoreRangeLower INT ,
    > CreditScoreRangeUpper INT ,
    > IncomeRange STRING)
    > ROW FORMAT DELIMITED FIELDS TERMINATED BY ',';
OK
Time taken: 1.009 seconds
```

图 8.2.5 在数据库 loan_db 中创建表 loan

8.2.2.5 将原始数据导入 loan 表

将 HDFS 上的数据 loan.csv 导入 loan 表中，命令如下：

```
hive (loan_db)> LOAD DATA INPATH '/usr/hadoop/loan_anas/loan.csv' INTO TABLE loan;
hive (loan_db)> SELECT * FROM loan;
```

loan.csv 中的 113 937 条数据全部导入 loan 表，运行结果如图 8.2.6 所示。

```
Completed       0.06790 NULL    Executive       Full-time       TRUE    760     779     $100.000+
Completed       0.18990 6       Other   Full-time       FALSE   740     759     $25.000-49.999
Completed       0.26390 3       Accountant/CPA  Employed        FALSE   660     679     $50.000-74.999
Current 0.16390 6       Professional    Employed        TRUE    680     699     $75.000-99.999
Current 0.12740 6       Analyst Employed        FALSE   800     819     $75.000-99.999
Current 0.18640 5       Food Service Management Employed        TRUE    700     719     $50.000-74.999
FinalPaymentInProgress  0.11100 8       Professional    Employed        TRUE    700     719     $75.00
0-99.999
Current 0.21500 3       Other   Employed        TRUE    700     719     $25.000-49.999
Completed       0.26050 5       Food Service    Full-time       TRUE    680     699     $25.000-49.999
Current 0.10390 7       Professor       Employed        FALSE   680     699     $50.000-74.999
Time taken: 2.434 seconds, Fetched: 113937 row(s)
```

图 8.2.6 数据导入成功

统计表数据行数，命令如下：

```
SELECT COUNT(*) FROM loan;
```

统计 loan 表中的行数，运行结果如图 8.2.7 所示。

```
hive (loan_db)> INSERT OVERWRITE DIRECTORY '/usr/hadoop/loan_anas/01'
              > ROW FORMAT DELIMITED FIELDS TERMINATED BY '\t'
              > SELECT COUNT(*) FROM loan;
WARNING: Hive-on-MR is deprecated in Hive 2 and may not be available in the future versions. Consider using a dif
erent execution engine (i.e. spark, tez) or using Hive 1.X releases.
Query ID = root_20240508225942_581bb1d4-1ab2-4a5e-9bb3-6f83d99f4a76
Total jobs = 1
Launching Job 1 out of 1
Number of reduce tasks determined at compile time: 1
In order to change the average load for a reducer (in bytes):
  set hive.exec.reducers.bytes.per.reducer=<number>
In order to limit the maximum number of reducers:
  set hive.exec.reducers.max=<number>
In order to set a constant number of reducers:
  set mapreduce.job.reduces=<number>
Starting Job = job_1715179751823_0003, Tracking URL = http://master:8088/proxy/application_1715179751823_0003/
Kill Command = /opt/hadoop-2.7.7/bin/hadoop job  -kill job_1715179751823_0003
Hadoop job information for Stage-1: number of mappers: 1; number of reducers: 1
2024-05-08 22:59:55,260 Stage-1 map = 0%,  reduce = 0%
2024-05-08 23:00:06,092 Stage-1 map = 100%,  reduce = 0%, Cumulative CPU 2.86 sec
2024-05-08 23:00:19,510 Stage-1 map = 100%,  reduce = 100%, Cumulative CPU 6.53 sec
MapReduce Total cumulative CPU time: 6 seconds 530 msec
Ended Job = job_1715179751823_0003
Moving data to directory /usr/hadoop/loan_anas/01
MapReduce Jobs Launched:
Stage-Stage-1: Map: 1  Reduce: 1   Cumulative CPU: 6.53 sec   HDFS Read: 7708726 HDFS Write: 7 SUCCESS
Total MapReduce CPU Time Spent: 6 seconds 530 msec
OK
_c0
Time taken: 37.83 seconds
```

图 8.2.7　统计 loan 表中的行数

将统计出的行数"113937"写入 HDFS 的"/usr/hadoop/loan_anas/01"文件夹下，命令如下：

```
INSERT OVERWRITE DIRECTORY '/usr/hadoop/loan_anas/01'
ROW FORMAT DELIMITED FIELDS TERMINATED BY '\t'
SELECT COUNT( * ) FROM loan;
```

运行结果如图 8.2.8 所示。

```
hive (loan_db)> select count(*) from loan;
WARNING: Hive-on-MR is deprecated in Hive 2 and may not be available in the future versions. Consider
using a different execution engine (i.e. spark, tez) or using Hive 1.X releases.
Query ID = root_20240508225015_0468f220-cf0e-4969-854b-50c9d970e110
Total jobs = 1
Launching Job 1 out of 1
Number of reduce tasks determined at compile time: 1
In order to change the average load for a reducer (in bytes):
  set hive.exec.reducers.bytes.per.reducer=<number>
In order to limit the maximum number of reducers:
  set hive.exec.reducers.max=<number>
In order to set a constant number of reducers:
  set mapreduce.job.reduces=<number>
Starting Job = job_1715179751823_0001, Tracking URL = http://master:8088/proxy/application_17151797518
23_0001/
Kill Command = /opt/hadoop-2.7.7/bin/hadoop job  -kill job_1715179751823_0001
Hadoop job information for Stage-1: number of mappers: 1; number of reducers: 1
2024-05-08 22:50:49,319 Stage-1 map = 0%,  reduce = 0%
2024-05-08 22:51:00,278 Stage-1 map = 100%,  reduce = 0%, Cumulative CPU 2.41 sec
2024-05-08 22:51:30,930 Stage-1 map = 100%,  reduce = 100%, Cumulative CPU 5.6 sec
MapReduce Total cumulative CPU time: 5 seconds 880 msec
Ended Job = job_1715179751823_0001
MapReduce Jobs Launched:
Stage-Stage-1: Map: 1  Reduce: 1   Cumulative CPU: 5.88 sec   HDFS Read: 7709125 HDFS Write: 106 SUCCE
SS
Total MapReduce CPU Time Spent: 5 seconds 880 msec
OK
_c0
113937
Time taken: 79.785 seconds, Fetched: 1 row(s)
```

图 8.2.8　将行数统计结果写入到 HDFS 文件夹"/usr/hadoop/loan_anas/01"

8.2.2.6 用 Hive 进行数据分析

1) 分析信用得分对借款的影响

在整体借款数据中，计算信用得分 ProsperScore 对于借款的影响。以信用得分为变量，统计借款次数，即以信用得分 ProsperScore 为变量，对借款进行计数统计，按降序排列，结果写入 HDFS 的"/home/hadoop/loan/loan_anas001/"文件夹中，即了解大多数借款人的信用得分。

SELECT 分析语句如下：

```
SELECT  ProsperScore,count(*)  AS  sum  FROM  loan
GROUP BY ProsperScore ORDER BY sum DESC;
```

运行结果如图 8.2.9 所示。

```
Hadoop job information for Stage-2: number of mappers: 1; number of reducers: 1
2024-05-08 23:04:36,136 Stage-2 map = 0%,  reduce = 0%
2024-05-08 23:04:47,827 Stage-2 map = 100%,  reduce = 0%, Cumulative CPU 2.25 sec
2024-05-08 23:04:55,365 Stage-2 map = 100%,  reduce = 100%, Cumulative CPU 3.99 sec
MapReduce Total cumulative CPU time: 3 seconds 990 msec
Ended Job = job_1715179751823_0005
MapReduce Jobs Launched:
Stage-Stage-1: Map: 1  Reduce: 1   Cumulative CPU: 3.88 sec   HDFS Read: 7708671 HDFS Write: 347 SUCCESS
Stage-Stage-2: Map: 1  Reduce: 1   Cumulative CPU: 3.99 sec   HDFS Read: 5743 HDFS Write: 322 SUCCESS
Total MapReduce CPU Time Spent: 7 seconds 870 msec
OK
prosperscore    sum
NULL    29084
4       12595
6       12278
8       12053
7       10597
5       9813
3       7642
9       6911
2       5766
10      4750
11      1456
1       992
Time taken: 75.647 seconds, Fetched: 12 row(s)
```

图 8.2.9　统计借款人的信用得分

结果写入 HDFS 的"/home/hadoop/loan/loan_anas001/"文件夹中，命令如下：

```
INSERT OVERWRITE DIRECTORY  '/home/hadoop/loan/loan_anas001/'
ROW FORMAT DELIMITED FIELDS TERMINATED BY '\t'
SELECT  ProsperScore,count(*)  AS  sum  FROM  loan
GROUP BY ProsperScore ORDER BY sum DESC;
```

运行结果如图 8.2.10 所示。

```
2024-05-08 23:06:31,131 Stage-2 map = 0%,  reduce = 0%
2024-05-08 23:06:38,429 Stage-2 map = 100%,  reduce = 0%, Cumulative CPU 1.1 sec
2024-05-08 23:06:49,285 Stage-2 map = 100%,  reduce = 100%, Cumulative CPU 3.56 sec
MapReduce Total cumulative CPU time: 3 seconds 560 msec
Ended Job = job_1715179751823_0007
Moving data to directory /home/hadoop/loan/loan_anas001
MapReduce Jobs Launched:
Stage-Stage-1: Map: 1  Reduce: 1   Cumulative CPU: 3.37 sec   HDFS Read: 7708671 HDFS Write: 347 SUCCESS
Stage-Stage-2: Map: 1  Reduce: 1   Cumulative CPU: 3.56 sec   HDFS Read: 5363 HDFS Write: 91 SUCCESS
Total MapReduce CPU Time Spent: 6 seconds 930 msec
OK
prosperscore    sum
Time taken: 67.485 seconds
```

图 8.2.10　结果写入 HDFS 的"/home/hadoop/loan/loan_anas001/"

2) 找出借款较容易的行业前 5 及对应借款次数

找出借款较容易的行业前 5 及对应借款次数。给出借款较多的行业前 5，结果写入 HDFS 的"/home/hadoop/loan/loan_anase002/"文件夹中。

SELECT 分析语句如下：

```
SELECT  Occupation,count(*)  AS  sum FROM LOAN
GROUP BY Occupation
ORDER BY sum DESC limit 5；
```

运行结果如图 8.2.11 所示。

```
2024-05-08 23:13:31,615 Stage-2 map = 0%, reduce = 0%
2024-05-08 23:13:39,952 Stage-2 map = 100%, reduce = 0%, Cumulative CPU 1.14 sec
2024-05-08 23:13:46,223 Stage-2 map = 100%, reduce = 100%, Cumulative CPU 2.73 sec
MapReduce Total cumulative CPU time: 2 seconds 730 msec
Ended Job = job_1715179751823_0009
MapReduce Jobs Launched:
Stage-Stage-1: Map: 1  Reduce: 1   Cumulative CPU: 3.93 sec   HDFS Read: 7708648 HDFS Write: 2477 SUCCESS
Stage-Stage-2: Map: 1  Reduce: 1   Cumulative CPU: 2.73 sec   HDFS Read: 8030 HDFS Write: 231 SUCCESS
Total MapReduce CPU Time Spent: 6 seconds 660 msec
OK
occupation       sum
Other    28617
Professional     13628
Computer Programmer      4478
Executive        4311
Teacher 3759
Time taken: 58.495 seconds, Fetched: 5 row(s)
```

图 8.2.11　统计借款较多的行业前 5

结果写入 HDFS 的"/home/hadoop/loan/loan_anas002/"文件夹中，命令如下：

```
INSERT OVERWRITE DIRECTORY '/home/hadoop/loan/loan_anas002/'
ROW  FORMAT  DELIMITED FIELDS TERMINATED BY  '\t'
SELECT  Occupation,count(*)  AS  sum FROM LOAN
GROUP BY Occupation
ORDER BY sum DESC limit 5；
```

运行结果如图 8.2.12 所示。

```
2024-05-08 23:15:18,163 Stage-2 map = 0%, reduce = 0%
2024-05-08 23:15:24,615 Stage-2 map = 100%, reduce = 0%, Cumulative CPU 1.38 sec
2024-05-08 23:15:33,136 Stage-2 map = 100%, reduce = 100%, Cumulative CPU 3.25 sec
MapReduce Total cumulative CPU time: 3 seconds 250 msec
Ended Job = job_1715179751823_0011
Moving data to directory /home/hadoop/loan/loan_anas002
MapReduce Jobs Launched:
Stage-Stage-1: Map: 1  Reduce: 1   Cumulative CPU: 6.43 sec   HDFS Read: 7708648 HDFS Write: 2477 SUCCESS
Stage-Stage-2: Map: 1  Reduce: 1   Cumulative CPU: 3.25 sec   HDFS Read: 7650 HDFS Write: 84 SUCCESS
Total MapReduce CPU Time Spent: 9 seconds 680 msec
OK
occupation       sum
Time taken: 63.891 seconds
```

图 8.2.12　结果写入 HDFS 的"/home/hadoop/loan/loan_anas002/"

3) 分析贷款状态为违约的贷款人就业信息

分析贷款状态为违约的贷款人就业信息，将结果前 3 写入 HDFS 的"/home/hadoop/loan/loan_anas003/"文件夹中。

SELECT 分析语句如下：

```
SELECT  EmploymentStatus,COUNT(*) AS sum  FROM loan
WHERE  LoanStatus='Defaulted'  GROUP BY  EmploymentStatus
ORDER BY sum DESC LIMIT 3;
```

运行结果如图 8.2.13 所示。

```
2024-05-08 23:17:14,465 Stage-2 map = 0%,  reduce = 0%
2024-05-08 23:17:20,749 Stage-2 map = 100%,  reduce = 0%, Cumulative CPU 1.07 sec
2024-05-08 23:17:37,081 Stage-2 map = 100%,  reduce = 100%, Cumulative CPU 4.28 sec
MapReduce Total cumulative CPU time: 4 seconds 280 msec
Ended Job = job_1715179751823_0013
MapReduce Jobs Launched:
Stage-Stage-1: Map: 1  Reduce: 1   Cumulative CPU: 6.72 sec   HDFS Read: 7709487 HDFS Write: 352 SUCCESS
Stage-Stage-2: Map: 1  Reduce: 1   Cumulative CPU: 4.28 sec   HDFS Read: 5930 HDFS Write: 170 SUCCESS
Total MapReduce CPU Time Spent: 11 seconds 0 msec
OK
employmentstatus        sum
Full-time        2217
Not available    1204
Employed         630
Time taken: 81.951 seconds, Fetched: 3 row(s)
```

图 8.2.13 统计违约的贷款人就业信息前 3

结果写入 HDFS 的 "/home/hadoop/loan/loan_anas003/" 文件夹中，命令如下：

```
INSERT OVERWRITE DIRECTORY '/home/hadoop/loan/loan_anas003/'
ROW   FORMAT   DELIMITED FIELDS TERMINATED BY  '\t'
SELECT  EmploymentStatus,COUNT(*) AS sum  FROM loan
WHERE  LoanStatus='Defaulted'  GROUP BY  EmploymentStatus
ORDER BY sum DESC LIMIT 3;
```

运行结果如图 8.2.14 所示。

```
2024-05-08 23:18:57,516 Stage-2 map = 0%,  reduce = 0%
2024-05-08 23:19:08,621 Stage-2 map = 100%,  reduce = 0%, Cumulative CPU 2.42 sec
2024-05-08 23:19:18,391 Stage-2 map = 100%,  reduce = 100%, Cumulative CPU 4.49 sec
MapReduce Total cumulative CPU time: 4 seconds 490 msec
Ended Job = job_1715179751823_0015
Moving data to directory /home/hadoop/loan/loan_anas003
MapReduce Jobs Launched:
Stage-Stage-1: Map: 1  Reduce: 1   Cumulative CPU: 3.89 sec   HDFS Read: 7709486 HDFS Write: 352 SUCCESS
Stage-Stage-2: Map: 1  Reduce: 1   Cumulative CPU: 4.49 sec   HDFS Read: 5544 HDFS Write: 47 SUCCESS
Total MapReduce CPU Time Spent: 8 seconds 380 msec
OK
employmentstatus        sum
Time taken: 67.849 seconds
```

图 8.2.14 结果写入 HDFS 的 "/home/hadoop/loan/loan_anas003/"

4) 对数据中收入范围进行分组统计

对数据中收入范围进行分组统计，以降序排列，查看贷款人收入情况，结果写入 HDFS 的 "/home/hadoop/loan/loan_anas004/" 文件夹中。

SELECT 分析语句如下：

```
SELECT IncomeRange ,COUNT(*) AS s FROM loan
GROUP BY IncomeRange
ORDER BY s DESC ;
```

运行结果如图 8.2.15 所示。

```
2024-05-08 23:20:23,248 Stage-2 map = 0%, reduce = 0%
2024-05-08 23:20:33,670 Stage-2 map = 100%, reduce = 0%, Cumulative CPU 2.39 sec
2024-05-08 23:20:41,055 Stage-2 map = 100%, reduce = 100%, Cumulative CPU 3.99 sec
MapReduce Total cumulative CPU time: 3 seconds 990 msec
Ended Job = job_1715179751823_0017
MapReduce Jobs Launched:
Stage-Stage-1: Map: 1  Reduce: 1   Cumulative CPU: 2.93 sec   HDFS Read: 7708648 HDFS Write: 352 SUCCESS
Stage-Stage-2: Map: 1  Reduce: 1   Cumulative CPU: 3.99 sec   HDFS Read: 5756 HDFS Write: 321 SUCCESS
Total MapReduce CPU Time Spent: 6 seconds 920 msec
OK
incomerange       s
$25.000-49.999    32192
$50.000-74.999    31050
$100.000+         17337
$75.000-99.999    16916
Not displayed     7741
$1-24.999         7274
Not employed      806
$0                621
Time taken: 60.064 seconds, Fetched: 8 row(s)
```

图 8.2.15　统计贷款人收入情况

结果写入 HDFS 的"/home/hadoop/loan/loan_anas004/"文件夹中，命令如下：

```
INSERT OVERWRITE DIRECTORY '/home/hadoop/loan/loan_anas004/'
ROW FORMAT DELIMITED FIELDS TERMINATED BY '\t'
SELECT IncomeRange ,COUNT( * ) AS s FROM loan
GROUP BY IncomeRange
ORDER BY s DESC ;
```

运行结果如图 8.2.16 所示。

```
2024-05-08 23:22:13,165 Stage-2 map = 0%, reduce = 0%
2024-05-08 23:22:17,373 Stage-2 map = 100%, reduce = 0%, Cumulative CPU 0.98 sec
2024-05-08 23:22:38,501 Stage-2 map = 100%, reduce = 100%, Cumulative CPU 4.21 sec
MapReduce Total cumulative CPU time: 4 seconds 210 msec
Ended Job = job_1715179751823_0019
Moving data to directory /home/hadoop/loan/loan_anas004
MapReduce Jobs Launched:
Stage-Stage-1: Map: 1  Reduce: 1   Cumulative CPU: 3.38 sec   HDFS Read: 7708649 HDFS Write: 352 SUCCESS
Stage-Stage-2: Map: 1  Reduce: 1   Cumulative CPU: 4.21 sec   HDFS Read: 5386 HDFS Write: 138 SUCCESS
Total MapReduce CPU Time Spent: 7 seconds 590 msec
OK
incomerange       s
Time taken: 81.77 seconds
```

图 8.2.16　结果写入 HDFS 的"/home/hadoop/loan/loan_anas004/"

5) 对信用得分上限及下限进行中间数求值作为信用得分

对信用得分上限及下限进行中间数求值作为信用得分，计算各职业中的信用得分最高分。要求按照信用的得分降序，职业升序，将结果前 5 写入 HDFS 的"/home/hadoop/loan/loan_anas005/"文件夹中。

计算各职业中的信用得分最高分，按照信用的得分降序，职业升序，SELECT 分析语句如下：

```
SELECT Occupation,MAX(CreditScore) AS c  FROM
(  SELECT    Occupation,    CreditScoreRangeLower,    CreditScoreRangeUpper,
(CreditScoreRangeLower+CreditScoreRangeUpper)/2  AS  CreditScore  FROM loan)  t1
```

```
    GROUP  BY  Occupation
    ORDER  BY c DESC,Occupation  ASC
    LIMIT 5;
```

运行结果如图 8.2.17 所示。

```
2024-05-08 23:24:05,860 Stage-2 map = 0%,  reduce = 0%
2024-05-08 23:24:12,154 Stage-2 map = 100%,  reduce = 0%, Cumulative CPU 1.04 sec
2024-05-08 23:24:18,499 Stage-2 map = 100%,  reduce = 100%, Cumulative CPU 2.39 sec
MapReduce Total cumulative CPU time: 2 seconds 390 msec
Ended Job = job_1715179751823_0021
MapReduce Jobs Launched:
Stage-Stage-1: Map: 1  Reduce: 1   Cumulative CPU: 6.09 sec    HDFS Read: 7710393 HDFS Write: 2854 SUCCESS
Stage-Stage-2: Map: 1  Reduce: 1   Cumulative CPU: 2.39 sec    HDFS Read: 8589 HDFS Write: 254 SUCCESS
Total MapReduce CPU Time Spent: 8 seconds 480 msec
OK
occupation        c
Administrative Assistant          889.5
Construction       889.5
Doctor   889.5
Engineer - Electrical   889.5
Executive        889.5
Time taken: 67.535 seconds, Fetched: 5 row(s)
```

图 8.2.17 计算各职业中的信用得分最高分

结果写入 HDFS 的"/home/hadoop/loan/loan_anas005/"文件夹中,命令如下:

```
INSERT OVERWRITE DIRECTORY '/home/hadoop/loan/loan_anas005/'
ROW  FORMAT  DELIMITED FIELDS TERMINATED BY  '\t'
SELECT Occupation,MAX(CreditScore) AS c  FROM

(SELECT     Occupation,     CreditScoreRangeLower,     CreditScoreRangeUpper,
(CreditScoreRangeLower+CreditScoreRangeUpper)/2  AS  CreditScore  FROM loan)  t1
    GROUP  BY  Occupation
    ORDER  BY c DESC,Occupation  ASC
    LIMIT 5;
```

运行结果如图 8.2.18 所示。

```
2024-05-08 23:25:47,056 Stage-2 map = 0%,  reduce = 0%
2024-05-08 23:25:54,535 Stage-2 map = 100%,  reduce = 0%, Cumulative CPU 1.18 sec
2024-05-08 23:26:02,872 Stage-2 map = 100%,  reduce = 100%, Cumulative CPU 2.64 sec
MapReduce Total cumulative CPU time: 2 seconds 640 msec
Ended Job = job_1715179751823_0023
Moving data to directory /home/hadoop/loan/loan_anas005
MapReduce Jobs Launched:
Stage-Stage-1: Map: 1  Reduce: 1   Cumulative CPU: 4.91 sec    HDFS Read: 7710405 HDFS Write: 2854 SUCCESS
Stage-Stage-2: Map: 1  Reduce: 1   Cumulative CPU: 2.64 sec    HDFS Read: 8209 HDFS Write: 107 SUCCESS
Total MapReduce CPU Time Spent: 7 seconds 550 msec
OK
occupation        c
Time taken: 65.183 seconds
```

图 8.2.18 结果写入 HDFS 的"/home/hadoop/loan/loan_anas005/"

6) 分析职业对于贷款违约的影响

数据挖掘。请根据 Apriori 关联规则算法的原理找出与违约最多的贷款(借款状态,后项)之间的关联度最强的职业(前项),并计算出其支持度与置信度。要求如下:

支持度写到 HDFS 的"/home/hadoop/loan/loan_anas006/"文件夹中(保留 5 位小数)；
置信度写到 HDFS 的"/home/hadoop/loan/loan_anas007/"文件夹中(保留 5 位小数)。

(1) 计算支持度。

支持度：表示同时包含 A 和 B 的事务占所有事务的比例,用 P(A&B)表示；包含 A 事务的比例用 P(A)表示,支持度计算公式为 Support = P(A&B)。

这里的 A 为前项,表示 loan 中的数据总行数；B 为后项,表示 loan 中违约最多的职业行数。

先计算 A,即统计 loan 表的总行数,命令如下：

```
SELECT COUNT( * ) FROM loan;        #结果 A 为 113937
```

统计结果如图 8.2.19 所示。

```
2024-05-08 23:26:39,637 Stage-1 map = 0%,  reduce = 0%
2024-05-08 23:26:50,988 Stage-1 map = 100%, reduce = 0%, Cumulative CPU 2.79 sec
2024-05-08 23:27:00,724 Stage-1 map = 100%, reduce = 100%, Cumulative CPU 4.93 sec
MapReduce Total cumulative CPU time: 4 seconds 930 msec
Ended Job = job_1715179751823_0024
MapReduce Jobs Launched:
Stage-Stage-1: Map: 1  Reduce: 1   Cumulative CPU: 4.93 sec   HDFS Read: 7709123 HDFS Write: 106 SUCCESS
Total MapReduce CPU Time Spent: 4 seconds 930 msec
OK
 c0
113937
Time taken: 32.723 seconds, Fetched: 1 row(s)
```

图 8.2.19　统计 loan 表的总行数

再计算 B,即统计 loan 表中违约最多职业的行数,命令如下：

```
SELECT occupation,count( * ) AS total FROM loan
WHERE LoanStatus = 'Defaulted'
GROUP BY occupation
ORDER BY total DESC limit 1;      #结果 B 违约最多的是 Other,有 1281 行
```

统计结果如图 8.2.20 所示。

```
2024-05-08 23:33:22,106 Stage-2 map = 0%,  reduce = 0%
2024-05-08 23:33:28,636 Stage-2 map = 100%, reduce = 0%, Cumulative CPU 1.39 sec
2024-05-08 23:33:37,340 Stage-2 map = 100%, reduce = 100%, Cumulative CPU 3.4 sec
MapReduce Total cumulative CPU time: 3 seconds 400 msec
Ended Job = job_1715179751823_0026
MapReduce Jobs Launched:
Stage-Stage-1: Map: 1  Reduce: 1   Cumulative CPU: 4.1 sec   HDFS Read: 7709469 HDFS Write: 2338 SUCCESS
Stage-Stage-2: Map: 1  Reduce: 1   Cumulative CPU: 3.4 sec   HDFS Read: 7886 HDFS Write: 110 SUCCESS
Total MapReduce CPU Time Spent: 7 seconds 500 msec
OK
occupation    total
Other   1281
Time taken: 64.246 seconds, Fetched: 1 row(s)
```

图 8.2.20　统计 loan 表中违约最多职业的行数

再计算支持度 B/A,结果用 ROUND()函数保留五位小数,存放在 HDFS 的文件夹"/home/hadoop/loan/loan_anas006/"中。合并上述语句,支持度计算的最终命令如下：

```
hive (loan_db)> SET hive.mapred.mode = unrestrict;
hive (loan_db)> INSERT OVERWRITE DIRECTORY '/home/hadoop/loan/loan_anas006/'
```

```sql
SELECT ROUND((t2.s / t4.s),5)
FROM (SELECT t1.occupation as c, COUNT(*) AS s FROM loan t1
WHERE t1.LoanStatus = 'Defaulted'
GROUP BY t1.occupation
ORDER BY s desc, t1.occupation ASC LIMIT 1
)t2
JOIN (select count(*) AS s FROM loan t3) t4;
```

运行结果如图 8.2.21 所示。

```
2024-05-08 23:40:20,512 Stage-6 map = 0%, reduce = 0%
2024-05-08 23:40:27,845 Stage-6 map = 100%, reduce = 0%, Cumulative CPU 1.54 sec
MapReduce Total cumulative CPU time: 1 seconds 540 msec
Ended Job = job_1715179751823_0030
Moving data to directory /home/hadoop/loan/loan_anas006
MapReduce Jobs Launched:
Stage-Stage-1: Map: 1  Reduce: 1   Cumulative CPU: 3.37 sec   HDFS Read: 7709484 HDFS Write: 2338 SUCCESS
Stage-Stage-4: Map: 1  Reduce: 1   Cumulative CPU: 3.53 sec   HDFS Read: 7708325 HDFS Write: 117 SUCCESS
Stage-Stage-2: Map: 1  Reduce: 1   Cumulative CPU: 4.13 sec   HDFS Read: 7129 HDFS Write: 116 SUCCESS
Stage-Stage-6: Map: 1             Cumulative CPU: 1.54 sec   HDFS Read: 4911 HDFS Write: 8 SUCCESS
Total MapReduce CPU Time Spent: 12 seconds 570 msec
OK
_c0
Time taken: 155.523 seconds
```

图 8.2.21　结果写入 HDFS 的文件夹/home/hadoop/loan/loan_anas006/

（2）计算置信度。

若前项为 A，后项为 B。置信度表示包含 A 的事务中同时包含 B 事务的比例，即同时包含 A 和 B 的事务占包含 A 事务的比例，计算公式为：Confidence = P(A&B)/P(A)。

这里的 A 表示 loan 表中 occupation = 'Other' 行数；B 表示 loan 表中 occupation = 'Other' 的行中违约的行数。

先计算 A，统计 loan 表中 occupation = 'Other' 行数，命令如下：

```sql
SELECT COUNT(*) AS s FROM loan  WHERE occupation = 'Other';    #A 为 28617
```

统计结果如图 8.2.22 所示。

```
2024-05-08 23:45:17,773 Stage-1 map = 0%, reduce = 0%
2024-05-08 23:45:25,506 Stage-1 map = 100%, reduce = 0%, Cumulative CPU 2.56 sec
2024-05-08 23:45:32,969 Stage-1 map = 100%, reduce = 100%, Cumulative CPU 4.14 sec
MapReduce Total cumulative CPU time: 4 seconds 140 msec
Ended Job = job_1715179751823_0031
MapReduce Jobs Launched:
Stage-Stage-1: Map: 1  Reduce: 1   Cumulative CPU: 4.14 sec   HDFS Read: 7709936 HDFS Write: 105 SUCCESS
Total MapReduce CPU Time Spent: 4 seconds 140 msec
OK
s
28617
Time taken: 44.044 seconds, Fetched: 1 row(s)
```

图 8.2.22　统计 loan 表中 occupation = 'Other' 行数

再计算 B，即统计 loan 表中违约最多的职业行数，同上节。

```sql
SELECT occupation, count(*) AS total FROM loan
WHERE LoanStatus = 'Defaulted'
GROUP BY occupation
ORDER BY total DESC limit 1;     #结果 B 违约最多的是 Other，有 1281 行
```

合并上述语句,置信度计算的最终命令如下:

```
hive (loan_db)> SET hive.mapred.mode=unrestrict;
hive (loan_db)> SELECT ROUND((t2.s/t4.s),5)
FROM (SELECT t1.occupation AS c,count(*) AS s FROM loan t1
WHERE t1.LoanStatus='Defaulted'
GROUP BY t1.occupation
ORDER BY s DESC, t1.occupation ASC LIMIT 1
)t2
JOIN(select count(*) as s from loan t3
WHERE occupation = 'Other') t4;
```

统计结果如图 8.2.23 所示。

```
2024-05-08 23:55:08,740 Stage-5 map = 0%, reduce = 0%
2024-05-08 23:55:18,540 Stage-5 map = 100%, reduce = 0%, Cumulative CPU 2.04 sec
MapReduce Total cumulative CPU time: 2 seconds 40 msec
Ended Job = job_1715179751823_0039
MapReduce Jobs Launched:
Stage-Stage-1: Map: 1  Reduce: 1   Cumulative CPU: 5.73 sec   HDFS Read: 7709502 HDFS Write: 2338 SUCCESS
Stage-Stage-4: Map: 1  Reduce: 1   Cumulative CPU: 5.65 sec   HDFS Read: 7709147 HDFS Write: 116 SUCCESS
Stage-Stage-2: Map: 1  Reduce: 1   Cumulative CPU: 2.32 sec   HDFS Read: 7129 HDFS Write: 116 SUCCESS
Stage-Stage-5: Map: 1              Cumulative CPU: 2.04 sec   HDFS Read: 5234 HDFS Write: 107 SUCCESS
Total MapReduce CPU Time Spent: 15 seconds 740 msec
OK
_c0
0.04476
Time taken: 149.05 seconds, Fetched: 1 row(s)
```

图 8.2.23　计算置信度为 0.04476

将统计结果保存在 HDFS 的"/home/hadoop/loan/loan_anas007/"文件夹中,命令如下:

```
hive (loan_db)> SET hive.mapred.mode=unrestrict;
hive (loan_db)> INSERT OVERWRITE DIRECTORY '/home/hadoop/loan/loan_anas007/'
SELECT ROUND((t2.s/t4.s),5)
FROM (SELECT t1.occupation AS c,count(*) AS s FROM loan t1
WHERE t1.LoanStatus='Defaulted'
GROUP BY t1.occupation
ORDER BY s DESC, t1.occupation ASC LIMIT 1
)t2
JOIN(select count(*) as s from loan t3
WHERE occupation = 'Other') t4;
```

执行结果如图 8.2.24 所示。

```
2024-05-08 23:52:02,018 Stage-5 map = 0%, reduce = 0%
2024-05-08 23:52:11,728 Stage-5 map = 100%, reduce = 0%, Cumulative CPU 2.07 sec
MapReduce Total cumulative CPU time: 2 seconds 70 msec
Ended Job = job_1715179751823_0035
Moving data to directory /home/hadoop/loan/loan_anas007
MapReduce Jobs Launched:
Stage-Stage-1: Map: 1  Reduce: 1   Cumulative CPU: 6.83 sec   HDFS Read: 7709484 HDFS Write: 2338 SUCCESS
Stage-Stage-4: Map: 1  Reduce: 1   Cumulative CPU: 5.27 sec   HDFS Read: 7709137 HDFS Write: 116 SUCCESS
Stage-Stage-2: Map: 1  Reduce: 1   Cumulative CPU: 4.02 sec   HDFS Read: 7129 HDFS Write: 116 SUCCESS
Stage-Stage-5: Map: 1              Cumulative CPU: 2.07 sec   HDFS Read: 4841 HDFS Write: 8 SUCCESS
Total MapReduce CPU Time Spent: 18 seconds 190 msec
OK
_c0
Time taken: 158.842 seconds
```

图 8.2.24　结果写入 HDFS 的/home/hadoop/loan/loan_anas007/文件夹

至此,完成了所有数据分析任务。可以查询一下保存在 HDFS 上的分析结果,命令如下:

```
[root@master /]# hdfs dfs -ls /home/hadoop/loan
```

执行结果如图 8.2.25 所示。

```
[root@master /]# hadoop fs -ls /home/hadoop/loan
Found 7 items
drwxr-xr-x   - root supergroup          0 2024-05-08 23:06 /home/hadoop/loan/loan_anas001
drwxr-xr-x   - root supergroup          0 2024-05-08 23:15 /home/hadoop/loan/loan_anas002
drwxr-xr-x   - root supergroup          0 2024-05-08 23:19 /home/hadoop/loan/loan_anas003
drwxr-xr-x   - root supergroup          0 2024-05-08 23:22 /home/hadoop/loan/loan_anas004
drwxr-xr-x   - root supergroup          0 2024-05-08 23:26 /home/hadoop/loan/loan_anas005
drwxr-xr-x   - root supergroup          0 2024-05-08 23:40 /home/hadoop/loan/loan_anas006
drwxr-xr-x   - root supergroup          0 2024-05-08 23:52 /home/hadoop/loan/loan_anas007
```

图 8.2.25 查看 7 个存放分析结果的文件夹

查询文件夹下的分析结果文件,命令如下:

```
[root@master /]# hdfs dfs -ls /home/hadoop/loan/loan_anas001
```

可见(1)的分析结果保存在 000000_0 文件中,如图 8.2.26 所示。

```
[root@master /]# hadoop fs -ls /home/hadoop/loan/loan_anas001
Found 1 items
-rwxr-xr-x   2 root supergroup         91 2024-05-08 23:06 /home/hadoop/loan/loan_anas001/000000_0
```

图 8.2.26 查看分析结果内容

查看 000000_0 文件内容,命令如下:

```
[root@master /]# hdfs dfs -cat /home/hadoop/loan/loan_anas001/000000_0
```

运行结果如图 8.2.27 所示。

```
[root@master /]# hadoop fs -cat /home/hadoop/loan/loan_anas001/000000_0
\N      29084
4       12595
6       12278
8       12053
7       10597
5       9813
3       7642
9       6911
2       5766
10      4750
11      1456
1       992
[root@master /]#
```

图 8.2.27 查看文件内容

单元总结

本单元通过简单介绍财务报表分析方法和贷款数据的分析方法,通过两个具体案例,运用 Hive 的 SQL 命令,针对具体分析要求,构建 Hive 的 SQL 语句,解决财务和金融的数据分析实际问题,并将查询结果存储于 HDFS 上。

单元习题

一、简答题

1. 简述财务比率分析方法。
2. 如何根据实际需要,在 Hive 工作表中建立相应的财务分析模型。
3. 查阅资料:Apriori 关联规则算法的原理是什么?
4. 使用笛卡尔积 JOIN 查询,需要设置什么参数?

二、技能训练题

1. 独立执行任务 8.1 和任务 8.2 中的所有步骤和查询命令,并将任务 8.1 的查询结果存入 HDFS,路径为"/home/hadoop/cwbb",文件名自拟。

2. 江苏财源有限公司 2022 年的资产负债表和利润表分别见表 8.1.5、表 8.1.6。参照任务 8.1 的 8.1.3.5 中的数据分析 Hive 语句,对 2022 年财务报表数据进行分析,计算以下各财务指标:

(1) 流动比率=流动资产合计.期末余额/流动负债合计.期末余额

(2) 速动比率=(流动资产合计.期末余额-存货.期末余额-预付账款.期末余额)/流动负债合计.期末余额

(3) 资产负债率=负债合计.期末余额/资产总计.期末余额

(4) 股东权益比率=所有者权益合计.期末余额/资产总计.期末余额

(5) 产权比率=负债合计.期末余额/所有者权益合计.期末余额

(6) 利息保障倍数=三、利润总额.本期金额/((应收账款.期末余额+应收账款.期初余额+应收票据.期末余额+应收票据.期初余额)/2)

(7) 应收账款周转次数=一、营业收入.本期金额/((资产负债表:应收账款.期末余额+应收账款.期初余额+应收票据.期末余额+应收票据.期初余额)/2)

(8) 存货周转次数=减:营业成本.本期金额/((资产负债表:存货.期末余额+存货.期初余额)/2)

(9) 固定资产周转次数=一、营业收入.本期金额/((固定资产.期末余额+固定资产.期初余额)/2)

(10) 总资产周转次数=一、营业收入.本期金额/((资产总计.期末余额+资产总计.期初余额)/2)

单元 9

大数据迁移工具 Sqoop

Sqoop 全称为 Apache Sqoop,是一个开源工具,能够将数据从数据存储空间(数据仓库、系统文档存储空间、关系型数据库)导入 Hadoop 的 HDFS 或列式数据库 HBase,供 MapReduce 分析数据使用,也可以被 Hive 等工具使用。当 MapReduce 分析出结果数据后,Sqoop 可以将结果数据导出到数据存储空间,供其他客户端调用查看结果。

教学目标

知识目标
1. 了解 Sqoop 架构。
2. 了解 Sqoop 数据导入和导出的过程。

技能目标
1. 掌握 Sqoop 的安装和配置。
2. 运用 Sqoop 在 HDFS、MySQL、Hive 之间的实现数据迁移。

单元任务

任务 9.1　Sqoop 的工作原理。
任务 9.2　Sqoop 的安装和配置。
任务 9.3　用 Sqoop 导入、导出数据。

任务 9.1　Sqoop 的工作原理

任务描述

大数据迁移工具 Sqoop 可以实现数据在 Hadoop、HBase 和 Hive 之间导入和导出,Sqoop 具有优良的架构特征和强大的数据转换能力。本任务学习 Sqoop 架构模式、数据导入过程和数据导出过程。

关键步骤

(1) Sqoop 架构。
(2) Sqoop 数据导入过程。

(3) Sqoop 数据导出过程。

9.1.1 Sqoop 架构

Sqoop 的出现使 Hadoop 或 HBase 和数据存储空间之间的数据导入和导出变得简单，这得益于 Sqoop 的优良架构特征和其对数据的强大转换能力。Sqoop 导入和导出数据如图 9.1.1 所示。

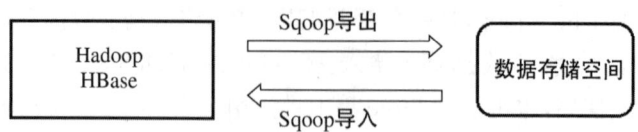

图 9.1.1　Sqoop 导入和导出数据

由图 9.1.1 可以看出，Sqoop 作为 Hadoop 或 HBase 和数据存储空间之间的桥梁，很容易实现 Hadoop 或 HBase 和数据存储空间之间的数据传输。

Sqoop 的架构也非常简单，主要由 Sqoop 客户端、数据存储与挖掘（HDFS/HBase/Hive）、数据存储空间三个部分组成，如图 9.1.2 所示。

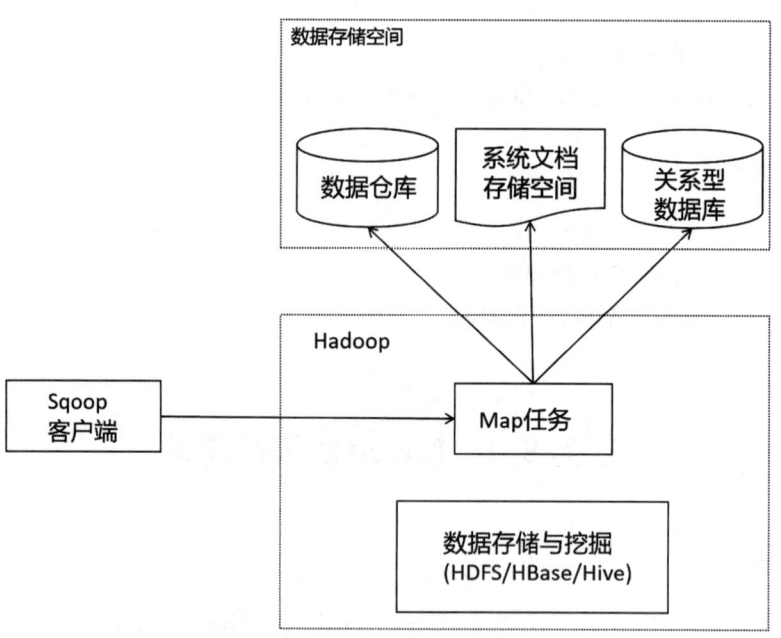

图 9.1.2　Sqoop 架构

由图 9.1.2 可以看出，Sqoop 协调 Hadoop 中的 Map 任务将数据从数据存储空间（数据仓库、系统文档存储空间、关系型数据库）导入 HDFS/HBase 供数据分析使用，同时数据分析人员也可以使用 Hive 对这些数据进行挖掘。当分析、挖掘出有价值的结果数据后，Sqoop 又可以协调 Hadoop 中的 Map 任务将结果数据导出到数据存储空间。

> **注意**
>
> Sqoop 只负责数据传输,不负责数据分析,所以只会涉及 Hadoop 的 Map 任务,不会涉及 Reduce 任务。

9.1.2　Sqoop 数据导入过程

Sqoop 数据导入过程:从表中读取一行行数据记录,经过 Sqoop 的传输,再通过 Hadoop 的 Map 任务将数据写入 HDFS,如图 9.1.3 所示。由图 9.1.3 可以看出,Sqoop 数据导入过程如下:

(1) Sqoop 通过 JDBC 获取所需要的数据库元数据信息,如表列名、数据类型等,并将这些元数据信息导入 Sqoop。

(2) Sqoop 生成一个与表名相同的记录容器类,记录容器类完成数据的序列化和反序列化过程,并保存表中的每一行数据。

(3) Sqoop 生成的记录容器类向 Hadoop 的 Map 作业提供序列化和反序列化的功能。

(4) Sqoop 启动 Hadoop 的 Map 作业。

(5) Sqoop 启动的 Map 作业在数据导入过程中,会通过 JDBC 读取数据库表中的内容,此时 Sqoop 生成的记录容器类同样提供反序列化功能。

(6) Map 作业将读取的数据写入 HDFS,此时 Sqoop 生成的记录容器类提供序列化功能。

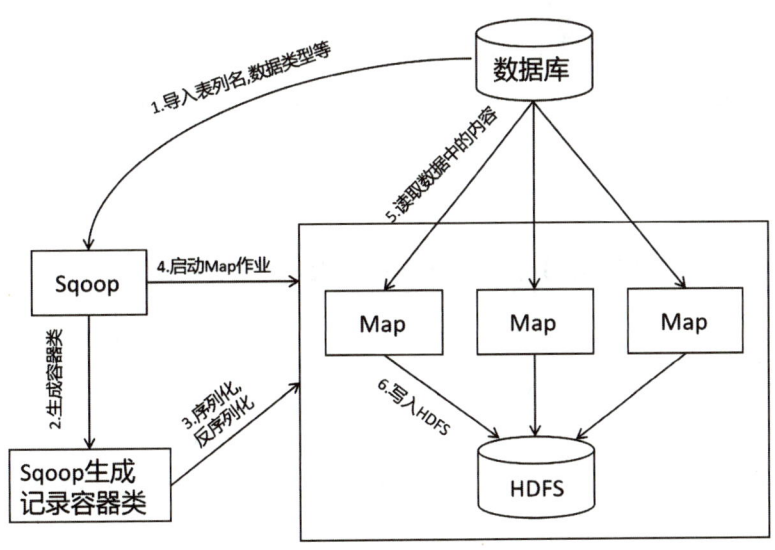

图 9.1.3　Sqoop 数据导入过程

9.1.3　Sqoop 数据导出过程

Sqoop 数据导出过程:将通过 MapReduce 或 Hive 分析后得出的数据结果导出到关系型数据库,供其他业务查看或生成报表使用,如图 9.1.4 所示。

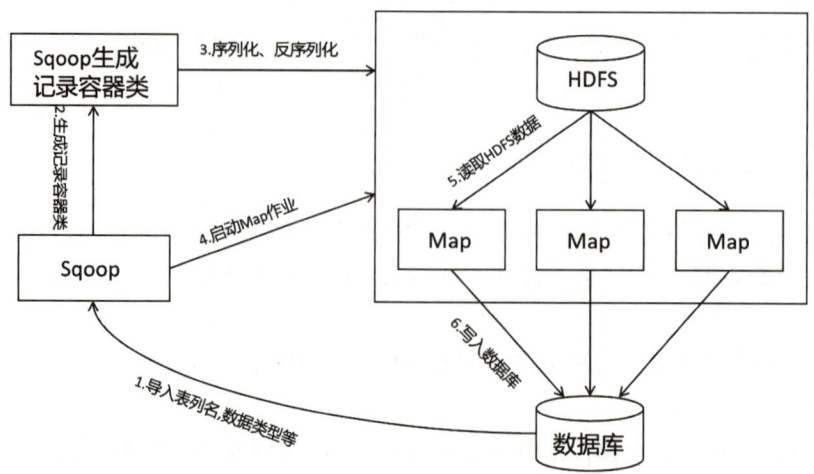

图 9.1.4　Sqoop 数据导出过程

由图 9.1.4 可以看出，Sqoop 数据导出过程如下：
（1）Sqoop 读取数据库的元数据信息（包括数据表列名、数据类型等）。
（2）Sqoop 生成记录容器类，该类与数据库的表对应，提供序列化和反序列功能。
（3）Sqoop 生成的记录容器类为 Map 作业提供序列化和反序列功能。
（4）Sqoop 启动 Hadoop 的 Map 作业。
（5）Map 作业读取 HDFS 中的数据，此时 Sqoop 生成的记录容器类提供反序列化功能。
（6）Map 作业将读取的数据通过一批 INSERT 语句写入目标数据库中，每条 INSERT 语句都会批量插入多条记录。

任务 9.2　Sqoop 的安装和配置

任务描述

大数据迁移工具 Sqoop 可以实现数据在 Hadoop、HBase 和 Hive 之间的导入和导出，Sqoop 具有优良的架构特征和强大的数据转换能力。本任务实际操作 Sqoop 的安装和配置过程。

关键步骤

（1）下载 Sqoop 安装包。
（2）解压 Sqoop 安装包到指定目录。
（3）修改配置文件 sqoop-env.sh。
（4）拷贝 MySQL 的 jdbc 驱动包到"sqoop/lib"目录。
（5）配置 configure-sqoop。

(6) 修改/etc/profile。
(7) 验证 Sqoop,安装成功。

9.2.1 下载 Sqoop 安装包。

用户可以到 Apache 官网下载 Sqoop,链接地址:https://archive.apache.org/dist/sqoop/1.4.7/。Sqoop 安装包下载界面如图 9.2.1 所示。

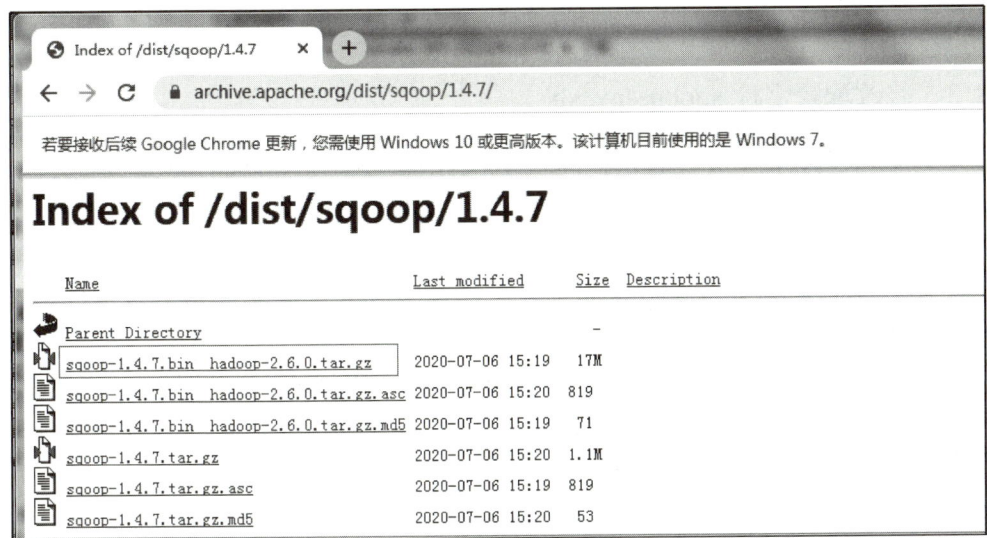

图 9.2.1 Sqoop 安装包下载

将 sqoop-1.4.7.bin__hadoop-2.6.0.tar.gz 下载到本地 Windows 系统中。再用 WinSCP 将 sqoop-1.4.7.bin__hadoop-2.6.0.tar.gz 上传到虚拟机 CentOS 7 的"/root"目录下,如图 9.2.2 所示。

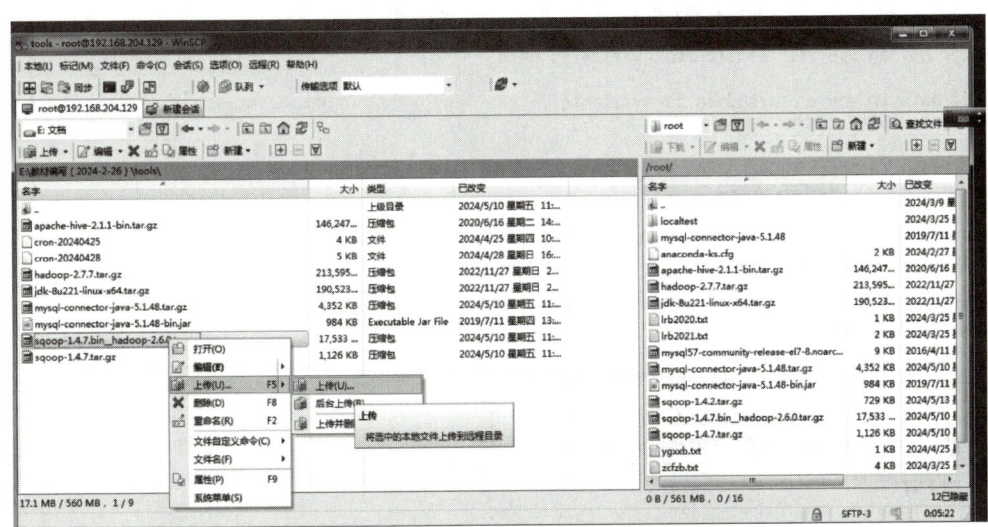

图 9.2.2 将 Sqoop 安装包传到虚拟机 CentOS 7

9.2.2 解压 Sqoop 安装包到指定目录

解压 Sqoop 安装包到指定目录,并重命名为"sqoop"。在虚拟机 CentOS 7 进行 Sqoop 安装操作,命令如下:

```
cd /root
tar -zxvf sqoop-1.4.7.bin__hadoop-2.6.0.tar.gz -C /opt/modules
cd /opt/modules
mv sqoop-1.4.7.bin__hadoop-2.6.0/ sqoop
```

9.2.3 修改配置文件 sqoop-env.sh

在 sqoop 文件夹的"conf"目录中,将配置文件 sqoop-env-template.sh 重命名为 sqoop-env.sh,命令如下:

```
cd /opt/modules/sqoop/conf
mv sqoop-env-template.sh sqoop-env.sh
vi sqoop-env.sh
```

对 sqoop-env.sh 进行配置,在 vi 编辑器的 INSERT 模式下,将"/opt/modules/hadoop"添加到"export HADOOP_COMMON_HOME ="和"export HADOOP_MAPRED_HOME ="语句后,或直接在文件末尾添加以下代码:

```
export HADOOP_COMMON_HOME=/opt/modules/hadoop
export HADOOP_MAPRED_HOME=/opt/modules/hadoop
```

修改结果如图 9.2.3 所示。

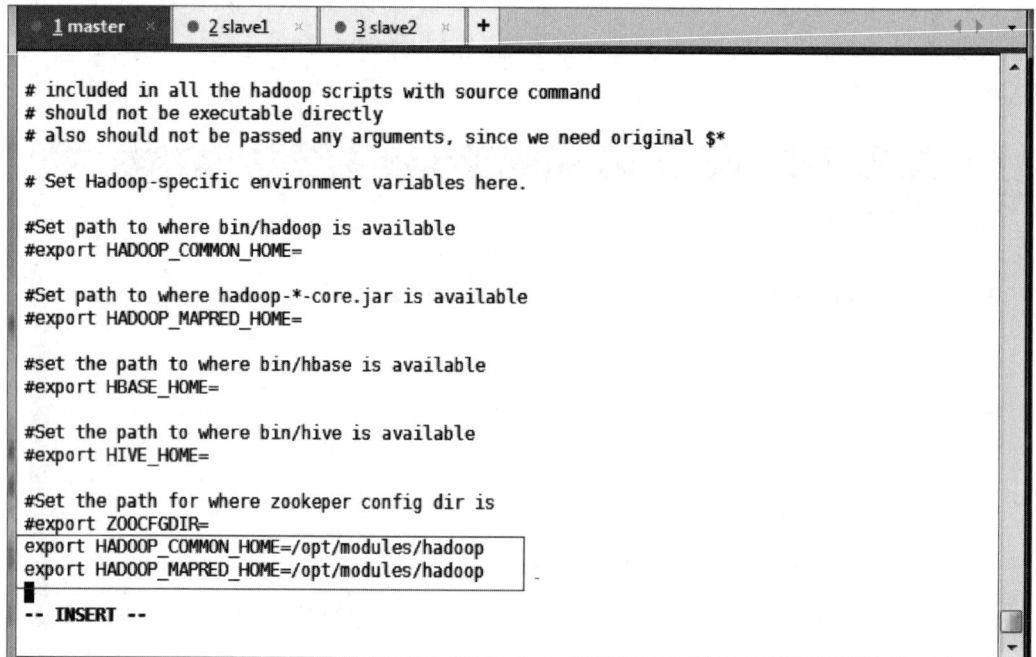

图 9.2.3 修改配置文件 sqoop-env.sh

按键盘上的 Esc 键,输入":wq"保存退出。

9.2.4 拷贝 MySQL 的 jdbc 驱动包到"sqoop/lib"目录

拷贝 MySQL 的 jdbc 驱动包到"sqoop/lib"目录下。查询已经安装的 MySQL 版本号,命令如下:

```
mysql --version
```

可见 MySQL 版本号为 5.7.44,如图 9.2.4 所示。

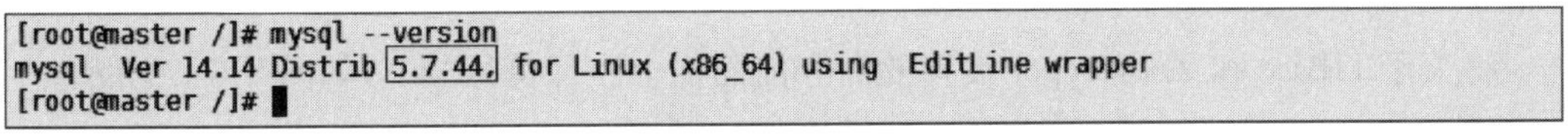

```
[root@master /]# mysql --version
mysql  Ver 14.14 Distrib 5.7.44, for Linux (x86_64) using  EditLine wrapper
[root@master /]#
```

图 9.2.4　查询已经安装的 MySQL 版本号

MySQL 5.7 对应的 JDBC 驱动是 mysql-connector-java-5.1.33 或更高版本。下载 mysql 驱动包 mysql-connector-java-5.1.33,下载地址为:https://downloads.mysql.com/archives/c-j/。下载 MySQL 驱动包界面如图 9.2.5 所示。

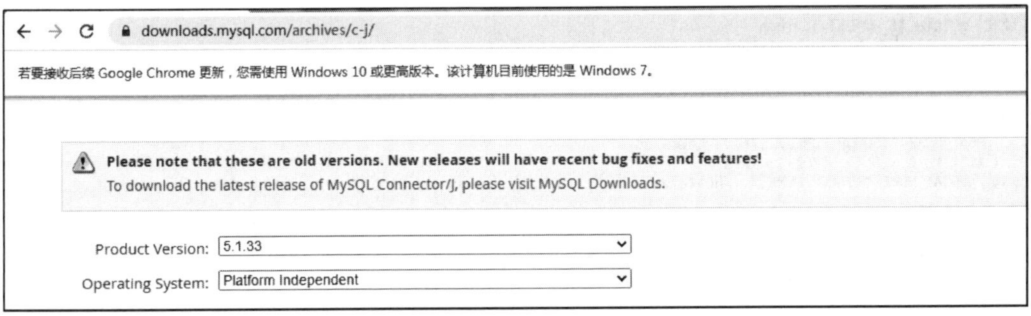

图 9.2.5　下载 MySQL 驱动包

将 mysql-connector-java-5.1.33.tar.gz 上传到 CentOS 7 的"/root"目录下,解压后得到 mysql-connector-java-5.1.33.jar,命令如下:

```
[root@master ~]#  cd /root
[root@master ~]#  tar -zxvf mysql-connector-java-5.1.33.tar.gz
[root@master ~]# cd mysql-connector-java-5.1.33
[root@master mysql-connector-java-5.1.33]#   ls
```

可看到文件夹中有 mysql-connector-java-5.1.33-bin.jar 文件,如图 9.2.6 所示。

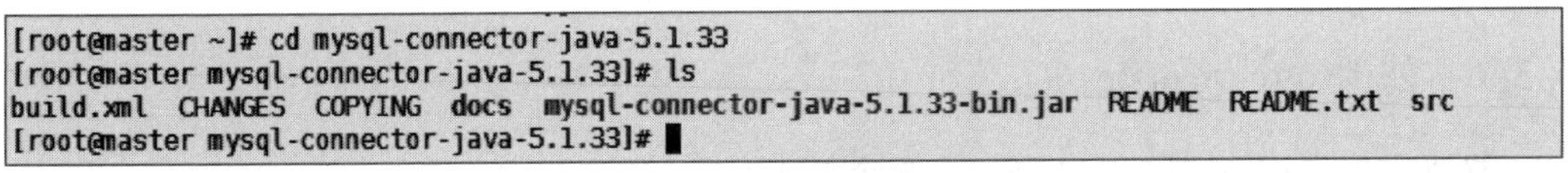

```
[root@master ~]# cd mysql-connector-java-5.1.33
[root@master mysql-connector-java-5.1.33]# ls
build.xml  CHANGES  COPYING  docs  mysql-connector-java-5.1.33-bin.jar  README  README.txt  src
[root@master mysql-connector-java-5.1.33]#
```

图 9.2.6　查询到驱动包

将 mysql-connector-java-5.1.33-bin.jar 文件拷贝到"sqoop/lib"目录下,命令如下:

```
cp mysql-connector-java-5.1.33-bin.jar  /opt/modules/sqoop/lib
```

9.2.5 配置 configure-sqoop

配置 configure-sqoop 时，应注释掉对于 HBase 和 ZooKeeper 的检查。因本系统没有安装 HBase 和 ZooKeeper，这里要对"/opt/modules/sqoop/bin/"目录下的配置文件 configure-sqoop 进行修改，注释掉对于 HBase 和 ZooKeeper 的检查，命令如下：

```
cd  /opt/modules/sqoop/bin
vi  configure-sqoop
```

将关于 HBase 和 ZooKeeper 设置的命令前面加上注释符号"#"，如图 9.2.7 所示。

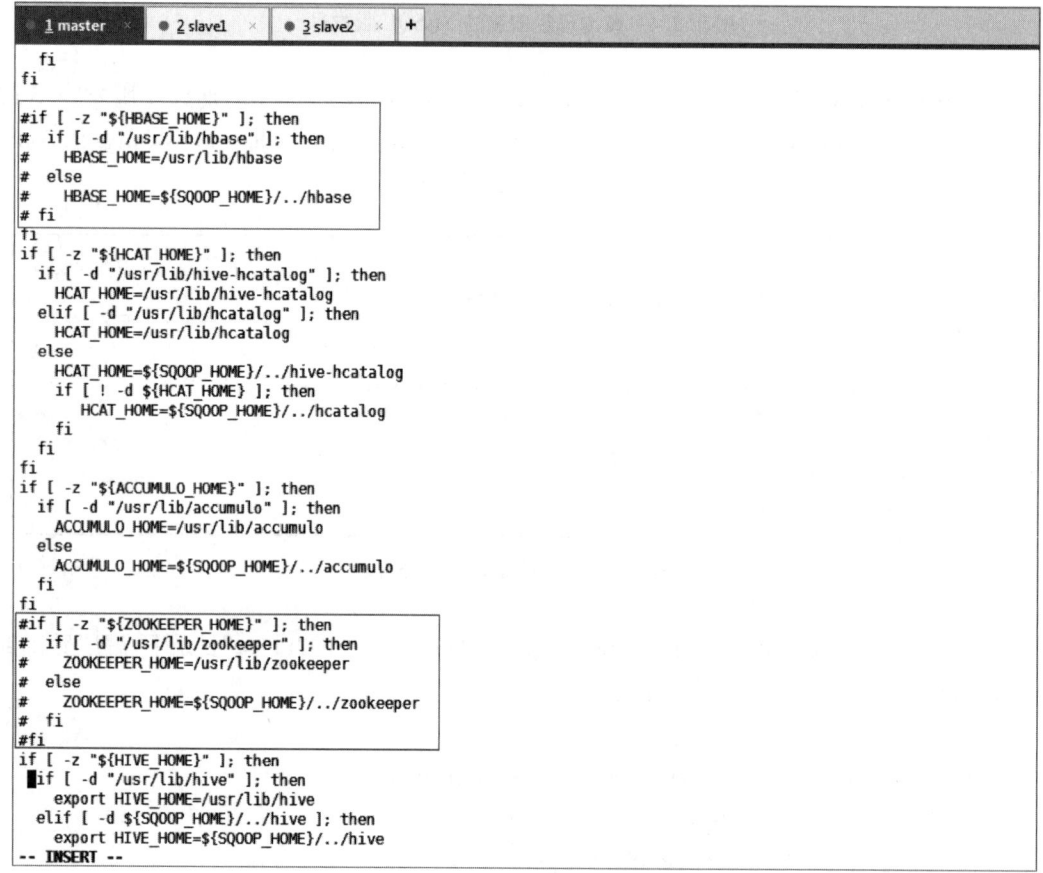

图 9.2.7　注释掉对于 HBase 和 ZooKeeper 的配置

9.2.6 修改/etc/profile

修改/etc/profile，添加环境变量，命令如下：

```
vi /etc/profile
```

末尾添加以下内容：

```
export SQOOP_HOME=/opt/modules/sqoop
export PATH=$PATH:$SQOOP_HOME/bin
```

保存退出。

配置文件生效,命令如下:

```
source /etc/profile
```

9.2.7 验证 Sqoop

执行"sqoop help"代码,验证 Sqoop 是否安装成功,命令如下:

```
sqoop help
```

执行结果如图 9.2.8 所示。

```
24/05/13 14:45:59 INFO sqoop.Sqoop: Running Sqoop version: 1.4.7
usage: sqoop COMMAND [ARGS]

Available commands:
  codegen            Generate code to interact with database records
  create-hive-table  Import a table definition into Hive
  eval               Evaluate a SQL statement and display the results
  export             Export an HDFS directory to a database table
  help               List available commands
  import             Import a table from a database to HDFS
  import-all-tables  Import tables from a database to HDFS
  import-mainframe   Import datasets from a mainframe server to HDFS
  job                Work with saved jobs
  list-databases     List available databases on a server
  list-tables        List available tables in a database
  merge              Merge results of incremental imports
  metastore          Run a standalone Sqoop metastore
  version            Display version information

See 'sqoop help COMMAND' for information on a specific command.
```

图 9.2.8 验证 Sqoop 安装成功

测试 Sqoop 是否能成功连接数据库,命令如下:

```
sqoop version
```

运行结果如图 9.2.9 所示,说明数据库连接成功。

```
[root@master mysql-connector-java-5.1.33]# cd /
[root@master /]# sqoop version
Warning:   does not exist! HBase imports will fail.
Please set $HBASE_HOME to the root of your HBase installation.
Warning: /opt/modules/sqoop/../hcatalog does not exist! HCatalog jobs will fail.
Please set $HCAT_HOME to the root of your HCatalog installation.
Warning: /opt/modules/sqoop/../accumulo does not exist! Accumulo imports will fail.
Please set $ACCUMULO_HOME to the root of your Accumulo installation.
Warning:   does not exist! Accumulo imports will fail.
Please set $ZOOKEEPER_HOME to the root of your Zookeeper installation.
24/05/13 14:48:34 INFO sqoop.Sqoop: Running Sqoop version: 1.4.7
Sqoop 1.4.7
git commit id 2328971411f57f0cb683dfb79d19d4d19d185dd8
Compiled by maugli on Thu Dec 21 15:59:58 STD 2017
```

图 9.2.9 验证 Sqoop 连接数据库成功

在使用 Sqoop 时,需要在 MySQL 赋予虚拟机用户的权限,这里的主机名为 master,MySQL 登录密码为 123456,先启动 MySQL,再进行连接操作,命令如下:

```
systemctl restart mysqld
sqoop list-databases --connect jdbc:mysql://master:3306/ --username root
--password 123456
```

该命令是与 MySQL 建立连接,并列出 MySQL 中的数据库,运行结果如图 9.2.10 所示。

```
24/05/13 14:11:17 INFO manager.MySQLManager: Preparing to use a MySQL streaming resultset.
information_schema
hive
hive_test
mysql
performance_schema
sys
```

图 9.2.10 列出数据库名称

可见,输入的命令显示出了 MySQL 中所有的数据库信息。

任务 9.3 用 Sqoop 导入、导出数据

任务描述

大数据迁移工具 Sqoop 可以实现数据在 Hadoop、HBase 和 Hive 之间导入和导出,Sqoop 具有优良的架构特征和强大的数据转换能力。本任务实际操作 Sqoop 进行数据的迁移,包含把 MySQL 数据导入 HDFS 和 Hive、把 HDFS 数据导出到 MySQL、把 Hive 数据导出到 MySQL 等。

关键步骤

(1) 将 MySQL 数据导入 HDFS。
(2) 将 MySQL 数据导入 Hive。
(3) 将 HDFS 数据导出到 MySQL。
(4) 将 Hive 数据导出到 MySQL。

9.3.1 将 MySQL 数据导入 HDFS

9.3.1.1 准备 MySQL 数据

仍以江苏财源有限公司数据为例。江苏财源有限公司员工基本信息表(部分)如表 9.3.1 所示,在 MySQL 中创建数据库 jscy_mysql,在该数据库中再创建表 ygxxb。

表 9.3.1　江苏财源有限公司员工基本信息表(部分)

职工编号	姓名	性别	部门	职务类别	基本工资
001	Wangboyu	male	office	manager	3 200.00
002	Qiming	female	office	assistant	2 500.00
003	Lihongmei	female	finance office	manager	3 000.00
004	Wangxiaoyan	male	finance office	accountant	2 000.00
005	Chengyanli	female	finance office	cashier	1 800.00

第 1 步:调用 MySQL 命令,创建 jscy_mysql 数据库。

命令如下:

```
mysql -uroot -p123456
create database jscy_mysql;
```

运行结果如图 9.3.1 所示。

```
[root@master /]# mysql -uroot -p123456
mysql: [Warning] Using a password on the command line interface can be insecure.
Welcome to the MySQL monitor.  Commands end with ; or \g.
Your MySQL connection id is 33
Server version: 5.7.44 MySQL Community Server (GPL)

Copyright (c) 2000, 2023, Oracle and/or its affiliates.

Oracle is a registered trademark of Oracle Corporation and/or its
affiliates. Other names may be trademarks of their respective
owners.

Type 'help;' or '\h' for help. Type '\c' to clear the current input statement.

mysql> create database jscy_mysql;
Query OK, 1 row affected (0.05 sec)
```

图 9.3.1　创建 jscy_mysql 数据库

第 2 步:在 jscy_mysql 数据库下创建表 ygxxb

在 jscy_mysql 数据库下创建表 ygxxb,命令如下:

```
use jscy_mysql;

CREATE TABLE ygxxb ( zgbh VARCHAR ( 10 ) PRIMARY KEY, xm VARCHAR ( 20 ), xb VARCHAR(10), bm VARCHAR(20), zwlb VARCHAR(60),jbgz FLOAT);
```

运行结果如图 9.3.2 所示。

```
mysql> CREATE TABLE ygxxb(zgbh VARCHAR(10) PRIMARY KEY, xm VARCHAR(20), xb VARCHAR(2), bm VARCHAR(20),
 zwlb VARCHAR(60),jbgz FLOAT);
Query OK, 0 rows affected (0.09 sec)
```

图 9.3.2　创建表 ygxxb

第 3 步:向表 ygxxb 里插入数据,支撑后续实验。

ygxxb 表结构建好后,给表插入一些数据。可以用"INSERT INTO"命令给表插入一行数据，命令如下：

```
INSERT INTO ygxxb(zgbh,xm,xb,bm,zwlb,jbgz) VALUES
('001','Wangboyu','male','office','manager',3200.00);
```

同样，将其余数据用"INSERT INTO"插入表中，命令如下：

```
INSERT INTO ygxxb(zgbh, xm , xb , bm, zwlb, jbgz) VALUES
('002','Qiming','female','office','assistant',2500.00);

INSERT INTO ygxxb(zgbh, xm , xb , bm, zwlb, jbgz) VALUES
('003','Lihongmei','female','FinanceOffice','manager',3000.00);

INSERT INTO ygxxb(zgbh, xm , xb , bm, zwlb, jbgz) VALUES
('004','Wangxiaoy','male','FinanceOffice','accountant',2000.00);

INSERT INTO ygxxb(zgbh, xm , xb , bm, zwlb, jbgz) VALUES
('005','Chengyanli','female','FinanceOffice','cashier',1800.00);
```

用 HiveQL 查询 ygxxb 数据，命令如下：

```
SELECT * FROM ygxxb;
```

查询结果如图 9.3.3 所示。

```
+------+------------+------+---------------+------------+------+
| zgbh | xm         | xb   | bm            | zwlb       | jbgz |
+------+------------+------+---------------+------------+------+
| 001  | Wangboyu   | ma   | office        | manager    | 3200 |
| 002  | Qiming     | fe   | office        | assistant  | 2500 |
| 003  | Lihongmei  | fe   | FinanceOffice | manager    | 3000 |
| 004  | Wangxiaoy  | ma   | FinanceOffice | accountant | 2000 |
| 005  | Chengyanli | fe   | FinanceOffice | cashier    | 1800 |
+------+------------+------+---------------+------------+------+
5 rows in set (0.00 sec)
```

图 9.3.3　查询表 ygxxb 数据

可见，5 行数据已全部插入 ygxxb 表中。

退出 MySQL 系统，命令如下：

```
mysql> exit;
```

9.3.1.2　导入数据

将 ygxxb 表里的数据导入 HDFS 的"/usr/sqoop/mysql_to_hdfs"目录下。

命令如下：

```
hdfs dfs -mkdir -p /usr/sqoop/mysql_to_hive

sqoop import \
```

```
--connect jdbc:mysql://master:3306/jscy_mysql?characterEncoding=utf-8\&useSSL=false \
--username root   \
--password 123456   \
--table ygxxb   \
--target-dir /usr/sqoop/mysql_to_hdfs \
--fields-terminated-by '\t' \
--num-mappers 1 \
--delete-target-dir
```

以上代码中的一些注释如下：

--connect 表示连接。

--username mysql 表示账号。

--password mysql 表示密码。

--table mysql 表示表名。

--num-mappers 1 表示执行 map 的次数为 1。

--fields-terminated-by 表示列的分割。

--target-dir 表示要导入 HDFS 上的目录。

运行结果如图 9.3.4 所示。

```
24/05/15 19:21:16 INFO mapreduce.Job: Counters: 30
        File System Counters
                FILE: Number of bytes read=0
                FILE: Number of bytes written=213064
                FILE: Number of read operations=0
                FILE: Number of large read operations=0
                FILE: Number of write operations=0
                HDFS: Number of bytes read=87
                HDFS: Number of bytes written=218
                HDFS: Number of read operations=4
                HDFS: Number of large read operations=0
                HDFS: Number of write operations=2
        Job Counters
                Launched map tasks=1
                Other local map tasks=1
                Total time spent by all maps in occupied slots (ms)=2905
                Total time spent by all reduces in occupied slots (ms)=0
                Total time spent by all map tasks (ms)=2905
                Total vcore-milliseconds taken by all map tasks=2905
                Total megabyte-milliseconds taken by all map tasks=2974720
        Map-Reduce Framework
                Map input records=5
                Map output records=5
                Input split bytes=87
                Spilled Records=0
                Failed Shuffles=0
                Merged Map outputs=0
                GC time elapsed (ms)=65
                CPU time spent (ms)=1010
                Physical memory (bytes) snapshot=219488256
                Virtual memory (bytes) snapshot=1951887360
                Total committed heap usage (bytes)=130547712
        File Input Format Counters
                Bytes Read=0
        File Output Format Counters
                Bytes Written=218
24/05/15 19:21:16 INFO mapreduce.ImportJobBase: Transferred 218 bytes in 32.5902 seconds (6.6891 bytes/s
24/05/15 19:21:16 INFO mapreduce.ImportJobBase: Retrieved 5 records.
```

图 9.3.4 将 ygxxb 表里的数据导入到 HDFS

9.3.1.3 查看结果

输入以下命令：

```
hdfs dfs -ls /usr/sqoop/mysql_to_hdfs
hdfs dfs -cat /usr/sqoop/mysql_to_hdfs/part-m-00000
```

运行结果如图 9.3.5 所示。

```
[root@jiangdaoxia-272-cbb56d66d-zgkt9 ~]# hdfs dfs -ls /usr/sqoop/mysql_to_hdfs
Found 2 items
-rw-r--r--   1 root supergroup          0 2024-05-15 19:21 /usr/sqoop/mysql_to_hdfs/_SUCCESS
-rw-r--r--   1 root supergroup        218 2024-05-15 19:21 /usr/sqoop/mysql_to_hdfs/part-m-00000
[root@jiangdaoxia-272-cbb56d66d-zgkt9 ~]# hdfs dfs -cat /usr/sqoop/mysql_to_hdfs/part-m-00000
001   Wangboyu      ma   office        manager    3200.0
002   Qiming        fe   office        assistant  2500.0
003   Lihongmei     fe   FinanceOffice manager    3000.0
004   Wangxiaoy     ma   FinanceOffice accountant 2000.0
005   Chengyanli    fe   FinanceOffice cashier    1800.0
```

图 9.3.5　ygxxb 表数据成功导入到 HDFS

9.3.2　将 MySQL 数据导入 Hive

9.3.2.1　导入数据

从 MySQL 向 Hive 导入数据无需事先建表，可直接导入。此处将 MySQL 的 jscy_mysql 数据库中的表 ygxxb 导入 Hive 的 jscy_hive 数据库的表 ygxxb 中。

第 1 步：先使用 Hive 创建数据库。

命令如下：

```
hive
CREATE DATABASE jscy_hive;
```

第 2 步：导入数据。

命令如下：

```
sqoop import \
--connect jdbc:mysql://master:3306/jscy_mysql \
--username root \
--password 123456 \
--table ygxxb \
--target-dir /usr/sqoop/mysql_to_hive \
--num-mappers 1 \
--hive-import \
--fields-terminated-by "\t" \
--hive-overwrite \
--hive-table jscy_hive.ygxxb
```

以上代码中的一些注释如下：

--hive-import 表示导入 Hive。

--hive-overwrite 表示覆盖表中原有数据。

--hive-database 表示 Hive 中的那个数据库。

--hive-table 表示 Hive 中的表。

--target-dir 表示要导入 HDFS 上的对应 Hive 表所在目录。

注意

该过程分为两步，第一步将数据导入 HDFS，第二步将导入 HDFS 的数据迁移到 Hive 仓库。

其中，第一步使用的是临时目录是"/usr/sqoop/mysql_to_hive"，通过--target-dir 来指定。

运行结果如图 9.3.6 所示。

```
24/05/15 19:31:13 INFO common.FileUtils: Creating directory if it doesn't exist: hdfs://localhost:9000/user/hive/warehouse/j
scy_hive.db/ygxxb
24/05/15 19:31:13 INFO ql.Driver: Starting task [Stage-1:STATS] in serial mode
24/05/15 19:31:13 INFO exec.StatsTask: Executing stats task
24/05/15 19:31:13 INFO hive.metastore: Closed a connection to metastore, current connections: 0
24/05/15 19:31:13 INFO hive.metastore: Trying to connect to metastore with URI thrift://localhost:9083
24/05/15 19:31:13 INFO hive.metastore: Opened a connection to metastore, current connections: 1
24/05/15 19:31:13 INFO hive.metastore: Connected to metastore.
24/05/15 19:31:13 INFO hive.metastore: Closed a connection to metastore, current connections: 0
24/05/15 19:31:13 INFO hive.metastore: Trying to connect to metastore with URI thrift://localhost:9083
24/05/15 19:31:13 INFO hive.metastore: Opened a connection to metastore, current connections: 1
24/05/15 19:31:13 INFO hive.metastore: Connected to metastore.
24/05/15 19:31:13 INFO exec.StatsTask: Table jscy_hive.ygxxb stats: [numFiles=1, numRows=0, totalSize=218, rawDataSize=0]
24/05/15 19:31:13 INFO ql.Driver: Completed executing command(queryId=root_20240515193113_c29a9d80-bf1c-4318-8b12-24a575a2c6
7d); Time taken: 0.601 seconds
OK
24/05/15 19:31:13 INFO ql.Driver: OK
Time taken: 0.804 seconds
24/05/15 19:31:13 INFO CliDriver: Time taken: 0.804 seconds
24/05/15 19:31:13 INFO conf.HiveConf: Using the default value passed in for log id: 5ea7403d-7f65-4c06-a43a-ca8c8fc8b4aa
24/05/15 19:31:13 INFO session.SessionState: Resetting thread name to main
24/05/15 19:31:13 INFO conf.HiveConf: Using the default value passed in for log id: 5ea7403d-7f65-4c06-a43a-ca8c8fc8b4aa
24/05/15 19:31:13 INFO session.SessionState: Deleted directory: /tmp/hive/root/5ea7403d-7f65-4c06-a43a-ca8c8fc8b4aa on fs wi
th scheme hdfs
24/05/15 19:31:13 INFO session.SessionState: Deleted directory: /ddhome/bin/hive/tmp/logs/5ea7403d-7f65-4c06-a43a-ca8c8fc8b4
aa on fs with scheme file
24/05/15 19:31:13 INFO hive.metastore: Closed a connection to metastore, current connections: 0
24/05/15 19:31:13 INFO hive.HiveImport: Hive import complete.
```

图 9.3.6　MySQL 数据导入 Hive

9.3.2.2　结果验证

启动 Hive，切换到数据库 jscy_mysql，查询表 ygxxb 中数据，命令如下：

```
hive
use jscy_hive;
select * from ygxxb;
```

运行结果如图 9.3.7 所示。

```
hive> use jscy_hive;
OK
Time taken: 1.103 seconds
hive> select * from ygxxb;
OK
001     Wangboyu       ma       office        manager    3200.0
002     Qiming  fe              office        assistant            2500.0
003     Lihongmei      fe       FinanceOffice manager 3000.0
004     Wangxiaoy      ma       FinanceOffice accountant           2000.0
005     Chengyanli     fe       FinanceOffice cashier 1800.0
Time taken: 1.353 seconds, Fetched: 5 row(s)
```

图 9.3.7　MySQL 数据成功导入 Hive

退出 Hive 系统，命令如下：

```
hive> exit;
```

9.3.3 将 HDFS 数据导出到 MySQL

大数据业务中经常涉及数据迁移操作，尤其是关系型数据库与大数据组件间的数据迁移操作。使用 Sqoop 操作使得数据迁移更加方便易行。

9.3.3.1 准备数据

在本地 CentOS 7 上备一份数据 hdfs_to_mysql，然后上传到 HDFS 的"/usr/sqoop/hdfs"目录下，命令如下：

```
mkdir /home/sqoop
cd /home/sqoop
vi hdfs_to_mysql
```

数据如下：

```
006    lindawei      male    R&DDepartment    manager   2200.00
007    zhuhanbin     male    R&DDepartment    RDpeple   2000.00
```

 注意

数据之间需要用 Tab 键隔开。

编辑界面如图 9.3.8 所示。

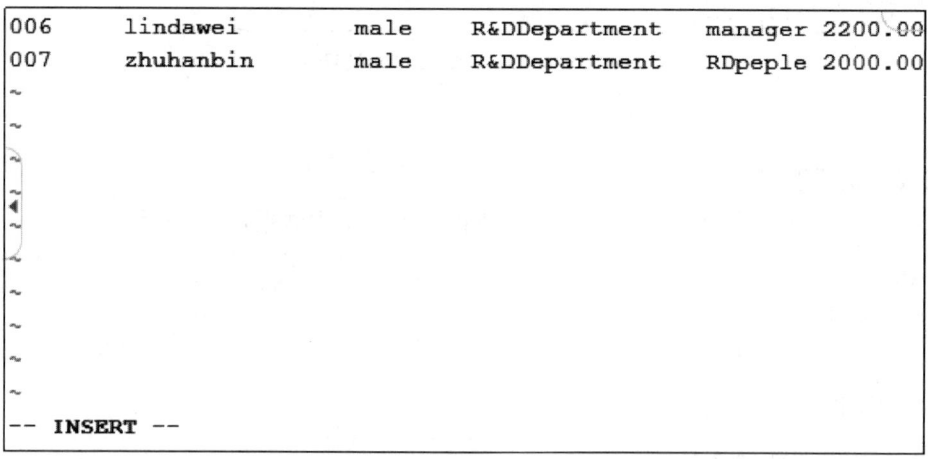

图 9.3.8　在本地创建数据文件 hdfs_to_mysql

按 Esc 键，录入":wq"保存退出，完成数据准备。

将刚创建的 hdfs_to_mysql 文件上传到 HDFS 的"/usr/sqoop/hdfs"目录下，若该目录不存在，就先创建，命令如下：

```
hdfs dfs -mkdir -p /usr/sqoop/hdfs
hdfs dfs -put /home/sqoop/hdfs_to_mysql   /usr/sqoop/hdfs
```

9.3.3.2 导出数据

在 Linux 下执行 Sqoop 数据迁移语句。将 hdfs_to_mysql 中的数据导出到 MySQL 中的 ygxxb 表中。

命令如下：

```
sqoop export \
--connect jdbc:mysql://master:3306/jscy_mysql \
--username root   \
--password 123456   \
--table  ygxxb   \
--num-mappers 1 \
--export-dir /usr/sqoop/hdfs    \
--input-fields-terminated-by "\t"   \
--columns="zgbh,xm,xb,bm,zwlb,jbgz"
```

运行结果如图 9.3.9 所示。

```
24/05/15 20:52:24 INFO mapreduce.Job: Job job_1715774632110_0009 completed successfully
24/05/15 20:52:24 INFO mapreduce.Job: Counters: 30
        File System Counters
                FILE: Number of bytes read=0
                FILE: Number of bytes written=212661
                FILE: Number of read operations=0
                FILE: Number of large read operations=0
                FILE: Number of write operations=0
                HDFS: Number of bytes read=231
                HDFS: Number of bytes written=0
                HDFS: Number of read operations=4
                HDFS: Number of large read operations=0
                HDFS: Number of write operations=0
        Job Counters
                Launched map tasks=1
                Data-local map tasks=1
                Total time spent by all maps in occupied slots (ms)=2972
                Total time spent by all reduces in occupied slots (ms)=0
                Total time spent by all map tasks (ms)=2972
                Total vcore-milliseconds taken by all map tasks=2972
                Total megabyte-milliseconds taken by all map tasks=3043328
        Map-Reduce Framework
                Map input records=2
                Map output records=2
                Input split bytes=131
                Spilled Records=0
                Failed Shuffles=0
                Merged Map outputs=0
                GC time elapsed (ms)=68
                CPU time spent (ms)=800
                Physical memory (bytes) snapshot=214245376
                Virtual memory (bytes) snapshot=1935933440
                Total committed heap usage (bytes)=131596288
        File Input Format Counters
                Bytes Read=0
        File Output Format Counters
                Bytes Written=0
24/05/15 20:52:24 INFO mapreduce.ExportJobBase: Transferred 231 bytes in 14.4714 seconds (15.9625 bytes/sec)
```

图 9.3.9　HDFS 数据导出到 MySQL

9.3.3.3 结果验证

登录 MySQL,查询 ygxxb 的数据,命令如下:

```
mysql -uroot -p123456
use jscy_mysql;
select * from ygxxb；
```

运行结果如图 9.3.10 所示。

```
MariaDB [jscy_mysql]> select * from ygxxb;
+------+-----------+------+---------------+------------+------+
| zgbh | xm        | xb   | bm            | zwlb       | jbgz |
+------+-----------+------+---------------+------------+------+
| 001  | Wangboyu  | ma   | office        | manager    | 3200 |
| 002  | Qiming    | fe   | office        | assistant  | 2500 |
| 003  | Lihongmei | fe   | FinanceOffice | manager    | 3000 |
| 004  | Wangxiaoy | ma   | FinanceOffice | accountant | 2000 |
| 005  | Chengyanli| fe   | FinanceOffice | cashier    | 1800 |
| 006  | lindawei  | male | R&DDepartment | manager    | 2200 |
| 007  | zhuhanbin | male | R&DDepartment | RDpeple    | 2000 |
+------+-----------+------+---------------+------------+------+
7 rows in set (0.00 sec)
```

图 9.3.10 HDFS 数据成功导出到 MySQL

9.3.4 将 Hive 数据导出到 MySQL

9.3.4.1 准备数据

在 MySQL 的 jscy_mysql 数据库中创建一张新表 ygxxb2。

命令如下:

```
mysql -uroot -p123456
use jscy_mysql;
CREATE TABLE ygxxb2（zgbh VARCHAR（10）PRIMARY KEY, xm VARCHAR（20）, xb VARCHAR(10), bm VARCHAR(20), zwlb VARCHAR(60),jbgz FLOAT）;
exit;
```

9.3.4.2 找到 Hive 表所在位置

在 Hive 的命令行下,在 jscy_hive 数据库中创建表 ygxxb1。

命令如下:

```
USE jscy_hive;

CREATE TABLE ygxxb1(zgbh VARCHAR(10), xm VARCHAR(20), xb VARCHAR(10), bm VARCHAR（20）, zwlb VARCHAR（20）, jbgz FLOAT) ROW FORMAT DELIMITED FIELDS TERMINATED BY '\t';
```

现有如下数据集:

```
001  Wangboyu     male    office  manager  3200.00
002  Qiminghong   female  office  assist   2500.00
```

```
003  Lihongmei    female  Finance  manager  3000.00
004  Wangxiaoyan  male    Finance  account  2000.00
005  Chengyanli   female  Finance  cashier  1800.00
```

将该数据集导入表 ygxxb1 中。在本地创建数据文件,命令如下:

```
cd  /home/sqoop
vi  hive_to_mysql
```

编辑界面如图 9.3.11 所示。

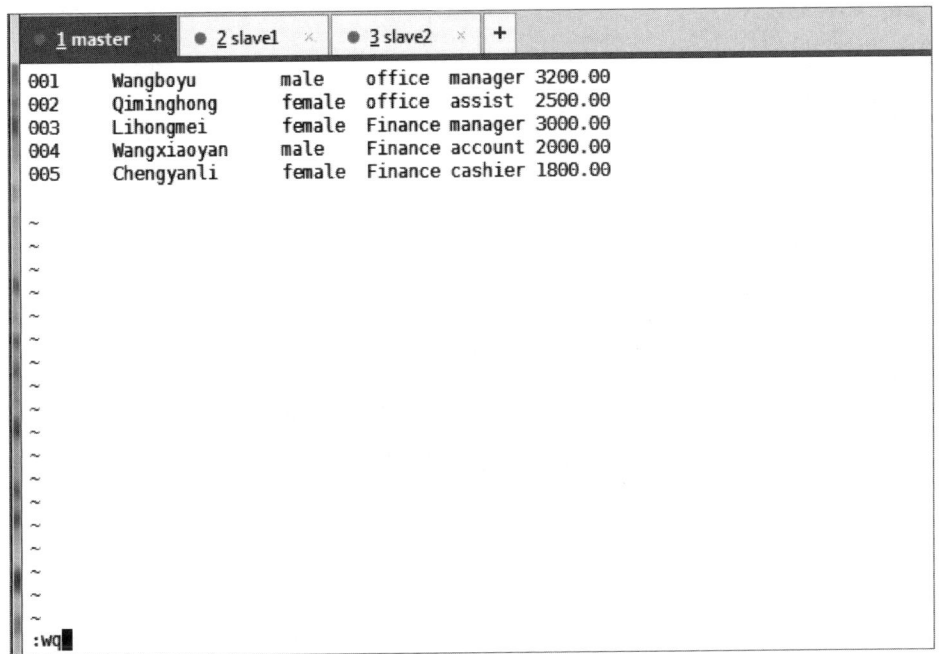

图 9.3.11　创建数据文件 hive_to_mysql

将 hive_to_mysql 文件内容导入表 ygxxb1 中,命令如下:

```
LOAD DATA LOCAL INPATH '/home/sqoop/hive_to_mysql' INTO TABLE ygxxb1;
SELECT * FROM ygxxb1;
```

运行结果如图 9.3.12 所示。

```
hive (jscy_hive)> LOAD DATA LOCAL INPATH '/home/sqoop/hive_to_mysql' INTO TABLE ygxxb1;
Loading data to table jscy_hive.ygxxb1
OK
Time taken: 1.71 seconds
hive (jscy_hive)> select * from ygxxb1;
OK
ygxxb1.zgbh     ygxxb1.xm        ygxxb1.xb     ygxxb1.bm        ygxxb1.zwlb     ygxxb1.jbgz
001     Wangboyu         male          office   manager 3200.0
002     Qiminghong       female        office   assist  2500.0
003     Lihongmei        female        Finance  manager 3000.0
004     Wangxiaoyan      male          Finance  account 2000.0
005     Chengyanli       female        Finance  cashier 1800.0
        NULL    NULL     NULL          NULL     NULL
Time taken: 1.856 seconds, Fetched: 6 row(s)
```

图 9.3.12　将数据导入到表 ygxxb1 中

要将 Hive 的数据导出到 MySQL,需要找到 Hive 表中数据存储的位置。通过以下命令查看表的存储位置 LOCATION:

```
SHOW CREATE TABLE ygxxb1;
```

运行结果如图 9.3.13 所示。

```
hive (jscy_hive)> SHOW CREATE TABLE ygxxb1;
OK
createtab_stmt
CREATE TABLE `ygxxb1`(
  `zgbh` varchar(10),
  `xm` varchar(20),
  `xb` varchar(10),
  `bm` varchar(20),
  `zwlb` varchar(60),
  `jbgz` float)
ROW FORMAT SERDE
  'org.apache.hadoop.hive.serde2.lazy.LazySimpleSerDe'
WITH SERDEPROPERTIES (
  'field.delim'='\t',
  'serialization.format'='\t')
STORED AS INPUTFORMAT
  'org.apache.hadoop.mapred.TextInputFormat'
OUTPUTFORMAT
  'org.apache.hadoop.hive.ql.io.HiveIgnoreKeyTextOutputFormat'
LOCATION
  'hdfs://master:9000/usr/hive_remote/warehouse/jscy_hive.db/ygxxb1'
TBLPROPERTIES (
  'numFiles'='1',
  'numRows'='0',
  'rawDataSize'='0',
  'totalSize'='222',
  'transient_lastDdlTime'='1715785552')
Time taken: 0.232 seconds, Fetched: 24 row(s)
```

图 9.3.13 查看表的存储位置 LOCATION

由图 9.3.13 可见,ygxxb1 表的存储位置在 HDFS 上的"hdfs://master:9000/usr/hive_remote/warehouse/jscy_hive.db/ygxxb1"上。

退出 Hive,命令如下:

```
Exit;
```

9.3.4.3 数据导出

登录 MySQL,创建一个表 ygxxb2。

命令如下:

```
mysql -uroot -p123456
USE jscy_mysql;
CREATE TABLE ygxxb2(zgbh VARCHAR(10), xm VARCHAR(20), xb VARCHAR(10), bm VARCHAR(20), zwlb VARCHAR(20),jbgz FLOAT);
```

运行结果如图 9.3.14 所示。

```
mysql> use jscy_mysql;
Reading table information for completion of table and column names
You can turn off this feature to get a quicker startup with -A

Database changed
mysql> show tables;
+-------------------+
| Tables_in_jscy_mysql |
+-------------------+
| ygxxb             |
| ygxxb1            |
+-------------------+
2 rows in set (0.00 sec)

mysql> CREATE TABLE ygxxb2(zgbh VARCHAR(10) , xm VARCHAR(20), xb VARCHAR(10), bm VARCHAR(20), zwlb VARCHAR(20),jbgz FLOAT);
Query OK, 0 rows affected (0.02 sec)
```

图 9.3.14　创建一个 MySQL 表 ygxxb2

退出 MySQL,命令如下:

```
Exit;
```

在 Linux 下执行 Sqoop 数据迁移语句,命令如下:

```
sqoop export \
--connect jdbc:mysql://master:3306/jscy_mysql \
--username root   \
--password 123456   \
--table   ygxxb2 \
--num-mappers 1 \
--export-dir /usr/hive_remote/warehouse/jscy_hive.db/ygxxb1 \
--input-fields-terminated-by "\t" \
--columns="zgbh,xm,xb,bm,zwlb,jbgz"
```

显示出来代表执行成功。

9.3.4.4　结果验证

登录 MySQL 客户端,查询 ygxxb2,进行结果验证,命令如下:

```
mysql -uroot -p123456
use jscy_mysql;
select * from ygxxb2;
```

单元总结

Sqoop 是在 Apache Hadoop 和关系数据库等结构化数据存储之间高效地传输批量数据的工具。本单元学习了 Sqoop 的概念、架构和数据导入、导出过程,详细操作了 Sqoop 的安装和配置过程,最后通过一个具体案例,学习了用 Sqoop 工具在 MySQL、HDFS 和 Hive 之间进行数据迁移的使用。Sqoop import 是指将关系数据库数据迁移到 HDFS 和 Hive,Sqoop emport 是指将 HDFS 和 Hive 数据迁移到关系数据库。

单元习题

一、简述题

1. Sqoop 产生的背景是什么？
2. Sqoop import、Sqoop export 的功能是什么？

二、技能训练题

1. 独立完成 Sqoop 的安装与配置。
2. 在安装好的 Sqoop 中完成 9.3.1 至 9.3.4 中所有导入、导出数据操作。

参考文献

[1] 林子雨.大数据技术原理与应用[M].3版.北京:人民邮电出版社,2021.
[2] 格物信息.会计如何利用大数据技术[EB/OL].(2023-12-14)[2024-04-02]. https://baijiahao.baidu.com/s?id=1785255760870404999&wfr=spider&for=pc.
[3] 韩敬敬,李卓键.大数据技术在会计工作中的应用研究[J].信息产业报道,2024,(1):147-149.
[4] 史佳璐.大数据技术在财务会计工作中的运用[J].今商圈,2024,(7):0164-0167.
[5] 刘圣前.大数据在财务会计中的应用及对财务报表的影响研究[J].财会学习,2023,(16):1-3.
[6] 微枫 Micromaple.为什么要使用虚拟机?VMware 安装使用[EB/OL].(2022-09-26)[2024-04-02]. https://blog.csdn.net/qq_41779565/article/details/127048791.
[7] 佚名.VMware 虚拟机原理及安装浅析[EB/OL].(2024-05-02)[2024-04-02]. https://eduai.baidu.com/view/3db2aa98de3383c4bb4cf7ec4afe04a1b171b056.
[8] leecy125.Centos7 安装 MySQL 详细步骤[EB/OL].(2024-05-02)[2024-04-02]. https://www.cnblogs.com/leecy/p/16328065.html.
[9] 冰河.海量数据处理与大数据技术实践[M].北京:北京大学出版社,2020.
[10] 书生-w.MYSQL 命令大全(详细版)[EB/OL].(2023-09-30)[2024-05-02]. https://blog.csdn.net/m0_53882348/article/details/130046194.
[11] 蔡清龙.Excel 在财务会计中的应用[M].6版.上海:上海交通大学出版社,2020.
[12] 张远录.财务报表分析[M].4版.北京:机械工业出版社,2023.
[13] Edward Capriolo, Dean Wampler, Jason Rutberglen HIVE 编程指南[M].曹坤,译.北京:人民邮电出版社,2015.
[14] 张素青.MySQL 数据技术与应用[M].2版.北京:人民邮电出版社,2023.
[15] 黑马程序员.Hive 数据仓库应用[M].北京:清华大学出版社,2022.
[16] 肖睿,兰伟,廖春琼.Hadoop 数据仓库实战[M].北京:人民邮电出版社,2021.
[17] 米洪,张鸽.Hadoop 平台搭建与应用[M].北京:人民邮电出版社,2020.
[18] Confluence Administrator, Stamatis Zampetakis. LanguageManual UDF[EB/OL]. (2023-09-15)[2024-05-02]. https://cwiki.apache.org/confluence/display/Hive/LanguageManual+UDF.